A HISTORY OF
CHRISTIAN THOUGHT

A HISTORY OF
CHRISTIAN THOUGHT

By

DR. J. L. NEVE

Professor Emeritus, Hamma Divinity School
Wittenberg College, Springfield, Ohio

———————

Volume One

HISTORY OF CHRISTIAN DOCTRINE

With Contributions by
the Reverend O. W. Heick, Ph.D.
on
The Middle Ages
and
Catholicism

———————

THE MUHLENBERG PRESS
PHILADELPHIA : PENNSYLVANIA

UB 172
Printed in United States of America

To the Faculty of Hamma Divinity School

A FOREWORD

to

VOLUMES ONE AND TWO

The History of Doctrine, or in wider conception the History of Christian Thought, is a study of great importance for theologians and pastors. It came into existence about the beginning of the nineteenth century. At that time of Rationalism its purpose was to show that the confessional heritage of the Church could not be maintained. But soon, with the revival of evangelical theology, the Conservatives also adopted this branch and put it into the service of theological conservatism.

We need a new History of Christian Thought in English. During a number of decades, it is true, the pre-eminent use of a common "text," in the hands of all students, has given way to the professor's lectures and to his reference to a larger literature. However, there can be no denial of the value of one comprehensive history to serve as a guide for the student through the pertinent problems of the ages, provided that a wider collateral reading be not neglected.

In many of our Theological Seminaries and Bible Schools the one-volume *History of Doctrine* by George Park Fisher has been much used since 1886 and has done good service; but it is not sufficient any more for the needs of this present day. The two-volume *Lehrbuch* by Reinhold Seeberg, translated into English by Charles E. Hay, 1902, but now out of print, also did good service for a full generation. But Seeberg, who died October, 1935, had developed this work into five large volumes (4 volumes and a double volume, of 3,166 pages).

It is at this time of waiting for a "Guide" in this field that we offer the services of a new History of Christian Thought, complete in two volumes. These lectures were offered to the students in Hamma Divinity School in mimeographed form. In the course of the development of this work, I found it advisable to associate with myself the Rev. Dr. Otto W. Heick, at one time professor in the former Martin Luther Seminary at Lincoln, Nebr. It was agreed that for Volume One Dr. Heick should take over the Middle Ages, continuing at the close of Volume One with brief reviews on the outstanding developments of Roman Catholicism at Trent and at the Vatican, and finish this subject in Volume Two. My special contribution to Volume One, then, has been on the Ancient Church and on the Reformation up to and including the theology of the Seventeenth Century.

It was agreed also that, for Volume Two, I was to contribute the eight chapters on the developments through the Eighteenth Century in Holland, England, and Germany; and that for the Modern Age in Volume Two I was to add the succeeding four chapters on Kant, on the Religion of German Idealism, on Schleiermacher, on Hegel and the Hegelian theologians. These twelve chapters, following those on the Reformation, describe the full inauguration of the Modern Age.

Upon this, then, Dr. Heick was to follow with the developed topics of the Modern Age into its more recent times: the Continental Theology (Germany, Holland, the Northlands); Great Britain in the Nineteenth and Twentieth Centuries; and America with its own contributions. All of these topics, worked out by Dr. Heick on the basis of a large modern literature, cover chapters in the second volume of this work. (Cf. the Table of Contents of Volume Two.)

Professors and students, in using this work, will keep in mind that the manuscript for Volume One was finished before the publication of Anders Nygrén's writings had appeared. See our review of his significance for the History of Christian Thought, page 13 ff. and our postscriptum references and interpolations in this volume. On the Lundensian theology compare especially Dr. O. W. Heick in Volume Two (Continental Theology).

With regard to the Ancient Church in Volume One, it should be added that the late Professor R. Seeberg, together with Professor W. Dress, who was associated with him at the Berlin University, read very carefully and critically this fundamental part of the manuscript, making a number of suggestions but approving that section of the work.

The reader will pardon a personal note. For many years Professor Seeberg, up to his departure on October 23, 1935, had been following with an unabated interest the maturing of this History of Christian Thought. Differences from him even on important subjects, such as the estimate of Theodore of Mopsuestia and the adoptionist Antiochean Christology, did not lesson his interest in the work. In one letter, after that critical reading of the manuscript, he wrote encouragingly: *Mit am besten hat mir Ihre Behandlung des Augustinus gefallen.* Standing in imagination at his grave, at the lonely cemetery near his summer home in Arenshoop on the Baltic Sea (Meklenburg), looking to his Baltic homeland, I express my deeply felt gratitude to this noble theologian and great historian!

In the cases of quotation from R. Seeberg and from the rest of the present-day Histories of Doctrine (A. von Harnack, F. Loofs, F. Wiegand and others) the title and the pages of their works have always been given for credit. Many of my footnote references, however, are not for giving "sources" but they are intended to lead the student into a reading of the present-day great Histories of Doctrine.

While both authors of this two-volume work have been writing in careful unity of organization and purpose, yet they have agreed that each must be responsible for the contents of his own historical contribution. A History of Christian Thought is not a Dogmatics, not an expanded Catechism, not a Comparative Symbolics; yet, together with Symbolics, as we have expressed it in our *Churches and Sects of Christendom,* it is an historical auxiliary to Christian Dogmatics or Systematic Theology. As such it is to serve all the Protestant Churches and, on every page, it must be open to the critique and the possible supplementations of thinkers everywhere. It does not claim to be a final delivery on the subjects discussed; but rather it seeks to provide attitudes and positions on the basis of which students may strive for something more perfect, just as one generation stands upon the shoulders of the one preceding it. And let it be understood that in the methodology and encyclopedia of a well ordered theological course there should be studied, first, the History of Christian Thought, and after that the doctrinal tenets of the Churches in their confessional differences and slowly growing agreements.

At pertinent places in this volume the author has found the occasion to express his deeply felt gratitude to certain men to whom he is indebted for special services in the creation of this work. In this connection he has to think of his friend, the Rev. P. M. Brosy, his assistant in the earlier stages of this endeavor. The counsel with his co-laborer, Dr. O. W. Heick, through the years, has been very helpful. A much appreciated service, similar to that of the professors R. Seeberg and W. Dress, was given by the scholarly and critical review of his manuscript by Professor W. Petersmann at that time in Eden Theological Seminary.

President Dr. R. E. Tulloss of Wittenberg College was untiring in encouraging and urging the completion of the whole two-volume work. My good wife, Charlotte, assisted both of the authors in the many technical features of their undertaking.

To the Rev. Dr. Paul Zeller Strodach, literary editor of the United Lutheran Publication House, we are deeply indebted for expert care given to these manuscripts which by the nature of this work had to include many technical matters.

Springfield, Ohio
1943

J. L. NEVE.

A HISTORY OF CHRISTIAN THOUGHT

Volume One: History of Christian Doctrine

TABLE OF CONTENTS

BOOK ONE

The Ancient Church

CHAPTER ONE

INTRODUCTORY MATTERS

CHAPTER TWO

PRECURSORY THOUGHT

CHAPTER THREE

CHRISTIANITY OF THE POST-APOSTOLIC FATHERS

x

xi

BOOK TWO

The Middle Ages

class. 3 Confessions under influence of Calvin: (a) Zurich Consensus (Tigurinus); (b) second Helvetic Confession, the Heidelberg Catechism in Germany, the Westminster Confession with Catechism in Great Britain; (c) the Canons of the Synod at Dort, the Confession by Episcopius in Holland for the Arminians.

ACKNOWLEDGMENTS

Credit with much care in quoting author, title, and page has been given throughout this volume to the histories of doctrine: to Adolf von Harnack's various editions, published by Mohr, Tuebingen (including the English translation by Buchanon); to Friedrich Loofs' work, published by Niemeyer, Halle; to Friedrich Wiegand's two small volumes, published by Quelle & Meyer, Leipzig. Special use has been made of R. Seeberg, 2nd and 3rd editions, published by the A. Deichert'sche Verlagsbuchhandlung, Leipzig (the same house from which our Philadelphia publishers secured the right to publish the English edition, now out of print).

Further grateful acknowledgment is made to the following publishers for their courtesy in granting permission to use a few quotations from books of which they control the copyright: To the Board of Christian Education and Publication, Philadelphia, publishers of Geo. W. Richard's *The Heidelberg Catechism;* to The Funk and Wagnalls Company, New York, publishers of the *New Schaff-Herzog Encyclopedia;* to Mrs. Sarah C. Birch, owner of the copyright of T. Bruce Birch, *De Sacramento Altaris;* to The Macmillan Company, publishers of V. Ferm, *What Is Lutheranism?,* and E. Brunner, *The Mediator* (Miss O. Wyon, translator); to the Harvard University Press for use of the text in Kirsopp Lake, *Apostolic Fathers.*

To Dr. O. W. Heick I express my appreciation for preparing the topical index.

BOOK ONE
The Ancient Church
Chapter One
INTRODUCTORY MATTERS

I. SUBJECT MATTER AND METHOD

1. *Are We Justified in Calling This Work a History of Christian Thought?*

In expressing himself on the subject matter to be dealt with in this work, the author must not limit himself to this first volume but must also consider the discussions planned for the second volume. Volume Two will be pre-eminently a *History of Protestant Theology* which is to include many theological developments aiming at a reconstruction of doctrinal theology, liberalistically or conservatively.

a. Much of this work on the "History of Christian Thought" concerns itself with the *History of the Confessions.* This relates primarily to the history of the Ancient Church and of the Reformation. It should not be overlooked, however, that a large part of the discussion of the Ancient Church had but a very indirect reference to the development of the dogma.[1] The section on the Middle Ages also must take in much material which is only distantly related to the dogma of the Church. This holds true in a high degree regarding developments following the post-Reformation age.

b. In distinguishing between dogma and general Christian thought, the following may be said: In the dogma, i.e., in the Confessions of the Church, we have the tangible results of fundamental Christian thought on matters of divine revelation. Such thought, crystallized into final formulated statements and received by the Church, is honored by the name dogma. The Church Fathers designated their reliable and authoritative doctrines of faith as dogmas over against the mere opinions, the δόξαι of the philosophers and heretics. Gradually the Nicene Creed came to be regarded as dogma in the strictest sense. The modern man is inclined to turn away from authorized doctrines, from a κανὼν τῆς ἀληθείας, from a *regula fidei,* that is, from doctrines claiming to be rules of faith. But we must think of the situation in which Christianity found itself. The message of salvation through Christ was to be brought to a world in which all the influences of a pagan philosophy and of religious heresies of every description were at work to oppose and to counteract that message.[2] Surely, the young Church was in need of confessional guides and of actual "rules" of faith. These, as expressions of the Church's experience, came to be recognized as public Confessions, and have through the centuries guided the peoples of many races in their religious life. Surely we would not put the Apostles' Creed, the Nicene Creed, the Augsburg Confession, the Thirty-Nine Articles, and the Westminster Confession on one level with general Christian thought.

---

[1] See for instance our portraits of some of the great theologians in Chapter VIII on the "Old Catholic Theologians."

[2] See Chapter V on the "Perversions of Christianity."

1

The title of this work has been chosen chiefly for the larger freedom it leaves to include matters of general theological interest. This freedom will be much needed in the study of the Middle Ages, and more so in the second volume, in which we must deal with the development of theological positions under the influence of modern philosophy.

   c. Argumentation with regard to the Problem of Method. Adolph von Harnack in his own way, Friederich Loofs and Reinhold Seeberg, preceded by others, have made "History of Dogma"—*Dogmengeschichte*—the standing title for the branch of theology here dealt with. This special interest in the "dogma" of the Church, even on the part of liberalism, is easily explained. Rationalism had overtaken the church of Germany in the eighteenth century and discredited the historic dogma as expressed in the so-called "ecumenical creeds of Christendom." In the struggle between the conflicting theological tendencies—the radicals, the conservatives, and the middle-of-the-road men ("Supra-naturalists")—there arose a need for tracing with historical criticism the genesis of this confessional quantity which claimed authority in the Church. This was the task which W. Muenscher, the "father of German *Dogmengeschichte*," set for himself, and in which he was supported by a number of like-minded historians who followed him. But there has been considerable reaction in Germany against limiting the subject matter of *Dogmengeschichte* to the Confessions officially recognized. Loofs gives a complicated discussion of the whole situation in his article on *Dogmengeschichte*, volume 4 of the *Protestantische Realencyclopaedie* [3] (*PRE*). See especially pages 760 ff.; cf. also G. Krueger: *Was heisst und zu welchem Ende studiert man Dogmengeschichte?* 1895. Prof. Carl Stange wrote on *Das Dogma und seine Beurteilung in der neueren Dogmen-geschichte*, 1898. He criticized, against Harnack, Loofs and Kaftan, the traditional conception of *Dogmengeschichte*. Then followed Otto Ritschl with his four volumes on *Dogmengeschichte des Protestantismus*, 1908-1927. See in his Prolegomena to this work the argument with which he turns against Loofs and Seeberg, who insist upon closing the History of Dogma with the Confessions of the sixteenth century and then call what follows a History of Protestant Theology.

   It is interesting to observe that the three American writers on this subject (W. G. T. Shedd, H. C. Sheldon and G. P. Fisher) all exchanged the title "History of Dogma" for that of "History of Doctrine," because they wanted to include in their treatment the movements that ensued in the time after the establishment of the dogma of the Reformation. On the point under consideration here, there is no essential difference between History of Doctrine and History of Christian Thought. Both include in their investigations much that has not yet crystallized into publicly recognized dogmas.

   d. But will not the title "History of Christian Thought" obligate us to deal not only with the history of doctrine, *but also with the history of Christian Ethics?* To this we ask in turn: Even though pre-eminence must be given to the doctrines of the Church in the parts of this work which are devoted to the history of dogma, is it not a fact that we must of necessity include the corresponding ideas of Christian Ethics? In the *Didache* we read of the "Two Ways," the way of life and the way of death. The Montanist, the Novatian, the Donatist movements, and the attitudes expressed respectively by the writer of Hermas, by Tertullian, Cyprian, Callistus and Augustine, were stimulated by an intense interest in the ethical purity of the Church. In the Middle Ages the problem of repentance became an outstanding concern. In this problem Luther found the starting point for the Reformation. Read in this connection Article XII of the Augsburg Confession, which concerns repentance, and the articles on the same subject in the other Protestant Confessions. In history the subjects of Dogmatics and Ethics are intimately related. Thus there can be no serious objection to our choice of title on the ground here referred to. In history, ethics is inseparable from dogma.

2. Ready, then, to write under the title "History of Christian Thought," we may ask the question: *How can we limit ourselves in the review of the seemingly limitless material that lies before us?* He who aims to tie himself to the history of the dogma alone has his convenient limitations in the history of the publicly recognized doctrines. But even in our broader field there are a few lines of limitation that seem serviceable.

a. Our title holds us to what is *history* of Christian thought. We must be on our guard against losing ourselves in dogmatizing and polemics. Our task is always an historical one. The aim of the historian of course will not relieve him from the duty of criticism. But there is a characteristic difference between polemicizing for dogmatic purposes and objective historical criticism.

b. Furthermore, it must be our aim to confine our critical historical reviews to the interest of *historic Christianity.* There are radical forms of religion that have abandoned entirely the foundations of the Christian Church. These must be dealt with as we have done in Chapter V of this book on the *Perversions of Christianity,* and as we must do in several of the chapters of Volume Two. Such discussions, however, must always keep in view the doctrinal interests of historic Christianity. We are not studying history of philosophy, even though we must frequently review developments in the field of philosophy; our aim is to trace the history of Christian thought and to draw the lessons from that study.

Note: On the "Lundensian Theology" see below, III, ii, and Volume II.

II. ORIENTATION WITH REGARD TO ORIGINAL SOURCES
(Concerning the Ancient Church)

1. *The Minutes of the Councils:* These frequently give not only resolutions, but also discussions. The following may be mentioned:
    a. HARDOUIN, J. *Collectio Maxima Conciliorium Generalium et Provincialium,* 12 vols., Paris, 1715.
    b. MANSI, J. DOM., *Collectio Sacrorum Conciliorum,* 31 vols., Florence and Venice, 1759-1798. Best collection. New print, 1903.
    c. BRIGHT, W., *Notes on the Canons of the First Four General Councils,* 2nd ed., Macmillan and Co., New York, 1892.
    d. FULTON, J., *Index Canonum,* New York, 1892.
    e. MITCHELL, E. K., *Canons of the First Four General Councils,* University of Pennsylvania, Philadelphia, 1898.
    f. BOYD, *The Ecclesiastical Edicts of the Theodosian Code,* 24 vols. The Columbia University Press, Macmillan and Co., Agents, New York, 1905.
    g. O'LEARY, L. E., *The Apostolic Constitution and Cognate Documents,* New York, 1906.
    h. SCHWARTZ, E., *Edition of the Councils,* Munich, 1937.
2. *Histories of the Councils:*
    a. HAMMOND, W. A., *The Six Ecumenical Councils,* Oxford, 1843.

     b. HEFELE, VON., *Konziliengeschichte,* 9 vols., 1855 ff.; 2nd ed., vols. 1-3, 1873-1890. French ed., 8 vols., Letuozay et Ane, Paris, 1907-1921.

     c. DU BOSE, *The Ecumenical Councils,* 4th ed., Scribner's Sons, New York, 1910.

3. *Writings of the Church Fathers:*

     a. MIGNE, J. P., *Patrologiae cursus completus - - - qui ab Aevo Apostolico ad Tempora Innocentii* III (anno 1216) *pro Latinis et ad Concilii Florentini Tempora* (anno 1439). *MSG—Series Scriptoresque Ecclesiae Graecae,* 161 vols., 1857-1904; *pro Graecia Floruerunt,* Paris, 1867. *MSL—Series Latina,* 221 vols., Paris, 1844-1904.

     b. *Maxima Bibliotheca Patrum,* 27 vols., since 1677.

     c. CSEL—*Corpus Scriptorum Ecclesiasticorum Latinorum,* Vienna ed., since 1866 (not yet completed).

     d. GEBHARDT, O. VON and HARNACK, A., *Texte und Untersuchungen (TU),* Leipzig, 1882 ff.

     e. *Texts and Studies,* following the *TU* ed., by J. A. Robinson, since 1891.

     f. *Die griechischen Schriftsteller der drei ersten Jahrhunderte,* edited by the Berlin Academy, since 1897.

     g. CAMBRIDGE, *Patristic Texts,* since 1899.

     h. LIETZMANN, H., *Kleine Texte,* since 1902.

     i. *The American Library of "The Ante-Nicene" and of "The Nicene and Post-Nicene Fathers,"* 1885 ff.

This last-named collection of 35 large volumes, which has wide circulation and is found in all ecclesiastical and in many private libraries in America and England, will be used more than any of the above mentioned sources. Many, even of the critically minded students, may want to use this translation for a temporary orientation before they go to a text in the original language which is not always available. Such students will appreciate the convenience of a connected view of a complete table of contents, *which otherwise could be had only by the inconvenience of going from book to book all through the 35 volumes of this set.* We therefore offer the following prospectus:[3]

Part One

    1. *The Ante-Nicene Fathers (ANF).* This *first section* of 9 volumes offers translations of the writings of the Fathers down to A.D. 325. Originally, the writings in these volumes were published in Edinburgh by T. and T. Clark in the "Ante-Nicene Christian Library" of 24 small volumes (1866-1872) under the editorship of Alexander Roberts and James Donaldson. The American reprint of this Edinburgh edition was "revised and chronologically arranged with brief prefaces and occasional notes" by A. Cleveland Coxe, and published in Buffalo (Christian Literature Company) 1885-1886.

    The contents, with date of publication of each volume, read as follows:

      I. The Apostolic Fathers with Justin Martyr and Irenaeus, including Clement of Rome, *Ep. to Diognetus* Polycarp, *Ep. of Barnabas,* Papias—1885.

      II. Pastor of Hermas, Tatian, Theophilus, Athenagoras, Clement of Alexandria —1885.

      III. Tertullian (25 writings) grouped in 3 parts—1885.

      IV. Tertullian, part 4 (9 writings), Minucius Felix, Commodianus, Origen (6 writings, including *De Principiis* and *Against Celsus*)—1885.

      V. Hippolytus, Cyprian, Caius, Novatian, Appendix, which includes Novatian in 31 chapters *On the Trinity*—1886.

      VI. Gregory Thaumaturgus, Dionysius the Great, Julius Africanus, Anatolius, Minor writers, Methodius, Arnobius—1886.

---

[3] It goes without saying that a work of this nature published between 1885 and 1900 cannot be up-to-date in its historical introductions and that also the translation of the texts in a collection of so many volumes has defects which are absent in the more recent endeavors, such as those of Kirsopp Lake, the TU and others in sectional publications of the Fathers. It also must not be overlooked that these translations date from a time when the ready use of Greek and Latin was not yet a lost art.

VII. Lactantius, Minor writers, *Teaching of the Apostles, Constitutions, Early Liturgies*—1886.
VIII. Patriarch, *Excerpts and Epistles, Pseudo-Clementine Literature, Apocrypha of the New Testament, Decretals, Syriac Documents, Remains*—1886.
IX. Appendix, Bibliographical Symposis and Index—1886.

Part Two

The *second section* of the American Library, which is the *First Series* of a "Select Library of the Nicene and Post-Nicene Fathers," was edited by Philip Schaff (New York, 1886-1889).

To complete the plan of an American Edition, Philip Schaff "in connection with a number of patristic scholars of Europe and America" (see the prefaces) in 1886 undertook the task of adding to the 9 previously described volumes containing the Ante-Nicene Fathers, the Nicene and Post-Nicene Library. The task was begun in 1886 and finished in 1890. This series contains the following writings:

I. Augustine: *Prolegomena, Confessions, Letters*—1886.
II. Augustine: *City of God, Christian Doctrine*—1887.
III. Augustine: *On the Holy Trinity, Doctrinal Treatises, Moral Treatises*—1887.
IV. Augustine: *Anti-Manichaean* and *Anti-Donatist Writings*—1887.
V. Augustine: *Anti-Pelagian Writings*—1887.
VI. Augustine: *Sermon on the Mount, Harmony of the Gospels, Homilies on the Gospels*—1888.
VII. Augustine: *Gospel of St. John, First Epistle of St. John, Soliloquies*—1888.
VIII. Augustine: *Expositions on the Psalms*—1888.
IX. Chrysostom: *On the Priesthood, Ascetic Treatises, Select Homilies and Letters, Homilies on the Statues*—1889.
X. Chrysostom: *Gospel of St. Matthew*—1888.
XI. Chrysostom: *Homilies on Acts and Romans*—1889.
XII. Chrysostom: *Homilies on First and Second Corinthians*—1889.

Part Three

The *third section* of the American Edition which is the *Second Series* of "the Select Library of the Nicene and Post-Nicene Fathers" was translated into English under the editorial supervision of Philip Schaff and Henry Wace, 14 volumes (New York, 1890-1900).

The following is the list of contents with the date of publication of each volume:

I. Eusebius: *Church History, Life of Constantine the Great, Oration in Praise of Constantine*—1890.
II. Socrates: *Church History*, and Sozomenus: *Church History*—1890.
III. Theodoret, Jerome, Genadius, Rufinus—1892.
IV. Athanasius: *Select Works and Letters*—1893.
V. Gregory of Nyssa: *Select Works and Letters*—1893.
VI. Jerome: *Select Works and Letters*—1893.
VII. Cyril of Jerusalem, Gregory of Nazianzūs—1894.
VIII. St. Basil: *Select Works and Letters*—1895.
IX. Hilary of Poitiers, John of Damascus—1899.
X. St. Ambrose: *Select Works and Letters*—1896.
XI. Sulpitius Severus, Vincent of Lerins, John Cassain—1894.
XII. Leo the Great, Gregory the Great—1895.
XIII. Gregory the Great, Ephraem Syrus, Aphrahat—1898.
XIV. *The Seven Ecumenical Councils*—1900.

j. The Oxford Library. In closing this section on the Sources it must not be left unmentioned, that as a predecessor to the writings of the Fathers in this American edition (besides the above mentioned contents of the first section) there is the so-called "Oxford Library." (Title: *A Library of Fathers of the Holy Catholic Church anterior to the Division of the East and West.*) This "Oxford Library" consists of 48 volumes which were translated and published under the direction of Edward B. Pusey, John Keble and John Henry Newman (1837-1845). Parts of this collection have supplementary value for the *ANF* and *PNF*, edited by Schaff.

In his preface to the "first series" of the *Select Library of the Nicene and Post-Nicene Fathers*, Vol. I, Dr. Schaff characterizes the Oxford Library as follows: "The Oxford Library was undertaken not so much for an historical as for an apologetic and dogmatic purpose. It was to furnish authentic proof for the supposed or real agreement of the Anglo-Catholic school with the faith and practice of the Ancient Church before the Greek schism. The selection was made accordingly. . . . It is very valuable as far as it goes, but incomplete and unequal. Volume followed volume as it happened to get ready. An undue proportion is given to exegetical works; six volumes are taken up with Augustine's *Commentary on the Psalms*, six with Gregory's *Commentary on Job*, sixteen with Commentaries of Chrysostom; while many of the most important doctrinal, ethical and historical works of the Fathers, as Eusebius, Basil, the two Gregorys, Theodoret, Maximus Confessor, John of Damascus, Hilary, Jerome, Leo the Great, were never reached."

k. A German Translation of the Fathers. Roman Catholic scholars in Germany, under the supervision of Dr. Valentin Thalhofer, formerly professor in Munich, translated many writings of the Fathers into German. They were published in Kempten by the Koeselsche Buchhandlung in over 400 small numbers, three or four in one volume (1869-1886). Seven volumes were devoted to letters of the popes. The selection has been made with special regard to the interest of the Roman Catholic Church. The World War I interrupted considerably the completion of a second edition, edited by Brandenhewer, Scherman and Weymann. (*K B²*.)

III. Brief Review of the History of Dogma as a Branch in the Study of Theology

Literature: F. LOOFS on *Dogmengeschichte* in HAUCK's *Protestantische Realencyclopaedie³* (PRE), Volume IV, 752-764. Cf. the *New Schaff-Herzog Encyclopedia* (NSH); also LOOFS, *Leitfaden zum Studium der DG⁴*, see the Introduction.

1. The Middle Ages saw no object in a study of the History of Dogma, because the teaching of the Church was held to have been believed "everywhere, always and by all" (*ubique semper et ab omnibus*). These were the words of Vincent of Lerins (d. 434). The dogma was there from the beginning of the Church. Only the assimilation of it had been gradual, and of this alone has there been a history. This is correct. But we must not overlook the intense historical, human development in the gradual working out of the principles and issues and in the final formulation of Christian truth. The mistake of the Church in the Middle Ages lay in its conception of tradition as a quantity that was handed down from age to age and that was not subject to the purifying process of criticism. Thus there was no room for a real history of the dogma.

2. The Reformation opened the path for a real history of the dogma. Luther established himself on the principle that dogmas have no authority in the decrees of the councils and popes, but only in the Scriptures (See his tract *"Von den Conciliis"* etc. W. Ed. 25, 240 ff.). This did away with the principle that creedal statements, because made by councils, must be adopted without investigation. The Lutheran Reformers at the outset had unbounded confidence in the doctrinal developments of the first five centuries. Nevertheless, Luther expressed a criticism of the ὁμοούσιος in the Nicene Creed. Melanchthon averred the observing of certain Platonic influences upon the early

Christian doctrines.[4] He found a strong adulteration of the Christian dogma in the ages following Leo the Great. Flacius, in his pioneer work on Christian History, characterized these Centuries (*Centurien*) as a continuous process of beclouding the specifically evangelical doctrines, with a lonely witness to the truth now and then, incapable, however, of arresting the fatal development. Such views stimulated inquiry and historical investigation. The conservatism of the latter part of the sixteenth century and of the seventeenth did not, however, encourage any critical attitude toward the "ecumenical creeds."

3. *Illumination and Rationalism.* G. Arnold, a theologian of the Pietist group, blazed the trail by his *Unparteiische Kirchen und Ketzerhistorie,* 1699 f., a work in which he made it his object to show that orthodoxy is fallible, and that the truer expressions of piety have come from the heretics and the sects. The men of the Enlightenment, then, declared the creedal statements of the past to be historical problems which must be investigated with regard to origin, development and validity for succeeding generations. It was his interest in this investigation that made Wilhelm Muenscher, a theologian of the rationalist school, the father of the modern History of Dogma. The interest that guided him in his presentation was: How and by what agencies has the Christian dogma gradually received the character and form in which we have it today? His writings on the subject were the following: *Handbuch der Christlichen Dogmengeschichte,* 4 volumes, 1797 ff. (covering the first six centuries); *Lehrbuch der Christlichen DG,* 3 editions, 1811-1832[5]. In the main it must be said that these men, in observing the changes in the development, failed to see and evaluate the abiding elements of truth in the dogmas of the succeeding ages.

4. *Schleiermacher's influence* upon the History of Dogma has also been felt. He was interested in the element of continuity in the new life of Christianity. This is an emphasis that can be observed of *A. Neander* (1857), and *K. R. Hagenbach* (1840). *Baumgarten-Crusius* (1832) and *E. M. Engelhardt* (1839) also belong to this class. To Engelhardt reference must be made below, section 7.

5. A contribution from Hegel's conception of history came through the writings of F. C. BAUR: *Lehrbuch der Christlichen Dogmengeschichte,* 3rd ed., 1847-1867. Back of the individual phenomena in history he saw and pointed to the great motives, to the idea of Christianity, which develops with an inner necessity.

Many of Baur's "results" were unacceptable to the men of the Church. It is of interest to observe that this same Hegelian principle of development offered itself as a workable basis to a group of confessional Lutherans. Thus T. KLIEFOTH in his *Einleitung in die Dogmengeschichte,* 1839, saw in the History of Dogma the organic unfolding of Christian truth in the life of the Church. In this conception is seen also the influence descending from Schleiermacher. Especially must be mentioned G. THOMASIUS, *Die Christliche Dogmengeschichte als Entwicklungsgeschichte des kirchlichen Lehrbegriffs,* 2 vols., 1874 ff.; supplemented and modified in a 2nd ed. by N. BONWETSCH and R. SEEBERG, 1886 ff. The aim of Thomasius was to describe the dogma as a development starting from the revelation of Scripture and issuing in the (Lutheran) Reformation of the sixteenth century. In the exhibition of the development there is a constant distinc-

---

[4] *Loci,* ed. Plitt-Kolde[3], 1900, p. 65.
[5] On further literature of the same kind see Seeberg in the various editions of his work; Loofs in *PRE*[3], IV. 752 ff.

tion between theological opinion and crystallized dogma. All the succeeding Histories of Dogma received much from this remarkably rich work of Thomasius. There are more writers on History of Dogma that were influenced by the Hegelian conception of history. We mention P. MARHEINEKE, H. SCHMID (4th ed. by A. HAUCK, 1887), K. F. A. KAHNIS (*Der Kirchenglaube historisch-genetisch dargestellt,* 1864), A. DORNER (*Grundriss der Dogmengeschichte,* 1889) who combined influences from SCHLEIER-MACHER and HEGEL, and F. NITZSCH (*Grundriss der Dogmengeschichte,* Vol. 1).

6. ADOLPH VON HARNACK wrote a work on the History of Dogma in three large volumes. This work is altogether in a class by itself and has become famous. It appeared between 1886 and 1890 under the title *Lehrbuch der Dogmengeschichte.* From the 3rd edition (1894-1897) it was translated into English in seven volumes by N. Buchanan (1894-1903). Harnack also prepared a *Grundriss* of his work which in 1922 saw its 6th edition, a book of 486 pages. Earlier editions of this volume were translated into English. This volume has been used much, first in its 4th and later in its 6th edition.[6]

Harnack developed under special influences from Albrecht Ritschl and was con-vinced that a confessional Christianity (*dogmatisches Christentum*) has no future in the Church. He admits that the History of Dogma is a witness to the unity of the Christian faith, because it shows that the central significance of Christ and the funda-mentals of the Gospel have maintained themselves in the face of all attacks.[7] Yet, as Bonwetsch remarks, Harnack has presented the History of Dogma as "issuing in the dissolution of the dogma" (*als in die Aufloesung des Dogmas muendend*).[8] Harnack himself closes his introductory review of the "conception and aim of the History of Dogma" with the statement that the History of Dogma is the best way of liberating the Church from the "*dogmatisches Christentum.*"[9]

By "dogma" Harnack means particularly the dogma of the Ancient Church, more especially the Christological dogma, as it found expression in the theology of the "Rules of Faith" in the Nicene and Apostles' Creeds and was completed in its fundamental outlines about the year 300—"a conception of the Greek mind in the realm (*auf dem Boden*) of the Gospel"—and was recognized by the Church in the fourth and fifth centuries.[10]

This dogma, Harnack insists, has become antiquated, as he undertakes to show by referring to its three distinct issues: (1) In the *Eastern Orthodox Church,* after a devel-opment that closed with John of Damascus, it became petrified; the life of this church today lies in its cultus. (2) For the *Roman Catholic Church* this Greek dogma under-went a modification through the Augustinian system, preserving, however, in the Decrees of Trent, its specifically Hellenistic character. But the later Vatican dogma of the infalli-bility of the pope practically shelved these decrees and made obedience to the hierarchy the controlling principle. (3) *The Protestant Reformers,* as Harnack continues, took over the Greek dogma, but in contradiction of their own principles regarding the matter

---

[6] As to a few estimates of Harnack while he was still living see Loofs in *PRE*[3], Vol. 739 f.; also in his *DG*[4], pp. 5-7; Bonwetsch, *Grundriss der Dogmengeschichte* pp. 7 ff.; R. Seeberg, *DG* I[3], 24 f., 13, 16; Wiegand, *DG* 1, 4 f. (cf. his popular edition of 1928 I, 9 f.); G. P. Fisher, *History of Doctrine,* pp. 2 f.

[7] On Harnack's meaning of the significance of Christ and the Gospel see his book *Das Wesen des Christ-entums,* 1900 ff. In English translation by Saunders, 1901.

[8] N. Bonwetsch, *DG*[2], p. 7.

[9] *Grundriss*[6], p. 6. He stresses the element of flux and constant development in doctrine and theology. ("*Das Dogma hat stets im Fortgang der Geschichte seine eignen Vaeter verschlungen,*" p. 5)

[10] Cf. Loofs in *PRE*[3], Vol. IV, 760, lines 21-25.

of doctrinal authority in the Church; for dogmas are admitted to be always subject to revision. The Lutheran Church particularly is at fault because of its adherence to a dogmatic Christianity.[11]

Upon the basis of his conception that the History of Dogma issues in its own dissolution, Harnack now naturally has no interest in following the history of confessional development in the age of the Reformation. So he stops his special investigation with the Council of Trent and with a brief report on Protestantism in its first stage of doctrinal development. The doctrinal "inconsistencies" of the Reformers and their differences among themselves are left by Harnack to be treated in a special department of Church History. It is of great interest to note that in this radical limitation of the History of Dogma to the particular dogma of the Ancient Church, its rise and dissolution, Harnack has had no successors, not even in the confessionally independent Loofs who dedicated his own work to him *in Dankbarkeit und Freundschaft*.

The popularity of Harnack's work has its explanation: (1) Its publication fell into an age of widest opposition to dogma and creeds. Harnack does not really deny the inner impulse of Christianity to express its faith and its convictions in public statements, but he looks upon the binding significance of such statements as something that has never generally functioned in the Church and is incapable of functioning. In his indifference to this interest and armed with an immense store of learning, he made himself the historian of anti-creedal attitude in the field of History of Dogma itself. In this he was bound to become the leader of many outside of the Lutheran Church, for there especially a milder conception of confessions of faith has always been recognized. (2) His work appeared at a time when the Ritschlian points of emphasis were an attraction to many theologians in Germany and abroad. (3) He offered an entirely new method in dealing with the History of Dogma as a branch of theology. The traditional categories for organization of the material were dismissed, the details of his outlines were dictated by the genetical development. Harnack takes much from the characterization of personalities and from the situation of the times. A conspicuous feature lies in the repeated attempts to view many individual events as an expression of conditions in the Church as a whole, often leaving the critical reader with the feeling that the author has risked too much in conjecturing.

We may close this review of Harnack with the following evaluation by R. Seeberg: "A many sidedness of historical viewpoints, unity and energy in raising questions, a vivid doctrinal interest and a fascinating manner of presentation have secured for this work a far-reaching influence upon future endeavors in the field of the History of Dogma."[12]

7. It is of interest to observe that the three authors next to be mentioned (Loofs, Seeberg and Wiegand) have not followed Harnack in limiting the History of Dogma to the special "Hellenistic" dogma of the Ancient Church and its supposed dissolution in the opening stages of the Protestant Reformation. They have continued rather and improved the historico-genetic method begun with Muenscher and further developed by Gieseler and Engelhardt, who were the first to succeed in liberating themselves from Hegelian influences introduced by Baur.[13]

---

[11] As to that much discussed "Hellenization" of the dogma in the early Church, Harnack soon saw his cherished emphasis swept into the background and overtaken by the syncretistic wave introduced by the "Historico-Religious School" with its doctrine that original Christianity (*Urchristentum*) had to share its identity with the oriental ideas and cults in the Roman world of this period. See in our Vol. II, *The Historico-Religious School.*

[12] *DG* I³, 24.

[13] See Loofs, *PRE* Vol. IV, 757, line 54.

It was in 1889 that FRIEDERICH LOOFS first published his famous *Leitfaden zum Studium der Dogmengeschichte*. Its fourth edition of 1906 presents a volume of 1002 pages. It was intended chiefly as a guide for students. Although differing from Harnack as to results, it follows him in method.[14] Especially does Loofs make large concessions to Harnack's way of picturing the contemporary history as a contributing factor in the evolution of the dogmas. There is that constant aim to derive the essentials of doctrine from an analysis of the leading personalities.

Outstanding in usefulness for the Church is REINHOLD SEEBERG's *Lehrbuch der Dogmengeschichte*. It was first published in 1895-1898 in two volumes, with an English translation by C. A. Hay. This work starts with the conception of the Scriptures as a foundation and standard of truth, and then it treats the dogmas as relatively independent developments. Seeberg was far more conservative than Harnack or even Loofs. This is noticeable not only in his organization of the material but especially in his fundamental harmony with the general confessional positions of Kliefoth, Thomasius and Schmid, even though in details we see in him the representative of a "modern-positive" movement. On this movement, however, see *RGG*,[2] Vol. IV, 126 f. While indebted to Seeberg in very many ways—he has been a personal friend to the writer and has aided him in many ways—I could not follow him in the Antiochean Christology of Theodore of Mopsuestia as developed in the later editions of his great work. But in other respects Seeberg has given to his History of Dogma the character of a practical guide, relating his material to the real problems of the Churches, even to the Denominations (*"Konfessionskirchen"*). Cf. his Vol. I[3], 8 ff. and so many places in all volumes; see especially Vol. IV[3] and the 4th ed, IV, A. There is an indescribable wealth of ideas discussed in this work of R. Seeberg. He has also published an outline (*Grundriss*) for instruction and review, 173 pages. The last (5th) edition of this little book appeared in revised form, 1927. He passed away October 23, 1935. (Highly interesting is Seeberg's personal estimate of his own theology in E. STANGE's, *Die Religionswissenschaft in Selbstdarstellungen*, Vol. I, 173 ff.) For the appreciation of Seeberg as a personality see the published address of his colleague, Prof. A. Deissmann, at his funeral.

F. WIEGAND with his *Dogmengeschichte* in two small volumes (1912, 1919) shares in many ways the characteristics of Loofs and Seeberg. He has many references to Harnack, but he covers the whole of the History of Dogma. The readable way in which he reviews the well organized material constitutes the pedagogical value of this little work (Volume I has 141, Volume II 176 pages). We call special attention to Wiegand's lucid orientation in presenting the sources. His remarkable gift for popularizing and still covering the essential issues, is seen in his three little volumes on *Dogmengeschichte* totaling 373 pages, published by Walter de Gruyter and Co., Berlin, 1928-1929 (*Sammlung Goeschen*).

In addition to the "Outlines" (*Grundrisse*) mentioned (Schmid, Hauck, Harnack, Seeberg, and Wiegand), there is one by N. Bonwetsch (206 pages, 1909, with a second edition in 1919). We mention also the one written in English by E. H. Klotsche (262 pages, Lutheran Literary Board, Burlington, Iowa, U. S. A., 1926).

8. We shall refer to three American writers on "History of Doctrine" and describe them as aiming at a discussion not just of the dogma, but of all doctrinal interests:

---

[14] See his comment on Harnack in *PRE* IV, 759, lines 15-21.

W. G. T. SHEDD (*History of Christian Doctrine,* in two volumes, 3rd ed., 1877) in the preface confesses his indebtedness to the historians of Germany, but also to the great lights of the English Church, such as "Hooker and Bull, Pearson and Waterland." He mentions especially Baumgarten-Crusius and Hagenbach as having "to some extent furnished the rubrics under which the generalizations have been made, as well as considerable material itself" (p. 8). On the Reformation Shedd writes as a strict Calvinist. Against his treatment of Lutheranism, CHARLES PORTERFIELD KRAUTH, in his *Conservative Reformation,* 1871, pp. 329-354, directed a searching critique. Shedd's method is the now generally abandoned topological one, with the special matters preceded by a general introduction. The history of each topic is followed through the ages up to the present, including Latitudinarianism and Unitarianism and closing with a history of the Confessions in the manner of an introduction to Comparative Symbolics.[15]

H. SHELDON (*History of Christian Doctrine* in two volumes, 3rd. ed., 1901) also uses the topological method. But he discusses the topics in a review of five periods: 90 to 320; 320 to 726; 726 to 1517; 1517 to 1720; 1720 to 1895. The categories for this topical treatment are always the same: (1) The Godhead; (2) Creation and Creatures; (3) Redeemer and Redemption; (4) Church and Sacraments; (5) Eschatology. In the last "period" he speaks with regard to *Germany* of Leibnitz, Wolff, Kant, Fichte, Schelling, Lotze, Hegel, Schleiermacher, Schopenhauer, v. Hartmann, Herbart; with regard to *France and England* of Comte, J. Mill, J. St. Mill, Spencer; so also of the Moravians, Methodists, Arminians, Baptists, Swedenborgians, Unitarians, Universalists, of the theological schools on the Continent and in England, of the denominations in America, etc. This shows how the author takes the liberty of departing from the History of Doctrine and makes his work a History of Christian Thought, even approaching a History of Philosophy of Religion.

G. P. FISHER in his *History of Christian Doctrine,* 1886 ff., abandoned the topological method. He also abandoned the traditional arrangement of the material under the heads General and Special Doctrinal History. The German precursor in this was Engelhardt.[16] To him Fisher feels himself indebted. In this way he also mentions Neander, Schaff, Moeller, Harnack, Loofs, Baur and the Ritschlian writers. Seeberg's great work was not yet in the field when Fisher wrote—not even in its first two volumes, not to speak of its present form in four large volumes (the double volume four alone has 989 pages). Nor had the work of Loofs seen its fourth much modified and amplified edition. The treatment of Fisher presents a natural history in distinct units. He had an appreciation of what Ritschl wrote against the "anatomical" procedure of the old topological method, and he followed his demand for a "physiological" procedure, by which was meant a treatment of the matter in the connections in which it actually and chronologically presented itself.[17] Fisher also, in dealing with all the modern schools of theology, made his work a History of Christian Thought, although his title is "History of Christian Doctrine." The work of Fisher must be supported by a lecturer with a wealth of additional information and an intuition for historical observation in order that the contents may be made sufficiently impressive for pedagogical purposes. Yet the painstaking fairness and moderation of Fisher in every respect has attracted many readers.

---

[15] As to precursors in this method in Germany cf. the article on *DG* by Loofs in *PRE* IV, 757, line 50; also p. 758, line 27.
[16] Cf. Loofs, *PRE* IV, 757, line 60.
[17] A. Ritschl in *Jahrbuecher fuer deutsche Theologie,* 1871, pp. 191 ff. Cf. Fisher, p. 16.

9. ARTHUR CUSHMAN McGIFFERT, first American student of Adolph Harnack, was a professor in Union Theological Seminary, New York. His book on *The Apostles' Creed* (1902) had in the main the position of Harnack as expressed in his article on this same subject in the *PRE*.[3] He was an independent, moderately liberal theologian of the Ritschlian type. His two books, *Protestant Thought before Kant* (1911) and *The Rise of Modern Religious Ideas* (1924) are written with the orientating judgments of a matured scholarship. A generation of students was moulded by the course of his subjects in Union Theological Seminary. Toward the end of his life he published a *History of Christian Thought* in two volumes. In the first volume (1932) he dealt with the New Testament origins of Christian Thought and with the Fathers of the Eastern Church; in the second (1933) with the developments in the West beginning with Tertullian and closing with Erasmus. He had intended to add a third volume on the history of Modern Thought, enlarging upon the contents of his above mentioned two smaller books along this line. But his departure came before this volume could be finished. He died in 1934. It should be added that McGiffert was also the author of a Life of Luther (*Martin Luther, the Man and His Work,* 1911) which has been widely appreciated.

10. Here we must pause for a moment and look at the *contributions from Great Britain*. The English theologians have written very ably on the same materials treated by the Germans, yet in a different way.

We have the book by J. F. BETHUNE-BAKER, *An Introduction to Early History of Christian Doctrine to the Time of the Council of Chalcedon,* 1903. The title at once characterizes this treatment as a monograph. And this is the British peculiarity to which we call attention. Most of the English writings in this field are monographs. We have referred to a number of them in this first volume. As a rule they deal with doctrinal problems such as Trinity, Christology, The Holy Spirit, The Sacraments, Predestination, preferably with the many questions in controversy between Conformists and Nonconformists.

English historians have liked especially to center their interest upon outstanding personages of the Ancient Church. Thus we have the *Theology of Justin Martyr* (E. R. Goodenough), *The Theology of Tertullian* (R. E. Roberts), *The Meaning of Homoousios* centering about the personality of Athanasius (J. F. Bethune-Baker), *Nestorius and His Teachings, Apollinarianism* (C. E. Ravens), *The Commentary of Pelagius on the Epistles of Paul* (A. Souter). There is a scholarship in these monographic productions that is not second to that of the Germans. The inclination to conduct the investigations in the form of monograph and biography may have its explanation in the aim of the Anglo-Saxon mind to present the varied things in units of tangible reality.[18]

It would be misleading, however, to think that the English writers have no aptitude for a larger combination of Christian thought; their monographs often present great combinations. True, they have not created Histories of Dogma such as those of Thomasius, Harnack, Loofs and Seeberg. But they have shown peculiar aptitude in presenting critical investigations which deal constructively with the materials of the whole field. The influence of Harnack is observable in most of them. We mention the following: PERCY GARDNER, *Growth of Christianity,* 1907. Cf. his book *Evolution in*

---

[18] This is the suggestion of W. Vollrath in his book *Theologie der Gegenwart in Grossbritannien,* pp. 142 ff.

Christian Doctrine, 1918; also *Christianity in History, a Study of Religious Development,* 1917, by J. V. BARTLET and A. J. CARLYLE; and earlier than these the very stimulating but much criticized book, written in America (Cambridge) by A. V. G. ALLEN on *The Continuity of Christian Thought: a Study of Modern Theology in the Light of its History,* 1884.

Note: This book by Allen grew out of an attempt to take refuge from the Augustinian and Western tradition by going back to Clement of Alexandria, Origen and Athanasius. See C. L. Slattery, *A. V. G. Allen,* 1911. In influential quarters of England there is, according to Vollrath (p. 143), a deep-going appreciation of religion and theology expressed by the Greek mind. We are told that "Origen is the greatest representative of a type of Christian thought which has not yet done its full work in the West." Here is determined opposition to the tenets of Augustine.

11. Closing these reviews, we must yet give a brief presentation of the much discussed *Swedish Lundensian Theology.* Here the reference must be introductory in character. With the review we step from the History of Doctrine (Dogma) over into the field of the History of Religion.

The Lundensian theologians point to the motif back of the development of the Christian teachings. They say: The motif of individual teachers and churches (instead of the teachings themselves) must be made the special object of investigation and discussion.

At the Lund University in Sweden Professor GUSTAF AULÉN (now bishop) published his book *Den kristna gudsbilden* (1927) which was translated, 1930, into German under the title *Das christliche Gottesbild in Vergangenheit und Gegenwart* (400 pages), published by C. Bertelsmann in Guetersloh. This book introduced itself as an *Umriss-zeichnung,* an outline. But in it the author offered a program which his colleague, Dr. ANDERS NYGRÉN, Professor of Systematic Theology in the same university, has developed in three volumes under the title *Agape and Eros.*[19]

What is it that Dr. Nygrén has in mind with the title *"Agape and Eros"?* For these two Greek words mean love, but, as the translator Hebert tells us in Vol. I, they are to express two completely different things. They are to indicate "the Christian and the Greek attitude to life." "Agape is primarily God's own love, manifested in the life of the Son of Man who came to seek and save that which was lost, above all in His death on the Cross." It includes the love which God through His Spirit enkindled in the Christian heart in response to God's love. "Agape is the downward movement of the self-giving Divine love"; but Eros, of pagan (Platonic) origin, is "the upward movement of the human soul to seek the divine." In the author's discussion of Eros the interest is neither biologically nor psychologically in the "sensual desire," not in the "vulgar Eros," of which there was so much in Greek art. But his interest is in Plato's "heavenly Eros" with "the endeavor of the soul to escape from the fetters of sense and seek the satisfaction in its highest spiritual needs in the eternal and true." By speaking of Agape and Eros, the author wants to discuss Grace and Nature as the two ways of salvation, observing them as contrasts or rather antitheses: Agape is the work of God's

[19] These volumes were published in Stockholm, Sweden. The first volume, *Den kristna kaerlekstanken* appeared in 1930, a German version being issued at the same time. The translation into English was made by A. B. Hebert, Kelham, Newark, who accompanied the book with a valuable "translator's preface." The succeeding two volumes, under the same general title, are a *History of the Christian Idea of Love* under the special title *Den kristna kaerlekstanken genom tiderna,* 1936, and were translated into English by Philip S. Watson of Wesley College, Leeds, who also wrote the very helpful preface, 1938, 1939. The common title for all three volumes is *Agape and Eros,* published in English by the Society for Promoting Christian Knowledge, London and New York (Macmillan).

grace to transform nature into His image. In the words of the "translator's preface" to Vol. I: "The history of Christian thought is the tangled story of the integration of the Biblical and Christian tradition with the Greek tradition, of Agape and Eros." Again in the words of the translator: "It is fundamental to Christianity that God is both Creator and Redeemer.[20] The God who created the world is the God of Agape. As creator He is the author of the natural world and of human life with its upward movement, which Aristotle describes in terms of Eros, and in this natural world and in the natural goodness of human life, God is present, and His glory is manifested. But it is only in Redemption, that is, by Agape, that He is personally revealed, both in the incomplete revelation of Agape in the Old Testament, and in the perfect manifestation by Christ" (p. XII). To this quotation from Hebert, our co-laborer Dr. O. W. Heick (in Vol. II, under Continental Theology) adds: "There can be no doubt that Lundensian theology represents a serious attempt to return to Luther and the New Testament. It strikes without mercy at the humanistic perversion of the Gospel in Neo-Protestantism. . . . Lundensian theology is a great eulogy of the sola gratia and sola fide in religion."

For purposes of illustration and education in the Divinity Schools, we add from Dr. Nygrén's Table of Contents to his first volume a few essential features and shall likewise epitomize the contents of the other two volumes.

In Volume I the author describes the Divine Agape in its difference from that of Nomistic Judaism and Pharisaic legalism (pp. 41 ff.); then follows the Pauline Agape: the Agape of the Cross (76 ff.); next the Johannine Agape: God is love (108). Then follows the Platonic Eros with the soul's ascent to the heavenly world (108); then the Eros of Aristotle and Plotinus (140); and in closing, the essential antithesis of the Agape and Eros (158).[21]

The Table of Contents of the closing two volumes is exceedingly interesting for one trained in the topics of the History of Christian Thought. We have the Nomos type in the Apostolic Fathers and the Apologists (II, 38 ff.); the Eros type in Gnosticism (II, 73); the Agape type in Marcion (II, 101); again the Nomos type in Tertullian (II, 119); then the Eros type in Alexandrian theology (II, 133); the Agape type in Iranaeus (II, 177); the compromise of the two in Athanasius, Gregory of Nyssa, and other Fathers (II, 197). Next comes the completion of the Synthesis in the long study of Augustine (Part II, Vol. II, 231-344). After this there follow the Middle Ages (445-448) issuing in the Eros "Motif" of the Renaissance (449-462). As last chapter the author offers "the Renewal of the Agape Motif in the Reformation." In this section there is a study of "Luther's Vital Problem: the Settlement of the Issue between the Eros and Agape Motifs" (II, 474 ff.).

To this extract from the contents of the last two volumes (which give the history of Eros and Agape), we add the following from Philip S. Watson's "Translator's Preface." He mentions as special questions to be discussed: How is fellowship with God conceived? How is it supposed to be realized? In what does it consist? It is within these questions that the "motifs" to be discussed must be seen. The interest is in man's salvation. It is the answers given by Judaism, by Hellenism and by Christianity that are

[20] Let us say: God in Christ is Redeemer.
[21] For an illustration of what Eros is, see Nygrén I, p. 54. The Eros features will appear also in such matters as legalism, unevangelical rationalism, pagan speculations, certain forms of mysticism and semi-Christian mediations along the lines of Pelagianism.

to be considered: by means of Nomos, Eros and Agape. These are the three different ways of fellowship with God.[22]

In closing we add the following observations:

1. The outstanding leaders in the Lundensian theology, Drs. Aulén and Nygrén, are established upon the thought that in the analysis of Christian teachings the theologian must not stop with the symbolically formulated dogma. He must aim to arrive at the "motif" (*Lebenstrieb, Grundmotiv*) and make this the starting point of his theological work.[23]

2. It is with regard to the estimate of Scripture and concerning Christology that evangelical Conservatism thinks it has found itself in disagreement with certain positions expressed in the Dogmatics of Bishop Aulén (*Den allmaenneliga kristna tron*). On this we refer the readers to our Vol. II, pp. 89-196, on Continental Theology. The *Motif-Forschung* has been applied chiefly to three great problems of Doctrine: the concept of God, and of the Atonement,[24] and the Christian idea of Love. Perhaps we may add the study of Eschatology (referring to Folke Holmstroem). It should not be overlooked that in the application of the topics mentioned in the above Tables of Contents these writers have given them very far reaching relationships.

3. Still it will seem to us that this motif method, when followed in teaching History of Doctrine, may lead the student to an unnatural limitation of interest which should be absent in a full History of Christian Thought, which is in organic connection with historical life in so many directions. In this estimate, however, it ought not to be overlooked that in the theological program of the schools there should be room, on the side, for the fascinating monographs of the *Motif-Forschung*.

4. Gustaf Aulén insists that the History of Christian Thought, as a work, must have a unified theme. In this respect, he says, Adolph Harnack's great work on History of Dogma was better than the more encyclopedic work of Reinhold Seeberg. Aulén is not in agreement with the Liberalism and Humanism of Harnack whose one aim it was to show that the (Christological) dogma of the Ancient Church and of the Reformation had met its defeat. Aulén and Anders Nygrén (with certain exceptions peculiar to their system, cf. our Vol. II) are decidedly on the conservative side, with outstanding merits in their critical discussion of theological Liberalism. But they criticize Seeberg's method, wishing he had, at the basis of his work, a Christian *Grundmotiv* with a "dynamic of love." To this permit us to say: True, Harnack had his own brilliant gift in picturing history. But the great four-volume work of Seeberg and the fine brief History of F. Wiegand have their great merit in the adaptability of their works to *the needs of the Church*. This is one great advantage of these last mentioned Histories of Doctrine.

The student on this section of Swedish thought must bear in mind that this Lundensian theology, while dealing with many topics of the History of Doctrine or Dogma, is a History (or Philosophy) of *Religion*. Instead of confining itself to the content of Christian doctrine, it seeks to define the relation of that doctrine (Agape) to the subjective or natural religious consciousness (Eros). *Morphologie des Luthertums*

---

[22] Much assistance for intelligent quotation and interpretation of Aulén and Nygrén can be received from Dr. N. F. S. Ferré's book on *Swedish Contributions to Modern Theology* (*with special reference to Lundensian Thought*). Harper and Brothers, New York and London, 1939. We also refer to Dr. W. M. Horton, *Contemporaneous Continental Theology*, 1939, also at Harper and Brothers.

[23] Cf. Aulén, *Das Christliche Gottesbild*, p. 54.

[24] We refer to Aulén's "Historical Study of the Three Main Types of the Idea of the Atonement" under the title *Christus Victor*, critically discussed by Dr. O. W. Heick in Vol. II.

speaks of the "Dynamis" of Lutheranism. And the late Karl Holl in his famous essay on *What is Religion to Luther?* applied something like this *Motif-Forschung* to his investigations of the development of the German Reformer. See his *Gesammelte Aufsaetze*, Vol. I, on Luther (4th and 5th photo-mechanic edition, published by J. C. B. Mohr, Tuebingen, pp. 1-110).

IV. THE HISTORICAL DOGMA

A. DOES THE DOGMA REPRESENT A DEVELOPMENT?

1. A Consideration: The Dogma— and by this we mean all the abiding truth of the various dogmas—is in the Scriptures. But the Scriptures do not offer this truth in formulated statements. Some of it is clearly expressed. But then there are matters which seem only to be indicated. That brings the need of a proper interpretation of Scripture, which is guided by the Analogy of Faith (cf. Rom. 12:7). Here not all of the Christian churches have reached the same conclusion. There are cases of wilful heresy (Titus 3:10). But can all failure to find the truth be so characterized? Occasionally there may be diversity of opinion with regard to the law of reasoning in arriving at a certain truth from Scriptures. Objectively, the truth of the dogma is in the Scriptures; but there is a subjective and a group element that has much to do with the expression of this truth. Here we have touched upon matters that call for a closer discussion.

2. The Question of Development. The statement of Vincent of Lerins has been quoted, namely, that the teaching of the Catholic Church has been believed "everywhere, always and by all." His reference was to what the Church of his time expressed in the Niceno-Constantinopolitan Creed and in the "Roman Symbol." The Roman Church of today would speak of the dogma as the progressive unfolding of the truth by divine, supplementary revelation through the "Church," that is, through the councils and through the pope.

If we look at the history of the Confessions that are accepted by the Lutheran Church (the "ecumenical" and the "particular"), and if we consider the confessional history of the Reformed Churches, then there can be no reasonable objection to saying that the whole content of these confessions represents a development. Later ages, in their confessional experience, have grown upon the shoulders of preceding ages. Let us point out a few of the prominent features in which we observe the development of the dogma.[25]

3. There has been a *logic in the succession in which topics of the History of Doctrine have come up for special consideration.* There was (1) the problem of the relation of the Son to the Father. Gradually the question of the relation of the Holy Spirit was added. Reference is to the Trinitarian problem, to Christ in His pre-existence. The truth on this subject is in the Scriptures. But the discussion began in the pre-Catholic age when the Scriptures did not as yet exist in the form of a recognized canon, at a time at least when the knowledge of scriptural truth was sporadic, when heresy (Ebionitism, Gnosticism) was at work to pervert the Apostolic tradition. The bishops, as guardians of the Church's tradition, were of great importance in this whole process of clarification.

---

[25] The evolution that we shall admit must not be confounded with an evolution of the naturalistic type which fails to see that in the beginnings of Christianity there were the elements of supranaturalism. See especially Seeberg's *DG* I³, 4 ff.

(Cf. our Book I, Chapter VII.) Then (2) there followed the endeavors to define the relation of the divine and human in Christ in His historical existence. We are reminded of the conflict between the Antiochean and the New Alexandrian School (Chapter X). After that (3) there came as a real problem the soteriological interest as it issued in the conflict between Augustine and Pelagius (Chapter XI). And finally (4) there were doctrines that were held in connection with impossible views concerning repentance, that age-long discussion of the admissibility of a "second repentance"; concerning atonement, that idea of a price paid to Satan; concerning the eucharist, that wavering between realism and spiritualism. On these subjects and others we see development and misdevelopment all through the centuries. Yet the logic of history in the succession of these topics is always noticeable.

4. There is also a development that comes from *the contribution of the nations.* The Greek, the Roman, the German, the Anglo-Saxon mind, each has made its special contribution. But they have all worked with the heritage coming from the Apostolic age. There is a unity of interest also in this: that one age and one race usually takes over the heritage from its predecessor. At times this heritage is translated into the individuality of the new race, but with certain eliminations and modifications that impoverish Christianity. At other times the new race offers conditions favorable to greater religious depth. Here we touch upon a matter that can be described more profitably below when we consider the interest in the purity of the dogma.

5. *Philosophical influences* have contributed their share in the development of Christian doctrines on their way toward the crystallization into dogmas: Neoplatonism and Stoicism in the Ancient Church, Nominalism and Realism in the Middle Ages and among the Reformers.

6. Nor should we overlook *the bent of mind and the individuality of certain leaders* in the development of Christian thought. We mention Irenaeus, Tertullian, Origen, Athanasius and the Great Cappadocians, Theodore of Mopsuestia and Cyril of Alexandria, Leo the Great, Augustine, Gregory the Great, Thomas Aquinas, Luther, Melanchthon, Zwingli, Calvin. Here is room for a psychological study of the individuals and of the races. Origen shows the Hellenistic type of mind; Tertullian, Cyprian and Augustine the Latin type; Luther was a German, Calvin a Frenchman. These are factors that must be considered, to be sure. Yet they are only contributory factors. There are other and very decisive elements that enter into the making of the dogma: the weight of Scriptural testimony in itself, and the providentially directed constellation of historical situations in critical moments of world events. Why was it that in spite of all the political intrigues in favor of Arianism at the Byzantine court, and even though at the time of the migration of the peoples Arianism was embraced by all the tribes destined to constitute future civilization, except the Franks,—why was it, we ask, that this Athanasianism which was almost crushed in the constant persecution of its standard-bearer, nevertheless kept the field and had the future? Was there no providence in that event at Toledo, 589?[26] Considerations of this nature are tabooed by the purely "scientific" historian; the Christian theologian cannot help but give them his thought.

B. THE PURITY OF THE CHURCH'S DOCTRINE: ITS CRITERION. Reinhold Seeberg in his introduction to Volume I of the third edition of his *Dogmengeschichte* makes

---

[26] See our remarks at the close of Chapter XI.

interesting observations on the question here indicated; we shall try briefly to epitomize them:

1. *The criterion* of religious truth must be seen in the religion of redemption as it was taught by the Apostles and is normatively and fundamentally expressed in the Holy Scriptures. This statement of Seeberg (I³, p. 3), leader once of the modern-conservative wing of German Protestantism, is encouraging and assuring to the many who cannot, and never will sacrifice the Scriptures as authority in the great questions of religious truth. Creeds and Confessions have always claimed to be Scriptural. This must be their test.

2. It belongs consequently to the task of the History of Christian Doctrine to ask *whether the purity of the dogma has not been lost in the development*. During this process there has been a constant danger of assimilating foreign elements such as extra-Christian mysticism, legalism, etc. It is interesting to watch the process of nationalization of certain doctrines. Let us emphasize that this very process may mean and in many cases has meant the rendering of a very important contribution. Luther and Melanchthon in their fine appreciation of teachings and practices of the past, recognized this thought. There are special heritages and endowments that must be watched, respected and treated with an open mind, though with most careful criticism. In the Ancient Church the Greek mind made a special contribution (Irenaeus, Origen, the Cappadocians, Cyril). In the transition to the Middle Ages (Tertullian, Leo the Great, Augustine, Ambrose, Hilary, Gregory the Great) the Roman mind is functioning and shaping the dogma. In the Reformation we have in Luther and in the influences behind him and about him the specifically German type of thought; in John Knox and the English Reformers, interpreting Calvin, the Anglo-Saxon type. The History of Doctrine is interested in the question whether dogmas have been Hellenized or Romanized, Germanized or Anglicized, and whether in such processes they have perhaps lost their purity. In themselves, Seeberg remarks, such processes of nationalization do not necessarily mean a corrupting of the dogma; they only indicate that "the thoughts of the Christian religion, at certain great epochs, were thoroughly digested" and entered into the very civilization of certain nations. "But," he continues, "the danger of these processes consists in this: that the respective peoples or ages do not merely translate Christianity into their own peculiar understanding, but they alter its contents and change it into a lower form of religion." Here the History of Christian Thought must proceed with criticism. And we add: where there has been actual adulteration of the dogma, there is a legitimate call for reformation. In such reformation, however, there is the possibility of new errors that may call for a second reformation.[27]

C. THE PLACE OF THE DOGMA IN THE LIFE OF THE CHURCH. Here, differently from A and B, above, we must take "dogma" to mean the accepted Creed or Confession. We think of the confessional standards in the historical churches.

But are there not anti-creedal churches? To this question Philip Schaff replies: "Experience teaches that those sects which reject all creeds are as much under the authority of a traditional system of a few favorite writers, and as much exposed to controversy, division and change, as churches with formal creeds."[28]

---

[27] See Seeberg in his retrospective review (*Rueckblick*) of the Ante-Nicene Age, I³, 667 ff., especially 674-676.
[28] *Creeds of Christendom* 1, 9.

1. Are Creeds or Confessional Denominational Standards infallible? What is here the difference between Rome and Protestantism? To Rome the creeds are only a part of the Church's tradition. The dogma, as part of this tradition, is infallible. Conservative Protestantism denies an infallible Church, and therefore can admit the truth of a dogma only in so far as its teachings are proven Scriptural in the experience of the investigating members of the Church. The convinced members of these churches will say that their Confessions are Scriptural in their essentials.

2. What is included in a confessional subscription to the Church's doctrine? The statement is frequently made that the theological form must not be included as obligatory, because it changes with the times. There is truth in this qualification, of course. But it is one that can leave out of consideration certain elements that should be seen. What do we mean by the *theological form?* Here we may distinguish between *terms* that are employed and the *frame* of a given article in which the terms occur.[29] Seeberg says that two things are essential in confessional subscription: (1) the rejection of a certain position or doctrine; (2) the affirmation of the religious tendency which excludes this doctrine. We will have to keep in mind that all Confessions are not alike; and within the Confessions the different articles may offer special cases. There are instances where the "frame" of the discussion and the "terms" employed should not be made binding on the subscriber. Again there are other examples in which the theological form is inseparable from the very substance of the confessional idea. "This very form grips or coins the thought in a very peculiar way; it expresses the thought once and for all. The form limits the confessional thought and determines its direction. It keeps this confessional idea from assimilating heterogeneous elements." [30] In this respect it may be remarked that certain terms in the Nicene Creed (cf. Art. I of the Augsburg Confession) such as "essence," "person," and the ὁμοούσιος, which our age had begun to discredit because of their Hellenistic origin and association, have after all their confessional significance. They convey to us the fundamental idea to be professed. Luther once said that he hated the ὁμοούσιος, but was holding to the fact (*Sache*). But we have no new forms and terms that would cover the idea. Those that are offered as substitutes fail to satisfy. J. Stier remarks: *"Diese Formen haben den Druck der Gegensaetze getragen der alten und der mittelalterlichen Welt."*

D. THE DENOMINATIONAL SITUATION. The conservative reformation (Lutheran and Reformed) took over the dogma of the Ancient Church with regard to Christology and the Trinitarian relation; also the heritage from Augustine with regard to sin and grace in its essentials. The Socinian and Anabaptist movements were opposed to binding creeds, and had their interest in the rationalization and spiritualization of the leading features in the content of the objective faith. Deism in England, Naturalism in France, Rationalism in Germany, as results of the new philosophy in a new age, had prepared the way for the abandonment of dogma.

What position are we to take on the question of truth where there are extreme differences among the Protestant bodies? We shall treat this point in detail later when we come to discuss the principles of the Reformation. Here we can afford only a few thoughts. Although the Protestants started with a common acceptance of the ancient

---

[29] See the article by W. Walther, late professor at Rostock, in *Neue Kirchliche Zeitschrift,* Oct. 13, 1912, Leipzig; reprinted in *Kirchliche Zeitschrift,* Dr. M. Reu, Nov., 1913.

[30] These were the words of J. Stier in an article in the *Ev. Luth. Kirchenzeitung,* April 28, 1911.

symbols, they separated into two camps, the Lutherans and the Reformed. On the surface, the differences seemed to be based on a disagreement concerning the means of grace. There is a similar difference with regard to the relationship of the divine and human in Christ. Neither were their positions alike in the adoption of Augustinianism. Fundamentally, both sides have felt that they were divided by "another spirit." This difference has been expressed in the Confessions which they produced. We may say that the Lutheran and Reformed Confessions reveal a different comprehension of the Gospel which has produced a different piety and a different church life. The viewpoints and controlling principles are not the same. Luther is guided for the most part by the question: "What must I do to be saved?" Calvin's leading interest reposes in the glorification of God in the congregation of believers. This is just *one* of the differences in point of view. Other definitions of distinctions may be adduced. Each of the two systems has an historically developed way of salvation with points of agreement, if individual tenets are taken by themselves, but with persisting differences permeating each system as a whole. The History of Doctrine must deal with this distinction in the study of the founders of these two Churches. But the truth, as well as the misapprehension of the truth, must be dealt with not polemically, but in such a way that their study simply presents the historical facts objectively. For further reading on this subject we refer to our *Churches and Sects of Christendom,* 1940.

Chapter Two

PRECURSORY THOUGHT

The thought here to be expressed must primarily characterize some pertinent features in Graeco-Roman philosophy. There must be a reference to conditions and ideas in Judaism. Then must follow a brief discussion of the New Testament foundations, which show us the starting point of the gradually developing doctrines of the Church.

I. GRAECO-ROMAN PHILOSOPHY

A selected literature will here be of service: The Histories of Philosophy. We mention especially WINDELBAND, WEBER, UEBERWEG-HEINZ, CUSHMAN, TILLY. In the way of special investigation: U. VON WILAMOWITZ-MOELLENDORFF, *Platon*, 2 vols., 1919. On Neo-Platonism see R. SEEBERG, *DG*, I³, 26 ff. and cf. 476 ff. and the literature there referred to. P. BARTH, *Die Stoa*, 1903. E. ZELLER, *Die Philosophie der Griechen in ihrer geschichtlichen Entwicklung* I⁵, 1892; II⁴, 1909 (with sectional English translations). We mention especially GOMPERZ, *Greek Thinker*, 4 vols., 1901 ff.; also, BURNET, *Early Greek Philosophy* 2, 1908. O. PFLEIDERER, *Vorbereitung des Christentums in der griechischer Philosophie*, 1904. A. HARNACK, *Die Mission und Ausbreitung des Christentums in den ersten drei Jahrhunderten*, in 2 vols., 1906, 1915. English translation in 2 vols., 1904-1908. J. GEFFCKEN, *Der Ausgang des griechisch-roemischen Heidentums*, 1920. CARL SCHNEIDER, *Einfuehrung in die Neutestamentliche Zeitgeschichte*, Leipzig, 1934. BENN, *The Philosophy of Greece*, 1898. CAPES, *Stoicism*, 1880. E. ZELLER, *Stoics, Epicureans, and Sceptics*, Eng. ed., 1892. At the basis of the following, covering Section I, lies a larger dissertation by the REV. P. M. BROSY, S.T.M.

Passing over the pre-Socratic philosophy, it is to be said that several of the ancient philosophical systems have left their marks upon the history of Christian Dogma. Epicureanism, of course, with its sensualism, materialism and eudemonism, declined under the attacks of Christian polemic. Aristotelianism, as a philosophy separated from Platonism, had no influence upon the Ancient Church. The time for the influence of this philosophy came in the Middle Ages when its realism was ardently embraced by some of the great scholastics (Anselm, Albert the Great, Thomas Aquinas). This leaves for our review, besides Socrates, only Platonism, Stoicism and Neo-Platonism as philosophical presuppositions of Christian thought in the Ancient Church. It will be found that some of this thought influenced the Christian thinkers in such a way that it more or less suggested or lent to them the form in which to present their Christian ideas, and that in certain cases it even supplied some of the essential materials which they took over. In most cases, of course, this thought constituted a tradition that was to be overcome by the specific message of Christianity.

1. Socrates connected absolute knowing with the absolute good. Clear knowledge, he taught, was bound to produce good actions; evil actions follow from ignorance. Virtues are teachable, they are innate in man, they need only to be brought into being. And God, though invisible, is the author of virtue in man. As he governs nature, so he also leads man in his conditions. Man's soul has a part in the divine only in so far as he participates in God's wisdom. Freed from the physical body his soul is immortal.

We can understand why Justin Martyr, that "philosopher in the mantle of a Christian," would speak of Socrates as having practically been a Christian. (*Apol.* I, 6). The early Christians referred to Socrates as a moral example. Here we are reminded of the moralistic trait in the Christianity of many of the Fathers of the first centuries, to which there must be frequent reference. And the identification of knowledge with goodness in the philosophy of Socrates reminds us of positions taken later by the Gnostics and by Clement of Alexandria, as well as of the stress that was laid upon knowledge by the Greek Church Fathers as the essential of Christianity.

2. Among the ideas of *Plato* the following are of interest in the history of Christian doctrine:

a. There is a *dual world:* the world of ideas and the world of phenomena. The only real world is that of ideas. The world of phenomena, which is constantly changing, is fundamentally non-existent; it receives real character only in so far as it partakes of the ideas. This metaphysical differentiation between the two worlds is, to Plato, at once an ethical one. The world of ideas only is the world of good. The summit of the world of ideas and the good is God.

b. Plato's *idea of God* is that He is "good" and therefore the source of all good and beneficial things. He cannot be the cause of evil. For our troubles we must seek some other causes. God is also "unchangeable." He is not a "sorcerer" who "appears designedly at different times in different shapes, deceiving us and making us conceive false opinions of him." Since God is the perfection of goodness and beauty and excellence, any change in Him would mean a change for the worse. In the *Timaeus,* God is called "creator," "father," and "artificer," who formed the universe after "an eternal pattern." Such ideas would naturally find favor with Christian thinkers, and would influence them in the fashioning of their own theology.

c. The human soul is assumed to be pre-existent. In the world of ideas it committed transgression. So for the purposes of expiation and purification, it has been sent into the world of phenomena and united with a body. It is the task of the soul to slough off this bodily prison and "house of correction" and to return into the world of pure spirit. The principal means for the accomplishment of this self-redemption are two: the theocentric contemplation of the world of ideas, and the practice of mystical asceticism. The soul remembers the ideas which it once viewed in its pre-existent state, and it is seized with a deep yearning for them. An enthusiastic, erotic homesickness lifts it up and prepares it for its return to the world of ideas. This intellectual and mystical ascent of the soul is accompanied by a curbing and repression of the body. Through asceticism the sexual desires are subordinated to the reasoning powers of the soul. This is accomplished either by harmonious union of body and soul, or by a complete repression of the former. From the process of harmonization arise the four cardinal virtues of wisdom, courage, temperance and justice, the natural virtues of medieval theology. But asceticism can also have for its aim the complete destruction of all sensual phenomena and world-relations. One of Plato's fundamental maxims was this: "By fleeing the world one becomes like God, so far as this is possible." Here we have that asceticism which is hinted at in the New Testament, and which resumed unnatural forms in the monasticism of the Church.

d. The pre-existent human soul belongs properly to the world of ideas and is therefore *immortal.* Plato was especially interested in the immortality of the soul; he provided an array of proofs which were used again by Christian theologians; immateriality, simplicity, vitality, ability to grasp eternal ideas, etc. In the *Phaedo* we read that "the soul is in the very likeness of the divine, and immortal and intelligible and uniform and indissoluble and unchangeable." Again: "If the soul be truly affirmed to be self-moving, then must she also be without beginning and immortal." Plato reports Socrates as saying shortly before his death: "I am confident in the belief that there truly is such a thing as living again, and that the souls of the dead are in existence, and that the good souls have a better portion than the evil. . . . You may bury me if you can catch me; . . . and be of good cheer, and say that you are burying my body only."

e. The soul's self-redemption, when successfully worked out, will result in the final attainment of the "beatific vision" of eternal beauty and goodness. For the bad there will be future punishments. But these punishments, after having continued for ages, will finally come to an end. Here is the germ of the later doctrine of purgatory, or even of the restoration of all things, of Origen. Some men, however, who have become so steeped in sin and wickedness, will prove to be beyond pardon; these will be "hurled into Tartarus, which is their suitable destiny, and they never come out."

3. *Stoicism,* of which Zeno of Citium (d. 264 B. C.) was the founder, was the noblest exponent of ancient pagan ethics. In many respects it made a close approach to Christianity, and even influenced the nascent religion. It built upon the ruins of pagan polytheism a system of practical ethics that was not without its points of worth, merit and excellence. It was represented by such men as Brutus, Cato, Cicero, Seneca, Epictetus and Marcus Aurelius.

a. In Stoicism we find features of a peculiar *materialism.* Like Aristotle, Stoicism taught that the world, as composed of spirit and matter, is the consequence of two principles. The spirit as the active principle is the mover, while the passive principle, namely the matter, is the moved. These two principles are, however, but different aspects of one ultimate reality. This reality is material and physical; pure spirit does not exist. In matter there are coarser and finer forms. Mind is a finer form of matter, the body a coarser form. Abstract qualities are also corporeal. Even God is thought of in the same terms. The world is actually His body. Here we have an underlying thought of Tertullian's theology.

b. Stoicism was naturally *pantheism.* What the soul is to the body, God is to the world. He is the great world-soul, the movement of matter, the fire which warms and animates it, the intelligence which guides it, the law which governs it, the *Logos* or reason, of which our reason is a part. Since all the seeds of life and development are present within the *Logos,* it is called the *"spermatic Logos."*

This identification of God with the living universe is pantheism. When viewed thus, God is the absolute mechanical *necessity,* the *destiny,* the fate which determines everything.

c. But Stoicism was also *theism.* As Weber states, the Stoics maintained "a kind of compromise between pantheism and theism." God is viewed as the benevolent *providence* which guides everything teleologically. He is the "good king and true father" of all things. He is perfect, kind, good, benevolent, a lover of mankind, who has rewards for the virtuous and punishments for the evil.

d. The *summum bonum* of Stoicism was virtue, and its chief ethical maxim was: Practice virtue for virtue's sake. Happiness is not the chief end of life but only an incidental by-product. Still the holy man will be the happy man. Hence the great law of life should be: Live according to nature or live according to reason. The holy man is able to accept with resignation and apathy anything and everything which may come to him.

e. The root of evil, or sin, is seen to lie in ignorance and in the absence of reason, as with Socrates. He who really knows the good will love it, is bound to love it. Sensuality is man's worst enemy and suppression of it is his first duty. Stoicism was not blind to sin as a general condition of mankind, and it aimed at conversion.

f. There was a *cosmopolitanism* about Stoicism that helped to prepare the soil for Christianity. Since there is one divine reason (the *Logos*) which pervades the entire universe and of which all men are partakers, it will follow that the human race is a solidarity. By the same token there can be only one law of nature and one rule of moral conduct. This applies to all men, whether slave or emperor, and all men are morally free. The idea of the universal fatherhood of God stands out clearly. We are all children of the same Father. Aratus said: "We are all His family"; and Cleanthus: "We, too, are His offspring" (Acts 17:28). The inevitable consequence is the universal brotherhood of men. As Seneca declared: "We are members of a great body." If it be true that all men are brothers, then we ought to aid and forgive even our foes. All men must work together for the highest good and for the welfare of the whole body. Still, as an exclusive philosophy of the upper classes, Stoicism fostered a haughty aloofness and self-sufficiency of spirit which were surely inimical to and incompatible with a faith which extolled Christian humility.

4. Neo-Platonism. The last philosophical phenomenon which we shall name, and that a most significant one for Christian theology, is Neo-Platonism. In it terminated both Greek philosophy and ancient religion, as it appeared in the mysteries. Neo-Platonism was a cosmopolitan philosophy in which were represented the fundamental tendencies of Platonism, the religious morality of later Stoicism, the ideals of Philo, and general oriental influences. In time Christianity also influenced it, and it in turn affected the early teachers of Christianity.

With Neo-Platonism we enter the third century of the Christian era. The characteristic defender of Neo-Platonism was Plotinus, who lived in the years A. D. 204-269. His system was epitomized by his pupil Porphyry in the six *Enneads.* "The fundamental conception of this important work," says Weber (*History of Philosophy,* p. 167), "is emanatistic pantheism. It looks upon the world as an 'overflow,' as a diffusion of the divine life, and upon its 'reabsorption' in God as the final goal of existence." This is the monistic trend in the system of Plotinus, in which the world first emanates from God and then returns to Him.

a. The emanation or overflow. God is a simple, perfect, absolute existence. He is One, and in Him there is no plurality or diversity. Furthermore He transcends all being and knowledge. His transcendence precludes any positive statement we may make concerning Him. If we attempt to say anything about Him by way of definition, we simply limit Him. Hence we can only say what He is not. We cannot even say that He thinks or feels or wills. Therefore we must be content with negative statements. So far as human knowledge, whether theological or philosophical, is concerned, Plotinus insisted very strongly upon God's unapproachableness and His differentiation from the world.

Although God is the source of all things, He nevertheless did not create the world. For one thing, He does not need the world; and for another thing, He does not will to create the world. The world is only an emanation or "overflow" from God. In this process of emanation or overflow, there are three stages: (1) the *Nous,* or pure in mind; (2) the *Psyche* or *Soul;* and (3) *Matter.* Through the union of the soul with matter arises the world of phenomena, and the soul thereby becomes bound up with mortality and evil. The entrance of the soul into the human body constitutes a genuine fall, caused by the soul fixing its gaze upon the earth rather than upon God. While the body is fundamentally evil, still the soul may be benefited by its period of tabernacling in the body. It will thus gain cognizance of evil, and learn to utilize its own powers, thus starting on its return to God.

b. The Return or Absorption. The process is now reversed, and the development proceeds from the lower to the higher. It is the task of the soul to return to God by severing its connections with the crass materiality of the body and by rising higher and higher in gradual stages. Failure to do this will send the soul after death into another body, either human or animal or vegetable, according to the nature and depth of its sin. The pure souls are colonized in the stars; only the very ripest may return entirely to God. The means by which this ascending development takes place are the mystical ecstasy and ascetic ethics. In the state of mystical ecstasy the soul transcends itself, rises to the world of ideas where it not only recognizes that it is God, but actually becomes God.

c. What was the effect of Neo-Platonism on Christianity? Traces of Neo-Platonism are to be found not only in the heretical excrescences of Christianity, but also in the teachings of the Church Fathers. The Neo-Platonic conception of the transcendence, unknowableness, spirituality and timelessness of God had its effect not only on Dionysius the Areopagite, but also on Augustine. Still more significant in their after effects on the Christian conception were the combination of monism and dualism, and the idea of a development from God to the world and from the world to God.

II. JUDAISM

In describing the Jewish thought precursory to the Christian dogma, we shall not mention the Old Testament writings. The religion of the Old Testament as expressed in the teachings of the prophets is inseparably connected with the New Testament, which is to be discussed later (sub 3). Here we are interested in the thought current among the Jews in the time "between the Testaments." On this there is a large and growing literature:

Literature: W. BOUSSET, *Die Religion des Judentums im Neutestam. Zeitalter,* 1903. R. H. CHARLES, *The Apocrypha and Pseudepigrapha of the Old Testament.* 2 vols., 1913. ADOLF DEISSMANN, *Licht vom Osten*[4], 1923. (Second English edition, *Light from the Ancient East,* by LIONEL R. M. STRACHAN, 1927). G. F. MOORE, *Judaism in the First Three Centuries of the Christian Era.* 2 vols., 1927. EMIL SCHUERER, *Geschichte des Jüdischen Volkes im Zeitalter Jesu Christi*[5]. 3 vols., 1920 (English translation by SOPHIA TAYLOR and PETER CHRISTIE, from the 2nd German ed. 5 vols. 1891). HERMANN STRACK and PAUL BILLERBECK, *Kommentar zum Neuen Testament aus Talmud und Midrasch,* 4 vols. 1922-6. Cf. R. SEEBERG, *DG,* I[3], 48 ff. and the literature there referred to. C. MONTEFIORE, *Judaism and St. Paul,* 1914. FOAKES JACKSON and LAKE, *Beginnings of Christianity,* 1920-33, has much material on this subject.

1. Situations in the Judaism of Palestine. In the message of the Old Testament prophets, the law of God as given to the people of Israel had occupied an important place. It was an exceedingly spiritual quantity. In the giving of the law God had revealed Himself as the living God of history to Israel as His own people. More and more the prophets had been showing that the aim of the Old Testament with its law written on stone was a new testament where the divine law would be written in the hearts of men (Jer. 31:31 ff.). Then came the time when the living word of prophecy ceased in Israel. After the exile there was a restoration of the Law. Gradually a new religion developed into the "Judaism" of Jesus' day. It was very different from the religion of the Old Testament, which is characterized by that personal relation of gratitude and confidence of the soul in God, as it is reflected in the Psalms. The religion of Judaism was one of peculiar legalism. The whole interest was in the painstaking fulfillment of the Law, to which was added a system of sacred legislation, including the oral tradition handed down by the elders. Here the exegetes of the Law found material upon which to work. All this made for a religion of externalism. Inward piety and moral veracity were lost. The Pharisees were in a special sense the custodians of this religion. It is this situation that explains many of the utterances of Jesus against the Pharisees. We can also understand much in the writings of Paul when we read of the work-righteousness that was taught in the book of Tobit (12:8; 14:9), Apocalypse of Baruch (45:2).[1] These views vitiated the conception concerning the mission of the Messiah. He was expected to bring the reward for the righteous and freedom from alien oppression. A highly developed eschatology was taught.

2. *The Jewish Diaspora* especially was of significance for the Christian Church. Here also the Jews watched over their identity, especially by maintaining synagogues for teaching the Law and by holding to monotheism. But the fact that the Old Testament could be read in the Greek translation brought Jewish and Greek modes of thought in touch with each other. As a result, we see, especially in Egypt, the interest of the Jew of the diaspora in Greek philosophy. First traces of such a union between Greek speculation and the belief of the Jew in revelation are found in the writings of Aristobulus and in the *Wisdom of Solomon,* which were quoted by the Christian theologians of the first centuries.

This Greek-Jewish philosophy reached its culmination in Philo at Alexandria, the contemporary of Jesus. He had an altogether abstract conception of God. This gave him the problem of God and the world, of spirit and matter. He bridged the chasm by mediating potencies, reminding one of the Platonic ideas, the Jewish angels, the Pythagorean numbers and the mythological demons. The *Logos* or Divine Reason, is the highest or the sum of these potencies. This middle being is called "the Son of God," "the First Begotten of God," "the Second God." This is a language recurring in the endeavors of the Church Fathers to describe the relation of Christ to God. This *Logos* was the organ for the world's creation. Man's soul is from God, but it fell and became imprisoned in the body, which offers the occasion for sin and evil. His task is the conquering of his sensuality and the suppression of his inclinations. For this he needs the assistance of God. The highest piety will manifest itself in an ecstatic relation of the soul to God. Philo's influence has been felt in the development of the Christian dogma.

III. THE FUNDAMENTAL TESTIMONY OF THE SCRIPTURES

Literature: G. B. STEVENS, *The Theology of the New Testament,* 1905. JAMES ORR, *Revelation and Inspiration,* 1910. SEEBERG, *DG* I³, 67 ff. P. FEINE, *Theologie des Neuen Testaments*⁴, 1922. A. SCHLATTER, *Die Geschichte des Christus²,* 1923; *Die Theologie der Apostel²;* 1922. TH. ZAHN, *Grundriss der neutestamentlichen Theologie²,* 1932. F. BUECHSEL, *Theologie des Neuen*

[1] See F. Weber, *System der altsynagogalen palaestinenischen Theologie,* 1880.

*Testamentes*², 1937   L. IHMELS. I. *Wer War Jesus?* II. *Was wollte Jesus?*⁶, 1921. H. OFFER-MANN, *Jesus, Wer er war, Was er wollte,* 1923. These last mentioned two pamphlets each contain two lectures of remarkable orientation for those open to carefully grounded positions of con-servatism. For a brief view of the whole situation, see W. B. SELBIE, *Aspects of Christ.* (Cf. A. M. FAIRBAIRN, *The Place of Christ in Modern Theology,* 1916.) FOAKES JACKSON and LAKE, *The Beginnings of Christianity,* Part I, Vols. I-V, 1920-33, also J. MOFFATT, *Love in the New Testament,* 1929, and *Grace in the New Testament.* F. C. PORTER, *The Mind of Christ in Paul,* 1930. SHIRLEY J. CASE, *The Social Origins of Christianity,* 1923. Cf. E. Brunner (below).

The development under the sway of the now more and more abandoned *Historismus*, cultivated by the era of Harnack, is indicated by names such as Wrede, Heitmueller, Juelicher, Weinel, Gunkel, Bousset. The work of A. Schweitzer, *Von Reimarus zu Wrede,* has the sub-title *Eine Geschichte der Leben Jesu Forschung,* 1906, 4th edition, 1926. The title of the English translation from the first German edition is, *The Quest of the Historical Jesus*², 1911. The literature of these scholars must be read with careful criticism; cf. the review of our colaborer Dr. O. W. Heick on *The Historico-Religious School* in Vol. II of our work.

In the preceding two sections we have been reviewing the ideas of noble thinkers who stood outside of Christian revelation—men whose writings created a large part of the literary atmosphere in the days of the early Church Fathers. Not only did they influence these Fathers, but there are passages in both of the Testaments with direct or indirect reference to extra-Biblical thought.[1] But the "Scriptures" have a significance for Christian dogma which cannot be claimed for the literature that has just been reviewed.

What is the relation of the Scriptures to the History of Dogma? The teachings of Jesus and the Apostles constituted the special object of thought for the early Christian Fathers. This teaching was at first a living Word, not confined to the New Testament writings. The latter were but partially known, and only gradually did they come into the possession of the whole Church. There were, in fact, special impulses for the creation of a recognized *canon*. The Gnostics aimed to prove the legitimacy of their peculiar speculations by an interpretation of writings which they claimed to be Christian and Apostolic. The question as to the extent of the canon therefore became a burning issue for the Ancient Catholic Church. And the Church Fathers had to interpret its writings in harmony with the tradition of the Church (*regula fidei*). Irenaeus is a typical repre-sentative of the Church's interest in this respect. To him the criterion of a truly Christian doctrine was its definitely biblical character.

To Christianity the teaching of the New Testament as the full fruit of the Old Testament development is the normative criterion of Christian truth. This does not mean that we would use individual passages of Scripture, irrespective of their historical connection, to prove or disapprove Christian truth. The sacred Scriptures, both Old and New Testament, as a history of redemption, represent an historical organism of Christian truth.[2] This must be held in view when we speak of them as normative and use them as criteria of truth. But while the Scriptures have a fundamental significance and are normative, there is in their whole background, in the *Urchristentum*, in the living Word of the New Testament age, the impulse and the starting point for Christian thought, which, under the guidance of the Holy Spirit (John 16:13), became crystallized into Confessions of Faith.

In this last part of our chapter on thought precursory to the dogma of the Church, we must speak very briefly of a few ideas and facts of Scripture, which soon became issues for Christian thought in the History of Doctrine.

---

[1] Cf. Ex. 20:23—23:19 with the Code of Hammurabi; Jude 4:14 with Enoch 1:9.

[2] J. C. K. Hofmann, the founder of the so-called "Erlangen School" wrote an epoch-making work on this subject. Reference is to his book *The Scripture Proof (Der Schriftbeweis),* 1852-56.

1. Who was Jesus? The early Church Fathers were forced to express themselves on this question against the Gnostics, Ebionites, Samosatenes and Arians. In the positive endeavor at formulating the conception of Christ's relation to the Father and later to the Holy Spirit, the arguments were all on this one question. (Cf. Chapter IX on the Trinity.) Here the teachings of the New Testament furnished the foundations.

Matthew speaks of Jesus the revealer of God (11:27). He has the authority to interpret God's law (5:22, 28, 34, 39); and is commissioned with the right to forgive sins (9:6). Before His death He established a new covenant (26:28).

These statements of Matthew are corroborated by Mark and Luke. According to their testimony, Jesus of Nazareth was the prophet of God, mighty in deed and word. While Mark emphasizes the Messianic power of Jesus by which He forgives sins (2:5), exercises authority over the Mosaic Law (2:28), and bestows upon the people that followed Him in great numbers the saving power of His ministry, Luke adds to this conception of Jesus the Friend of sinners, who has come to restore that which is lost of Israel (4: 16 ff.; 5: 8 ff.; 7: 37 ff.; 19: 1 ff.; 23: 39 ff.).

With this picture of the Synoptics, the teachings of the Fourth Gospel are in full harmony: Jesus is He of whom Moses and all the Scriptures testify (John 5:39, 46), and Whose day Abraham rejoiced to see (8:58). Jesus calls to repentance and faith both the Pharisee (3:1 ff.) and the sinners (4:1 ff.; 5:14), manifesting His power amidst a diversity of human want and misery (2:1 ff.; 5:1 ff.; 6:1 ff.; 9:1 ff.; 11:1 ff.). He also is, in the conception of John, Lord of the Sabbath (5:9; 9:14) and of the sacerdotal precepts of the Pentateuch (2:19 ff.; 4:23). As the servant of the Lord (Deutero-Isaiah) He is the Lamb of God bearing the sins of the world (1:29).

The deeds and words of the earthly Jesus constitute also for Paul the foundation of his faith (I Cor. 2:2), from which he has not omitted and to which he has not added any essential incident. But he has faithfully delivered to his congregations what he also received through the tradition of the first Christian community (I Cor. 15:3). According to the gospel of Paul, Jesus, though being in the form of God, was made in the likeness of men (Phil. 2:6 ff.), born of a woman under the Law (Gal. 4:4). John the Baptist, preaching the baptism of repentance to all Israel, bore witness of Jesus as the coming Saviour (Acts 13:23 ff.). The fact that Paul believed in the miracles of Jesus is shown by his belief in the miraculous power of himself and of the other apostles in their service of Jesus (Acts 14:3; 15:12; Rom. 15:19; II Cor. 12:12). The transitory though divine character of the Law which Paul emphasizes so emphatically in his letters to the Romans and Galatians, he has learned from no one else but Jesus Himself. Jesus also, according to the message of Paul, in the night preceding His death, established a new covenant by virtue of His blood, giving the disciples His body to eat and His blood to drink (I Cor. 11:23 ff.). And in regard to his teaching on the crucifixion of Jesus under Pontius Pilate, His death, burial and resurrection, Paul is in full harmony with the other apostles.

The resurrection of the dead is, according to the unanimous witness of the New Testament, the proof of the worth of the claim of Jesus. This great fact made Jesus the "Lord" (*Kyrios*) which, as is stressed by R. Seeberg against Bousset, means the Lord of glory (Acts 4:33; 10:36; I Cor. 2:8; I Peter 1:21; James 2:1). Here is also the basis for the promise of a continued presence of Christ with His believers and of His final return for judgment (Matt. 28:20; John 16:22).

The facts here expressed direct our attention to the two terms "Son of Man" and "Son of God." The real foundation for speaking of Jesus as the Son of God is in His incarnation as taught in the prologue to John's Gospel. It is said that the Synoptics, which stress the human side of Christ, offer the earlier testimony, and that John's Gospel is of a later date. But let us note (1) that John says nothing on this point out of agreement with the Synoptics. Two of these have the story of the Virgin Birth.[3] And let us note (2) that the later date of John's testimony has the additional advantage of larger perspective. Christ Himself did not begin by announcing Himself as the Son of God, but educationally aimed to lead to a gradual conviction by experience.

The uniqueness of Jesus is further expressed in the Pauline Epistles and the General Letters. Paul speaks of Him as "the second Adam," the new federal head of humanity (Rom. 5:12; I Cor. 15:45-49); "the firstborn of all creation" (Col. 1:15); "the firstborn from the dead" (Rom. 8:29); "the image of the invisible God" (Col. 1:15); and "on an equality with God" (Phil. 2:6). Paul thus clearly sets forth the pre-existence of Christ. In I Peter Christ is represented as "a lamb without blemish and without spot" (1:19); "the shepherd and bishop of souls" (2:25); "a chief cornerstone" (2:6); and "the just" who died for the "unjust" (3:18). The writer of Hebrews designates Him "a priest forever after the order of Melchizedek" (5:5, 6) and "the new and living way" (7:19; 10:20). These designations provided for the early Christians the basis for the Christological development of the Church (Brunner, *Mediator,* 316-54).

2. *What was the Mission of Jesus?* Closely associated with the doctrine of the person of Christ is that of His work in the world. This question includes the ideas of atonement, justification, and the establishment of the Church, about which numerous controversies centered.

a. The Atonement is set forth in the peculiar patterns of the different New Testament writings. In Mark 10:42-45 Jesus speaks of giving his life "a ransom for many." Exegetes have differed widely as to the significance of this statement, yet it is to be associated with redemption. The words of institution of the Lord's Supper embrace the idea of forgiveness, "This is my blood of the New Testament, which is shed for many for the remission of sins" (Matt. 26:28). In foretelling His death, Jesus implied that it was voluntary and vicarious (Matt. 16:21). The Apostolic tradition clearly associated the death of Jesus with the forgiveness of sins and salvation. Paul claims that he received from the early Apostles the teaching that "Christ died on behalf of our sins according to the Scriptures" (I Cor. 15:3).

The problem with which the early Church was confronted in this connection was how to reconcile the ignominious death of Christ on the cross with the exalted mission of the promised Messiah, for the Jews readily argued that such a death proved that Jesus was not the Messiah. This, however, was interpreted as a great crime on the part of the Jews who rejected Him, yet as a power and a blessing to those who accepted Him. The "stumbling block of the cross" (I Cor. 1:23) was, after all, the culmination

---

[3] There are the critical scholars who decline to accept the New Testament testimony as to the earthly beginnings of our Lord. The story of the Virgin Birth, according to Matthew and Luke, is the product of the imaginative mind of the primitive Christian community. It was these early Christians, they say, who raised Jesus of Nazareth to the proportion of a heavenly, supra-mundane being, born of a virgin and coming again upon the clouds of heaven. But in the New Testament testimony itself the consideration referred to is without real foundation; the conclusions are reached by conjecture. The critical attitude of these men seems to be rooted in the naturalistic bent of their own minds (cf. Vol. II, Book V, as referred to).

of Christ's saving work and the crown of His Messianic mission. The early Christians found the Old Testament in harmony with this idea.

The theme of Paul's preaching was "Jesus Christ and Him crucified." (I Cor. 2:2.) In Gal. 3:13, the Apostle presents Christ's death as vicarious, "having become a curse for us." The atonement was effected logically and in harmony with the divine justice and mercy in that Christ suffered as a sinless saviour and voluntarily on behalf of men who could never pay the penalty for sin, and thus effected reconciliation between man and God (II Cor. 5:21; I Thess. 5:10; Gal. 1:4; Rom. 4:25; 8:32; Col. 1:13; II Cor. 5:18 . In becoming a curse for us, Christ did not become the curse of the law. Rather did He become the substitution for us in revealing and vindicating the divine righteousness. This is far more than retributive justice, and it exalts the righteousness of God (Rom. 324-26).

In I Peter the death of Christ is likewise clearly set forth as redemptive (3:18), but is presented in relation to moral cleansing rather than to legal acquittal from guilt. This Epistle does not enter into the involved arguments of the Pauline theology, but rather sets forth as a ground of comfort and hope the vicarious character of the suffering of Christ, who offered Himself once for all (1:18; 3:18) for sinners.

The writer of Hebrews sets forth the atonement under the figure of the priesthood. The fact of the imperfection of the old Levitical priesthood (7:11) called for a new priesthood of perfect and perpetual significance. This change was effected in Christ, who abolished the old order and opened up the new and living way unto God. His sacrifice thus once for all atoned for sin (9:28), and offered to men a testament of His benefits (9:20).

In the Apocalypse the death of Christ is redemptive. It is in "the blood of the Lamb" that saints receive purification from sin (1:5; 7:14; 22:14). The symbol of the Lamb is one of vicarious suffering, mercy and love (5:12).

According to John, Christ, the righteous One, fulfills a twofold function: He not only delivers us from sin, but is our advocate with the Father. (I, 2:1) His blood "cleanses us from all sin" (I, 1:7). The atonement from sin unto righteousness is clearly expressed in the designation "propitiation" (I, 2:2, I, 4:10). Salvation is a present blessing as well as a future reality (6:47).

We see, therefore, that the New Testament presents and develops the idea of the atonement as a distinct part of the Messianic mission of Jesus in terms of His death, blood, resurrection, suffering, propitiation and the like. (Brunner, 475 ff).

b. *Justification* is a doctrine which received special development and emphasis in the writings of the Apostle Paul in the new Testament. The roots of the forensic conception of righteousness lie in the Old Testament (Hab. 2:4), but in Judaism the Law was conceived of as making man good. Righteousness came by the Law. For Paul the Law can serve only to make man conscious of guilt. It can never take away sin (Rom. 7:7; I Cor. 15:56). Since the whole race is under the condemnation of sin, the righteousness of God is required to take away sin. How is this brought about? God freely pronounces righteous the unrighteous man because of Christ, through faith as the receiving hand. Justification is therefore a forensic act. The idea stands in contrast with the teaching of the Pharisees who posited righteousness by works. It is by faith alone that man apprehends the righteousness achieved by Christ (Gal. 2:20; 3:3). It is not that God recognized faith as meritorious, but it is conditional. "Of faith" means "according to grace" (Rom. 4:16). But this "righteousness of God by faith" is not imputed apart from Christ. It is for Christ's sake that believers are declared righteous. Justification, therefore, grows out of atonement. Christ's death is, therefore, called a propitiation (*see ante*). "He was delivered for our transgressions and raised again for our justification." From justification then flows peace, sanctification and the new life (Rom. 5:1; Eph. 5:25; Titus 2:14).

While this idea of justification is Pauline, yet other New Testament writers are in accord with it. According to the writer of Hebrews God produces good works in us (13:21; 11:7), though not in the sense of meritorious works. Peter recognizes moral integrity as a divine requirement (I Peter 2:24; 3:14), but this is not in terms of the law, for the law is only a "law of liberty" (I Peter 2:16). James, however, emphasizes works, basing the edict of justification not exclusively upon faith. Yet the works of which he speaks are the works which follow faith. While he seems to differ from Paul, he nevertheless avoids clearly the legalism of Judaism (James 2:20 ff.).

Neither in the Pauline Epistles nor in other writings of the New Testament is the doctrine of justification thoroughly systematized. It remained for the teachers of the Church to formulate and develop the scattered conceptions and points of emphasis into consistent representations in which frequently the one is supplementing the other.

c. The establishment and organization of the Church constituted a distinct part of Christ's mission. The implications expressed in the founding of the Church, particularly in respect to polity, have occasioned unlimited controversies in the history of dogma.

The Synoptic Gospels teem with statements concerning the "kingdom of God" or the "kingdom of heaven." This theme was uppermost in Jesus' thought. Analyzing what Christ meant, we must guard against overemphasizing its external significance. To Pilate He said: "My kingdom is not of this world" (John 18:36). The true program for the coming of the kingdom is to work for regeneration in the hearts of men by the power of the Holy Spirit through the means of grace. The kingdom is a process comparable to the leaven in the meal (Matt. 13:33). The character of the kingdom depends upon a condition in the hearts of men. Briefly, the kingdom, according to the teachings of Jesus, lay in the experience of the forgiveness of sin and in the reign of divine love in the hearts and lives of those who receive His grace and yield cheerful and devoted service (Matt. 4:17 ff.; 13:44 f.). Jesus established it as a growing process with the design of universality. The parables reflect this idea (Mark 4:26 ff.). The principles of the kingdom are to permeate all social relationships of life. On this subject theology presents the many works on Christian Ethics, Christian Sociology and on the practical life of the churches. This is not the place for details except to say that it is possible to overlook the claims of Christian Sociology as the fruit that must follow faith.[4] However, the kingdom, in the teachings of Jesus, transcends every temporal, ultra-mundane achievement. It is, in the last analysis, an eschatological entity, the "wholly other."[5]

While Jesus appointed disciples and gave promise of the organization of the Church, yet it remained for history to develop the forms for external organization. The word "Church" (*ecclesia*) appears only twice in the Synoptic Gospels.

[4] Cf. C. H. Dodd *et al, The Kingdom of God in History,* Oxford Conference volume, 1938. And also E. F. Scott, *The Kingdom of God in the New Testament,* 1931. For our own position on the subject see our *Churches and Sects of Christendom* in Chapter VII on the "Methodist Church Family and its relatives," pp. 412 ff. and cf. Chapter IV on the "Lutheran Church," 218 ff.
[5] The eschatological aspect of the Kingdom has received consistent emphasis in the works of the Historico-Religious School and more recently in the writings of the Dialectical Theologians.

In the historical narratives of the Acts, the necessity for a development of the organization of the Church is seen. At first the early Christians conducted the actually established new Church in a somewhat elastic manner, meeting together from house to house (Acts 4:31-37). However, the growth of the movement called for the appointment of deacons to assist in daily ministrations (6:5).

Paul speaks far more frequently of the Church than of the kingdom of God, not because he was primarily interested in external organization, but it devolved upon him to see that the various communities of believers were properly organized and equipped for service. He thought of the kingdom as "righteousness and peace and joy in the Holy Spirit" (Rom. 14:17). He conceived of the Church as local communities of believers and followers of Christ (I Cor. 1:2; 12:28; 15:9). The early Epistles of Paul do not refer to ecclesiastical officers (cf. Galatians and I Corinthians). In all probability the party factions in Corinth grew up because of the fluidity of organization. It is in his first Epistle to the Corinthians that the Apostle speaks so extensively of the *charismata*. The later Epistles show that there has been a development in the organized life of the Church, for official leaders appear as deacons, presbyters and bishops. It is generally conceded that the office of bishop and presbyter was the same in New Testament times. The Pastoral Epistles especially portray a highly developed organization (see Chapter VII). While the Apocalypse speaks of the seven churches of Asia and refers to the general community of elect from all tribes and nations, yet it does not add anything essential to the Pauline teaching concerning the organization of the early Christian communities. It has remained for history to deal with the problems of church polity.

3. The Sacraments have occasioned no small part of the controversies which were waged in the development of Christian doctrine. According to the testimony of the New Testament, Jesus established the two sacraments of Baptism and the Lord's Supper.

a. Baptism as a rite was practiced by the Jews and by the devotees of the mystery religions, as well as by the early Christians. John the Baptist introduced new connotations in the rite he employed. But Jesus instituted Christian baptism, differing in significance from the purification of the Jews and the rite of John the Baptist. In the narratives of the Acts, this baptism was practiced "in the name of Jesus." However, there appears even in Matthew (28:19-20) a triadic formula, supported also by many other references (I Cor. 6:11; 12:4; II Corinthians 13:13; Rom. 15:16, 30; Eph. 2:19-22; II Thess. 2:13). Apparently there was in the early Church a definite tradition or course of instruction connected with baptism. Its confessional character called for the formulation of the belief and practice. Accordingly, a baptismal confession was crystallized (Rom. 6:3; Acts 19:2; Heb. 10:22; Eph. 4:5). This Baptismal Formula and tradition served as a basis for the Rule of Faith and later the Apostles' Creed. (Cf. our Book I, Chapter IV). Anglican scholars call attention to the fact that baptism, in the early church, was preceded by penitence and was often followed by the practice of laying on of hands (confirmation); (Acts 8:14 ff.; Heb. 6:2). They see in the apostolic custom a legitimate basis for speaking of other rites besides the Supper and Baptism as sacraments.[6]

b. In addition to the Baptismal Formula, there was also a tradition concerning the Lord's Supper (I Cor. 11:23 ff. and in the Synoptic Gospels), which was likewise associated with Christian instruction and confession. With the exception of the diffi-

---

[6] Cf. *Essays, Catholic and Critical*, 1926, p. 376.

culties which grew out of the Agape feasts as related to the Lord's Supper, little insight is given in the New Testament to the Communion feast other than the repeated references and words of institution. In the development of doctrine, the Sacraments, both in the East and in the West, came to be more and more crystallized into definite means of grace (cf. *ibid.*, Chapter XII).

4. *Eschatology* occupied a unique place in the thought of the *Urchristentum*. It accounts, in fact, for the delay in the production of Christian literature and also for much of the literature which appeared. On the one hand, early Christians, mindful of the promise of Christ's early return and eagerly expectant of this event, were satisfied with the oral gospel and the dominance of the Spirit. They felt no need for a written New Testament. On the other hand, when His coming seemed unduly delayed, confusion arose and it became necessary for the Apostle Paul with his far-reaching faith to write admonishingly concerning this doctrine (cf. I and II Thess.).

Jesus Himself inaugurated the hopes upon which the disciples meditated after His death. In the book of Acts those hopes appear very vivid (Acts 1:11). Paul endeavored to coordinate this tradition with his program of world-wide missions (II Thess. 3:5). The writer of the Apocalypse elaborated upon this doctrine in terms of Jewish apocalyptic symbolism and in the light of the Roman imperial powers. The symbolic character of this book gave rise to many conflicting opinions in the development of Christian doctrine. Augustine (*De civitate Dei*), at a later time, to a very large extent, clarified Christian thinking along this line.

5. In addition to the above named doctrine which grew up on New Testament soil there are *other traditions*. For example, in the house-tables of the Pauline Epistles we note the development of definite traditions of an ethical character, particularly with respect to virtues and vices (cf. Rom. 12; Eph. 6; Col. 5:18 ff.). Likewise we note numerous admonitions concerning the offices, regulations of worship, and the like (I Tim. 3:1; Titus 1:7; I Cor. 14; Heb. 6:1-2). Some of these traditions became crystallized in the *Didache* (cf. the "Two Ways").

The early Christians became conscious in their Church life of various problems which called for solution, questions of doctrine and practice. In the Pauline Epistles particularly, we see the efforts of the inspired Apostle to establish standards of conduct and teaching. For example, he deals with marriage, the sacraments, the doctrine of resurrection (I Cor.), and other questions troubling the local community of believers. Thus we note a growth and development of Christian tradition, sometimes very fluid, at other times more or less definite. These constitute, as has been indicated, the starting point for the development of Christian doctrine. However, the New Testament does not offer formulated and systematized doctrines for the Church, but it supplies the principles and sets the standards for working out the doctrines needed for the guidance of the Church.

Chapter Three

THE CHRISTIANITY OF
THE POST-APOSTOLIC FATHERS

Sources: The *Patres Apostolici*, ed. by FUNK, 2 vols., 2nd ed., 1901. (Small ed. in KREUGER'S *Quellenschriften*). HARNACK in *Texte und Untersuchungen* (*TU*), small ed., 1886. *The Texts and Studies* edited by J. A. ROBINSON (1891 ff.) have their foundation in the *TU*. Both of these editions include the *Didache*. The same is the case with the Greek text with brief introductions and an English translation of the *Apostolic Fathers* by KIRSOPP LAKE, 2 vols., 1917-19. To these publications we add: E. HENNECKE, *Neutestamentliche Apokryphen²*, 1924. The readers of English are referred to M. R. JAMES, *The Apocryphal Books of the New Testament*, 1924. To this literature of sources we add the very helpful reader *Dogmengeschichtliches Lesebuch* by H. RINN, 1910 and *Die Apostolischen Vaeter* by A. BIEHLMEYER, in *Sammlung ausgewaehlter Kirchen und dogmengeschichtlicher Quellen schriften*, 1924.

Literature in the form of investigation: Besides the above mentioned introductions by KIRSOPP LAKE, we call special attention to A. HARNACK, *Geschichte der altchristlichen Literatur bis Eusebius*, 3 vols., 1893-1904. G. KRUEGER, *Geschichte der altchristlichen Literatur*, 1895, also in English translation, 1897. O. BARDENHEWER, *Geschichte der altchristlichen Literatur*, 4 vols., 1902 ff. H. JORDAN, *Geschichte der altchristlichen Literatur*, 1911. FARRAR, *Lives of the Fathers*, 2 vols., 1889. FOAKES JACKSON and KIRSOPP LAKE, *The Beginnings of Christianity*, 1920 ff., Part I, Vol. I, Prolegomena. H. LIETZMANN, *Handbuch zum N. T.* As an addition, *Die apostolischen Vaeter* 1920-1923 (a commentary). See the Histories of Doctrine. We refer especially to HARNACK, LOOFS, R. SEEBERG and WIEGAND. As to ANDERS NYGRÉN, *Agape and Eros*, see Part II, Vol. I, 38 ff.

I. BRIEF ORIENTATION ON THE EARLIEST OF THE FATHERS
AND THEIR WRITINGS

The so-called *Apostolic* or *Post-Apostolic Fathers* were those early Christian writers who immediately succeeded the Apostles, and whose period of activity extended over the years A. D. 90 to 140. The expression *Apostolic Fathers* originated in the belief that these men had been pupils of the Apostles. Since some of the Fathers were not contemporaries of the Apostles, the designation is not strictly accurate. The significance of these men lies in the fact that they formed the connecting link between the time of the Apostles and the Old Catholic Age, and thus furnish the starting point for the History of Doctrine.

It may be imagined that the few of these Fathers of whom we have any knowledge exhibit only individual opinions, and hence they possess no value for the History of Doctrine. The scanty writings however, which have come down to us are the specimens of a much larger literature which must have been influential in its day. What GROTE says of the classical literature of Greece is applicable to the literature of the early Church: "We possess only what has drifted ashore from the wreck of a stranded vessel."[1] These writings were so significant in their day that some of them came very near being admitted into the New Testament Canon. There is no doubt that they afford us a cross-section of the mode of religious thought in the Gentile-Christian congregations of that time.

---

[1] Cf. G. P. Fisher, p. 41.

The writings which are available for a study of this period are the following:

1. The so-called *First Letter of Clement;* written in 96 or 97 A. D. by CLEMENT of Rome, and addressed to the Church at Corinth. It contains general moral and doctrinal instructions and also particular admonitions with regard to a quarrel which had arisen between the presbyters and certain rebellious laymen of that church.[2] Although CLEMENT accepted the doctrines of Paul, he failed to fathom them but lost himself in legalism.[3]

2. The Shepherd of Hermas, written by a member of the Roman Church. This is an exhortation to repentance, and is composed of five Visions, twelve Mandates and ten Similitudes. In this document the Church appears as an ancient lady, while the "Angel of Repentance" is represented by a shepherd. The Ancient Church regarded the *Shepherd of Hermas* as a canonical book until the warning was issued not to "count it among the prophets nor the writings of the Apostles." The objection was that it had been written *"in our times"* (middle of the second century) by a certain HERMAS whose brother was Pius, bishop of Rome (139-154). The book is supposed to have been written around 140; but because of Vision II, 4, it has been dated as early as the year 97.[4]

3. The Seven Letters of Bishop Ignatius of Antioch addressed to the congregations in Ephesus, Magnesia, Tralles, Rome, Philadelphia and Smyrna, and to the bishop of Smyrna. The date of composition is placed between 110 and 115 A. D. In these letters there are extremely interesting thoughts on Christ's pre-existence, or the reality of His incarnation, on the Christian as a "Godbearer" (Θεόφορος) and on the Church and the bishop as representative of the Church's unity.[5]

4. The Letter of Bishop Polycarp of Smyrna. This was written to the congregation at Philippi close to the date of the seven letters of Ignatius, probably 155.

5. The so-called *Letter of Barnabas* was written by some unknown author, not by St. Paul's companion. There is no agreement as to the date of composition. Some place it as early as 70 A. D., while others date it as late as 117-138. This writing, which is characterized by a strong opposition to Judaism, interprets the Jewish ceremonial law as an allusion to Christ and His redemption.[6]

6. The so-called *Second Letter of Clement* was written about 150 by some unknown author and is the most ancient homily that has been preserved. It is strongly legalistic in tone.

7. The Exposition of the Oracles of the Lord, consisting of five books, was written about 125 by Bishop PAPIAS of Hierapolis. Only a few fragments of this work have been preserved. These are especially significant because of their chiliastic descriptions drawn from the Jewish apocalyptic books.

8. The Didache, or Teaching of the Twelve Apostles, is a church manual for catechists and congregations. The first part, which is catechetical, presents moral precepts in the form of the two ways—the Way of Life and the Way of Death. The second part contains instructions for church worship and rules for the congregational life. A

---

[2] For the situation as it existed in Corinth see our discussion in Chapter VII, Sec. I, 1c.

[3] For reading: R. Seeberg, Eng. ed., p. 56. W. Wrede, *Untersuchungen zum ersten Klemensbrief,* 1899. G. Uhlhorn, *PRE,* IV, 169; cf. *NSH.*

[4] G. Uhlhorn, *PRE,* VII, 718. Seeberg, Eng. ed., I, 58 ff.; cf. *DG³,* Th. Zahn, *Der Hirt des Hermas,* 1886.

[5] R. Seeberg, Eng. ed., I, 66; cf. 67. Fisher, 70 ff. Th. Zahn, *Ignatius von Antiochien,* 1873. E. v. d. Goltz, *Ignatius von Antiochien als Christ und Theolog,* 1894.

[6] Seeberg, Eng. ed., I, 70-73; cf. *DG, I³.*

review of these instructions is given by Harnack.[7] The document closes with eschatological statements. Seeberg places the date of the writing at the beginning of the second century, while Harnack locates it somewhere between 120 and 165.[8]

9. *The Preaching of Peter* (*Praedicatio Petri*) is the so-called missionary sermon of Peter. It is really a pseudonymous work which originated between 110 and 130. Only fragments of this writing remain.[9]

II. DOCTRINAL CONCEPTIONS OF THE CHRISTIAN FAITH AS PRESENTED
BY THE APOSTOLIC FATHERS[10]

1. *On God.* We cannot speak of theology which these Fathers had in common. For this there was not yet the needed distance and perspective. Furthermore, no need was felt for formulated doctrines. These early Christians stood under the powerful impression of the personal relation to Christ, of His life and sufferings, in the face of which there were no impulses for the creation of doctrinal statements. Their chief interest was in the demands of the new Christian life. They formulated decisive principles on the "two ways" (cf. the *Didache*). Their doctrinal expression was sporadic and accidental.

In contradistinction to the polytheistic faith of heathenism, the Post-Apostolic Fathers adhered tenaciously to monotheism in the Old Testament sense. HERMAS begins his book with the command: "Above all things believe that there is One God, Who created and ordered all things, Who brought everything to existence from nothingness, and Who comprehends all things, although He Himself is incomprehensible." To all of them God is the Almighty Lord, the Creator, Upholder, and Ruler of the world. Although He created the world, He Himself is not a part of it. He is invisible, incomprehensible, uncreated, everlasting, and in need of nothing. At the same time He is the merciful Father Who manifests Himself as love to men and especially to sinners. He created the world for men and the Church. These thoughts are mainly of Old Testament and Jewish origin, and hence exhibit scarcely any Hellenic influence.

That a kind of *Trinitarian Relationship in the Godhead* was recognized by some of these Fathers is indicated by remarks such as the following: *The First Letter of Clement* speaks of God and the Lord Jesus Christ and the Holy Spirit.[11] In *Similitudo* VI Hermas has an approach to a trinitarian relation when he speaks of the Father, Lord of the farm, of the Son as servant, and of the flesh as bearing the Holy Spirit.[12] The following passage from Ignatius is very interesting. He speaks of Christians as being stones of the temple of the Father, made ready for the building of God our Father, carried up to the heights by the engine of Jesus Christ, that is the cross, and using for a rope the Holy Spirit.[13] It need hardly be stated that the Post-Apostolic Fathers were familiar with the baptismal formula and its crystallization of the Trinitarian relationship. The Trinity, however, was not made a subject of speculation. This was particularly the

---

[7] *PRE*, I, p. 713.
[8] Harnack, *PRE*, I, 711-730; cf. *NSH*.
[9] G. Ficker in Hennecke.
[10] In quoting the texts we follow Kirsopp Lake as referred to at the beginning of this chapter.
[11] LVIII, 58, 2; XLVI, 6.
[12] Cf. V and VII.
[13] *Eph.* IX, 1.

case with regard to the Holy Spirit. There was the natural difficulty of conceiving of the Spirit hypostatically. Furthermore, in view of the fact that the Church still had its charismatics and pneumatics, as the media through which the productive and creative activity of the Spirit was transmitted, there was little occasion for discussing the Holy Spirit.

2. *Concerning Christ.* The Divinity of Christ was an accepted fact among these Fathers. To Ignatius, Christ was "my God" and "our God." *The First Letter of Clement* speaks of Christ as "the sceptre of the majesty of God," and the *Homily of Clement* declares: "We ought so to think of Jesus Christ as of God, as of the Judge of the quick and the dead" (I, 1). Governor Pliny reported that the Christians "are accustomed to sing a hymn to Christ as God" (*Christo quasi Deo carmen dicere soliti sunt*) in his letter to the Emperor Trajan.[14]

At the same time the *humanity* of Jesus was just as clearly recognized. The *Didache* characterizes Jesus not only as the Chosen and Beloved of God, but also as the Servant of God. Ignatius speaks of Him as "conceived by Mary" and as being "of the seed of David."[15] And the *Homily of Clement* says: "Christ the Lord Who saved us, though He was originally Spirit, became flesh and thus called us." (IX, 5.) But concerning the relation between Christ's divinity and humanity, and the relation of His divinity to that of the Father, the Apostolic Fathers did not yet speculate.

The *pre-existence* of Christ was also clearly and positively asserted. Ere time and space began, Christ was God, exalted above the angels; and yet He was differentiated from the Father. He assisted at creation, Who later appeared in the flesh to open the kingdom of God to the ransomed.[16] Hermas says: "The Son of God is older than His creation so that He was the counsellor of His creation to the Father."[17] Hermas also designates the pre-existent Christ as the Spirit, and calls His incarnation a tabernacling in the flesh. Owing to this, the impression has arisen that Hermas identified the Son of God with the Holy Spirit, and so espoused a Binitarianism instead of a Trinitarianism. But more exact investigations lead to another result. Zahn declares: "It is certain that Hermas assigns a pre-historic, i.e. an external, existence to the Son of God as personally differentiated from the Holy Spirit."[18]

3. *On Salvation.* In the conception of these Fathers concerning the saving work of Christ, there is less clarity than we found with regard to the person of Christ. It is true that concerning the atonement such statements as the following are found: "Let us fix our gaze upon the blood of Christ and let us know that it is precious to His Father, because it was poured out for our salvation, and brought the grace of repentance to all the world."[19] And: "For it was this reason that the Lord endured to deliver up His flesh to death that we should be sanctified by the remission of sin, that is, by His sprinkled blood."[20] "Christ gave His blood by the will of God for us, and His flesh for our flesh, and His soul for our souls."[21] In the *Epistle of Diognetus* we have a beautiful testimony to the vicarious significance of the death of Jesus for man: "He

[14] Mirbt, *Quellen*[4], No. 23.
[15] *Ad Eph.* XVIII, 2; *Ad Tral.* IX.
[16] Cf. Ign., *Ad Magn.* VI, 1; Hermas, *Similitudo* V, 6.
[17] *Similitudo* IX, 12, 2.
[18] *Der Hirt des Hermas*, 1868, p. 261.
[19] *I Clement*, VII, 4.
[20] *Barnabas*, V, 1.
[21] *I Clement*, XLIX, 5.

gave His own Son a ransom for us, the Holy One for transgressors, the Blameless One for the wicked, the Righteous One for the unrighteous, the Incorruptible One for the corruptible, the Immortal One for them that are mortal. For what other thing than His righteousness was capable of covering our sins? By what other One was it possible that we, the wicked and the ungodly, could be justified, than by the only Son of God? O sweet exchange! O unsearchable device! O benefits surpassing all expectation! That the wickedness of many should be hid in a single Righteous One, and that the righteousness of One should justify many transgressors!" [22] Polycarp, Justin Martyr, Irenaeus and all the Fathers speak of the vicarious suffering of Christ. But there is no reflection upon the question why and how Christ's work has redeeming power. The Fathers liked to speak of the *gifts* which God had brought to mankind. Among these is *the forgiveness of sins,* but in the fashion of the Greek mind; the pre-eminent gifts are the *"knowledge of the truth"* and *"eternal life."* *The Homily of Clement* calls Christ the Redeemer and the Captain of immortality, "through Whom God revealed the truth and the heavenly life to us." [23] It is clear that the Apostolic Fathers took as prominent only those elements of the Christian revelation which were of special value to them and their times. The result was this one-sidedness and this meagerness of conception which impress the reader of today. While we see no error in these views, we cannot help but feel the absence of a unified and systematic teaching.

A positive error occurred when the gift of Christ came to be viewed principally as the revelation of a new law (*nova lex*). Christ was taken to be the new lawgiver. In the *Shepherd of Hermas* there are many statements expressing this sentiment. As a result, there is scarcely any trace of the Pauline doctrine of justification in the writings of these Fathers. They viewed man's relation with God as being regulated, not by faith, but by works. It is true that the *First Letter of Clement* has a passage which is strongly reminiscent of Paul: "All of them were therefore glorified and exalted, not through themselves, or their own, or the righteous actions which they had wrought, but through His will. And therefore we who by His will have been called in Christ Jesus are not made righteous by ourselves—but through faith, by which Almighty God has justified all men." [24] But this passage is without parallel in the rest of the Apostolic Fathers, and even Clement himself says in other places: "Blessed are we, beloved, if we perform the commandments of God in the concord of love, that through love our sins may be forgiven." [25]

Much has been written on the question, how to explain this preaching of moralism in the Post-Apostolic age, so shortly after the Gospel note of Paul had been heard.[26] There are the scholars who have suggested that it was an influence from the widespread Stoic philosophy which laid such great stress on the moral law and its observance. Others have spoken of Jewish influences. There is truth in both of these views. R. Seeberg remarks: "The legalism which here appears is not of the Jewish sort, but it nevertheless, without awakening suspicion, prepared the way for the intrusion of Judaic influences. The moralism is that of the heathen world, particularly in that age, and it has its origin

[22] Chap. IX.
[23] XX, 5.
[24] XXXII, 3, 4.
[25] L, 5.
[26] Read the interesting review of J. H. Kurtz, *Church History,* Eng. ed., 1888, sect. 30, 2. The writer has quoted the pertinent passages in his *Introduction to the Symbolical Books of the Lutheran Church*², 1926, pp. 149 f.

in the state of the natural man as such. The misconceptions of the Gospel may be traced directly to the fact that the Gentile Christians did not understand the Old Testament ideas presupposed in the apostolic proclamation of the Gospel. But moralism always serves the interests of legalism. Making much of man's own works, the age accepted (e.g. from the Book of Tobit), the legalistic works of the later Jewish piety." [27] In his 3rd edition R. Seeberg expresses himself on this whole situation in an entirely re-written discussion. He calls attention to the task that was upon the Church in that age of first steps into history. The Christian religion as a religion of redemption was not to be sacrificed, but there was the necessity of establishing among the newly converted the habit of an ethical life. So it came to that emphasis upon the "law of Christ." But since the whole atmosphere of life, through Stoicism and Judaism, was saturated with moralism, the emphasis upon the Christian life led back into these channels in such a way that the redemption through Christ was not clearly held in view.

With all this explanation, however, it is obvious that the emphasis has already begun to fall upon works and their merit. A far-reaching road was being prepared for a subsequent development. This is evidenced by statements like the following: "If you are able to do what is good, do not delay, for alms have power to release from death" (Polycarp). "Work with thy hands for the ransom of thy sins." [28] "If ye turn to the Lord with your whole heart and work righteousness the remaining days of your life, and serve Him strictly according to His will, He will heal your former sins." [29] "Almsgiving is therefore excellent as a repentance for sins; fasting is better than prayer; but almsgiving is better than either,—for almsgiving becomes lightening of the burden of sins." [30] Due to Jewish and heathen impulses, the idea also arose that it is possible to perform an *excess of good works,* which is made the foundation of a higher morality. The *Didache* declares: "If you will wear the entire yoke of Christ, you will be perfect; if not, then do what you can." [31] And Hermas says: "If you can do more than what God commands, you will earn more glory for yourself and you will have more honor before God." [32]

Thus we see that the errors connected with moralism have already begun to insinuate themselves. Grace, faith and forgiveness have yielded the ground to the new law and good works.

Postscript. The manuscript for this section was written long before Dr. Nygrén published his chapters on "Nomos, Eros and Agape" (pp. 31 ff.) and "The Nomos Type in the Apostolic Fathers and the Apologists" (38 ff.) in Part II, Vol. I of his work *Agape and Eros,* 1938. (See our review of the three volumes in the Introduction to our book.) We want to refer here to these above mentioned two chapters. It is the Jewish "Nomos Type" and its relation to the idea of Agape, in which the student will be interested. The "Two Ways" in the *Didache* "were fitted into the Jewish framework of Nomos," says Dr. Nygrén (p. 41). The Nomos functions as a motive in legalistic directions (p. 43 ff.).

4. The Church. The Post-Apostolic Fathers regarded the Church in terms of the highest appreciation.

---

[27] Eng. ed., 81 f.
[28] *Barnabas,* XIX, 10.
[29] Hermas, *Mandata,* XII, 6, 2.
[30] *Homily of Clement,* XVI, 4.
[31] VI, 2.
[32] *Similitudo* V, 3, 3.

To Clement of Rome it is the company of saints, the flock of Christ, and God's own possession. Even pre-existence is attributed to it. The *Homily of Clement*[33] declares that the first Church, the Spiritual Church, was created before the sun and moon. Hermas says that it was created first and before all things. The Church is the real goal of creation. Its connection with Christ is as intimate as that of the body with the soul. According to its being, the Church can only be "one" and "holy." Such was the case in the beginning, and such will be the case at the end. We belong to the Church if we do the will of our heavenly Father. But the Church is also historical and empirical. As such it contains within itself *objectionable elements*. Hermas expresses that idea in the following simile: "As the trees are all alike in winter, when they have cast their leaves, and it is not evident which ones are dead and which ones are full of vital energy, so in this world neither the righteous nor the unrighteous are recognized, but all appear alike." [34] But Hermas anticipates that it will not always be so. Again: "After these (i.e. the wicked) are cast out, the Church of God shall become one body, one understanding, one mind, one faith, one love; and then the Son of God shall rejoice exceedingly among them and receive His pure people." [35]

Ignatius likens the personal union between Christ and the believer to the relationship of the congregation to the bishop. He thus makes an easy transition from soteriology to ecclesiology. The bishop is the *centripetal point* of the congregation. Just as wherever Christ is, there is the Church Catholic, so "wherever the bishop appears, there let the people be." [36] The bishop is likewise the best weapon and protection against heresy. With this in mind, Ignatius says: "Shun divisions as the beginning of evils. Do ye all follow your bishop as Jesus Christ followed the Father, and the Presbytery as the Apostles, and to the deacons pay respect." [37] Although Ignatius never wearied of reminding the congregations to adhere to the bishop in view of the threatening dangers of heresy, he did not intend his statements to be understood in an hierarchical sense. The episcopate was still congregational, and not diocesan. Nevertheless his statements were soon to be used in the interest of the hierarchy.

It is also important to note that Ignatius thought of the Church not only as a local congregation, but also as a universal institution, extending throughout the whole world. He was the first to our knowledge to use the word "Catholic" to express the Church's universality.

Thus, statements on the dogma of the Church were already being made. The Church appears on the one hand as an ideal, eternal magnitude belonging to the sphere of God. On the other hand it is viewed as an empirical product which not only exists in the world, but which is also rendered peccant by the influences of the world.

5. *The Holy Scriptures.* To the Church belongs the Word of God. For the Apostolic Fathers the following may be mentioned as comprising that Word:

a. The Old Testament. The Apostolic Fathers depended upon the Old Testament in its entirety and recognized it as an absolute authority. Wherever we find "the Scripture" mentioned or quotations introduced with "it is written," we may be sure the Fathers were thinking of the Old Testament. It was regarded as "the revelation of the

---

[33] XIV, 1.
[34] *Simil.* III, 2; 3.
[35] IX, XVIII, 4.
[36] *Ad Smyrna* VIII, 2.
[37] *Ad Smyrna* VII, 2—VIII, 1.

past, present and future." [38] There were some who believed that Christianity had become the true Israel and hence the only custodian of the Old Testament after the rejection of the Jews, while others, like Barnabas, believed that God never made any revelation at all to the Jews; but all were agreed that the Old Testament now belongs to the Christians and not to the Jews. The Old Testament was interpreted entirely in terms of Chris-·ianity and the present. Gradually Old Testament institutions—especially the priesthood and the sacrificial idea—came to be looked upon as emblematic of the Christian congregation. Such a conception and interpretation of the Old Testament naturally destroyed any historical insight into it. With few exceptions this conception and its application continued to prevail until the Reformation.

b. The incipient New Testament. First there were the *Words of Jesus* which occupied a high position of authority with the Fathers. It is comparatively seldom, however, that we find an exact and solemn quotation of them. Next to the words of Jesus stood *those of the Apostles.* The First Epistle of Clement cites the books of the "prophets and apostles" as doctrinal authorities. It also admonishes the Corinthian congregation to read again the letter which the blessed Paul wrote to them, and to permit themselves to be instructed thereby. Zahn rightly says: "The possibility that an Apostle could have erred in the doctrine and instructions which he directed to the congregations had obviously no place in the circuit of ideas in the Post-apostolic Age." [39] Careful investigations have proved that the *thirteen Pauline Epistles and the four Gospels* were known to the Apostolic Fathers. But it must remain an open question whether or not they used these writings in the form of a closed collection as a sort of Canon; this is the claim which Zahn has made in his *History of the Canon* in contradiction to other investigators. It should be noted in passing that the formation of a New Testament was not precipitated in the first instance by heretical antitheses such as Gnosticism. It was due first of all to normal impulses which proceeded from motives lying within Christianity itself. The Church's struggle with heresy simply strengthened the incipient New Testament Canon and brought it to a formal conclusion sooner than would otherwise have been the case. The subject will be discussed more at length in Chapter VI on the Source and Norm of Truth.

6. The Sacraments. To the Church belong also the Sacraments. These had not yet been influenced by the ancient mysteries, and hence remained true to the spirit of primitive Christianity. We need not identify ourselves with the position of the Historico-Religious School that the Sacraments in the New Testament were a product of the mystery religion. We refer to the larger part of the literature quoted in connection with Chapter XII and to our statement at that place.

a. Baptism. First in the name of Jesus, but gradually in the name of the Triune God, Father, Son and Holy Spirit, baptism was thought of as the real instrument for imparting the gift of Christianity.[40] Barnabas says: "We go down into the water laden with sins and filth, and rise from it, bearing fruit in the heart, having reverence and hope in Jesus in our spirits." [41] Hermas declares: "There is no other repentance than this, that we go down into the water and receive the forgiveness of past sins." [42] Thus,

---

[38] *Barnabas,* I, 7.
[39] *Geschichte des Kanons,* 1888 ff., I², p. 804.
[40] *Didache* VII, 1-3.
[41] XI, 11.
[42] *Mandata* IV, iii, 1.

baptism confers the forgiveness of sins. It is also the "seal" that we have received the Holy Spirit and with Him the assurance of a new life of faith and hope in Christ. With the forgiveness of sins man receives a new heart and also the obligation to live according to Christ's commandments. On the meaning of baptism as a seal for the gift of the Holy Spirit, Hermas and Second Clement especially, moved entirely in the language of Paul (II Cor. 1:22; Eph. 1:13; 4:30).

b. We noted that baptism secures the forgiveness only of *past* sins. But what about those of the future? It was concern over this question which started a development that later led to the *sacrament of repentance.* There was living in these early Christians a deep-going recognition of sin, but with a marked distinction between the unavoidable sins of daily occurrence and some special sins of a graver nature that must absolutely be absent in the life of a real Christian. Here we have the beginning of the later theory of "venial" and "mortal" sins. The prevailing idea of the time was that repentance for sins is an inner experience gone through once and for all time when one enters the Christian life. It had been the teaching of Judaism that in the last Messianic times there would be no further opportunity for repentance because the Lord will function as judge.[43] Where was the hope for the many among the Christians who after baptism had fallen into grave sins? It was concern over this that drove many Christians into extraordinary despair and pangs of conscience. It can easily be imagined that passages such as I John 5:16 f. and Hebr. 6:4-6; 10:26 f.; 12:17, etc., had been used falsely to limit repentance as a grace. How should troubled souls find relief? It was to this problem that Hermas devoted himself. He announced that in an exceptional way God is willing to permit even a second repentance. But he exhorted the fallen to earnest repentance as the *condition* of participation in this present and final revelation of God's grace.[44] R. Seeberg points out the fundamental error when he says: "The chief defection from the Biblical standard lies in the failure to understand grace as the forgiveness of sins extending continually throughout the whole of life."[45]

b. The Eucharist. In the Lord's Supper the coming and presence of Christ are prayed for and experienced. The growing realistic conception of this sacrament is indicated by the following statement of Ignatius: "The Eucharist is the flesh of our Saviour Jesus Christ, which suffered for our sins, which the Father in His goodness raised from the dead." He speaks of the "breaking of the one bread, which is the medicine of immortality, an antidote that we might not die, but live in Jesus Christ forever."[46] The Eucharist still meant a "thankoffering." The sacrificial conception had not yet appeared. The celebration of the Supper was charged with a strong eschatological significance, as is indicated by the famous Eucharistic prayers with their petition: "Let grace come, and let the world pass away."[47] Among the Apostolic Fathers there was no speculation on the meaning of the words of institution. One needs to read the critical review by Loofs in the *PRE,* I, 39-41 of the endeavors to interpret the meaning both of Ignatius and of Justin in their expression on the Eucharist, to despair of all possibility of arriving at anything of practical value for the future teaching of the Church on this sacrament. The Post-Apostolic Fathers considered the Lord's Supper a mystery of greatest importance,

---

[43] *Apocalypse of Baruch,* LXXXV, 12; IV Esdras, VII, 112-115.
[44] *Mand.,* IV.
[45] Eng. ed., I, *DG,* I³, 157-164. We shall return to this subject in Chapter VII, II, a.
[46] *Eph.,* XX, 2.
[47] *Didache,* X, 6.

but they had no mature thoughts on the subject. For a more comprehensive review of the whole situation on the sacraments in the early Church and later, see Chapter 12.

7. *Eschatology.* The time of the Apostolic Fathers, like that of primitive Christianity, was thoroughly eschatological in tendency. Men had the consciousness that they were living in the last times. The immediate return of Jesus was anticipated. It was this expectation which held the congregations together. Men considered it their imperative task to keep an eye on the approaching end and to work for their moral betterment, so as not to be surprised by its appearance. In looking for the consummation, men learned to observe the signs of the times and to watch for definite indications which would precede Christ's coming. The precedent signs were to take the form of false prophets and seducers, increase of wickedness and persecutions, Anti-Christ, signs and wonders, the resurrection of the dead. Chiliasm was defended by Papias in a very gross and materialistic form. He spoke of a thousandfold fruitfulness of vines and crops. According to Barnabas, the return of Christ would be followed by His temporal reign for a thousand years. Although the historical Church comprises both good and bad, the final judgment will bring about a separation of the righteous and the unrighteous. The resurrection is defined in a decidedly Jewish and anti-Grecian sense, as the resurrection of the flesh. The chief thing remained the final judgment of the world, and the certainty that the holy shall go to heaven to God, and the unholy to the place of eternal punishment.

Chapter Four

THE GREEK APOLOGISTS

I. ORIENTATION

Literature: The writings of the Apologists here under consideration are found in Greek in the *Corpus Apologetarum,* ed. Otto, 9 vols. (1844 ff. and 1876 ff.) In *Texte und Untersuchungen* by GEBHARDT, HARNACK and SCHMIDT, we have Tatian, Athenagoras and Aristides (*T. U.*). See *Texts and Studies* (*T. and St.*), edited by J. A. ROBINSON since 1917. The *ANF*, Vols. I, II, and IX contain English translations of the Greek Apologists. R. SEEBERG, R. RAABE, E. HENNECKE and J. GEFFCKEN have written on Aristides in special investigations; M. VON ENGELHARDT, A. STAEHLIN, W. FLEMMING and E. R. GOODENOUGH on Justin Martyr; SCHWARTZ and HAR-NACK on Tatian. P. CARRINGTON wrote on *Christian Apologetics of the Second Century in its Relation to Modern Thought,* London, 1921. See the titles in the theological encyclopedias of late editions. For references to and quotations from the Apologists see H. RINN, 1910, pp. 20 ff. Of special importance are the Histories of Doctrine in their latest editions. See especially SEEBERG, I³, 331 ff. Cf. NYGRÉN, *Agape and Eros,* Part II, Vol. I, 49 ff.

1. *Occasion for the Rise of Christian Apologists.* The second century was an age of severe conflicts for Christianity. It was exposed to the attacks which came from Judaism and the Gnostic movements. Of this we shall treat in Chapter V. Here we call attention to an attack of a different sort. Heathenism as a whole, backed by the Roman Empire, turned against Christians. The latter were looked upon as a menace to the state. Both their morals and their faith were impugned. Consequently, Christianity had of necessity to prove its right to exist. Defenders were needed who were equipped with the scholarship necessary to meet this foe. These came to the front in a whole group of writers which we shall now study. It is a study at once interesting and important, because it is in these *Apologists* that we have the first attempt at a system of Christian theology.

2. *Their Aims.* Two tasks occupied the attention of the Apologists. (1) They aimed to defend Christianity against the gross calumnies and misrepresentations of the heathen writers and against the rumors current among the people of that time. Heathen-ism had made a significant attack on Christianity through the medium of the philosopher Celsus and his work *The True Word,* which appeared in A. D. 178. Of this work we possess only fragments. Celsus, the most typical spokesman of heathenism, declared the entire Christian teaching to be utter folly and pure myth. He claimed that numerous discrepancies and fabrications were to be found in the Christian Scriptures. Especially repugnant to him was the idea of the incarnation of God. These objections were answered by the Christian Apologists, who sought to formulate for the first time a *science of Christian truth. On the one hand,* heathenism as viewed from the standpoint of ethics and history, was sharply criticized as a religion of demons. *On the other hand,* the Apologists recognized copious elements of truth in the heathen religions and especially in the Greek philosophy. These elements of truth, they said, were derived *historically* from the Old Testament, or *metaphysically* from the *seminal logos* (λόγος σπερματικός) which appeared in Christ as the *entire logos* (ὁ πᾶς λόγος) or *psychologically* from the soul which is by nature Christian, or *ethically* from the sense of morality which is inborn

in every man. By the application of the contemporary philosophical conception of the *Logos,* Christianity was set forth as the true philosophy. In writing thus, the Apologists offered a positive doctrine in the form of a Christian philosophy, especially in reference to the *Logos.* Where it was possible and suitable to their purpose, they justified the Christian doctrine by drawing certain analogies between Christianity and heathenism. From apologetics some of the Apologists turned to polemics and pointed out the folly, immoral character, and intolerance of heathenism. (2) Next to the religion of heathenism, and quite inseparable from it, stood the menace of the empire. The growing intolerance of Rome and the increasing taste of the emperors for Christian blood, were matters which called loudly for literary defenders.

Note: Our present discussion is limited to the *Greek Apologists.* The most important of these, and likewise the most frequently quoted are the following: Aristides, Justin Martyr, Tatian, Athenagoras and Theophilus of Antioch. Of these Justin is an especially outstanding figure. The time of their activity was from about A.D. 130 to 180. Of course, Irenaeus, Origen, Minucius Felix, Cyprian and Tertullian were apologists too. But for the History of Doctrine they must be reserved for later consideration.

II. REVIEW OF THEIR WRITINGS

1. MARCIANUS ARISTIDES addressed an *Apology* to Emperor Antonius Pius (150). *See Texts and Studies* (I, 1) edited by J. A. Robinson; cf. description by A. Harnack in the *New Schaff-Herzog Encyclopedia,* I, 283.
2. JUSTIN MARTYR wrote in the same year an *Apology* with a supplement, known as the *Second Apology* to the same emperor. This was the most important of all these Apologies. He further wrote a *Dialogue with Trypho the Jew* and a treatise *On the Resurrection.* See the texts in G. Krueger, *Quellenschriften,* 1891 (last ed. 1904). We have an English translation of his writings in the *Library of the Fathers,* edited by E. B. Pusey, J. Keble and J. H. Newman (Oxford, 1861). Cf. the Edinburgh series of the *Ante-Nicene Fathers,* Vol. I, 194 ff. The necessary information about his life and writings is given by N. Bonwetsch in the *New Schaff-Herzog,* IV, 282. There has been an interesting conflict about the type of Justin's theology between M. v. Engelhardt (*Das Christentum Justins des Maertyrers,* 1878) and A. Staehlin (*Justin der Maertyrer und sein neuester Beurteiler,* 1880). For a list of literature see the encyclopedias (*PRE., NSH., HE., RGG.*).
3. TATIAN of Syria wrote an *Address to the Greeks* (150), which contained a severe criticism of paganism. For his life and writing we refer the student to the article by E. Preuschen in the *New Schaff-Herzog,* XI, 274. Cf. the article in the *Encyclopedia Britannica,* (11th ed., XXVI, 450).
4. ATHENAGORAS wrote (c. 177) a *Petition for the Christians,* which was addressed to Marcus Aurelius and Commodus. In this work he refuted the current accusations. He wrote also a treatise, *On the Resurrection.* See the *New Schaff-Herzog,* I, 347 (cf. *HE.* and *RGG.*).
5. THEOPHILUS, bishop of Antioch, wrote three books *To Autolykos,* a heathen friend.
6. *Lost Writings.* With the exception of a few remnants, the following writings have all been lost. QUADRATUS, *To Emperor Hadrian;* B. CLAUDIUS APOLLINATIÚS of Hierapolis. *To Marcus Aurelius, To the Greeks,* and *Of the Truth;* MILTIADES, *To the Greeks, To the Jews,* and *To the Secular Prince Concerning the Christian Philosophy;* B. MELITO of Sardis, *To Marcus Aurelius; Ariston of Pella,* an anti-Jewish *Dialogue between Jason and Papiscus.*

III. A FEW OF THE ESSENTIAL THOUGHTS OF THE GREEK APOLOGISTS

1. Their Conception of God. The Apologists emphasized that God is one. He has created the world out of nothing and He preserves it.[1] In their description of the Divine Being they spoke in negative terms: He is "invisible," "unbegotten," "incomprehensible," etc.[2] What is best in God they hesitated to express, for fear that the Divinity

---

[1] Justin 1:6; Ath. 8; Theoph. III, 9.
[2] Arist. 1; Justin *Apol.* I, 10, 13, 25, 49, 53; II, 6; *Dial.* 127; Tat. 4; Ath. 10, 13, 16, 44, 21. Theoph. I, 4, 3; II, 10, 3, 22.

might be dragged down into the sphere of the creature, as was done in the mythologies of the heathen world.

They taught that it was through the *Logos* that God created the world. God is spaceless and infinite, and therefore was in need of the *Logos* as a middle being to bridge the gap and chasm between Him and the world. What had the Apologists to say on this much discussed topic of their age?

2. *The Logos*

a. Let us ask first: *Why did the Apologists speak of Christ in terms of "Logos"?* The answer of Seeberg is worthy of quotation: "This was a favored term of the cultured classes. Whenever it was mentioned the interest of all was at once secured. But that precisely this term was chosen proves how entirely the thoughts of the Church were centered in the exalted Christ. If they had thought chiefly of the man Jesus, they might easily have characterized Him as a second Socrates. But they thought of Him as God, in God and with God; and hence selected a term such as *Logos* in order to make the matter plain to the heathen" (English ed. I[2], 113; German ed. I[3], 344 ff.).

b. The Eternal Pre-existence of the Logos. The *Logos* existed before He became incarnate. He existed as the divine reason (νοῦς) in God, just as a thought exists in man before it issues forth in verbal utterance. To this pre-existent *Logos* Theophilus applied the word ἐνδιάθετος, which was used by the Stoic philosophers and also by Philo.[3] Thus the Logos was the divine immanent reason.

c. The Work of the Logos was seen in this, that he was operative at the creation of the world and later in the prophets and wise men.[4] According to Justin the *Logos* has a most intimate relationship with the reason of man, and man's perception of truth is derived from the *Logos*. He is the *seminal Logos* of whom all men partake. From this source heathen philosophers received all the truth which was contained in their systems. It was the *Logos* who spoke through the prophets of the Old Testament.[5] In the fulness of time the *Logos* was born of the Virgin Mary and became Man, took unto Himself flesh, blood and a human soul. He still remained God. The purpose of the incarnation of the *Logos* was to teach mankind the higher philosophy which embraces the one God, the "New Law" requiring a righteous life, and immortality, or, more strictly speaking, the resurrection, bringing with it rewards and punishments.[6]

d. The Personal Differentiation of the Logos from God. From all eternity the Father was simply *logos-natured.* But for the purpose of creation the *Logos* was projected as an independent personal being. By an exercise of God's will, the *Logos* sprang forth as the thought is uttered in speech (λόγος προφορικός). This involved no separation or violence or loss in the Godhead, but was like unto the fire which is not diminished by kindling another from it. (Justin, *Dial.* 61 et al; Theophilus, *Ad Autol.* II, 10, 22.) To express the idea of how the *Logos* became differentiated the word γεννηθῆναι was used, and the word κτίζεσθαι avoided. The *Logos* was called "the first production of the Father," "the first-born work of the Father." [7] He appeared as the angel of the covenant in the Old Testament, and in the fulness of time He took upon Himself our

[3] *Ad Autolykon,* II. 10.
[4] Justin, *Apol.*, I. 44.
[5] *Apol.*, II. 8, 13, 14.
[6] *Apol.*, I. 12-19.
[7] Tatian, c. 5.

nature. This *personal differentiation* of the *Logos* from God was something new, and it was Christian when considered in the light of the Stoic philosophy. Still it should be noted that according to the Apologists there was no personal differentiation of the *Logos* before the creation. And although Christ and the *Logos* were identified, nevertheless the *historical Christ* was pushed somewhat into the background, and the Son of God was understood to be the pre-existent *Logos*.

e. *Subordinationism.* The Apologists, especially Justin, taught the subordination of the Son to the Father. From Justin's *Dialogue* (Cf. Seeberg, Eng. ed., 113) the Father alone is the real God; the *Logos* is only a Divine Being of second rank. With respect to the Father the *Logos* is something else (ἕτερόν τι) and another (ἄλλος τις). He is the Father's organ and servant, and is dependent on Him. He is different also in this, that while the Father is eternal, infinite, incomprehensible, unchangeable and transcendent, the Son is not (Justin, *Dial.* 56, 62, 128 f.). Loofs remarks that the Apologists outside of Justin were not so strong in their insistence upon subordination. However, it was a tenet which continued to trouble the developing Christian Church. See our Chapter X on the Trinity.

3. *The Trinity.* The Apologists were familiar with the triadic baptismal formula. Theophilus was the first to use the term τριας.[8] Nevertheless the Godhead was a Triad rather than a Trinity with the Apologists. This is seen in the fact that while the Spirit was distinguished from the *Logos* and the Father, He was subordinated to both. Due to the idea that the *Logos* inspired the prophets and was now at work everywhere, there was little room left for the activity of the Holy Spirit. Fortunately the Apologists had no occasion to speak to the heathen about the Holy Spirit. As yet they themselves had not clarified their ideas on the subject.

4. *Anthropology.* The Apologists rejected the Stoic fatalism. On the contrary, they taught, man is endowed of God with freedom of the will. By means of this freedom he is able to make decisions in favor of goodness and truth. Through Jesus' teaching man learns the correct use of his freedom, and is thus enabled to be victorious in his struggle with carnal weakness and demonic temptations. Thus he finally arrives at union with God.[9] But with these conceptions the Apologists failed to perceive the powers of man's natural depravity.

5. *Church and Sacraments.* The *Church of Christ* is the true Israel, the People of God, a new generation, a generation of the pious, etc. When the Christians were blamed for not serving in the army, the Apologists replied that the Christians do a much better thing—they pray that the emperor may be successful and victorious. Instead of being dangerous to the empire, the Christians are really the ones who hold it and the world together.[10]

Baptism in the name of the Holy Trinity, was considered a washing of forgiveness and a regeneration. It brings pardon and the new life, and is therefore necessary to salvation.[11]

The Eucharist as conceived by Justin was this: "We have been taught that the food blessed by the word of prayer employed by Him, from which our bodies and blood are

---

[8] II. 15.
[9] Justin, *Apol.* II. 6, 13; *Dial.* 30:1 a.
[10] Theoph. II. 14.
[11] Justin, *Dial.* XXX. 19.

by its transformation nourished (κατὰ μεταβολήν), is also the Body and Blood of the same Jesus who was made flesh." [12] Because of the phrase here quoted, Justin has been cited as teaching transubstantiation. But these words cannot be taken in this sense. Yet we have here the idea that "the divine *Logos* is mysteriously present in the bread and wine, as in the Incarnate Christ" (Fisher, p. 68). All through Church History there run two conceptions of the Eucharist: 1) the *realistic* which sometimes culminates in the metabolic view; and 2) the *spiritualistic* or *symbolic*. Justin belongs to the line of realists, just as Augustine, later, is found on the symbolic side. As to a view of the whole development see Chapter XIII, B.

6. *Eschatology*. In eschatology the Apologists restricted themselves to the thoughts of primitive Christianity as opposed to Hellenism and Gnosticism. Since the body as well as the soul had chosen righteousness on this earth, it was only natural that the body would be expected to share in the imperishable character of the soul. The Apologists therefore looked for an immortality of the body along with that of the soul. The emphasis with which they championed this point was occasioned by the opposition they met at the hands of the Gnostics. The Apologists taught also the Parousia of Christ and the Millennial Kingdom. At the appearing of Christ, both good and bad will stand before Him to receive the reward of their deeds.

7. *Christianity a Philosophy*. To the Apologists Christianity appeared as a true philosophy. Some of them declared Christianity to be the absolute truth, of which heathenism was the direct antithesis. Others thought of heathenism as being only the imperfect bud, while Christianity was the full-blown and perfect flower. At any rate, all of them pointed to Christianity as a higher and more reliable philosophy. In heathenism and Christianity the aim is identical, namely, to arrive at a trustworthy knowledge of the true God, virtue and immortality. But Christianity is a better, an absolutely reliable philosophy, *because it rests not upon its own speculation, but upon perfect revelation.*

The channels through which this perfect revelation has come are twofold. The first is the *Scriptures of the Old Testament*. Since they are inspired by God and the *Logos*, they are inerrant. From this source the philosophers derived many of their ideas. Such a presentation stimulated a lively interest in the Old Testament in the churches. The second channel of this perfect revelation is the *Logos*. Before His incarnation the *Logos* had spoken through the prophets and wise men. When He had become man, He continued His work directly in person. The Apologists often took the teachings of Christ, proved them from the Old Testament, and then compared them with the corresponding thoughts of heathen philosophy. Such comparison and contrast had great apologetic value.

IV. ESTIMATE

It seems to be a *fait accompli* with the histories of doctrine that rationalism and moralism are the distinctive marks of the Christianity of the Apologists. Said Moritz von Engelhardt in his pioneer work *Das Christentum Justins des Maertyrers (1878)*: "Justin wishes to be, and according to his faith is, a Christian. But he is a Christian who shows in everything his dependence upon the world-view as held by heathenism" (Cf. p. 210). And again: "Justin is at once a Christian and a heathen" (p. 485). In

[12] Just. *Apol.* I, 66.

the opinion of Harnack, the Apologists made Christianity a "deistical religion." In *content* their theology differs hardly from the idealistic philosophy of their contemporaries. Their religion, he held, is a rationalistic religion with emphasis on one God, virtue, and immortality (*DG*[4], II, 224 ff.) Over against this severe criticism, A Nygrén has come out to make an act of reparation to the Apologists, and especially to Justin. Upon the background of the Lundensian *motiv-forskningen,* Nygrén refuses to be led astray in his judgment by the apparently philosophical language of the Apologists. When these speak of Christianity as a "New Philosophy" and "New Law," Nygrén maintains that they have not surrendered the essence of the "Agape-type" (see our Introduction) of religion. In later antiquity philosophy was occupied, Nygrén points out, "not with pondering theoretical, rational problems, but with the cure of souls, to bring help to a troubled and suffering generation." [13] Accordingly it is not a theoretical, but a practical, religious interest which drives Justin to philosophy, and for him its task is to give instruction about God and set man in relationship with Him" (p. 52). That Christianity is the True Philosophy means to him that it is "the true religion, the right Way of salvation, the only one that can lead to real fellowship with God" (p. 53). This Way is possible for man "solely as God in Agape comes down to man and meets him *through revelation*" (p. 54).

Likewise, as regards Justin's definition of Christianity as a "New Law," Nygrén holds that it has no legal meaning. The New Law, according to Justin, is the New Covenant; it is not a sum of new commandments, but Christ Himself Whose Agape is manifest in the Cross which, as Nygrén insists, holds a central part in Justin's thought.

In passing critical judgment upon the Apologists, it must be remembered that every practical apologetic proof forced them to accommodate themselves to the language of their opponents. Thus, in contrast to Harnack, we would say that the theology of the Apologists is philosophical in *form,* but that there is a great wealth of genuine New Testament piety back of their philosophical terminology. Such a method, however, always breeds danger. In the course of time, language will inevitably affect the content of its message. In this respect the Apologists set a bad example for succeeding generations. Nygrén is steering in the right direction, as can be seen from a statement previous to his discussion of Justin: "The post-apostolic period shrank from accepting its (i.e. Paul's message of Agape) consequences; and although Paul's message of the Agape of the Cross might have shown the way, there is hardly a trace of Paulinism in this early period." It is the Nomos-type which "is mainly found in the Apostolic Fathers" (p. 35).[14]

---

[13] *Agape and Eros,* Part II, Vol. I, 51.
[14] The observant reader will notice that the two statements of Nygrén are little short of contradictory.

Chapter Five

PERVERSIONS OF CHRISTIANITY

In Chapters VI and VII, and especially in Chapter VIII and the following chapters, our studies will be on the Catholic Church ("Old Catholic," "Ecumenical Catholic"), its norms and foundations, its government, its theology, its historical faith, its church practice.

Our present Chapter V is given this place for the purpose of starting us in a study of some of the earliest of sectarian aberrations from the Church Catholic (or the Church Universal).[a]

There are other sectarian movements besides the four here to be discussed: the Novatians, Donatists (concerning the Church); Sabellians, Samosatenes, Arians, Nestorians, Eutychians or Monophysites—all on the Person of Christ and on His relation in the Trinity; Pelagians and Semi-Pelagians, on nature and grace. These all will be spoken of later in their historical connection.

Most of these "Sects" do not exist under the old names, but many of their principles still live as historical tendencies in present-day Comparative Symbolics (*Konfessionskunde*) and in the History of Religion.

Literature: H. SCHMID, former professor in Breslau University, *Handbuch der Symbolik,* 1890 f., offered a thoroughgoing discussion of the *Haeresen* in the Ancient Church (pp. 460-488). Cf. J. L. NEVE, *Churches and Sects of Christendom,* 1940 ff. See especially the section on the Distinction between Church and Sects, pp. 33-41. Cf. the theological and religious encyclopedias; also E. T. CLARK, *The Small Sects in America,* 1937. (Many American sects have their roots in heretical tenets of the Ancient Church.)

In considering the heretical perversions of Christianity in the Ancient Church it is to be observed that they took their rise from two chief sources. The first source, which was at once Jewish and Gentile in character, lay outside of Christianity. The second was found within Christianity itself. The chief representatives of these various perversions may be classified as follows: (1) Judaizing Christianity, which was essentially Jewish in its origin; (2) Gnosticism, which was of heathen parentage; (3) Marcion, whose ideas were derived, half and half, from heathenism and Christianity; and (4) Montanism, which was rooted mainly in Christianity.

I. EBIONITISM

Primary Sources: JUSTIN, *Dialogus cum Tryphone,* c. 47. IRENAEUS, *Adversus haereses,* I, 26, 2. ORIGEN, *Contra Celsum,* II, 1, 3; V, 61, 65. EPIPHANIUS, *Panarion haer.,* 29, 30. EUSEBIUS, *Historia,* III, 27. HIERONYMUS, *Epistulae,* 112-113. HIPPOLYTUS, *Philosophumena,* VII, 34; IX, 13-16.

Literature: in *German:* E. PREUSCHEN, *Antilegomena,* 1901 and 1905. E. KLOSTERMANN, *Apokrypha,* I, II, 1908. T. ZAHN, *History of the N. T. Canon,* II. G. HOENNECKE, *Judentum im 1 u. 2 Jahrhundert,* 1908. W. BRANDT, *Elchasai,* 1912. E. HENNECKE, *Neutestamentliche Apokryphen²,* 1924. In *English:* A. NEANDER, *Christian Church,* I, 344-364. P. SCHAFF, *Christian Church,* II, 428-432. Cf. J. B. LIGHTFOOT, *Galatians,* Dissertation III, London, 1890.

---

[a] Spoken of by the apostles as hairesis. Cf. II Peter 2:1; Gal. 5:20; I Cor. 11:19. The Latin fathers said "haereses." So in the title to the great work of Irenaeus (Chap. VIII).

Our discussion of a heretical Judaizing Christianity needs only touch upon those points where this perversion maintained principles that were incompatible with Christianity. Nationality and the Law were two such principles. Hoennecke in his exhaustive work on Jewish-Christianity, gives us this definition: "The peculiar conception of the Gospel, which was characteristic of the Christianity of Jewish origin, consisted in this: (1) it was opposed to Paul's universal preaching and his law-free Gospel and (2) it had for its significance: Complete salvation can be secured only through the medium of Judaism. Thus in connection with the declaration of Jesus' Gospel, this Jewish national-principle was urged and the bond uniting religion and nationality was maintained" (p. 18).

These Jewish Christians had already been in evidence in the Apostolic age; and although their presence was still felt in the post-Apostolic age, they were gradually losing their influence, so far as the prevailing Gentile-Christian Church was concerned. In Ebionitism, however, they began to take on an increasingly pronounced heretical character. The varying accounts of the Church Fathers make it difficult for us to present a clear picture of Ebionitism. Justin's delineation is the most lucid. Justin was acquainted with two classes of Jewish Christians. The one deemed that the Law had binding authority only on those who were Jews by birth. The other insisted on imposing the Law upon Gentile Christians as well. It is probably correct to call the stricter of these two groups "Ebionite."

In addition to the principles we have already mentioned, the Ebionites represented a *heterodox Christology*. To them Jesus was merely a man. They rejected the Virgin Birth, and insisted that the Holy Spirit, who was curiously thought of as a female, had descended upon Jesus for the first time at His baptism. The Messianic work of Christ was looked upon as that of a prophet and a teacher, in consequence of which He wrought miracles and enlarged the Law by precepts of greater strictness.

This Jewish Christianity received also an influx of Gentile ideas, and so resulted in a kind of Jewish-Christian Gnosticism. This was emphasized in a certain book written by Elkasai in the reign of Emperor Trajan. Angelic powers played a great role. The Virgin Birth was rejected. Christ Himself was thought of as the Primal Man who was continually becoming incarnate. The Law was to be retained, but the sacrificial system was abrogated. Its place was taken by all kinds of lustrations and by an ascetic mode of life. The Gnostic views of Jewish Christianity influenced a species of Ancient Church-literature—the so-called *Pseudo-Clement's writings*. Under the name of Peter and his alleged pupil Clement of Rome, these writings set forth the principles of Judaizing Christianity in a strongly polemical fashion.

By the fifth century Ebionitism had practically disappeared. If it had any effect at all on the Church, it was to force the Church toward the formulation of a correct Christology.

II. GNOSTICISM

Literature: Our knowledge of Gnosticism is derived chiefly from the reports of its opponents, the Church Fathers, such as Justin, Irenaeus, Tertullian, Hippolytus and Epiphanius. These, however, do not always agree with each other; indeed, contradictory statements are often made by the same reporter. In addition to these writings we have some few original documents, as for instance the *Letter of Ptolemaeus to Flora*, the *Pistis Sophia*, and a number of fragments. The student will find valuable orientation in HAUCK, *Protestantische Realencyklopaedie* and in the *New Schaff-Herzog*, especially in the most up-to-date review in *Religion in Geschichte und Gegenwart*, II, 1272-1281. If he wishes to make a careful study of the various systems, he will find a great deal of material conveniently arranged in W. SCHULTZ, *Documents of Gnosticism*, 1910. The deductions of this book, however, must be read critically. As sources for general reading in English we mention the Church Histories of SCHAFF and NEANDER. NEANDER also wrote a genetical history of the leading systems of Gnosticism under the title *Genetische Entwicklung*, etc. (1818). D. R. S. MEADE, *Fragments of a Faith Forgotten*, 1906. Also W. BOUSSET, *Die Hauptprobleme der Gnosis*, 1907. In our brief survey we shall not take the space to quote the ancient sources. Our references will be to the larger Histories of Dogma, such as those of THOMASIUS, LOOFS and SEEBERG; to Church Histories of KURTZ, WALKER; to texts as published by H. RINN. We have used HARNACK in the one volume edition (6th) of his *Dogmengeschichte, Grundriss*, 1922, and shall occasionally point to other editions.

The following statements will summarize in brief the *general features* of Gnosticism:

1. The Origin and Rise of Gnosticism. The investigations of Bousset have made it clear that Gnosticism began as a movement within paganism. It was one of the results of that process of religious fusion which had begun before the advent of Christianity. Following the religious syncretism of the time, Gnosticism approached Christianity with the intention of adding it to the long list of contributing religions.

The whole movement, as it appears in the light of history, had for its explanation a number of interesting reasons. (1) The ancient world had exhausted its resources and was now dying of a terrible hunger—a hunger for salvation. Only a powerful stimulant could ward off its imminent death. (2) Although many of the ancients rejoiced over the salutary and rejuvenating influences which Christianity had introduced, some of them were not at all satisfied with a religion which proclaimed the Divinity of Christ and the foolishness of the Cross. (3) The intellectual and cultivated minds of the day felt that the Church did not make as much of philosophical thought and principles as it should. (4) To those who were acquainted with the elaborate and mysterious ceremonies of heathenism, the worship of the Church seemed strangely dry and barren.

Led by these considerations, Gnosticism proposed to remedy the situation by forming an alliance between the religions of paganism and that of the Church. This desperate endeavor to rejuvenate the ancient world, favored by the syncretistic drift of the age, resulted in the boldest and grandest syncretism the world had ever seen. All the previously isolated and heterogeneous elements of religion, philosophy and culture were to be blended in one. Revelation was to be combined with the "wisdom of the world," and Christianity was to be made a truly modern religion. This gigantic undertaking was decidedly favored by the "all-prevailing drift of the age in the direction of syncretism, the disposition to amalgamate mythology with philosophy, to explain and assimilate, as far as might be, Oriental religions, systems and cults." Seeberg calls this the first attempt in the history of the Church to bring the world into subjection to the Church by interpreting Christianity in harmony with the world.

2. The Elements Represented in Gnosticism. Gnosticism was an eclectic movement in which cosmological myths, the philosophical thoughts of Greek and Oriental paganism, and the truths of Christianity were represented. The religions of Babylonia, Syria, Asia Minor, Persia and India, the Judaism of Philo, and the Christianity of Jesus and the Apostles were all fused in the Gnostic crucible. Gnosticism possessed certain features in common with Christianity, as for instance the divine plan of salvation, the Christian tradition, and the centrality of Christ in human history. But these features were badly distorted. As a rule heathenism predominated. The student should note the emphasis which was placed on the idea of evolution, the cosmogonic theories, and the pagan mystery-worship.

3. Knowledge versus Faith (Gnosis versus Pistis). In the Christian system, faith was held to be the faculty through which salvation is acquired. For the Gnostics, however, "gnosis" or higher knowledge was the channel of salvation. This "gnosis" did not mean a mere intellectual knowledge acquired by mental processes, but rather a supernatural knowledge which came from divine revelation and enlightenment. In harmony with the claims of Greek philosophers who asserted the existence of a race of intellectual patricians, the Gnostics claimed to possess a deeper knowledge of divine things than did the ordinary believer. Hence the name *gnostikoi*—"the men who know"—as used in certain Gnostic circles. This esoteric system of Gnosticism naturally appeared more profound than did current Christianity with its popular creed. But in spite of its much vaunted claim to a higher knowledge, Gnosticism never attained to a higher goal than the precincts of its ancient mythology.

4. A Way of Salvation. (Cf. points 5 and 9; also Nygrén, Part II, Vol. I, 77 ff.) Although the Gnostics were deeply interested in the fabrication of speculative religious philosophies, this was not their chief concern. In fact, philosophical considerations were really a secondary affair with them. The underlying idea of Gnosticism was the avowed purpose to present a way of salvation to a sick world. Loofs says: "All these speculations are ancillary to the idea of redemption." Being fundamentally redemptive in purpose, Gnosticism sought to establish not merely a religion, but rather the universal religion. In addition to its speculative and mythological aspects, Gnosticism claimed to have a divine revelation from God. Divine revelation, mystical experience, symbolical forms of enchantment, and the practice of asceticism—these were the means by which the higher life was to be achieved. The heathen mysteries were imitated and employed to impart saving knowledge. Religious organizations with elaborate rituals were even established.

5. Gnostic Problems. The problems which engaged the minds of the Gnostics were of a highly speculative nature. In one sense they were simply the old philosophical questions to which the mind of man has ever been devoted. But in a far deeper sense they were the serious problems which, if happily solved would give men a satisfactory answer to the great question: "What shall I do to be saved?" In other words, the end of these problems was the solution of the problem of man's redemption. Hence it was that Gnosticism was ever querying: Whence God? Whence the world? Whence man? Whence evil? How are we to explain that mysterious commingling of spirit and matter in man, or how did man become fettered in the chains of matter? How is redemption effected? Who is the Redeemer? How do we attain immortality?

Let us now proceed to point out a few of the characteristic features of Gnosticism:[1]

6. The Dualistic Theory. It is important that we understand this dualistic conception, because it is here that we find the origin of the world and man, of sin and woe, and hence the resultant necessity of redemption.

Gnosticism derived its dualism from the *Syrian systems* which had been shaped under *Parsee influences.* Persian dualism was physical and consisted of two antagonistic principles—light and darkness. In Gnosticism this physical dualism of light and darkness became a metaphysical dualism of spirit and matter. Here the world of matter (ὕλη), which is under the governance of the evil principle, is from all eternity in violent opposition to the world of spirit (πλήρωμα) which is ruled by the good God. In the

[1] Read critically the interesting enumeration of these points by Harnack in the *Grundriss*⁶, p. 74 ff.

conflict some of the spiritual elements became imprisoned in the world of matter. Such was the beginning of the world and man, and likewise of sin and misery.

The more Hellenistic systems (Basilides and Valentinus of Alexandria) were inclined to Platonic ideas. Here the dualistic opposition was not hostile, but "non-essential and non-substantial." This dualism, which was pre-eminent in the realm of ideas, was modified by the emanation theory; but it remained dualism nevertheless.

7. *The Emanation Theory.* This theory which was held especially by the Alexandrians and was extensively developed by them, served to explain how the world and man came into existence. The system of Valentinus in particular had a highly fantastic and speculative process of cosmogony and theogony. From the hidden God there emanated a long series of divine essences (*aeons*) whose inherent divine power diminished inversely with the distance of removal from the original divine source. This process of depotentialization continued until a point was reached where the spiritual element came into contact with matter and was imprisoned in a material body. Thus man and the world were created.

8. *The Creator.* The last link in the theogonic chain was the Creator or demiurge. He was thought to occupy a middle position between the world of spirit and the world of matter, and was usually identified with the Jehovah-God of the Old Testament. Although not absolutely hostile and evil, he was an inferior and antagonistic being—a blind intelligence, who was ignorant of the good God and who had unwittingly brought the world and man into existence. Arguing from the characteristics of the Jewish Law as described by Jesus, the Valentinian Ptolomaeus maintained that they could not have originated from the devil. It must have come from the demiurge—the "middle God" or "just God" (Epiphanius *Pan.*, h. 31:3-1), who was regarded as an angelic being not free from malice and who governed with a loveless external justice.

9. *The Problem of Redemption.* The chief problem of Gnosticism was: How can man be liberated from the world of matter and be made a partaker of the world of light? Man deserves to be emancipated because something of the spiritual world still remains within him. How, then, is redemption effected? The origin of redemption is to be looked for in the world of spirit. The demiurge had brought about the creation of the world and man, with their concomitant sin and woe, thus necessitating a redemption of the spiritual elements in man. But the demiurge would not and could not carry out the plan of redemption. Therefore the Highest Aeon came as a redeemer to secure perfect emancipation. The Redeemer was Jesus Christ.

A high estimate was attached to the person of Christ and His appearance was praised as a great turning-point in history. It was this note in their teaching which deceived so many Christians. An atonement for sin through the death of Christ was not considered necessary. All that Gnosticism needed was a teacher "to dispel ignorance and to abrogate death." [2] The attention of men was directed away from Christ's specifically soteriological work and fixed upon His teaching. Christ's teaching, said Gnosticism, is intended to help us overcome the material world, whether it be by the practice of asceticism or by fleshly libertinism. It gives man an insight into the world-relations, and familiarizes him with the mysterious formulas of enchantment by which he may transcend the planetary spheres, mount to God, and obtain entrance into the realm of light.

---

[2] Irenaeus, I, 15, 2

10. Docetism. Christianity knows of no doctrine of atonement save through the Incarnate Son of God. But Gnosticism rejected the doctrine of Incarnation. It declared that Christ could not possibly have a body: (1) because the absolute cannot enter into a real union with the finite; and (2) because matter is evil, and the spiritual world is ever in conflict with it. It was thought that the Christ had joined Himself for the time being with the body of a profoundly spiritual man called Jesus. As Fisher puts it, the divine was merely "in temporary juxtaposition with humanity." This union was effected either at the birth or at the baptism of Jesus, and it was dissolved shortly before the crucifixion. It followed, therefore, that the Christ was not really crucified. The crucifixion of Christ was an optical illusion in which the man Jesus was the real sufferer. Thus Gnosticism with its docetic conception denuded the Redeemer of any real humanity and destroyed the historic Person of Christ. The trouble with Gnosticism was that it derived its ideas of the Redeemer from pagan mythology. Hence it was never able to effect any genuine union between the Christ and Jesus of Nazareth.[3]

11. The Classification of Men According to Natural Inclination. Earlier Gnosticism divided men into two classes, but later Gnosticism saw three. According to the proportion of spirit in their natural constitution, men were said to be either spiritual, or psychical, or carnal. The first class was represented by the true Christians or Gnostics, of whom there were but few. The second class was composed of the Jews and Christians, who had faith but not "gnosis." And the last was identified with heathenism. Thus inclusion in the first class was considered to be the chief object of redemption. It was taught that "these are not only by practice, but also by nature pneumatic, and will necessarily be saved." The psychics, or ordinary Christians, might be saved through faith and good works; but the carnal or hylics, to whom the majority of men belonged, would all be lost. (Irenaeus, I, 6, 2). Regeneration was defined as the separation of the spiritual from the sensual, and it was thought of as a chemical rather than an ethical process. This was one of the glaring points of difference between Christianity and its Gnostic perversion. The Gnostic system was never interested in ethics and morality as such. All ethical and moral considerations were pushed aside in the interest of the one all-absorbing idea—the emancipation of the spirit from the thraldom of matter. Hence the practice of the Gnostics was never uniform in the ethical realm. Some demanded strict abstinence from sensual pleasures, while others went to the opposite extreme and lived according to the principle that the flesh can be mortified only by excessive gratification. Vegetarianism was also a feature of the system.

12. No Resurrection and No Final Judgment. Because of its belief in the inherent evil of matter the Gnostic system had no place for a bodily resurrection. Neither was there to be any final judgment. Gnosticism taught that the emancipated soul would simply ascend to the place of its origin—the kingdom of light—where it would present itself, repeat the mysteries, and finally be reabsorbed into the fulness of the Godhead. Thus Gnosticism held out no hope for a personal immortality of the individual. The souls which had not received the mysteries would be thrown back into bodies. The worst sinners would be cast into the outer darkness of complete annihilation.

13. The Mysteries. These are symbolic rites, mystic ceremonies, magic formulas, etc., which were used to popularize the cosmic theory and to give assurance of salvation. Inasmuch as they had their origin in the heathen mysteries of the time, they served to

[3] In this connection read the fine observation in Martensen's *Dogmatics,* Sec. 128.

place a heathen construction on the Christian idea of redemption. These esoteric features were part of the scheme to ethnicize Christianity and to make it the universal religion of the enlightened. For a special study of the symbols that were employed and the mysteries in their details, see W. SCHULZ, *Dokumente der Gnosis* (1910).

14. Attitude Toward Scriptures. The Old Testament was either totally rejected or interpreted allegorically in the interests of the Gnostic system. The Apostolic writings were received, but interpreted in accordance with Gnostic thought. Thus the Gnostics became the first exegetes. Frequently, however, the documents commented upon were altered to conform to the predilections of the commentators. A great deal was made of the unwritten Apostolic traditions and teachings. In addition, a voluminous literature of apocryphal and pseudonymous books was published for the dissemination of Gnostic doctrines.

15. Effects of Gnosticism on the Church. The intimate acquaintance of the Church with Gnosticism was productive of several distinct results. (1) The claim of Gnosticism to be the universal religion led the Church to assert the catholicity of her own position. (2) Since Gnosticism had concerned itself so greatly with the Old Testament and the Apostolic writings, it became the imperative duty of the Church to settle forever the inspiration of the Old Testament and the contents of the New Testament Canon. (3) To the contention of Gnosticism that Christianity was fundamentally a doctrine, the Church replied by stating what that doctrine really was. (4) In order to standardize the doctrine of the Church, appeal was made to the Rule of Faith (*regula fidei*). From this rule, varying somewhat in the different localities, sprang the ancient Creeds of Christendom. (5) When Gnosticism began to assume alarming proportions, the Church was obliged to call for able defenders. The bishops came forward and fought the heresy throughout the entire realm. In this way the prominence of the bishops was secured, and added impetus was given to the development of episcopal polity. (6) Although defeated in the end, Gnosticism succeeded in imparting some of its own mysticism to the Church. (7) Finally, the asceticism of Gnosticism prepared the way at least in part, for the monasticism of the Church.[4]

16. The Significance of Gnosticism. In this connection it will be of interest to consider two estimates. *First,* we shall give one of Harnack, which is surely a gross overestimate of the Gnostics. He says: "They were simply the theologians of the first century. They were those Christians who sought to make a rapid conquest of Christianity for the Hellenic culture, and vice versa." (*DG*[4], I, 251.) He refers especially to the Basilians and Valentinians who refused to separate themselves from Christianity. But these schools were *de facto* not Christian, and their representatives were no Christian theologians. Insisting on this judgment, we may yet admit with Harnack—in his *Grundriss*[6], p. 71 in one volume—that it was in these circles where the pioneer work was done in the creation of critically written books on the tradition of the Church, on the text and contents of the New Testament writings, and on Dogmatics and Ethics. It was theology, but surely in no respect a Christian theology. *Second,* we have the judgment of Bousset who, on the other hand, sees in Gnosticism a movement which was essentially retrogressive and extra-Christian—"the reaction of the ancient syncretism against the rising universal religion."[5]

---

[4] On the influences which Christianity received from Gnosticism, see Harnack, in the various editions.
[5] *Hauptprobleme der Gnosis*, p. 7.

Today there is a strong inclination to revive the fundamental thoughts of the ancient Gnosis. This is due to the modern interest in the Orient and to an exaggerated application of comparative religion. For example, we refer to E. H. SCHMITT'S work in two volumes on *Gnosticism* (Diderichs, Jena), the interesting sub-title of which is *"The Fundamental Principles of a World-View as Held by a Noble Culture."* In this work Gnosticism is traced through the centuries up to the present day.

Note: Attention must be called to the full discussion by Nygrén of Gnosticism as contrasted with the position of the Church in his work on *Agape and Eros,* Part Two, Vol. I, pp. 19 ff. and pp. 73-100: Eros starts with self, with desire; the human soul with its divine origin is to be raised to the divine. The soul is homesick for that higher world from which it came. Agape, Christian love, is of a wholly different nature: "The human is not here raised to the divine, but the divine, in compassionate love, descends to the human, unveiled at its deepest in the cross of Christ" (p. 20). Nygrén refers to Paul's polemic against the Gnostics among his opponents. But, says Nygrén, Christian Agape and Hellenistic Eros are not always separate: "Now one, now the other predominates, but in general there is a mixture of the two," although they "are at the beginning historically quite distinct." Nygrén leads here into an interesting observation: It is vain, he says, to seek an "earliest form of Christianity," that was absolutely free from Hellenistic influences (pp. 21 and 22). We know that these influences, this spirit, gained an entry into Christianity. Here we meet Harnack's cherished idea of the Hellenization of the early Christianity. But, objects Nygrén in agreement with Aulén: This "Hellenization" should not have been interpreted as an adulteration of Christianity *in its substance.* The Lundensian theologians speak of Creation, Incarnation and Resurrection as the fundamental dogmas of the Early Church. Cf. G. AULÉN, *Die Dogmengeschichte im Lichte der Lutherforschung,* 1932; and Nygrén goes into details in discussing (1) Gnosis and the Eros-Motif, (2) the Gnostic Way of Salvation, (3) the Transformation of Agape into Vulgar Eros. (See pp. 73-100.)

III. MARCION'S ATTEMPTED REFORMATION

The special sources are: TERTULLIAN, *Adversus Marcionem,* II, V. JUSTIN, *Apologia,* I, c. 26, 58. IRENAEUS, *Adversus Haereses,* I, 27, 2-4; *Philosophumena,* VII, 29-31. EPIPHANIUS, *Haereses,* c. 41, 42. We refer to the following monographs: Marcion's New Testament in ZAHN, *History of the N. T. Canon,* Vol. I, HARNACK, *Marcion: Das Evangelium vom fremden Gott,* 2nd ed. 1924.

1. Marcion's Place. How is Marcion to be classified? The Church Fathers looked upon him as a Gnostic. Indeed, certain features of his system justified this view: (1) His dualism of the just God and the good God; and (2) his rejection of the real incarnation of Christ (Docetism). Furthermore, it is known that Marcion was more or less influenced by the Syrian Gnostic Cerdo who taught that "the God, proclaimed by the Law and the prophets, was not the Father of our Lord Jesus Christ. For the former was known, but the latter was unknown; while the one also was righteous, but the other was benevolent" (Irenaeus, *Haereses,* I, 27, 1).

The investigations of Zahn and Harnack have made it clear that Marcion should be placed in a class by himself. As proof of this we cite the following reasons: (1) Marcion was guided exclusively by a soteriological and not a metaphysical interest; according to him the way of salvation was through faith instead of through Gnosis. (2) He did not acknowledge the emanation theory and the Gnostic explanation of the origin of sin. (3) The Canon, which was limited to a mutilated gospel of Luke and to ten Pauline writings, was the source of truth. (4) He did not aim to form within the Church mystic associations holding speculative tenets; rather, he sought to reform the Church by establishing rival congregations in opposition to the Catholic parishes. Marcion was thus a reformer who desired, on the basis of Paul's writings, to free the

Church from the Law and to plant it squarely on the Gospel. In Marcion we observe a reaction against the legalism which was characteristic of most of the Church Fathers.

2. His Theory of Opposites. Marcion assumed that there were two Gods. The God of the Old Testament was the creator of the world. He was also the just God who cared only for His people Israel, although He ruled them with rigorous justice and maltreated them with His Law. This just God was ignorant of the Good God—the Unknown God, the Highest God, the God of love and mercy, whom Christ, the Bringer of the Gospel, came to reveal.

Marcion held that the Old Testament and the New Testament, the Law and the Gospel, were as distinct from each other as was the just God from the God of grace. While intending to follow Paul, Marcion nevertheless ignored Paul's conception that the Old Testament was a preparation for the New. He further overlooked Paul's declaration that the Law was "the pedagogue to lead us unto Christ"; and likewise the statement in Galatians 4:4: "When the fulness of the time was come, etc."

In Marcion's judgment the twelve Apostles were opposed to Paul. They had handed down a false and spurious tradition. It was Paul who restored the Gospel.

3. His Conception of Christ. Marcion failed to clarify Christ's relation to the good God. "Christ is distinguished from the Father in name only, for in Christ God was revealed through Himself (*in Christo Deus per semetipsum revelatus est*). The Father and the Son represent just such an equation as do the Son and the Gospel. Marcion was a Modalist as were other ancient Christian teachers; but he was probably a more conscious one than they." [1] As a rule Christ was identified with the good God. He abrogated the Law, and by way of retaliation the just God secured His crucifixion at the hands of the Jews. But Christ, who had a docetic body, did not really die. He merely went into Hades where He liberated the Gentiles. The pious of the Old Testament were passed by.

4. Man's Salvation. Man is saved, Marcion taught, not by any effect resulting from the death of Christ, but simply by believing what Paul teaches about the good God. By this kind of faith love is enkindled, which in turn leads man to a life of asceticism.

5. Marcion's Canon. Marcion repudiated all of the Old Testament. So far as the New Testament was concerned, he admitted only a mutilated Gospel of Luke and ten corrected epistles of Paul. The Pastoral Epistles and the Epistles to the Hebrews he excluded. Marcion's attempt at such an early time (c. A. D. 160) to set up a recognized canon of Apostolic writings stimulated the Church to clarify its own views on the subject. His rejection of the allegorical interpretation of Scripture had a beneficial effect on the Church.

Note: One would expect, naturally, that the *Motif-Forschung* of Dr. Nygrén *would point* to some of the conceptions of Marcion for the illustration of the Agape type, against the Nomos and the Eros Type in religion. But he regrets that with Marcion's denial of the creation, of the incarnation and also of the resurrection of the body he had proclaimed "a strange Christianity." (Cf. Vols. I and II.)

6. Effect on the Church. The Marcionite controversy led the Church to the clearer apprehension of the thoughts: that the Creator and the Redeemer are the same God, and that in God justice and mercy are combined.

---

[1] Harnack, *Marcion: Das Evangelium vom fremden Gott²*, 1924, p. 162.

IV. MONTANISM

Primary Sources: The Montanistic writings of TERTULLIAN: *De virginibus velandis, De corona militis, De fuga in persecutione, De exhortatione castitatis.* The following are especially radical: *De monogamia, De jejunia adversus psychicos, De pudicitia.* See also EPIPHANIUS, *Haereses,* 48, 49. P. DE LABRIOLLE, *Les sources de l'hist. du Montonisme,* 1913; also *La crise Montanists,* 1913. Later writings: N. BONWETSCH, *Geschichte des Montanismus,* 1881, 197 ff.; also *Texte zur Geschichte des Montanismus,* 1914. E. ROLFFS, *Urkunden aus dem antimontanistischen Kampfe des Abendlandes,* 1895. H. WEINEL, *Die Wirkungen des Geistes und der Geister im nachapostolischen Zeitalter bis auf Irenaeus,* 1889. J. DE SOYRES, *Montanism and the Primitive Church,* Cambridge, 1878.

Montanism marked the transition from the extra-Christian heresies to the reactionary and reformatory movements within Christianity. About the year 156, Montanus, a pagan priest but recently converted, appeared upon the scene. He claimed to be possessed of the spirit of prophecy which still operated actively in the Church and which was acknowledged as such by the Church Fathers. Later he was joined by two women, Maximilla and Priscilla, who had deserted their husbands with Montanus' sanction. Montanus professed to represent a special form of prophecy in which he declared himself to be the manifestation of the Paraclete promised in John 14. The period of revelation was closing, said Montanus, and with its conclusion would come the end. Indeed, one of the prophetesses maintained: "After me there will be no further prophecy; then shall the end be." Montanism thoroughly recognized the previous stages of revelation in the Old and New Testaments and likewise the ecclesiastical doctrine which had developed therefrom. Up to this point it was entirely orthodox and far removed from every Gnostic heresy.

The new feature, which the Paraclete had now to reveal, was concerned with the sphere of ethics and ecclesiology. "The present task of the Paraclete is to bring to completion what is lacking in the sphere of morals. He now institutes what Christ and the Apostles did not command out of consideration for the weakness of flesh. By intensifying the discipline the new prophecy will perfect the new law." In the sphere of morals and discipline Montanism represented the sternest rigor, surpassing entirely that of the New Testament. This program was carried out in detail by Tetullian after he had become a Montanist. He prohibited second marriages, and in the main even marriage itself. He ordered the strictest fasting, unreserved preparation for martyrdom, and separation from the world. Only those Christians who met these demands of the Paraclete, were pneumatic. Only these constitute the true Christians, the communion of saints. This Church alone, and not the externally organized Church, possesses the full power of absolution. In consequence of this, Tertullian, who joined the Montanists, wrote: "Therefore the Church will indeed forgive sins; but only the Church of the Spirit can do this through the Spirit-filled people, and not the Church which consists of a number of bishops." [2] Thus Montanism manifested an ecclesiastical reaction as well as a reform-movement.

Bonwetsch says that Montanism was "the first movement of any distinction that was called forth by the problem of the Church's worldliness" (*Montanismus, Vorwort*). It protested against the incipient secularization of the Church and sought to restore the Church to its original status. On the other hand, it overdid itself by making harsher and more radical moral demands and by seeking to make the saints only the real Church.

---

[2] *De pudicitia,* 21

Montanism paved the way for a series of movements which have continued down through the entire history of Christianity. We refer to the Novatians, the Donatists, the Waldensians, the fanatics of the Reformation period, and the modern holiness movements.

Finally, Montanism was a reaction and an attempt to preserve the eschatological mood of early Christianity which was rapidly disappearing at the end of the second century. The movement represented a synthesis of pneumatics, ethics and eschatology.

"The expulsion of Montanism from the Church contributed greatly to freeing the Church from the reproach so often advanced against it of being a narrow sect." [3] Loofs says: "The elimination of Montanism reacted mightily upon the Church. It strengthened the prestige of the Canon. It sanctioned the spirit of conniving at moral laxity, and as a result the differentiation between a higher and lower morality. It raised the position of the bishops, and promoted the development which changed the Church from a communion possessing the assurance of salvation to an institution which must guarantee salvation" (*Leitfaden zur DG*[4], p. 175).

[3] Kurtz, Sec. 40. 5. p. 231.

Chapter Six

SOURCE AND NORM OF TRUTH, OR FOUNDATION OF THE DOGMA

In Chapters IX, X, and XI we shall study the special Dogma of the Ancient Church: Trinity, Christology and Soteriology. Before this can be done preparatory developments must be observed. In this present Chapter we come to the point where we must ask: What constituted the source and norm of the Early Church? Upon what foundation was the dogmatic system of the Church to be erected? By way of introduction, these questions may be answered briefly in the following manner:

As early as the first part of the second century the Church was accustomed to refer to the authority of the Old Testament, of the words of Christ and the Apostles, and of the Sacred Scriptures soon to be gathered into a *recognized Canon*. Next, the fundamentals of the Christian religion which were used in the parochial and missionary work, were being crystallized into *creedal statements*. And finally, in that day of incessant struggle with heresy, the *episcopate* came to be looked upon as the powerful guardian and the reliable interpreter of the Scriptures and the Rules of Faith.

All three of these factors require a more detailed exposition. The first two, the Canon and the Rule of Faith, will be dealt with in this chapter. The third—the development of the episcopate—is so closely related to the conception of the Church that it must be treated in connection with this more general subject (Chapter VII).

I. THE CANON OF THE HOLY SCRIPTURE

Literature: T. ZAHN, *Introduction to the New Testament* (translated from the third German edition, 3 vols., 1909). Also his article on *Glaubensregel* in the *PRE*, VI, 682 ff. (cf. *NSH*). R. SEEBERG, *Dogmengeschichte*, I³, 192 ff. A. HARNACK, *Dogmengeschichte*, 3rd (English) and 4th editions, I; his *Grundriss³*, pp. 84 ff. See also his *Entstehung des Neuen Testaments*, 1914. J. MOFFATT, *Introduction to the Literature of the New Testament* (4th ed., 1920) : F. K. KENYON, *Our Bible and the Ancient Manuscripts*, 1911. A. SOUTER, *The Text and Canon of the New Testament*, 1913. H. SMITH, *Ante-Nicene Exegesis of the Gospels*, Vols. I and II, 125, 126.

1. Formation of the Canon. Our discussion of this subject must be studied in connection with what was said in Chapter III, about the views and positions of the Apostolic Fathers. There we saw that, besides the Old Testament and the *Words of the Lord,* the Post-Apostolic Fathers knew the Gospels (the *four-fold Gospel*) and the writings of Paul.

a. Unclarified views hindered the formation of a Canon of Scripture. On the one hand, some of the Post-Apostolic writings, such as the Shepherd of Hermas, the Epistles of Barnabas and Clement, the Apocalypse of Peter and the Acts of Paul, had come to be regarded as having equal value with the writings of the Apostles. On the other hand, the Epistle to the Hebrews, the Epistle of James, and Second Peter, were not in the Bibles of the Occident until about the middle of the fourth century. From then on the word *Canon,* which in the second century had been applied to the Rule of Faith, was used to designate the accepted body of Holy Scripture.

b. There were, however, *several influences* at work which forced the Church to settle what books should constitute the Canon. The following are worthy of mention: (1) *Marcion* had created for his followers a Canon of sacred writings which omitted those books that did not support his special conception of the Gospel. (2) *The Muratorian Fragment* (cir. 170 or 180), represented another attempt to formulate a Canon of Scripture. (3) *The Peshito* appeared, at the end of the second century as the Canon of the Syrian Church. (4) *The Pneumatics,* with their unbounded enthusiasm led the Church to scrutinize all alleged revelation in the light of the words of Christ and the Apostles as deposited in a recognized Canon. This institution of the Early Church, which had the sanction of Paul (I Cor. 14: cf. I Thess. 5), came in time to be greatly abused in individual cases. The Church gradually found itself engaged in a real struggle with pneumatics of all kinds (*Geistesmenschen aller Gattungen,* Seeberg) with men and women who claimed to be organs of the Holy Spirit. The Epistle of Clement to the congregation at Corinth was directed at this evil. Especially did this wild enthusiasm of the Montanists show what would happen to the Church, should it give free rein to the Pneumatics. (5) The speculations of the *Gnostics* and their efforts to prove the same from the Apostolic writings constituted a powerful inducement to the Church to establish an authoritative and actually recognized Canon of the New Testament. (6) Finally, an *apocryphal literature,* such as the *Acta of the Apostles,* and numerous apocalyptic writings (*Sibyllines*), were shooting up like weeds in a rich garden. In these the great past was magnified by the report of wonderful miracles. The Apostles were portrayed as being essentially "workers of miracles who, without exception, raised the dead, made dogs and donkeys speak, healed broken statues, put life into smoked fishes, and killed demons." [1]

c. The Test of Canonicity. When a book was being considered either for admission into or for exclusion from the Canon, a twofold test was applied. (1). There was the *historical test.* The age had a deep consciousness of the fact that it was the Apostles to whom Christ had committed the preaching of the Gospel and that in them was the selfsame Spirit Who had been operative in the writers of the Old Testament (Irenaeus). The writings to be admitted into the Canon were tested by asking the question whether the authors had been Apostles and if not, whether they had had such a relation to the Apostles as to warrant the placing of their writings on a level with the Apostolic books. (2) There was the *internal test.* This test was made by asking whether "the *internal appeal* of a given book had such a character, such a spirituality and elevation, as to make it worthy of the rank of an Apostolic writing." Thus it was that, by using these tests, certain books of the Post-Apostolic Age were finally dropped from the number of those which were being considered for incorporation in the Canon.

2. As to the *Contents of the Canon* in the Early Church, we wish to record the findings of the scholars who have given themselves to a life-long investigation of the subject. Zahn says that the Canon, as used by the Early Church, comprised the four Gospels, the thirteen Pauline writings, the First Epistle of Peter, the First of John, perhaps also Jude, and the Apocalypse.[2] Harnack writes: "Thus there arose a collection of Apostolic-Catholic writings which did not differ extensively nor materially from the

---

[1] R. Seeberg, *DG,* I³, 358.
[2] *Kanongeschichte,* I, 432.

number of those which were used and preferred by the churches of the previous generation."[3]

3. *Inspiration* was claimed for the New Testament writings, just as it was believed that the Old Testament was inspired. At first inspiration was thought to be a state of ecstasy in which the sacred authors wrote as purely passive agents. Athenagoras compared the soul of the prophet, while engaged in prophesying, to a flute. In his *Cohortatio ad Graecos,* Justin Martyr likened the prophet to a lyre which is struck by the Holy Spirit as the plectrum, etc. The Montanists held to ecstatic inspiration, and Tertullian made the ecstatic condition an essential of inspiration. This theory was first brought into disrepute by the Montanist prophets. It was against them that the Apologist Miltiades directed this statement: "The prophet does not need to speak in ecstasy." Irenaeus rejected the passivity of the New Testament writers. Although he believed in verbal inspiration, he accounted for the transposition of words in Paul by the "velocity" of his utterance and the vehemence of his spirit. A modification of the doctrine of inspiration may be observed in the Alexandrians. Origen, for instance, ascribed the peculiarity of style in the New Testament authors to their individuality. He even went so far as to speak of a variation in the measure of inspiration of the Bible. Nevertheless, he shielded the New Testament from every kind of error.

II. THE RULE OF FAITH

Sources: T. ZAHN, article on *Glaubensregel* in the *PRE,* VI, 682 ff.; cf. the *NSH.* The article on *Apostolisches Symbol* by A. HARNACK in the *PRE,* I, 741; cf. the *NSH.* A. E. BURN, *The Articles of the Apostles' Creed,* 1899. F. KATTENBUSCH, *Das Apostolische Symbol,* 2 vols., 1894, 1900. A. C. McGIFFERT, *The Apostles' Creed,* 1902. J. KUNZE, *Glaubensregel, Heilige Schrift und Taufbekenntnis,* 1899. P. SCHAFF, *Creeds of Christendom,* 1899. W. A. CURTIS, *History of Creeds.* H. B. SWETE, *The Apostles' Creed,* 1908. P. FEINE, *Gestalt des Apostolischen Glaubensbekenntnisses in der Zeit des N. T.,* 1925. R. SEEBERG, *DG,* I³, 192 ff., 371 ff. For a brief review of the situation compare J. L. NEVE, *Introduction to the Symbolical Books²,* 1926, on Apostles' Creed. R. SEEBERG, *Zeitschrift fuer Kirchengeschichte* 40, 1922, pp. 1 ff. A. HARNACK, K. HOLL and A. LIETZMANN in SBA, 1919. D. McFAYDEN, *Understanding the Apostles' Creed.*

1. *What was the Rule of Faith?* In our discussion of the Post-Apostolic Age we learned of a *Rule for Faith and Life,* to which the *Didache* makes especial reference, but which can be traced back even to the later books of the New Testament literature. It has been a much debated question among the special scholars on this subject (Zahn, Harnack, Kattenbusch, McGiffert and Kunze) as to what the Church Fathers really meant by the Rule of Faith (κανὼν τῆς ἀληθείας, *regula veritatis,* κανὼν τῆς πίστεως, *regula fidei*). According to Zahn it was merely the profession made at baptism (PRE, VI, 682 ff.). Kattenbusch, who is seconded by Harnack, Loofs and others, takes it to be the Church's interpretation of the Baptismal Formula.[4] J. Kunze emphasizes the thought that it was an antiheretical profession supplemented and interpreted by Scripture.[5] We may conclude from this that the Rule of Faith was a brief expression in creedal form of all the fundamentals of the Church's entire teaching.[6] It is important to refer at this point to a work of Irenaeus (᾽Επίδειξις) which shows in a vivid way the large range of

---

[3] Seeberg, *HD* (Eng.) I, 82; cf. *DG,* I³, 199.
[4] Harnack, *DG³,* 320 ff. Kattenbusch, *Das Apostolische Symbol;* Loofs, *DG⁴,* 131-134; cf. his *Symbolik.*
[5] *Glaubensregel, Heilige Schrift Taufbekenntnis.* J. Hausleiter, *Trin. Glaube u Christusbekenntnis,* 1920.
[6] Cf. R. Seeberg, *DG,* I³, 211 ff.

these fundamentals; it even transcends the doctrinal sphere and touches upon numerous matters of an ethical devotional nature.

2. Next we come to the *Baptismal Formula*—that brief epitome of the Faith upon which the Church was establishing itself.[7] It may be traced back to a fixed doctrinal tradition as found in the following expressions taken from the New Testament Epistles; Seeberg illustrates: profession (I Tim. 6: 12; Hebr. 10: 23; 4: 14); things that have been committed (I Tim. 6: 20; II Tim. 1: 12, 14); faith (Jude 3: 20; Tit. 1: 13; Col. 1: 1); word of truth (I Peter 1: 22; cf. Col. 1: 5); form of doctrine (Rom. 6: 17; 16: 17; II John 9 ff.; Hebr. 6: 2); the Gospel (Rom. 2: 16; 16: 25; Gal. 2: 2; I Cor. 15: 1); sound teaching (II Tim. 1: 13); words of faith (I Tim. 4: 6).

We may have to distinguish between a wider and a narrower conception. (1) Expressions such as Gospel and Faith seem to comprise the whole Christian teaching, namely Christ's descent from David, His Divinity, His suffering, resurrection, ascent to heaven, His session at the right hand of the Father, the work of the Spirit, baptism and the eucharist. (2) There seems to have been a difference between this catechetical material and the profession (ὁμολογία) which was made at baptism. What Paul writes in I Cor. 15: 3-4 sounds like the echo of the Baptismal Formula: "For I have delivered unto you first of all that which I also received," (and now follows that ὅτι which is identical with our quotation marks), "how that Christ died for our sins according to the Scriptures: and that He was buried, and that He rose again the third day according to the Scriptures; and after that He was seen by Cephas, then of the twelve." I Tim. 6: 20 may refer to a similar form.[8]

Professor P. Feine reconstructs from the New Testament writings the following formula as an existing rule of faith:

"I confess one God, the Father, the Creator of the World (or: of Whom the world is, or: by Whom and through Whom and to Whom the world is, or: Who has made heaven and earth, or: One God and One Father of the world, Who is over all and in all). And (I confess) Jesus Christ, the Lord (or: our Lord), the Son of God (the only begotten), born of the seed of David. . . . Who suffered under Pontius Pilate (or: Who was crucified under Pontius Pilate), died for our sins, was buried, preached the Gospel to the dead (or: Who descended to the dead), was resurrected the third day sitting at the right hand of God after having entered heaven, to Whom are subject the angels and the powers, Who shall judge the living and the dead (or: Who shall come to judge the living and the dead, or: Who is ordained by God as Judge of the living and the dead) through Whom we receive forgiveness of sins and the gifts of the Holy Ghost and the hope of resurrection of the dead (or: the resurrection of the dead and the eternal life, or: and the hope of eternal life)."[9]

While this perfectly Trinitarian Faith may be taken as the matrix from which there eventually issued a recognized formula for baptism and also the so-called *Apostles' Creed*, yet it does not mean that at that time baptism was being administered in the name of the Triune God. At first baptism was in the name of Christ.[10] The emphasis was always placed upon faith in Christ "from the seed of David, born of the Virgin, suffered under Pilate, raised from the dead by the Father, sitting at the right hand of God whence

---

[7] R. Seeberg, *DG*, I³, 82.

[8] Special investigations along this line have been made by A. Seeberg in his *Katechismus der Urchristenheit*, Leipzig, 1903. Cf. R. Seeberg, *DG*, I³, 371 ff.

[9] *Gestalt des Apostolischen Glaubensbekenntnisses in der Zeit des Neuen Testaments*, 1925. Cf. Harnack in *Theol. Literaturzeitung*, 1925, pp. 392 ff. Like constructions by Seeberg and Lietzmann should be compared with this one by Feine.

[10] Ignatius *ad Trall.* IX, 1-2; *ad Smyrn.* I, 1-2; *ad Magn.* XI; *ad Romanos*, VI, 1; *ad Phil. inscrib. Eph.* XVIII, 2; Polycarp *ad Phil.*, II, 1.

He shall come for judgment." This is easily explained. Since the earliest Christians were Jews who already believed in God, it was not necessary for them to reaffirm that faith. The essential thing for them was to confess their faith in Jesus the Christ. Hence the use of the older Christological form. But gradually we find the Post-Apostolic Fathers mentioning the fact that baptism was administered in the Name of the Triune God.[11] In view of the contemporaneous testimony of Irenaeus and Tertullian we come to the conclusion that from about 130-140, the Baptismal Formula had become Trinitarian for the whole Church. The most recent investigator on this subject is Feine. By reconstructing the baptismal formulae which were used in certain localities, as in Egypt for instance, he shows that the Trinitarian formula of Matthew was employed about the year 100 (in the work mentioned above). This change from the Christological to the Trinitarian form is readily explained. The Gentiles were coming into the Church. It was necessary for them to confess their faith, not only in Christ as their Redeemer, but also in the One God and the Holy Spirit as well. Therefore it was natural to follow the express command of Christ in administering baptism. In connection with this Trinitarian form we soon hear of Eastern Creeds which varied in their expressions, but which resembled more or less our so-called *Apostles' Creed*. Kunze reconstructs the Creed of Antioch, and Zahn another Creed from the *Didascalia*.[12] The question may be asked why these creeds or rules of faith were not freely recorded. The answer is that in the Old Catholic Age the Christians were pledged to silence regarding the mysteries of the Christian faith (*disciplina arcani*). Tertullian said: *"Symbolum nemo scribit."* Therefore, instead of exact literary quotation, we have only periphrastic and explanatory references. These, however, are all integral parts of original documents.

3. *The Old Roman Symbol* now attracts our special attention. It was quoted as a whole for the first time by Marcellus of Ancyra (348) and then by Rufinus (400).[13] All agree that this Symbol is much older than the others. Kattenbusch undertakes to trace it back to about 100. Seeberg admits that it goes back at least to the beginning of the third century. McGiffert traces it back to the latter part of the second century. The following is the text of the Old Roman Symbol as translated into English.[14]

> "I believe in God the Father Almighty.
> And in Jesus Christ, His only Son, our Lord;
> Who was born by the Holy Ghost of the Virgin Mary;
> Was crucified under Pontius Pilate and was buried;
> The third day He rose from the dead;
> He ascended into heaven; and sitteth on the Right Hand of the Father;
> From thence He shall come to judge the quick and the dead;
> And in the Holy Ghost;
> The forgiveness of sins;
> The resurrection of the body (flesh)."

The Relation of the Old Roman Symbol to the Creeds of Asia and the East in general presents a perplexing problem. The question is, whether the Eastern Creeds came into existence independently of the Old Roman Symbol, or whether this Roman Creed was the source of all the ancient forms, even of those in the East. On this question

---

[11] Justin, *Apol.* I, 61; cf. *Didache*, VII, 1.
[12] See Hastings, *Dictionary*, IV, 237-238; also Neve, *Introduction to the Symbolical Books²*, 1926, p. 49 ff.
[13] Marcellus' quotation of it is preserved by Epiphanius, *Panarion Haereseon*, 72; cf. Kattenbusch, I, 64 f.; McGiffert, 40. For Rufinus' reference to it see the *Nicene and Post-Nicene Fathers*, 2nd series, III, 544. f.
[14] See the Greek and Latin texts as given by McGiffert, pp. 42-43; also in *PRE*, article by Harnack, 1, 744. Cf. the *NSH*.

we have an unsettled controversy with the scholars sharply divided into two camps. Kattenbusch, Harnack and McGiffert insist that the Roman Symbol is the parent of all other forms including those of Asia Minor. On the other hand, Zahn, Burn, Sanday Kunze and Seeberg (following Caspari) defend the independence of the Eastern Creeds. Interesting as it is, the argumentation cannot be incorporated in our text.[15] As to the origin of the Old Roman Symbol we know nothing definite; everything is conjectural. Neither do we know anything reliable about the common source of the Creeds of Asia Minor.

4. *From the Roman Symbol to the Textus Receptus.* Our present Apostles' Creed is not identical in all respects with the Old Roman Symbol. Additional phrases have been inserted. Knowing that up to the fifth century Rome had been maintaining a jealous watchfulness over the integrity of her Creed, we are forced to ask how a change could have taken place.

It must be remembered that it was only up to the fifth century that the Roman Church used the Apostles' Creed as the Baptismal Confession. Then a remarkable change took place. The Ostro-Goths under Odoaker brought their Arianism into dangerous contact with Rome. Straightway the Roman Church decided to use the Nicene Creed in place of the Old Symbol because of its clear antithesis to Arianism.[16] Three centuries later the Roman Church returned to the use of the Apostles' Creed in baptism and in the services of the sanctuary.[17] But in the meantime the present form of our Creed had developed in Western Gaul, due to the habit of the extra-Roman Churches of adding some phrases of particular significance. This altered form of the Creed was then accepted by Rome because the additions had indeed an historic right; in fact, most of them had been used in the earliest times by the churches of various localities.[18] The form which now came into use was soon accepted in the whole West, and in this form it was later taken into the Catechism of Luther and the Heidelberg Catechism.

5. *Regarding the contents of the Apostles' Creed* we shall refer only to a few particulars which in one connection or another have been matters of interest in the history of dogma:

Article I in the Old Roman Symbol read: "I believe in God the Father Almighty." The Creed of Aquileia added "invisible and impassible" against Sabellianism and Patripassianism. At a time when heathenism was the chief opposition, the Eastern Creeds inserted "one" before "God." The present text has the additional phrase "Creator of heaven and earth"; but the same, or a like phrase, was contained in the Rules of Faith in the ante-Nicene Creed as a confession against the Gnostics, who made a distinction between the true God and the Demiurge who was considered the real Maker of the world.

Article II. It is to be admitted that the phrase "conceived of the Holy Ghost" was not used by the earlier form of the East, neither was it in the Old Roman Symbol. It appeared as a creedal statement for the first time in a confession of orthodox bishops in 359; and because it was taught in Luke 1:31, 35, it was taken into the *Textus Receptus.*

---

[15] See Harnack, article on *Apostol. Symbol* in PRE, I, 741; cf. *NSH.* Hastings' *Dictionary*, IV, 237; Kattenbusch, Zahn, McGiffert, *ut supra.*

[16] A hundred years earlier the Nicene Creed had replaced the Apostles' Creed in the East.

[17] See the reasons as given by Harnack in *PRE*, I, 754.

[18] See Harnack in *PRE*, I, 754, 25; cf. Oehler, *Symbolik*, p. 58. It may be mentioned here that the Apostles' Creed did not come back into use at the same time in the East. This explains why the Nicene Creed is used in the Greek Catholic Church to this day.

"Of" (*ex*) the Virgin Mary came to be preferred to "dia," because it brought out more clearly the reality of Christ's incarnation and life in opposition to the docetic heresies. Some form had "truly born."

"Suffered" (*passus*) and "dead" (*mortuus*) are additions to the *Textus Receptus*, but we meet these expressions even in the Eastern Symbols. There was no doctrnial tendency in these amplifications; the aim was merely at greater completeness.

The same can be said of the phrase of the present text "He descended into hell," which was not in the Old Roman Symbol, but was to be found in the Aquileian Creed. The meaning is that Christ descended into the abode of the dead before the resurrection, which on the basis of Scripture was already believed in the first century.

Article III. The word "Catholic" in the sentence "I believe in the Holy Catholic Church" is an addition to the *Textus Receptus*. It is first found in the Creed about 450 in Southern Gaul, but it had already been used by Irenaeus (d. cir. 200). The meaning is this: The Church is co-extensive with the dissemination of the Christians. This was indeed the meaning of the term "Catholic" as used by Ignatius and the early Christians. It concurs also with the meaning of the term "Church" (*ecclesia*) in the New Testament, which Luther always translated as "congregation" (*Gemeinde*).

Though the phrase "the resurrection of the flesh," is identical in the Roman form and in the received text, it cannot be dismissed without a few explanatory remarks, because it has been a subject of discussion throughout the centuries. In both forms we have "resurrection of the flesh" (Latin: *Carnis,* Greek: *sarkos*). The terminology of Paul in I Cor. 15, favors the use of the term "body." But the early Church, in its struggle with Marcion and the Gnostics, insisted upon employing the word "flesh." [19] McGiffert offers the following remark (p. 167) : "This insistence upon a fleshy resurrection over against the denial of it was due not only to the feeling on the part of many Christians that the future life was impossible without a resurrection of the material body, but also to the fear that the loss of the belief in the resurrection of the present flesh for judgment would lead to immorality and impurity." [20]

6. *The Old Nicene Creed, like the Apostles' Creed,* represents a development of the Rules of Faith—those creeds which arose in different localities of the East and which, while differing from each other, were shaped by the Eastern mind. The Creed of Caesarea was used as a basis for the Creed which was formulated at Nicea in 325 against Arianism.[21] Like the Roman Symbol, it was intended to be a confession of faith on the part of the catechumens. These Eastern creeds differed from those of the Western Church. While the latter were brief, practical and static, the former were, as Schaff rightly describes them. "more metaphysical, polemical, flexible, and adapting themselves to the exigencies of the Church in the maintenance of her faith in conflict with heretics." [22] These characteristics were unavoidably accentuated in the Creed which was formulated at Nicea. The fact is, this Creed was not intended, nor was it suitable, for baptism because of its theological and unliturgical nature. It was created chiefly for the purpose of representing a Christological Rule of Faith. The Biblical expressions of

---

[19] Tertullian, *De Carne Christi,* Chap. I, and *De Resurrectione Carnis,* against Marcion, IV, 37; V, 7, 9 f.; also Irenaeus II, 29 f.; V, 1, 18; V, 2 f., 11 f., 31 f.

[20] Cf. e.g., II Clement, IX; Hermas, *Sim.* V, 7, 2; Tertullian, *Adv. Marc.* V, 7.

[21] See W. A. Curtis, p. 123; and compare the review over the gradual construction and history of the Nicene Creed in Neve's *Introduction to the Symbolical Books*², 1926, pp. 61-71.

[22] *Creeds of Christendom,* I, 25.

the Caesarean Creed were not sufficiently definite and exclusive with regard to heresy; hence it was necessary to substitute theological terms and phrases not contained in the Scriptures. This had to be done in order to meet the subterfuges of Arianism. While the phrases and terms (such as the *homoousios*) were not derived from the Scriptures, nevertheless their content and meaning were fundamentally Scriptural. Under the circumstances the theological and polemical form was necessary. But such a form naturally affected the practical use of the Symbol in the services of the Church. The feeling existed that the Nicene Faith should be confessed at the solemn act of baptism and also in the liturgical worship of the Church. It was this consideration which gave us the present *Textus Receptus,* or the so-called *Niceno-Constantinopolitan* form of the Creed.[23]

7. *In Conclusion:* We have traced the source of the Baptismal Formula, as it gradually evolved into the Apostles' and Nicene Creeds. The contents of these creeds show that there were now two great problems before the Church: (1) Father and Son, and yet one God; and (2) Jesus the Son of God, and yet the Son of Mary. The solution of these problems marks a large part of the History of Dogma in the Ancient Church.

---

[23] For details see Neve's *Introduction,* pp. 67-70.

Chapter Seven

THE EPISCOPATE AS GUARDIAN OF THE TRUTH AND THE CHRISTIAN LIFE. EARLY IDEAS OF THE CHURCH

Literature: The Post-Apostolic Fathers as quoted. The Church Fathers of the Old Catholic age as quoted: Particularly IRENAEUS, *Adversus Haereses;* TERTULLIAN, *De Poenitentia* and *De Pudicitia;* HIPPOLYTUS, *Philosophumena* IX; CYPRIAN, *De Unitate Ecclesiae* and the *Epistolae.* AUGUSTINE'S *Antidonatistic* writings.

See the Church Histories, especially KURTZ, MOELLER, SCHAFF II, 132-63. With one of these works of older orientation compare the most modern among the larger Church Histories, namely, K. MUELLER I², 1924, sections 8, 21, 25. Also the Histories of Doctrine. THOMASIUS I², by N. BONWETSCH; SCHMID-HAUCK⁴, HARNACK, English translation from the third German edition. LOOFS⁴; SEEBERG, *HD,* English; *DG,* I³, 192 ff., 228 ff., 356 ff., 382 ff., 595 ff. The articles on all the pertinent topics in the *PRE* and *NSH,* in the *RGG* and in *HE,* especially the article on Church Polity. Among the books we mention: O. RITSCHL, *Cyprian und die Verfassung der Kirche,* 1885; E. PREUSCHEN, Tertullian on the above-mentioned two writings, 1890; E. ROLFFS, *Das Indulgenzedikt des Bischofs Kallist,* 1893; E. W. BENSEN, *Cyprian, His Life, Times and Work,* 1897; E. HATCH, *Organization of the Early Christian Churches,* London, 1881; J. REVILLE, *Les Origenes de l'episcopat,* Paris, 1895.

For investigations reaching over into the post-Reformation and present-day developments we mention: R. HOOKER, *Ecclesiastical Polity,* London, 1594-1662, best edition by J. KEPLE (3rd edition), 3 vols. 1845: G. T. LADD, *Principles of Church Polity,* New York, 1882; R. SOHM, *Kirchenrecht,* Leipzig, 1892; P. HERGENROETHER, *Lehrbuch des Katholischen Kirchenrechts,* Freiburg, 1905. There is a large English literature that has sprung up from the conflict between Conformity and Nonconformity. We mention H. W. CLARKE, *History of English Nonconformity,* 2 vols., 1911-1913.

INTRODUCTORY DISCUSSION

1. Before Cyprian and Augustine very little was done to formulate a doctrine of the Church. Serious reflection on the nature of the Church is necessary for the creation of a dogma of the Church; and such reflection is confined chiefly to those times when there is an occasion for discussing the relation of the *Una Sancta Ecclesia* to the historical appearances of the Church, as was the case at the time of the Reformation. Although this question was involved in the conflict with Novatianism and Donatism, still the Church of the first centuries was inclined to identify the essential Church with its external existence as established on the Rule of Faith and the authority of its leaders. Those utterances were indeed exceptional which suggested the distinction we have in mind when we hear of the visible and the invisible Church, or the Church *late et stricte dictu.* It is true that the earlier centuries were not entirely devoid of motives for making certain small contributions to the dogma of the Church, as the whole of the following discussion will show. But errors, such as the extravagances of the Pneumatics (Montanists, Novatians, and even the Donatists), were not sufficiently important to challenge fundamental thought for an exhaustive treatment of a doctrine of the Church. There were, however, other considerations which stood in the way. For one thing, the Church had not had enough actual experience to warrant a conclusive treatment of so practical a topic. Again, the theologians of the Catholic period were too much occupied with

such subjects as the Trinity, Christology, and Anthropology, to find time for fundamental
discussions of the Church. And finally, the Christians of the first centuries were so aware
of the reality of the Church that there was little cause for doctrinal reflection.

2. *A "Catholic Church."* Ignatius, Bishop of Antioch (cir. 115), was the first to
use the term "catholic."[1] Here, then, was a new expression of the unity of the Church
as taught by Paul: "There is one body and one Spirit . . . one Lord, one Faith, one
Baptism" (Eph. 4: 4f.). This teaching was much emphasized by the Apostolic Fathers.
Ignatius saw the unity of the Church in the *Eucharist*.[3] To this may be added: (1)
Baptism in the Name of the Triune God, as enjoined in the *Didache* (c. 7) and reported
as a general practice by Justin Martyr;[4] (2) the *Disciplina* in accordance with the ethical
requirements of the Lord; (3) the observance of *fasting* and of *prayer,* especially the
regular use of the Lord's Prayer (cf. *Didache*); and (4) the *Rule of Faith* with its
crystallization in the Baptismal Formula. Those who adhered to these things were
regarded as being in the unity of the Catholic Faith. The catholicity of the Church's
character was asserted again and again by the Fathers of the Catholic Age, especially by
Irenaeus, Tertullian, Origen, and their successors. Irenaeus wrote: "No matter how
different the languages of the world, the contents of tradition are the same everywhere
and neither the Churches founded in Germany have another faith or another tradition,
nor those in Spain, Iberia, Gaul, nor those in the East, Egypt, and so forth; but as God's
sun is one and the same for the whole world, so the preaching of the truth enlightens
all men who are willing to see the truth."[5] For special reading, see below.[6]

3. *The Two Motives Underlying the Development.* In the development of the
dogma of the Church there were two interests which served as guiding factors. *First,*
there was the interest in the *purity or apostolicity of the Church's teaching.* This interest
led to a recognition of the bishop for the purpose of safeguarding the truth as expressed
in the Scriptures, in the Rule of Faith, and in the Baptismal Formula, as we have seen
in Chapter VI. It led first to a recognition of the bishop-presbyters as over against the
Pneumatics; next, to a recognition of one bishop in each congregation; then to a special
recognition of the bishops located in places where the Apostles had labored; after that,
to the recognition of a college of bishops; and finally, to the recognition of a monarchical
episcopate at Rome. *Second,* there was the interest in the *holiness of the Church,* or the
purity of the Church's life, or let us say, the interest in repentance as an institution of
the Church. These questions—purity of teaching and purity of life—have been the two
outstanding motives for developing the Church and its institutions. It is interesting to
observe that the East, generally speaking, had a special bent for formulating a dogma for
the Catholic Church, whereas the Western part of the Church preferred to devote itself
to the establishment of institutions which would cultivate and safeguard the Christian
life of its members. As to time, these two interests are constantly running parallel, and
they frequently overlap. The distinction between East and West is not always exclusive;
yet, in the main, the two lines can be clearly traced.[7]

---

[1] See *Ad Smyrn.* 8, 2; cf. *Mart. Polyc.* inscp., and VIII, 1.
[2] I Clement XLVI, 7; XXVII, 1; LVII, 2; Ignatius *ad. Eph.* V, 1; *ad. Philad.* IX, 1.
[3] *Philad.* 4.
[4] *Apol.* I, 61.
[5] *Adversus Haereses* I, 9, 5.
[6] Thomasius-Bonwetsch[2] I, 108 ff. Schmid-Hauck[4], pp. 189 ff. Loofs[4], p. 163. Seeberg, English ed., 86,
147 ff.; *DG*, I[3], 230-48. Harnack, English ed.[3], III, 212, 235 ff.
[7] See the interesting observations of Seeberg, *DG*, I[3], 624 ff. Cf his English edition, I, 175 ff.

Let us now turn to a

DETAILED DISCUSSION OF THE TWO INTERESTS OR MOTIVES

I. APOSTOLICITY OF TEACHING THE MOTIVE FOR DEVELOPMENT

1. The Responsibility for Teaching in the Church Changes from the Pneumatics to the Bishop-Presbyters.

a. The Pneumatics in the Early Church. Originally the preaching and spiritual leadership of the Christian congregations were in the hands of a class of men who were recognized as being in a special sense the organs of the Spirit. We refer to the Apostles, prophets, evangelists, pastors, and teachers (Eph. 4:11; I Cor. 12 and 14). From the *Didache* we learn that the Apostles and Evangelists traveled from place to place, while the prophets, pastors, and teachers were permitted to settle in one congregation. The prophets differed from the teachers in this, that they had the charism of prophecy. According to Paul and John, their messages were subject to trial by the Church (I Thess. 5:21; I Cor. 12:10; 14:29; I John 4:1). The *Didache* says that, if the prophets' lives are Christ-like, their messages are not to be tried; to try the messages of these would constitute a sin against the Spirit. The unknown author of the Epistle attributed to Barnabas regarded himself as a Pneumatic teacher and accordingly claimed authority on that account. At the time of Paul and also in the earlier decades of the Post-Apostolic Age (*Didache* 13, 13; 15, 1), these prophets and teachers were the real leaders in things spiritual.[8] The prophets offered free prayer at the Eucharist.[9]

b. The Bishop-Presbyters in the Early Church. As yet the office of the bishops or presbyters was far from being what it later became. We are here reviewing the time when bishop and presbyter meant one and the same thing, and when in each local congregation there was to be found a number of men, appointed or elected, who were called either bishops or presbyters (Cf. Tit. 1:5, 7; I Tim. 3:1; 4:14; 5:17, 19). In Phil. 1:1, Paul addresses himself not to one, but to a number of bishops. According to Acts 20:17, 28, all presbyters of the Ephesian Church were appointed bishops. The Post-Apostolic Father, Clement of Rome (cir. 96), knew of no distinction between bishops and presbyters; and the *Didache* (about the beginning of the second century) speaks of only two classes of officers who were elected by the congregation:—bishops and deacons.[10]

What was the work of these bishop-presbyters in the Early Church? It was that of "oversight" ἐπισκοπεῖν). Such work naturally fell to men of experience—the "presbyteroi" or elders. The men appointed or elected to this office were held responsible for good order in the conduct of the congregational services, as demanded in I Cor. 14:40. It must have been their duty to see to it that services were held in which the prophets and teachers would edify the congregation. Originally, then, the bishop-presbyters were not the regular preachers and teachers of the Early Church, but simply directors and overseers. Their position, which was much like that of the rulers of the synagogue (Acts 13:15 and see also Luke 4:17, 20), demanded good judgment and executive ability in matters of church government.

---

[8] Cf. the ἡγούμενοι in Heb. 13:7 with Acts 15:22.
[9] *Didache*, 10, 6.
[10] Seeberg, *DG*, 1³, 192-95, 321-30

c. It was natural for the Bishop-Presbyters gradually to add the work of the Pneumatics to their own duties. This was indeed a change which Paul himself had favored. It was the task of the bishops to preserve not only good order, but also sound doctrine (Acts 20: 28-31). This gave them the right, and even made it their imperative duty, to "try the spirits" by applying the test of orthodoxy to the messages of the prophets (I Cor. 14: 29). Furthermore, in the absence of a prophet one of the presbyters or bishops would be obliged to take his place (I Tim. 5: 17; Tit. 1: 9; cf. Did. 13, 4: 15: 1-2). Therefore the bishop himself had to be sound in doctrine and "apt to teach" (I Tim. 3: 2). Thus it came about gradually that it was one of the college of bishop-presbyters who took the exclusive title of bishop.

Clement, one of the bishop-presbyters, wrote a letter to the Corinthian Church which has interesting information on this subject. We learn that at Rome, around the year 96, the Pneumatics did their work under the authority of the bishops, and that the latter also preached and taught and even offered free prayer at the Eucharist.[11] At that time the Corinthian Church was involved in a troublesome dispute due to the fact that two prophets of that place demanded the entire leadership of the church. Such a situation was, to use Clement's words, an "unholy revolution." In his letter Clement appealed to the Old Testament, declared the bishops to be the successors of the Apostles, and insisted upon the superiority of the bishops over the prophets *jure divino.* He even tried to establish the *apostolic succession* with the following argument: "As Moses gave the right of the priesthood to the family of Aaron, so the Apostles arranged that the bishops should be followed by others." It must be understood, of course, that the assumption of sacerdotal functions by the bishop-presbyters cannot be dated from any particular time *for all parts of the Church.* It was a gradual development.

2. The Monarchical Episcopate.

Bishop Ignatius of Antioch, who died about 115, was not only the first man, so far as we know, to employ the term "catholic," but also the first to speak of one bishop at the head of the presbyters and deacons in each congregation.[12] He urged the monarchical episcopate as a necessity for the Church.

a. The demand was for one bishop in every congregation. As yet there was no thought of one bishop for the whole Church. Ignatius urged the congregation to be loyal to its bishop and to the presbyters under him. He compared the bishops to Christ and the presbyters to the Apostles. The burden of his exhortation was that "as the Universal Church has its center in Christ, so the separate congregation should find its center in the bishop. What the Apostles are to the Church at large, the presbytery is to the individual congregation . . . . The individual congregation, subject to the bishop and the presbytery, is a copy of the Church Universal which is led by Christ and the Apostles. Christ and the preaching of the Apostles, therefore — not the episcopacy — condition the unity of the Church Universal." [13]

b. How did this arrangement for one bishop at the head of a local church originate? The most natural answer to this question is that it came from the Church at Jerusalem. From Acts 15, we learn that James, the brother of our Lord, presided over the council of Apostles and presbyters in Jerusalem; or at least he spoke for them. According to a

[11] 40, 41.
[12] *Smyr.* 8, 2; *Mart. Polyc.* 8, 1; Justin, *Dial.* 81, 102.
[13] Justin, *Ad Tral.* 2, 1; 3, 1; *Magn.* 2; *Smyr.* 8; *Eph.* 6.

report from Hegesippus,[13] James was succeeded by Simeon, who was also a relative of the Lord. So a kind of episcopacy had become a tradition in Jerusalem. From there it was easily carried to Antioch. The origin of this episcopate should not be sought for in Rome. Clement of Rome indicates, in his above-mentioned letter to the Corinthians (cir. 96), that he was only one of the bishop-presbyters.[14] The Shepherd of Hermas, which was written in Rome about 150, likewise knows of no monarchical episcopate. And we know that Marcion held a conference at Rome about 140, not with a bishop, but with a college of presbyters.[15] Regarding the monarchical episcopate, which by the time of Irenaeus and Tertullian was recognized throughout the entire Church, we have only to remember that its introduction came about by gradual steps.

c. The reason for supporting the bishops at this time is found in the necessity of presenting a fixed authority against the Gnostic tendencies then spreading through Asia Minor. The unity of the Church in one faith had to be preserved. This was always the chief motive in urging the monarchical episcopate, as can be seen from the writings of the Anti-Gnostic Fathers.[16] The bishops of the individual churches co-operated with each other in the task of keeping all the Christian Churches in the unity of the faith. Bishop Polycarp of Smyrna traveled to Rome to confer with Bishop Anicet (150). At the same time Hegesippus visited Rome and Corinth. About the year 170 the Corinthian Bishop Dionysius sent a number of *catholic letters* to the congregations in Athens, Nicomedia, Crete, Pontus, and Rome.[17] The bishops also wrote credentials and letters of recommendation, with certain marks, for itinerant Christians. These, together with many other things, were the means of preserving the unity of the faith.

3. The Bishops of "Mother-Churches."

a. The Unbroken Chain of Succession. The Church, in its struggle with heresy, depended absolutely on the teaching of the Apostles. The endeavor was to receive, preserve, and transmit the *Apostolic Tradition* in its purity and integrity. The heretics, who were the first exegetes of the New Testament writings, claimed to have received from the Apostles secret commissions to interpret the Scriptures. What was the Church to do in order to defend its conception of the Apostolic teaching as expressed in the Rule of Faith and in the Baptismal Formula? This is what it did. It pointed to the bishops of the "Mother-Churches" where the Apostles themselves had labored—Smyrna, Ephesus, Jerusalem, Corinth, Philippi, Thessalonica, and especially Rome. It was claimed that there were such churches all over the world, wherever the martyred Apostles or their co-laborers had taught.[18] The argument was that in these "Mother-Churches" the purity of the Apostolic Tradition had been guarded with extraordinary care.[19] Tertullian spoke to the heretics in the following fashion: "Let them therefore produce the origins of their churches; let them display the order of their bishops, running through succession from the beginning in such a way that the first bishop had as his teacher and predecessor some one of the Apostles or of the Apostolic men who were closely associated with the

[13] Eusebius, *Historia ecclesiae*, II, 23, 4; IV, 22, 4.
[14] Cf. Fisher, p. 77.
[15] Epiphanius, *Panarion*, 42, 1.
[16] Irenaeus, *Adversus Haereses*, I, 10; IV, 26, 2-6; V, 20. Tertullian, *De praeser*, 20; *De Virginibus Velandis*, c. 2. Clement Alex., *Strom.* V, 6; VII, 17. Origen, *Homily on Genesis*, II, 3.
[17] Eusebius, *Hist. Eccl.* IV, 23.
[18] Irenaeus III, *Op. cit.*, 3, 2-3; 12, 5. Tertullian, *De Praescr.*, 32, 36.
[19] Irenaeus IV. *Op. cit.*, 33, 8.

Apostles." [20] The center of interest was in the unbroken chain of episcopal succession Hegesippus devoted himself to the succession of bishops in Rome and other places.[21]

b. The Special Charism of the Bishops. In attributing a special charism of truth to the bishops, the Anti-Gnostic Fathers went beyond Ignatius. According to Irenaeus the bishops in the succession had received "a sure gift of truth" (*charisma veritatis certum*); and they were regarded as the possessors of a trustworthy tradition.[22] But more than this, it was believed that they possessed a special charism which guaranteed a correct interpretation of the Apostolic Tradition. Their office, then, was that of mediating to the Church the correct interpretation of the final revelation contained in the New Testament. There was no claim to special revelations, as was the case with the Montanists.[23] It should be observed that in the view of Irenaeus the charism functions through the tradition as handed down by those in the succession.[24] Tertullian, after he had become a Montanist, desired to recognize as bishops only those who could be counted among the *spirituales*.[25] And Cyprian, slightly modifying the view of his teacher, said: "All bishops are *spirituales*; if they are not, they have no real right to be bishops." He actually taught that the bishops are guided in their decisions and writings by inspirations and visions. This has reference to special illuminations granted for special duties.[26] So then the Church once more had its pneumatics; only now it was claimed that the bishops were the possessors of the charisms formerly held by the prophets.[27]

c. The Episcopate for the Whole Church. We have seen that there was a bishop at the head of each church and that there was no thought of one bishop for the Church at large. Yet every one of these bishops had a significance for the whole Church Universal, because all were engaged in the task of preserving the Apostolic doctrine in its integrity for the Church of all places and of all ages. Fisher says: "The bishop is no longer the mere head of a local church; he has a relation to the Church Universal. He has a part in the episcopate which is one and single." [28] As centers of the Church, the bishops constituted an organism, and as such they represented the whole Church.

d. Among the Mother-Churches Rome was regarded as Pre-eminent. It was here that the great Apostles Peter and Paul had taught and died. The Apostolic Tradition, as it was preserved by the Roman bishops, was considered as being especially trustworthy. Men did not believe it possible that reliable traditions in any of the "Mother-Churches" could disagree with what was preserved in Rome.[29] The Roman Church was also in possession of a form of faith, called the "Roman Symbol," which was accepted by the other churches in the West. In Rome heretics were kept out of the Christian communion with better success than was the case in Alexandria and Constantinople. Thus it came about that Rome was looked upon as a guardian of the Church's unity. The Roman bishops were conscious of the position they occupied. Bishop Callistus (217 to 222) presented himself to the Church with such titles as "Pontifex Maximus" and

---

[20] *De Praescr.* 32; cf. 21, 36, 37.
[21] Eusebius, IV, *Op. cit.*, 11, 22.
[22] Irenaeus, *Adversus haereses*, IV, 26, 2.
[23] IV, 26, 5. Cf. Tertullian in the pre-Montanist period of his life, *Adv. Prax.* 2.
[24] Irenaeus IV, *Op. cit.*, 26, 2.
[25] *De Pudicitia*, 21.
[26] *Ep.* 11, 3, 4; 57, 5; 68, 5; 66, 10; 63, 1; 73, 26.
[27] Cf. our investigation sub. 2a.
[28] Cf. Cyprian, *De Unitate Ecclesiae*, 5.
[29] Cf. Irenaeus, *Adversus Haereses* III, 1, 2.

"Episcopus episcoporum." [30] Tertullian himself, as well as Irenaeus, had spoken of the Church at Rome as the *"radix"* and the *"mater"* of the Catholic Church;[31] but he was far from recognizing a special authority of the Roman bishop over the other bishops of the Church. His position can be derived from the following words: "If you are near Achaia, you have Corinth. If you are not far from Macedonia, you have Philippi . . . . . If you can turn to Asia, you have Ephesus. If you are bordering on Italy, you have Rome where also we have a convenient authority." [32] We now come to Cyprian's position on the subject. He appealed to Matthew 16: 18-19: "Thou art Peter, and upon this rock I will build my Church . . . . And I will give unto thee the keys of the kingdom of heaven; and whatsoever thou shalt bind upon earth shall be bound in heaven; and whatsoever thou shalt loose on earth shall be loosed in heaven." Cyprian's teaching was as follows: "The other Apostles were also altogether (*utique:* positively, certainly) what Peter was, endowed with an equal share of both honor and power; but the beginning proceeds from unity, in order that the Church of Christ may be shown to be one." [33] So then, the commission was given to Peter, as a representative of the Apostolate, for the purpose of expressing the unity of the Apostles (*monstretur*). But let us follow Cyprian's conception in its application to the Church of Rome. Cyprian shared the general belief that Rome was the Church where Peter had been bishop. His view was as follows: Rome represents (*monstretur*), so to speak, the unity of the Church Universal, as Peter represented that unity among the Apostles; the Church of Rome is the representation of the great idea of the Church's unity. Cyprian therefore directed the Church of his day to the See of Rome "where priestly unity had taken its beginning" (*ad Petri cathedram atque ad ecclesiam principalem unde unitas sacerdotalis exorta est. Ep. 48: 3*).[34] But with all this emphasis upon the idea of which Rome was the outward symbol, Cyprian refused to recognize any special authority of the Roman bishop over the other bishops.[35] He quoted the words of Christ: "He who hears *you* hears me;" [36] and he even drew the attention of those who were so interested in Matthew 16, to the error of Peter as recorded in Galatians 2. All of which shows that to Cyprian's mind the special significance accorded the Roman Church did not include any such claims as Bishops Callistus and Stephen were making.[37] But Cyprian's peculiar conception was too speculative and too idealistic to maintain itself in the praxis of church-life; the tendency of the age was in the direction of a powerful authority concentrated in a hierarchy.[38]

II. THE INTEREST IN THE PURITY OF LIFE THE MOTIVE FOR FURTHER DEVELOPMENT

1. The settlement of the problem of repentance proved to be an occasion for advancing episcopal authority. We have seen how the interest in the apostolicity or purity of the Church's teaching had led to the recognition of the episcopate. We shall

---

[30] See Tertullian's sarcastic reply in *De Pudicitia* 1; cf. 15, 21.
[31] See Cypr. *Ep. 95,* 14.
[32] *Praescr.* 36.
[33] *De Unitate Ecclesiae* 4.
[34] See Kattenbusch in *PRE*, XVII, 79, 19 ff.
[35] Cf. *Ep.* 74; 59, 2, 14; 67, 5.
[36] *Ep.* 66, 4.
[37] Cf. also Eusebius, *Op cit.,* V, 24.
[38] Cf. Seeberg, *DG,* I³, 612 ff.

now se⸱ ⸱ow the conflict, which was waged over the problem of maintaining the holiness of th⸱ Catholic Church, led to the advance in the conception of the Church which has jus⸱ been described.

a. *Public opinion on the doctrine of repentance* started with the view of the early Christians that grave sins committed after baptism could not be forgiven.[39] The Shepherd of Hermas had already made the distinction between mortal and venial sins. Yet he claimed to have received a special revelation to the effect that the chance for a "second repentance" was to be offered in view of the imminent consummation of the world. "The Church never lost sight of this idea" (Seeberg). The Montanists were unyielding in their rigorous church-discipline. Before joining the Montanist ranks, Tertullian reluctantly accepted the theory when he said: "I am afraid of the second chance; I should rather say, the last hope." [40] The reference of the stricter party, which later came to be known as the "Novatians," [41] was to sins of a "serious and destructive" nature, such as the following: homicide, idolatry, fraud, denial of the faith in times of persecution, blasphemy, adultery, and fornication. Sins of this kind were regarded as "irremediable," requiring excommunication from the congregation of saints.[42] Novatian wanted to build up a congregation of the pure[43] in opposition to Cornelius and the milder practice which had come into vogue since the issuing of Callistus' special ordinance, of which we shall hear immediately. And since he was surrounded by churches of a differing practice, he even insisted upon the rebaptism of those who were joining him, and also upon the appointment of opposition-bishops in other places. Thus he maintained a schism in the Church which had already been in evidence under Bishop Hippolytus.

b. *Callistus,* Bishop of Rome (217-222), was the one who, as we have just said, publicly sanctioned and established the milder practice. The conflict between the two parties as to what sins could not be forgiven by the Church, had been narrowed down to about two offences: "in times of peace, especially fornication; in times of persecution, denial of the faith and apostasy." While matters were standing thus, Callistus published a new penitential order in which he allowed the second repentance in case of fornication. He defended this step (against Hippolytus) with Biblical arguments which we, from our viewpoint, do not hestitate to accept.[44] But the chief point of interest for us in our present investigation is this: *Callistus settled the problem as a "conscious hierarch."* He took the position that the Church—which thus far had been regarded as being made up of the holy people of God who held in common the faith of the Apostles, i.e. the faith of the bishops—is *an institution which is subject to the control of the bishop who pardons or retains sins by divine authority in his own sovereign judgment.* "He whom the bishop recognizes belongs to the Church. The bishop is lord over the faith and the life of the Christian world by virtue of an absolute supremacy divinely bestowed upon him. Callistus was the author of the Roman Catholic conception of the Church" (Seeberg). But we should note the significance of the manner in which Callistus

---

[39] See Chapter III, II, 6, b.

[40] *De Poenitentia,* 7.

[41] Here we must be referred to Church History for information concerning the conflict between Cornelius and Novatian as rival candidates for the See of Rome, cir. 251; the former representing the milder, the latter, the stricter party.

[42] Cf. Tetullian, *De Pudicitia,* 19.

[43] Cf. Eusebius, *Op. cit.,* VI, 43, 1.

[44] Cf. Seeberg, *HD,* p. 176.

defended his penitential order: (1) he insisted that the regulation of repentance belonged to the council of bishops; and then (2) he appealed to the power of the keys (*potestas clavium*) given to Peter as representing the bishops of the Church. Since it was already believed that Peter had been the first bishop of Rome, it only remained to draw the obvious conclusion — namely, the monarchical episcopate with its visible culmination in the Roman See. For this step the way was fully prepared.

c. The Conception of Cyprian. It was Cyprian, bishop of Carthage (248-258), who laid the doctrinal foundation for the conception of the Church in the Post-Nicene Age and for the development of the Church into the Roman hierarchy. He did this especially in his book *De Unitate Ecclesiae,* and in the letters he wrote. His thinking was stimulated by the contemporary conflict over the regulation of repentance. Tertullian, his great teacher, who had joined the Montanists, was bitterly opposed to the penitential order of Callistus against which he published his most radical writing *De Pudicitia* (cir. 220). But the practice introduced by Callistus had become universal by about 250. It was then that the violent persecution broke out under Emperor Decius. Many Christians denied the faith, either by making offerings to idols, by buying certificates showing that they had done so, or by making false statements regarding their relation to Christianity. The question which now forced itself upon the Church's attention was whether they should be readmitted or not. So it came about that apostasy from the faith was added to the sins of the flesh with which the order of Callistus had been dealing. Cyprian decided that the lapsed should be admitted into the Church again, providing they showed signs of real repentance and made public confession. But a peculiar situation developed which stimulated Cyprian to his fundamental utterances on the position of the bishops. There were presbyters who took the matter into their own hands and admitted the backsliders. Cyprian at once took the position that such presbyters should be excluded from the Church. He worked in harmony with Bishop Cornelius in Rome, directing his efforts against Novatian. In 252 an assembly of bishops was held in Carthage to settle this matter. It should be understood that the bishops alone were called upon to make the decision.

2. Cyprian's leading thoughts have been referred to above (cf. 3 b ff.). In his system he took the position that the Church is an institution for the salvation of mankind, which comprises the good and the evil alike. Admitting that in individual cases God may judge differently, he insisted that the Church alone can guarantee salvation. Orthodoxy constitutes no guarantee when the individual is outside of the Church. *Extra ecclesiam nulla salus. Si quis ecclesiam non habet matrem, Deum, non habet patrem.* The Church is established upon the bishops. They can be judged by no one except by God. To criticize the bishop is rebellion. Cyprian did not stress apostolic succession as a test of the validity of the episcopal office; but he emphasized the idea that the bishop is the successor of the Apostles, and hence is the legitimate interpreter of the Apostolic Tradition. As we have seen (supra 3 c), he further emphasized the college of bishops (episcopate) as the authority of the Church, and he willingly recognized the pre-eminence of Rome (cf. 3 d). He had no intention of favoring a Roman hierarchy, but that very thing resulted on the basis of his utterances. The Cyprian theory of safeguarding the unity of the Church was soon overtaken by the actual development which established the bishop of Rome as the visible head of the Church.[45]

---

[45] E. W. Bensen *Cyprian,* 1897. The *NSH,* vol. III, 81. Lōofs⁴, pp. 204 ff. Seeberg, *HD,* I, 178 ff.; *DG,* I³, 612 ff., cf. 595 ff., 532 ff. Harnack, *Grundriss⁴,* pp. 97 ff.

Chapter Eight

OLD CATHOLIC THEOLOGIANS. FIRST STEPS INTO THE ECUMENICAL AGE

A. TEACHERS AND THEIR CHARACTERISTICS IN THE OLD CATHOLIC AGE

a. Characteristics: The Old Catholic Age (170-325), the age after the Greek Apologists, may be characterized as follows: A Church theology was being established, (1) against Ebionitism; (2) against the religious philosophy of the Gnostics; (3) against Marcion; (4) against the views of the Monarchians, i.e., the Samosatenes (dynamistic) and the Sabellians (modalistic). Other characteristics of this age were: (5) Development of the Rules of Faith; (6) Establishment of the Canon of the Holy Scriptures; (7) First conscious steps in the creation of an episcopal organization were taken; (8) Montanism was refused, an act which kept the Church from becoming a narrow sect. (9) As to the outward situation the Church was under persecution.

b. Schools and Teachers:
1. *The School of Asia Minor,* with Irenaeus (who died about 200) and his pupil, Hippolytus, as leading teachers;
2. *The School of Alexandria,* represented by Clement (d. before 216) and Origen (d. 254);[1]
3. *The School of North Africa,* led by Tertullian (died about 225) and Cyprian (d. 258).

Christianity's most dangerous opponent in the Old Catholic Age was Gnosticism. The objections which the Old Catholic teachers raised against Gnosticism are summarized by Harnack (in his *DG*) as follows: (1) that the God of the Old Testament is the Creator of the world and is identical with the God of redemption; (2) that the whole Gnostic dualism takes away, not only the omnipotence of God, but also the very conception of God; (3) that the unity of God is endangered by the Gnostic emanation-theories which constitute a mere playing with ideas; (4) that the endeavor to discuss conditions in the Divinity is a frivolous undertaking; (5) that the Gnostics are compelled to place the origin of sin in the kingdom of light (*pleroma*); (6) that criticizing the constitution of the cosmos is impudent because it judges the wisdom and goodness of God; (7) that the docetic conception of Christ is tantamount to fastening a lie upon the Deity; (8) that man's freedom cannot be denied, etc.[2]

I. IRENAEUS THE FOUNDER OF A BIBLICAL THEOLOGY OF FUNDAMENTALS

Literature: Irenaeus wrote much more than has been preserved. But his great work against the Gnostics, *Adversus haereses,* has come down to us, only in a Latin translation. It consists of five books written at the request of a friend who desired information on Valentinian Gnosticism.

---

[1] Kurtz, *Church History,* Eng. ed., par. 31; cf. German, 14th ed., par. 28.
[2] Harnack, *DG⁴,* 1905, p. 115.

'or the text of this work the student is referred to the edition by W. W. Harvey, Cambridge, 1877,
vols., and also to the *ANF*, Vol. I. In addition to the *Adversus haereses* there is also his *Epideixis*.
As valuable literature on Irenaeus we cite the following: T. ZAHN'S article in *PRE*, IX, pp.
'01 ff., and an abbreviation of the same article in the *NSH*, VI, 28 ff. A HARNACK, in *Geschichte
'er Christlichen Literatur*, 1891, I, 263-288. T. ZAHN, *Forschungen zur Geschichte des Kanon*,
V, 247-283. J. KUNZE, *Die Gotteslehre des Irenaeus*, 1891. N. BONWETSCH, *Die abend-
aendische Theologie um 200 nach Christo*, Part I: Irenaeus, 1925. J. WERNER, *Der Paulinismus
'es Irenaeus*, 1889, in *TU*, VI, 2. The Histories of Dogma or Doctrine as referred to for special
eading at the close of this study on Irenaeus. F. R. M. HICHCOCK, *Irenaeus of Lugdunum, A Study
'f His Teaching*, 1914. J. A. ROBINSON, *St. Irenaeus and the Apostolic Preaching*, 1920, in *Trans.
f Christian Lit.*, Ser. IV. A. DUFOURCQ, *Saint Iréné*, 1926 W. BOUSSET, *Kyrios Christos,
'eschichte des Christusglaubens von den Anfaengen des Christentums bis Irenaeus³*, 1926 (in chap.
'0 on Irenaeus, 333-362). Cf. NYGRÉN, *Agape and Eros*, II, I, 177 ff. H. RINN, pp. 31 ff.

1. Historical Orientation. IRENAEUS, who was bishop at Lyons in Southern Gaul
ut the time of his death (cir. 200), had lived in Asia where he knew Polycarp personally.
'n theology, Irenaeus was typical of the School of Asia Minor. This School was "the
outcome of John's ministry, and was distinguished by a firm grasp of Scripture, solid
aith, conciliatory treatment of those within, and energetic polemics against heretics." [3]
Although the Johannine origin of Irenaeus' theology is worthy of emphasis, it must not
be forgotten that Irenaeus was filled with the spirit and thoughts of Paul more than was
he case with any other of the leading theologians of his age.

Note: It is interesting to note the relation of the School of Asia Minor to the two other
schools of the Old Catholic Age which we shall review presently—the Alexandrian School (Origen
nd Clement) and the North African School (Tertullian). The *Alexandrian* started with the
.*ogos*, much after the manner of Philo and the Greek Apologists. "Their special task was the
onstruction of a true ecclesiastical gnosis over against the false heretical gnosis, and so the most
elebrated teachers of this school have not escaped the charge of unevangelical speculative tendencies.
. . *The North African School* by its realism and a thoroughly practical tendency, formed the direct
ntithesis of the idealism and speculative endeavors of the Alexandrian School. It repudiated
lassical science and philosophy as fitted to lead into error, but laid special stress upon the purity
f Apostolic tradition, and insisted with all emphasis upon holiness of life and strict asceticism"
(Kurtz).

As to the relation of these schools to each other this may be said: *Irenaeus* represented an
arlier stage as compared with Origen and Tertullian as two extremes. *Origen*, with his use of the
Alexandrian Logos-speculation as the principle of Christian science, barely escaped degrading
Christianity to the level of a philosophy, and he lost himself in the mazes of an unbounded spir-
tualism. On the other hand *Tertullian*, who fastened his whole attention upon nature, aimed at
ubstantializing even God and the soul. So he settled upon a one-sided realism. *Irenaeus* avoided
he dangers of both by his thoroughly sound Biblicism, by his sound attitude to tradition, and by
is Christo-centric theology.

2. Like Tertullian, *Irenaeus was opposed to philosophical speculation in matters of
'eligion.* Gnosticism shows, he said, where we shall arrive if we follow philosophy.
Being of an intensely practical turn of mind, Irenaeus was averse to every kind of *a priori
speculation, and his theology was therefore a theology of Biblical facts. God is known
o us, not through speculation, but through revelation. Hence we should not concern
ourselves with idle questions, such as what God did before creation. Christ is understood
o be the revelation of God. As such He is pre-existent and co-eternal (*semper
coexistens*). The Father and the Son belong together from all eternity. Just as Christ
is the revelation of God, so God has always been revealing the Son; and the relation

---

[3] Kurtz, Eng. ed., par. 31, 1. As was mentioned above, Harnack denies the existence of a *School of Asia
Minor.* But we fail to see the validity of this denial in the light of what Loofs tells us (p. 140) of a preceding
heology of Asia Minor to which Irenaeus gave comprehensive expression. Read Loofs, pp. 139-146.

between the two includes the personal differentiation.[4] The manner in which the Father generated the Son is altogether incomprehensible.[5] We should therefore abide by the language of Scripture and not depart from the Rule of Faith. Irenaeus began with the historic Christ Whom he regarded as the revelation of God the Father. He thus transcended the viewpoint of the Greek Apologists. His thinking was Christo-centric not Logos-centric. In other words, his interest was centered in Christ the God-Man as the Mediator of our salvation,[6] and not in the Logos as the Mediator between God and the world. It is not our present intention to take up the details of the development of the doctrine of the Trinity; this belongs to Chapter IX. We may say, however, that Irenaeus made but a small contribution to a scientifically articulated dogma of the Trinity. This was chiefly due to his refusal to deal with speculative questions.

3. *The Structure of Irenaeus' Theology.* Soteriology (*Goettliche Heilsoekonomie*) was the material principle of his entire theology. Against Gnosticism Irenaeus raised the fundamental thought that the God of creation is the same as the God of redemption.[7] Christ the God-Man, Who is the personification of the eternal self-revelation of God, is the Mediator of man's salvation. The first Adam misused his free will and disobeyed God, in consequence of which he fell, and with him all mankind. Through the fall man lost the divine image and became the victim of death. Thus the divine plan of leading man gradually to actual Godlikeness was interrupted. Physical death constituted a certain negative remedy. But God immediately inaugurated a positive plan for the salvation of man and for leading him to the intended goal—actual Godlikeness. So he entered into a fourfold federation with man. The first covered the time from Adam to the flood; the second, the time after the flood under Noah; the third, the giving of the Law under Moses; and the fourth is the period in which man is to be renewed and everything brought to completion and perfection through the Gospel (II, 2, 8). Under this fourth federation God became Man in Christ, Who, as the second Adam, entered into solidarity with our sinful race. He proved His holiness in the hours of temptation, overcame the common enemy, and thus regained for man the possibility of Godlikeness. In this way Christ restored the interrupted development and led it to a conclusion in Himself. This is the so-called ἀνακεφαλαίωσις or *recapitulation-thought* of Irenaeus. The term is found in Ephesians 1:10. Christ appeared as the Second Adam. As the First Adam who fell had produced a generation of sinful men, so Christ, the Second Adam, produces a new generation of righteous men in whom the divine image is restored. In Christ the new man becomes immortal. *Quando incarnatus et homo factus, longam hominum expositionem in se ipso recapitulavit. In compendio nobis salutem praestans, ut quod perdideramus in Adam, id est, secundum et similitudinem esse Dei, hoc in Christo reciperemus.*[8] Through His obedience Christ did what Adam had failed to do. He thus destroyed sin and Satan. All stages of human life, from infancy onward, are sanctified by the life of the Second Adam. This thought of Christ's works and sufferings for us is carried out even to His descent into Hades, into which His followers shall likewise descend and from which they shall come forth at the resurrection of the body.

---

[4] *Adversus haereses*, II, 30, 9; III, 18, 1; II, 25, 3; 28, 2.
[5] II, 28, 4, 5.
[6] II, 13, 8; 28, 5.
[7] IV, 20, 2; 6, 2.
[8] III, 18, 1. The English translation of this remarkable statement can be found in the *ANF*, Vol. I, p. 446.

as Christ did.[9] After all has been completed and the mission of Christ is accomplished, Christ's special position in the economy of the Trinity will cease. The hosts of redeemed mankind will then occupy the place of Christ, and God will be all in all.[10] Harnack characterizes the view of Irenaeus by the remark: "He sees the Redeemer in Christ, merely because He is the Incarnate God." This is correct. Christ, the God-Man, occupied the center of Irenaeus' thinking, and not Christ the Teacher, as was the case with the Apologists. Irenaeus raised the question: *"Cur Deus homo?"* and then answered it thus: 'In order that we might become Gods, that is, Godlike."

4. *The Epoch-Making Significance of Irenaeus' Theology.* Zahn says: "Irenaeus is the first writer of the Post-Apostolic Age who deserves the name of a theologian." [11] Loofs calls his theology "the Catholic form of an older theological tradition" which had its home in Asia Minor (p. 139). Harnack expresses a certain dislike at connecting Irenaeus (through Polycarp) with the ministry of the Apostle John. The objection is that in this way "Irenaeus is given authority which he cannot claim by virtue of the character of his theology." Seeberg remarks that it is the theology of Irenaeus which aids us in best viewing the heritage (*das geistige Kapital*) bequeathed to the Church by the Apostolic Age. But Harnack also admits that the conception of Christianity as expressed in Irenaeus' theology has become "a deciding factor in the History of Dogma." [12] This is surely the case. There are leading elements in his doctrinal system which the Church could not avoid adopting and using as the basis for the further development of a system of Christian truth. Thomasius passes a correct judgment when he cites Irenaeus as "the most conspicuous representative of the Church's consciousness," and when he characterizes his theology as "sound to the core" (*grundgesund*).[13] The truth of this latter statement is seen particularly in these three things: (1) his theology is Biblical; (2) it sustains a deep reverence for the Apostolic tradition; (3) it is Christocentric.

Concerning the Biblicism of his theology it may be said that in Irenaeus we have, for the first time, a consideration and an understanding of the Scriptures as a whole. The relation of the Old Testament to the New is indicated, and the teaching of Paul is understood. From the trying conflict with fundamental heresies there has come a classification of views with regard to many of the fundamentals of Christianity. There is a Scriptural and even an evangelical ring in the system of Irenaeus. We have the feeling that a truly *Catholic* theology has appeared. It is a theology which the Reformation of the 16th century recognized as *Catholic* over against the *Roman* Catholic innovation of later times.

5. *Shortcomings.* A closer study of Irenaeus' writings shows that his teaching was not without erroneous elements, especially in the field of Soteriology. Like the Anti-Gnostic Fathers, he emphasized the freedom of man's will, and therefore could not free himself from that ethical apprehension of the Gospel which we have noticed in the Apologists. He lacked the evangelical note also, as can be seen from the way in which he spoke of sins committed after baptism, and again from the way in which he under-

---

[9] Loofs locates all the pertinent passages in footnote 3, page 145.
[10] Cf. Loofs, 145.
[11] *PRE*, IX, 410.
[12] *DG*⁴, I, 556.
[13] I³, 145.

stood faith to be a doing of God's will.[14] Likewise the teaching of the *deification* of man as a result of the *incarnation* of God reveals, as Nygrén remarks (II, I, 193 ff.), a serious limitation of the Agape-motif in his theology.

II. CLEMENT AND ORIGEN AS REPRESENTATIVES OF THE SCHOOL OF ALEXANDRIA

1. Orientation. Our attention is now drawn to the School of Alexandria which was represented by Clement and particularly by Origen. In this school it was the speculative tendency which was dominant. Theology was viewed as a science and expressed in terms of philosophical thought. Beyond creating the background for this type of theology, Clement's contribution to the dogma was small. But the theology of Origen, while prolific of much that was negative, was, nevertheless, rich in helpful suggestions and even in solution of the Trinitarian and Christological problems. To theology in general Origen proved to be a great stimulus.

2. The Catechetical School of Alexandria: Its Teachers—Their Writings. The city of Alexandria in northern Egypt had been founded in 332 B. C. by Alexander the Great from whom it took its name. Originally intended to be a commercial center, it succeeded in becoming an intellectual center also. And this is not strange. When men come together to trade their material possessions, it frequently happens that they are apt, at the same time, to trade their intellectual property. So it turned out that Alexandria became the common meeting-ground for Greek philosophy, ancient Egyptian thought, the Oriental cults, and the religion of Judaism. It would have been strange if Christianity had not entered the intellectual and scholastic life of the city. At any rate, this is what happened. The existence of the numerous differing schools in Alexandria conspired to give rise to a Christian School. By about 185 there existed in Alexandria a famous catechetical school which prepared catechumens for baptism. The pronounced scholastic character of the school may be accounted for in two ways. It may have been caused either by conscious imitation of, or by direct opposition to, the various systems found in that place.[15]

Pantaenus was the first teacher of this school, so far as we know. He had formerly been a Stoic philosopher. But very little is known of him.

CLEMENT (died before 216), of whom we know more, had also been a learned pagan philosopher. In his search for knowledge he came to Alexandria where he placed himself under the influence of Pantaenus whom he later succeeded as teacher. As compared with the methodically proceeding Origen, Seeberg says that Clement was a "talented dilettante with the virtues and vices which belong to such character."[16] This can be substantiated by a study of Clement's writings.

Some of these writings have been lost, especially his interpretation of the Scriptures in eight volumes. But a large work composed of three parts has been preserved. The first part of this work is a *Word of Admonition to the Greeks;* in this part, which is at once apologetic and polemic, Clement exposes the foolishness and vanity of heathenism.

---

[14] Comp. Werner, *Der Paulinismus des Irenaeus*, in *TU*, by Gebhardt and Harnack, IV, Heft 2.

[15] See *PRE*, I, p. 356. Later we shall hear of a *New Alexandrian School* (see our introductory note to this chapter).

[16] Eng. ed., 141; cf. *DG*, I³, 489 ff. His reference is to the *Panegyricus* on Origen by Gregory Thaumaturgus, c. 6-15.

The second part, which is entitled the *Instructor,* offers in three books a guide for the Christian life of those who are destined to be *gnostikoi.* This may well be called the Church's first comprehensive work on Christian Ethics. To it Clement added a monograph on the question: *Which rich man may be saved?* The third part, which comprises eight books, is entitled *Stromateis,* meaning *Patchwork* or *Miscellanies;* it takes its name from the aphoristic style and the variety of its contents, and aims to present an introduction to the perfect Christian knowledge (*gnosis*). It discusses the relation of Christian truth to philosophy, and of faith to knowledge, and thus delineates the ideal of the Christian Gnostic. This part lacks unity of thought. It is indicative of Clement's type of mind. He was not a systematic thinker.

Texts: A much used edition of Clement's works is that by J. POTTER, 2 vols., Oxford, 1715. Seeberg quotes from this edition. It is reproduced by MIGNE, VIII-IX. The best modern text is that by O. STAEHLIN, *Leipzig,* 1905-06. In Vol. II of the *ANF,* 1885, we have a good English translation which follows Potter. Cf. H. RINN, pp. 57-61.

Literature in the form of Discussion: C. BIGG, *The Christian Platonists of Alexandria,* Oxford, 1886, 1913. F. J. A. HORT, *Six Lectures on the Ante-Nicene Fathers,* London, 1896. C. MERK, *Clement Alex, in seiner Abhaengigkeit von der griechischen Philosophie, Leipzig,* 1879. W. SCHERER, *Clement Alex. und seine Erkenntnissprinzipien,* Munich, 1907. R. B. TILLINTON, *Clement of Alexandria, A Study in Christian Liberalism,* 1914. I. PATRICK, *Clement of Alexandria,* 1914.

Clement was a thoroughgoing eclectic. He praised Plato, but followed the ethics of the Sota. Still he contributed more than any other to the creation of that attitude of mind which formed the background and foundation of the systematic theology of the Greek Fathers.[17]

ORIGEN (d. 254), who was the pupil of Clement, was the greatest among the representatives of the Alexandrian School. So universal was his mind that he has been "celebrated as a philosopher, philologist, critic, exegete, dogmatician, apologist, polemicist." He was a man "whom posterity has with equal right honored as the actual founder of an ecclesiastical and scientific theology, and reproached as the originator of many heretical opinions." [18] In 203 he became teacher at the School of Alexandria. After his excommunication, which was probably due to the jealousy of Bishop Dimetrius, he taught at Caesarea.

A large part of Origen's work was in the field of *Biblical criticism.* In this field there was his *Hexapla* comprising fifty volumes—a work in which he placed in parallel columns all the then known texts and translations of the Old Testament, indicating the agreements and variations and adding in many cases his own critical remarks. This work, on which he labored continuously for twenty-seven years, disappeared when Caesarea was destroyed by the Arabians. But fragments of it have been collected by Montfaucon, and these represent Vols. 15 and 16 in Migne. [19] It should be mentioned that much of Origen's work was devoted to an *exegetical investigation in the sphere of interpretation and application.* [20] Worthy of special mention is Origen's *dogmatic work* Περὶ 'Αρχῶν which has been preserved in a Latin translation entitled *De Principiis* (4 vols.). This was the first attempt to present a comprehensive system of Christian doctrine by founding it on the Scripture and the Apostolic Tradition, and then building it up with the philosophical knowledge of the age. Although this work abounds in many impossible tenets, nevertheless, by reason of its creative character it has exerted a great influence upon the Christian dogma both positively and negatively.[21]

---

[17] Read Seeberg, *DG,* I[3], 489-500.

[18] Kurtz, par. 31, 4; cf. par. 51; par. 52, 6; par. 53, 6.

[19] Cf. the two vols. by F. Field, Oxford, 67-74; also E. Klostermann, *Analekten zur LXX.*

[20] The *Semeioseis* or *Scholia* are interpretations of difficult passages of Scripture; the *Timpi* are commentaries on books of the Scripture, especially Matthew and John; and the *Homilies* are expository addresses.

[21] The edition by Lommatzsch, 183 ff., has it in vol. 21.

The eight books, *Contra Celsum*, also contain important material for an exposition of Origen's system of theology. Vol. 3 of the *ANF* includes none of Origen's writings but *De Principiis* and *Contra Celsum*. The only complete edition of all of Origen's writings is the one by Charles de la Rue (Paris, 1733-57) in four large volumes. C. H. E. Lommatzsch's edition of twenty-five small volumes (Berlin, 1831-48) is a reprint of this, and has been reproduced by Migne (*MSG*). Cf. Rinn, pp. 73-93.[22]

3. The Philosophical Character of the Alexandrian Theology. The theology of Clement and Origen differed greatly from that of Irenaeus and Tertullian. Pre-Catholic conditions maintained themselves longer in Alexandria than in Asia Minor and Carthage. This situation in which Clement found himself explains the Hellenic form of much of his theology. By Origen's time the Catholic tradition had also become established in Alexandria; but it did not do away with the peculiar type and tendency of theology in the School. Clement regarded philosophy as having the same pedagogical significance for the Greek world which the Law had for the Hebrews. Philosophy is the light of reason which the Logos has imparted to mankind. It is the preparation for the higher light which shines in the Gospel. Through the Greek philosophy the soul is prepared beforehand for the reception of faith on which the truth builds up the edifice of knowledge.[23] Philosophy is the means by which the real nature of Christianity is disclosed to the thinking man. Even today philosophy will do this service for man. Such were the thoughts of Clement which lay also at the foundation of the system of Origen, his greater pupil. He looked upon Christianity as a higher philosophy. Christ towers above Zeno and Plato (1) because He overcomes polytheism, and (2) because His religion is at once the religion for the common man and for the thinker. The Alexandrian School was a continuation of the principles which were expressed by Philo and by the Greek Apologists after him. Little wonder that this school marked the first consistent synthesis between the Biblical revelation and philosophical speculation. In the words of Nygrén, the Christian and the Hellenistic views of love were merged into a real synthesis with the effect that Agape was interpreted in the lines of Eros (II, I, 175).

4. Is Philosophy a Legitimate Factor in the Work of Theology? This age-old question, which men have continued to ask up to the present time, was suggested by the peculiar type of Alexandrian theology. It cannot be denied that what Clement and Origen were aiming at was an inner necessity for Christian theology. Christianity is universal in character, which means that it is the religion which is destined to exercise the controlling influence over the world's thought. Kurtz says: "When once the substantial truth of divine salvation had cast off the Judaistic husk in which the kernel had ripened, those elements of culture, which had come to maturity in the Roman-Greek world, were appropriated as the means for giving to Christian ideas a fuller and clearer expression. The task now to be undertaken was the development of Christianity on the lines of Graeco-Roman culture."[24] The Apologists began the work along this line. Tertullian did a great deal of it without intending to do so. The Alexandrians dealt with

---

[22] *As literature in the form of discussion* we mention the following: Westcott's fine article in the *D. C. B.,* 4, 69-142. C. Bigg, *The Christian Platonists of Alexandria,* 1913;, pp. 115-268, Oxford, 1886. J. Patrick, *The Apology of Origen in Reply to Celsus,* London, 1892. C. Klein, *Die Freiheitslehre des Origenes,* Strassburg, 1894. W. Fairweather, *Origen and Greek Patristic Theology,* Edinburgh, 1901. F. W. Farrar, *History of Interpretation,* pp. 187-203, New York, 1889. A. Zoelling, *Die Inspirationslehre des Origenes,* Freiburg, 1902. The article on Origen in *PRE,* XIV, 467 ff.; cf. *NSH,* 8, 268 ff. The Church Histories accessible in English are: Neander, Kreuger, Schaff, Kurtz, Moeller. As to the Histories of Doctrine the reference is especially to Harnack's *Grundriss⁶,* pp. 140 ff., to Loofs, 192 ff.; and to Seeberg, DG I⁸, 500 ff. Cf. Nygrén, Pt. II, Vol. I, 133 ff.

[23] *Strom.,* 3.

[24] *Par.* 19; cf. par. 7, 25 f.

philosophy in such a way that it appeared to be an integral part of the whole system. The Gnostics had also done this, but without any consideration for the Apostolic Tradition and the Rule of Faith. When Origen opposed his "Christian gnosis" to a "pseudonymous gnosis," he did so with the intention of being guided by the Scriptures, although he frequently failed in this because of his allegorical exegesis and his philosophical trend of mind. But what we wish to state here is that, no matter how impossible his system was as a whole, no matter how much we may reject his many errors and his synthesis of religion and philosophy in its practical details, nevertheless, Christianity does possess the inner impulse to establish itself as a system and to pour its contents into the mental forms which have been developed by the work of philosophy. In this sense Origen was a pioneer in the quest for theological method. Irenaeus' refusal to recognize philosophy prevented him from making any contribution to the solution of the Trinitarian problem. But the contribution of Origen and his successors was great.

5. *Pistis and Gnosis.* The peculiar theology of both Clement and Origen pivoted about the relation of faith to a deeper knowledge of the contents of faith. Clement said: "To know is more than to believe." [25] Faith is the outward acceptance of God and of the doctrine of Christ in the literal sense; but the Christian Gnostic possesses an initiated vision which apprehends salvation inwardly and comprehends it. [26] This attitude or experience gives the Gnostic a higher motive for his ethical functioning. He does not do the Christian's work for reward, but for its own sake and out of love to God. [27] In faith there is already an element of that knowledge ($\gamma\nu\tilde{\omega}\sigma\iota\varsigma$), and therefore faith is sufficient for salvation. The simple believer has already received in his baptism the needed perfection and the assurance of salvation. The believer is one who is taught by God, and as such he is a pneumatic. These thoughts separated Clement from the views of the Gnostic who said that men from their birth are either hylics or pneumatics and that the latter alone can be saved. But the simple faith is to be lifted to something higher—to a vision of the divine mysteries. And it is here that philosophy comes in to aid. But even here Clement was opposed to an *unlimited speculation.* A true Gnostic, said he, is one who bases his thinking on the faith of the Church. [28] In these thoughts Origen agreed entirely with Clement. The cultured man, who sees the Logos in Christ, is the perfect Christian. He sees divine truth in all things. Every fact is merely a symbol to him of abstract teachings which express higher truth. So we may say with Seeberg that from this theology "there resulted two forms of Christianity. In contrast with the barely believing and uncultivated beginner, inclined to externalties, stands the Christian who beholds the mysteries of God and who with heart and understanding receives God to abiding fellowship. The Stoic discrimination between the wise and the advancing is here transferred to Christianity. . . . The 'Gnostic' of Clement stands higher than his 'believer'." [29]

6. *Origen on the Interpretation of Scripture.* The allegorical interpretation was more or less common to the Church Fathers of this and the following periods. But it was Origen who systematically developed this method of interpretation in Vol. IV of his *De Principiis.* And his book *Contra Celsum* is full of references to this way of inter-

---

[25] *Strom.*, VI, 14.
[26] VI, 11, 12; V, 1; VII, 12; VI, 10.
[27] IV, 18; IV, 22.
[28] Cf. VII, 7.
[29] English ed., I, 142.

preting Scripture. It has been fittingly remarked that it was "this method which enabled him to conceal the foolishness of the Gospel and to glorify it as wisdom." [30] Origen needs this allegorical method in order to establish the system of his peculiar doctrines. According to him, the Cosmos—God's first revelation—is threefold: *spiritual, psychic,* and *material.* In the same way the Scriptures, which constitute God's second revelation, are threefold. First, the Scriptures have a *somatic or literal sense* upon which the simpler souls of the multitude depend. Exegesis is to find that sense, but must remember withal that it is intended only to conceal the true sense. Second, the Scriptures have a *psychical or moral sense* which refers "to the individual soul in this life and to its ethical relations, including its relations to God." And third, the Scriptures have a *pneumatic or speculative sense.* Here we have the real spiritual content of Scripture—the profounder meaning which is sealed to all save the mature believer.[31] There are cases where the literal sense must be rejected altogether (as for instance, Gen. 19; 20 ff.; 25:1 ff.; 29:27 f.; 30:3, 9). The literal sense is intended to conceal the spiritual sense in order that pearls may not be cast before swine. But the mature believer will press beyond the literal sense and discover the esoteric tenets of the divine Word.

7. *Origen on the Trinitarian Relation in God.*

Note: In presenting this and the following special topics of Origen's positive teachings (7-12) we shall not aim at more than to give glimpses of his very elaborate and unified system. The reader would be helped by seeing how Harnack in his comprehensive grasp of this system has succeeded in picturing Origen's world of thought. We refer especially to the description of his latest—the sixth—edition of his *Grundriss,* pp. 144-54. Cf. Rinn, pp. 73-93.

a. God. In Neo-Platonic fashion Origen saw reality only in the spiritual as opposed to things material and visible. This led him to an abstract conception of God. As the Father, God is one and is opposed to the many things. These have their cause in Him. He alone is really being. Anthropomorphic expressions are carefully avoided. God is Goodness and Omnipotence, and for this reason He presses toward a revelation which takes place through the *Logos.* God cannot be thought of without revelation. Creative activity belongs to His very being. His being appears in the many things which He is creating. But revelation includes limitation. In creating man a free agent God limited himself.[32] Origen was Platonic in his abstract conception of God.

b. The Son reveals the Father to us. Origen followed Neo-Platonism, which taught that from the Divine Being proceeds the *Nous.* The Son proceeds from the Father somewhat as the will proceeds from a human being.[33] This procession is expressed in the conception of a generation (*genesis*) of the Son from the Father. But Origen made a larger contribution to the dogma of the Trinity by speaking of an *eternal generation.* The Father *is always begetting* the Son.[34] Origen was thus a strong opponent of Monarchianism, which had its supporters in Rome. He looked upon the *Logos* as a Person, and taught that the Son, begotten of the Father from all eternity, was also from all

---

[30] For example see VI, 7; V, 60. Cf. the estimate of Porphyry in Eusebius, *Hist. Eccl.,* VI, 19, 4, 7 f., and also *Celsus,* IV, 38.

[31] *De Principiis,* I, 1, 2.

[32] For a lucid description of Origen's conception of God see the article in the *NSH* (VIII, 272) on the basis of E. Preuschen in the *PRE.*

[33] *De Princ.* I, 2, 6.

[34] I, 2, 4.

eternity an hypostasis.[35] Origen's teaching differed thus from all previous conceptions of a *hypostatic Logos;* especially was this true with reference to the Apologists who took the position that the hypostasizing of the *Logos* occurred *in time* for the purpose of creation and incarnation. Kurtz says: "The generation of the Son took place not simply as the condition of creation, but as of itself necessary, for where there is light there must be the shedding forth of rays. But because the life of God is bound to no time, the objectivizing of His life in the Son must also lie outside of all time. It is not, therefore, an act of God accomplished once and forever, but an eternally continued exercise of living power."

This was the first advance made towards stating the Son's co-eternity with the Father which is expressed in the ancient creed. This thought—that the Son is co-ternal with the Father, opened the way to that other and equally important term of the creed—ὁμοούσιος.[36] Still it should be remembered that Origen did not wholly succeed in overcoming his subordinationism.[37] He even maintained that prayer should be addressed to the Father alone.[38] But Origen's subordination was somewhat modified. "He restricted it within the narrowest possible limits." He rejected the expression that the Son came "from the essence of the Father," but he did this, we must remember, in opposition to the Gnostic theories of emanation. In opposition to the *homoousios* as used in the Patripassian sense, he maintained that the Son is different in His being from the Father. He taught the generation of the Son from the Will of God, but only because he saw in Him the objectified Divine Will. He called Him a creature (κτίσμα), but only in so far as He is generated of God and does not have a life independent of God. Thus, what Origen taught was not a subordination of essence or nature, but only of existence or origin.

c. The Holy Spirit. Origen felt obliged to express himself on the Holy Spirit since the Rule of Faith assigned Him the third place in the Trinity. In describing the relation of the Son to the Father Origen made use of analogies suggested by the philosophers.[39] But he proceeded differently with regard to the Spirit. Here he aimed to rely altogether on revelation.[40] Although the Spirit is a production of the Son, nevertheless He is a *hypostasis* and is divine in character. He is active, not like the Logos in all intelligent things, but only in the souls of the saints. The Spirit's sphere of activity is the smallest. The Father governs in the sphere of being, the Son in that of the reason, and the Spirit in the souls of the Christians (Church). The spirit's work is therefore the most important.

Thus, according to Origen the *Trinity* can be represented graphically by three concentric circles of which the Father is the largest, and the Spirit the smallest. The Trinity is at once economic and ontological. God reveals Himself, but He cannot be thought of without constantly revealing Himself in that way.

8. Origen on Cosmology and Anthropology. There was a *history before history.*[41] Since God has been revealing Himself from all eternity, the world also is eternal; that

---

[35] I, 2, 9 f.; IV, 28; *Contra Celsum* V, 37.
[36] *Contra Celsum* VIII, 12; *De Princ.* I, 2, 12.
[37] *Contra Celsum* V, 39; VI, 60; II, 9.
[38] VIII, 13; cf. VIII, 26.
[39] The Neo Platonian Plotinus spoke of the *Nous* proceeding from God as Origen spoke of the *Logos.*
[40] *De Princ.* I, 3, 1-4.
[41] *De Princ.* II, 8, 3; 9, 2.

is, the world of spirits is eternal, not this visible world.[42] The Mediator in God's creative activity is the Son. The spirits, whom He originally created all alike, were created free agents, and their destiny was to be fixed by their own determination. The spirits were intended to arrive at a condition of constancy and were then to make room for new creations. But the world of spirits became the scene of a fall into sin. Some of the spirits did not participate in the fall (such as the soul of Jesus and others), while others did in a greater or lesser degree. Their condition in the world of creation was fixed by their abstinence from, or by their participation in, the fall.

The creation, which is recorded in Genesis, was for the purpose of punishment and purification. In the creation the spirits received bodies which corresponded with their merits. Their attitude toward good and evil showed itself even in their external appearance. On the one hand, there were those who had attained to the heights of goodness; these appear now as divinities, as thrones, or as stars which are looked upon as living beings. On the other hand, there were the creatures, namely, Satan and the devils, who fell first and deeper than the others; these appear now in dark and coarse forms. Between these two classes are the spirits or souls of men in their own form of corporeal being; it was for these that the world was created.[43] Man is to be purified in and through a terrestrial life. For this he is endowed with freedom, by the use of which he may attain to the position of the angels.

The souls of men, then, are fallen spirits. In the pre-existent world, from which he came, man had received his *nous* or intellect from the *Logos.* But by reason of the fall that *nous* had lost its participation in the divine fire and had cooled down into a soul.[44] The freedom of the soul in its material body is emphasized. Still, in spite of this, the soul comes into this world polluted with sin and is surrounded by temptations from the demons.[45] Man is therefore in need of redemption. The following thought of Origen is of interest since he speaks of the advantages which help, or the disadvantages which hinder, redemption. He said that the actions of the souls in their pre-existent state determined also the situations of men in the world of history, even with regard to such things as parental origin, place of birth, region and environment in which this earthly life is to be spent, etc.[46]

9. *Origen on Soteriology.* After Origen had developed the prehistoric part of his system which may be called "the prelude in heaven," he proceeded to Biblical history. The revelation contained therein is for man's redemption. To the natural law there is added the Mosaic Law. Next comes the Gospel—first the *literal* Gospel and then the *eternal* Gospel which needs no covers or illustrations. From what we have learned of Origen's distinction between *pistis* and *gnosis,* and between the external and internal sense of Scripture, we know what he meant by these stages in his historic revelation.

The significance of Christ is twofold. On the one hand, there are the uncultivated beginners who cannot believe without externalities and who must therefore be impressed. To these Christ had to bring a redemption in fact by paying a ransom for the deliverance of man from the devil. On the other hand, there are the real Gnostics, the real Christians

---

[42] I, 2, 10; II, 9, 6.
[43] III, 4, 5; II, 1-4.
[44] II, 8, 3.
[45] *Contra Celsum,* III, 62.
[46] II, 9, 8.

who behold the mysteries of God. To these Christ appeared as a priest to open the depths of knowledge and to make them participants of His divine life, so that they might become gods themselves.

There was a difference between the Christian gnosis of Origen and the pseudo-gnosis of the Gnostics. The latter denied the historicity and reality of the facts of redemption, while Origen believed and taught them. According to him, however, these facts are needed only by the uncultivated beginner (νήπιος); the real or Christian Gnostic requires neither Christology nor soteriology, i.e., a doctrine in which the historic facts of redemption are accounted for. The Christian Gnostic has Christ in an immediate way. Divinity and humanity present no problem to him. In other words, the historic facts of revelation represent *real truth,* but they are not *the* truth. This reminds us again of Origen's distinction between faith and theology.

In dealing with the work of Christ, Origen again proceeded with his characteristic distinction between two classes of Christians, the Christians of simple faith and the Christians of advanced knowledge. To the first class Christ had to present Himself as the God-Man and the Physician. To the second class He is the Teacher and the Divine Principle. The latter, whom we may call the Christian Gnostics, no longer require the Physician, for Christ has taught them the deeper mysteries. "Blessed are they who have arrived at the point where they do not need the Son of God as the Physician who heals the sick, nor as the Shepherd, nor as the Redeemer, but who have Him as Wisdom and Reason." [47] The highest work of Christ, then, consisted in His doctrine of the divine mysteries. In this work the *Logos* used the Man Jesus as His organ.

Origen accepted what the Scriptures teach concerning the redemptive significance of the *passion and death of Christ.* But it is only *the Christians of simple faith who need this.* The object is to liberate men from the dominion of the demons. Here the Christians of simple faith are to be helped by objectifying this redemption in the doctrine of the death of God's Son in which an atonement was made and a ransom paid.

What are the elements of Origen's doctrine of atonement? Through sin the souls of men had come under the sovereignty of the devil. So Jesus offered His soul unto death as an exchange (ἀντάλλαγμα) or ransom λύτρον in order that they might be redeemed from the devil. But the devil was not aware that he was unable to endure the presence of a sinless soul. He was deceived into accepting the ransom, because he did not possess the *touchstone* whereby possession of the ransom might be retained (John 16:8). Again, Origen expressed himself as follows: "But to whom did He give His soul as a ransom for many? Surely not to God! Perhaps to the Evil One. For he reigned over us until the soul of Jesus had been given to him as a ransom—to him who deceived himself, thinking that he could be master over it, not realizing that it did not suffer the agony which he applied to hold it down" (Commentary on Matthew 16:8). Thus the souls of men became free from the power of the devil and his demons.[48] Origen was the first to interpret Christ's death as a deception of the devil, which was the view of so many of Anselm's predecessors. Nevertheless it is of interest to note that the necessity of a propitiation before God was recognized. Christ bore in our stead the penalty which rightfully belonged to us. Thus God was reconciled to us and we to God. To these Biblical thoughts Origen added his own peculiar ideas that

[47] III, 61, 62.
[48] II, 47; VIII, 54, 27, 64.

the work of reconciliation extends even beyond the world of men to the realm of angels, and that Christ continues His redeeming work all through the ages.

10. Origen on Christology. It was for the sake of the simple and imperfect Christian, the Christian who is not capable of deeper knowledge, that Christ had to become the God-Man. To satisfy his religious need the doctrine of Christ had to be put in a form which excludes the errors of Docetism and Ebionitism.

Christ had a human soul which formed the connection between the *Logos* and the body of Jesus.[49] This soul was a pure spirit which had not participated in the prehistoric fall. It was this soul, together with the human body, which suffered; and not the Logos who is incapable of suffering. Origen was careful to leave to each of the two natures of Christ *its natural property.* The Man Jesus was really mortal, He really suffered, and really died. Against Celsus' accusation that the Christians considered the dying Jesus to be God, he insisted that the Logos is incapable of changing and therefore cannot die. When it is said that the God-Man really died, then such an expression must not be understood to mean what it seems to say. Here we have an anticipation of Zwingli's *Alloiosis* in which he treated such an expression as a *phrasis loquendi.*

And yet Origen felt obliged to insist upon a *real union* of the two natures of Christ. And what kind of union is it? Is it not merely a communion (κοινωνία) between the two natures, but a real union (ἕνωσις). But what kind of union is it, positively speaking? It is a *spiritual or mystical union,* much like that which exists between Christ and the believer. The *Logos*—the all-permeating reason or *nous*—has a controlling influence over the Man Jesus. The influence of the *Logos* deifies the humanity of Christ more and more. Origen went so far as to say that, because of its virgin-birth, the body of Christ was from the act of incarnation even more divine than our bodies. So Origen arrived at a union of the Divine and the human in Christ by teaching a moral influence of the *Logos* over the Man Jesus which led to a gradual deification of His body. The union between the *Logos* and the soul and body of Christ became so close that Scripture applies the predicates of divinity interchangeably. The *Logos* gradually absorbed the body of Jesus until finally He was transformed into spirit and admitted into union with the Godhead.

Harnack says of Origen's Christology: *"All imaginable heresies* have here been touched upon, though limited by precautions. . . . The only exception is modalism." The last reference is to Origen's fundamental opposition to modalistic Monarchianism. In the Epitome to Article VIII on the Person of Christ, found on page 517 ff. of the "People's Edition of the Book of Concord" by H. E. Jacobs, there is an enumeration of erroneous teachings which is helpful in pointing out the special errors charged against Origen's Christology.

11. Origen on the Sacraments. Baptism is for the forgiveness of sins. But the act of baptism is a symbolic exhibition of the soul's purification through Christ, just as Christ's healing miracles were symbolical of man's continual liberation from the demons through the *Logos.* The actual benefit which the individual derives from baptism comes from the prayers connected with the act. For Origen's expressions on the subject see the references in Seeberg.[50]

---

[49] On Origen's Christology read *De Principiis* II, 6, 3, 4. Cf. *Contra Celsum* I, 66; II, 9, 64; III, 28; V, 39; VII, 16; VIII, 42. Many of the references on this subject are in the exegetical writings. Since the location of these is not given in vol. IV of the Ante-Nicene Fathers, we refer the student to Loofs and Seeberg.

[50] *DG,* I³, 531 f.

Next comes the institution of *Repentance*. Baptism is the sacrament through which sins are forgiven. But for sins committed after baptism there is a forgiveness which is available through repentance. In this connection Origen has some beautiful and really evangelical thoughts. "Repentance consists primarily in the confession of one's sins to God, since He is the true Physician of souls; but also to one's fellow men. In the latter sense it is necessary, however, to find a man, whether clerical or lay, who has the Spirit, who is devoted to the service of God, and who is like the merciful High-Priest Christ, as were the Apostles." [51] This sounds different from the legal view on repentance as held in the West.[52]

Regarding Origen's view of the Lord's Supper we shall have a special discussion in Chapter XII of this volume.

12. Origen on Eschatology. The goal to be reached is the union of man with the *Logos* and the deification of human nature. All that has been mentioned is merely the means to that end.[53] Complete redemption comes with death and the things which follow. In eschatology Origen broke with the tradition of the Church. His spiritualizing method permitted him to put forward a different interpretation of these things. Those who are saved receive a pneumatic body and enter Paradise. The place for the rejected is hell. There they experience the fire of judgment which Origen understood to be the individual's conscience tortured by the sense of its sinfulness. But this is a purifying fire, and even the wicked, including the devil, will finally reach the intended goal, although it be only after infinite ages.[54]

III. TERTULLIAN THE FOUNDER OF WESTERN THEOLOGY

1. His Writings. Tertullian wrote mainly in Latin. Only a few of his first writings were in Greek. The edition of his works, which is generally used, is by F. OEHLER, 3 vols., 1853-54. The *Corpus Scriptorum Ecclesiasticorum Latinorum* (begun 1866) is not yet complete on Tertullian. In English we have the writings of Tertullian in Vols. III and IV of the Ante-Nicene Fathers, Buffalo ed., 1887. Those writings which have a special doctrinal significance are in Vol. III: *Against Hermogenes* (on the power of God as the Creator and against the eternity of matter); the five books *Against Marcion* (the Old Testament and New Testament revelations belong together; the humanity of Christ was real, and Docetism is to be rejected); *Against Praxeas* (in which the subordinationist conception of the Trinity is defended against Monarchianism); *De Carne Christi* (against Docetism); *De Resurrectione Carnis* (which defends the resurrection of the body against the heathen Gnostics); *De Anima* (which deals with the doctrines of traducianism, original sin and the substantiality of the soul); *De Poenitentia*, and *De Baptismo*. In *De Praescriptione Haereticorum* he suggests a method of argument against the heretics, in which he denies their right of appeal to Scripture and tradition. Vol. IV of the *Ante-Nicene Fathers* contains Tertullian's practical writings: *The Apparel of Women, The Veiling of Virgins, To His Wife, Exhortation to Chastity, On Monogamy, On Fasting, On Flight in Persecution.*

---

[51] Seeberg, Eng. ed., I, 158; cf. German ed., I³, 532 ff.

[52] Compare our discussion of this matter in the treatment of Art. XI of the Augsburg Confession, *Introduction to the Symbolical Books*, 2nd. ed., p. 288 ff.

[53] Loofs, 200 f.

[54] ἀποκατάστασις τῶν πάντων. Acts 3: 21; *Contra Celsum*, V. 15; *De Principiis*, II, 10, 4; I, 6, 3.

Literature: H. KELLNER gives, in the *Bibliothek de Kirchenvaeter*, a careful German translation of all the writings of Tertullian. The English reader will make use of the American edition of the *ANF.* Among the publications of Tertullian we refer the student to: the article by N. BONWETCH in *PRE*, and the corresponding article in *NSH*, IX, 305 ff J. DONALDSON, *Critical History of Christian Doctrine.* A. HAUCK, *Tertullians Leben und Schriften*, 1887. N. BONWETCH, *Die Schriften Tertullians*, 1878. K. HOLL, *Tertullian als Schriftsteller*, Preus. Jahrbuecher, 1897, pp. 262 ff. Cf. HOLL, *Gesammelte Aufsaetze zur KG*, vol. 3. J. STIER, *Die Gottes- und Logos-Lehre Tertullians*, 1899. G. ESSER, *Die Seelenlehre Tertullians*, 1893. K. H. WIRTH, *Der Verdienstbegriff bei Tertullian*, 1892. Special attention should be paid to the Histories of Dogma, especially those by THOMASIUS. HARNACK, LOOFS, and SEEBERG. A. D'AILES wrote a Theology of Tertullian in French, 2 vols., 1905. Compare also BARDENHEWER, *Patrologie* Eng. trans., St. Louis, Mo., 1908, pp. 157-167. R. E. ROBERTS, *The Theology of Tertullian* (London, 1928). A. NYGRÉN, *Agape and Eros*, Part II, Vol. I, 119 ff. (Read in RINN, pp. 44-57.)

2. Orientation. Tertullian was born about 150 and died about 225. He never was more than just a presbyter. Like Cyprian who revered him as his teacher,[55] he belonged to the School of North Africa. His writings indicate the various influences to which he had been subjected. For one thing, there was his own training in Stoicism. Next, there was his reading in the early apologetic literature of the Church. And then, there was the strong influence of the tradition of Asia Minor transmitted through Irenaeus.[56] Tertullian was very outspoken in his emphasis upon tradition as the authority for the Church. In his writing, *De Praescriptione*, he advised the Christians not to argue with the heretics on the basis of Scripture, but rather to deny them the right of appeal to that source. The reason which he advanced was that the heretics had lost all legitimate connection with the Church. He pointed to the churches of the Apostles as the depositories of apostolic teaching, and to the succession of bishops as the custodians of a reliable tradition. It is one of the remarkable instances of historical irony that this same man became a schismatic himself in the latter part of his life and joined the Montanists. It should be remembered of course that Montanism, which was an aberration in matters of practice only, did not really depart from the Rule of Faith.[57]

Was Tertullian a jurist before his conversion? Such is the information which is given us by all Church Histories and Histories of Dogma. These in turn derive their knowledge from passages in Eusebius and Jerome. But Seeberg declares, on the basis of a special investigation by S. Schlossman,[58] that "Tertullian was no jurist." The History of Dogma has had an interest in this question because of Tertullian's language, method of argumentation, and various legal views expressed in his writings. Seeberg explains that these points only serve to show how much the cultured people of the West were saturated with the juridical spirit.[59]

3. Tertullian's Personality as a Writer. There were various traits in Tertullian's personality which both attracted and repelled. Fisher says: "His genius and eloquence atone for the faults of temperament." Seeberg remarks: "Easily excited, he inclines to virulent and biting witticism, and is not always master of the dark emotions of his nature. He works with all the exaggeration of the orator, but at the same time he never fails in the originality of Christian feeling. In his speech he climbs to expressions of burning wrath, but even at such moments he succeeds in closing with points of sharp

---

[55] Jerome relates that no day passed in which Cyprian did not say to his servant: *"Da magistrum*—hand me the teacher."

[56] Cf. Loofs. 152 f.

[57] See Chap. IV.

[58] "*Tertullian im Licht der Jurisprudenz*" *in Zeitschrift d. Kirchengeschichte*, XXVII, 252 ff., 407 ff.

[59] *DG*, I⁸. 435 ff.

logic. His is a practical mind, more rich than deep, employing a multiplicity of means and methods, and yet never for a moment losing sight of the goal of his effort."

In his theologizing Tertullian was moved by practical motives. He knew of no interest in theological or philosophical knowledge for its own sake. His thinking moved in paradoxisms. No one of the Church Fathers was so extreme in emphasizing the Church's positivism. "To know nothing of the things that may be in conflict with the Rule of Faith," he exclaimed, "is to know everything" (*adversus regulam nihil scire omnia scire est*).[60] Faith is consent in a state of absolute obedience. The more unreasonable the articles of faith are, the more opportunity there is for faith to develop its strength. The more impossible the object of faith is, the more certain it is.[61] On the basis of such an expression Tertullian has been epitomized in the sentence: *Credo quia absurdum est*. This, however, is not an expression of his own creation. But on the other hand the same Tertullian, who built everything upon authority and paradox faith, declared in his apologetic writings that the proof of the truth of Christianity lies in its reasonableness, and he proceeded to use rational-psychological methods in offering his proof. We see something here of the dualism of faith and knowledge (*Glauben und Wissen*) which was present in the medieval scholasticism and which has always been a problem with us in Protestant theology.

4. The Practical Religious Trait in His Theology. Tertullian belonged to the North African School which we discussed and of which we learned that it was opposed to the speculations of Origen and Clement. Philosophy was looked upon as the guide which leads into the paths of error. The points stressed were the apostolicity of the Church's teaching as expressed in the Rule of Faith, and holiness of life. In these matters both Tertullian and Bishop Cyprian after him were leaders. The practical trait of Tertullian's religion is seen in many of his writings, as in the fact that he later joined the Montanists. Here we desire to call attention to his objection to speculation as it was employed by the Gnostics and the Alexandrian theologians. When Tertullian wished to prove the truth of Christianity, he did not marshal together the concessions of heathen philosophers, as did the Greek Apologists. He rather invoked the untutored, unsophisticated soul to give its witness to the existence of God. "Its unpremeditated expressions—such as 'Which may God grant,' 'If God will,' 'May God repay,' 'God shall judge between us'—spring out of the depth of the heart and are the best attestation of truth." [62] Tertullian styled the philosophers, and Plato as their chief, "the patriarchs of the heretics." [63] He went so far as to call the serenity of Socrates in the presence of death "a forced or affected composure." He exclaimed: "What have Athens and Jerusalem, the Academy and the Church, the heretics and the Christians in common with each other? Our doctrine comes from the hall of Solomon who himself commanded us to seek the Lord in simplicity of heart. Those who teach a Platonic, Stoic, dialectic Christianity may be responsible for what they are doing." [64]

5. His Principle of Realism. And yet Tertullian himself was not independent of philosophical thought. The influence of Stoicism, in particular, is quite apparent in some of his theological conceptions. According to his view, all that exists is corporeal,

---

[60] *De praescriptione,* 14.
[61] *Prorsus credibile est quia ineptum est . . . certum est quia impossibile est. De Carne Christi,* 5.
[62] *Adv. Marcionem* I, 11-13.
[63] *De anima,* 3.
[64] *De praescriptione,* 7, 10-14; *Adv. Hermog,* 8; *De anima,* 3, 23.

even God and the soul. Much of his theology rests upon the principle that there is nothing spiritual without corporeity. *Omne quod est, corpus est sui generis.*[65] *Quis negabit Deum corpus esse, etsi Deus spiritus est?* [66] *Corpus est anima.* [67] It can easily be seen why a theologian devoted to this principle should have been a teacher of traducianism. So we have in Tertullian a theologian whose position tended to be fundamentally opposed to the Alexandrians as well as to the Gnostics. *Realism* was his fundamental principle. The reality of nature and the visible world, the reliability of the senses, the significance of the corporeity and the substantiality of the spirit—these things constituted the basis of his thoughts. With a keen sense he detected the Divine in the creation, the Divine Reason shining through the orders of creation. He delighted to study nature, to trace the Creator and the inscriptions of truth in the cosmos, and to analyze the soul for the purpose of discovering in it the witnesses to God's existence. This realism, then, was the basis of Tertullian's theology, and his weapon in the struggle with Gnosticism and a one-sided spiritualism. It was from this starting-point that he argued for the substantiality of God, for the unity of the race and its history, for the origin of sin in the soul of man, for the historicity of revelation, for the truth of the Divine-human Person of Christ, and for the facts of redemption and the resurrection of the body.[68] In arguing for the existence of God he placed much stress upon the cosmological and physico-teleological proofs.[69]

6. *His Relation to Irenaeus.* As a systematic theologian Tertullian did not succeed in presenting a unified theology on the basis of one great leading thought, such as we observed in our study of Irenaeus. He was in essential agreement with Irenaeus on the doctrine of redemption through Christ the God-Man, in emphasizing the significance of the Incarnation, in adopting the Old Testament as well as the New as sources of truth, and in recognizing the Rule of Faith. But Irenaeus' entire theology was organized around the Christo-centric principle, while in Tertullian's theology certain things have the appearance of being added elements. It was more in the isolated discussion of individual topics that Tertullian showed his creative force (see Section 7).

Tertullian has an interesting thought in his "economic conception of the Trinity." Although the monographic method of this book calls for a treatment of Tertullian's doctrine of the Trinity in a separate chapter (IX), still the thought, in which we are interested at this point, is one in which Tertullian moved on ground occupied by Irenaeus. Like Irenaeus, Tertullian taught that there is a Trinity for the purpose of revelation only. After all has been accomplished, the distinction between the Persons will cease.[70] This reminds us of Irenaeus' recapitulation-theory. But Tertullian differed from Irenaeus in going back to the thoughts expressed by the Greek Apologists: "The disposition of God, in which He unfolds Himself, is for the purpose of bringing the world into existence" (*Realisation der Weltidee*). The existence of the Son as a separate Person in the Trinity became necessary because of the creation of the world. With Tertullian, as with the Apologists, this conditioned a subordination of the Son to the Father.[71]

---

[65] *De carne Christi,* 11.
[66] *Adv. Prax,* 7.
[67] *De anima,* 5.
[68] Thomasius, I, 142 f.
[69] *Adv. Hermog.* 35; *Adv. Prax.* 7; cf. *De anima,* 11.
[70] *Adv. Prax.* 4 with reference to I Cor. 15.
[71] Compare Seeberg, *HD,* I, 121; *DG,* I⁸, 426 f.; *PRE,* XIX, 548, lines 2-28; also Thom.-Bonw., I, 191-193.

7. *Tertullian the Founder of Occidental Theology.* The terms which he employed offered an apparatus of formulas which were soon found to be helpful when the dogmas of the Trinity and Christology were crystallized into their final form.

a. It was Tertullian who first used the word *"Trinity"* and introduced the terms *substantia* and *persona* to describe the relation of the three Persons in the Trinity to each other (*Adv. Prax.*). With Origen and, later, Athanasius he was a pioneer in paving the way for the Church's conceptions of the Trinity, even though he did not succeed in avoiding subordinationism. The details of his teaching on this subject belong to Chapter IX, which is to trace the developments of the Trinitarian relation of the Deity.

b. And it was also Tertullian who, in struggling with the Docetism of Marcion and the Gnostics, coined terms to describe the *two natures of Christ* and their relation to each other. These terms sound like an anticipation of the formulas employed in the Chalcedonian and Athanasian Creeds. "Each nature contains its own attributes"; there is "no confusion, but a conjunction of the human and the Divine." Against Docetism he emphasized that Christ was really Man, possessed of a rational human soul and spirit.[72] His suffering was in the "human substance" of His Person; but because of the union of the human and the Divine, Tertullian spoke of the "sufferings of God," and said that God was "truly crucified." [73] Tertullian had the same significance for the Christology of the West that Origen had for the East.

c. Even on *sin and grace* (in connection with repentance and baptism) Tertullian was the pioneer theologian along lines which became more or less normative for the Western Church (largely through Cyprian). We do not refer especially to his theory of traducianism, which was not really adopted by the Western Church, but to his doctrine of original sin.[74] In this he was generally followed by the Fathers of Augustine's time. The reason for his emphasis on the freedom of the will, which seems out of harmony with his teaching on original sin, is to be found in his conflict with Gnosticism and Manichaeism. In stressing the freedom of the will he taught that even after the fall man was able to choose between the opposites of good and evil.[75] This teaching led him to arrive at views concerning the way of salvation which were in entire accord with the teachings of the later *Roman Catholic Church.* It is true that he completely recognized the importance of Christ's death which he made the foundation of man's salvation.[76] He even knew of grace as a creative principle which changes man's heart.[77] But his description of grace did not fit into the system which was developed by Augustine. The entire religious and moral life of the Christian was viewed from the angle of obligation. He liked expressions which pictured man as God's debtor, and which spoke of a meriting and of a rendering of satisfaction. Christ is pre-eminently the Bringer and Interpreter of the New Law, the *nova lex.*[78] The relation between God and man is that of two private persons in which the one has offended the other and therefore owes a satisfaction, such as was required by the Roman Law. Tertullian wrote: "You have offended Him,

---

[72] *De anima,* 10-13.
[73] *Adv. Prax.* 27, 29. *De Carne Christi,* 5.
[74] *De anima,* 39.
[75] *De anima* 21; *Adv. Marc.* 11, 5, 6, 8, 10.
[76] *De virg.* 16.
[77] Cf. Thomasius, I, 496.
[78] *Adv. Jud.* 3, 6, 7; *De Mon.* 8, 14; *De orat.* 11, 22; *De poenitentia* 3.

but there is a way of reconciliation. You have one to whom you can render satisfactio
and who will be glad to accept it." [79] For a summarizing estimate of Tertullian as
pioneer for Roman Catholicism see our closing Chapter XIII, section II.

d. By *Baptism* guilt and punishment are removed; but man earns his salvation i
baptism by *repentance*. This Sacrament of Baptism, which in Kattenbusch's judgmer
is *eine durch und durch kultische Groesse,* imparts the power of sanctifying grac
The sanctifying power is attached to the water. Through it the Holy Spirit is obtainec
Whom Tertullian, true to his realism, conceived to be something material. If we si
after baptism, satisfaction is to be rendered. This is done by repentance which consis
of a deep sorrow, of confession in which the sinner humbles himself, and of sighin;
weeping, and fasting. Thus man atones for his transgression, makes satisfaction to Goc
and earns forgiveness for himself. By such punishment of himself man liberates himse]
from the eternal punishments.[80] The most valuable satisfaction man may offer to Go
is martyrdom. The Sacraments of Baptism and Repentance stand out as the savin
elements.[81]

e. Not only are the Divine commandments to be observed with scrupulous care
the "evangelical counsels" must also be carried out. Abstinence from marriage wa
praised and practiced by Tertullian.[82]

He taught that men are justified through faith; but by faith he meant not onl
acknowledgement of Christ as Saviour, but also fulfillment of the Divine commandment:
Tertullian was a remarkable anticipation of Roman Catholic theology. In fact, Nygré
is right when he passes the judgment on Tertullian that his "outlook united Old Testa
ment nomism and Roman moralism and jurisprudence. The result is a *theology of mer*
whose influence on the later history of Christianity was calamitous. . . . In Tertullia
Nomos has taken form as nowhere in the history of Christianity" (II, I, 131 f.).

Note: We shall dispense with a special treatment of Cyprian because we have discussed *i*
extenso his leading interest and significance in another connection (Chapter VII). And it shoul
be admitted, as Kurtz remarks, that "in originality, profundity, force, and fullness of thought, a
well as in speculative and dialectic gifts, the practical-minded bishop stands far below the somewha
eccentric presbyter."

B. THE ECUMENICAL CATHOLIC AGE

a. *Characteristics:* It is the time between the first and the last of the ecumenica
councils (325-787). There are the following *characteristics:* (1) Settlement of th
Trinitarian, Christological and Soteriological problems; (2) Completion of the episcopa
hierarchical organization; (3) Maturing of the Western and Eastern types of Catholicism
For fuller characteristics see Chapter XIII on *The Christianity of the East and the Wes*
b. *Schools and Teachers:* 1. The *Antiochean* School (Theodore of Mopsuestia, d. 429
Theodoret, 457; Ephraem, the Syrian, 387; John Chrysostom, 407; Nestorius, banishec
432). 2. The *New Alexandrian* School (Athanasius, 373; the Great Cappadocians
Basil of Caesarea, 379; Gregory Nazianzus, 390; Gregory of Nyssa, 394; Cyril of Alex

[79] *De poenitentia,* 7, 1.
[80] *De poen.,* 9.
[81] *De Orat.,* 18.
[82] *Adv. Marc.,* 11, 17; *Ad Uxorem,* 1, 3; 11, 1.

andria, 444; Eutyches, deposed 448). 3. The *Occidental* School (Ambrose, 397; Jerome, 420; Augustine, 430; Leo the Great, 461).[83]

The fathers here mentioned were the leading theologians in the Christological controversies. Theodore of Mopsuestia and Nestorius, Athanasius and the three Great Cappadocians together with Cyril of Alexandria and Leo the Great contributed negatively or positively to the formulas expressed in the Creed of Chalcedon.

At the end of this remarkable doctrinal development which has controlled Christian belief in Trinity and Christology stands a man who had a far greater lasting influence than all his predecessors. This man, *Aurelius Augustinus* (d. 430), in addition to his intense interest in the doctrine of the Trinity, became the leading genius in a temporary solution of the anthropological and soteriological problems, raising questions which constituted the central interest of the Reformation in the sixteenth century (cf. Chapter XI). The Church Father Augustine, Bishop at Hippo Rhegius, was of such a significance that this chapter on the outstanding theologians of the Ecumenical Catholic period must offer a connected description of

IV. AUGUSTINE IN SPECIAL PHASES OF HIS DEVELOPMENT

The review here given cannot cover all features in the theological interest of this religious genius. To complete the picture there are to be added the conception of Augustine on the Trinity, at the close of Chapter IX, and especially the part in Chapter XI, which reviews his conflict with Pelagianism and also his expression on the Sacraments in Chapter XII.

Primary Sources: The *MSL* (J. P. MIGNE, *Patrologiae Cursus Completus Seria Latina*), in the parts pertaining to Augustine (vols. 32-47), is a reprint of his works by the Maurine Congregation of the Benedictines in eleven volumes.[84] In the *CSEL* (*Corpus Scriptorum Ecclesiasticorum Latinorum*, 1867 ff.), intended as an especially critical text, the writings of Augustine are not yet complete. So far the *Confessions*, the *Retractions*, the *Letters*, the *City of God* and the *Anti-Donatist Writings* are among the things that have appeared. The American edition of the *Post-Nicene Fathers* (first series, Philip Schaff, editor), in the following to be cited as *PNF*, which is part of the *Ante-Nicene, the Nicene and the Post-Nicene Fathers*, offers a selection of Augustine's writings in eight volumes. It reproduces in revised form the 15 volumes of the Edinburgh edition (M. Dods, editor), and three vols. of Augustine on the New Testament and the six vols. on the Psalms in the Oxford Library (with treatises not previously translated). For a reading on Augustine on all phases of his development and on all conflicts cf. H. Rinn, pp. 172 to 231.

For an estimate of Augustine's life and development the *primary sources* are his *Confessions*, his *Retractions* and the *Vita Augustini* by his pupil Posidius.

General Literature in the form of investigation and discussion: C. BINDEMANN, *Der heil. Augustinus*, 3 parts, 1844-1869. F. BOEHRINGER, *Aurelius Augustinus; Bischof von Hippo*, Stuttgart, 1878². U. J. C. BOURKE, *Life and Labours of St. Augustine*, Dublin, 1880. R. W. BUSCH, *St. Augustine, His Life and His Times*, London, 1883. H. C. COLLETTE, *St. Augustine, His Life and His Writings as Affecting His Controversy with Rome*, 1883. W. CUNNINGHAM, *Augustine and His Place in the History of Christian Thought*, 1886. J. HUDSON, *St. Augustine, Bishop of Hippo*, 1899. J. McCABE, *St. Augustine and His Age*, New York, 1903. W. MONTGOMERY, *Saint Augustine, Aspects of His Life and Thought*, 1914. W. THIMME, *Augustins geistige Entwicklung in den ersten Jahren nach seiner Bekehrung*, 1908. H. BECKER, *Augustin, Studien zu seiner geistigen Entwicklung*, 1908. The same, *Augustin, ein Lebens und Characterbild auf Grund*

---

[83] Kurtz, English ed., par. 47; German, 14th ed., par. 55.

[84] The editions have been as follows: The first at Paris, 1679-1700; the second at Antwerp, 1703, and Venice, 1720-34; the third at Venice, 1797-1807, in 18 quarto vols. (with reprint in Germany).

seiner Briefe, 1910. H. WEINAND, Die Gottesidee der Grundzug der Weltanschauung de Augustinus, 1910. E. TROELTSCH, Augustin, die Kirchliche Antike und das Mittelalter, 1916 P. ALFARIC, L'evolution intellectuelle de Saint Augustin, I, 1918. K. HOLL, Augustins inner Entwicklung, 1923. M. I. HOERREGARD, Augustins Bekehrung, 1923. And see H. DOERRIES Fuenfzehn Jahre Augustin-Forschung in Theologische Rundschau, 1929, Heft 3. Especially shoul we also call attention to the Histories of Dogma or Doctrine. SEEBERG in the latest edition o his work, devotes 195 pages to Augustine. Among the Encyclopedias the following offer valuabl articles on Augustine: PRE, with a very thorough-going article by LOOFS, which is abbreviated an popularized in the New Schaff-Herzog Encyclopedia. The article on Augustine in HASTINGS Encyclopedia was contributed by B. B. WARFIELD. See also the discussion of Augustine in th Catholic Encyclopedia. And cf. A. NYGRÉN, Part II, Vol. I, 231-344. The reader will understand that the place for literature touching special features in the experience of Augustine must be given below in connection with the specific discussion of these. On Sin and Grace and on Predestinatior there has been a large literature in England.

1. *Augustine's Significance.* Tertullian and Cyprian were the first to contribute positive direction and the distinctive characteristics to Western theology. But it wa the influence from the writings of Augustine which determined decisively the specia character of Occidental (Roman) theology. His influence upon Western theology is comparable to that of Origen upon the theology of the East, but it was far greater. He was indeed the father of Occidental Christianity. Many features of Roman Catholicism must be traced back to ideas, principles and suggestions in his theology. In the Donatist controversy he gave to the *formula* of Cyprian a meaning of the *unitas ecclesiae*, which Protestantism cannot accept. Schaff says of his anti-Donatist works: "They are the chief patristic authority of the Roman Catholic doctrine of the Church against the sects. They are thoroughly Romanizing in spirit and aim, and least satisfactory to Protestant readers. Augustine defended in his later years even the principle of forcible coercion and perse- cution against heretics and schismatics by false exegesis of the words in the parable, 'Compel them to come in' (cf. Luke 15: 23)." [85] There is hardly a dogma of the Roman Catholic Church that does not bear in one or another way the marks of Augustine's influences. The best in the theology of Scholasticism was also stimulated by his thoughts. Even in method the old Scholastics had learned from Augustine.[86] The mysticism of the Middle Ages also, in its conservative as well as in its radical forms, functioned under influences from Augustine. Then there is the dogma of the Trinity, which was com- pleted by Augustine for the West with all the specific features that contributed to the later schism between the East and the West. But Augustine's theology along this line was accepted by the Reformation. Furthermore, his doctrine of sin and grace, with its determined aim at emphasizing the *sola gratia*, in which he was not in entire harmony with the fundamentals of Rome, made him a teacher not only of the Reformers of the sixteenth century, but also of the conservatives among their followers in succeeding generations.

2. It is possible to make too much of *the moral defects in the life of Augustine before his conversion.* His *Confessions* in 13 books, written in 397, are the true mirror of a saint's sincerity. But in fastening our attention upon his relation first to one woman in Carthage for fifteen years, and shortly before his conversion in Milan to another (in both cases with faithfulness to each), we must remember, as Loofs has pointed out,[87] that outside of the Church such relations were without ethical reproach among the pagans

---

[85] See PNF, preface to Vol. I of Augustine series, p. 16.
[86] See Loofs in PRE, II, 277, 34.
[87] PRE, II, 261, 41 ff.

of that day. Augustine was still not a Christian. It was a relation of monogamic concubinage, which was distinguishable from a legitimate marriage, first in this, that the wife was not of equal social position, secondly, that the relation was soluble, and thirdly also in this, that the "natural" children of such a union were not legitimate heirs of property left by the father. Augustine visited with his "wife" and child in Thagaste, and was received by his mother Monica. Later, of course, Augustine condemned his own life in this relationship in strongest terms, as we would expect of a sincere Christian. In the severity of his repentance he was prompted by his growing appreciation of the monastic life, which to the Church Fathers in that day was the bridge from the impurity of heathenism to the ethical standards of Christianity. But Augustine's character, even before his conversion, was not as questionable as some historians have painted it.

In his search for truth, salvation and satisfaction, Augustine became a *Manichaean* for nine years (373-384). Christianity had not appealed to his speculative mind. But the natural-philosophical character of Manichaeism attracted him. First there was in the form of a phantastic mythology that conflict between light and darkness. Then there was a redemption that consisted in the liberation of the elements of light from the embrace of darkness, namely by cultivating an ethics of ascetic abstinence from the matters connected with darkness, which included a merely graded continence, according to the degree of saintliness that had been attained in the progress from the *auditores* to the *electi*. Augustine always remained in the class of the former. But about the year 382, he began to turn away from the fantastical cosmological systems of the Manichaeans, and in the end he separated himself from them in a series of writings that mark an important stage in his inner development.[88]

3. It was at this time that Augustine came *under the influence of Neo-Platonic writings*. In place of the dualistic conception of God and evil among the Manichaeans, he learned to think of God as the eternal real substance and of evil as the *voluntary* turning from the good which alone is being. It was the coming into this attitude of mind, into this renunciation of all and everything that cannot claim to have divine authority or reality, which in the *Confessions* (VI) he has later called his "conversion." The year 386 brought him under the influence of Bishop Ambrose of Milan. That generally known occurrence in the garden of Milan, where in the most receptive mood of his mind his attention was called to Romans 13: 13, 14, was the moment of his life when God first enabled him to turn his whole will against the powers of sensuality, which so far had been depriving him of the spiritual freedom for which he was longing. His new and intense interest in the Neo-Platonic world of thought, however, gave a highly philosophical character to his thought and meditation at this time. We know that it was on philosophical subjects that he wrote in the *Cassisiacum* near Milan, where he had retired with his son Adeodatus and friends to prepare for baptism.[89]

The following writings cover the period up to 391: The Roman numbers here given refer to the volume numbers of the works of Augustine in the *MSL*: Three letters *Contra academicos, tomos* 32, I, pp. 905-958; *De beata vita* (t. 32, I, 959-976); *De ordine libri duo* (t. 32, I, 977-1020); *Soliloquiorum libri duo* (t. 32, I, 869-904, compare *PNF*, VII, 537-560); *De immortalitate animae* (t. 32, I, 1021-1034). Soon afterwards in Rome he added: Two books *De moribus ecclesiae catholicae et de moribus Manichaeorum* (t. 32, I, 1309-1378); *De quantitate animae* (t. 32, I,

[88] See these writings in *MSL*, t. 32, 34, especially 42; compare the Manichaean writings in the *Post-Nicene Fathers*, first part of volume IV.
[89] *PRE*, II, 268, 25: 30.

1035-1080); book one of *Libri tres de libero arbitrio* (t. 32, I, 1221-1240). In Thagaste he wrote the *Epp.* 5-20 (t. 33, II, 67-87; compare Augustine's letters in the *PNF*, I, and read "prefatory note" on page 212); also *Libri duo de Genesi adv. Manichaeos* (t. 34, III, 173-220); *De magistro*, (t. 32, I, 1193-1220); *De vera religione* (t. 34, 121-172); and most parts of the *Liber de diversis quaestionibus octoginta tribus* (t. 40, VI, 11-100).

4. We agree of course with Harnack, Loofs and Seeberg in stressing the greatly Neo-Platonic character of Augustine's religious views at this fundamental time in his life. Still, when all this has been admitted, we must think of it that Augustine was preparing himself for Christian baptism, that he tells of impressions from reading the Psalms,[90] that he surely knew the contents of the baptismal formula in the form of the "Apostles' Creed," and that all through his life the liturgy and hymns of the Christian services in the Church at Milan resounded in his soul.[91] To all this we should add Augustine's growing recognition of the authority of the Church in the great messages such as Ambrose was offering on the basis of the generally accepted Rule of Faith. Therefore the contemporaneous deep interest in the problems of a philosophy which at this time seemed to Augustine to have so much in common with Christianity, should not be used to minimize the specifically Christian ideas that had their existence in the heart of this candidate for Christian baptism. The beginnings of a new life are shrouded in mystery. This is not less the case with the beginning of our spiritual life (John 3:8). Seeberg has not closed his mind to the need of harmonizing the purely philosophical and the genuinely Christian elements in Augustine at this time of his development. He covers the situation by this one remark: "The authority of the Church has furnished Augustine the soul-contents of his faith, but philosophy gave him the form." [92] We would indeed overlook an important factor in the religious convictions of Augustine if we should pass by his growing recognition of the authority of the Catholic Church in interpreting Scripture for establishing the institutions for man's salvation.[93] He even took the position that this authority must precede the operation of reason: *Crede ut inteligas*. Knowledge is necessary for the perfecting of faith.[94] The results of this first stage under the special influence of Neo-Platonism are seen in his writings.[95] Here we have a recognition of the historical Christ. But it is the teacher with His example that attracts Augustine's attention. There is not yet the evangelical appreciation of His death and resurrection.[96]

5. In 391 Augustine became *presbyter* of the Church in Hippo Rhegius, and in 395 he became *bishop*. This relation to the Church as teacher and leader offered impulses for his development as a churchman. He felt keenly his lack of maturity in doctrinal ways. This feeling drove him into a diligent study of the Scriptures, an interest which soon began to color his language. From now on he speaks less of reason and almost exclusively of the faith, following the authority of the Church. Tracing the

---

[90] *Conf.* IX, 4, 8.

[91] *Ibid.* 6, 14.

[92] *DG*, II³, 409.

[93] *De ordine* II, 5, 16; 9, 24; 19, 26. *Contra Academicos* III, 20, 43; *De Vera Religione* 26, 48.

[94] *De Moribus Ecclesiae* 1, 47; *De Utilitate Credendi*, 13, 29; *Ep.* 89, 6; *Serm.* 43, 4. 118, 1; *De Magistro* 11, 37; *Ep.* 120, 8. On Augustine's attitude to Scripture and tradition see Seeberg II³, 411 f.

[95] E.g. *De Vera Religione*, as referred to.

[96] Cf. the writings *De Magistro*, *MSL*, t. 32, 1193-1220 and others as used especially by Loofs, p. 367, and in special investigations by O. Scheel, *Die Anschauung Augustins von Christi Person und Werk*, 59 ff. As to later writings, see our presentation of the various controversies in which he became involved, especially the anti-Donatistic and the anti-Pelagian.

evelopment in some details, we call attention to the following points: *First:* To the
Neo-Platonic conception of God as an absolute Being, in distinction from the conditioned multiplicity and variableness of the world,[97] Augustine now adds an emphasis
upon God as the personal Creator and Governor of the world.[98] *Second:* Under the
influence of Neo-Platonism he had given much thought to the analysis and definition
of evil (*malum*), of which he had spoken as lacking in real being, with much interesting
distinction between reasonable and unreasonable creatures.[99] On this topic he learned
in the language of Scripture to take sin as the voluntary yielding of man to the temptations from the devil. On this he has expressed himself in his *De Libero Arbitrio*,
written about 388-395.[100] It is the will of man that governs all faculties of the soul,
puts them into motion, and forces them to operate.[101] Faith, in the last analysis, is an
act of the will.[102] *Third:* Extricating himself more and more from Neo-Platonism,
Augustine grew away from the merely aesthetic enjoyment of God to find such enjoyment in the living of a life of obedience. This was in line with what we have observed
in his estimate of the will as the governing faculty of the mind. *Fourth:* The Augustinian
teaching of redemption has always been a matter of much interest. Two great scholars
have written in searching investigations on this subject, and have arrived at opposing
conclusions. O. Scheel wrote on *Die Anschauung Augustins von Christi Person und
Werk*, 1901, and J. Gottschick on *Augustins Anschauung von den Erloeserwirkungen
Christi* in *Zeitschrift fuer Theologie und Kirche*, 1901, pp. 97-213, with reply by
Scheel: *Zu Augustins Anschauung von der Erloesung durch Christus*, in *Studien und
Kritiken*, 1904, pp. 401-433; 491-554. Scheel sees in the Augustinian theory of redemption chiefly the influence of Christ upon the sinner. He says that Augustine's peculiar
philosophical conception of Christ's divinity had kept him from an ethical-soteriological
estimate of the death of Christ. J. Gottschick, on the other hand, starting from Augustine's strong emphasis on the forgiveness of sins, undertakes to show that Augustine
meant redemption as a reconciliation of God in the sense of Anselm: placating God,
satisfying God.[103] It will have to be admitted that Augustine, when speaking of the
death of Christ as a satisfaction offered to God,[104] did not mean a satisfaction of God
in the sense of Anselm, but in agreement with the general view of that day, looked upon
the death of Christ as a price paid for releasing man from the rightful claims of the
devil. It will not be possible to reduce all of Augustine's statements on the subject of
redemption to a consistent theory. Still the following facts are outstanding: (a) Augustine's piety never lost the deep sense of guilt.[105] (b) This conviction led him to a
grateful appreciation of the remission of sins in baptism. (c) In this state of mind
he put a high estimate on the cross of Christ. While stressing the significance of Christ
as our king, Augustine never tires of praising Him as the Saviour of sinners.[106] The

---

[97] *De Civitate Dei* XI. 10. 1.
[98] *De Civitate Dei* XII, 25; V., 9, 4. It appears in his thoughts on the Trinity. See Loofs in *PRE*, II, 270 f.
and *DG⁴*, pp. 365 ff.
[99] For a lucid description we refer to *PRE*, II, 271 f.
[100] In *MSL*, t. 32, I, 1221-1310.
[101] *De Trinitate* X, 11, 17.
[102] *De Spiritu et Littera* 57.
[103] Cf. Seeberg, II³, 428.
[104] *Serm.* 152, 11.
[105] Cf. Loofs in *DG⁴*, with reference to *Gottschick*, pp. 115, and to many places in Augustine's writings, p. 396.
[106] Cf. Seeberg II³, 425 with many references; also Wiegand I, 99.

continuation of these thoughts must be followed in Chapter XI in our study of the soteriological problems, particularly in the conflict between Augustine and Pelagius.

6. *Augustine's Views on the Church.* (The Conflict with Donatism.)

Literature: OPTATUS, *De Schismate Donatistarum* in *MSL*, t. 11, 883-1104, in *CSEL*, t. 26 (written probably about 368). For an enumeration of Augustine's anti-Donatistic writings, see below. F. C. BURKITT, *The Book of Rules of Tyconius in Texts and Studies*, III, 1. T. HAHN *Tyconius-Studien*, 1900, in *Studien zur Geschichte der Theologie und Kirche* by N. BONWETSCH and R. SEEBERG. H. SCHMIDT, *Des Augustinus Lehre von der Kirche*, in *Jahrblatt fuer Deutsche Theologie und Kirche*, 1861, pp. 197-225. TH. SPECHT, *Die Lehre von der Kirche nach den heiligen Augustin*, 1892. N. BONWETSCH, *Donatismus* in *PRE*, IV, 788-798. Cf. *NSH.* LOOFS *DG*, 369-377; his article *Augustinus* in *PRE*, II, 281 ff. SEEBERG, English ed., *HD*, I, 312 ff.; German, *DG*, II³, 437-449. WIEGAND I, 101-106.

a. Augustine's part in the Donatistic controversy became *the occasion* of developing further the popular ideas about the Church which we have traced historically in Chapter VII, and which we followed up to Cyprian.

The Donatists were opposed to the election of Archdeacon Caecilian as bishop in Carthage because he had been the candidate of the party favoring readmission of the lapsed into the Church (during the Diocletian persecution). The party of a stricter discipline elected Majorinus, and it was under his successor Donatus (d. 355) that the whole conflict became an issue for the Church. The Church dealt with the difficulty at the Synod of Arles, 314. The Donatists took the position that the Church must be a communion of real saints. The bishops, like the apostles, must be holy men. It was an element of the old pneumatics that was reviving itself in the Donatists. The Novatians, before them, had demanded the holiness of the members, and the Montanists had established themselves on the principle that the Church, as the communion of saints, must not defile itself with the readmission of the excommunicated that had fallen into grave sins. So the Donatists insisted that the Church as the bride of Christ must be holy. For this reason she must not have bishops that betrayed the truth in times of persecution. A Church of such bishops loses the validity of the sacraments; first of all of the sacrament of ordination, and with it even baptism, which now must be repeated.[107] Not all of the Donatists were that radical. Tyconius was such an exception.[108]

After 370, Optatus of Mileve wrote from the standpoint of the Catholic Church on *The Schism of the Donatists.* But it was chiefly Augustine, after he had become bishop, who used his whole influence for the reconciliation of the contending parties which were of about equal strength. His writings against the Donatists are found in volume IX of the *MSL*. The conflict which was confined to the African Church, covers the time between 393 and 420, in the life of Augustine.[109]

b. The Catholics Acknowledge the Orthodoxy of the Donatists, and at the Synod of Arles, 314, they recognized also their sacraments. They established themselves upon the position that the validity of the sacraments does not depend upon the moral con-

---

[107] *Optatus*, V, 6. For a fuller description see Seeberg *DG*, II³, 442 f.

[108] Cf. *Bonwetsch* in *PRE*, IV, 795.

[109] For an enumeration of his Anti-Donatist writings see *PRE*, II, 281 f. and IV, 788; Seeberg *HD* (Eng. ed.) I, 313; *DG*, II³ 437; Wiegand I, 102; Cf. the "table of chief events in the life of Augustine" in the *PNF*, vol. I of his works, p. 25. They cover vol. IX in the Benedictine edition as taken over by *MSL*, cf. t. 43. Outstanding are (1) *Contra Epistulam Parmeniani;* (2) *De Baptismo Contra Donatistas;* (3) *Contra Litteras Petiliani;* (4) *Contra Cresconium;* (5) *De Unico Baptismo contra Petilianum;* (6) *Breviculus collationis cum Donatistis;* (7) *Ad Donatistas post collationem;* (8) *Contra Gaudentium.* In the *CSEL* they occupy t. 51-53. Of these the English Schaff edition (*PNF*) in the second part of volume IV, offers No. 1, No. 2 and a *Treatise on the Correction of the Donatists* (his letter 185).

dition of the administrating person.[110] Still Augustine would not admit that the Donatists were a real representation of the Church. He called them a *quasi-church,* because they were occupying a sectarian position and building a partisan wall which is not resting upon the cornerstone. To him they were outside of catholicity.[111] While admitting, against the general tradition of the North African Church, the validity of their sacraments, so that when returning to the Church they needed not be rebaptized, he nevertheless strenuously insisted that outside of the Catholic Church the sacrament of baptism is "of no avail for the forgiveness of sins." [112] The Donatists' charge of "unholiness" against the Catholic Church, because a few bishops at the time of the Diocletian persecution had not been faithful, was to him a matter of indifference in this controversy.[113] Absolute holiness of the Church cannot be expected in this life. The passages of Scripture referring to such holiness speak of the future and the state of perfection.[114]

c. *Augustine's conception of the Church combined in itself several considerations: First:* He started with a strong emphasis upon our duty to recognize *the Church Catholic;* it is a visible appearance. This Church alone, as possessing the Faith of the Apostles, the sacraments and the ministry, is in a condition to expand all over the world and to save and to sanctify its members. Outside of this Catholic Church, which is the body of Christ, there is no truth, no salvation.[115] Separation from it is sacrilege.[116] *Second:* From the Church as an outward organization Augustine distinguishes the Church as a *communion of the saints,* (*Communio sanctorum, congregatio sanctorum, societas credentium, Christiana societas, bonorum societas*).[117] In this "invisible union" we have those that love God and one another, and that pray for the Church. [118] He distinguishes between those that are only outwardly in the Church and those that really belong to her.[119] *Third:* He adds a third feature to his conception of the Church by pointing to the distinction between the predestinated and the non-predestinated. The "invisible union of love" is not identical with the "number of the predestinated." In the end that man alone can maintain himself as a true member of the Church who is predestinated and has the gift of perseverance. [120] And among these there may be some who do not even belong to the Catholic Church. [121]

We must not close this study of Augustine's views on the Church without adding a brief review of the ideas expressed in his great work, *De civitate Dei,* which covered thirteen years of intensive thought (from 413 to 426).[122]

As a first philosophy of history this work of twenty-two books has often been

---

[110] *Contra Litteras Petiliani* III, 68.

[111] Here Augustine accepted the position taken by *Optatus* III, 7, 10

[112] *De Baptismo* I, 12-18; V, 8-9; VI, 5-7.

[113] Augustine in *Breviculus Collationis cum Donatistis,* III, 19 ff.

[114] *Ibid.* III, 9; *Optatus* II, 20.

[115] *Ep.* 141, 5.

[116] It is interesting, however, to observe in this connection that Augustine, though acknowledging the primacy of the apostolic chair (*Ep.* 43, 7) and seeing in it a "representation of the unity of the Church," knows nothing of a special authority vested in Peter or his successors.

[117] See Seeberg's *HD,* Eng. ed., I, 324; cf. *DG,* II³, 465 ff.

[118] *De Baptismo* III, 19, 26; *De Unitate Ecclesiae* 21-60.

[119] *De Baptismo* I, 26; III, 26; IV, 4; VII, 100; *Contra Litteras Petiliani,* II, 247; *De Unitate Ecclesiae* 74.

[120] *De Corruptione et Gratiae,* 9, 22; *De Dono Perseverantiae* 2, 2.

[121] Cf. Seeberg, English ed. I, 352.

[122] The student will find it in t. 41 of the *MSL* (Vol. VII of Augustine's works in the *MSL*). A very readable and accurate translation into English was prepared by M. Dods for the Edinburgh edition, and has been taken over into the *PNF,* Vol. II. In the late sixteenth century J. Healey furnished a translation which was recently reprinted in the *Ancient and Modern Theological Library.*

mentioned as reminding of Hegel's *Philosophie der Geschichte*. It is erected upon the conception of two states differing fundamentally in their principles, but continually touching each other—the people of God and the people of this world. These two states are described as having had their prototypes in the separation of the evil angels from the good. The historical development appears in the descendants of Cain and Abel, continuing in the contrast between the followers of Christ and those of Anti-Christ (the city or state of God and of this world: *civitas Dei, et civitas terrena huius mundi*).

By the state of this world as the counterpart of the City of God, Augustine thinks generally of what we understand by the political state, as the natural order aiming at the maintenance of peace and welfare (XIX, 12, 16, 17). Along this line Augustine was decidedly conservative. He emphasized that Christians need the state even though earthly things are not their goal. Wars also, though evil in themselves, may serve "the necessity of protecting life and liberty" (III, 10).

But Augustine, in his idea of contrasting the two states, had especially in mind the pagan state. The occasion for his work was the charge of the pagans still living and holding to their religion that Christianity had resulted in the fall of Rome through the Barbarians (410). Augustine now wanted to show that the cause of this fall was the deterioration of righteousness in the old Rome. By this procedure he secures the foundation for describing the genius of the state as contrasted with that of the true Church of Christ. There is in the state no real righteousness, no true justice, might makes right. The large states, especially with their policies of imperialism, are unrighteous (XIX, IV, 4). Augustine recognizes the necessity of the state, but because of man's sinfulness the ideal of righteousness cannot be realized, for it is erected upon the foundation of pride, love of self, and the flesh (XIV, 28; cf. 13).

There is a wonderful sublimity of expression in Augustine's description of the "City of God" as the family of the redeemed and pilgrims of the heavenly city (I, 35; XV, 1, 2; XIX, 11). While its members are not of the world, they are living in the world. The family life leads to a larger social life and so on to the necessary relations in the state. Generation follows generation. In all of it is the hand of God for the education of the human race (X, 14). Here we must quote from Seeberg *DG,* II³, 475: "What takes place on earth becomes a preparation for the eternal life (XXI, 15). According to the divine plan everything in this comprehensive development has been appointed its place, the evil as well as the good. For this reason we may compare the order of the ages of history with a beautiful poem (*pulcherrimum carmen*) in which the manifold antitheses produce a wonderful harmony (XI). In this great compass even the evils of this life must serve for the further maturing of the children of God. Suffering and persecution bring patience, opposition by wicked thought results in wisdom (XVIII, 51)." [123]

NOTE. Seeberg also investigates the question (p. 480 f.) to what extent the hierarchs of the Middle Ages were justified in appealing to the authority of Augustine for making their claim of rulership over the state. He comes to the conclusion that there was indeed a dualism in Augustine's conception of the Church as the "Kingdom of God." While he looked upon it eschatologically as comprising not only the Church militant but also the Church triumphant (XIX, 17), he did include in the former the Church in its empirical existence as presided over by the bishops (*praepositi,* XX, 9, 2). This was an illogical feature in the execution of Augustine's great work, because his plan was to contrast "the people of this world" with "the people of God," the latter of which he has taken throughout to be God's true people (XIV, 28). Augustine did

123 Cf. *PNF* Augustine's works. Vol. II, p. 392.

ot teach, nor even suggest, a rulership of the Church over the state. But inconsistently he offered foundation that was used by the hierarchy after his time.

Here we close our study of Augustine so far as this chapter is concerned. The tudent will look for the completion of this biographical picture by continuing to study Chapter IX, Augustine's contribution to the doctrine of the Trinity, and Chapter XI, his onflict with Pelagianism, and Chapter XII, his conception of the sacraments.

Chapter Nine

THE DOCTRINE OF THE TRINITY

Introductory Considerations: The term "Trinity" is not in the Scriptures. This does not mean that the doctrine which historically has come to be expressed by that term cannot be Scriptural and Christian. The fact is that the trinitarian conception of God is the underlying and governing thought of the Biblical history of redemption. In addition to that the trinitarian faith expresses a doctrinal experience of the Church, the necessity of which has been tested by the practical needs of piety through a life of many centuries. The problem already presented itself unconsciously in the Baptismal Formula of earliest Christianity. It was soon felt as a burning problem in all parts of the Church. The interest was not just metaphysical, it was *religious.* At times—in the Apologists and in Origen—the philosophical interest blended with the religious. But Athanasius was not a philosopher; he was a churchman. Even Augustine, a real philosopher and a dialectician, in discussing the trinitarian "relations," was prompted after all not by the speculative but by the religious interest. This is an unfailing impression received from the reading of his *De trinitate.* The problem of the Trinity was a practical interest of the Church as the congregation of believers. It began with the overwhelming conviction, confirmed by Scripture, that the presence of Christ in the Church is like that of God the Father Himself. The early Christians prayed to Christ as they prayed to God. Very naturally they had to do some thinking on the relation of Christ to the One God. Then there was in Matthew 28:19 that trinitarian formula for baptism, which included the Holy Spirit. If in that age of intense monotheism Christ had not been deeply experienced as the reality of God Himself, the trinitarian formula would have died a natural death as other purely philosophical doctrines have done. The problem persisted and grew in intensity even up to the close of the ancient period of the Church when finally John of Damascus and St. Augustine each undertook to say temporarily a final Word for the East and the West, respectively, on this matter. Purposely we call it a temporary settlement. The Trinity is a mystery and as such it is open for expression in all the ages of the Church. It will never do to dismiss the historic significance of the work of the ancient Church on the trinitarian problem by treating it as useless speculation of the Greek mind. The Latin mind which functioned as the regulative factor in this process was intensely practical and frequently counterbalanced the speculation of the Greeks. But with even this admission we would not say that the statements of John of Damascus and Augustine are beyond criticism. We refer especially to the humble language of Augustine at the close of his *De trinitate.*

I. FIRST STAGES IN THE DEVELOPMENT OF THE TRINITARIAN CONCEPTION OF GOD

1. The Post-Apostolic Fathers. The early writers of the primitive Christian Church were not given to doctrinal speculations about the Baptismal Formula; they used the trinitarian formula; but this formula did not provoke them to a discussion of the relation of the three to each other. Concerning Christ's relation to the Father we can only say that they regarded Christ as the Son of God, and ascribed to Him those attributes which can be predicated of God alone. And with Father and Son, the Holy Spirit is mentioned in so many cases.[1] Baur and Harnack say that the first Christians, particularly Hermas, held Ebionitic or adoptionistic views. But even so independent an investigator as Loofs who dedicated his work to Harnack admits that this position is not convincing.[2] It must be admitted that the language of the Post-Apostolic Fathers was frequently binitarian. The Spirit was taken as the Spirit of Christ, as in 2 Cor. 3:17. But with this they did not mean an actual identification of the Spirit with the Son. It was simply an abbreviation in expression. There was the natural difficulty of speaking of the Holy Spirit in hypostatic terms.[3]

2. The Early Apologists, in their aim at creating a Christian theology, discussed more or less the relationship between Father and Son. About 180 Theophilus wrote as follows concerning the Godhead: "In like manner also the three days, which were before the luminaries, are types of the Triad (τριας) of God and His Word and His Wisdom." [4] Although the meaning of this passage is rather vague, nevertheless Seeberg assures us that "the Trinity is certainly an article of the common faith. . . . Although the Apologists find little occasion to speak of this mystery, the apprehension of it constitutes for them the profoundest problem and supreme desire of their hearts." [5] He then quotes from Athenagoras who characterizes the Apologists as being "carried away with this desire only, to see God and the Logos with Him. What is the unity of the Son with the Father? What the fellowship of the Father with the Son? What the Spirit? What the union and difference of those who are thus united—the Spirit, the Son, and the Father?" For a fuller discussion of this situation see our Chapters III (II, 1) and IV (III).

In discussing the relation of the Son to the Father, the Apologists introduced the Logos-term from St. John's Gospel. This was attended, however, with the danger of identifying St. John's Logos with that of Philo. The Apologists did not altogether escape this danger, as is evidenced by the fact that they failed to recognize a personal differentiation of the Logos from the Father before the creation of the world, which led them to subordinate the Son to the Father. They did not yet think in terms of a co-equality between Father and Son. "Adopting Philo's distinction of λόγος ἐνδιάθετος and λόγος προφορικός, they for the most part regarded the hypostasizing as conditioned first by the creation of the world, and as coming forth not as a necessary and eternal element in the very life of God, but as a free and temporal act of the divine will." [6]

3. Irenaeus in his conflict with Gnosticism taught without speculation and simply on the basis of the Rule of Faith that Son and Spirit participate in the Divine substance.

4. Tertullian. Tertullian defined God as Father, Son, and Holy Spirit, and to express his thought he used the word trinitas. He championed hypostasianism against the monarchianism of Praxeas. The following citations will illustrate his thought. "Everywhere I hold one substance in three cohering." [7] "All are of one, by unity of substance; while

---

[1] We refer especially to H. B. Swete, The Holy Spirit in the Ancient Church (1912), 11-21.
[2] See his DG⁴, p. 182, footnote 4.
[3] See Seeberg, DG, I³, 143 ff., footnote 2.
[4] Ad Autolyeus 11, 15.
[5] English edition, I, 114.
[6] Compare our discussion in Chapter IV.
[7] Adversus Praxeam, 12.

the mystery of the dispensation is still guarded, which distributes the Unity into a Trinity, placing in their order the three, the Father, the Son, and the Holy Spirit; three however . . . not in substance but in form, not in power but in appearance; for they are of one substance and one essence and one power, inasmuch as He is one God from Whom these degrees and forms and aspects are reckoned under the name of the Father and of the Son and of the Holy Spirit." [8] To make his meaning clearer he drew analogies from nature; The Father, Son, and Holy Ghost are to each other as the root, shrub, and tree; and as the fountain, stream, and river.[9] This language shows that subordinationism was still in the mind of Tertullian. The Father is the whole substance, while the Son is only a derivation who participates in the divine substance in a lesser degree than the Father. And again, as with the Greek Apologists, the hypostasizing of the Son as the Logos did not take place until the time of the creation.[10]

5. *The Problem.* The immediate problem, which the Church had to solve, was stated in two questions: (1) How could the Church escape from subordinationism? or how could it get away from viewing Christ as a kind of "second God" (ἕτερος Θεός)? (2) How could the Trinity of special persons (hypostasianism) be maintained without sacrificing Christian monotheism? Thus far subordinationism had been the safeguard of monotheism.

6. *Origen's Helpful Suggestion.* It was the many-sided genius of Origen that helped to solve the problem. Origen, like Tertullian, was strongly opposed to Monarchianism with its emphasis on monotheism to the exclusion of hypostasianism and tri-personality. Abandoning the view of the Apologists and of Tertullian who conceived the Logos to be a person only from the time of the creation, Origen declared the Logos to have been a person from all eternity.[11] "His generation is as eternal and everlasting as the brilliancy produced by the sun." "The Father did not beget the Son and set Him free after He was begotten, but He is always begetting Him." This suggestion of an *eternal generation* was a needed contribution. It was unconsciously a step in the direction of the *co-eternity* and *co-equality* of the Son with the Father, as expressed in the Church's doctrine of the Trinity. Thus Origen arrived at the same terminology as Irenaeus; the former by philosophical speculation; the latter by following the Scriptures and the Apostolic Tradition.[12]

II. THE ELIMINATION OF MONARCHIANISM

Literature: On Paul of Samosata and Sabellius only we take space to refer to original sources. See the article on "Monarchianism" by A. HARNACK in *PRE*, XIII, 303-36; cf. the *NSH.*

General Remarks. The word "Monarchian" was first made use of by Tertullian [13] to designate those defending the monarchy or sole government of God. The aim of Monarchianism was to be commended. It sought to save the Unity of God (i.e., monotheism) by rejecting hypostasianism and tritheism. "Monarchianism," says Seeberg, "made an effort to reconcile monotheism, the most precious treasure of Christianity, as

---

[8] *Ibid.,* 2.
[9] *Ibid.,* 8.
[10] Cf. Seeberg, *DG,* I³, 413-27. See our discussion of Tertullian in Chapter VIII, C.
[11] See our discussion of Origen with sources in Chapter VIII.
[12] Seeberg, *DG,* I³, 508-15.
[13] *Adversus Praxeam,* 3.

ontrasted with the heathen world, with the divinity of Christ without resorting to the xpedience of the 'second God.' In this consists its historical significance." [14] The Monarchians, in addition, were opposed to a philosophic Christianity and the Logos Christology.[15]

There were two types of Monarchians—the *Dynamistic* and the *Modalistic*. The first type is called *adoptionistic* by Harnack; *humanitarian* by Fisher. The dynamistic Monarchians regarded the divinity in Christ as a mere power or influence ($\delta\acute{u}\nu\alpha\mu\iota\varsigma$). Their starting point was the human person of Jesus who was eventually deified. The second type, on the other hand, thought of Christ as a *mode* or epiphany or manifestation of God the Father. Both rejected the Logos-Christology as being Gnostic: The first in the interest of the historic or synoptic Christ; the second in the interest of the monarchy and divinity of Christ.[16] Thomasius fittingly calls these two types *Ebionitism and Docetism in a higher form*. He also points out their differences: "The one maintains the personality of the historic Christ and sacrifices His essential divinity; the other maintains His essential unity with the Father and sacrifices the personal differentiation. The one starts from below with the historic-human person of Christ and degrades Him to a mere man; the other begins with the celestial Christ who has complete divinity dwelling within Him and so endangers His true humanity."

Both types of Monarchianism seem to have originated in Asia Minor. But as Rome was the great centripetal force in those days, they were soon in evidence there. For a time, indeed, it seemed as if a modified form of Modalism would eventually prevail in Rome. But in Carthage it was Tertullian who fought the battle against the modalism of Praxeas.

1. Dynamistic Monarchianism. Although a historic connection with Ebionitism cannot be proved, nevertheless Dynamism resembled the Ebionite conception which contended that Christ was a mere man who was chosen, inspired, and exalted by God. The emphasis was placed upon the excellence of His character. He was the Son of God solely by adoption.

a. Before referring to the chief representative of this group the following should be mentioned: (1) The *Alogoi*. Their entire interest was centered in the human synoptic Christ, born of the virgin, divinely adopted when the Spirit descended upon Him at baptism, and exalted at the resurrection;[17] (2) The *Theodotians* and the *Artemonites* who held similar views.[18]

b. Paul of Samosata, metropolitan of Antioch in Syria, was the most conspicuous of the dynamistic Monarchians. He has been described as unspiritual, worldly, imperious, vain, pompous, insidious, sophistic, covetous, and even immoral.[19] Briefly summarized, his teaching was as described in Art. I of the Augsburg Confession. God must be thought of as One Person. It is permissible to speak of a Logos or Son and a Wisdom or Spirit in God; but these are nothing more than attributes of God. God has been projecting this divine reason or Logos from all eternity; still it is merely an impersonal influence ($\delta\acute{u}\nu\alpha\mu\iota\varsigma$). Jesus who was born of the Virgin, was a man ($\kappa\acute{\alpha}\tau\omega\theta\epsilon\nu$) upon

[14] Eng. ed., I, 163.
[15] Cf. H. B. Swete, Ch. VI. *The Holy Spirit in the Ancient Church*, 1912.
[16] Cf. Loofs, 183.
[17] See Loofs, 243; Kurtz, Eng. ed., par. 33, 2; Fisher, 100; Zahn, *Alogoi* in *PRE* and *NSH*.
[18] Loofs, 184. Kurtz, *ibid.*
[19] Sources: Eusebius, *Church History*, VII, 27-30. Epiphanius, *Panarion*, 65.

whom God exercised his Logos-influence. The indwelling of this divine wisdom from above (ἄνωθεν) made the man Jesus the Son of God. A parallel to this is seen in the indwelling of wisdom in the prophets, except that this indwelling occurred in a unique way in Christ as the temple of God. Thus Jesus exhibits merely a *moral union* between God and man. "Through immovable steadfastness in this relationship He united Himself intimately with God by the influence of the spirit and unity of will, thus securing the power to perform miracles and fitness to become the Redeemer, and in addition attaining a permanent oneness with God." [20]

Such was Paul's doctrine. In spreading his views he went so far as to remove the hymns of praise addressed to Christ as Lord. This especially was offensive to the minds of sensitive Christians. The condemnation of Paul's doctrine was not secured until three synods had been held between 264 and 269. The first two were without result. For he knew how to conceal the heterodox character of his views. It was only at the third synod that the presbyter Malchion, a practiced dialectician and formerly a rhetorician, succeeded in unmasking him at a public disputation. The word *homoousios* was here rejected because Paul had used it to designate God and the Logos as one Person.

Paul of Samosata exemplified Dynamism at its height, and the rejection of him and his doctrine marked a turning-point in the history of Christology in the Church. Harnack observes: "With the deposition of Paul of Samosata, it was no longer possible to gain a hearing for a Christology which denied the personal, independent pre-existence of the Redeemer." [21]

2. Modalistic Monarchianism.

Dynamistic Monarchianism, which we have just discussed, was largely a tendency in a few of the Church's leaders. But the very opposite was true of Modalism which affected the vast body of the Church's membership. Modalism appealed very strongly to the ordinary believer who saw in it a veritable safeguard of monotheism. Tertullian saw the situation in its true proportions, when he wrote: "For some simple persons—not to say inconsiderate and ignorant, as is always the majority of believers—since the Rule of Faith itself leads us away from the many gods of the world to the one and true God, not understanding that he is to be believed as being one but with his own economy, are terrified at this economy. They think that the number and order of the Trinity implies a division of the unity" (*Adv. Prax. 3*). Hence it turned out that Modalism became very widespread and influential in the West. So Harnack remarks: "The really dangerous opponent of the Logos-Christology between 180 and 300 was not 'Adoptionism,' but the doctrine which saw the Deity Himself incarnate in Christ, and which conceived Christ to be God in a human body." [22]

The chief interest of Modalism was to maintain Christian monotheism without sacrificing the divinity of Christ. So the Modalist sought to solve the problem by identifying Christ with the Father and by regarding Him as one of the successive forms in which the Father manifested Himself. This led, on the one hand, to Patripassianism

---

[20] Harnack, Eng. ed., III, 40 ff.; his article on *Monarchianism* in PRE, XIII, 303; cf. NSH; Thom.-Bonw., I, 181; Seeberg, Eng. ed., I, 164 ff.; his DG, I³, 566-69; Fisher, 104; Loofs, 218 f.; G. Bardy, *Paul de Samosata*, 1923. F. Loofs, *Paulus von Samosata*, TU, 44, 1924. H. Rinn, pp. 71-73.

[21] *Grundriss⁶*, p. 48. Loofs, in the above-mentioned investigation "Paulus von Samosata" (1924) tried to prove that Paul was not a dynamistic Monarchian. The reliability of this result depends upon whether a certain document is genuine or not. Harnack replied in *Theol. Literaturzeitung* that the genuineness of that document cannot be contested.

[22] Eng. ed., I, 51.

which taught that it was really the Father who suffered and died; and on the other hand, to Docetism, although in a higher form than the docetism of the Gnostics.[23]

Let us add a few notes on a few of the various exponents of Modalism:

a. Noetus of Smyrna. One of the first representatives of the modalistic Monarchians was Noetus of Smyrna. These statements by him characterize Modalism: "When the Father had not yet been born, He was rightly called the Father; but when it had pleased Him to submit to birth, having been born, He became the Son, He of Himself and not of another." [24] "Christ is Himself the Father, and . . . the Father Himself was born, He suffered and died." [25] "For Christ was God and suffered for us, being the Father Himself, in order that He might be able also to save us." [26]

b. Praxeas. About 190 Praxeas, an adherent of Noetus, came to Rome, bringing with him the doctrines of his teacher. While Praxeas agreed in the main with Noetus, yet he admitted more of a distinction between the Father and the Son. "The Son indeed suffers, but the Father suffers with Him." [27] Thus we may say that Praxeas represented a certain blending of the Modalist with the dynamitic type of Monarchianism. Praxeas' teaching even recruited followers in Carthage, which caused Tertullian to write his great work *Adversus Praxeam.*[28]

c. Sabellius. The most significant of all the Modalists, however, was Sabellius.[29] Seeberg remarks: "As we have called Paul of Samosata the only real Dynamist among the Monarchians, so Sabellius is the only real Modalist among them." [30] The year 215 saw him teaching his doctrines in Rome. He differed from Noetus and Praxeas in this, that in a trinitarian conception he gave the Holy Spirit a place with the Father and the Son.[31]

His system may be outlined as follows: God is a Unity (μονάς). There are no distinctions in the divine Being, but God the divine Unity reveals Himself successfully in three different modes or forms (ὀνόματα, πρόσωπα). In the Father God reveals Himself as creator; in the Son, as redeemer; and in the Spirit, as sanctifier. But these are not three hypostases; they are rather three roles or parts played by the one person. In other words, all three are one and the same Person. The thought may be illustrated by a figure from the stage. One *persona dramatis* will impersonate three different characters or roles before the audience, and yet there is in reality only one person. Or to use a Sabellian analogy: Man has three names, body, soul and spirit; but there is only one person. The one sun possesses light, heat and roundness; but there is only one sun. So God has three names, Father, Son and Holy Spirit; but there is only one Person. The Father, Son, and Holy Spirit are identical; and it was this supposed identity which lay at the bottom of the entire system. The God of Sabellianism was therefore a Unity, a Monas, a single Person viewed under three different forms. After the πρόσωπον of the Father accomplished its work in the giving of the law, it fell back into its original condition; advancing again through the incarnation as Son, it returns by the ascension

---

[23] Thom.-Bonw. I, 179 ff.; Harnack, *Grundriss*⁶, 161-67; Eng. ed., III, 51 ff.; Seeberg, Eng. ed., I, 168; DG, I³, 570-76.

[24] Hipp. *Refut.*, ix, 10.

[25] *Contra Noetum*, 1.

[26] *Ibid.* 2.

[27] Tert. *Adv. Praxeam*, 29.

[28] Seeberg, *DG*, I³, 575 ff., Eng. ed., I, 167. Harnack, Eng. ed.³, III, 66.

[29] As sources we mention Hippolytus, *Refutation*, IX, 11, 12; Epiphanius, *Panarion*, 62; cf. 69, 7; Athanasius, *Orationes contra Arianos*, III, 4, 36; also IV (probably not by Athanasius), 2, 3, 9, 13, 17, 25.

[30] *DG* I³, 575 f.

[31] Epiph. *Pan.* 32, 1. Cf. H. Rinn, pp. 69 f.

into the absolute being of the Monas; it reveals itself finally as the Holy Spirit, to return again, after securing the perfect sanctification of the Church, into the Monas that knows no distinctions, there to abide through all eternity. This process is characterized by Sabellius as an expansion and contraction.[32]

Although Sabellius was ultimately excommunicated and his teaching rejected, nevertheless he unconsciously prepared the way for the *homoousios* in the orthodox Christology of a later time. While his absolute identification of the Three Persons in the Trinity was a positive error, he hinted at a more positive truth, namely the co-essence, co-equality, and co-eternity of the Three Persons.

3. *The Modified Monarchianism* of the Roman bishops from Victor to Callistus should also be noted. The situation in Rome was both confusing and detrimental to the Church. On the one hand stood Hippolytus, the champion of hypostasianism and subordination; on the other hand was Sabellius, advocate of modalistic Monarchianism. Bishop Callistus regarded it as his task to discover some formula of compromise by which Hippolytus and Sabellius might be excluded and the strife ended. To this end he taught that the Father, Son, and Holy Spirit are the names of the *one indivisible Spirit* and that they are one and the same thing. The divinity of Christ is identical with the Father; yet the flesh of Jesus should be called the *Son*, since it is inhabited by the God-Spirit who deified the man Jesus.[33] Hippolytus correctly called this doctrine a combination of the teaching of Sabellius and Theodotus.[34] But it should be observed that Callistus really labored to avoid *Patripassianism* by teaching that the Father did not suffer except in and with the Son. Kurtz remarks fittingly "Decidedly monarchian as this formula of compromise undoubtedly is, it seems to have afforded the bridge upon which official Roman theology crossed over to homoousian hypostasianism."[35] While his deification of the man Jesus seems to smack of Dynamism, still Callistus created a kind of Godlike hypostasis for the Son, which proved helpful in the subsequent Nicene theology.[36]

III. FURTHER STRUGGLE FOR CLARIFICATION OF VIEWS

Of the two types of Monarchianism, it was Modalism which was attended with the greater success. But even Modalism gave way gradually to the Logos-doctrine. In the Orient it bowed to the form as represented by Origen; in the West to that of Tertullian. The old problem, however, was still before the Church: How was Subordinationism to be overcome? It will be remembered that Origen had suggested the idea of the eternal generation of the Son from the Father; and this thought had not been lost sight of by the Church's teachers. In the struggle for the elimination of Monarchianism it is interesting to note how the various views were being clarified. In studying this process of clarification we note:

1. *Novatian.* This was the learned presbyter who, after Cornelius had been elected bishop of Rome (251), headed the revolt in favor of applying the strictest discipline

[32] Thom.-Bonw., I, 185-187. Seeberg, *DG*, I[3], 573 ff. Harnack, *Grundriss*[6], 166; Eng. ed.[3], III, 84 ff. Loofs, 186. Fisher, 103.
[33] *Refut.* 9. 6.
[34] *Refut.* 23.
[35] 33, 5.
[36] Seeberg, *DG*, I[3], 576 f. Harnack, *Grundriss*[6], 166; Eng. ed.[3], III, 69.

o the lapsed. We shall now hear him on the Trinity. [37] His treatise *De Trinitate*, written sometime between 240 and 250, shows how completely Tertullian's views had replaced the modified Modalism which had reigned in Rome from Victor to Callistus. The writing is as decided against the Monarchians as it is in favor of the Trinity. Novatian declared that the Son was "always in the Father, else the Father would not always be the Father." [38] Yet he was extremely careful to avoid the charge of *Ditheism* which was made by the Monarchians. The best way to do this, he thought, was to admit that the Son had a beginning, and that in a certain sense the Father precedes the Son. The Father alone is eternal and unborn, while the Son is a personal derivation from Him. Thus, subordinationism was still present. Novatian is interesting to us (1) because he placed himself squarely on hypostasianism, and (2) because in his system the Holy Spirit appeared as the third person of the Trinity.

2. *The Controversy Between the Two Bishops Dionysius.* Bishop Dionysius of Alexandria was a pupil of Origen and, like his teacher, was the head of the Alexandrian catechetical school for some time. He adhered to the Logos-doctrine and believed in the personal differentiation of the Son from the Father. The errors of subordination, which usually attended hypostasianism, did not trouble him greatly.

As a hypostasianist, Dionysius rejected the modalistic doctrine of Sabellius, which had gained many recruits in Libyan Pentapolis. In writing against Sabellius his zeal carried him too far in the opposite direction, and he was charged with declaring that "the Son of God is a creature . . . in essence alien from the Father, just as the husbandman is from the vine, or the shipbuilder from the boat; for that, being a creature, He was not before He came to be." [39] Athanasius admits that, although the charge was correct, yet it was based on but a fragment of Dionysius' teaching, which could not properly be construed as the foundation for a true judgment. But this teaching gave offense to intelligent Christians in Alexandria in whose consciousness the eternal existence or generation of the Son was firmly lodged. They accordingly brought complaint against their bishop before *Dionysius of Rome* (c. 260).

In his reply the Roman Dionysius did not condemn the erring colleague; but he did declare himself opposed to any attempt to destroy the monarchy of the divine Being. The Son and the Spirit must be held in close connection with the Father. "It must needs be that with the God of the universe the Divine Word is united, and the Holy Ghost must repose and habitate in God." [40] The divided Trinity is to be brought together and summed up in one God, the Almighty Ruler of all things. The Son is not to be regarded as a creature, it must not be taught that He had a temporal beginning. The Church must defend the *homoousios* and believe simply in "God the Father Almighty, and in Jesus Christ His Son, and in the Holy Ghost."

In a voluminous *Refutation and Defence,* designed to clear himself of heresy, the Alexandrian Dionysius replied that he had not been entirely understood. He agreed with his opponents, he declared, and had no intention of denying the *homoousios,* although the expression is not Biblical. In stating his own views of the Trinity, he said:

---

[37] The student will keep in mind that we are still in the pre-Nicene period of development.
[38] *De Trin.* 31.
[39] Athanasius, *De Sent. Dion.,* 4.
[40] *Ibid.,* 18.

"We expand the monad undivided into the Trinity, and again combine the Trinity undiminished into the monad."[41] Such an explanation was apparently satisfactory, and the controversy was not revived. The agreement between the two parties was an auspicious omen. All parts of the Church were gradually coming together on the subject.

IV. ARIANISM VERSUS ATHANASIANISM

Literature: The special sources regarding Arius and Athanasius will be given below. Here we refer to valuable information in the Histories of Doctrine: THOMASIUS-BONWETSCH, I, 212 f.; SCHMID-HAUCK[4], 52 f.; LOOFS, 236; SEEBERG, English ed., I, 201 ff.; DG, II[3], 21 ff.; HARNACK, *Grundriss*[6], 210 ff.; English, IV, 3 ff. 21-24. WIEGAND I, 70-74. FISHER, 135 ff. Cf. RINN, pp. 115-134.

The two men who fought the great battle over Arianism were both from the Church at Alexandria—the archdeacon Athanasius who earned the title *father of orthodoxy,* and his opponent, the presbyter Arius. The systems they taught were diametrically opposed to each other, and their fundamental ideas admitted of no compromise. The Church was obliged to decide between them.

1. The Genesis of Arianism. It is interesting to note the relation of Arius to certain teachers of the past. There was, indeed, little originality about the doctrine of Arius. On the one hand, he was vastly indebted to Paul of Samosata with whom his teacher, Lucian of Antioch, had acquainted him. Says Harnack: "This school (i.e. Antioch) is the nursery of the Arian doctrine and Lucian, its head, is the Arius before Arius." [42] Like Paul of Samosata, Arius was opposed to modalistic monarchianism, and strongly in favor of hypostasianism of the subordinationist type. Athanasius was right when he accused the Arians of teaching the Samosatene doctrine without having the courage to admit it. On the other hand, Arius drew some of his ideas from certain uncautious remarks of Origen; as for instance, the latter's reply to Celsus, in which he said that the Logos is "intermediate between the nature of the uncreated and that of all created things." Fisher remarks: "Arianism was not really a new doctrine. The springs of it can easily be seen in one class of Origen's statements, taken apart from his teachings as a whole, and in expressions like those of Dionysius of Alexandria" (p. 135).

2. Arius labored with a twofold purpose in view. With the Church he wished to preserve the Logos-Christ as an independent being. With the Monarchians he desired to save the monotheistic principle of Christianity. In combining these two interests he was compelled to emphasize subordinationism to such an extent that the eyes of the Church were opened wide to a fact that had long remained concealed, namely that the idea of a decided subordination of the Son to the Father constituted a danger to the full conception of the divinity of Christ. Arianism was only subordinationism heretically developed.

3. The Teaching of Arius. Arius was evidently a skillful practical psychologist. In spreading his doctrines he wisely put them into verses ($\theta \acute{\alpha} \lambda \epsilon \iota \alpha$) which the people might sing at their work and so be indoctrinated the more easily.

Sources: A few fragments of three letters, one to Eusebius of Nicomedia, one to Alexander of Alexandria and one to Emperor Constantine, together with the writings of Athanasius and with the following literature, enable us to reconstruct the teachings of Arius: From Bishop Alexander

[41] *Ibid.,* 17.
[42] Harnack, *DG,* IV[4], 3

n Alexandria we have two circulars, one to Bishop Alexander in Constantinople and another which s the document of deposition of Arius addressed to all Catholic bishops (published in Greek by , P. Migne in *MSG, tom.* 18, 547-84). On the works of Athanasius, see below.

In addition to these sources we should mention the *Reports on the Council at Nicea* by :usebius, Socrates, Sozomenos, Theodoret and Philostorbius (cf. *PRE*) in Mansi, *Acta Concilii,* II, ¡35-1082.

In the way of investigation and discussion we refer to the Histories of Doctrine and add: :. F. HEFELE, *Conciliengeschichte²,* I, 282-443 (English translation, Edinburgh); W. KOELLING, *¡eschichte der arianischen Haeresie,* 2 vols., 1874, 1893; J. H. NEWMAN, *The Arians of the ²ourth Century,* 1876; H. M. GWATKIN, *Studies of Arianism²,* 1900; the same ((popularizing), *ĩhe Arian Controversy²,* 1901; P. SNELLMAN, *Anfang des Arianischen Streites,* Helsingfors, 1904.

In his endeavor to explain Christ, Arius introduced a mythological figure—a *tertium juid,* half-God and half-man—something like the *demiurge* of the Gnostics. This ĩhrist was not a mere man. He was a demigod: divine indeed, but not co-equal with he Father. True, this had been taught by the subordinationists of the past, such as the Apologists and in a way even Tertullian. But Arius was arguing the idea that there is ι real difference in essence between the Father and the Son. The Father alone is a real livine Being, while the Son is only a creature (κτίσμα). The idea of co-eternity was :ejected. There was a time when the Son was not. To the Son belong all predicates hat belong to the creature. After Arius had established the difference in essence (ούσία))etween the Father and the Son, he proceeded to point out the differences between the ĩon and other creatures, and to explain the Son's mission in the world. The Son was :reated before time and space, in order that He might mediate in the creation of the world and that He might also reveal God to the World. For this purpose He was ≥ndowed in advance with a special divine glory—a glory which He deserved in view of :he virtuous life He was going to lead. The Son, to Arius, was not God, but divine.

4. Estimate of Arius' Doctrine. With Paul of Samosata it was the man Jesus who)ecame divine. But Arius taught that the Son or Logos was a finite being who was made divine because God foresaw His future ethical achievements. The background of :his teaching was an abstract conception of God, according to which God is an absolute monadic unity without differentiation in Himself, and hence unable to create the world without the mediation of the highest created Being. Seeberg remarks: "Thus a mytho-logical element was introduced into Christianity, and bare monotheism is transformed into the polytheism of heroes and demigods." [43]

5. The First Ecumenical Council. Alexander, bishop of Alexandria, was irrevocably opposed to the views of Arius, and at a large synod held in 321 at Alexandria he had Arius deposed and excommunicated. But Arius was not without sympathizers. Many, like the influential Eusebius of Nicomedia, openly favored him. Others, like Eusebius of Caesarea, were for tolerating Arius, although they did not agree with him. Emperor Constantine, who had heard of the situation, was disposed to treat the matter as an inconsequential church quarrel in which nothing essential was involved. But his trusted adviser, Bishop Hosius of Cordova, was of a different mind. It is likely that it was Hosius who persuaded the emperor to see the seriousness of the controversy. So it came to pass that Constantine called in 325 at Nicea the first General Council, which was attended by about 300 bishops and many others of lower rank. To the scene of battle journeyed Alexander, and with him came his archdeacon Athanasius who was to become the mighty champion and bulwark of orthodoxy in the Arian controversy.

---

[43] Eng. ed. I. 204.

Three parties were represented: (1) The *Homoousians,* weak in numbers, but strong in their conviction, led by Alexander and Athanasius; (2) the Arians, headed by Eusebius of Nicomedia; (3) a large group embracing those who did not understand the situation and whose main interest was peace. To this group belonged Eusebius of Caesarea.

Alexander placed himself firmly on the eternal generation of the Son (Origen). The birth of the Saviour from the Father is without beginning. To deny this would be to deny the eternity of the Father's light. The Sonship of Christ, being eternal, is therefore different in kind from that of human beings. The Son is truly a necessary part of the Father's being.

Eusebius of Nicomedia first presented an Arian creed which was promptly voted down. Then Eusebius of Caesarea offered his creed in which Christ was called the "created image." This creed would have satisfied the Arians, and indeed most of the assembled bishops. But Athanasius and Alexander could not subscribe to it. Hosius of Cordova suggested that the word *homoousios* be used in speaking of Christ. This term was finally agreed upon. Thus it was the Creed of Caesarea out of which the new confession of faith was formed. The characteristic phrases of the new creed were these: "Out of the essence of the Father, generated, not made, of like essence with the Father." [44] To the whole creed was appended the following damnatory clause: "But the holy and apostolic Church anathematizes those who say that there was a time when He was not, and that He was made from things not existing, or from another person or being, saying that the Son of God is mutable or changeable." [45]

6. *Athanasius* (d. 373) was not a man of great originality in opening up new springs of religion as did Augustine or in conceiving a method of such a universal sweep as can be observed in the highest sense of this term. He saw the practical essentials in religion and theology and organized the fundamental interest of the Church about the religion of redemption. He brushed aside the purely philosophical interests of the followers of Origen and established the Church upon Christ as the Redeemer. It was from this specifically religious position that he secured the rejection of Arianism at the Council of Nicea.

In addition to this theological position it was the strong unfaltering determination of Athanasius, during a long life of persecution and oppression, which was the deciding factor in the final overthrow of all mediating attempts that threatened the victory of homoousianism. The life of Athanasius reads like a page from fiction. He was exiled five times, and yet he proved victorious in the end. At Nicea his eloquence was so convincing that the small minority of the Homoousians prevailed over the large and influential majority of Arians and Semi-Arians. And equally strong was he in the literary conflict that followed the action of Nicea.

Sources: The works of Athanasius were published by MONTFAUCON, 1608, and are printed in Greek in the collection by J. P. MIGNE, parts 25-28. The main dogmatical works are given by THILO in *Bibl. patr. graec. dogmat.,* I, 1853; the historical works by W. BRIGHT in his *Historical Writings of St. Athanasius,* 1881. The student will find the leading thoughts of Athanasius in his *Orationes Quattuor Contra Arianos.* As to a full enumeration of all his writings see SEEBERG, *DG,* II³, 51 f., and his *Grundriss* (1927), 40. The *APNF,* in the second series, Vol. IV, 1893, offers a

[44] On the history of the creed in the different stages of its development, see our Chapter VI on "Sources and Norms of Truth."

[45] Harnack, English ed., IV, 50-59; the same in *PRE,* XI, 12-28 on Konstantinopolitanisches Symbol (cf. NSH). Schaff, *Creeds of Christendom,* I, 29. See Neve, *Introduction to the Symbolical Books of the Lutheran Church³,* 66-71. On the *present* form of the Nicene Creed, the "Niceno-Constantinopolitan Symbol," see the same, *Introduction,* etc., 57 ff. F. Loofs, *Der authentische Sinn des Nicaenums,* 1905.

selection of the works and letters of Athanasius in English (64 writings). The *prolegomena* of this volume open with a complete review of all the editions. There is also a German translation of selected writings by KEMPTEN in the *Bibliothek der Kirchenvaeter* (*BKV*²).

Literature in form of discussion: F. LAUCHERT, *Die Lehre des heil. Athanasius,* 1895. H. M. SCOTT, *Origin and Development of the Nicene Creed,* Chicago, 1896. L. L. PAINE, *Critical History of the Evolution of Trinitarianism,* 1900. BETHUNE-BAKER, *The Meaning of Homoousios,* Vol. VII in *Cambridge Texts and Studies,* 1901. L. H. HOUGH, *Athanasius, the Hero,* 1906; H. B. SWETE, *The Holy Spirit in the Ancient Church,* 1912, pp. 171 ff., 211 ff. E. WEIGH, *Untersuchungen zur Christologie desheil. Athanasius,* 1914.

The leading thoughts of Athanasius are as follows:

a. Arianism leads to practical polytheism. If Christ is not co-eternal and of one essence with the Father and at the same time not just a man, as was admitted by Arius, then He is a middle being or demigod, comparable to the *demiurge* of the Gnostics. Then we would be worshiping a creature. Why should there be any need for such a Middle Being? Is God, the Creator, too proud to come into direct contact with His creatures? And furthermore, if it was impossible for Him to create the world without a Middle Being then it was also impossible for Him to create the Son without a Middle Being. [46]

This was directed not only against Arius, but also against the Logos-speculations of the Apologists. The Logos-doctrine in the old philosophical form disappeared from this time on. Harnack calls attention to the fact that the word Logos, which was contained in the Symbol of Eusebius, was accordingly omitted from the Nicene Creed.

b. The full divinity of Christ must be admitted. Athanasius insisted that, if Christ is in any sense divine, as Arius taught, then He belongs to the unseparated and undivided monad of the Deity. The Son existed personally from all eternity. The three hypostases, however, are not to be separated from one another. "The relation between the Father and Son is like that between a fountain and a stream that gushes from it. Just as a river springing from a fountain is not separated from it, although there are two forms and two names, so neither is the Son from the Father, nor the Father from the Son." [47] Thus the co-eternity and the co-equality of the Son with the Father must follow. Such a Son is different in origin and nature from created beings. He is the "other-natured" (ἑτεροούσιός) with regard to created beings, but is "same-natured" (ὁμοούσιος) with the Father. This is the co-essence of the Son with the Father. If then the Son, who is "same-natured" with the Father, differs from the Father in person, then the Son cannot have been created; He must have been generated. If the Father has always been the Father—which is obviously necessary since there can be no change in the Godhead—then the Son must have been generated from all eternity. In other words, the Son must have been eternally the Son. [48]

c. It was upon these thoughts that Athanasius based his insistence upon the full divinity of Christ, upon a real Trinity expressive of a carefully guarded monotheism. Upon these thoughts only could he base prayer to Christ, the administration of baptism and, above all, the redemptive character of the Christian religion with the forgiveness of sin and the hope of resurrection.

d. Athanasius saw in the Scriptures and in the Rule of Faith the *authority* for the teaching of the Nicene Faith. Against the objection of the Arians that the terms of

[46] *Contr. Arianos* II. 25. 25. 29 f.
[47] *Expos. fid.* 2; *Contr. Ar.* III 4.
[48] *Ibid.,* I. 14; cf. III. 66; I. 27.

the Nicene Creed are not in the Scriptures, he replied that they do express the substance of Scripture teaching.[49] He interpreted the Bible in the light of what it says on Christ and on redemption. He even had the appeal to Christian experience on this subject. And finally he saw an expression of all these essentials in the apostolic teaching of the Church.[50]

7. *The Temporary Defeat of Homoousianism.* Although the Nicene victory seemed complete, it was nevertheless far from permanent. The majority of those who voted for the *homoousian* creed had but a meager conception of its real meaning. Consequently the sixty years, which followed the Nicene Council, were all confusion. Athanasius had been appointed bishop of Alexandria in 328, and for a time all went well. But in 335 at the synod of Tyre, Eusebius of Nicomedia preferred charges against him with the emperor, and he was deposed. Time and time again the bishop was forced into exile and then permitted to return. When Athanasius died in 373, it seemed that the great things for which he had fought had been completely defeated. All of these sixty years were dark hours for Homoousianism, and apparently Arianism was to gain the ultimate victory.

8. *The Final Victory of Homoousianism.* From the very beginning victorious Arianism had within it the seeds of defeat. The statement of faith, which had been formulated at Nicea in the "old Nicene Creed," had been opposed by two parties. The first was the small group of Arians. The other however was a large group, more conservative in principle. This latter group regarded the word *homoousios* as an echo of Sabellianism. It preferred to use the word *homoiousios.* (Note: *Homoiousios* should not be translated with "similar" in comparison with *homoousios* as having the meaning of "equal." By using the term *homoiousios* this group wanted to safeguard the real *hypostasis* of the Son over against any tendency towards Modalism.) These two parties were agreed in two things: (1) in their aversion to the word *homoousios,* and (2) in their hostility to each other. This state of affairs in the ranks of the opposition was destined to work out well for the cause of Athanasius. The Arians gradually became more radical, while the Homoiousians became more conservative. The result was that under Emperor Valens, an outspoken Arian, the Homoousians and the Homoiousians were driven together, and gradually constituted an alliance for Athanasianism.[51]

In addition to the effect produced by this fusion of the Homoousians and the Homoiousians, the powerful influence of the three great Cappadocians in the East— Basil of Caesarea, Gregory of Nazianzus, and Gregory of Nyssa—and of Ambrose in the West, was another factor in directing the Church's attention to the truth of Athanasianism. Note below our critical remarks on Eastern Christology as compared with that of the West. Seeberg remarks: "The modification, which has been made in the ancient Nicene doctrine, is very evident. Athanasius (and Marcellus) taught the one God, leading a threefold personal life, who reveals Himself as such. The Cappadocians think of three divine hypostases which, as they manifest the same dignity, are recognized as possessing one nature and the same dignity." Athanasius starts with the one divine nature (οὐσία, or ὑπόστασις) indicating the threefold personal life. The Cappadocians begin with the three divine hypostases (or πρόσωπα) and they labor to bring these under

[49] *De decretis synodi Nicaenae,* 21. 18.
[50] *Contr. Arianos Orat.* I, 4; 8; II, 34; III, 28; ad Serap I, 28; 33.
[51] The details in this part of the investigation with sources are reviewed by Seeberg, *DG.* II³, 87 ff.

he one divine οὐσία. Each hypostasis has its peculiarity or property (ἰδιότης) or attribute. The Father is unbegotten, the Son generated, the Spirit proceeding. But all have the same divinity, energy and power, the same divine substance and nature and, therefore the same dignity and glory. The mystery for Athanasius lay in the Trinity; for the Cappadocians in the Unity. "It was with labor and difficulty that the latter guarded themselves against polytheism. But it was only in this way that the Nicene doctrines were, for the Orientals, freed from the taint of Sabellianism, and that the personality of the Logos appeared to be sufficiently assured. The Cappadocians interpreted the doctrine of Athanasius in accordance with the conceptions and underlying principles of the Logos-Christology of Origen. They paid, however, for their achievement a high price, the magnitude of which they did not realize—the idea of the personal God. Three person-alities and an abstract, impersonal essence are the resultant. In this form the *ousia* and *physis* are a heavy weight upon the doctrine concerning God, for they are in conflict with the personality of God. It was a partial corrective of this that they after all—inconsistently—identified the Deity with the Father, which was again a relic of the earlier Subordinationism. . . . Thus, in place of the conception of the *one-natured, threefold* God, had come the doctrine of the *like-natured, triune* God." [52]

9. *Clarification of Views on the Holy Spirit.* Arius and his followers in connection with their conception of the Son as the highest of all creatures, took the Holy Spirit as the first creature brought forth through the Son. The Nicene Creed of 325 said no more on this subject than simply: "We believe in the Holy Spirit." This recognition was taken of the Spirit because of Matt. 28: 19, the Trinitarian expression in the early baptismal creeds and the early doxologies and hymns which glorified the Spirit with the Father and the Son. [53]

Gregory of Nazianzus tells us that there was a great diversity of opinions among the theologians concerning the Spirit, who was variously regarded as an energy or influence, a creature or angelic being. Some deemed it best not to make any definite statements concerning the Spirit.

Athanasius, now in a later period of his life, again proved to be of service in the solution of this problem. He had become convinced that, if we are to hold to the Baptismal Formula, the Spirit cannot be a creature. If the Spirit is a creature, then something of a different nature is introduced into the Godhead, and we have a Diad instead of a Trinity. The Spirit, like the Son, must be *homoousios* (co-essential, con-substantial, same-natured). This he undertook to prove from His work of sanctification. Athanasius wrote on this subject in four letters *Ad Serapionem.* [54] Bishop Macedonius of Constantinople opposed this position and declared that the Holy Spirit is a creature subordinate to the Son. But a synod at Alexandria (362), presided over by Athanasius, established the *homoousia* of the Holy Spirit who was declared to be a person like the Father and the Son. The disciples of Macedonius were styled *Pneumatomachians* and later were called *Macedonians.* The leading theologians, such as the three Cappadocians and Didymus the Blind, followed in the footsteps of Athanasius. It was now the Baptismal Formula, taken directly from the Scriptures, which was the real moving factor in this

---

[52] Seeberg, Eng. ed., I, 232 f., 228. In his *DG*, II², 132 ff., Seeberg reviews in a most interesting way the religious motives back of this theology. Cf. also, Wiegand I, 77 ff. The reference is to expressions such as by Basil, *Epist.*, 38, 3, 4; 52, 2; Gregory of Naz., *Orat.*, 31, 9; 28, 31.

[53] Cf. H. B. Swete², 231 ff., as quoted below.

[54] See especially I, 1, 2, 4 ff. 9, 10, 14, 17, 21, 24, 25, 28; III, 7; IV, 20, 25. Cf. also his letter *Ad Afros*, II.

direction. Cyril of Jerusalem had already taught the divinity of the Spirit as a person.[55] The Cappadocians aided with detailed argumentation.[56]

Thus it came to pass after the death of Athanasius (373) that the expressions on the Holy Spirit, as we have them in the present form of the Nicene Creed, were sanctioned at the so-called second ecumenical council at Constantinople (381). At a synod held in Rome (380) the Occident had already decided against all expressions of doubt with regard to the deity of the Spirit. The Spirit was now understood to be an *hypostasis* like the Father and the Son. The Spirit's work was interpreted as the completion and application of Christ's redemptive work. The difference between the Son and the Spirit is this: The Son is generated and sent forth, while the Spirit proceeds. For a detailed study of the conception of the Holy Spirit in the age of the Fathers, see H. B. Swete, *The Holy Spirit in the Ancient Church*, 1912.

10. Voices from the West. The Latin theologians stood always on the side of Athanasius. As we saw in that *modified Monarchianism* of the Roman bishops from Victor to Callistus, Western theology recognized the element of truth pointed to by Modalistic Monarchianism. They emphasized the unity in the Godhead. With this they combined the Alexandrian distinction between persons without resorting to a Logos speculation that would militate against the co-eternity, and the co-equality of the Son.

Hilary (d 367), in his *De trinitate,* defended with Biblical terms the independency of the persons and the unity of their being, and (in *De Synodis*) aided the union between the East and the West by admitting the *homoiousios* with the *homoousios.* He pointed to the distinction between the persons by referring to John 5:25: the Father gives; the Son receives. The Father, therefore, is another than the Son, for He generates Him, while the Son is generated. With Origen he takes the generation as an eternal act. But because of such generation the nature common to the two spells the unity of being.[57]

Ambrose (d. 397) followed the Cappadocians. He thinks of three persons being one in one substance, divinity, will, operation (*De fide ad Gratianum*).

We have now traced the development of the dogma of the Trinity up to the time when our present Nicene Creed replaced the original form of 325.

As it was the imperial power which had bestowed victory first upon the Nicene Faith and then upon Arianism, so now it was also the imperial influence which was to act decisively in favor of the Neo-Nicene faith. In 380 Emperor Theodosius issued an edict establishing the new orthodoxy. In 381 he convened the second ecumenical council at Constantinople at which the Nicene Creed was confirmed and adopted, and Arianism suppressed.

Note: As has already been indicated, the original creed, adopted at Nicea in 325, is not identical with that which we use today. Nor was the present form of the Nicene Creed, the so-called Niceno-Constantinopolitan Creed, created at the Council of Constantinople in 381. That this old view is erroneous, has been fully demonstrated by the investigations of Caspari, Hort, Harnack, Kattenbusch, and others. The situation is rather like this: What has been called the Niceno-Constantinopolitan Creed is according to Hort and Harnack a modification of the Baptismal Formula which was used in Jerusalem, and into which were incorporated the most significant phrases of the

---

[55] Cf. his *cat.* 17, 5; 13.33 f.

[56] Basil, *De Spiritu Sancto*, see 29, 72; Greg. of Naz., *Orat.* 31.

[57] The writings of Hilary are *De Trinitate* and *De Synodis.* See the article on Hilary by Loofs in *PRE,* p. 60 ff.; cf. *NSH* J. H. Reinkens, *Hilarius v. Poitiers,* 1864, p. 173 ff. J. Gummerus, *Die homoousianische Partei,* 1900, p. 109 ff. A. Beck, *Die Trinitaetslehre de heil. Hilarius,* 1903.

Nicene Creed, together with an additional statement regarding the Holy Spirit. How it came to be regarded as the creed made at Constantinople cannot be explained with certainty. All we know is that from about 500 this form came to be used in place of the original Nicene Creed. The Niceno-Constantinopolitan form does not have the highly significant words "out of the essence of the Father." The damnatory clauses are also omitted. The *filioque* is still a later addition.[58]

V. THE COMPLETED DOCTRINE AS CONTAINED IN THE "ATHANASIAN" CREED

The Doctrine of the Trinity was practically completed by the Council of Constantinople (381). There were two later theologians, however, who gave the final expression to this doctrine as it was held in the East and the West respectively. John of Damascus (d. cir. 754) represented the Eastern Church, and Augustine (d. 430) the Western.

1. *John of Damascus* was not a productive genius like Augustine. His significance lay in the fact that he summarized the dogma of the Trinity as it was held in the East. In the third part of his standard work, *De fide orthodoxa*[59] he presented God as One substance and three hypostases—Father, Son and Spirit. The three hypostases, however, are not related to each other after the manner of three men. "They are one in all respects . . . except those of non-generation, generation, and procession" and their relation is that of a mutual permeation (περιχώρησις or *permeatio*) or interpenetration without any commingling. Although John rejected subordinationism, he spoke of the Father as the source of the Godhead and the Spirit as proceeding from the Father through the Logos. Thus he exhibited after all a remnant of the old Greek subordinationism. He found his justification in two words of the Nicene Creed—"One God"—words which are indeed subject to misunderstanding. Thus the way was prepared for the later controversy over the *filioque*.[60]

2. *Augustine* (d. 430), representative of Western theology, restated the Latin view of the Trinity in his great work *De Trinitate*.[61]

With Augustine the emphasis lay upon the *unity* of God. The Trinity is the one God. In substance, nature, energy, and will God is one. This was carried out with great consistency. For instance, the Son is represented as taking part in His own sending and incarnation.[62] The Persons of the Trinity are not different from one another; with respect to the entire divine substance they are identical with each other.[63] In this sense Augustine used the word *homoousios*. The Son and the Spirit are not sent because they are in any sense inferior or subordinate to the Father, but because they proceed from Him.[64] Each of the three Persons is equal to the entire Trinity, and the entire Trinity is not more than one of the persons. Augustine spoke as though the essence of Being is after all a Person. Yet Augustine, in agreement with the Church's tradition,

---

[58] Kurtz, German, 14th ed. §61, 2; English, §56, 2; also §67, I and §91, 2. Seeberg, *DG*, II³, 165. For an exposition of the situation in English see Neve, *The Symbolical Books of the Lutheran Church²*, 1926; Schaff, *Christian Church* III, 616-49.

[59] See *MSG* 94 ff.

[60] Kattenbusch, *Konfessionskunde*, I, 323 ff.

[61] *De Trinitate*, Libr. 15, Ep. 120. For reading we refer to the *Histories of Doctrine*. Cf. Thom.-Bonw. I, 281 ff.; Dorner, *Augustinus*, 1873, p. 3 ff.; T. Gangauf, *Augustinus spekulative Lehre von Gott*, 1865. O. Scheel, *Die Anschauung Augustinus ueber Christi Person und Werk*, 1901. W. S. Bishop, *The Development of Trinitarian Doctrine in the Nicene and Athanasian Creeds*, 1910.

[62] *De Trin.*, II, 5. 9.

[63] VII, 6.11; VIII, 1; VI, 7.9.

[64] IV, 20.27.

insisted on the three Persons in the Trinity. How, then, was he able to do this after his previous statements on the unity? Simply by introducing the logical category of the relationship.[65] In the One God there are three forms of existence, and the one cannot be without the other. The three Persons are not related to God as the species to the genus, nor as properties to the substance.[66] Quantitative and qualitative distinctions are carefully excluded.. There is the relation of mutual dependency between the Persons. Father, Son and Spirit behold in themselves the entire undivided unity which belongs to each of them under a different point of view, as generating, generated, or existing through spiration.[67]

Augustine's analogies, taken from the human soul, are as interesting as familiar (1) *Sight*—the thing seen, vision, and the intention of the will uniting the two (2) *Thought*—the thing in memory, the inner vision, and the will uniting the two (3) *Spirit*—memory, intelligence, and will. (4) *Love*—the lover, the beloved, and the love itself. These analogies express the idea of a harmonious spiritual entity, impelled and controlled from a threefold center, and also the thought that three are equivalent to one.[68]

Augustine's chief interest was to make it impossible to think of the God of redemption without thinking of Him at once as Father, Son, and Spirit. This thought called for emphasis on the unity and demanded the reduction of the hypostases to relative Trinitarian distinctions within the divine monad. Augustine was aware of the inadequacy of human language as a medium of expressing absolute truth. "Nevertheless, when it is asked, What are the three? human speech at once toils with great insufficiency. Yet we say three persons, not in order to express it, but in order not to be silent." [69]

The closing words of Augustine's great work are beautiful and worthy of remembrance. "Lord our God, we believe in Thee, the Father, the Son and the Spirit. For truth would not have said, Go, baptize, etc. (Matt. 28: 19), unless Thou be a Trinity . . . I would remember Thee, I would love Thee. . . . Lord, Thou One God, Divine Trinity, whatsoever I have written in these books by suggestion of Thee the One, mayest Thou the Three accept; if anything of myself, mayest Thou the One and Thou the Three overlook it." [70]

The fundamental features of Augustine's doctrine of the Trinity were crystallized in the *Symbolum Quicunque*, popularly known as the Athanasian Creed. This Creed has been recognized by the Western Church alone.[71]

VI. Summarizing Observations

To aid the student we shall express ourselves in numbered paragraphs:

1. There are those who insist upon seeing the origin and rise of the Trinitarian idea in the early Christians' exalted estimate of the man Jesus. They say he was looked

---

[65] V, 11.12.

[66] V. 5.6; VII, 3.6; VIII. 1.

[67] XV, 14.23.

[68] XI, 2; cf. XV, 3.5; IX, 22.

[69] V, 9.10.

[70] XI, 21.51.

[71] *Literature:* E. F. Foulkes, *The Athanasian Creed*, 1872. C. A. Swanson, *The Nicene and the Apostles Creeds; together with the Creed of Athanasius*, 1875. G. D. W. Ommanney, *The Athanasian Creed*, 1875. By the same author, *Early History of the Athanasian Creed*, 1880. A. E. Burn, *The Athanasian Creed and Its Early Commentaries*. See Schaff. *Creeds* I, 29-42. Neve. *Intr.*², 1926, pp. 71-82.

pon as a hero, as a semi-divine being or demigod. Gradually His admirers exaggerated his idea so that Christ stood before them as God. This forced upon them the question s to His relation to the Father-God. If this were a correct estimate of Jesus then the 'rinitarian conception would simply have to be recorded as an aberration. To those hat hold this the admission of the Trinity would constitute an element incompatible vith pure monotheism.

2. The Conservatives, even the progressives among them, [72] look upon the doctrine f the Trinity as the very foundation for the Biblical history of redemption. It is in the nission of Christ that they begin with an explanation of the Trinity; not with God as he absolute. The Trinity is to them not a matter of speculation, but of religion. Even he untutored Christian in his prayer-life moves unconsciously in the truth of the Trinitarian relation of the Godhead. It is a conviction also which is in harmony with the elf-consciousness of Christ (Cf. Luke 4:18. Matt. 11:27; 16:27; 19:28; 28:19; 24:25; 1:17, 31. John 5:15 ff.; 8:29; 10:17, 29 f., 33, 38; 14:9 ff.; chapter 17).

3. We have emphasized the religious character of the position of Athanasius in his efusal of Arianism. The permanent truth in his argumentation lies in two things: 1) Christ is God because He is the Redeemer. At the same time (2) the Being essence) of God is one; in no sense can Christianity admit in the Godhead a second nd a third subordinate Being; when speaking of God, it must always be the One God vho at the same time is Father, Son and Spirit, not successively as the Sabellians had it, ut de facto as the Athanasian Creed expresses it.

4. There is an abiding truth in the Greek emphasis upon the hypostases in the Trinity as it was insisted upon especially by the three Cappadocians and John of Damascus, even if we may admit with Seeberg in his searching criticism[73] that, as a system it cannot stand the test of logic. The abiding truth lies in the relation of the one Trinitarian God to mankind in an actual history of revelation, redemption and communication.

5. Augustine starts with the Western emphasis upon the unity in the Trinity. We earned that Roman bishops leaned to a modified Monarchianism in the Sabellian direction. The three persons are not to be denied, but Augustine sees them only in "relationhips." With Athanasius he is carefully on his guard against taking Christ as a "second God." But in describing the relations of the One to the Three, refusing even qualitative listinctions such as employed by Hilary, [74] and only reluctantly employing the term "person," his aim at harmonizing the persons with the unity results in a speculative system which is in constant danger of losing the relation to the reality of the divine evelation through history. Still there is a great historic significance in the really fundamental features of the Augustinian statements as expressed in the Athanasian Creed: they have served as safeguard against the degeneration of the Trinity into critheism.

6. In closing we call attention to two historic moments when Athanasianism was at the point of losing to Arianism, but still came out victoriously.

When under Emperor Contantius, after 350, even the West was forced to yield to the condemnation of Athanasius, and the third Sirmian Synod (357) displaced the

---

[72] R. Seeberg, Dogmatik[1], 1924, I, 133 ff. K. Girgensohn, Grundriss der Dogmatik, 1924, 82 f. W. Elert, Die Lehre des Luthertums im Abriss[2], 1924, p. 96 f.   English translation; An Outline of Chr. Doctrine, 1925. C. Stange Dogmatik, 1927, I, 231 ff.
[73] DG, II[3], 162 ff.
[74] De Trin. II, 8. 29.

Nicene Creed by a semi-Arian formula, Athanasianism seemed to be crushed. But the conflict that followed, first between the Semi-Arians and the Arians and then between the Semi-Arians among themselves, resulted in an agreement between the Athanasian and the Semi-Arians, in consequence of which the Church experienced a re-establishment of the Nicene Faith. This was a remarkable event. In addition to this, the Church has witnessed another remarkable development.

In the migration of peoples from the East to the West, about the fourth and fifth centuries, the Ostrogoths, the Visigoths, the Vandals, Burgundians, Suevi, and Longobards accepted Arianism. It was at the time when the old Roman Empire was crumbling. The future of Europe belonged to these tribes. Were they to be Arian on the Trinity? The conversion of the soon powerful Franks to the Catholic Faith in the form of Athanasianism (496) turned the tide. This was another great event in the history of the Church. We have before us the historical fact that all the human elements in this whole development united with the voice of Scripture and the experience of the Church in testifying to the fundamental significance of the doctrine of the Holy Trinity.

Chapter Ten

THE DOCTRINE OF TWO NATURES AND ONE PERSON IN CHRIST

INTRODUCTORY OBSERVATIONS

The superscription which we have chosen is more fitting than that which is often found, namely, the "Christological Controversies." Such a caption as the latter ignores the fact that, in discussing the Trinitarian controversies, we have been dealing constantly with Christological problems. Before going any further, let us endeavor to present the matter in its proper orientation.

1. The *first stage* of real Christological development began with the attempt to solve the Trinitarian problem. The starting-point of the development was this consideration: If Christ is really our Redeemer, then He must be God. But in order to avoid the appearance of polytheism the question had now to be answered: How is the Christ or Logos related to the One God? As the result of much debate and controversy, the doctrine of the Trinity finally emerged: There is One Divine Being in three distinct Persons—Father, Son, and Holy Spirit—all participating in the same Divine Essence and differing only in functions. Thus the first stage decided definitely the *real Deity* of Christ.

2. The *second stage* of the Christological development was reached, when men turned their attention to the *humanity* of Christ. It was necessary and inevitable that they should do so. It was all the more necessary since, as Harnack says, "no single outstanding church-teacher really accepted the humanity in an unqualified way."[1] It is true that the Church, in dealing with Docetism, had learned to insist upon the real humanity of Christ. But much was still to be learned on this subject. In emphasizing the humanity of Christ against the docetic conception the Church had used expressions which referred chiefly to the genuineness of His corporeality. Tertullian and Origen had spent their genius upon this problem; but it was Apollinaris who was to precipitate the issue by propounding seriously and suggestively the Christological problem.

3. The *third stage* of the development came when men, satisfied as to the divinity and humanity of Christ, were compelled to ask the next question: What is the *relation* between the divine and the human in Christ? Tertullian, with fine prophetic intuition, had anticipated the final Christological result when he said: "We see His double state, not intermixed but conjoined in one person Jesus, God and man."[2] But it is our task to trace the development as it proceeded gradually and painfully, sometimes even violently, toward the truth.

Our present study will deal with the second and third stages of the development. Whereas our former treatise (Chapter IX) dealt with Christ's prehistoric existence and divine nature, our immediate interest will be turned in the direction of His *historical* existence as that of the incarnate Son of God, of the connection of the divine nature

---

[1] Harnack, *IV*, 129.
[2] *Adv. Praxeam*, 27.

with the human nature of the Son of Mary, and of the mutual relations of both to on
another. We may well say with Thomasius that this is really *Christology in the strict*
sense of the word.

I. The Problem as Proposed by Apollinaris

Literature: J. DRAESEKE, *Appollinaris von Laodicea, sein Leben und seine Schriften,* Leipzi
1892; in GEBHARDT and HARNACK'S *Texte und Untersuchungen.* H. LIETZMANN, *Apollinaris v*
Laodicea und seine Schule, Tuebingen, 1904. The fragments here given constitute the origin
source for the teaching of Apollinaris described below. C. P. CASPARI, *Alte und Neue Quelle*
1879. G. VOISIN, *L'Apollinarisme,* Louvain, 1901. J. F. BETHUNE-BAKER, *Introduction to ti*
Early History of Christian Doctrine, London, 1903. C. E. RAVEN, *Apollinarianism,* 1923.

The first one to propose and deal with the Christological problem in a serious an
suggestive way was Apollinaris, bishop of Laodicea (d. cir. 390). He was a man of
fine intellectual gifts, a voluminous writer, a capable and enthusiastic defender of th
Nicene Christology, and at one time a bulwark of orthodoxy. For a while at least, h
was the friend of Athanasius. Let us endeavor to grasp briefly his reasoning, mistake
and historical significance.

1. *His teaching:* To Apollinaris the Christological problem was fundamentally
religious one. Like Athanasius, he viewed Christ's soteriolgical work as changing man
sinful mortality into sinless immortality. With the thought of redemption constantl
before him Apollinaris said that Christ is both God and man; if Christ is only man, H
did not save the world; and if only God, He did not save it through suffering. If Chris
was only man, or if only God, He was not a mediator between man and God. Thu
Apollinaris was convinced that Christ, in order to be our Redeemer, must be God an
man. But this conviction raised the important and puzzling question. How can perfec
humanity and perfect divinity be maintained in one person? "If a perfect God wer
united with a perfect man," reflected Apollinaris, "then there would be two (sons), on
by nature the Son of God, and the other by adoption."[3] The personal unity of Chris
must be maintained. Also, if we hold to the perfect humanity of Christ, then Hi
sinlessness is not guaranteed, neither is there any way of establishing harmony betwee
the two wills. Christ would therefore be a peccable and mutable being, unfit for carryin
out the work of redemption. How was the problem to be solved? Arguing from th
trichotomic view as presented by Aristotle and supported by 1 Thess. 5: 23, Apollinari
taught that the humanity of Christ consisted of body (σῶμα) and animal soul (ψυχή)
the mind (νοῦς) being taken by the Logos. For this certain Scriptural passages, suc
as John 1: 14 and Romans 8: 3, were quoted. This meant then that Christ was huma
according to the body only, and that the Son of God had assumed the flesh of Mary'
son and absorbed it into His divinity. Although this exalted the divinity of Christ, i
did so only by denying His real humanity. Apollinaris was paving the way fo
Monophysitism.

2. The *mistakes* of Apollinaris' Christology were clearly seen by the orthodo
fathers of that day, especially by the Cappadocians. *First,* in objecting to the mutilate
humanity of Christ, they pointed out that in such a being the facts of the Gospel histor
cannot be harmonized, e.g. the absence of omniscience, and the struggle of the huma
will with the divine will in Christ (Luke 22: 42); and that Apollinaris would necessaril

[3] Athanasius, *Contra Apollinarium* 1, 2.

e driven to Docetism. Their *second* main objection was that the Apollinarian Christ
s incapable of effecting redemption. Sin has affected not only our bodies and animal
ouls but likewise our minds. Hence a complete and perfect redemption demands a
uman as well as *divine* Redeemer whose body redeems our bodies, whose soul redeems
ur souls, and whose mind redeems our minds. Only by becoming what we are in all
he parts of our being could Christ bring humanity into communion with God. [4] If
nyone imagines a man without a mind, such one is really inconceivable and altogether
nworthy to be saved. For that which cannot be added to, cannot be cured; but that
vhich is united to God, is already saved. If the half of Adam fell, it was the half also
vhich was added to and saved; but if the whole Adam fell, the addition was made to
he whole that was born, and he was wholly saved." [5]

3. What is the *historical significance* of Apollinaris? Looking at the question in a
road and general way, his significance lies in the fact that he proposed for the Church's
onsideration the Christological problem of the two natures in Christ. Loofs says:
Apollinaris set forth the questions here involved with such acumen and with such
ompleteness that the discussion, which lasted for more than three hundred years up to
he ecumenical synod at Constantinople in 680, could add to the debate but few points
f view that were really new. Even the technical terms of the later controversies are
ound, for the most part, with him." [6]

4. Apollinaris, his teachings and his followers, were condemned at Rome in 377,
t Antioch in 378, by the so-called Second Ecumenical Council at Constantinople in 381,
nd by Rome again in 382. The Apollinarians were excluded from the Church; they
ater joined the ranks of the Monophysites. The Decree of Chalcedon (451) was very
xplicit in its rejection of Apollinarianism. It declared that Christ is "true God and
rue man of a reasonable soul and body (ἐκ ψυχῆς λογικῆς καί σώματος)," and that He
s "of the same substance with us according to his manhood." And even in 691 the
Quinisextum Synod remembered to condemn "Apollinaris, leader of wickedness, who
mpiously declared that the Lord did not assume a body endowed with both soul and
mind." [7] C. E. Raven, a thoroughgoing scholar on this subject, says: "Apollinaris can
nly be condemned by those who are prepared to allow that the whole Greek school
rom Justin to Leontius and John of Damascus is similarly at fault, since the divergences
etween them and the heresiarch are merely verbal and superficial." The fact is that
none of the Greek theologians succeeded in seriously establishing the perfect humanity
f Christ, Cyril of Alexander included. [8]

As to aims the Church had completed two stages in its Christological growth. In
he Arian controversy it had established the true divinity of Christ; and in the Apol-
inarian conflict, His true humanity. It was now ready for the third stage, and its
roblem was to discover correct terms with which to express the relation of the divine
nd the human in the God-Man. The solution of the problem was attempted from two
lirections. Two schools—the Antiochean and the Alexandrian—were to devote their
nergies toward answering the question: How are the divinity and the humanity related
n Christ?

[4] Greg. Nyss. *Contra Eunomiuni* II.
[5] Greg. Naz. *Ep. ad Cledon*, 1, 7, cf. *Ep.* 10, 7, 3.
[6] *DG*⁴, p. 266.
[7] Mansi, *Collectio*, XI, 936.
[8] Compare W. Vollrath, *Theologie der Gegenwart in Gross-Britanien*, 1928, p. 145.

Cf. Kurtz, English ed., §52, 2; Schmid-Hauck[4] (82 ff.) offers a large quotation of source Thom.-Bonw., I, 314 ff.; Harnack, Eng. ed., IV, 119 ff.; Seeberg Eng. ed., I, 243 ff.; *DG*, I[2], I[3] 174 ff.; Wiegand I, 80 ff.; Fisher, 148 ff.

II. THE PROBLEM AS DEBATED BY THE SCHOOLS OF ANTIOCH AND ALEXANDRIA

KURTZ (*Church History*) describes the situation fittingly when he says: "Each o these two schools represented one side of the truth of the Church's doctrine; in th union of the two sides the Church proclaimed the full truth. On the other hand th two schools proceeded more and more one-sidedly to emphasize each its own side c the truth, and so tended toward positive error. Thus arose two opposite errors, th separating of the natures and the confusing of the natures, which the Church rejecte one after the other, and proclaimed the truth that lay at the root of both." [9]

A. THE ANTIOCHEAN SCHOOL

Literature: On *Theodore of Mopsuestia*, see his commentaries and dogmatic fragments i MIGNE (*MSG*, 66, 1-1020); cf. *Theod. Mops.* in *epistolas b. Pauli commentarii*, ed. H. B. SWETE 2 t. Cambridge, 1880-82; cf. SWETE in *Dict. of Chr. Biogr.*, IV, 934 ff.; HARNACK, *History o Dogma* (English edition), Vols. III and IV; cf. his *Grundriss*, 6th edition; also his article on th *Antiochenische Schule* in *PRE*, I, 1896; LOOFS, *DG*[4], SEEBERG, *DG* II[3], 168 ff., 242 ff.; FISHEI WIEGAND. J. F. BETHUNE-BAKER, *Intr.;* DORNER, *Doctrine of the Person of Christ*, II; LOOF§ article on *Theodor von Mopsuestia* in *PRE*, XIX, 1907; SWETE, article on *Theodore of Mopsuesti* in the *Dictionary of Christ. Biogr.;* KUEHN, *Theodor von Mops. und Jun. Africanus als Exegeten* 1880; the article on *Theodore of Mopsuestia and Modern Thought* in the *Church Quarterly Review* 1875; F A. SPECHT, *Der exeget. Standpunkt des Theodor von Mops., und Theodoret*, 1871; th articles on *Theodoret* in *Dictionary of Christian Biography* and in *PRE; N.* GLUBOKOWSKI, *De selige Theodoret, Bischof von Cyrus, sein Leben und seine schriftstellerische Taetigkeit*, 2 vols Moscow, 1890. Cf. H. RINN, pp. 144-147.

The Antiochean School (cf. Loofs, p. 277) in its later history was represented firs by Diodorus of Tarsus (d. 378), but chiefly by Theodore of Mopsuestia (d. 428), an subsequently by Theodoret (d. 457). This school was marked by an aversion to meta physical speculation and to the deeper mystical element in Christianity. It rejected th allegorical exegesis and established a grammatico-historical method of Scriptural inter pretation. The men whom we have named were diligent exegetes who studied th life of the historical Christ, especially His human and moral development. They wer thus naturally opposed to Docetism and Apollinarianism. Their chief emphasis wa upon the humanity of Christ without intending in the least to deny His divinity. [10]

1. Christ is indeed possessed of a *perfect humanity* which consists of a body and . reasonable soul. He is also endowed with a free will or "power of self-determination. But the humanity which Christ assumed was subject to mutability, physical weakness and sinful affections. By the use of His human will Christ overcame the tempter, sir and all fleshly lusts, and so arrived at perfection. The process of divinization which took place in the humanity of Christ has a saving and sanctifying effect on the humar race which is connected with Him. Kurtz describes it thus: "The historical developmen of the God-Man is with him (i.e. Theodore of Mopsuestia) the type and pattern o

---

[9] Eng. ed., §52, 2.
[10] Cf. Kurtz, 47, 9. Seeberg, *DG*, II[3], 186 ff.; cf. Thom.-Bonwetsch, I, 331; Harnack, Eng. ed., IV, 163 Loofs, 279 ff.

he historical redemption of mankind. Christ assumed a complete human nature with all its sinful affections and tendencies; but He fought these down and raised His human nature by constant conflict and victory to that absolute perfection to which by the same way He leads us through the communication of His Spirit."

2. But, according to the Antiocheans, *what is the relation between the divine and the human in Christ?* These writers were very careful to exclude any confusion of the two natures. Since Christ is both divine and human, it follows that the divinity has its residence ('ενοίκησις) in the humanity. The *Logos* resides in the man Jesus as in a shrine; this indwelling is also compared to Christ's indwelling in the hearts of believers. The relation is therefore a connection or conjunction (συνάφεια). This does not constitute a union according to essence, nor according to energy, but rather a union according to grace. The *Logos* entered into an intimate relation with the humanity of Jesus because He was pleased with it. It is therefore a moral union. Knowing in advance what would become of the man Jesus, the Logos entered into fellowship with His person in the womb of the Virgin Mary. As the man Jesus succeeded more and more in the struggle with sin and became sanctified by the Spirit of God, the fellowship grew closer and closer; it finally reached its highest degree of intimacy in the resurrection and ascension of Jesus.

3. How, then, are these two natures to be brought into the unity of one person? Here is the difficulty, and it is here that the Antiochean theology has been condemned. *One is given the impression that there are two persons.* Theodore of Mopsuestia realized this, and he labored to avoid such an accusation. He said: "The Son is rightly confessed to be one, since the distinction ought of necessity to remain, and the unity of person ought to be guarded without interruption." [11] Nevertheless, this unity meant no more than the harmonious adjustment of the will of Jesus to the will of the *Logos,* so that Jesus became the perfect organ of the willing and acting *Logos.* Thus Theodore seemingly secured the unity of the two natures. "When we distinguish the natures," he observed, "we maintain that the nature of God the Word is perfect; perfect, too, the person—for it is not possible to speak of a distinct existence which is impersonal; perfect, too, the nature of the man, and the person likewise. But when we look to the conjunction of the two, then we say that there is one person." [12] He illustrated the thought by the words of Christ concerning a nuptial pair: "They are no longer twain, but one flesh" (Matt. 19: 6). To summarize, the reasoning of the Antiocheans was simply this: If we fasten our attention exclusively upon the two natures, both of which are personal, we observe two persons; but if we keep in mind the perfect and harmonious union of will into which they have entered, then we have only one person.

This was the argumentation of the Antiocheans. But the observation of Loofs (p. 380 ff.) will be correct that they did not succeed in really meeting the objection of their opponents, the Cappadocians and later Cyril of Alexandria. The Antiocheans expressed the relation between the two natures in Christ by the word συνάφεια. The union, then, is not a genuine personal union. While Theodore of Mopsuestia used the phrase "two natures and one person," still the term "person," meant no more than the appearance of one being—a πρόσωπον under which the *Logos* and the man Jesus pursued their common existence. In this view there is no room for a real incarnation of the

---

[11] *De Incarnatione,* XV, 1.
[12] *De Inc.,* VIII.

Logos in the sense of John 1: 14, *"The word was made flesh."* Theodore said that this verse must not be taken literally; the *Logos* simply adopted the flesh of Jesus and made it His habitation. The judgment of the Church has been that the separation between the two natures as insisted upon by the Antiocheans is too radical. The human nature developed independently of the divinity; therefore a real participation of the divinity in the experience of the human life is not admissible. Contrary to the intention of the Antiocheans, this destroyed the real union of the two natures in the person of Christ Mary is therefore only ἀνθρωποτόκος in the literal sense; only by metaphor may she be called theotokos (Θεοτόκος) or Mother of God, as the worshipers of the Virgin had begun to style her. [13]

B. THE ALEXANDRIAN SCHOOL

Literature: The Church Histories. HARNACK, III and IV. LOOFS, *DG*[4]. SEEBERG, *DG*, II[8] 221 ff., 168 ff., 210 ff. DORNER, *Doctrine of the Person of Christ.* J. F. BETHUNE-BAKER, *Introduction to the Early History of Christian Doctrine*, 1903. H. WEISS, *Die Kappadocier als Exegeten*, 1872. KRUEGER, *Basilius von Caesarea*, in *PRE*, II, 1897. ULLMANN, *Gregor von Naz.*, 1867. LOOFS, *Gregor v. Naz.* in *PRE*, VII, 1899; also *Gregor v. Nyssa* in *PRE*. BARDENHEWER, *Gregory Nazianzus and Gregory of Nyssa*, in *Patrologie*, 1901.

The Alexandrians moved in a different direction from the Antiocheans. The starting-point of this school was the divine side of Christ's Person and the incarnation of the *Logos*, as it had been taught by the orthodox teachers of the Church, and given a doctrinal expression particularly by Athanasius in his controversy with Arianism.

1. The Teachings of Athanasius. [14] Athanasius had insisted upon a complete humanity—one that remains essentially different from the divinity of the *Logos*. The states of humiliation and exaltation affected only the humanity of Christ. The *Logos* really became "flesh" (John 1: 14) by taking upon Himself flesh and soul from the Virgin Mary and making them His own. As a result, the two natures became one person in an abiding union of divinity and humanity. By reason of the incarnation the real subject of this union is the *Logos* who has the flesh as His organ of revelation and work. With this union in mind Athanasius went on to teach that the divinity and humanity enjoyed equal participation in the works of Christ during His earthly pilgrimage, since they were the works of one subject. The divinity had a part even in the sufferings of Christ, though with the restriction that the divinity did not suffer in itself but in the flesh. The suffering of the body was transferred by the *Logos* to Himself. He suffered the weakness of the flesh, because the flesh was His own body. Mary is also spoken of as "Theotokos."

Note 1: In the interests of chronological precision it should be remembered that Athanasius wrote before the time of the Antiocheans. But we have dealt with his position at this point, because the Alexandrian theologians started with his Christology. It should also be kept in mind that Athanasius did not deal intentionally with the person and natures of Christ. In the West Tertullian had spoken of "two substances and one person," and this formula was destined to aid Eastern speculation in solving the problem.

Note 2: Harnack makes the criticism that Athanasius did not succeed in escaping Docetism in every form. His conception of the divinity of Christ forced him to special interpretations of the historic Christ and His history. The subject of his Redeemer is the God who, it is true, became man, but who in reality only accommodated Himself to the human nature, its limitations

---

[13] Cf. Thomasius-Bonwetsch, I, 321 ff.; cf. Loofs, 280 f.

[14] Our special reference here is to the letter of Athanasius to bishop Epictet of Corinth, written about 372. See *MSG*, 26, 1049-69. (Eng. in *APNF*, 2d series, IV, 570 ff.)

nd sufferings. But whenever Athanasius dealt seriously with Christ's humanity, then the history of the Redeemer was divided into what God and what man had done.[15] Let us remark right here that Docetism has always been the charge made against the theologians who have followed a course different from that of the Antiochean School.

2. After the time of Athanasius the system of the Alexandrian School received its first contributions from the Cappadocians, especially from the two Gregories. Completed and rounded out by Cyril of Alexandria (d. 444), it betrayed its heretical tendency in Eutyches and Monophysitism. The emphasis of this school was upon the union of the two natures and upon the person, as the means of safeguarding the validity of Christ's redemption.

Gregory Nazianzus (d. 390) took the position that in the incarnation the humanity of Christ had, by a process of mixing or commingling (*synkrasis, anakrasis, mixis*), entirely disappeared in the divinity. He compared the divinity and humanity of Christ to the sun and stars; the sun shines with such brilliancy as practically to extinguish the stars. *Gregory of Nyssa* (d. cir. 400) also said that Christ's passive body had mixed with His active divinity, that the human had been transformed into the divine. He likened the divine and human to the sea and a drop of vinegar which is completely enveloped and absorbed in the oceanic vastness. These theologians founded their doctrine of incarnation on the principle: *Natura humana capax divinae*. When the objection was made that the perfect God cannot unite with an imperfect humanity, they responded with the argument that the mutable and peccable body was in itself perfectly dignified, since birth, growth, and nourishment of the body are only processes of life established by the Creator Himself; sin and death did not touch Him. So strongly did these theologians emphasize the union of both natures, that the two natures actually seemed to disappear. They seemed to continue only *in abstracto*. Yet Gregory Nazianzus spoke of the body of Christ as continuing its life in heaven. And Gregory of Nyssa spoke of the *idiomata* of both natures and of a free-will in Christ's humanity which was guided and determined by the will of His divinity. It is evident that the great Cappadocians had not yet arrived at a consolidated theory or system with regard to the two natures and one person in Christ. This came with Cyril of Alexandria.

III. The Problem as Debated by Nestorius and Cyril

A. Nestorius

Literature: J. D. MANSI, *Sacr. Concil. Socrates Scholasticus, Historia Ecclesiastica,* VII, in *Nicene and Post-Nicene Fathers,* Oxford, 1891. C. F. HEFELE, *History of the Councils of the Church,* 1894-96. Edinburgh translation. LOOFS, *Nestoriana, Halle,* 1905 (which contains the fragments of the works of Nestorius). See his article on *Nestorius* in *PRE* (cf. *NSH*); also his book *Nestorius and His Place in the History of Christian Doctrine,* Cambridge, 1914. L. FENDT, *Die Christologie des Nestorius,* 1910. G. T. STOKES, article on *Nestorianism* in the *Dictionary of Christian Biography.* J. F. BETHUNE-BAKER, *Nestorius and His Teaching,* Cambridge, 1908. Also the Histories of Dogma. C. H. PESCH, *Nestorius als Irrlehrer,* 1921.

Nestorius, who became the Patriarch of Constantinople in 428, was of the School of Antioch. It is always interesting to see how scholars of differing type have judged a historic personage. Kurtz describes him as "an eloquent and pious man, but hasty and imprudent, with little knowledge of the world and human nature, and immoderately

---

[15] See Harnack's final judgment of Athanasius, in his *Grundriss*[6].

severe with heretics." [16]   Harnack calls him "naively self-conceited, storming and short-sighted, but sincere and not without noble traits." [17]   Seeberg, in the 3d German edition of his *Dogmengeschichte*, characterizes him as a man of *pedantry*, equipped with the dogmatic fanaticism that is usually peculiar to the later generations of schools." [18]

In his zeal for orthodoxy Nestorius not only persecuted the Arians, Apollinarians, Novatians, and Macedonians, but he also started a crusade against those who spoke of Mary as "mother of God."   "To speak correctly," said Nestorius, "Mary is only the mother of Christ."   His position, which was perfectly correct, was that a human mother could not give the divine nature to the *Logos,* and hence the divinity of Christ had not originated from Mary.   But it does not follow from this, as Luther pointed out,[19] that it is wrong to say that God was born of Mary.   Luther argues that it would be the same as if we said: This woman has given birth to a child; the child's soul, however, is not of her nature but of God, and therefore she cannot be the mother of the child.   But says Luther, a woman is the mother of the entire child including the soul, although the soul has in a special sense its origin from God.   For this reason, Luther continues, we are justified in saying that Mary is the Mother of God.   Because of the position from which Nestorius argued, Luther scolds him as "a proud, coarse, and unlearned man."

There was nevertheless a deeper reason why Nestorius was opposed to the word "Theotokos."   As pupil of the Antiochean School, he objected to the transference of the *idiomata* of Christ's human nature to the *Logos.*   Luther saw this clearly, and so continued his discussion along that line.

Nestorius was condemned at the Third Ecumenical Council in Ephesus (431) for dividing the one Christ into two persons or two *hypostases.*   Luther defends the accused against this charge.   On the basis of the historical material that was accessible to him he insists that Nestorius meant to teach, and did teach, a Christ of two natures in one person only.   This cannot be denied. [20]   But what was the foundation for this unjust charge?   As a pupil of the Antiochean School which emphasized the reality of the two natures in Christ, Nestorius defined the relation of the one to the other as a *synapheia,* a mere connection or conjunction. His teaching was like that of Theodore of Mopsuestia. Beginning with the conception in the womb of Mary, the *Logos* enters into a relation with a complete man; this relation becomes so intimate that it results in one person. Yet the *Logos* only resides in the man Jesus as in a shrine.   It is not a physical or an essential union.   Each nature has its own properties and we must ever distinguish between the created and the uncreated.   Only the human nature can be born, suffer, and die, be raised from the dead, etc.; and only the divine nature is eternal, omnipotent, omniscient, omnipresent.   In thinking of Christ there must be a constant distinction between the two natures.   This, then, made Christ appear to be not a real God-Man, but a *God-bearing man.*

True to the divisive character of Antiochean Christology, Nestorius rejected the *communicatio idiomatum.*   His real reason in rejecting the *Theotokos* was this: It is impossible for the *Logos* to be born.   Nothing human must be predicated of the divinity. But of the *heresy* of Nestorius we can say nothing more than that he taught the theology

---

[16] §52, 3; cf. Loofs in *PRE,* XIII. 737, 53 ff.
[17] *Grundriss*[6], p. 250.
[18] II, 214.
[19] See Luther's writing of 1539 *Von den Concilien und Kirchen,* Erl. ed., XXV, 302 ff.; W. ed. 50, 509 ff.
[20] Cf. Loofs in *PRE,* XIII, 741, 34-44; Seeberg, II, 217 ff.

of the Antiochean School. It was a Christology that could hardly avoid an emphasis upon the humanity of Christ, that endangered the unity of His person.

We shall now try to show that the Alexandrian Christology, as systematized by Cyril, was in line with the development of orthodoxy in the Church, and that it did indeed help to establish important elements of truth in the Christological dogma as it was finally crystallized in the Creed of Chalcedon and in Part Two of the Symbolum Quicunque. (Cf. pp. 121 f.)

B. CYRIL OF ALEXANDRIA

Literature: The works of Cyril, in Greek, are found in MIGNE (*MSG*), 68-77. For the Nestorian controversy our chief interest is in the following among his many writings: (1) The *second* of his three Letters addressed to Nestorius (*MSG* 77, 44-49); (2) *the Five Books against Nestorius* addressed to Bishop Celestine I in Rome (76, 9-248); (3) *three doctrinal letters de recte fidei* addressed to Theodosius II and the ladies of his court (76, 1133-1420); (4) the *third* of the above mentioned letters to Nestorius, *ep. synodica*, to which there are attached the twelve Anathemas against Nestorius and the defense of these (315-452).

In the way of discussion: A. BEHRMANN, *Die Christologie des h. Cyrillus v. Alex.*, 1902; G. KRUEGER in *PRE*, IV, 377 ff. See the Church Histories and Histories of Doctrine.

1. *Cyril of Alexandria* (d. 444) was unrelentingly opposed to Nestorius whose heresy consisted in teaching the Christology of the Antiocheans, especially that of Theodore of Mopsuestia which, up to the appearance of Cyril, had had a legitimate place in the Church's endeavors to solve the Christological problem.

It is true that there were certain personal elements which were involved in the conflict between Cyril and Nestorius. The charge is that Bishop Cyril was a man who used questionable means to establish and to further the cause for which he stood. Kurtz refers to him as a *tricky prelate* (*ein raenkevoller Kirchenfuerst*). Even Luther expresses his disgust with the Third Ecumenical Council at Ephesus (431) at which Cyril succeeded in bringing about the condemnation of Nestorius (see *ante*). Loofs remarks that the modern historian, with his wider knowledge of the older sources to which Luther had no access, is compelled to render even a more severe verdict.[21] Ecclesiastical rivalry between the two Sees of Alexandria and Constantinople played an important part in the whole controversy. The emperor, who was favorably disposed to Nestorius, had intended to investigate charges against Cyril at a council. But Cyril turned the tables, preferring charges against the patriarch of Constantinople and using violence. He had the good fortune, in connection with his church politics, to fight in the interests of piety, like Athanasius in his day. "Cyril offered," says Loofs, "a further development of the traditional line, represented by the Apologists, by Clement and Origen, by Methodius, Athanasius and Gregory Nazianzus, which was running parallel with the trend of popular piety" (292). Fisher calls him "sincere in his opinions," and Thomasius remarks that Nestorius had rejected the *Theotokos* so emphatically that it was generally felt the attack was directed against the Christological conception which was connected with that term.[22] Harnack remarks: While Cyril was offensive in the methods he used, yet he was honest in the principles for which he stood. It must not be overlooked that he wrote his work *De Incarnatione Unigenite* before the outbreak of the Nestorian controversy.[23]

---

[21] *PRE*, XIII, 736, 60; see p. 741 ff.
[22] I, 337.
[23] Cf. *MSG*, 75, 1189-1253.

2. *The teaching of Cyril* is now to be presented. Cyril did not start with the historic Christ, but, like Athanasius and Gregory Nazianzus, with God the *Logos* who became man. This *Logos-God,* who is unchangeable, assumed the impersonal human nature including the mind, without Himself sacrificing anything to the same. *In Deum non cadit mutatio.* In this union the *Logos* became the subject. The religious interest in these assertions of Cyril was that the activity of the Redeemer had to be the work of the unalterable God Himself; otherwise the death of Christ could not have effected our redemption. By thus employing the conception of the two natures, the human which is impersonal and the divine as the subject of both, Cyril avoided using the word *mixture* which the Cappadocians had used.

With Cyril the emphasis is upon the personal union of the two natures of the God Man. Before the incarnation, abstractly, there were two natures, but after the incarnation there was only one, a divine-human nature. Cyril was wont to say that Christ was *one from two natures* (ἐκ δύο φύσεων εἷς). The position of Cyril is described in the following statement: Only before the union and *in abstracto* can we speak of two natures; after the incarnation and *in concreto* we can speak only of one divine-human nature. In this respect the Monophysites have claimed Cyril.

On this basis a *communicatio idiomatum* is taught. While the *Logos* Himself is incapable of suffering, yet He suffered in the human nature which became His own in the incarnation. Because of this doctrine Nestorius accused Cyril of dragging the divinity into the sphere of the finite.

Such was the Christological system of Cyril. There are two natures and yet a unity. The one is not changed into the other, nor are the two confused with each other. Neither is there an adjoining of one nature to the other (συνάφεια), nor an indwelling of the divinity in the humanity (ἐνοίκησις). Each nature preserves its attributes. Cyril's system really offered no reasonable solution of the problem. But did Cyril intend a real solution of the problem? The fact is, he simply stated the *mystery of godliness* (I Tim. 3: 6) in harmony with the orthodox traditions of the Church as expressed by Athanasius and the Cappadocians, avoiding at the same time the mistakes of his predecessors, and completing the system.

IV. EUTYCHEANISM, MONOPHYSITISM, AND THE FINAL SETTLEMENT IN THE CREED OF CHALCEDON

Literature: HEFELE, *History of the Councils,* German, II, 320 ff., 564 ff.; Eng. III, 186 ff. Cf. MANSI, *Acta concil.,* VI-XI. Cf. DORNER, *Person of Christ* (transl. from German, Edinburgh), II, 1-11; 150-93. SCHAFF, *Ch. History* III; *Creeds,* vol. I. LOOFS, *PRE,* V, 635 ff. KRUEGER, *PRE,* XIII, 372 ff., 401 ff. KUH, *Christologie Leos,* I (1894). HASSE, *Patriarch Dioskur* (1909). HARNACK, German, 4th ed., II, 368 ff., 400 ff. LOOFS, 297 f. SEEBERG, *DG,* II³, 242 ff., 267 ff. and his *Abriss,* 1927, p. 57 ff. FISHER, 155.

1. *The Situation:* In the Nestorian controversy both Cyril and Nestorius had been deposed from office through the decision of Emperor Theodosius II (431). But in 433 a truce between the Antiochean and Alexandrian Schools was proclaimed by means of a confession which harbored nothing antagonistic to the opinions of the Antiocheans. This confession was prepared by the Antiocheans and signed by Cyril. Thus Cyril was able to retain his office and influential position in the Church. The confession represented concessions on both sides, and hence the union of the two schools was not based on any doctrinal settlement of the Christological problem. Such a situation was keenly

It, even among the adherents of Cyril. Cyril died in 444, and was succeeded by
ioscurus who continued the policy of his predecessor to make the Alexandrian See the
ominating institution in the Church of the East. He persecuted the Antiocheans, labored
do away with the *two natures,* and favored creeds which had an Apollinarian bias.

2. At this juncture *Eutyches,* the abbot of a monastery near Constantinople and an
lherent of the new Alexandrian School, came forward with an extreme opinion in
hich we can observe the heretical element which may easily emerge when the Alex-
adrian Christology is pressed too far. He taught that after the incarnation Christ had
aly one nature. Eutyches said: "Christ is *of* two natures, but not *in* two natures," thus
ying undue emphasis on what Cyril had said: "Of two natures Christ is one." He
so said that the body of Christ, which is the body of God, is not consubstantial with
ar own.

Eutyches was condemned and deposed by a synod at Constantinople over which
ae Patriarch Flavin was presiding (448). Leo I of Rome sided with Flavian, and in
famous letter (usually called Leo's *Tome*), addressed to Flavian in the summer of 449,
e asserted the doctrine of one person and two natures in Christ. In August of the
ame year the emperor convoked an ecumenical council at Ephesus which was presided
ver by Dioscurus. This council in a high-handed manner undertook to purify the
hurch of the leaven of Antiochean Christology. The clarifying utterance of Leo was
ot permitted to be read. On the contrary, the doctrine of the two natures was con-
emned, Eutyches was restored, and Flavian, Eusebius, and Theodoret were deposed.

3. Leo branded the convention with the name *Robber Synod,* condemned its resolu-
ions, and demanded a new council under the influence of the Roman See. In the
aeantime he secured for his cause the influence of Pulcheria, the emperor's sister. The
mperor died in 450 and was succeeded by Pulcheria and her husband Marcianus. Both
vere hostile to Dioscurus of Alexandria and in sympathy with Leo. A new Ecumenical
Council was called in 451 to meet in Nicea; but to suit imperial pleasure the place of
aeeting was changed to Chalcedon. At this council Dioscurus was deposed, the doctrine
f the two persons and its defenders were anathematized, and Theodoret was reinstated.
yril was declared to have been orthodox; and on the basis of Leo's *Tome,* Christological
efinitions were formulated which have always been regarded by the Latin, Greek, and
onservative Protestant Churches as the final solution of the Christological problem. It
vill be of interest to read the final verdict as pronounced by the Creed of Chalcedon:

"We, then, following the holy Fathers, all with one consent, teach men to confess one and
ae same Son, our Lord Jesus Christ, the same perfect in Godhead and also perfect in manhood;
uly God and truly man, of a reasonable soul and body; consubstantial with us according to the
aanhood; in all things like unto us, without sin; begotten before all ages of the Father according
o the Godhead, and in these latter days, for us and for our salvation, born of the Virgin Mary,
ae Mother of God, according to the manhood; one and the same Christ, Son, Lord, Only-begotten,
a two natures, inconfusedly, unchangeably, indivisibly, inseparably, the distinction of natures being
y no means taken away by the union, but rather the property of each nature being preserved, and
oncurring in one person and one subsistence, not parted or divided into two persons but one
ad the same Son and Only-begotten, God the Word, the Lord Jesus Christ; as the prophets from
ae beginning have declared concerning Him, and the Lord Jesus Christ Himself has taught us,
ad the creed of the Holy Fathers has handed down to us." [24]

The leading ideas of this Chalcedonian Christology were embodied in the second
art of the Athanasian Creed.

---

[24] Hahn (3) §146, p. 166 f.; Schaff, *Creeds* I, 29 ff. Neve, *Introduction to the Symbolical Books of the
atheran Church* 2d. ed., 76 ff.: Loofs on *Athanasian Creed* in *PRE,* II, 177 ff. (cf. *NSH*).

4. The Settlement Unsuccessfully Challenged by Monophysitism and Monotheletism

a. Monophysitism. The so-called *Monophysite struggles* began immediately after the Council of Chalcedon. Those who opposed the Creed of Chalcedon with its recognition of the two natures, were now called Monophysites. A great hubbub took place chiefly in Egypt and Palestine. The whole Church was in a feverish excitement. (For details consult Church Histories.) Monophysite sects were formed in Egypt, Syria, and Armenia; they exist to this day, and are known as the Coptic, Jacobite, Ethiopian, and Armenian Churches. Strongly opposed to the two natures in Christ, they sought to defend their position by rejecting Eutyches and by appealing to the teaching of Cyril. As to positive teaching they soon split among themselves. One class (Severians) although opposed to a human nature in Christ as contrasted with a divine nature, held that the body of Christ was corruptible before the resurrection. Another class (Julianists) declared the opposite to be true. Still another faction was willing to accept the Chalcedonian Creed with a Cyrillian interpretation. None of these views succeeded in bringing about any change in the Chalcedonian settlement.

b. Monotheletism. A second attempt to change the decision of Chalcedon was made in the *Monothelite controversy* (633-680). Emperor Heraclius, persuaded by certain Monophysite bishops of Armenia and Syria, endeavored to reconcile the contending parties by saying that "Christ accomplished His work of redemption by the exercise of one divine human will." [25] The one Christ works the human and the divine things through a divine human energy. Some of the Catholic bishops saw nothing unorthodox in this view, and the movement received the support of Patriarch Sergius of Constantinople and even of Bishop Honorius of Rome. But opposition arose on the orthodox side. The monk Sophronius, who was soon to become Patriarch of Jerusalem, raised his voice in protest, and a new controversy arose. Theodore I and his successor rejected the Monothelite doctrine which Emperor Heraclius had espoused and promulgated, and the West severed church-fellowship with the East. Finally, at the Sixth Ecumenical Council at Constantinople (680), it was decided on the basis of a letter by Bishop Agatho of Rome that Christ has "two natural wills or willings . . . not contrary one to the other. . . . but His human will follows, not as resisting or reluctant, but rather as subject to His divine and omnipotent will."

We have followed, in a cursory manner, the course of the Christological development. In conclusion, let us repeat the conciliar decisions by which the Christological problem was finally solved and crystallized into a dogma: Nicea, 325—Christ is Divine; Constantinople, 381—Christ is human; Ephesus, 431—Christ is one in Person; Chalcedon, 451—Christ is two in nature.

Failing to see the religious interest in this controversy this whole story may seem to some a reflection of mental perversion. But it is upon this Christology that a very large part of deep Christian thought in the liturgies and the hymns and in the devotional language of the Church is founded. The Church wants a Christ of whom the believer can say as does Paul in Ephesians 2: 14 ff.: (For he is our peace, . . . and to them that were nigh. For through him we both have access by one Spirit unto the Father.) There are features in this Christology which sound like a theory, but back of it is a fundamental truth of Scripture and of Christian experience.

---

[25] Mansi XI. 564-568.

Chapter Eleven

THE PROBLEMS OF ANTHROPOLOGY AND SOTERIOLOGY

I. The East on Man's Original State, the Fall and Its Consequences

Literature: The Histories of Doctrine up to the last edition have their usual value. Special attention for sections I and II of the following investigation is called to HAGENBACH, *History of Doctrine,* English ed. THOMASIUS-BONWETSCH also offers important contributions. In the *PRE* we have the following articles: CREMER on the *Image of God in Man,* V, 113 ff.; also KIRN, article on *Original Righteousness in Man,* VI, 546 ff.; also KIRN, article on *Sin,* XIX, 138 ff. The special sources will appear in the following investigation. Cf. H. RINN, pp. 167 ff.

Introductory Remarks: The Eastern thought was not the leading agent in discussing the problems of sin and grace; this was a sphere of Christian thought, in which the practical mind of the West had the chief interest. The dominating interest of the East, so much inclined to speculation, was in the doctrine of the Trinity and in Christology.[1]

The condition of man's will, however, in its relation to saving grace (anthropology), did become a matter of interest in the East because of a threefold opposition: There was (1) *Stoicism* which reduced free will to a minimum by teaching that man is in the hands of fate. (2) There was *Gnosticism* with its teaching that men are by nature either spiritual, physical, or carnally minded, being inexorably doomed to a life of sin and excluded from the capability of regeneration; also with the teaching that regeneration is not an ethical but a natural process. There was (3) *Manichaeism* with its doctrine that man had come into being as the creature of the devil, and, therefore, was evil from the beginning.

Against these influences the Greek fathers emphasized strongly man's freedom and his accountability. Stimulated by this interest in the freedom of the will in spiritual things there were a number of matters belonging to the field of anthropology that came up for occasional discussion. As such we mention two subjects: (1) the original state of man, and (2) the fall and its consequences. We shall, however, not take space for a full review of the discussion along these lines, but we want to call the student's attention to helpful literature on the matter. The first mentioned subject, the original state of man, included (a) the problem of *the image of God in the first man* (reason and free will, moral perfection, immortality of the soul). As to the literature, see the footnote below.[2] And closely connected was (b) the exact conception of the East concerning *man's Original Righteousness.* On this interesting subject pertaining to the later discussion by the Reformers of the material contents of the image (knowledge, righteousness, holiness, Eph. 4: 24, Col. 3: 10) we refer in the footnote[3] to an informing literature.

---

[1] Thomasius-Bonwetsch I, 455, 461 f.; Schaff, *Creeds,* I, 25.

[2] Hagenbach, in his History of Dogma (English), has interesting passages on this subject: I, 207, 214 ff., 21-29; Thomasius-Bonwetsch, I, 455, 465; Cremer on the *Image* in PRE, V, p. 114, (lines 30-34), 115, 2-21; F. Delitzsch, *System of Biblical Psychology*[2] (English), p. 79 ff.; Seeberg, English ed., I, 122, 316.

[3] Besides the above mentioned article by Cremer on the *Image* we mention his article on *Original Righteousness* in PRE, VI, 546 ff. Cf. Hagenbach, I, 229; Thomasius I, 461.

The second of the above mentioned subjects, *The fall and its consequences,* h
reference to the effect of the fall on the will. Man's knowledge (reason) was darkene
his judgment on right and wrong became increasingly uncertain. He came under th
dominion of sensuality, and his will became weakened, a condition which became gener
in the human race. The thought of the Greek fathers on original sin is well describe
by two older historians in the field of the History of Doctrine.

Hagenbach remarks: "Opinions were not as yet fully developed concerning the moral depravi
of each individual, and the sin of the race in general was considered as the effect of the first si
They were so much disposed to look upon sin as the free act of man's will that they could hard
conceive of it as simply an hereditary tendency transmitted from one to another. The sin of eve
individual, as found in experience, had its type in the sin of Adam, and consequently appeared
be a repetition, rather than a necessary consequence of the first sin. In order to explain th
mysterious power which drives man to evil, they had recourse to the influence of the demons, stror
but not absolutely compulsory rather than to a total bondage of the will as the result of origin
sin" (I, 231). While the Greek fathers admitted the universality of sin and even emphasize
the first sin as an act in which the whole race had participated, yet they would not admit that th
sinful condition was necessarily universal among men, for fear that such an admission might detra
from the guiltiness of sin.

The other historian to be quoted is Kurtz. He says: "Opposition to Gnosticism and Manichaeis
led the elder fathers to emphasize as strongly as possible the moral freedom of men, and induce
them to deny inborn sinfulness as well as the doctrine that sin was imprinted in men in creatio
and to account for man's present condition by bad training, evil example, the agency of ev
spirits, etc." [4]

But Irenaeus, as we have seen, expressed his belief in original sin, and Grego
of Nyssa also made strong statements in this direction. Still the consequences of
consistent doctrine of original sin were not drawn. On the contrary, in men lik
Athanasius, Gregory of Nyssa, Clement of Alexandria, Cyril of Alexandria, etc., we me
with expressions which plainly imply a rejection of original sin. Thomasius quote
Clement of Alexandria as saying: "We baptize the children, although they have no sin

II. WHAT KEPT THE EAST FROM LEADING IN THE PROBLEMS OF SOTERIOLOGY?

1. The East was not especially interested in the discussion of divine grace as relate
to man's freedom. Grace, i.e. redemption through Christ, liberation from the old sinf
life, and regeneration by baptism, was such a powerful factor in the consciousness
the early Christians that a dogmatic reflection was not especially invited. On this poi
all were in general accord. As Christians they felt the powers of the Spirit so pulsatin
within them and furnishing them the strength for their ethical tasks that there seeme
to be no need for dogma-making along that line.[5]

2. A further explanation of why it was the West and not the East which cultivate
the field of soteriology for future doctrinal decisions must be seen in a characterist
difference between the Greek and Latin parts of the Church, a difference which can k
traced back as far as the Greek Apologists. The Greek fathers, unlike the practical Latin
were attracted by speculative subjects, and from the time of the Apologists they regarde
Christianity chiefly as a revelation of truth. It was looked upon as a higher philosop
or as absolute truth when compared with the relative truth found in Judaism ar
heathenism.

[4] *Church Hist'y,* Engl., §53, 1.
[5] Thom.-Bonw., I, 461 f.; cf. 455.

3. Furthermore, with the Hellenic idea of the *Logos* there came in, as Thomasius
points out (I, 462), a certain accommodation to the Hellenic conception of reason and
freedom as possessed by the natural man. This was not without influence upon the
soteriological views of Greek Christianity according to which man was regarded as
possessing the power to act comformably to the light of reason. Yet the Greeks, particularly the Anti-Gnostic fathers, were not thoroughgoing Pelagians. They admitted that
man's will had been weakened by the fall and that the assistance of grace was needed
(Irenaeus, Clement and Cyril of Alexandria, Origen, Athanasius, Basil, the Gregories,
Cyril of Jerusalem). According to them freedom and grace stand side by side in
producing the acts of goodness; or, more correctly, man's free will begins and grace
follows in a supplementary manner (Semi-Pelagianism). Faith is man's own work. A
real regeneration as a creative act of divine grace, including a renewal of man's will,
was not and could not be taught in consistency with these views. There were, of course,
individual voices which spoke in other tones. Origen sometimes spoke of a kind of
prevenient grace, and the great Cappadocians expressed themselves occasionally with
biblical correctness. But Chrysostom again employed Semi-Pelagian terms; "it depends
upon us and upon God," he said. "We must first choose the good, then God will do His
part. God does not anticipate our will that our freedom may not suffer; but after we
have chosen, He grants much help." [6]

III. The Teaching of the West

As has been remarked repeatedly, the Latin fathers were different from the Eastern.
The more practical questions and not the speculative problems, occupied the chief place
in their interest. While the Latin Church also discussed and advocated human freedom,
its emphasis was upon the facts of sin and grace. The difference in tendencies was of
latent nature; in the main the two parts of the Church were in agreement with each
other. But for the provocation of a conflict it only required the overemphasis of one
of the two tendencies. In the course of time the conflict came. But before we shall be
ready to discuss the peculiar situation in that event, we must consider the view of man's
natural depravity as it was developed by the Latin Church fathers.

1. Tertullian's Doctrine of Original Sin. It must be admitted that the Church
fathers of the East did approach the doctrine of man's natural depravity as inherited
from his ancestors; they had even spoken of a guilt that is common to the whole race.
But TERTULLIAN, in his *De anima,* was really the first to teach original sin. Loofs, who
points to his dependence on Stoic views, calls it *a kind of original sin* (163). As an
advocate of Traducianism, Tertullian believed that the individual soul consists of a human
substance and that it comes into existence with the body in and through generation as
transmission from the seed of Adam. Thus the way was prepared for the recognition
of inherited sin. The soul has its sinful condition as a result of its relation with Adam.
Our race is infected, not only with Adam's death, but also with sin which has become,
so to speak, a natural element in mankind, a second nature, a *malum animae, a vitium
originis.*[7]

2. But Tertullian did not succeed in drawing the evangelical conclusions from his

---

[6] Cf. Thomasius, with references to many of the Fathers, I, 488-491.
[7] Thom.-Bonw., I, 482 f., 494. Hagenbach I, 211; Loofs, 163; Fisher, 93.

doctrine of natural depravity. His conception of grace does not fit into a system
soteriology such as was later constructed by Augustine. His opposition to Gnostici
led him to lay strong emphasis upon man's free will even before conversion. But
was especially his legalistic conceptions regarding the relation between God and m
that kept him from an evangelical view of grace. God is the offended judge, and m
is the offender and debtor who must settle with the divine majesty through works
satisfaction in self-humiliation, asceticism, and, if possible, through martyrdom. Th
he will experience grace which as a creative principle is infused into his heart.
Tertullian was a forerunner of occidental catholicism.

3. And yet it must be stated that in Tertullian and other teachers of the West the
was *a larger emphasis upon man's real sinfulness and a corresponding emphasis up*
grace. Cyprian (258) defended infant baptism on the ground that the child also
sinful and therefore needs regeneration. [8] Hilary was strong in his expressions on t
universality of man's natural depravity and he recognized divine grace as preceding
meritorious work. Ambrose was even more outspoken on both sin and grace. He spo
of man's sin as a contagion which he traced back even to conception, and which
described as a guilt that needs to be forgiven. In his teaching of grace he was deep
than any of his predecessors, and he was the first to express his belief in prevenient gra
He pointed to the first turning of man's will as an effect of divine grace. [9]

4. It is to be noted, however, that *the difference between the East and the West*
this whole subject had not yet become disruptive. On the one hand, the East had
thought of denying altogether the universality of man's sinfulness and the need of gra
for his salvation; and, on the other hand, the Latin fathers were far from denying t
personal responsibility of man and his free will in accepting or rejecting the gracio
influences of God. As was stated above, there was a difference in tendency in the tw
sections of the Church, but this was as yet latent in character. Up to this time there ha
existed no occasion for a conflict, since neither of the two tendencies had been assert
strongly enough to exclude the other. We shall now discuss the period when that can
to pass.

IV. AUGUSTINE AND THE PELAGIANS

Literature: Outside of the Histories of Doctrine we refer to the monographic treatments
Augustine and Pelagius. We mention: G. WIGGERS, *Augustinismus und Pelagianismus, Versu
einer pragmatischen Darstellung,* two vols., 1821, 1833 (English translation at Andover, 1840
this is a standard work. LUTHARDT, *Die Lehre vom freien Willen und sein Verhaeltnis zur Gnad*
1863. MOZLEY, *The Augustinian Doctrine of Predestination,* 1878. KLASSEN, *Die inne
Entwicklung des Pelagianismus,* 1882. B. B. WARFIELD, *On Augustine and the Pelagian Contr
versy* (an introductory essay of 61 pages to Volume V of the *PNF*). ROTTMANNER, *Augustinism
1892. E. JAUNCEY, *The Doctrine of Grace up to the End of the Pelagian Controversy, Historical
and Dogmatically Considered,* 1900. CUNNINGHAM, *Augustine and His Place in the History
Christian Thought* (the Hulsean Lectures of 1885). H. RINN, pp. 172 ff.

A. A PRELIMINARY STUDY OF PELAGIANISM.

1. *The Leading Pelagians and Their Writings.* Pelagius, who died after 418 was
British or Irish monk of much ability and learning. He left behind him a considerab
number of writings of which, besides a few fragments in Augustine's works, only

[8] *Ep. ad. fid.*
[9] *De Paenitentia,* I, c. 3. *Apologia Davidis,* XI. 56.

nmentary on the thirteen Epistles of Paul,[10] a letter to Demetrius,[11] and an address
bellus fidei ad Innocentium)[12] have been preserved.[13] Two of Pelagius' most enthusi-
ic supporters were Caelestius and Julianus of Eclanum (d. 450). The latter was
effective advocate of Pelagian views which he developed into a system by adding
ionalistic and naturalistic elements.[14] The most pertinent of his writings are his
ra IV ad Turbantium and *Libra VIII ad Florum*, of which we have many fragments
Augustine's *Contra Julianum*[15] and especially in the *Opus imperfectum.*[16]

2. *Literary Orientation regarding the Anti-Pelagian Writings of Augustine.* See
ir enumeration below, under B. In Latin they will be found in the *MSL*, t. 44-45,
, 993 ff., or in Vol. X of the special works of Augustine. Translated into English, they
nstitute Vol. V of Augustine's works in the *ANPF* (which is Vol. 26 in this whole
rary). Two large writings, however, the one "Against Julian" (*Contra Julianum*)
d the "Unfinished Work" (*Opus Imperfectum*) have not found place in this collection
d therefore must be read either in the *MSL* or in the German translation of the
MPTEN *Bibliothek der Kirchenvaeter* (2d. ed.). W. BRIGHT published a *Selection
the Anti-Pelagian Treatises* (1880). Two Oxford scholars (Woods and Johnston)
ve us an excellent translation of the three treatises: *On the Spirit and the Letter, On
iture and Grace,* and *On the Proceedings* (*De Gestis*) *of Pelagius* (D. Nutt, London,
86). For a further account of the sources we refer the student especially to the articles
LOOFS in the *PRE* on *Augustine* and *Pelagius and the Pelagian Controversy*, which
e reproduced in the *NSH*. Compare the literature prefaced to the larger Histories of
octrine (HARNACK, LOOFS, SEEBERG). See also WIEGAND, who gives a good
ientation on the fundamental sources.

3. We can cover *the teachings of the Pelagians* by briefly describing their concep-
n of human freedom of sin, of the universality of sin, and of grace.[17]

a. *Freedom of the will.* Does man come into harmony with God by making the
ght use of his natural ability to choose from case to case between good and evil? Or
this harmony to be expected, fundamentally, by an influence of divine grace upon
e life of man so that in consequence of this influence the will of the regenerated now
nctions in true freedom in the direction of the good? This was the problem in the
ntroversy. The Pelagians affirmed the first of these two questions. Pelagius stressed
e power of contrary choice (*possibilitas utriusque partis*) or what we call formal
eedom.[18] He never tired of praising the inalienable power of man's nature to do
iat is right (*bonum naturae*). He argued that since God has enjoined His law upon
an, therefore man must have the power to fulfill it.[19] There is nothing in man that
mpels him to sin. That *bonum naturae* has enabled many in paganism to develop the
ghest virtues. It is even not impossible for man to lead a sinless life.[20]

---

[10] *MSL*, t. 30, pp 645-902; cf. A Souter, *The Commentary of Pelagius on the Epistles of Paul;* 1907, Vol. I
itroduction), 1922; Vol. II (text and apparatus criticus), 1927. Compare H. Zimmer, *Pelagius in Ireland,* 1901.
[11] In the works of Jerome (*MSL*, 30, 15-45).
[12] Hahn *Bibliothek der Symbole*[3], pp. 228 ff.
[13] Cf. Loofs, *PRE* XV, 747 ff.
[14] N. Bonwetsch in *PRE*, IX, 603 ff.
[15] *MSL*, t. 45.
[16] *MSL* t. 45.
[17] Cf. Seeberg, II[3], 488-496.
[18] Pelagius, *Ad Demetr.*, 3. Cf. Augustine in *De Grat.*, Ch. IV, 5.
[19] Pelagius, on *Rom.* 11: 8.
[20] On *Rom.* 8: 3; cf. Aug., *De Nat. et Gratia*, VII, 8; *De Grat.*, Ch. IV, 5; *De Gestis Pel.*, VI, 16.

b. Sin. This conception of man's freedom as the natural power to choose fre case to case and in act after act indicates the Pelagian conception of sin. Sin is not se in a condition of man's nature, in an inclination, in tendencies of the will. This led Pelagians to reject the doctrine of an original sin or of a sinful inclination as transmitt from parents to children; the position was taken that not the soul (*anima*) but only flesh (*caro*) is traceable to Adam.[21] The fall of Adam was looked upon as an ins nificant act, with no meaning for his posterity.[22] Man's sensual nature, his concupiscen was regarded as entirely indifferent. On this Julian had a severe conflict with Augusti (cf. below). Physical death, also, was not the consequence of sin, but merely a necess of the human organism, while it was admitted that spiritual death (*mors animae*) h passed from Adam to his children. But this would not justify our speaking of imputation of guilt from an inherited sinful condition, which would constitute injustice of which God would be incapable.[23] Children, therefore, do not need to baptized for the forgiveness of sins.[24]

c. The apparent universality of sin was explained by pointing to man's sens nature which, although entirely innocent in itself, becomes the occasion for temptati and sinning.[25] In addition to this, Pelagius mentions the attraction of evil examples the occasion for the sinning of individuals. And these again have their power in t continued practice of sinning, the *longus usus peccandi*, the *longa consuetudo vitiorum* so that Pelagius is compelled to admit even a necessity of sinning.[27] This is a ve significant admission! The universality of sin is to be explained, after all, out of sinful condition in the human race which defeats the original assertions of the *hum natura.* He does not really want to make this admission. For his interest does not beyond isolated individuals and isolated human acts. He fails to see the ethical un of the race and the ethical unity in the individual.

d. The Pelagian teaching *on grace* corresponds with these views of human natu and free will. The Pelagians did not believe in a real grace, i.e., in a grace conceiv of as the divine influence in man, much less in a creative divine influence upon spiritual powers. To them grace was first of all an enlightenment of man's reaso enabling him to see the will of God so that he in his own powers can choose and a accordingly.[28] Then grace consists in the revelations of the divine will through t Law, especially as given in the New Testament by Christ Himself in precept a example, and also in promises, discipline, warnings, trials, etc.[29] But all this is mer for the purpose of assisting man, who chooses and acts in perfect independence. Sin grace is nothing but an assistance and since man can do the right without such a Caelestius argued that grace is not absolutely but only relatively necessary. In His wo of grace God merely facilitates the right action of man's will.[30] The requirement man's part is that he should make himself worthy of such aid.

[21] Pelagius, on *Rom.* 7: 8. Julian, in *Opus Imperf.* I, 61; IV, 14, 19 f.
[22] VI, 11 f.
[23] Pelagius, on *Rom.* 5: 12, 15.
[24] Caelestius, quoted by Augustine in *De Pecc. Orig.*, VI, 6.
[25] Pelagius, quoted by Augustine in *De Grat.*, X, 11.
[26] Pelagius, *Ad Demetr.*, VIII, 17.
[27] On *Rom.* 7: 20.
[28] *Ad Demetr.*, 2, 4 ff., 8.
[29] *Ad Demetr.*, 8. Augustine in *De Peccato Orig.* 26, 30.
[30] Pelagius, quoted by Augustine in *De Grat.*, I, 26.

Note: Loofs[81] has called attention to the fact that Pelagianism was not a new doctrine with which at the outbreak of that controversy the Church under the theological leadership of Augustine was unexpectedly confronted. Pelagius, with Caelestius and Julian, simply gave blunt and systematized expression to certain tenets in the vulgar-Catholicism of that day; we have the elements of that theology in the Greek Apologists of the second century and in the whole moralistic-intellectualistic and rationalistic popular-philosophy of the centuries before Augustine. The moralizing influence of Stoicism especially is observable.

On the basis of the rediscovered text of *Pelagius' Commentary on Paul to the Romans* by A. Souter and the investigations of H. Zimmer, Loofs has also called attention to the energy with which Pelagius has stressed the *justification by faith alone.* W. Walker in his *Church History,* page 186, seconds Loofs[82] by remarking, "No man between Paul and Luther so emphasized justification by faith alone." On this question the student will be interested to hear Seeberg. He admits that Loofs has correctly quoted the teaching of Pelagius on justification. But he insists that in the case of Pelagius that formula *justification by faith* does not have the meaning that it appears to have simply for the reason that in the Pelagian conception of Christianity it is impossible to find a logical place for that teaching of Paul. He adds, "Pelagius was rationalist and moralist, and he had no understanding of the inner relation between sin and grace."[83] Loofs agrees practically with this when, in connection with a criticism of both Augustine and Pelagius, he says that the latter "was prevented by his moralism from appreciating the religious significance of faith" (DG, I. 420). Still we have learned from this whole investigation that Pelagius was a man of personal piety, that for his salvation he wanted to rely upon the forgiveness of sins through Christ,[84] and that he had a deeper conception of the guilt of the sinner than the history of the past warrants us to believe.[85]

This discovery, however, does not change the fundamental structure of Pelagian theology as pictured above. In this theology the divine law appears too much as a collection of moral demands merely, and sin was thought of, so to speak, as a heap of separate stones with no organic unity in a depraved nature. Christian perfection was likewise viewed as a cluster of individual virtues and works, with no demand of a regenerated heart as the necessary source of the truly Christian life. Fisher[86] remarks correctly that Pelagius' "conception of character is atomistic." The historical fact is that in the conflict between Augustine and the Pelagians two fundamentally different conceptions of Christianity clashed with each other. It is a conflict that will never be entirely settled.

B. AUGUSTINE AND HIS TEACHING

In an earlier period of his life before he was converted Augustine defended human freedom in opposition to the Manichaeans. But on reflecting how his own conversion had come to pass, he came to the conviction more and more that man in his natural condition is incapable of any positive co-operation with divine grace in conversion and that the enkindling of faith depends solely upon the grace of God. He found himself unable to change his will; and now it had come as a gift. It is a mistake to believe that the change in Augustine's conviction was caused by the Pelagian controversy. We know that already in 396, before he knew of Pelagius, he had been moved by exegetical reasons (Rom. 9: 16; 1 Cor. 4: 7; Phil. 2: 13) to believe that faith also is the gift of God. [87]

---

[81] See his article on Pelagius and the Pelagian Controversy in the *PRE,* XV, 747-774 (cf. *NSH*), as also in his *Leitfaden zum Studium der DG*[4], 417 ff.

[82] *DG*[4], 419.

[83] *DG,* II[3], 495.

[84] See *Ad Demetr.,* 8; cf. Julian in *Opus imperf.,* I, 171.

[85] Cf. the interesting characterization by Harnack, Eng. ed., V, 172.

[86] *History of Doctrine,* p. 190.

[87] *MSL,* VI, 1, 2, 9, 102-27.

And even before that time, 386, he prayed for faith as a gift: *Da fidem!*[38] Neithe should we leave out of consideration that, on sin, grace and faith, Ambrose was in man ways a precursor of Augustine with passages which "do not fall a whit behind th famous statements of Augustine." [39]

The following works of Augustine are of chief importance for the study of this fundamenta experience in his life: *Liber de 83 Quaestionibus* (388-396). *De Libro Arbitrio* (388-395) *Quaestiones ad Simplicianum* (397). *Confessiones* (400). In connection with the Pelagian con troversy: *De Peccatorum Meritis et Remissione* (412). *De Spiritu et Littera* (412). *De Natur et Gratia* (415). *De Perfectione Justitiae Hominis* (415). *De Gestis Pelagii* (417). *De Grati Christi et de Peccato Originali* (418). *De Nuptiis et Concupiscentia* (419). *Contra Duas Epistula Pelagianorum* (420). *Contra Julianum* (421). *De Gratia et Libero Arbitrio* (427). *De Cor reptione et Gratia* (427). *De Praedestinatione Sanctorum* (428). *De Dono Perseverantiae* (429) *Opus Imperfectum Contra Julianum* (until his death).

The following is an endeavor to Present Augustine's views on sin and grace ir form of a brief outline. But the wealth of Augustinian theology is such that from thi summarizing study little is gained unless we add a reading of the sources to which there shall be constant reference. Almost all of these are found in the eight volumes o Augustine's works in the *PNF* (which lack, of course, the long *Opus imperfectum* an the work against Julian). Vol. V, containing the *Anti-Pelagian Writings*, is of chie importance.

1. *Man's Original State.* In his conflict with Manichaeism Augustine had learnec not to look for man's sinfulness in natural qualities received at the creation. The origina man was just, and his will was in harmony with God as well as with himself. The will was master over the carnal impulses. There was no suffering. To this God hac added the help (*adjutorium*) to remain in this blessed state.[40] He was in the state of not needing to sin and to die. (*Posse non peccare et non mori*, not a *non posse peccare et non posse mori*.) But it lay in the freedom of his will that he was not compellec and, therefore, if he should use his freedom in the wrong direction his state woulc become one in which it was impossible for him not to sin and not to die (*non posse non peccare et mori*).[41]

2. *The Fall* of Adam was a great sin (*De Nuptiis* II, 58). Pride was the motive.[42] He wanted to be his own master and, therefore, refused to obey God. This fall was not just a single act but his will became evil. Turning from God he had turned tc himself. It had made Adam a sinner with a sinning will.[43] The soul lost that above-mentioned *adjutorium* and with it the control over the body: the mind became carnal and was turned to things low, changeable, mutable and uncertain.[44]

3. *Consequences for the Race.* The sin of Adam was the sin of the whole human race. For this Augustine quoted Rom. 5: 12 (where the Vulgate uses *in quo* for ἐφ' ᾧ). We all were in Adam, and all were he (*in illo fuimus omnes*, and: *Omnes ille unus fuerunt*).[45] Augustine taught that human nature in its totality was present

[38] *Soliloquia*, I, 1, 5. MSL, I, 872.
[39] Harnack, Eng. ed., V, 49 referring to Deutsch, *Des Ambrosius Lehre von der Suende und Suendentilgung* 1867.
[40] *De Corrept.* XI, 31, 32.
[41] Cf. *De Corrept.* VI, 10; VII, 11; XI, 32; X, 28; XII, 33.
[42] *De Nat. et Grat.* XXIX, 33.
[43] *Opus Imperf.* I, 71; *De Civ.* XIV, 11.
[44] *De Lib. Arb.* I, 16, 35.
[45] *De Peccat. Mer. et Rem.* I, 11; III, 14; *De Nupt. et Conc.* II, 15; *Opus imperf.* II, 176.

eminally in the first man.[46] "As a personal act, the first sin was not our act but the ct of another; yet it was truly the common act of mankind in their collective or undistributed form of existence." We sin willingly. (*Non inviti tales sumus.*) Therefore guilt is imputed to the whole race. It is the guilt of the entire race by right, because n Adam's sin the will of his posterity was operative. Children are included in this ondition of sin, though actual sins have not been committed; their salvation in case f death can be admitted only if they were baptized.[47]

Such was Augustine's conception of original sin. The means for the transmission f sin from parents to child was seen in the impure character of the sexual desire which, n his view, is not separable from sin. He wrote: "When it shall come to the act of generation, it is not possible that allowable and honorable intercourse should occur without the burning of lust, so that what springs from reason might be transmitted and not what springs from lust." [48] We have touched upon a point where Augustine differed rom Luther. While to Luther inherited sin, as a condition, was essentially unbelief (cf. Art. 2 of the Augsb'g Conf.), to Augustine it was the dominion of sensuality over he spirit. "The corruption of the body which oppresses the soul is not the cause, but he penalty of the first sin; neither does the corruptible flesh make the soul a sinner, but the sinful soul makes the flesh corrupt." [49] It has often caused surprise that Augustine could not decide whether traducianism or creationism was right.[50] One would expect him to have been a traducianist.

4. Man's Restoration comes through grace alone. This grace is in no sense just elatively, but absolutely necessary. It attaches itself to the remnant of the divine image n man, in his need of redemption and in the capacity for salvation.[51] Grace begins with baptism which is the first act through which God establishes a relation between Himself and man who needs grace. As we remarked, even children cannot be saved without baptism. Through baptism man's guilt of original sin is removed.[52] Grace received by faith does what the law with its demands was unable to do, namely to overcome concupiscence. Now the motto is: "Grant what Thou commandest;" not any more: "Do what I command." [53] Grace operates as a divine creative act.[54] In this process of renewal the Holy Spirit works faith in man, dispelling the spiritual ignorance which had come over him through the fall. So man assents to divine truth and arrives more and more at a higher knowledge of spiritual things.[55] But faith as mere assent does not save; it must become a faith in Christ, in which "both hope and love are added." [56] Through this "infusion of love" the will of man is liberated more and more so that concupiscence loses its power over him. In this way nature is repaired and man is transformed. It is of greatest importance to observe what was already indicated that the transformation of the natural man into a spiritually minded man is not the result

[46] II, 5, 12.
[47] De Civit. Dei XIII, 14; De Peccatis Mer. et Rem. I, 10, 11; Ep. 186, 6.
[48] De nupt. 1, 24, 27. Cf. De Pecc. Mer. et Rem. 2, 22, 36.
[49] De perfectione justitiae 8, 19. De Civ. XIV, 3.
[50] De Anima et Ejus Origine II, 14, 20; 15, 21. Retract. 1, 1, 3.
[51] De Civ. XXII, 24; De Spiritu et Littera, XXV, 47.
[52] Sermo 158, 5.
[53] De Spiritu et Littera XIII, 22.
[54] De Grat. Ch. XXIV, 25.
[55] Sermo 43. On John 27, 7; 22, 5; 29, 6.
[56] On John 29, 6.

of a natural psychological development as the Pelagians had it, but that it is the result of a supernatural divine influence upon his will. It is this process for which Augustine has the term "justification" (besides the terms *renovatio, vivificatio, regeneratio, sanctificatio*). By this term he means that, after the beginning of the new life has been made with the forgiveness of his sin[58] he becomes actually righteous.[59] Augustine needed this emphasis upon forgiveness as the first gift of grace in order to secure peace for the sinner who has not yet had any opportunity to exercise his faith in works of love. But so closely does he connect with this act of forgiveness the anticipated renovation[60] that it amounted to a failing in interpreting Paul as the Reformation succeeded in doing. There is a deplorable absence of an emphatic distinction between justification and sanctification as Paul and Luther had it. Grace to Augustine was essentially an inspiration of a good will[61] in the form of a gradual process.

Note. Both Rome and Wittenberg have appealed to Augustine. The followers of Luther (likewise the followers of Calvin) can claim him on the doctrine of natural depravity and free grace in the forgiveness of sin with no meritorious works preceding this remission. Rome can claim Augustine in much of the language in conceiving of justification as a gradual process of making man actually righteous. However, when this is admitted we must not forget (1) that Augustine, like Luther, saw in the forgiveness of sins, through baptism, a divine act of justification preceded by no meritorious work (comp. with this the Roman Catholic *meritum de condigno*), and (2) that the principle of justifying love was always regarded by Augustine as a work of the Holy Spirit.[62] It was this that took Augustine near to the Reformers.

In this connection Nygrén's conception of Augustine will be of special interest. Augustine so he maintains, came to Christianity with a Hellenistic prepossession; i.e., the Eros-motif, man's ascending desire for the *summum bonum* was the dominant feature in his thought. In his study of Paul he became confronted with the Agape motif of Christianity, i.e., with God's descending love for men. This meeting of the Eros and Agape motifs produced "a characteristic third which is neither Eros nor Agape, but *Caritas.*"[62a] *Caritas* to Augustine is primarily love *to* God, not God's love. It is love directed upwards, the means to posses in the Creator the *summum bonum.* But has any man power to raise himself to God? To this question Augustine answers: By grace only. Thus *gratia* became the key-word of Augustine's interpretation of Christianity. "Everything in our life depends ultimately on God's grace" (p. 308). "It is at this point," Nygrén says, "that Augustine is furthest from the Hellenistic theory which served as a starting-point for his doctrine of *Caritas.* . . . Without grace there is no access to God. Without grace, *Caritas* has no air beneath its wings for its flight to God." But *"the end is and remains the ascent of Caritas to God"* (p. 309).

So far Nygrén. His illuminating analysis of Augustine's thought is a confirmation of what we have said above. The emphasis on grace took Augustine near to the Reformation; but in his definition of justification as vivification or sanctification he remained essentially on a Roman level. His Paulinism was limited to the *sola gratia,* because he looked upon Agape as a means to the end, to make possible man's ascent to God.

5. Predestination. Grace, in Augustine's view, is irresistible and predestinating. This doctrine, in its completed form, was added after he had developed his doctrine of sin and grace. This was finished before the pelagian controversy began in 412. Not until 416, in his letter to Pauline of Nola, did he offer his teaching of predestination.

Seeberg remarks correctly: "Many lines of thought are concentrated in this term: the Neo-Platonic tincture of Augustine's doctrine of God, his personal religious experi-

---

[57] *De Spiritu et Littera* XXIX, 50, 51.
[58] *De Peccatorum Meritis* 7.
[59] *De Spirit. et Lit.* XXVI, 45.
[60] Cf. *Sermo* 158, 4, 5. *De Spir. et Lit.* XXIX, 51.
[61] *De Corr.* II, 3.
[62] *Epist.* 194, 5, 19.
[62a] *Op. cit.,* Part II, Vol. II, 233.

ice, his recognition of the sole agency of grace, and exegetical considerations." [63] In race, says Augustine, we have the will of God with regard to man's salvation. If grace ys hold of man, there can be no resistance, for God carries out His will in the human eart no less than in nature.[64] But He does not do this against man's will but through is will, by restoring the same to freedom from the old servitude so that he now hooses the good.[65] Thus man is liberated from the power of concupiscence. In these tatements Augustine would not deny the freedom of the will. He would explain this s follows: the will makes its choice always with freedom. But it depends upon the nclination of the heart what it will choose. As long as the inclination is toward the atural it *cannot,* but it also *will* not choose the spiritual. But grace changes the heart, nd now the will chooses with freedom the spiritual things.[66] But in the work of hanging the heart grace acts in such a way that man's will cannot resist.[67] Thus we an say: Man is converted, not because he wills, but he wills, because he is converted.

To this Augustine added that God gives to the elect the gift of perseverance, the *onum perseverantiae.*[68] Man needs this gift if he is to be saved and God grants it. according to the psychology of Augustine, the granting of the gift of perseverance annot have reference to the individual acts from case to case, but to the keeping of man in the state of grace out of which the individual acts will follow as a natural result.[69]

But why do not all who are called yield to grace? Augustine answers this question y the doctrine of predestination. From eternity some men have been predestined to alvation, while others have been predestined to punishment. The number in each roup is fixed and unchangeable, and no one can pass from the one to the other. To he predestined (*electi*) God gives the grace of perseverance as a special effect of pre- lestination. These may stumble and fall, but they cannot do so permanently, because God's grace is irresistible. It is just the opposite with the unpredestined. Even if they ppear to be true Christians, called, justified, regenerated through baptism, renewed, hey will not be saved, because they have not been elected. To the question, why he hooses some and leaves others to their fate, the only answer is, "I so will," at which he creature must humbly bow before his Creator. Yet Augustine avers that God cannot e blamed for the rejection of the non-elect; the fact is, they fall by their own will, and God simply passes them by.[70]

The religious element in Augustine's teaching of predestination is fittingly expressed y Seeberg in this remark, "In tones that can never be forgotten it taught the Church: There is only one thing to be feared—rebellion against God, or evil in the heart; and here is only one thing good and great—the effectual grace of the living God." In ddition let us remember that Augustine argued out of an inner need for the assurance f salvation.

---

[63] Eng. ed I, 350. Cf. *DG*³, II, 534.

[64] *De Corr. et grat.* XIV, 45.

[65] *De Spiritu et Lit.* XXX, 52; *Ep.* 157, 2, 10; 177, 4; *Enchir.* 25, 105.

[66] *De Grat. et Lib. Arbitr.* XV, 31, II, 4.

[67] *De Corr. et grat.* XIV, 45.

[68] *De Dono Pers.* I, 1; *De Corr.* XII, 34.

[69] Cf. Seeberg, *DG*, II³, 536 f.

[70] Here we refer generally to Augustine's two writings, *De Predestinatione* and *De Dono Perseverantiae,* pub- shed in 428 and 429. For an exhaustive discussion of Augustine's doctrine of predestination see Seeberg, *DG,* l³, 534-45.

V. Semi-Pelagianism and the Temporary Settlement of the Controversy

The crudities of Pelagianism were rejected by the Church when in 412 at a Synod in Carthage it excommunicated Caelestius, the friend of Pelagius; and likewise when it condemned Pelagianism at a General Synod in Carthage in 418, as again at the Third Ecumenical Council at Ephesus (431). But the rejection of Pelagianism did not mean the acceptance of everything in the Augustinian system. It was Augustine's doctrine of predestination which gave offense, to those even who otherwise favored him in his controversy with Pelagius. We now come to a series of conflicts known as the Semi-Pelagian Controversies.

1. The Controversies.

a. Due to Augustine's doctrine of predestination, there was *a considerable agitation* among the monks in Egypt. By pushing the doctrine of predestination to its two logical conclusions some had relaxed into a state of optimistic but rash confidence; some became the victims of distressed consciences and were plunged into the abyss of hopeless despair and others fell into the error which ascribes merit to the human factor in salvation. In 427 Augustine wrote two books—*De Gratia et Libero* and *De Correptione et Gratia*— in which he endeavored to counteract the disastrous consequences of his doctrine.

b. More violent was the opposition which arose in Southern Gaul. At Massilia there was a monastery which was presided over by John Cassianus, a disciple and friend of Chrysostom. The monks of this monastery and the theologians belonging to the same school protested against Augustine's doctrine of predestination. Among them was the famous Vincent of Lerins who set forth in his *Commonitorium pro Catholicae Fide Antiquitate et Universatate* (434)[71] the criteria of Catholic doctrine, insisting that only that is genuinely Catholic and orthodox which has been "believed always, everywhere and by all" (*semper, ubique et ab omnibus*). An application of this principle to Augustine's theory of predestination made it very evident that on this point Augustine was far from being Catholic.

These opponents of Augustine's doctrine of predestination were called *Semi-Pelagians;* but the most of them could with more precision be styled Semi-Augustinians. In matters outside the predestination problem they were great admirers of Augustine. They strongly emphasized man's sinfulness, particularly its sensual aspects. The sin of Adam was regarded as a hereditary disease. Since the fall there prevails a weakness in the human will. This they found to be their starting point in Augustine's teaching of the natural depravity of man.

But they abhorred his doctrine of predestination. They characterized it as new, in conflict with tradition; as dangerous, because it defeats the end of preaching, weakens the moral energy or leads into despair; it supposes that God, the Creator, is of diverse natures. In opposition to all this they declared that grace is absolutely general, that Christ died for all, that predestination must be based upon foreknowledge.

The *Semi-Pelagian features* of these Semi-Augustinians, however, were not absent. They taught that, while in the fall man had suffered a great weakening of his spiritual powers and was therefore unable to free himself by his own will, yet he was able to wish to have the Physician and to believe on Him. So God comes to the assistance of the

---

[71] *MSL*, 50 ff.

weakened human will. Grace is concomitant and not prevenient to human merits. Grace co-operates with man's free will. Cassianus approached Pelagius when he said that grace is an enlightenment and instruction through the law of which a spiritual understanding is given. As to who would take the initiative in the working out of our salvation, Cassianus said that sometimes God takes the first step, and sometimes man does. But in all cases it is co-operation. The *sola gratia*—Augustine's best contribution —was sacrificed. He wrote against the Massilians his *De Praedestinatione Sanctorum* and also his *De Dono Perseverantiae*.

 c. *Outspoken Defenders of Augustinianism.* After the death of Augustine in 430, Prosper of Aquitania (d. 460) raised the standard in behalf of the Augustinian doctrine and waged a stern warfare with all its opponents. His chief work *Liber Contra Collatorem* and his polemical *Carmen de Ingratis* were written against those who do not attribute all good to divine grace. [72] He characterized Semi-Pelagianism as an impossible *tertium quid* arising from Augustinianism and Pelagianism. Whereas Pelagius had taught that man takes the initiative and the Church teaches that grace makes a beginning, the Semi-Pelagians ambiguously straddle the fence. Prosper also criticized their attitude on original sin. On the one hand, he said, they admit that man's sinful condition is inherited, and on the other hand they speak of seeds of virtue in man: which shows that the sin from Adam is not regarded as a total depravity.

 d. *In another writing which came from the Augustinian circle* and which appeared anonymously under the title of *De Vocatione Gentium,* [73] an attempt was made to construct a doctrine on sin and grace on the basis of Augustinian conceptions. Care was taken, however, to avoid the most objectionable features. It is not the human will, by its merits, that makes the beginning toward salvation, but the elective will of God, which does not exclude the free exercise of man's will.

 In order to save the universality of grace (I Tim. 2: 4) along with the Augustinian conception of a special election of a limited number, the author of this work introduced the distinction—peculiar to himself—between general and special grace. By *general grace* the writer meant God's dealing with individuals and peoples independently of His special revelation, namely through the voice of nature, endowments, providence, traditions and influence of the Spirit (Acts 17: 28; 14: 14). This revelation is sufficient to induce men to turn to God and seek Him. But for those who are really saved, there is the *special grace* through the revelation in Christ. The general grace has a pedagogical significance in that it leads men to the special grace of revelation. This special grace, however, is enjoyed by only a part of humanity. The best co-operation of such general and special grace is seen in people under the influence of Christianity. Grace in its manifold forms of influence (invitation through examples, dangers, miracles, intuitions, suggestions) takes the initiative everywhere and influences the will in its relation to salvation in Christ. Back of it stands God's irrevocable decree of election with regard to certain individuals. Why are not all men saved? Here the writer takes refuge in theological mystery. It is certain that the lost perish only by their own fault. [74]

 e. Among the defenders of Augustinianism belongs also the unknown author of the *Hypomnesticon,* quoted by Article XVIII of the Augsburg Confession. The aim of the

---

[72] His writings are in *MSL*, 51. Cf. G. F. Wiggers, *Augustinismus und Pelagianismus*, II, 163 ff.
[73] *MSL*, 51.
[74] See the excellent review in Thomasius, I, 563-570. Cf. Seeberg, *HD*, I, 373; *DG*, II², 575 ff. Weigand, I, 120 f.

writer was to reinstate the doctrines of Augustine, but at the same time, to remove the
offensive features of the system without endangering anything that was essential to the
sola gratia. Through the fall man's free will was lost in things spiritual and in things
pertaining to salvation. Freedom of will was retained only with regard to what touches
upon this present life, i.e. with regard to *purely external matters* (*res externae*) such as
building a house, and with regard to *external things in the moral sphere*—civil righteousness and its opposite—such as murder, theft, etc. Freedom in spiritual things is restored
through prevenient grace which flows from the wounds of Christ and works in man
faith and the power for good works. It is, however, within man's power to resist God's
gracious influences. Predestination is here distinguished from prescience or foreknowledge. God foresaw who would accept Christ, and these he predestinated to salvation
before the foundation of the world. He also foresaw who would continue in godlessness.
But He did not predestinate them to their doom.[75]

f. The *Praedestinatus*[76] is another anonymous writing, dated about 450; this title
was given to the work by its first editor. It seems to have been composed by a Semi-
Pelagian whose aim was to satirize and thus bring into disrepute the Augustinian doctrine of predestination.[77]

g. A very outspoken Semi-Pelagianism was taught by Bishop Faustus of Reji who
was born in Britain and died about 495. He went beyond Cassianus and was the most
promising spokesman of the Semi-Pelagians. His principal writing is *De Gratia Dei et
Humanae Mentis Libero Arbitrio* which was written soon after the Synod of Arles in
475. It may be called the program of the Semi-Pelagians.[78]

Faustus spoke in strong terms against Pelagius, calling him *doctor pestifer.* He
criticized him for regarding the natural powers of man as sufficient to attain salvation
and for denying original sin. Holding the monastic idea, he taught that original sin
had its source in the sexual desire.[79] Death came as a consequence of the fall. The
free will, while not extinct, is *infirmatum et attenuatum.* Man cannot exercise it for his
salvation without the aid of grace. Faustus rejected decidedly the predestinarian conception of a divine monergism and taught that the will of man, by virtue of the freedom
left in him, makes the beginning (II, 10). Salvation is accomplished by the co-operation
of the human and the divine factors, the latter taking the initiative. But it is emphasized
that the Lord invites only the willing and seeking ones. But what did Faustus understand by grace (*adjutorium divinum*)? It is the illumination of his will, the preaching
with its promises and warnings, and God's guiding hand in man's life,[80] it is not, as
it was with Augustine, the regenerating power of grace in the heart.

2. The Temporary Settlement. Both sides had received a thorough hearing. The
voice of Faustus was decidedly Pelagian, and his book was approved by many because
of its rationality. A strong reaction against Augustinianism appeared, even after fifty
years, among the Scythian monks of Constantinople (cir. 520). Fulgentius of Ruspe
in the name of a Council, replied with an able apology (*De Veritate Praedestationis et
Gratia Dei*) for the doctrine of Augustine. He was followed by two able Gallic Bishops

[75] Seeberg, Eng. ed. I, 374. Loofs, 440, Note 1
[76] *MSL,* 53.
[77] H. v. Schubert, *Der sog. Praedestinatus,* 1903.
[78] See his writings in the *CSEL* 21; also in the *MSL,* 58. Cf. the article by R. Seeberg on Faustus in *PRE*
V. 782 ff.; his *DG* II³, 577 ff.
[79] *De Gratia* I, 1, p. 11 ff.; cf. Seeberg, *HD,* I, 374, note 3. *PRE,* V, 786, 30.
[80] Seeberg in *PRE,* V, 785, 50.

Avitus of Vienna and Caesarius of Arles, who won at the Synod of Orange (529) a decided victory over Semi-Pelagianism. [81]

What doctrine was accepted at Orange? A predestination of man to perdition was rejected. Beyond this statement no utterance was delivered on the doctrine of predestination. Neither did the synod accept Augustine's doctrine of irresistible grace. But regarding sin and grace, the utter inability of the natural man in things spiritual, and the necessity of attributing every good movement to grace, was clearly confessed. Grace was declared to be prevenient. Not only sanctification but even the first impulses of our willing belong to the work of grace. [82]

The following paragraphs are given as a summary of the consensus upon which the followers of Augustine (such as Prosper, Fulgentius and Maxentius in harmony with the Roman See) stood united:

a. God foreknows all things, both good and evil. But His prescience as such is not causative. He wills and foreordains only what is good. Predestination, therefore, has reference exclusively to the children of God.

b. While God foreknows all evil persons and influences, He does not foreordain them. Evil is not present in God; hence it cannot be the object of divine predestination.

c. When the regenerated fall, it is not because they were not earnestly called, but they fall by reason of their own perverted will. Grace is universal and the election is through Christ. When man perseveres in grace unto the end, it is to be attributed to the grace of God alone. It is therefore impossible that a child of God should through predestination become a child of the devil. God, however, did not predestinate unto salvation those who would resist Him and fall. [83]

d. The grace of God and the merits of Christ are for all. God earnestly desires and wills the salvation of all men (I Tim. 2: 4).

e. But, to use the language of the Scythian monks, "We believe that the natural free will is able to do nothing but to distinguish and to covet the fleshy things or the things of this world; but as to the things of the eternal life it can neither think the same nor will them nor covet them nor do them; it be then that the Holy Spirit is poured out in our hearts and works inwardly in it." [84] This doctrine was approved by Bishop Boniface II of Rome.

It was a great heritage that the Church received in the statements of the Synod at Orange. It was the teaching of man's complete depravity, of the loss of his spiritual freedom, of the absence of any merit in his salvation which is by grace alone. Faith and the new life are produced by grace. This grace is attached to the sacrament of baptism with the admission that grace may also work independently of the sacraments, through the Word. The double predestination of Augustine was passed by. Our treatment of the Middle Ages will show us the return of Semi-Pelagianism and the establishment of principles that made the Reformation necessary, as we shall see. In all these developments we continue to have a history of Augustinianism.

---

[81] C. F. Arnold, *Caesarius von Arelate und die Gallische Kirche seiner Zeit,* (1894).
[82] Mansi, *Acta Conciliorum,* VIII, 711-26, Canons 1, 7, 22, 3, 8, 20, 28.
[83] Prosper, *Ad Objectiones Vincentii,* c. 12.
[84] Maxentius in *Libellus Fidei,* in *Biblioth. Max Patrum,* IX, 539.

Chapter Twelve

THE SACRAMENTS

In the following we shall confine our review to the development of the sacraments of Protestantism in the Ancient Church, that is, to Baptism and the Lord's Supper. Tertullian was the first to speak of the *Sacramentum baptismatis et eucharistiae*. [1] But at occasional moments only did synods charge themselves with the task of giving authoritative definitions of baptism and of the eucharist. [2]

I. Baptism

1. Baptism in the Name of the triune God was looked upon as the door of admission into full membership with the Christian family. It was considered as the means of the forgiveness of all past sins, and as the sacrament with which, according to later views, the Holy Spirit is received for illumination and for regeneration. [3] The first demand for the administration of the sacraments by clerics came from Justin Martyr when he spoke of them as belonging to the special work of the bishops. [4]

Baptism, of course, was not meant to work magically. Without repentance, it would be without value, declares Tertullian. [5] The back must be turned upon sin, says Origen. [6] The connection of the gifts of baptism with the administration of it is not in the view of all absolutely simultaneous, there may be spiritual life before the act; but there is an inner logical connection between the two. [7]

2. Later in the catholic age the original use of water only was supplemented by an anointing with oil. The use of water now symbolized the removal of sin, the anointing with oil the positive gift of the Spirit. This double act was preceded by a declaration of renunciation of the devil (a natural result of the view that non-Christians stood under the influence of demons) and by the profession of faith through the baptismal formula. After exorcism there followed somewhat later the ceremony of breathing the Holy Spirit (cf. John 20: 22). During the first centuries adult baptism was practiced. The act itself was by thrice-repeated immersion. In Spain the immersion was only once. In a varying practice during the centuries since Tertullian other symbolical features were added. The sign of the cross was made on the forehead and breast. Later a grain of salt was put into the mouth (Mark 9: 50). Eye, nose, ear, and tongue were touched with spittle and the words spoken: *Ephphatha*, Be opened (Mark 7: 34).

---

[1] *Adv. Marc.*, 4, 34.
[2] On the term *sacrament* see the article by Kattenbusch in *PRE*, XVII, 349 ff. Cf. *NSH*. Loofs, *DG⁴* 211. H. C. Sheldon, *History of Doctrine*, I, 136.
[3] Just. Mart., I, *Apol.*, 7, 5; 61. Tert., *De Bapt.*, 1. Iren., III, 17. *Epideixis*, 3. Clem. Alex., *Paed*, I, 6. Gregory Naz., 3. *Hom.*, 40.
[4] Loofs, *DG⁴*, p. 213.
[5] *De poenitentia*, 6.
[6] *Homily*, 21, on Luke. Cf. also Cyril. *Cat.*, 3. 15.
[7] Thus even Tert., *De poenit.*, 6.

n Italy, occasionally a piece of money was laid into the hand as a symbol of the entrusted alent (Luke 19: 12), and so on. [8]

3. The strongly realistic tendencies of Tertullian which we have described in Chap. VIII, Sec. III, 5, led him to speak of the Spirit as a fine material substance influencing he water of baptism. [9] The Spirit is spoken of as the *substantia baptismatis*. [10] This, however, was not yet a unified theological position. [11] Later, after the Cappadocians, the Greek Fathers speak more generally of a power imparted to the water itself through nvocation. Cyril of Alexandria says that by the Holy Spirit the water is metamorphosed (μεταστοιχοῦνται) into a certain divine and ineffable power. [12] The intention was not o teach a literal transubstantiation of the water. But there were those among the Greek Fathers who in both sacraments (see on Lord's Supper below) inclined to a consubstantiation in the meaning of a combination (mixture) of the heavenly and the earthly elements into a *tertium quid*.

4. As to the gift of baptism there was formally still the original conception of the New Testament writers that it was the sacrament of the forgiveness of sin and of the communication of the Spirit. [13] But in the meantime the adult baptism had changed to infant baptism. At first this practice was exceptional, but with Constantine it had become the rule. Now we must remember that the Greeks had not been speaking of original sin. [14] That meant there was now an unconscious lessening of the emphasis on the forgiveness of sin as the gift of baptism. While the words *forgiveness of sin* do occur (following the terminology of the old formulas), they are frequently given a meaning to correspond with the conception referred to above (close of Sec. I), namely that the injury of sin is above all a certain corruption of nature which conditioned the loss of immortality. This injury was to be overcome by a *removal* of that corruption (καθάρσις). The way is to be prepared for a gradual restoration of the divine image and of immortality. As part of a system, we see this idea in the *recapitulation-thought* of Irenaeus (Chap. VIII, sec. I, 3).

5. *Influences of Adjustment.* But that above-mentioned lessening among the Greeks of the emphasis upon forgiveness of sin as the gift of baptism was effectively counteracted by the soteriology of the Latin Church. We have already heard the voice of Tertullian (Chap. VIII, Sec. III, 7, d). In the East and in the West, however, there was after all unanimity in stressing three stages in baptism: Forgiveness of sin, communication of the Spirit, and the obligation to fulfill the commandments of Christ. Gradually the Church had also arrived at the conviction that forgiveness of sin and the receiving of the Spirit are not separate, but go together. Both are received through baptism. In the case of adults there was to be the evidence of repentance. It was difficult to find the adjustment when infant baptism came to be the practice.

Cyprian, the pupil of Tertullian, sees in baptism the means of God's saving work in man. With this position he combines elements of the peculiar realism that was

---

[8] As to sources see Seeberg, I³, 441 ff.; Loofs, DG⁴, p. 212. W. Rohnert, *Lehre von den Gnadenmitteln,* 1886, p. 76 ff. For my orientation regarding pertinent literature concerning Baptism and the Lord's Supper I owe much to this monograph by W. Rohnert.
[9] *De bapt.,* 4 A. Schweitzer, as referred to in *RGG,* I, 15, is more up to date.
[10] *Pud.,* 9.
[11] Cf. Seeberg, *DG,* I³ 448.
[12] *MSG,* 73. 245 f.
[13] Cyril, *De Fide* to Theodosius, *MSL,* 76, 1188.
[14] See Chapter XI, Sec. I.

characteristic of the North African School. But upon this basis he made contribution
to the meaning of baptism that have always held a place in conservative theology, and
by which the above-mentioned shortcoming of the Greek Church was counteracted and
supplemented. The details must be read in the scattered expressions of his letters where
he protests against the validity of baptism administered by heretics. The statements of
Cyprian on baptism which have not been endorsed by the conservative Reformation are
those that grew out of his conflict over the validity of baptism, in which he had an
interest in stressing the charismatic gift of the bishop in true apostolic succession, insisting that it was the Spirit-endowed bishop that made the consecrated water the effectual
water of baptism. [15]

It is interesting to observe the manner in which *Origen* discusses the relation
between baptism and repentance: Baptism appears as a symbol of the continuous purification of the soul. Now the symbolical view is introduced. Still baptism is the
beginning and the source of the divine gifts. [16]

6. *Augustine* on Baptism. In Chap. VIII, Sec. IV, 6, a, the question was raised:
What according to Augustine is a sacrament? We here confine ourselves to his views
on baptism. These are important, because in them we have the materials for the
recognized teaching of the Catholic Church, systematized later by the scholastics, and in
certain features also a foundation for the teaching of the conservative Reformation
Augustine's definition of a sacrament as *a visible sign of an invisible grace* does not put
him into a class with the *Spiritualists* of the Reformation age, because he makes the
Word a constituent part of the sacrament and says that the *divine, invisible things* are
honored. [17] The sacrament as such is to Augustine a real means of grace.

Among his writings the reference is especially to *De Baptismo,* against the
Donatists, Book 7. There is also his answer to letters of Petillian. In his anti-Pelagian
writings, later, he wrote much on this subject. Kattenbusch remarks (*PRE,* XIX, p. 408,
line 38) that Augustine was the first who felt baptism as a problem. Against the
Donatists he insisted upon the validity of baptism even when administered by unholy
men and by schismatics.

The historically Augustinian teaching appears especially in his writings against the
Pelagians. He taught that it is the guilt of man's natural depravity, first of all, that is
removed by baptism: *Concupiscence* which, before baptism, constitutes man's special and
real guilt is not imputed to him any more. It is admitted that in connection with the
forgiveness of the guilt, as attached to the general sinful condition, the sins of act,
committed by heart, mouth, and hand, are also forgiven (*per accidens*). But it is
especially the inherited guilt which baptism removes. This was the new thought that
was introduced by Augustine. Up to this time it was the sinful acts committed before
baptism that were spoken of as the special objects of removal through the forgiving
grace of baptism. This just-mentioned Augustinian thought soon took hold of the
Church. In it there was a lasting truth, which has served not only to complement but
to counteract the insufficient conceptions of the Eastern Church on this subject.

With this we do not mean to stamp all the details of the later Augustinian system
as unalterable gospel: (1) While he insisted that baptism, when administered in the

---

[15] *Epist.,* 70, 1.
[16] See the investigation by R. Seeberg, *DG,* I³, 531 ff.
[17] *De Catechizandis Rudibus,* 26, 50.

name of the Holy Trinity or of Christ is identical and valid everywhere, his conception of the Church as the Church Catholic would not allow him to admit this above-mentioned gift of the sacrament when used by schismatics. The Spirit can work only in the Church. And while he frequently defines this Church as the fellowship of real believers, yet to him and under the condition of the times, it was the Catholic Church in distinction from schismatic associations. [18] Yet Augustine has to some extent covered the sternness of this principle by calling attention to the fact that even within the Catholic Church unrepenting sinners are baptized, who cannot be recipients of the gift of baptism. [19] (2) His belief regarding the fate of infants dying without baptism was arbitrary and artificial. (3) The manner in which he singled out concupiscence, i.e., sexual desire, as the special expression of the sin not to be imputed in baptism is beset with a one-sidedness that has always been open to criticism. But he offered lasting truth in the following points: (1) Baptism is the sacrament for removing the guilt of the sinful condition with which man is born. (2) The inherited sinful desire remains after baptism as an *affectus malae qualitatis,* as a morbid leaning to sin (*languor*). But (3) with baptism the Holy Spirit is received for the beginning of a renovation in a continued forgiveness of the daily sins, in which that languor is more and more reduced. (4) There is an element of truth in Augustine's emphasis upon the Church in connection with baptism. Taking the (Catholic) Church as the *body* of Christ, Augustine was led to speak of the saints (later the predestinated) as constituting the authority for bringing children to baptism. [20] The confessional thought of the Reformed Churches does not exactly cover the situation here discussed, but it reminds one of it. A. Ritschl, speaking of the efficacy of the means of grace, laid special stress upon the environment created by the Church. Lutheran theology also has here made concessions. (5) The objective character of baptism was safeguarded by insisting that while baptism does not bring salvation to the unconverted, it does stamp them with a *character dominicus* in which the Lord claims them as His property. For this reason they are not to be rebaptized when they become converted or return to the Church, but their original baptism is simply to be recognized. [21] (6) Children, also, when they later come to consciousness of the meaning of baptism are not to be rebaptized, but they simply step into conscious possession of the forgiveness of sin and of the gift of the Spirit.

The materials here reviewed were later systematized by the scholastics, especially by Peter Lombard and by Thomas Aquinas. Here, however, they were accommodated to the Roman Catholic conception of the effect of the fall upon the image, which the Reformers of the sixteenth century found in need of purification from a Semi-Pelagian background. It was taught by the scholastics that in the fall man had not suffered a real corruption of his whole spiritual nature, but had simply lost some superadded gifts (holiness, immortality, wisdom, dominion), which left him with a weakness only, not with an actual corruption, as taught in Art. II of the *Augsburg Confession.* (This Semi-Pelagian doctrine of the scholastics was later symbolized in the Roman Catechism, I, 2, question 18. For a critical review see Melanchthon's *Apology of the Augsburg Confession,* Art. II, *Smalcald Articles,* III, 1; and the *Formula of Concord,* Art. I in both parts.) It was not inconsistent, therefore, when Rome taught that in baptism original sin is not only forgiven (as is taught by conservative Protestantism), but is *removed,* because *original sin* is nothing more than the loss of those superadded gifts, therefore only something negative. Original sin, that natural depravity which manifests itself in general concupiscence, was to Rome something indifferent, neither good

---

[18] *De Baptismo,* I, 10, 11; IV, 1, 17, 22, 23; V, 21, 29; *Ep.,* 93, 8, 46.

[19] See VI, 12.

[20] We refer to the above mentioned article of Kattenbusch in the *PRE,* XIX, 408 f, and to the writings of Augustine there referred to.

[21] *De Bapt.,* III, 16, 21; VI, 3, 5; 5, 7.

nor bad and, properly speaking, not sin. It only becomes sin if not resisted, and if it develops into sinful acts. One can easily see that this conception of man's spiritual nature detracts from the real need of baptism, as taught by Augustine. He taught the necessity of baptism not only because it incorporates us into the Church, but because in the Church there is the salvation through the Spirit. And as to original sin, he taught that only the inherited guilt is removed, and that the guilt of the inherited evil desire (concupiscence) is not imputed.

II. THE LORD'S SUPPER

A. THE USE OF THE LORD'S SUPPER IN THE EARLY CHURCH.

1. A Re-examination of the Biblical Reports Concerning the Lord's Supper.

a. Paul's Report in I Corinthians 11: 23 ff. is admitted to be of all the oldest. This we shall keep in mind.

In recent decades there has been among the conservative theologians of the modern type an endeavor to throw new light upon the original meaning of the Lord's Supper. The Church of the past had become accustomed to look upon *body* and *blood* in the words of institution as the two co-ordinate constituents of the heavenly element (*materia coelestis*) in the Lord's Supper. It was expressed in the phrase of Article X of the Augsburg Confession, "That the body and blood of Christ are truly present and are distributed to those who eat in the Supper of the Lord"; also in the words of distribution, "Take and eat, this is the body of Christ, given for thee," and "Take and drink, this is the blood of the New Testament, shed for thy sins." Now we are told that body and blood must not be taken as correlated conceptions in the words of institution. For it must not be overlooked that in the institution proper, at the beginning of that last supper, Christ spoke only of His body. The reference to His blood occurred later, *after the supper* (I Cor. 11: 25). By *body* as used in the institution proper Christ meant Himself as person. He Himself, now at the point of parting from His disciples, promised to be present with them in a new form whenever they come together to break the bread in the Supper that He was now instituting. But for what purpose did Christ later, *after the meal*, come back to the matter once more to speak of the cup as the new covenant in His blood? Not, so we are told, to introduce His blood as a second constituent element of the Holy Supper. The giving of His blood was included, of course, in the giving of Himself in His body. As he declared (Matt. 20: 28), He gave *His life* a ransom for many. But when Christ here, *after the supper,* spoke of His blood, He simply meant to call attention to the giving of His life as a *new testament* for the forgiveness of sins. We have here been reviewing a most interesting discussion of Seeberg (*DG,* I³, 165-167).

Literature on the Eucharist:
A. EICHORN, *Das Abendmahl im Neuen Testament,* 1898. A. SCHWEITZER, *Das Abendmahl auf Grund der wissentschaftlichen Erforschung des neunzehnten Jahrhunderts und der historischen Berichte,* 1901. HEITMUELLER, *Taufe und Abendmahl bei Paulus,* 1903. J. HOFFMANN, *Das Abendmahl im Urchristentum,* 1903. R. SEEBERG, *Das Abendmahl im N. T.,* 1905. A. ANDERSEN, *Das Abendmahl in den zwei ersten Jahrhunderten,* 1906. B. FRITSCHKOPF, *Die neuesten Eroerterungen ueber die Abendmahlsfrage,* 1921. G. P. WETTER, *Das Christliche Mysterium, Studie zur Geschichte des Abendmahls,* 1921. K. L. SCHMIDT, article *Abendmahl* in *RGG,* I, 6 ff. H. LIETZMANN, *Messe und Herrenmahl,* 1926. C. STANGE, *Die Bedeutung der Sakramente²,* 1927, pp. 55 ff. A. JEREMIAS, *Die Abendmahlsworte Jesu,* 1935. The following English titles are to be added: J. P. LILLEY, *The Lord's Supper, Its Origin, Nature and Use,* 1891. PERCY GARDNER,

*rigin of the Lord's Supper, 1893. LAMBERT, *The Sacraments of the New Testament*, 1903.
aDAMSON, *The Christian Doctrine of the Lord's Supper*, 1905. D. STONE, *History of the Doctrine
f the Holy Eucharist* (*Vol. I*), 1909. J. E. SIMPSON, *The Sacrament of the Gospel*, 1914.
.. ANGUS, *The Mystery Religions and Christianity*, 1925. A. B. McDONALD, *Christian Worship
n the Primitive Church*, 1934. Y. BRILIOTH, *Eucharistic Faith and Practice*, 193. M. REU, *Can
We Still Hold to the Lutheran Doctrine of the Lord's Supper?* (*Kirchliche Zeitschrift*, Columbus,
)hio. As monograph, 1941). See O. W. HEICK in our work, Vol. II, Book V, Section Two,
Chapter IX.
    A part of this literature reflects the overdone endeavor of the Historico-Religious School to
)icture Baptism and Eucharist as resultants from the mystery cults of pagan religions. (Cf. in our
Churches and Sects of Christendom, page 79).
    If Christ in the establishment of the religion of redemption included also the two "sacraments"
vith their appeal to the senses and made them "means of grace" for his followers in Christian
vorship then such an institution must not be put into one category and on one level with those
»agan cults. Psychologically those cults may aid as illustrations to explain the efficacy, but his-
orically they are of an independent origin.

    There is indeed an element of truth in the results of this investigation. It is
)ossible so to think and so to speak of body and blood in the Supper that the two
ippear in the necessary distinction of correlated conceptions so that in the distribution
)f the bread we are forced to think of the body of Christ in the form of the solids
(flesh and bone) and in the receiving of the blood of the fluid element. And then the
:ommunicant will easily be led to the other also objectionable idea, namely to think
)f both as separated from his living person as the organizing factor. It is Christ Himself,
1ot separated and dead particles of His physical, earthly appearance, that we are receiv-
ng in the Lord's Supper. In the mentioning of the blood after the body has been spoken
)f in the words of distribution, we refer, in the meaning of Christ, once more to the
:act that He gave His very life for the forgiveness of our sins by establishing a new
:estament. This does not do away with the need for the Church of using the cup and
·eferring to the wine in the Lord's Supper. In a real supper eating and drinking go
:ogether. And in the use of bread and wine in the sacrament we have a symbolical
iction, the actual and communicated reality being the God-Man Christ Himself, not only
n His divinity, but also in His humanity.
    b. The contribution from John must not be overlooked. Our reference is to John
5:53-56, in which Christ speaks of the eating of His "flesh" and the drinking of His
'blood." Luther and others, in conflict with Zwingli, were not willing to admit that
John 6 was speaking of the Lord's Supper. But many of the best theologians, Seeberg
imong them, have insisted that in John 6 there is reference to the Supper in the same
way as in John 3 the Lord was referring to baptism. If this is true, then we have here
1 New Testament passage which speaks of the flesh (σάρξ) and blood of Christ in the
Supper. We need not here discuss the meaning that was in John's mind.[22] All we are
interested in here is the employment of the terms which continued to be used in the
Church. Ignatius, pupil of John, spoke with much energy of the Eucharist as the flesh
)f our Saviour, and he praises it as an antidote against death.[22a]
    2. The Practice of the Holy Communion in the Early Church.
    a. The early Christians celebrated the Eucharist (in the *Didache*, IX, 5, the name
εὐχαριστία occurs for the first time) at evening, choosing the time of the original institu-
:ion. Of this we are still reminded in some churches by the use of candles. At first,

---

[22] Cf. Seeberg, *DG*, I³, 168. W. Rohnert, in his *Dogmatik* (1902), p. 447 ff. has given a remarkably
exhaustive and lucid review of the problems of John 6.
[22a] *Ad. Eph.*, 20. 2.

when the Christians were few, the service had had the form of a Christian fellowship meeting, which was called the *agape*. But the growth of the Church soon necessitated the separation of Eucharist and agape. [23] The first step was taken in letting the Eucharist precede the agape. The next one was to celebrate the Eucharist in the morning and the agape in the evening. About the end of the fourth century the agape was taken out of the churches and held in private homes, which soon led to its entire discontinuance.

b. At first when the Christians had no houses of worship the liturgical form was very simple. The bishop, or the leader, began with a prayer of praise and thanksgiving spoken over the bread and wine (εὐχαριστίαν ποιεῖται). [24] The congregation answered with "Amen." Next followed the brotherly kiss (φίλημα ἅγιον) to indicate the recon ciliation of hearts. Then the broken bread and the cup were passed. After the third century the liturgy was further developed and used in the *Missa fidelium* which gathered the baptized members of the Church and separated them from those still under cate chetical instruction (*Missa catechumenorum*). We have this more developed liturgy for the Lord's Supper in the *Apostolic Constitutions* (cf. the American edition of the *Nicene and Ante-Nicene Fathers,* VII, 25; VIII, 12-15). [25] According to the liturgy (of James) used in Jerusalem about the third and fourth centuries, the service began with the reading of several prayers. Then followed the offertorium, i.e., the gifts of the com municants in bread and wine, which were gathered by the deacon. The loaf chosen for the celebration was called *hostia.* Now the liturgy continued with a benediction, the brotherly kiss, the washing of hands on the part of the administering clergyman, the warning of the communicants against receiving the sacramental gift unworthily. There followed the preparation of the elements which were guarded against insects by fans used by two sub-deacons. Then the bishop, or the presbyter as his substitute, in an impressive garment, continued with the words *Lift up your hearts,* the congregation answering, *We lift them up to the Lord.* Bishop: *Let us give thanks to the Lord, our God.* Congregation: *This is worthy and right.* Next followed a prayer for the sancti fication of the gifts. After another prayer the bishop said: *The holy to the holy,* answered by the congregation with *One is holy; One is God; One is Jesus Christ, to the honor of God the Father, blessed in all eternity. Amen. Glory be. . . .* During the com munion Psalm 34 was sung. The distribution took place with the simple words, *The Body of Christ, The Blood of Christ, the Cup for eternal life,* the communicant answer ing, *Amen.* Certain localities developed their own liturgies which, however, show their dependency upon the original one. At Alexandria we have the Liturgy of Mark, at Constantinople the Liturgy of Basil, which, in more abbreviated form, issued into the widely used Liturgy of Chrysostom, is in use even today in the Eastern Orthodox Church. Among the Western liturgies the one by Gregory the Great was recognized more and more. [26]

B. GRADUALLY DEVELOPING DOCTRINAL CONCEPTIONS.

Regarding the Lord's Supper and Baptism we cannot speak of a gradually develop ing dogma such as we have concerning the trinitarian relations, the two natures of

---

[23] About A. D. 150. Cf. *PRE,* I, 234, 36 ff.
[24] Cf. I Cor. 11: 24; 10: 16. Just Mart., *Apol.,* I, 66.
[25] On the *Apostolic Constitutions,* their constituent parts and their editions see *PRE,* Vols. VII (734 ff.) and XIII (105 f.); also the *Apostolic Church Orders* in these same volumes.
[26] Cf. W. Rohnert, *Op. cit.*

Christ, and sin and grace. The history of conceptions on the Lord's Supper in the ancient Church does not present a doctrinally logical development, in which the fathers, one taking up the work of the other, had aimed to create a *dogma*. [27] The Middle Ages did produce a *dogma* such as the Roman Catholic Church has today—a dogma which to Protestantism is objectionable not only because of the transubstantiation, but especially because it is converted into a repeated offering of the body of Christ by the priest of the mass. Realism and spiritualism as alternatives, or a certain combination of both, were the heritage of the past when the Reformation came in the sixteenth century. The conflict that took place between Lutheran and Reformed theologians on this subject is a story to be told in Book Three of this work. But for the sake of presenting to the readers all the phases of that realism and spiritualism we shall at least sketch the developments up to the time of the completion of the Roman Catholic dogma in the tenth century.

Literature: We shall make much critical use of the exceedingly profound and complicated article by F. LOOFS in the *PRE*, I, pp. 38-64. With this article we compare the related materials in the *DG⁴*, by the same author. SEEBERG'S *DG*, I³ and II³ has also been frequently consulted. In the same way we mention W. ROHNERT, as referred to; also his *Dogmatik* (1902), pp. 437-483. The investigation of G. E. STEITZ should be mentioned: *Die Abendmahlslehre der griechischen Kirche in ihrer geschichtlichen Entwicklung (Jahrbuecher fuer deutsche Theologie IX-XIII)* (1864-1868). On the problem of the influence of the ancient mysteries, a work was written by G. ANRICH: *Das antike Mysterienwesen in seinem Einfluss auf das Christentum* (1894). Cf. G. WOBBERMIN, *Religionsgeschichtliche Studien zur Frage der Beeinflussung des Christentums durch das antike Mysterienwesen* (1896). The article by KATTENBUSCH in *PRE*, XVII, 351 ff. discusses this question. H. B. SWETE, *Eucharistic Belief in the 2nd and 3rd Centuries (Journal of Theological Studies*, 3, 1900, 161-178). G. REUSCHEN, *Eucharistie und Bussakrament in den ersten 6 Jahrhunderten*, 2nd ed., 1910. H. VON SODEN, *Mysterium und Sacramentum in den ersten zwei Jahrhunderten* in *Zeitschrift fuer Neutestamentliche Wissenschaft* 1911, pp. 188 ff. P. J. DOELGER, *Die Eucharistie nach Inschriften fruehchristlicher Zeit*, 1922. J. GEISELMANN, *Die Eucharistielehre der Vorscholastik*, 1925.

1. Among the Post-Apostolic Fathers and among all the fathers of the ancient Church, excepting the old Alexandrians, one is impressed by their natural and unconcerned realism. The Eucharist was to them in some sense body and blood of Christ. The *Didache* speaks of it as *spiritual food for eternal life* (10, 3). Ignatius, by pointing to John 6: 54, calls it a remedy for immortality, an antidote against death, and the *Docetists* are censured because they deny that the eucharist *is the flesh of our Lord Jesus Christ, which suffered for our sins*. Justin Martyr says: "We receive it not as common bread (κοινὸν ἄρτον) or common drink." It is "the flesh and blood of that Jesus Christ who became man." [28]

2. In reading *Irenaeus* (IV, 17 and 18) we observe a strange emphasis upon the Eucharist as an offering of bread and wine. To this we shall have to return later. Here we are interested in the question whether Irenaeus can be taken as a representative of a realistic conception of the Eucharist. Historically it is a fact that the old distinction in Protestant theology between an earthly and a heavenly matter in the Lord's Supper (*materia terrestris* and *materia coelestis*) goes back, through Luther (E. 30, 116 ff.) to Irenaeus who spoke of a matter ἐπιγείου τε καὶ οὐρανίου. Loofs subjects the meaning of this phrase to a sharp criticism. [29] But finally (cf. *DG*) he himself agrees the Irenaeus

---

[27] Loofs *PRE*, I, 47, lines 12 ff.; cf. 44, 38 ff.
[28] Ignatius, *Ad Eph.*, 20, 2; *Ad Smyrn.*, 7; Justin, *Apol.*, 1, 66.
[29] *PRE*, I, 47 (25)-50 (50); cf. *DG⁴*, 212, note 6.

had a *realistic-dynamic* view. Irenaeus in the above quoted passage argues against the Gnostics: "Because our flesh is nourished in the Eucharist by the body and blood of our Lord therefore it is not possible for our bodies to fall victims of death and decay." But now the meaning of Irenaeus is this, through the prayer of the Church (ἐπίκλησις) the Holy Spirit unites the *Logos* with the elements, bread and wine, and makes them something that they were not before, namely, body and blood of Christ.[30] This was not meant to be transubstantiation, but it is the union of the *Logos* with the elements that makes these the body and blood of the Lord.

3. Concerning *Tertullian,* the question has been much debated whether he represented the realistic or the symbolical view of the Lord's Supper. But are we justified in asking the question in this form which is so natural for us as students of the Reformation and post-Reformation conflict? In the day of Tertullian, of Irenaeus and their predecessors it was altogether possible that a symbolical and in a certain sense realistic conception of the gift in the Supper were not exclusive the one of the other.[31] In those days it was altogether the opposition against the tendency of Docetism in the Gnostic systems that colored the expression of the Catholic fathers. Tertullian sees in the bread a *figura corporis*[32] and remarks that it represents (*representat*) the body.[33] This indicates the symbolical conception.[34]

4. *Origen* (d. 254) was the first who taught consciously the purely spiritualistic symbolical view of the Lord's Supper: The σῶμα in the Eucharist is the body of Christ in a typical and symbolical sense, a pointer only to the true eating of the *Logos,* the living bread." [35] The bread and the wine are symbols of the Word of Christ and the apostles. This Word alone brings benefit to the soul and is of profit to him who approaches the Eucharist with a pure mind and conscience. In the reading of the words of Christ's apostles we drink His blood. This is done outside of the Supper. But in the Eucharist there is added to the Word the symbol.[36] None of the fathers that followed Origen were *spiritualists* to such a degree. Still it is a fact that Eusebius of Caesarea, Basil and Gregory of Nazianzus stood under the influence of Origen.[37] In Athanasius also this influence can be seen, but this father had a stronger inclination to the realism of Irenaeus.[38]

5. The *Antiocheans,* owing to their peculiar Christology in which they declined the organic unity of the two natures in Christ, leaned toward the symbolic conception. Theodore of Mopsuestia, in interpreting I Cor. 11: 34 (cf. *MSG*, 66, 889), spoke of the elements as symbols of the death of Christ.[39] Theodoret (d. 457) said of the elements: "These remain what they are, but in the pious consideration they become body and blood of Christ." In the details of his position, however, he, the master of union

---

[30] See Seeberg *DG*, I³, 458 f.
[31] Cf. Loofs in the *PRE*, I, 44.
[32] *Adv. Marc.*, IV, 40.
[33] *Loc. Cit.*, I, 14.
[34] As to Tertullian's view in all respects, see Leimbach, *Beitraege zur Abendmahlslehre Tertullians* (1874) who saw in Tertullian a representative of the Lutheran view (to which Harnack agreed in his *DG*, I⁴, 477); but compare with these Loofs, *PRE*, I, 59 f. and Seeberg, *DG*, I³, 462 f. who insist with certain qualifications that, after all, the position of Tertullian is the symbolical one.
[35] Loofs *ut supra*, p. 49, line 51.
[36] See the references to Origen's writings as given by Loofs, p. 49 f.
[37] For the details we refer to Steitz, X, 97 ff.; 127.; 133 ff.
[38] Cf. Thomasius-Bonwetsch, I, 431.
[39] Loofs *ut supra*, p. 55, lines 46 ff.

formulas in the field of Christology present a kind of *mixtum* of the realistic-dynamic with the symbolical, also regarding the Lord's Supper. [40]

6. *The Final Development into Transubstantiation in the East.* Here it is necessary to distinguish precursory expressions from the final result.

a. We have spoken of the *Didache,* of Ignatius and Justin and of Irenaeus as being realists without teaching transubstantiation. The Eucharist was taken to be the body and blood of Christ. Up to Irenaeus there was no theorizing on the manner. Irenaeus and Tertullian theorized in the manner we have tried to describe (cf. pp. 42, 96).

b. In our tracing the whole development we have, so far, avoided discussion of a rather innocent idea that had been functioning from the beginning, but which in the end became a strongly contributing factor in preparing the way for transubstantiation —the conception of the Eucharist as being essentially an *offering.* Originally the Eucharist had the significance of an offering of praise (*sacrificium laudis*), an offering of the lips (Acts 5: 8; 8: 3 f.; Hebr. 13: 15; cf. Hosea 14: 3; Ps. 50: 25 and 116: 17) on the part of the participating congregation for the gifts of God in bread and wine which are now brought as offerings, even for the need of the poor. But soon the saying of these Eucharistic prayers over the oblations were made the special duty of the officers of the Church, [41] namely the bishops (or presbyters) and the deacons who were compared with the priests and the Levites of the O. T. and their offerings. Soon the real act of offering was seen, not in the offering of the congregation, but in the dedication of those gifts for use in the Eucharist. Gradually the τοῦτο ποιεῖτε, the words of Christ in the institution of the Supper (*this do*), had the meaning that was later given this phrase in the Decrees of Trent (*sessio* 12, *can.* 1). The next step in the development is seen in the words of Cyprian: "The bishop now imitates that which Christ did, and he offers the true and full sacrifice in the Church to God the Father." [42] This seemed natural, because bread and wine were held to be the body and blood of Christ. Cyprian simply stated what was already the belief of his age.

c. Transubstantiation is now in sight. The spiritualistic conception of the Origenists was discredited. This was the natural result of the Christological conflicts as we have described them in Chapter X. Four theologians must here be mentioned:

(1) Cyril of Jerusalem (d. 386). There was an emphasis upon the mysterious. The bread was looked upon as actually being the body of Christ. Cyril addressed the baptized in his church in his *Mystagogical Catechizations.* In the fourth and the fifth of these (*MSG,* 33, 1097 ff.) he deals with the mystery of the Lord's Supper. The object of worship is the Christ as He is prepared for an offering (5, 10, p. 1117). The significance of this sacrament is seen in the words, *this is my body.* Bread and wine are changed into body and blood. It is a μεταβολή, brought about through a calling (ἐπίκλησις) upon the Holy Spirit (5, 7, p. 1113). Now that which seems to be bread is not bread anymore, but body of Christ.

(2) Gregory of Nyssa (d. 394) wrote on the Lord's Supper in a certain catechization (C. 37 MSG 45, 93 ff.). Here he is also interested in the question of how our bodies may become liberated from the poison that makes us victims of death. His answer is that this can be expected only when, through the Eucharist, Christ's body is

---

[40] Cf. Loofs, 56, 4.
[41] 1 Clem., 44, 4.
[42] Ep., 63, 14.

received as food by the digestive organs of our body. The bread becomes, through consecration (sanctification), the eucharistic body of Christ, which now has that above mentioned effect upon our body. The theory reminds us of Justin Martyr (see above). Here we cannot enter into the detailed explanations by Loofs in PRE, I, 54, but simply want to call attention to the physiological character of Gregory's so-called *transformation theory.*

    (3) *Chrysostom* (d. 407) indulges in a description of a very coarse and sensual kind of real presence. [43] He speaks of a preparation (μετασχευάζειν) of the elements through which the bread becomes the real body of Christ so that we can see it and eat it with the teeth.

    (4) *Cyril of Alexandria* (d. 444),[44] drew the consequences of his Christology that stressed the absolute union of the two natures, which kept him in the main from the crass-sensualistic language of Gregory of Nyssa and of Chrysostom. But he reveals the common drift of the age to transubstantiation when he says that what lies on the altar is the real body of the *Logos* (IV, 6), even though it is covered by the form of the bread and wine (on Matt. 26: 26-28). But he reconciles us again when he speaks of the effect of the Eucharist, stating that it is through the Spirit of the *Logos,* which is not different from the work of the Holy Spirit upon man. [45]

    (5) *John of Damascus* (d. 750) became the formulator of the transubstantiation dogma for the Eastern Church.

    There was an old statement that had always been respected: Bread and wine in the Eucharist are the types of the body and blood of Christ. [46] At the iconoclastic synod (Constantinople, 754) it was declared that these are the *only* types of Christ's humanity. But John of Damascus, strong advocate of the images, had discredited this statement. [47] If some of the holy Fathers (for instance Basil in the liturgy) had so spoken, then they had not meant the consecrated (ἁγιασμόν) but the unconsecrated elements. This declaration was adopted at the second synod of Nicaea (787). [48] In other words, through the consecration the body and blood of Christ is created (μεταποιοῦνται εἰς τὸ σῶμα καὶ αἷμα τοῦ Χριστοῦ). [49] In his explanation of this transubstantiation dogma John uses the word μεταβάλλονται.[50] Loofs[51] offers reasons for calling this a transubstantiation theory in which ideas of Gregory of Nyssa and of Cyril of Alexandria are combined. We cannot go into the details of a further explanation here. The Roman Catholic Church later insisted upon the term μετουσίωσις (instead of μεταποίωσις), to which the Eastern Church (1274 and 1277) consented. [52]

    7. *The Developments in the West preparatory to the adoption of Transubstantiation as a Dogma.*

    a. *Ambrose* (d. 397) is the first to be considered. In his *De fide,* 4: 10, 124 he speaks of the Eucharist as an offering. Is there symbolical meaning to this? Some of

---

[43] *De sacerdote,* VI, 5. Cf. *Hom.,* 45, 2 on John, 6.

[44] See *Adv. Nest.* IV, 5, 6.

[45] *MSG,* 76, 376; 73, 601 f., 604.

[46] ἀντίτυπα τοῦ σώματος καὶ αἵματος τοῦ κυρίου. Gregory of Nazianzus, *Oration,* 8, 18.

[47] *De fide orthodoxa,* 4, 13.

[48] Mansi, XIII, 266.

[49] *De fide,* IV, 3.

[50] See Mansi, XIII, 270.

[51] *Ut supra,* p. 57.

[52] For explanation of the difference see Loofs, *PRE,* I, p. 57, line 51; cf. p. 54, line 15, 29.

his utterances have the symbolical ring. That offering is to him an *imago veritatis*.[53] But with this symbolical conception he combines the realistic-dynamic one of Irenaeus and his successors, and in his *De fide*, IV, we find the idea of a transubstantiation.[54] This would presuppose a real presence of the body of Christ at the altar. The same is suggested in the two writings *De Sacramentis* and *De Mysteriis*. These are not considered to have had Ambrose as their real author. But Loofs, whom we have here again been following (p. 61), suggests that for this reason these two writings are the much more characteristic of the transubstantiation sentiment also in the West, because they give expression to the fact that this sentiment was a general one.

b. *Augustine* (430) is of special interest regarding the conceptions of the Lord's Supper in the West. His teaching, however, presents a peculiar dualism. Again we must remind ourselves of his definition of a sacrament: *a visible sign of an invisible grace.*

(1) The body of Christ is to Augustine only a *sign* of the body. It is the mystical body by which he understands the Church, the fellowship of the saints. It is the Church that is symbolized in the Lord's Supper. Therefore the real Christians only receive the benefit. The benefit consists in this that it symbolizes our union with Christ, the spirit of love proceeding from Him and operative in the Church.[55] This is Augustine's symbolical conception of the Eucharist. It is to remind us of Christ's suffering and to stimulate us for the union of love as members of His body which is the Church.

(2) There is also another strain in the language of Augustine on the Lord's Supper. He speaks of a manducation of the flesh of Christ, of a drinking of the blood. The elements are called *corpus et sanguis Christi* (*Sermo* 234, 2). The bread is made the body through the benediction of Christ (*Sermo* 234, 2; 227). The converted Jews drink the blood which once they poured out (*Sermo* 77, 3.4.). Loofs and Seeberg insist that all such expressions are not irreconcilable with Augustine's symbolical conception,[56] and they refer to the fact that he denies repeatedly the ubiquity of the body of the glorified Christ; to him it is confined in one place in heaven.[57]

(3) Augustine also makes use of the idea of his age that the Eucharist is an offering. It is to remind the Christians of the original offering.[58] And it has the significance *of asserting the redeeming power of Christ's offering before God.* Occasionally Augustine would say that the congregation of believers, in the union with Christ in the Supper, brings itself as an offering to God.[59] The aim is to express (1) the consciousness that Christ's offering was for our redemption, and (2) to remind us of the duty to offer our own lives to Christ.[60]

8. It is historically of greatest importance that the most outstanding teacher of Western Catholicism occupied about the same position on the Lord's Supper which later was taken by *heretics* such as Berengar, Wyclif, (Zwingli), Calvin and their successors.

---

[53] On Ps. 38; cf. opp. Ambr. in the edition of the Benedictines, IV, c. 25.

[54] Cf. 9, 50; *Natura ipsa mutatur.*

[55] These observations of Seeberg, *DG*, II[3], 459 are supported by the following references: *Sermons on John,* 26: 10, 13, 15, 17, 18; *De Civ.*, XXI, 25, 2; *serm.*, 272; *ep.*, 185, 11, 50.

[56] Cf. however, the remark of Kattenbusch, *PRE*, 356, lines 48-60.

[57] *Ep.*, 187, 12, 41; 3, 10; *De Civ.*, XXII, 29, 4; *De agone Chr.*, 20.28; *Ad Catech.*, IV, 11; on John, 50, 4, 13. These references by Seeberg.

[58] *Contra Faust.*, XX, 18; *De 83 Quest.*, 61, 2; 20, 21.

[59] *De Civ.*, X, 6, 20.

[60] Seeberg, *DG*, II[3], 463.

It was Augustine who threw back for centuries the development in the West toward transubstantiation. And it was the authority of this church father that has kept transubstantiation from being a unanimously adopted dogma absolutely in the Roman Catholic Church.

 c. The real doctrine of transubstantiation with stressing of the actual alteration of the elements through the act of consecration, finally appeared in the *Canon of the Mass* issued by Gregory the Great (d. 604). Here we hear of the sacrament of the altar as a continually repeated sacrifice (*quotidinum immolationis sacrificium*) of Christ for our redemption. Still the heritage from Augustine had its adherents.

 9. *The Final Victory of Transubstantiation in the West,* came through a double conflict in the Middle Ages, in the ninth and the eleventh centuries. We refer to the Radbertus-Hrabanus-Ratramnus controversy in the ninth century and the protest of Berengar against transubstantiation two hundred years later. This is a story to be told in the review of the Middle Ages.

Chapter Thirteen

CONCLUDING OBSERVATIONS: THE CHRISTIANITY OF THE EAST AND OF THE WEST

In the preceding chapters, the dogma of the ancient Church has been traced in its development from the first elementary statements in the *Rules of Faith* (Chapter VI) into the more matured expressions of the so-called *Ecumenical Creeds* of Christendom, namely: the *Nicene,* or more correctly, the *Niceno-Constantinopolitan Creed;* and the *Creed of Chalcedon.* In addition to these two creeds which cover (1) Christ in His trinitarian relation or His *pre-existence* and (2) His historical *postexistence* as *God-man,* we may also mention (3) the decisions of the Synod of Orange (529) on the relation of the saving will of God to the spiritual power of man in the acts of his salvation.

Note: The twenty-five canons of this synod have not been counted among the *ecumenical* creeds of Christendom. They do not cover the whole doctrine of sin and grace in all the lessons from the great conflict between Augustine and Pelagius. The fuller religious experience of the soteriological sphere of Christian belief belongs to the Reformation of the sixteenth century. But the statements of the synod of Orange, as the result of the Semi-Pelagian controversies, present to us a remarkable anticipation of evangelical teaching on God and man as factors in the appropriation of salvation.

These creedal deliverances, as they have been traced and as they gradually found a more popular form in the so-called Apostles' Creed, started and developed in conflict with fundamental errors: Ebionitism, Gnosticism, Marcionism (Chapter V); Monarchianism, Arianism (Chapter IX); Nestorianism and Eutychianism (Chapter X); Pelagianism and Semi-Pelagianism (Chapter XI). Was this activity in the formulating of creeds nothing but the work of speculating theologians? The catechists of the Church, surely, had to speak on these things in a positive way, and they had to show the unity of the catholic faith. The rules of faith and the creeds were a necessity. If the theologians had not spoken, the laymen would have. And let it not be overlooked that the truth of the Christian dogma was prayed and sung before it was formulated (see Chapter I).

The special dogma of the Church must be seen in the statements on the full divinity and humanity of Christ (Chapters IX and X). The profession of Christ's divinity was enlarged and developed into the dogma of the trinitarian relation of Father, Son and Holy Spirit. It was the dogma in this sense that was later taken over by Luther and all the Reformers.

With this faith as a common possession, the East and the West differed remarkably in many of the religious views in the type of their theology and in their piety. In Chapter IX we have described in comparative discussion the differences between East and West on the problems of anthropology and soteriology. The sections 1 and 2 of this chapter ought here to be reviewed by the reader. But the difference in the Christianity of the East and the West as a whole can be pictured best in separate description:

I. EASTERN CHRISTIANITY

1. The direction for Greek theology was received from Origen. While much in the details of his teaching was refused, there was, nevertheless, something in his theology that continued to be characteristic of Christian thought among the Greeks. The significance of Origen lay in his combination of a threefold interest. He was interested in the Church's tradition, in the authority of the Scriptures, and in the Hellenistic philosophy. His allegorizing method in the interpretation of Scripture opened to him the way for a speculation in which he aimed to show the unity of Christianity and philosophy. But his regard for Christian tradition helped him to a certain conservatism in the admission of the topics for speculation. His high regard for the Scriptures and his own example as the first real exegete, brought impulses for an extensive interpretation of the New Testament, and it stimulated the growing interest in a recognized canon. Chief in urging such a Canon of Holy Scriptures was Athanasius (see his Easter letter of 367). This was accidental. But the permanent trait which Greek theology received from the school of Alexandria was that endeavor of Origen to unite the Gospel in the form of apostolic tradition with the Hellenistic philosophy in the form of Neo-Platonism. It was the conviction that Christianity and Hellenism agree in the main. In the eyes of the Alexandrians God was both *Agape* and *Eros*. This relation to Neo-Platonism characterized also the teaching of so prominent a theologian as Methodius of Olympus (d. 311), who otherwise rejected decisively the many spiritualistic heresies of Origen and his allegoric method of Scripture interpretation, and who corrected him by referring to the sane theology of Irenaeus.

2. The meaning of salvation in Greek theology must have brief consideration. It was not fully the same as in Latin theology. This explains certain characteristics which must not be overlooked. Among the Greeks, as remarked by Fisher, the *guilt* of sin was not felt with the same intensity as was its *effect,* which was seen in the corrupting influences of sin, particularly in the blinding of man's spiritual vision to the knowledge of God. Jesus, as Saviour, was taken to be more the restorer of sin's injury than the remover of its guilt. His work was for the bestowal of incorruption ($\dot{\alpha}\varphi\theta\alpha\varrho\sigma\acute{\iota}\alpha$). This must not be taken to mean that the idea of Christ's death as a ransom ($\lambda\acute{\upsilon}\tau\varrho\upsilon\nu$) was absent; it is professed by John of Damascus (III, 27). But the stress was upon Christ as giver of divine life, the remover of the corruption wrought by sin, the restorer of the real God-likeness in a $\theta\epsilon\upsilon\pi\upsilon\acute{\iota}\eta\sigma\iota\varsigma$ and in the communication of God's $\delta\acute{\upsilon}\xi\alpha$.[1] The idea of Christ's death bringing the forgiveness of sin has no stress among the Greeks. They failed to appropriate the Pauline idea of justification. Thus they overlooked the causal connection between the regeneration of the heart and the good works that are to follow. Thus also faith lost its Scriptural meaning of a personal attitude, i.e., of a *fiducia* in the forgiving grace of God, and it became an orthodoxy with regard to the formal statements of dogma.

For reading: E. SCHOLZ, *Die Lehre des heil. Basilius von der Gnade,* 1881. F. K. HUEMMER, *Des heil. Gregor von Nazianz Lehre von der Gnade,* 1890. K. HOLL, *Enthusiasmus and Bussgewalt beim Griech, Moenchtum,* 1898. E. WEIGEL, *Die Heilslehre des heil. Cyril von Alexandrien,* 1905. J. AUFHAUSER, *Die Heilslehre des heil. Gregor von Nyssa,* 1910. SEEBERG, DG, II³, 307 ff. Cf. F. KATTENBUSCH, *Konfessionskunde* I, and F. LOOFS, *Symbolik* I. Cf. G. AULÉN's treatment of the work of Christ in the Greek Fathers, *Christus Victor,* 1931. See our discussion of him in *Introduction* and in Vol. II, Book V, Sec. I, Chapter IX.

---

[1] Didymos, *De trin.,* III, 2; II, 12.

3. The Mystagogical Trait in Eastern Theology—(The writings of Dionysius the
reopagite and Related Literature).

a. There was a double trait in Eastern theology that must here be discussed in its
elation of the one to the other. The Greek mind had a deep interest in truth. To
ocrates virtue was practically knowledge. Paul writes (1 Cor. 1: 22): "The Greeks
ek after wisdom." The Gnostics sought real religion in a higher knowledge and they
onstructed it with faith. (See Chapter V, sec. II, 3). Clement and Origen took faith
• be the lower stage in religion, it is to be developed into knowledge (Chapter VIII, sec.
I, 6). The task of the Greek theologians was to reduce the essentials of religion to
andamental statements, to dogmas.

But closely related to this interest a seemingly opposite interest was already observ-
ole among the Greeks of the pre-Christian era. It was found that philosophical truth,
fter it had been seen and expressed in formulated sentences (dogmas) is in danger of
•sing its influence upon the life of its followers. This observation produced the culti-
ation of the Greek mysteries. They were intended to reveal and to communicate the
uth more fully, and to keep the faculties of the worshipper in a continued activity.
he intellectual, discursive activity of the soul is submerged into a state of immediate
eholding by means of the mystery in allegory, symbol and representation. The Gnostics
1ade much of this (cf. Chapter V, sec. II, 8). But it also affected the Church, especially
1 the East. We refer to the Mystagogical Catechizations of Cyril of Jerusalem.[2] The
hristian theologians are advised to use the mysteries as symbolizations of heavenly
1ings. The Trinity and the doctrine of incarnation, especially, were represented in
orms of the mysteries. But while the pagan mysteries did grow out of the interest to
afeguard the continued life of the philosophical principles, it must be said that in the
hurch of the East the embodiment of Christian truth in mystery forms issued into a
itualism through which Christian life became petrified and lost its creative power.[3]

b. The Writings of Dionysius the Areopagite and Related Literature. A factor
•hich contributed to making the Eastern Church a peculiar denomination was the
1fluence exercised upon it by the writings which in the last quarter of the fifth century
ppeared under the name of *Dionysius the Areopagite.* When the teachings of this
•riter were accepted, it was believed that they were from a pupil of Paul (Acts 17: 34).
Ve know now, and have known for a long time that these writings are of pseudonymous
rigin, dating from the fifth century, (about 482) and written, probably, by a Syrian.
hey are composed of four tracts: (1) The Names of God; (2) The Mystical Theology;
3) The Heavenly Hierarchy; and (4) The Church's Hierarchy. In their contents they
eveal the ideas of Proclus (d. 485), one of the last representatives of the Neo-Platonian
chool at Athens. It seems to have been their aim to incorporate Neo-Platonism into
he teachings of the Church and thus to remove it as an opponent. The text of these
vritings is found in the *MSG,* tom. 3, 4; translated into German in *BKV.*

On the basis of a Neo-Platonic abstract conception of the Godhead, in which the
rinitarian relation and the incarnated Christ in union with the Father is recognized, a
loctrine as follows was proposed: The Divine Being, which cannot be expressed in
oredicates and attributes, is to be thought of as the center of hierarchies of created

---

[2] *MSG* 33, 1065-1128; cf. *NPF,* Vol. VII.
[3] See Loofs, *DG*[4], 318; especially the most interesting discussion by H. Schmidt, *Symbolik,* pp. 43-52.
eeberg *DG,* II[8], 307 ff.

beings. Closest to God, in a first periphery, is the *heavenly hierarchy* represented b
three orders of angels ranging from the highest to the lowest. Then follows the *eccles*
astical hierarchy which again has three orders—bishops, priests and deacons. Final
comes the *lay hierarchy* which extends from the monks down to the other laity. At th
head of these orders stands Christ as the highest Hierarch. The Word, Sacraments, an
the gifts of the Spirit are the means through which the process of a gradual deificatic
is to go on. These theories of the *Areopagite* served as the frame for expressing cha
acteristic elements in the piety of Greek Christianity which were continued in th
Christianity of the West. The aim is to arrive at a union with God in a mystical fashic
without employing intellect and understanding. Here the influence proceeds from th
highest hierarchy, the angels, and through the priesthood down to the laity, by employir
a whole system of initiations. By a worship that stimulates spiritual devotions the so
is to be lifted up into a participation of the divine ($\theta\varepsilon o\pi o \acute{\iota}\eta\sigma\iota\varsigma$). It is the hierarcl
that effects the union of man with God. Christ himself is the source and power of th
hierarchy. Here is the authority. We know how this principle has been abused in
system which converted Christianity into a cultic institution to be directed by th
priesthood. But it must be admitted that this whole mystagogical theology was expre
sive of a deep-seated trait in the religious practice of devotion among the Eastern race

There is a large literature of the same character that grew out of the mystagogical tendenci
of the Eastern Church and extended deep into the Middle Ages. As a movement it represents
kind of parallel to the age of scholasticism in the Roman Church, except that it is exclusive
mystical. We cannot here go into a detailed description. But we refer the student to H. Koc
Pseudo-Dionysius Areopagita in his *Beziehungen zum Neuplatonismus und Mysterienwesen*, 190
And to NYGRÉN'S discussion in *Agape and Eros*, Part II, Vol. II, pp. 345 ff. See also the illuminatir
article of KATTENBUSCH on *Mystagogische Theologie* in Vol. XIII of the *PRE*, 612-622. It was upc
this basis that the mystagogical and, in connection with it, the mystical-liturgical character of th
Eastern Orthodox Church reached its full development.[4] Cf. SEEBERG, *DG*, II³, 307 ff. R. M. JONE
Studies in Mystical Religion, chap. 6, 1909. C. E. BOLT, *Dionysius the Areopagite on the Divir
Names and the Mystical Theology*, 1920. H. F. MUELLER, *Dionysius, Proklos, Plotinos*, 191
H. BALL, *Byzantinisches Christentum*, chapter 2, 1923.

4. A Dogma Concerning the Veneration of Images. Loofs calls attention to th
peculiar observation that, parallel with the adoption of the ecumenical creeds, in th
field of practical piety a lower Christianity was in the process of development. We ma
call it a paganized religion. It manifested itself in the worshiping of saints, angels an
of the Virgin Mary, of the cross, of images and relics. Since about the fourth centur
this *Christentum zweiter Ordnung*, as Harnack has called it[5] had become so strong tha
in the Greek Church, with the seventh ecumenical council at Nicaea (787), it resulte
in a dogma that sanctioned the veneration of images. The report of the circumstanc
in that conflict in which the theologians and especially the monks advocated the vener
tion of images, while the emperor with the soldiers violently opposed the practice, ma
be left to Church History. It seems that the state looked upon the worship of imag
as an indulgence in a private mystical piety that tended to have a weakening influenc
upon the virility of a nation that found itself in a life and death struggle with the forc
of Mohammedanism. On the other hand, the following may be enumerated as a
explanation of the advocacy of image worship: (1) Neo-Platonism with its persister
influence upon the theologians of that day stood for the principle that the heavenl

---

[4] *PRE* Vol. iv. 694 ff.
[5] *DG*⁴. II. 441; cf. *Grundriss*⁶, p. 272.

rces work through earthly symbols and images. (2) Monophysitism, as taught by the
:er Alexandrian School, particularly by Cyril, was a strong undercurrent of Greek piety.
nd now a picture of Jesus as man was looked upon as the symbol of His Deity. John
amascus contributed much to the final decision by his three orations on the images.[6]

II. WESTERN CHRISTIANITY

As Origen was in a special way the father of Eastern theology, so Tertullian and
ugustine have been the special makers of Western theology and Christianity. Our
terest here must be first in the pre-Augustinian and in the pre-Gregorian expressions
Western Christianity.

A review of the situation must recall the teachings of Tertullian, in which he laid
undations for the theology of the West. These were touched upon in Chapter VIII, C.
'ith Tertullian must be mentioned Cyprian and the bishops of Rome. There were
her theologians who also contributed. Some of them had been under the influence
Greek scholars: Hilary, Faustinus, Victorinus, Rhetor, Rufinus, Jerome, Ambrose.
hese have been channels for the transmission of Origen's exegesis and the theology of
e Cappadocians into the West. Others were more Latin in character: Optatus, Pacian,
·udentius, Zeno and others. Among all Western theologians before Augustine, Ambrose
as the most influential.

Literature: Some of the men here mentioned have biographers, or they are covered by articles
the encyclopedias. See the enumeration of literature by HARNACK, *Grundriss*[6], p. 286; LOOFS[4],
333; SEEBERG, *DG*, II[3], 363.

In the following we shall enumerate a number of factors that constituted the char-
·teristics of Western Christianity and theology.

Western Christianity was governed by the interest of creedal authority, the authority
a recognized creed, namely the so-called "Roman Symbol" (cf. Chapter VI). The
ıte was sounded by Tertullian when he demanded that *crede quod traditum est.*[7] He
lls the symbol "a law of faith" (*lex fidei, in Virg.* vol. 1—Spect. 4). In the mind of
:rtullian, furthermore, there goes with this demand to submit to the rule of faith the
·nception that the Biblical foundations for the Symbol are rational, comparable to the
ıtural knowledge of God. Reason and faith, therefore, are not antithetical. Tertullian
as a believer in what was later expressed as, *Credo, ut intelligam.* Like the Apologists
· believed that Christianity is the truly rational religion.

With this was associated that peculiar legalism which soon appears as a character-
tic of Western Roman Christianity. As the East inclined to speculation, so the West
as interested in moral righteousness, which, as Seeberg observes, had its first orientation
ı a peculiar combination of Stoic moralism (Seneca, Cicero) with Judaistic legalism.[8]
·race, to Tertullian, comes through the law which teaches man to do the good, and to
ırn eternal life as a reward. In his description of the process of the soul's salvation
e moves in legal terms. There is man's deficiency in consequence of an inherited sinful
ɔndition. In Baptism man is judged as one who has been forgiven. Now there is
ιe demand upon the Christian to fulfill the law and even to accumulate merits before

---

[6] Sources: Mansi, *Acta concil.* XII, 951, seqq. XIII, 1-820. Hefele, *Conciliengeschichte*[a] III, 441-490.
[7] *De Carne Christi,* 2.
[8] Cf. Seeberg *DG, I*[3]. 642 f.

God. His shortcomings call for a repentance which must express itself in satisfaction
A question that troubled the Church for a long time was whether after Baptism it we
admissible for all sins, and whether after Baptism the way were open to more than or
repentance. In the principles advocated by the Roman bishop Callistus, foundation
were laid for repentance as an institution on the basis of a further development of th
teaching of Tertullian and Cyprian. The gradual result was an elaborate system o
legalism.

At the same time we note as a characteristic of Western Chrisitianity the intere
in the institutional features of the Church. This was natural. The Romans expresse
their highest ideals in the state with its organization, it rights, it authorities, its offic
and laws. We have seen how legalism dominated in the field of soteriology. This
followed in the Church by an interest in the institutional conceptions of Christiani
with their aim of providing for tangible assurances of salvation in absolution and mult
plied sacramental acts. The development into the institutional introduced the proble
of the relation of the spiritual forces within the Church to the hierarchically organize
Church. We have traced the whole development in Chapter VII. It was a problem fo
the East as well as the West, but in Western Christianity the movement is characterize
by the interests of nascent Roman Catholicism.

The contribution to Western theology and Christianity from Tertullian has bee
discussed. Augustine, however, was also a powerful factor: (1) Concerning the doctri
of the Trinity he stressed the unity, thus recognizing a legitimate element in Monarchia
ism to which Rome had been holding. It found expression in Part One of the so-calle
Athanasian Creed which originated and came into use in the West. The devotion wit
which Augustine dealt with this problem in his *De Trinitate,* impressed upon the Churc
a lesson that this dogma must be forever a fundamental in the Christian Church. A
the Reformers were in agreement on this point. And even we of today take no excep
tion because the conception of God as the Triune is in true agreement with Christia
experience. (2) In the conflict of Augustine with Pelagianism and Semi-Pelagianis
the soteriological interest of Western theology came to a thorough discussion. Th
special problem of the West was: What shall I do to be saved? The chief message o
the theologians about the time of Augustine, and already before him (Ambrose an
Hilary) was on the way of salvation. And (3) through the Donatistic controvers
the objective character of the means of grace and of the Church had been safeguarde

Along the lines here reviewed we observe tenets of Western Christianity whic
were not so much discussed by the theologians of the East.

Both the Eastern and the Western form of Christianity represent the beginning o
denominational types with further characteristics to be developed during the Middle Age

BOOK TWO

The Middle Ages

By Dr. O. W. Heick

Literature: The reader will continue to be guided by some of the fundamental literature which ıs presented and described in Book One on "Introductory Matters."

Orientation with Regard to Original Sources. The references are to HEFELE, *Konzilienschichte,* vol. 3; J. D. MANSI, *Sacrorum Conciliorum nova et amplissima collectio,* latest print 03, and especially to the corresponding volumes in *Migne (MSL).*

As to the works of historical investigation, we refer to such standard works of Histories of octrine as J. BACH, R. SEEBERG, A. HARNACK, F. LOOFS, and the condensed two editions by WIEGAND (in the original larger edition Volume Two). Among the American Histories of octrine compare G. P. FISHER and the second volume of A. C. MCGIFFERT (subtitle: *The West om Tertullian to Erasmus*). Special attention, however, must be called to the already mentioned ɔlume Three of R. SEEBERG'S *Dogmengeschichte*[4], 1930 (797 pages). Very much History of ıristian Thought is found in the *Cambridge History of the Middle Ages* (12 vols.) and HAUCK'S *Kirchengeschichte Deutschlands.* The interpretation of the social implications of ıristianity in the Medieval Church is discussed by E. TROELTSCH in the *Social Teachings of the* bristian *Churches,* Volume One, 1931. On the Middle Ages in general, see H. O. TAYLOR, *The* assical *Heritage of the Middle Ages*[3], 1919 and the *Medieval Mind*[4], 2 vols., 1925, by the same ıthor; also J. FICKER and H. HERMELINK, *Das Mittelalter,* 1929, and the *Cambridge Studies in* edieval *Life and Thought,* edited by G. G. COULTON, (3 vols.). As to selected passages from iginal sources in an English translation, we want to direct the student to F. A. OGG, *Source Book Medieval History;* G. G. COULTON, *Life in the Middle Ages;* O. J. THATCHER and E. N. CNEAL, *Source Book for Medieval History;* and O. J. THATCHER, *Ideas That Have Influenced* ivilization (vols. 4 and 5). For selected passages in a German translation see H. RINN, *Dogmen- schichtliches Lesebuch,* 1910, pp. 227-329. Finally, much information may be gained from the ıcyclopedias such as A. HAUCK, *Protestantische Realenzyklopaedie* (PRE), the *New Schaff-Herzog ıcyclopedia of Religious Knowledge* (NSH), HASTINGS, *Encyclopedia of Religion and Ethics,* ıd the *Catholic Encyclopedia,* and *Die Religion in Geschichte und Gegenwart* (RGG).

INTRODUCTORY NOTES

(1) Transition from the Ancient Church to the Middle Ages. In the closing ıapter of Book One an estimate was given of the theological work in the Ancient .hurch. A Christological dogma had been worked out, which constituted the central ıd integral part of a Trinitarian conception of God and his relation to man. In addition, ıe conflicts concerning the doctrine of sin and grace had yielded certain evangelical ɔnceptions. At this status of the development the classical countries of Christianity xperienced the Mohammedan invasion. Both the Christian life and the spirit of the- logical work were quenched by the invasion. New objects for Christianization appeared ı the settling of the Germanic peoples that had emigrated from the East. From the .rianism which they had adopted in passing the gates of Constantinople they soon ırned to Athanasian Christianity. By and by they began to produce theological scholars. Ve read of them at the court of Charlemagne, in Spain, and in England. In the main, owever, they were yet like children, just wondering at the dogmatic creation of the ast. Still they gradually began to do a thinking of their own. All theological thought, owever, was a starting at the foot of the hill. The philosophy in the East, that potent

factor for the stimulation of dogmatic work, had been suppressed under the Isla
invasion. In theology, Rome had nothing to contribute. Its contribution to the a,
beginning with Gregory the Great, was the education of the new races in the elementa
matters of religion.

(2) The rise and the degeneration of the papacy and of scholasticism furnish
objects for interesting studies. The conception of the Church, the interest of t
hierarchy, legalism, asceticism, repentance, sin and grace, mysticism, the interactio
between philosophy and theology—all these will claim much of our attention in th
very brief review of the Middle Ages. Neo-Platonism and Aristotelianism again becan
objects of interest and constituted new temptations for the adulteration of Christi
doctrine. This was the complaint of the Reformation.

Chapter One

THE THEOLOGY OF GREGORY THE GREAT

Literature: Sources: *MSL* 75-79. Gregory's letters, edited by P. EWALD and L. M. HARTMANN. idies: H. K. MANN, *Lives of the Popes in the Middle Ages,* 1902 ff.; vol. 1, 1-250. F. H. JDDEN, *Gregory the Great, His Place in History and Thought,* 2 vols., 1905; H. H. HOWARTH, *egory the Great,* 1912; SNOW, *St. Gregory the Great,* 1924.

1. Gregory the Great may be compared to the doubleheaded Janus of the Romans. e looked backward upon six centuries and at the same time forward upon a new age hich derived its character from the tasks growing out of the collapse of antiquity and e migration of new races into Europe.

This man, who ruled dogmatic thought in the Church undisputedly for five hundred ars, and whose theology is still dominant in the Roman Church, was born about 540. ne son of a Christian senator at Rome, he began public life as a Roman prefect. He ok monastic vows, founded cloisters, became an abbot, and was elected pope in 590. s such he sought political independence and security for the papacy, and by his political gacity safeguarded the secular interest of the curia. In England he is remembered for e missionary expedition he sent to the Anglo-Saxons in 596. Through untiring cor- spondence, through his writings and liturgical reforms, he made his influence dominant pecially along practical lines. Chief among his writings are: *Exposition on Job* in 35 oks called *Moralia* and *Dialogue on the Life and Miracles of Pious Fathers in Italy,* ith appended thoughts on the immortality of the soul. He died in 604.

Gregory was a wise and energetic churchman, a shrewd politician, a lovable and nperative shepherd of souls. His theology issued into regulations for church life. nder forms familiar to Augustinianism he brought into the dogmatic storehouse of e Church the popular type of religious thought, adding many superstitious elements e original source of which was paganism.[1] His theology though variously described hodge-podge, or a *mixtum compositum,* remained within the bonds of the orthodox id down in the first four ecumenical councils.

2. A brief review of Gregory's teaching reveals the following: *a.* The Scriptures, cluding the four Gospels and Tradition covering the four Ecumenical Councils from icea to Chalcedon, constitute a full and equal dogmatic authority.[2]

b. God exists of three persons in one divine substance.[3] Christ is the God-Man, nly God, of one essence with the Father, also true Man, joined to us.

c. Christ, being sinless, became for us Mediator and Redeemer through His incar- ntion and by His dying, in order to remove God's wrath against sin. But the redemption also considered a price paid to Satan who was deceived in the bargain and could not ntrol the sinless God in Christ. Christ is moreover also Teacher, Revealer of God, of is will, of our sinfulness, and an example for us.[4]

---

[1] Cf the *PRE,* VII, 88 f.
[2] *Epist.* i, 25, p. 515.
[3] *Moralia* 33, 10, 20; 22, 17, 42; 3, 14, 26.
[4] *Ibid.* 9, 38; 61.

d. In his teaching on sin [5] Gregory was theoretically Augustinian. He stressed consequences of the fall and spoke of original sin, of an inherited guilt, and of de as the punishment for sin. He held to Augustine's teaching concerning the condem tion of children who died without baptism. His doctrine of grace also had an Aug tinian stamp. Through baptism sin is forgiven and faith is implanted. Faith throu the preached and inwardly digested Word produces the love and will for the good. H Gregory furnished a point of contact for the Reformers.

e. At heart, however, Gregory was a Semi-Pelagian, as may be seen from statement that God justifies man by imparting His commandments which man has fulfill and might even surpass. [6] This teaching submerged that monergism of gr which Augustine's doctrine of predestination had championed. Similar in consequer was the differentiation between prevenient and subsequent grace of God. In the teachi of penance also the Gregorian emphasis was Semi-Pelagian. He defined penance contrition, confession, absolution, and satisfaction. The argument was: The unsearchal God leaves no sin unpunished: in baptism the inherited original sin is forgiven; but all actual sins there must be "satisfactions." The "satisfactions" of the ancient Chur were a testimony of true sorrow for sin; Gregory made them self-inflicted tempo. punishments by which to escape eternal punishment. The merit of Christ and the pow of the Church centered in the ability to convert eternal punishments into temporal on and to decrease or do away with temporal ones through the intercession of Christ a the saints, through masses (for the living and the dead), and through the use of rel and amulets. The stimulus for the employment of these powers was the fear of losi salvation. The invention of an elaborate casuistry introduced the theology of fear a of ethical conceptions that have no root in Scripture. Thus we have with Gregory t sacrament of penance in an already finished form. [7]

f. The *Eucharist* also was changed by Gregory upon this Semi-Pelagian backgrou where man is doing instead of God, from a sacrament into a sacrifice for our redem tion. [8] Cyprian and others had spoken before Gregory of the Eucharist as a drama representation of Christ's original sacrifice. [9] As to the benefits received from the ma Ambrose was the first to employ this term—it is not especially the forgiveness of si as with Luther, but it is also bodily blessings, magically communicated. [10] Even the de can be partakers of such blessings, if the mass is offered for them.

g. Through his doctrine of *Purgatory* (only hesitatingly indicated by Cyprian a Augustine), Gregory expanded time and space to make more room for the working his system. His Scriptural proof for the existence of purgatory was Matt. 12: 32. [11]

h. The *Church* properly speaking was held, at least theoretically, by Gregory belong to the saints of all ages. But in the concrete the Church was to him as to Ron today a *civitas Dei,* a temporal state with the pope at its head, therefore a *corpus mixtu* comprising naturally the good and the bad. In this sphere the priesthood rules over

---

[5] *Ibid,* 12, 6, 9.
[6] *Ezekiel,* I h, 7, 16.
[7] See Gregory's *Canon of the Mass.*
[8] Cf. pp. 161 ff.
[9] *Moralia,* 23, 21, 40 et al.
[10] *Dialogue,* 4, 58.
[11] *Loc. cit.*

cluding the state, over body and soul, through the sacraments and magic rites, and
through the power of dispensing the spiritual treasures which the Church possesses.[12]

3. To summarize the estimate of Gregory the Great: (1) He was the guardian of
traditional orthodoxy on the Trinity and on Christology, but offered nothing new to
theology except perhaps through his accentuation of popular beliefs. (2) He put
tradition on an equal basis with the Scriptures. (3) On anthropology and soteriology
he was Semi-Pelagian and gave to repentance and the Eucharist an interpretation in
harmony with this view. (4) On church and priesthood he was hierarchical.

Gregory transformed virtues into rites and ordinances and religious acts. Humility
became monkery, repentance became penance. He made the miracle a characteristic
trait in religion, classified angels, devils, sacraments and saints, emphasized fear and hope
rather than a sure trust in God through Christ. He opened wide the door for what
Harnack has called "the Christianity of a second order" (*das Christentum zweiter
Ordnung*) by legitimatizing martyrs and saints and their intercessions, and thus he
crystallized many elements of religious superstition, which in that day of passing paganism and demigods made its way into the Church, by systematizing them into dogmas.[13]

He externalized internal graces into acts and ceremonies after the fashion of the
mysteries, and extended the power of the Church beyond earth through purgatory to the
very gates of heaven.

---

[12] *Evangelia* II h. 38. 7 f., et al.
[13] Cf. Harnack. *Grundriss*⁶. p. 334.

Chapter Two

THEOLOGICAL MOVEMENTS IN THE CAROLINGIAN RENAISSANCE

From Gregory the Great to the time of Charlemagne the Western Church show
no theological enrichments. Islam had conquered territories rich in theological lo
and the East had shaken off the powerful influence of Greek philosophy. In the sever
and eighth centuries Arianism was crushed through the conversion of England (es
cially through Gregory's mission to the Anglo-Saxons) and through the conversion
Germany to Rome and to Athanasianism (especially through the influence of Chlodwi
Theology now centered in the northern lands which had no doctrinal background.
sought only to absorb and learn from the past to which they were heirs. In the E
the monergistic and monotheletistic controversies ran their course with no visi
participation by the West which was engaged chiefly in making compendiums, excer
and in fashioning institutions. Under Charlemagne, however, a revival took place.

This emperor dominated the history of this period, not only in the state but a
in the Church. He felt it to be his call to exercise judgment and power in Chu
affairs, even in such detail as Church discipline, liturgical arrangements, education of t
clergy, Church art, missions, the placing of bishops and settling of papal affairs, a
therefore also in matters of doctrine. His determinations were practical and pragmati
throughout, rather than visionary. They concerned four major issues: Adoptionism
Spain, veneration of images in the East, the *filioque* of the Nicene Creed, and t
miraculous Virgin birth.

Later, under the reign of his successors, two other issues attracted the interest
the Frankish theologians: the teaching of a double predestination by Gottschalk, a
the teaching of transubstantiation by Radbertus.

I. THE ADOPTIONISTIC CONTROVERSY

Literature: Sources: *MSL* 96, 99, 100, 101, 104; MANSI, *Acta Concilii* 12, 13; H. FLOR
Espana sagrada 1750, vol. 5, 543 ff. Studies: C. J. HEFELE, *Conciliengeschichte²*, vol. 3, 642-6

The Adoptionistic Controversy was merely a repetition on a Spanish backgrou
of the old Christological controversy concerning the divine and human in Christ.[1] T
Spanish theologians Elipandus of Toledo and Felix of Urgel, on the basis of theologic
developments up to Augustine, defended the Christological conception which emph
sized the human in Christ and determined his divinity as the result of an act of adopti
by God.[2] They were opposed by the Asturians Beatus and Heterius of Libana (785
who centered upon *the divine Christ made man for us*. With the thought of safeguardi
the mystic-realistic conception of the Lord's Supper they accused the Spaniards
Nestorianism. The teaching of the two Spanish scholars was condemned by three syno

---

[1] Nestorian diophysitism against Eutychian monophysitism.
[2] Cf. the Mozarabic Liturgy containing Augustine's formula: *Passio filii adoptivi.*

ader Charlemagne, who probably desired to make himself felt as Ruler and Preserver the Church pertaining to orthodoxy. Pope Hadrian I agreed. The teaching of John Damascus was declared orthodox. But a sound refutation of Adoptionism was never ade. Therefore it cropped out again among scholars of the later Middle Ages. Our ference is to Alcuin's *Seven Books against Felix.*

II. THE ICONOCLASTIC CONTROVERSY

Literature: Sources: MSL 98; MANSI, *Acta Concilii* 12, 13. Studies: C. J. HEFELE, *Conliengeschichte²*, vol. 3, 604-712; J. B. BURY, *A History of the Later Roman Empire*, 1889, l. 2, 428-438.

After a long and fierce controversy the seventh ecumenical synod at Nicea (787) signed to the images of Christ and the saints *salutation and respectful reverence.* The nod had been convened by the Empress Irene of Constantinople, and delegates of ope Hadrian I took part in it. Charlemagne had not been consulted and no one repre-nting him was present. Resenting this omission, the emperor directed a critical xamination of the decrees of the synod and found cause for censure and disapproval the above mentioned matter, all the more because the Latin translation of the decree scribed to the images *adoration and divine homage, adoratio* and *servitium.* With arp criticism the *Libri Carolini* (790), rejected both the adoration and veneration of nages and likewise their destruction. They declared that adoration belongs only to iod, and veneration to the saints and their relics. The significance of images lies in ie fact that they beautify the Churches, awaken the memories of the past, and take the lace of the Scriptures for the illiterate. This view was reasserted in 794 at Frankfort ver against the diplomatic vacillation of the pope. With the breaking up of the mperial power of the Carolingians it was inevitable that this genuinely evangelical iewpoint should then give way to the image worship approved by Nicea and Rome. Iowever, the West was never willing to admit the veneration of images to be the per-ection of the Christological dogma and the climax of the religious life of the believer. Iere we have the beginning of a cleavage between the East and the West.

III. THE FILIOQUE CONTROVERSY

Literature: Sources: MSL 101, 105; MANSI, *Acta Concilii* 14. Studies: C. F. HEFELE, *Coniliengeschichte²*, vol. 3, 749-755; H. B. SWETE, *The Holy Spirit in the Ancient Church*, 1912.

In the doctrine concerning the procession of the Holy Ghost the cleavage between he West and the East was widened. On the basis of an Augustinian Modalism, as xpressed in Part One of the Athanasian Creed, the West conceived the procession of he Holy Ghost from the Son in like manner as from the Father. Gradually this teaching, without official act, caused the insertion of the *filioque* into the Nicene Creed. Its presence there was defended by BISHOP THEODULF OF ORLEANS in his book *De Processione Spiritus Sancti.* The Synod of Aachen (809), accepted the insertion with half-hearted approval of Pope Leo III, who discredited Charlemagne's right to alter by his own decree an ancient symbol of the Church. The *filioque,* though never popularized, became the accepted formula of the West, while it was roundly condemned in the East.[3]

---

[3] Cf. the old controversy between hypostasianism and subordinationism, also modalistic monarchism.

IV. The Controversy Over the Miraculous Birth of Jesus

Literature: Sources: *MSL,* 120, 121.

The controversy concerning the miraculous birth of Jesus centered in the perpetu virginity of Mary. The question was treated along more conservative lines by the mor Ratramnus. He conceded the virginity of Mary even after the birth of Jesus, but warn against docetism that would make Christ a phenomenon instead of a true man, l denying all natural processes in connection with his birth. His teaching was oppos by Radbertus, a fellow monk, who followed the miracle-seeking, mystical trend of l day in the way prepared by Augustine[4] and Ildefonsus of Toledo. (*Liber contra eos q disputant de perpetua virginitate Sanctae Mariae et de eius barturitione* in *Bibl. M* 12, 565). Ratramnus insisted upon a supernatural birth as well as a supernatural co ception of Jesus in every respect. The interest of the age in safeguarding the holine and sinlessness of Mary lent support to Radbertus, and directed the way for futu developments in such matters.

V. The Controversy Over Predestination

Literature: Sources: *MSL,* 112, 115, 119, 121, 122, 125, 345 ff.; Mansi, *Acta Concilii,* 14, 1
Studies: C. J. Hefele, *Conciliengeschichte,* vol. 4, 130-223.

The conflict between the received practice of the Church and genuine Augustinia ism had led the Church to a position not far removed from Semi-Pelagianism. T Carolingian theology had taken over this attitude. How blindly it proceeded is show by the *Libri Carolini* which endeavored to prove its orthodoxy by translating Pelagiu *Libellus fidei ad Innocentium.* This confession retained great influence throughout th entire Middle Ages. It went by the name *Sermo Augustini.* (Even history itself pla jokes!) Consequently, when the genuine Augustinianism was revived in the 9th centu by Gottschalk, it was either falsely interpreted or resolutely cast aside. The spirit Gregory and the needs of ecclesiastical practice, i.e., Semi-Pelagian tendencies, triumphe anew, and triumphed with finality.

The monk Gottschalk of Orbais had not only studied Augustine, he had al experienced him in the miseries of his life. It was for this reason that he recognize that the Church carried a Semi-Pelagian heart beneath its deceiving cloak of Augustinia formulas. His attacks upon the prevalent doctrine and practice of the Church we passionate and vehement, and they aimed at nothing less than a reformation. Brief stated he taught: The unchangeable God has definitely settled the course and destin of the world from all eternity. Election and rejection are due to an inscrutable decre of God. He has not determined some for salvation and others to death, because H foreknows the attitude which men will take toward His grace. Foreknowledge and pr destination rather are of a contemporary concurrence in God. The significance of fore knowledge consists in explaining the act of divine rejection as a just act. The evi however, is of man's will. God determines him not to evil, only to punishment. Sa vation is not through merits but through grace only. The work of Christ is efficaciou only for the elect; but no one knows who they are. On the other hand, Augustine emphasis on the psychological and formal freedom of man has no place in his system.

---

[4] *De Natura et Gratia,* 36, 42; *MSL* 44, 267.

The antagonists of Gottschalk saw in this doctrine no place for good works, priest or sacrament, nor for the whole ecclesiastical system. Through the preaching of Gottschalk, now a priest, on a journey into upper Italy, affairs reached a crisis, and complaints against him were made to Hrabanus, his abbott, by the bishop Nothing of Verona. In 848, the Synod of Mayence, dissatisfied with the confession laid down by Gottschalk and with his accusation of Semi-Pelagianism against Hrabanus, condemned him. The Synod of Chiersy (849) did likewise, and Hinkmar, the archbishop of Rheims, imprisoned him. He died (869) without recanting.

The Augustinian doctrine of predestination had however been brought favorably to the attention of scholars, even of Gottschalk's antagonists. It was treated in a manner halfway between Gregory and Gottschalk by four theologians of Alcuin's school: Prudentius of Troyes, Remigius of Lyon, Lupus of Ferrieres, and Ratramnus of Corbie. The mutual antagonism of the Alcuin and Hinkmar coteries played a large part in the controversy. A compromise decree was reached at the Synod of Valence (855), which accepted the double predestination of Augustine and at the same time the validity of the sacraments. In 859, at Savonières and Langres, and in 860, at Toucy, further compromises were made, and an academic peace restored on the following basis. God has assuredly predestined to life; in accordance with this purpose Christ died for all; the free will of man was weakened through the fall, but not destroyed. Pure Augustinianism was rejected in favor of practical piety.

VI. The Controversy Over the Lord's Supper

Literature: Sources: MSL, 112, 120, 121, pp. 1510-1518. Studies: DAWELL STONE, *A History of the Doctrine of the Holy Eucharist,* Vol. I.

Up till that period the theology of the West had been concerned occasionally only with the Lord's Supper. Ambrose and Gregory had expressed themselves realistically, while Augustine had strictly rejected a corporeal presence of Christ in the Sacrament. Popular piety, however, increasingly inclined to the view that in the mass the actual body of Christ was received. This tenet was rooted first of all in the general craving for the miraculous and in the crude conception of religion at that time. In addition to this, men with their exceedingly vivid consciousness of sin believed themselves to be entirely certain of forgiveness only if the mass were an actual repetition of the sacrifice on Calvary.

The treatise of Radbertus, a learned and courageous monk, who was abbot of the monastery at Corbie 842-853, *On the Body and Blood of the Lord,* is the first monograph on the subject. The author attempted a compromise between the theory of Augustine and the religious conceptions of the Church of his day, and propagated for the first time a real, though internal and mysterious, transubstantiation.

At the words of the priest God, who can do everything He wills, causes a miracle to take place: the consecrated elements are really changed into the historical body of Christ. The empirical observation that the accidents of color, form, and taste do not change is explained by the assertion that the change takes place not as an outward but as an inward mystery. The lack of visible proof is intended to confirm the faith of the Christian. In a remarkable contrast to this Radbertus then contends that whereas all do truly receive the sacramental elements, only those who spiritually comprehend Christ receive His body and blood. This is truly Augustinian. Radbertus, therefore, sought to co-ordinate the miracle with faith, and was not yet ready to separate the communion from the sacrifice of the mass.

The first opposition to this doctrine was raised by Hrabanus, the aged archbishop of Mayence. He was significantly more influenced by Augustine. The effect of the Supper consists in a spiritual union of the individual with the mystical body of Christ. Bread and wine are not the body of Christ Himself, but only a symbol of it. His symbolism, however, is no longer as pure as it was with Augustine, for even he recognized a certain change of the elements after the consecration.

Ratramnus, also a monk of Corbie, was drawn into the controversy by the emperor Charles the Bald, who asked him for an "opinion" on the matter of a real or mysterious reception of the Lord's body by believers. Ratramnus answered in a treatise, bearing the same title as that of Radbertus, that bread and wine are not changed into the historical body and blood of Christ. The sacramental elements are only a symbol. The presence of Christ, though real and true, is purely spiritual, and the effect of participation consists in a spiritual communion with the Lord.

The Augustinian spiritualism of Ratramnus could not maintain itself against the practice of the Church which supported the conception of Radbertus. Bishop Haimo of Halberstadt first formulated a theory of transubstantiation in the present Roman sense, entirely free from Augustinian symbolism or spiritualism.

Chapter Three

THE DEVELOPMENT OF PAPAL SUPREMACY

Literature: Sources: MSL, 161, 162: *Corpus Juris Canonici*; C. MIRBT, *Quellen zur Geschichte es Papstums und des roemischen Katholozismus*,' 1924; Studies: J. F. SCHULTE, *Geschichte der Quellen des Kirchenrechts*, vols. 1 and 2, 1875; T. GREENWOOD, *Cathedra Petri*, 6 vols., 1856 ff.; A. R. VINCENT, *The Age of Hildebrand*, 1896; M. RULE, *The Life and Times of St. Anselm*, vols., 1883; H. BOEHMER, *Kirche und Staat in England und in der Normandie im 11. und 12. Jahrhundert*, 1899. J. W. BOWDEN, *Life and Pontificate of Gregory VII*, 1840; T. T. TOUT, *The Empire and the Papacy*, 9th printing, 1921; R. W. and A. J. CARLISLE, *A History of Medieval Political Theory*, 2 vols., 1903; G. KRUGER, *Das Papstum, seine Idee und ihre Traeger*, Eng. Trans. 1909, 2nd German edition, 1932.

1. Religion in the Christian sense was a matter of national concern in the Middle Ages. Roman Catholicity fell heir to the Roman empire. As nations both the Germanic and the Slavic peoples accepted Christianity. National churches were the result. Gregory the Great in his days met with little success to bind all the new churches to Rome. The close relationship of the Carolingians with the papacy since the 8th century resulted in imperial theocracy, and not in papal hierarchy. When the imperial power disintegrated and the Church remained the only bond of union between Christian peoples, the old ways of Gregory were chosen once more. The sovereignty of the pope was soon established. And though it was not yet dogma, it became a demand of Church law that the pope be also held superior to the emperor. This was the trend of development during the Middle Ages.

2. The *Pseudo-Isidorean Decretals* (about 845) present as ancient papal rights all the claims ever advanced by the papacy concerning the independence from the laity of the Church and its subsidiary organs as well as the supremacy of the pope over the bishops and the national churches. The authority of the pope in his future conflicts with the emperor, his claims to supremacy over church and state and to the right to appoint bishops and other church dignitaries, though bolstered up by decree after decree, found its final authority in the Pseudo-Isidorean Decretals. In the desires of the popes to build up a new system of church jurisprudence with the authority of the pope as central, they placed the decretals on a par with the decrees of the ancient councils. And yet a *quasi* mistrust lingered about them for a long time.

3. The situation required a papacy regenerated from the immorality and inefficiency of the 10th century and a comprehensive church movement to carry through the ideals of Pseudo-Isidore. The aim was attained successfully through the emperors with the support of Clugny.

The Cluniac movement had in mind at first only a reform of the monasteries. However, gradually it developed into a general church movement. As this was first of all a purely ethical movement, it received the ready support of the emperors. The zeal of Clugny was directed against the immorality in the monasteries, marriage of the priests, simony, etc. But this zeal soon discovered that a check had been placed upon it and that that check was the state which wished to rule the Church according to its own laws and will. This recognition awakened the curialistic tendency of Pseudo-Isidore: the

Church is secularized because it is controlled by the State! Therefore the Church and the bishops must be withdrawn from the emperor and placed under the authority of the pope; the canon law of the Roman Church must take the place of the laws of the national Church. The right of investiture is to be given to the pope; fees paid to the emperor in return for bishoprics are to be branded as simony (Acts 8: 18-24). Thus *detachment from the world* was understood to mean *detachment from the state;* an ecclesiastical political program resulted from what started as an ethical one. A tragic fate willed that the emperors themselves should create the necessary premises of the conflict. Henry II and Henry III reformed the morally degenerate papacy (Synod at Sutri, 1046). Immediately the regenerated papacy began to strike at the very foundation of the state.

4. That which was only germinal in Pseudo-Isidore, was proclaimed with perfect candor by Gregory VII (1073-1085). The Church is of divine origin, while the state is rooted in the sinful order of the world (according to Augustine's *City of God*). The pope is the universal head of the Church. The bishops are his representatives and responsible to him alone. Their nomination and ordination are his exclusive privilege. The pope who has the power of the keys in heaven, has that power all the more on earth. The princes are his liegemen. They must kiss his feet, not the feet of the emperor. The emperor receives his glory from the pope as the moon from the sun. While the pope may depose the princes and the emperor, no human authority can depose the pope.

One should not trace these monstrous demands back to a sacerdotal craving for power in Gregory. Gregory felt that he was called of God to establish His kingdom on earth. Within himself he felt God thinking and working; for that reason he was convinced that he could shake the world to its foundations. There was a peculiar religious heroism lying behind this delusion of his. His dramatic conflict with the emperor Henry IV belongs to Church History.

5. After the death of Gregory, the representatives of the reform movement lacked the spiritual fervor of this great pope. The terms of the Concordat of Worms (1122) show that the curialists were forced to content themselves with a compromise. It is true that the pope now invested the bishops, but they were chosen under imperial influence. The bestowal of secular sovereignty remained the exclusive right of the emperor.

The later struggle between Frederick I and Alexander III, and between the last emperors of the house of Hohenstaufen with Innocent III, was a mere struggle for secular supremacy in Italy. As a lasting *status quo,* neither the supremacy of the state nor that of the Church was ever completely or factually established.

6. In this conflict the papacy rested its claim to sovereignty upon a legal basis. To attain their purpose, they fostered collections of synodical canons and papal decrees which might serve as binding sources of law. Ivo of Chartres (d. 1116) was one of the greatest jurists who took this matter in hand. At Bologna the study of canon law was made an independent discipline. At this university GRATIAN (d. 1140) wrote his *Decretal,* the most complete collection of canon law up to that time. Its importance lies in the fact that it assigned to the dogma and sacraments of the Church a place in the lawbooks, and established the Scriptures, tradition, the decrees of the

---

[1] Otto I (936-973), on account of his experience with the rebellious dukes of the empire, had created the institution of ecclesiastical principalities. The unmarried bishops were expected to be more loyal to the emperor than the dukes who only too often strove for political aggrandizement of their own dynasty.

councils, and the pope as the binding doctrinal authorities. In his *Sic et Non*, Abelard imitated for the first time the canonical method of placing together views which affirm or contradict an article of faith and then adjusting them dialectically. That was scholasticism! Anselm stressed the juridical point of view in his theory of atonement, the priest in the sacrament of penance, the pope in building up his supremacy. Thus the Church became a courthouse, then along the same line of development, a house of merchandise and "a den of thieves." Luther's burning of the papal bull was only a side issue to the main event of the conflagration of the books of canon law by the Reformation. It was due to the rise of a new piety that the religious zeal of the earlier Cluniac movement was not quenched by this rising tide of legalism.

Chapter Four

THE AWAKENING OF THE NEW PIETY

Literature: Sources: The Works of SCOTUS ERIGENA, *MSL*, 122, of RATHERIUS, *MSL*, 136, of OTHLOH, *MSL*, 146, of HUGO, *MSL*, 175-177, of BERNARD, *MSL*, 182-185.

1. The Carolingian theology and the new piety are related to each other as are mechanical learning and the inner understanding of that learning. In the early Middle Ages men were content to accept the Church's doctrines as they were, and to conserve them with slavish dependence. The mass of the people saw in Christianity not a new divine, spiritual life of the individual, but rather an external institution. In the eleventh and twelfth centuries, however, the maturing spirit of the young nations took on a new understanding of Christianity. It is true that the doctrines themselves remained undoubted. But a genuinely religious need was striving to liberate forces and treasures which lay bound in the Church's teaching, striving to establish through them a life of inward, personal piety. Men desired to strike water from the rock. They wanted to experience what until then they had only subscribed to. Thus there broke forth an impetuous, outspoken, religious subjectivism which asked with Augustinian seriousness about sin and grace, about God and the certainty of salvation. Certainty, experience and conversion are the three characteristics of this new piety.

The impulse to the new piety arose in the monasteries of Loraine and Clugny. It was supported by the laity more than by the clergy because of the heavier demands which it made on the priests. It is most clearly visible in the enthusiasm it engendered for the crusades and the innumerable monastic foundations it fostered. It aimed at a strict discipline for the monasteries, monastic regime for the secular clergy, supremacy of the Church over the nations, rulers and subjects, and the subordination of the present to the future life. By a peculiar twist of logic, freedom from and victory over the world were held to be attainable solely through the dominion of the Church over the world. Thus such antagonistic qualities as ambition and humility, sensuality and self-denial, brutality and sentimentality, characterize the period. Basic to the development of the new piety was the growth of mysticism. This, added to the ascetic ideals of monasticism, produced the new piety.

2. Mysticism was a constituent part of philosophical Christianity from the beginning. It had a strong hold especially on the theology and piety of the Eastern Church. Its first exponent of importance in this period was John Scotus. [1]

The background of this scholar who was not a cleric but a sort of court philosopher and independent thinker, was not only Augustine and Gregory, but also Philo and Neo-Platonism. He was well versed in classical Greek, using the Septuagint by choice, and had a deep sympathy for the speculation of the East. The writings of Dionysius the Areopagite he translated into Latin.

John's chief work *De Divisione Naturae* bridges the way from Neo-Platonism to the speculative mysticism of the Middle Ages. According to his system God created an

---

[1] Gardner, *Studies in John the Scot,* 1900.

ideal world, from which the real world emanated with man at its center. Man contains in himself all the properties of all creatures of the world. In this man sin is found without cause; it separates him into two sexes and a multitude of individuals. In Christ the original man is restored to unity and resolved into the original world of ideas and absorbed into God.

The influence of John Scotus was not discernible in his own day and age. He met with little opposition to his teachings because he was diligent to refrain from attacking the doctrine of the Church. Moreover he was not understood by his fellow theologians, nor did he understand the needs and problems of his day. His theological efforts were thoroughly disappointing to those who appreciated his learning. In the matter of Gottschalk and predestination, he absolutely identified predestination with foreknowledge and denied the reality of sin, so that his work *De Divina Praedestinatione* (849) was of no value to Hinkmar. In the controversy concerning the Eucharist, he emphasized the symbolic value of the elements, and he lent no support to the realists. John Scotus' works reveal the beginnings of scholastic investigation. After his death they were repeatedly condemned. He was not a mystic in the complete sense of the word, lacking the religious experience and yearning of the true mystic. His chief contribution to the age was the foundation he laid and the stimulation which he gave to mystical thinking in the future.

3. There were other representatives of the movement before Bernard. The mysticism that led to piety was fostered by Ratherius (d. 974), a speculative thinker with a large following. Classical expression was given to the aims and the movement by Othloh of Emmeram (d. 1083). He gave subjective treatment to all the materials of doctrine and faith, and popularized the mystic attitude. From this time on the laity welcomed contemplation, if not speculation. New monastic orders arose with a rigorous discipline. Even the papacy was won over and sanctioned the movement. One of the immediate results was the enthusiasm engendered for the Crusades.

The new piety and the Crusades interacted upon one another. From the intimate connection of many thousands through the Crusades with the land of the Gospels, new attitudes were developed. Chief among these was the desire to follow Christ in all the stages of His sufferings. The man Jesus was found again, and the goal of Adoptionism secured in another way. Negative asceticism, employing self-denial and emphasizing self-abnegation received a positive purpose: to follow Jesus and to become like Him. Mysticism, embracing Christ, as indicated by Augustine and enlarged by John Scotus, became a mighty current. The Church now possessed a threefold Christ: the transcendental, the sacramental, and the historical. Christian piety embraced the humble, holy, patient, sacrificing Lord, and to serve Him called forth ultimate resources of human invention.

In the teachings of Hugo (d. 1141), preceptor of the abbey school of St. Victor near Paris, we find the first oustanding representative of the new piety. A survey of his system of contemplation, based primarily on Augustine, is found in his work, *Commentary on the Heavenly Hierarchy*. Here he emphasized the three stages through which the soul attains knowledge of divine things. The first stage is sensual perception, the power for which has not been greatly diminished in man through the fall. The second stage consists in a search after the secret spiritual meaning of that which is perceived. In this the faculties of man are much more beclouded. The third stage consists in an untrammeled vision of the essence of things, which is possible alone through the Spirit of God. The motive behind Hugo's scheme was the personal experience of salvation and of union with Christ. "We can come to Christ only on the same path on which He came to us, through humility and suffering."

4. Bernard of Clairvaux (d. 1153),[2] the most powerful personality and the greatest religious genius of his time, gave classic expression to the general mood of the new piety. He created a coherent system of the order of salvation, which was Christ-centered, built on religious experience, and ended in mystic ecstasy.

It was the Man Jesus whom the Crusades had rediscovered for the Western World, in whom Bernard was interested. The metaphysical *Logos-Christ* or the sacramental Christ was of no concern to him. Even Augustine had recognized the significance of the Man Jesus and His humility for faith. But Bernard devoted himself to Jesus in a far more determined and glowing manner. Jesus the joy of his heart, is the great king —not in spite of His humility, lowliness and obedience, but because of them. In them, as well as in the patience, love and purity of Jesus, the divine reality is revealed to pious experience. Here every one can become sure of God in an immediate vision. That reminds us strongly of the conception of Luther who actually praised the monk of Clairvaux as one of the best saints of the Middle Ages. Bernard linked this fundamental idea in a unique manner with Augustine's Neo-Platonic stages of contemplation, which recall memories of Origen, Methodius and Ambrose. Nevertheless the whole system is an independent and new creation which rests upon one man's own experience. The chief sources of Bernard's mystic piety are his eighty-six sermons on the Song of Songs.

The first presupposition of the spiritual life is the believing recognition of the Church's doctrines. If one meditates profoundly (*sedula meditatio*) on the holiness and purity of Jesus, there breaks forth the mighty consciousness of one's sinfulness, and at the same time one feels the wrath of God in all its severity. But then, if one gazes at the sweetness of Jesus and His mercy, he becomes certain of forgiveness at the hands of a God Who does not impute sin. That is the first stage of the mystical way to God, which is at the same time the way of conversion. According to an illustration used by Bernard, contrition is a kissing of Jesus' feet. This is followed by repentance which is a kissing of His hands. By reflecting on the love of God in Jesus the impulse is awakened to imitate Jesus' love, patience, humility, etc., and above all His obedience. The perfect surrender of the will of the individual to the will of God is the most distinctive mark of the imitation of Christ.

Then follows the kissing of Jesus' lips which is the climax of ecstasy. This forms the third and highest stage. It is an absolutely spiritual experience of God which is not transmitted by sensuous means, but which is enacted spontaneously in the soul. Nor is it always a mere psychological impression or agitation of the soul, but an ascent of the soul to the Godhead.

In following the mysticism of the ancient Church, especially of Augustine, Bernard ran the risk on the one hand of degrading the historical consideration in religion to a transitory stage, and on the other hand of losing himself in pantheism, as was the case before him with Methodius of Olympus and after him with Amalrich of Bena and the sects of the Free Spirit. Bernard met these dangers by placing less emphasis upon the Augustinian differentiation between common faith which reaches only to the Man Jesus,

---

[2] J. C. Morrison, *St. Bernard*, 1868 and other editions. E. Gilson, *The Mystical Theology of St. Bernard*, 1940.

and the mystical vision of the Godhead. The way to pantheism is blocked according to Bernard's advice, in that one is to devote oneself more to God's will than to loving contemplations of Him. Besides, the different stages of mystical experience, according to Bernard, are of equal value in so far as the same thing is experienced in the previous stages as in the ecstasy, except that in the third stage the experience is immediate and stronger. The certainty of forgiveness is dependent on the complete devotion of the will. Bernard's mysticism received thereby a specifically Christian character. Finally, the ecstasy is not to be an end in itself. Like the Sadhu of late, Bernard received in the ecstasy a mighty impulse to manifest the powers of grace he had been given in works of love to his brethren. The active life (*Vita activa*) follows the contemplative life (*vita contemplativa*).

Not only was Bernard's Christianity adapted to the Church, it frequently reached to evangelical heights. Everything, the breaking out of the primal feeling of guilt, fear and love, as well as the desire for holiness, is traced back to the working of grace. It is genuinely Pauline when Bernard absolutely denies the possibilities of merits, and asserts that the forgiveness of sins and the granting of eternal life is by grace only. The only merit which a man may have is to hope in his Saviour and to have a humble readiness to recieve God's grace. "The righteousness of man consists in the pardon of God."

Bernard's subjectivism was indeed strong; but his ecclesiastical and hierarchial consciousness was just as strong. Church history does show that. Bernard was convinced that the individual comes in touch with the gracious influences of Christ only through the medium of the Church (sacraments). He is a firm believer in the Gregorian principle that it is the duty of the ecclesiastical hierarchy to compel all the world to serve the interest of the heavenly and divine. Thus Bernard is at one and the same time the greatest mystic as well as the most influential church diplomat of his age.

Chapter Five

THE BEGINNING AND RISE OF SCHOLASTICISM

Literature: Sources: The writings of Boethius, *MSL* 63-64, of William of Champeaux, *MSL* 163, of Anselm, *MSL* 158, 59, of Abelard, *MSL* 178, of Hugo, *MSL* 176, of Rupert of Deutz, *MSL* 167, of Honorius Augustodunensis, *MSL* 172, of Peter Lombard, *MSL* 192. Studies: H. Rashdall, *The Universities of Europe in the Middle Ages,* 3 vols., 1895; R. L. Poole, *Illustrations of the History of Medieval Thought,* 1920; M. de Wulf, *Histoire de la philosophie medievale,* 2 vols., 1924 f.; English translation by E. C. Messenger, 1926. J. Reiners, *Der aristotelische Realismus in der Fruehscholastik,* 1907; *Der Nominalismus in der Fruehscholastik,* 1910. M. Grabmann, *Die Geschichte der Scholastichen Methode,* 2 vols. 1909, 1911; C. H. Haskins, *The Renaissance of the Twelfth Century,* 1927; A. J. Macdonald, *Authority and Reason in the Early Middle Ages,* 1933; E. Gilson, *The Spirit of Medieval Philosophy,* 1936; K. Adam, *The Spirit of Catholicism,* 1937.

1. That which next to the new piety kept the Church from a more rapid decline in its seeking after earthly might, was the revival of a new interest in philsophy and theology known as scholasticism. Its beginnings date from about 1100; its period ends with the Reformation.

Scholasticism grew out of the same roots as the new mystic piety. Man wanted to know in order to become inwardly certain of salvation. By knowledge scholasticism understood the rational understanding, while the new piety understood it to be a spiritual experience. While with the new piety the interest was personal and subjective, with scholasticism the interest was more scientific and objective. The instrument of the rational understanding and proof was dialectics, as men had learned from Aristotle. Dialectics was the art of proving a thing through logical considerations. At this point the peculiar character of medieval thought becomes evident. Men thought from the inside out and not empirically. That is, the presuppositions from which men proceeded, were settled by authority and not by a critical and observant research. The authority of the Scriptures, the Fathers, the Councils, and the papal decrees were inviolable: they were considered a divine law. Men were not concerned about seeking the truth, but only about proving it and systematizing the divinely revealed metaphysics through a methodical reflection.

Scholasticism was not merely an unfruitful formalism. It was a truly creative movement. It fused the theology of revelation and the ancient philosophy into a natural theology and produced a world-view of remarkable breadth and completeness. It was remarkable in spite of its open character of compromise (revelation and philosophy), for it derived everything from God and then summarized everything again in Him. Theology became the only possible world-view, and philosophy was made only the *handmaiden* of theology.

The rise of scholasticism definitely curbed the growth and power of the monastic orders. It raised new units of influence in the schools, attracted prominent teachers and directly caused the development of modern universities.

2. In their attempt to prove the reasonableness of the Church's doctrines the school

men were confronted with the philosophical problem of the relationship between the idea of a thing and its reality, between thinking and being. And according to the solution proposed by the schoolmen, Nominalism and Realism became the names of opposing schools of thought.

The terms are based on the different conceptions of the reality of generic ideas (universals) by Plato, Aristotle, and the Stoics. The problem is: Do the universals exist only as subjective conceptions, or do they exist as objective realities? And, if the latter be the case, do they exist separately from the individual things or in them? Furthermore, are they corporeal or incorporeal? Is for instance, the general conception *man* a reality, or is it only the intellectual abstraction derived from the common properties of individual beings called men? According to Plato man carries within himself a conception of the idea of an absolute good and beautiful. He cannot have attained this impression by experience, since the absolute good does not exist in this sensible world. Rather, the soul has viewed this idea in its pre-existence and has retained a memory of it. Reason is the immortal part of the soul and constitutes its very essence. The rational perceptions of the soul, the ideas (universals), therefore, possess reality, since they are recollections of eternal and unchangeable corporeal though spiritual objects: *Universalia ante rem.* Whatever is truly reasonable, that also is truly real.

Plato's teaching of the ideas underwent a certain modification by Aristotle. He reduced the ideas to mere spiritual forces (energies) which are active in matter: *Universalia in re.*

Either type of realism was welcomed by the Church for its apologetic value. For the reality of the Church's doctrines seemed to be guaranteed if their reasonableness could be effectively demonstrated. The moderate realism of the Aristotelian type, however, was found to be best conformable to the interest of the Church and the needs of the time.

The ancient conception of the universals had suffered a further modification through the teachings of the Stoics who maintained that the ideas were mere intellectual abstractions (*nomina*) derived from the common attributes of things: *Universalia post rem.* This nominalistic theory was branded dangerous and destructive. It could find little favor with the Church for it endangered the objective reality of fundamental beliefs of the Church, as for example the doctrine of the Holy Trinity.

The chief champion of nominalism during this period is Roscellinus of Compiegne (d. about 1125). His theory was more orientated along the line of logic; its metaphysical significance he did not fully realize. Roscellinus found a stern opponent in Anselm of Canterbury who demonstrated to his contemporaries the pagan consequences of this pagan theory. But likewise the extreme realism of William of Champeaux met with little success. The main current of thought was supplied by the moderate realism of the Roman philosopher Boethius. By his translation of the *Categories* of Aristotle and the *Isagoge* of Porphyry, he provided the scientific tools with which to solve the problems of scholasticism.

3. The four outstanding scholars of this period are: Anselm, Abelard, Hugo and Peter Lombard.

a. Anselm was abbot in the monastery of Bec in Normandy, and from 1093, archbishop of Canterbury. He died in 1109 after a bitter conflict with King Henry I.[1]

---

[1] J. M. Rigg. *St. Anselm of Canterbury,* 1896.

Anselm's theological and religious conflict made it necessary for him to oppose th
nominalism of Roscellinus. This scholar's denial of the reality of the generic idea
would lead to the dissolution of the Church's doctrine of the Trinity. Instead of th
one triune God, we would have three gods. In his *Monologium,* therefore, Ansel
taught a moderate realism. The philosophical problem, however, was but a side issu
with him. His real interest was centered around theological speculation. He leane
heavily upon Augustine. The teaching of the Church laid down in the Bible an
the three ecumenical symbols possessed inviolable authority for him. But unlike th
older school, Anselm wanted to become inwardly certain of its truth by religious exp
rience. This tendency he had in common with the new piety. And by rational thinkin
he tried to demonstrate the truth of the Church's dogma to Christians, Jews and Ge
tiles (*Cur Deus homo?*). "I believe in order to understand." This progress from simpl
faith to religious knowledge is very momentous. By combining in this way faith an
knowledge, practical piety and theological speculation, he became the foremost pat
finder of scholasticism.

b. Abelard, a pupil of the nominalist Roscellinus, even surpassed the influence an
importance of Anselm. He was born in 1079 at Palais, Bretagne, the son of a Frenc
knight. In Paris he became the youthful rival of William of Champeaux and create
a real sensation in his lectures on Ezekiel. His brilliant personality and his pre-eminen
intellectual gifts conquered the hearts of youth for him and his mode of teaching. Afte
his love affair with Heloïse, he entered the abbey of St. Denis, and again caused diffi
culties with his treatise *Concerning the Divine Unity and Trinity,* which was condemne
as Sabellian at Soissons. He could boast of enthusiastic followers but also of un
compromising persecutors, the most prominent of the latter being Norbert and Bernar
of Clairvaux. Bernard the mystic saw in Abelard the rationalist, the principle of ev
himself. At the Synod of Sens (1141), he procured the condemnation of some o
Abelard's statements. Even an appeal to Rome did not save him. However, Peter o
Clugny offered him a place of refuge at his monastery, where he died in 1142. Othe
prominent works of Abelard are his *Christian Theology, Introduction to Theology, Si
et Non,* and his *Commentary on Romans.*[2]

In spite of his rationalistic tendencies he was not a rationalist after the fashio
of the 18th century. He never questioned the authority of the Bible. His position i
best defined as a type of mediating theology. His mediating view in the conflict betwee
realism and nominalism has been designated under the name of *conceptualism.*

In his defense against the radical scholars of the time he employed the true an
genuine dialectics by making it the scientific instrument of theology. In this he wa
guided by the optimism of the genuine scholastic who believed that reason could no
contradict revelation. The duty of the scholarly theologian, according to him, is t
"come through doubt to inquiry, and through inquiry to truth." "I understand in orde
to believe." But he never invades the right of authority. Reason has only the task t
support the doctrines, as far as possible.

In his *Sic et Non* he was the first to apply the dialectic method to the treatment o
theology. A long list of isolated questions of doctrine are taken, and then there ar
grouped around them concordant or contradictory opinions from the Bible, the Fathers
the decrees and canons. The thesis itself does not come up for discussion. Only th

---

[2] J. G. Sikes, *Peter Abailard,* 1932.

alue of the different authorities is weighed by the application of rational investigation. And while statements from the Fathers, from the decrees or canons may be false or istorically spurious, a quotation from the Bible is absolutely inviolable.

The question is, how does Abelard compare with Anselm? While Anselm demanded as the *conditio sine qua non* the willing surrender to the doctrinal system as a whole, Abelard thought of a gradual trial by reason, by which the theologian arrives at complete comprehension of doctrines. Anselm says, *Credo ut intelligam*, because he considers the doctrine to be supernatural and feels that it can be comprehended only through a science of experience (*experientis scientia*). Abelard says, *Intelligo ut credam*, because he considers a reasonable perception of the object of faith possible and necessary. Anselm works comprehensively. He experiences the doctrine in its entirety. Abelard is clever while Anselm is gifted with genius. With Anselm human reason creates or produces a new reason from the doctrine. Abelard is content to show that the individual doctrine is reasonable. In him there lived the old conviction of the apologists that Christianity is the climax of all philosophy.

One cannot value highly enough Abelard's significance for scholasticism. The characteristic feature of scholasticism appears clearly in his theological work. Ecclesiastical positiveness is brought into close union with a sober dialectic and scientific method. This combination forshadowed the great change which the thirteenth century was to bring; the displacement of Plato (the pure Neo-Platonic idealism in Augustine's theology) by Aristotle (the critical and empirical tendencies in later scholasticism). Though Abelard was mercilessly condemned by the Neo-Platonic authorities of his times, the immediate future thought differently of him. In Alexander III, a pupil of his, ascended the papal throne (1159-1181).

c. Hugo was the son of a noble of northern Germany. While traveling in France he was attracted to enter the Monastery of St. Victor at Paris. He died in 1141 at the age of forty-four as rector of the monastery's famous school.

Under the influence of his German training[3] Hugo followed a historical biblical outline in his discussion of theology. His book *De Sacramentis Christianae Fidei*[4] is the first important textbook on dogmatics in the Western Church revealing as it does the brilliant systematic ability of its writer.

The significance of Hugo consists in the fact that he knew how to unite the lines which came from Anselm, Abelard and Bernard. He summarized the speculative, rational and mystical elements into the establishment of a strictly ecclesiastical theology. The sting was pulled out of dialectics when the rationality of the dogma was subjected to the super-rational background of faith. In this limited sphere theology could mix with philosophy without endangering itself.

d. Peter with the surname the Lombard, was born at Navarra in Italy. He studied at Bologna, Rheims and Paris. In France he came into personal contact with Bernard, Abelard and Hugo. He later taught at the cathedral school of Notre Dame, and was finally made bishop of Paris. There he died about 1160.

Peter combined the dialectical method of Abelard with the orthodoxy of Hugo from whom he also inherited the systematic talent. As he collates together the various

---

[3] Rupert of Deutz and Honorius Augustodunensis are forerunners of his in Germany.

[4] It is best translated "Concerning the Mysteries of Christian Faith," for it is no discussion of sacraments in our sense of the word. By *sacramentum* Hugo understands everything that God has done for men.

pronouncements on the dogma, he compares and weighs them, and finally sets forth th
Scriptures as the highest authority. Reason has only a formal meaning. It is only use
as "a means of salvation against the contradictions of the authorities" (Abelard).

His *Four Books of Sentences* were written in Paris before 1150. In the four division
he treats of God, creation, original sin, Christ, the Holy Spirit, the sacraments an
eschatology. The present division into 182 distinctions is of a later date.

The *Sentences* became the medieval textbook on dogmatics. The objective treatmer
of the material made it a suitable guide for divergent theological schools. The *Sentence*
are marked by the absence of a true conception of the Gospel. Augustine also is inter
preted in the spirit of the day. The teaching of the Church concerning the sacrament
is preserved and fixed according to the conception that prevails at the time. Thus thi
conception attained dogmatic value, and Peter Lombard is held in high esteem by th
Roman Church for his important contribution in this field.

Chapter Six

DOCTRINAL ISSUES IN THE ELEVENTH AND TWELFTH CENTURIES

The period of early scholasticism has contributed to the discussion of theology proper, original sin, the Christological problem and the teaching concerning Mary; it has been especially instrumental in clarifying the conception of the sacraments and of the Church. The conflicting tendencies, while creating some disturbances of minor importance, directly caused two very bitter and pointed controversies: the Berengar-Lanfranc controversy over the Lord's Supper, and the conflict over the doctrine of the atonement which involved Anselm, Abelard and Bernard.

I. THE BERENGAR-LANFRANC CONTROVERSY

Literature: Sources: BERENGAR, *Liber de sacra coena adversus Lanfrancum*, edited by A. F. and T. Vischer; the works of LANFRANC, *MSL*, 150, of GUITMUND, *MSL*, 149, of ALGER, *MSL*, 180, of PETER LOMBARD, *MSL*, 192; MANSI, *Acta Concilii*, Vol. 19; HEFELE, *Conciliengeschichte*, Vol 4, 740 ff., 777 ff., Vol. 5, 126 f., 129.

1. Since the first medieval conflict over the Lord's Supper Radbert's realistic conception of the sacrament had gained ground more and more. The Augustinian tradition was unable to check this. With the beginning of the new learning a fresh scientific interest in this problem became manifest. A last, though futile, objection was raised in the name of reason to curb the crude massiveness of the doctrine.

2. Berengar (d. 1088), a pupil of Fulbert of Chartres, was the man to renew the attack upon the theory of Radbertus. Confident in his dialectics and convinced of the right reason, he uncovered the logical contradictions of the doctrine of the transubstantiation. Appealing to the Scriptures, his religious interest compelled him to reject the idea that the communicants receive only *pieces of Christ's flesh*. He demanded the entire Christ. So he came to revive the Augustinian-Ratmnian tropical conception of the sacrament. The corporeal presence is denied, for Christ's body exists undivided in heaven. The substance of the elements remains unchanged. Bread and wine are merely emblematic of the body and blood of the Saviour. But they receive a new relation to the invisible body of Christ. His body, passion and death can therefore not be comprehended by the senses. The union with Christ takes place inwardly and spiritually. With this spiritualization the presence and reception of the entire Christ, as demanded in the interest of true piety, is conceivable. Thus only believers receive the body of Christ. Only they experience the matter of the sacrament.

3. The alarmed Roman authorities forced from Berengar a confession of transubstantiation in its crassest form in 1059. He soon tired of submission and placing his confidence in the archdeacon Hildebrand who was well disposed toward him, he revived his view. There then broke forth a passionate literary feud. Now appear the chief writings: LANFRANC's *On the Body and Blood of the Lord,* against Berengar, BERENGAR's reply *On the Holy Supper,* against Lanfranc. Other opponents of Berengar were Hugo of Langres and especially GUITMUND OF AVERSA in his treatise *Three Books on the*

Truth of the Body and Blood of Christ in the Eucharist. For a few years Hildebrand was able to protect Berengar. But when he became Pope Gregory VII, he could do so no longer. In 1079 Berengar had to surrender again at Rome.

4. The new doctrine of the sacrament was scientifically elaborated by the opponents of Berengar. But there was not much new in the result; for the theologians were bound to the Roman confession of 1059. Transubstantiation was now the official teaching of the Church i.e., the substance of bread and wine is actually changed into the body and blood of Christ. Only the accidental properties (color, taste and form) of the element remain. In every host is the entire body of the historical Christ which believers and unbelievers alike receive.

5. A number of problems, however, remained to be solved. Starting with Christology, the first attempts were made to solve the problem of ubiquity. Alger of Liege said that "by virtue of the divine omnipotence which extends even to the flesh of Christ, the body of the Saviour can be everywhere at the same time." And Guitmund emphasized that in a thousand simultaneous masses all the hosts contain the entire Christ in all their parts.

A further consequence of the transubstantiation was the sentence of Lanfranc: "Even those who partake unworthily receive the real body of Christ." (*MSL*, 150, 436.) Lanfranc added, however, that the unworthy communicant receives it only according to its essence, not as a saving power. In this sense then, Alger and Lanfranc made a distinction between the communion of the believing and the unbelieving. Though the latter receive the true body of Christ, only the former enter into a spiritual communion with Him. Therewith the Augustinian distinction between the sign and the matter of the sacrament was taken over from Berengar.

Some followers of Berengar tried to take a mediating viewpoint by advancing the theory of impanation. They admitted that Christ is really, even bodily, present in the sacrament, but without any change in the elements. Just as in the incarnation the human nature remained unchanged, so in the impanation the bread and wine are substantially unchanged. And just as in the man Jesus the true Godhead was present in the closest union with Him, so it is in the bread and wine. This theory, while being condemned at its time, developed during the later Middle Ages into the theory of consubstantiation.

6. The Church gave its definite approval to the doctrine of transubstantiation at the fourth Lateran Council at Rome in 1215. This doctrine with the other sacraments, was placed alongside the dogmas of the ancient Church. It was considered a dogma of the same importance as the doctrine of the Trinity and Christology. In the first chapter of the confession called *Innocentium*, it says: "The Body and Blood are truly (*veraciter*) contained in the Sacrament of the Altar under the appearance of bread and wine, after the bread has been changed into the Body, and the wine into the Blood, through the power of God. Only the rightly ordained priest can perform this sacrament."

II. THE DOCTRINE OF THE ATONEMENT

Literature: Sources: The works of ANSELM, *MSL* 158, 159; of ABELARD, *MSL* 178; *Epistola 190* of BERNARD, *MSL* 182.

1. ANSELM OF CANTERBURY was the first to present a harmonious and consistent doctrine of the atonement in his epoch-making book, *Cur Deus Homo?* He rejected

he popular conception of Christ's work as a lawsuit with the devil and substituted a
ew theory on the subject.

2. The key to the understanding of Anselm's range of ideas is the fundamental idea
f the Kingdom of God. God is the Lord and the King of the world. In the beginning
He created the angels to inhabit His kingdom. After their fall, God created man as a
ubstitute for the loss which He had suffered. But through a wilful disobedience Adam
lso sinned and refused God's purpose. Sin, therefore, is embedded in the will and
onsists of the lack of righteousness which man owes God. God's honor is thus offended.
'or His honor consists in this that His will and plan should come to completion and
very creature should subject itself to Him. Since Adam and mankind constitute a unity,
n him and with him all men have sinned.

It is impossible for God in mercy simply to remit this sin, because such action
would bring disorder into His kingdom. Therefore there must be either punishment or
atisfaction. But punishment, that is eternal condemnation, would have defeated God's
wn eternal plan of man's salvation in His kingdom. So, then, there had to be satis-
action. But was man able to render an adequate satisfaction? The fact was that he
ould not. What he might have been able to do by means of contrition would not have
een an equivalent. Neither would any new obedience have atoned for the transgressions
f the past. Still it had to be man's own satisfaction.

It was this that made necessary the incarnation of the Son of God. Only as God-
Man (Deus-Homo) could Christ take our place and render that satisfaction. The
atisfaction, however, did not consist in Christ's earthly life of obedience, for as one
iving in this world He owed such obedience to God. The significance of a real satis-
action lay exclusively in the giving up of His life. To this He was not obligated, because
He was sinless and needed not to die. The value of Christ's death was heightened by
His voluntary submission. Such a voluntary self-sacrificing death of a sinless one God
ad to reward. But for Himself the God-Man was in need of no reward, for anything
hat the Father has is already His, and in His sinlessness He owes no debt that might be
emitted. Therefore He gives His reward, the fruit of His work, to those for whose salvation He became man, namely to His brethren who are burdened with debt.

3. Anselm's system is presented too much in a judicial fashion. The relation
etween God and man appears as that of a ruler to his subjects. There is a stress upon
he term satisfaction that makes the New Testament conception of God's love fall too
much in the background. Another defect of Anselm's system lies in the neglect to include
lso Christ's active obedience in His work of redemption. Furthermore, the application
f Christ's merit to the individual lacks evidence that justifying faith is the appro-
priating factor. Here the special contribution was to be made by the Reformation. But
it was the merit of Anselm, in this endeavor at a systematization of the doctrine of the
atonement, that he recognized the fundamental truths of Scripture and of Christian
experience involved in man's sin, namely God's justice and the means of redemption.
With all its imperfection of expression, lines were drawn that have served as a foundation
for arriving at more evangelical forms of teaching.

In modern times Anselm's theory became the special target for the criticism of the
Ritschlian and Harnackian bent of mind. On the other hand, so modern a theologian as
E. Brunner "has set himself to make to Anselm an act of reparation."[1] Aulén in his

---
[1] *The Mediator,* 1934, p. 440.

book *Christus Victor* (1931) has a special chapter on Anselm (pp. 100 ff.). He offers the criticism that Anselm's theory is a deviation from what he calls the "classical" idea of the Atonement as held by the Greek Fathers in that according to Anselm, "God is no longer regarded as *at once* the agent and the object of the reconciliation, but as *partly* the agent, as being the author of the plan, and *partly* the object, when the plan comes to be carried out" (p. 104 f.). We must agree that there is some justification in this statement. Anselm shares with the whole Latin theology the danger of making redemption partly a movement upward from man to God and only partly a downward movement from God to man.

4. Abelard's teaching of sin is subjectivistic and relativistic. It charms the modern mind. Sensual appetites, sexual desires, and man's deeds are morally irrelevant in themselves. They become sinful only through a willing consent to evil. The essence of sin therefore consists in a conscientious, disobedient contempt of God.

It is evident that such a conception of sin does away with the Church's doctrine of original sin. And indeed, Abelard reduced the significance of original sin to a mere hereditary punishment inflicted by God upon all descendants of Adam.

5. Abelard's view of the atonement is perfectly in line with this superficial conception of sin. The only thing which he has in common with Anselm is the rejection of the claim of the devil upon mankind. As for the rest, he severely criticized Anselm's position. In order to forgive Adam's sin, shall God be pleased with a crime which would far surpass Adam's sin, i.e., the slaying of His Son? The case of Mary, whom God exempted from the curse of original sin demonstrates that God can forgive without Christ. Rather, Christ's birth, passion and death reveal God's infinite love to mankind which awakens in us a reciprocal love and gratitude. This disposition of love is the basis both of justification and the forgiveness of sin (*caritas justificat;* Luke 7: 47).

Strange to say, with this subjective or moral conception of the atonement, Abelard held another view which was the nearest approach that he made to the objective view of the atonement. "Through His merits He has obtained for us everything good that we have." (*MSL* 178, 863.) Christ's merits, however, are not His death, but His perfect love. Inasmuch as our love is insufficient, so our merits are insufficient. They are supplemented by Jesus' instruction, His complete fulfilling of the law, and His effective intercession for us. Besides, Abelard also built the sacramental idea into his teaching of the atonement. Through the sacraments the love which is efficacious for the forgiveness of sin is infused into us. Thus along with the rational-psychological way to forgiveness there is opened up the sacramental supernatural way which is independent of the first. One recognizes the mediating theologian who, convinced of the right reason, still will not give up the genuine faith of the Church.

6. The larger stress of God's love in the teaching of Abelard is correct. But it is just as one-sided as that system of Anselm. While Anselm failed to make clear the subjective application of Christ's merits through faith, Abelard practically reduced the work of Christ to an incitement of trust and love in man's heart toward God. Christ is not the originator of man's redemption; He only is the teacher and herald of the redemption completed through God's love.

7. The greatest antagonist of Abelard was Bernard of Clairvaux. He like Abelard, stressed the need for meditating upon the love of Christ so that our hearts may be aroused to responding love. But it was unbearable for him that in the teaching of Abelard there

as no place for the blood of Jesus and His cross. To him the idea was shocking that Abelard should teach that Christ was only a teacher. As it was not the example of Adam that made us sinners, just as little does the example of Christ suffice for our redemption. The mystical element in his theology came to express the view that Christ was the second Adam who suffered vicariously and wrought our redemption as the head of a new spiritual race.[2]

8. According to Hugo, sin is disobedience to God, for which man suffers the punishment of spiritual ignorance and carnal concupiscence. Christ came to placate the offended God, and through the sacraments He communicates to us His renewing and sanctifying grace.

9. It is of the greatest significance that Peter Lombard followed Hugo in his teaching of original sin. The voluntaristic conception of Anselm and Abelard is pushed to the background, and carnal concupiscence is made the essence of sin. Through sexual pleasure this corruption of human nature is transmitted to the child and it also infects the soul, separately created by God in each individual.

In his teaching of the atonement Peter unites in an unsatisfactory way nearly all the theories of the work of Christ which tradition offered him, even the theory of the deception of the devil. However, like Anselm, Abelard and Hugo, he denies any claim of the devil upon the sinner. As a perfect sacrifice Christ was able to procure salvation for us.

In a more concise statement of how that happens,[3] Peter takes first the subjective view: God's love is revealed in Christ's death. Through the cross, responding love for God is kindled in us, and we are thereby justified. Next to that stands the objective view: God Himself was made flesh, since a mere man or angel might easily have sinned. The God-Man conquers the devil, redeems us from eternal punishment, and through the sacraments infuses into us His grace.

Thus the Lombard's doctrine of the atonement indicates a mere summary of various theories, but no settlement of the same.

---

[2] H. Williams, *The Mysticism of St. Bernard of Clairvaux*, 1931.
[3] *Sententiae*, book 3, dist., 18-20.

Chapter Seven

THE CHURCH AND THEOLOGY IN THE THIRTEENTH CENTURY

Literature: Sources: Letters and Writings of INNOCENT III, *MSL*, 214-217; ALEXANDER OF HALES, *Summa universae theologiae*, Venice, 1475, Cologne, 1622; BONAVENTURA, *Opera* Strasburg, 1495, Rome, 1588-96, Quaracchi near Florence, 1882-1902; ALBERTUS MAGNUS, *Opera* Lyon, 1651; THOMAS AQUINAS, *Opera*, Rome, 1570, Venice, 1594, Antwerp, 1612, Paris, 1660 Venice, 1775-88, Parma, 1852 ff., Rome, 1882 ff.

1. The thirteenth century was the golden age of Roman Catholicism. The church party of Gregory VII had attained its purpose. The pious expectation of Biblical eschatology had become materialized on earth. The church militant was also the church triumphant. "The kingdoms of this world are become the kingdom of our Lord and his Christ" (Rev. 11: 15), for the vicar of Christ was the undisputed sovereign of kings and bishops, church and state, the lord over temporal and eternal welfare of men There never was a pope more powerful than Innocent III (1198-1216), and except for the Vatican decree of 1870, no pope has ever uttered such great boasts and blasphemies as he. "The pope holds a position between God and man. Though he is less than God, yet greater than man. He judges everybody, but is himself judged by none."[1] Into passages like Isaiah 42: 8, John 1: 16, and Romans 8: 29, Innocent read reference to himself.

2. These unparalleled claims of the papacy were seconded and defended in the name of piety and theology by the new mendicant orders and the great teachers of the high scholastic period.

At the time when some of the heretical groups began to call attention to the contradiction between the simple earthly life of Jesus and the might and splendor of His vicar in Rome, these new orders made their appearance to demonstrate to the world that a genuine imitation of the poverty of the Saviour still had a place within the limits of the Church. The idea of this new type of monastic life originated with Francis of Assisi (1182-1226).[2] Born as the son of a wealthy Italian merchant, he left all he had and followed Jesus in His lowliness with the greatest sincerity. In him the Bernardian mysticism found its noblest representative in this period. As St. Bernard had been instrumental in fostering the new piety among the nobility, so through Francis the new piety was promulgated among the populace of the then efflorescent cities. A monastic order that wants to live in principle on alms, cannot establish itself in romantic solitude The headquarters of mendicant friars had to be among the hurly-burly of city life. This also offered the mendicant friars a splendid opportunity to take advantage of the teaching positions at the new centers of learning, the universities.

3. Theological thought in the 13th century received a strong impetus from a new and intensified study of Aristotle by the scholars of the West.

---

[1] *MSL*, 217. p. 568.
[2] J. Joergensen, *Saint Francis of Assisi*, 1912; T. Cuthbert, *Life of St. Francis of Assisi*, 1913; P. Robinson *The Writings of St. Francis of Assisi*, 1906, an annotated translation.

Hitherto merely a portion of Aristotle's logical writing had been known in the West, and that in the translation of Boethius. From 1150-1210 there was a gradual introduction of his Natural Philosophy, Politics, Metaphysics and Ethics. The translations were made not from the original Greek, but from the Arabian. For this activity special credit goes to the Spanish and Sicilian Jews who performed their work by order of the Archbishop of Toledo and the emperor Frederick II. Not until later when the Latin Empire was established in Byzantium, was it possible to obtain Latin translations from the original Greek.

It was significant that the West became acquainted with the works of Aristotle in their entirety not only from Arabian translations, but also from Arabian commentaries. For this reason the Church at first put the blame of the Neo-Platonic-pantheistic speculation of the Jewish-Arabian scholars on Aristotle himself, and his philosophical writings were prohibited under pain of excommunication as late as 1210 and again in 1215. The change came when the genuine Aristotle was distinguished from the Arabic Aristotle. By 1231 the study of Aristotle was generally permitted, insofar as he was purified "from every suspicion of error." After that the ban was broken. In 1255, the study of Aristotle was made obligatory by the University of Paris. He now was often spoken of as the *praecursor Christi in naturalibus* and compared to John the Baptist as the *praecursor Christi in gratuitis.* Albertus Magnus even declared him to be the *rule of truth, the highest perfection of human reason.*

The new material and problems as raised by this study of Aristotle also called for a new scientific method. Hitherto the systematic work had mainly been the writing of a commentary on the *Sentences* of Peter Lombard. This method was now replaced by the *Summa,* a very elaborate but carefully balanced treatment of all the objects of theology, resembling the superb Gothic architecture of the age.

4. With incomparable strength and an acumen never again attained the best talents of the Middle Ages devoted themselves to the work of welding the Augustinianism of the Church and the ecclesiastical law on the one hand and the Aristotelian philosophy on the other. At the same time the scholars held to the presupposition that both parties exist by equal right and that nothing dare be broken off from either natural and revealed theology.

a. The older Franciscan school had precursors of a kind in theologians like Praepositinus of Cremona, William of Auxerre and William of Auvergne. They started with the theology of the twelfth century and their chief authority was Augustine. At the same time, however, the modern tendencies asserted themselves in the new style of problematics and the more intensive use of dialectics.

The real founder of high scholasticism and the foremost exponent of the older Franciscan school was Alexander of Hales (d. 1245). His colossal *Summa universae theologiae* probably signifies the deepest cleavage between the theology of the twelfth and that of the thirteeenth centuries.

Alexander attempted to produce a homogeneous system upon the threefold foundation of the strictest orthodoxy, the new piety, and the Aristotelian philosophy. It was not a superficial arrangement of differentiating theses, but a search for the truth from the cognition of the principle. In this Alexander adhered to Augustinianism and permitted Aristotle only to determine his method of thought. Many of his new transpositions and solutions later became historically significant and are partially effective today: the dis-

tinction between the *fides informis* of the natural man which relies on authority, miracle
and rational arguments, and the *fides formata* or *infusa* when man is so illumined by the
divine light that he comes without further proof to the immediate certainty of God and
divine things; the doctrine of the primitive state; the combining of the Aristotelian
conception of form with the doctrine of grace, the differentiation of the *meritum de
condigno* from the *meritum de congruo,* the introduction of "attrition" (imperfect sorrow
for sin, such as arises from fear of punishment), and the preference given to the study
of the *Sentences* at the expense of Bible study.

Bonaventura, *doctor seraphicus,* was born in the Papal States in 1221, and died as
cardinal and general of the Franciscan order in 1274. He was the second great theologian
of the older Franciscan school. For him Augustine is the chief authority; Plato ranks
before Aristotle; the real Aristotle remained undisclosed as before. His theological position is characterized by three catch-words: illumination, voluntarism, and positivism, i.e.
the mystic contemplation of God, the enjoyment of God (*frui Deo*) by a voluntary
submission of the intellect in obedience to Christ, and the blind surrender of the conscience to the laws and commandments of the Church. Thus arose the strange alliance
between the boldest and most absolute mysticism and the most scrupulous and ingenious
traditionalism, as it can be observed in St. Bernard and later in Duns Scotus and Occam.

b. It was the Dominicans who brought the scholasticism to its height. Albertus
Magnus (*doctor universalis*) the son of a German nobleman (died in 1280 as professor
at Cologne) was the leader in this movement. He was in every part a teacher and is
described as the greatest philosopher of the Middle Ages. The perfection of scholasticism
however is reached in Thomas Aquinas, who was by birth an Italian aristocrat.[3] In 1243
he entered the Dominican order and studied under Albertus at Cologne. He later labored
at Paris, Naples and Rome. He died in 1274 on his way to the Council at Lyons. This
accomplished scholar of mature Romanism was a great literary genius with all-
embracing interest. He wrote commentaries on Aristotle, on books of the Old and the
New Testaments, and provided a dogmatic and ethical *Summa.* To theology he gave a
modern reworking and provided it with clarity before unknown. He was inclined to
mysticism but at the same time he recognized philosophy: reason and revelation were
both praised as divine and declared to be in nowise contradictory. Things mysterious
in theology may be above reason, but cannot be against reason. He and his school found
an implacable opponent once and for all in the Franciscan order. In this conflict Thomas
remained the victor. After he had been made the official theologian of the Dominicans
the Church also decided in his favor. In 1323 he was canonized; in 1567 he was proclaimed *doctor ecclesiae* and in 1880 *patron of all Catholic schools.*

In the problem of the universals, Thomas teaches a moderate realism. In his teaching of God, the fundamental issue of scholasticism, the harmonization of revelation and
reason, of Augustinian Biblicism and Aristotelian (or Platonian) realism, reached its
culmination. God is to Thomas the first cause and the absolute substance. Reason may
lead the way, but revelation alone can complete it. The *fides infusa* is required for the
reception of revelation, but the scholastic *fides infusa* is in itself merely an enhancement
of the rational powers of man.

---

[3] For important studies of Thomas we refer to: M. Grabmann, *Thomas von Aquin,* 5th ed., 1926, Eng.
1928: also his *Einfuehrung in die Summae Theologiae des hl. Thomas,* 2nd ed., 1928, Eng., 1930; E. Gilson,
Philosophy of St. Thomas, 1929; M. C. D'Arcy, *Thomas Aquinas,* 1931; T. Geheen, *The Problem of Matter in
the De Ente et Essentia of Thomas Aquinas,* 1940.

The disruption of this artificial combination was effected in two different ways. On the one hand, the humanists detached themselves from the Augustinian heritage of the Church and deepened an independent view of the world in the Hellenic fashion. On the other hand, Luther struck violently at this artificial edifice. Rediscovering the personal God of the Bible, he shattered the structure of the scholastics into fragments. This is the real and abiding significance of the Reformation. [4]

As to soteriology, Thomas, unlike Anselm, denied the absolute necessity of Christ's Passion. Christ suffered out of love and obedience. Hence he obtained a merit, and His sanctification is not only sufficient, but superabundant.

5. But in spite of the great advance in ecclesiastical power and theology the opposition against the Church became very noticeable during the thirteenth century. Through the Crusades the West had come into contact with the flourishing scientific and impressive social life of the Arabian countries. This created a sceptical sentiment as to the absolute truth of the Church. Men were beginning to arrive at the proposition of a twofold truth according to which a doctrine may be possible in theology, but impossible in philosophy. In Palermo, at the brilliant imperial court of Frederick II, probably, originated the notorious saying of the three imposters of mankind: Moses, Jesus and Mohammed. The pitiless conflict of the popes with Frederick II and the last rulers of the imperial dynasty of the Hohenstaufen was void of any spiritual objective; it was a mere struggle for political hegemony in Italy. No wonder that the papal ban could neither impair nor change the plans of the emperors. In the Church's desire to rule the world it forfeited its spiritual power and became a part of the world.

The rising tide also of nationalism in the Western world began to oppose the international and supernatural claims of the Church. The Latin of the Church was beginning to lose its exclusive position. A new national literature came into existence composed in the vernacular of the various countries. Poets like Walther von der Vogelweide (d. about 1230) and Dante (1265-1321), strongly sided with the emperors in their conflict with the popes and unhesitatingly assailed the unscrupulous and immoral strategy of the papacy.

Furthermore, the growth of the universities (Bologna eleventh century, Paris and Oxford twelfth century, Heidelberg 1396), added to the disintegration of the solidarity of the scholastic world-view. The study of Aristotle fostered a new interest in the natural sciences (Roger Bacon, died 1292). To be sure, these tendencies could fully succeed and mature only much later.

But the Chuch was also attacked and opposed in the name of genuine piety. Old heresies were revived as in the case of the dualistic-manichaeistic Cathari, and new heretical groups [5] sprang up, e.g., the Waldensians, who taught a Biblicism pure and simple. The Church tried to win them back or to exterminate them by a ruthless oppression. Thus it revived the dreadful pagan persecutions of the first centuries. Thereby the Church itself gave reason to belief that the papacy is the seven-headed beast of Revelation, and never since has this belief been without its advocates. With the pope a prisoner at the mercy of the French king and the grand intellectual structure of Thomas undermined by Duns Scotus, thus ended the golden age of Roman Catholicism.

---

[4] Cf George S. Hendry, *God the Creator*, 1937, pp. 60 ff.
[5] Cf. H. J. Warner, *The Albigensian Heresy*, 1922.

Chapter Eight

THE TEACHING OF SIN AND GRACE.
THE SACRAMENTS

Literature: In addition to the literature of the foregoing chapter reference may be made
MANSI, *MSL* 31, 1047-70; G. L. HAHN, *Die Lehre von den Sakramenten*, 1864; J. BACH, *D
Siebenzahl der Sakramente*, 1864; P. SCHANZ, *Die Lehre von den heiligen Sakramenten*, 189
N. GIHR, *Die heiligen Sakramente der katholischen Kirche*, 2 vols., 1902 f. D. STONE, *A Histo
of the Doctrine of the Holy Eucharist*, vol. 1, 1909. D. J. KENNEDY, article of *Sacraments .
Catholic Encyclopedia*, vol. 13, 295-304. A. J. MACDONALD, *Berengar and the Reform of Sacr
mental Doctrine*, 1930; H. C. LEA, *A History of Auricular Confession and Indulgences in t*
Latin Church, 3 vols., 1896.

1. As genuine scholars of the West the scholastics have made the greatest contr
bution to theology along the practical lines of anthropology and soteriology.

In describing the original state of man, they distinguished between the natur
endowment of man, i.e., a harmony of his natural powers and the absence of col
cupiscence, and the additonal endowment of grace to control the inferior sensitivene
in him (*donum superadditum*). Through this additional endowment man was also abl
to make himself acceptable in the sight of God.

As to the conception of sin the Franciscans strongly favored the traditional Sem
Pelagian tenets of the age, whereas Thomas kept himself closer to the Augustinia
heritage of the Church.

Original sin was defined as something negative, the lack of original righteousnes
the loss of the additional endowment. Hence no important alteration in man's natur
took place. According to Thomas, however, this natural depravity is also somethin
positive: it is concupiscence and it involves both guilt and punishment. Since creatior
ism is considered the only orthodox view, concupiscence has its seat in the flesh and i
propagated by generation.

The conditioned original sin is materialized through actual sin. The chief source
for this are seven: pride, covetousness, lust, anger, gluttony, envy and sloth. These ar
the capital sins (*peccata capitalia*). They again are subdivided into *peccata mortali*
and *venialia*. A sin is mortal if it is a wilful transgression of the law of God, and i
separates from God. Venial sins are only a *version*, a deviation from God withou
sufficient reflection or full consent of the will. They may be atoned for by tempora
punishments. The mere natural possibility of sinning is of God as the cause of every
thing; the depravity of the action, however, is of the free will of man. Though th
universality of sin was generally conceded, the scholastics made an exemption in th
case of the Virgin Mary. Whereas they all were agreed that Mary was exempte
from actual sin, the Dominicans objected to denying also original sin in Mary. N
formal decision was reached until 1854, when Pope Pius IX sanctioned the belief in th
immaculate conception of Mary.

On grace, Thomas, following Augustine, taught that God is the moving power i
effecting man's conversion. Still he insists that man is free in the use of his will as t

the preparation for grace. Grace is viewed from the standpoint of Aristotelian form which is at first a disposition in God and then becomes active in its object. By its infusion into man, he is restored and his nature is repaired. Thus justification is not a judicial act of God; it rather is a gradual process of human recovery.

Through the infusion of grace man also receives love which changes his attrition to contrition, and the *fides informis* to *fides formata*. Also his good works are so perfected in him that he now can justly claim eternal life from God (*meritum de condigno*), while before this infusion took place it only seemed appropriate that God should recompense the honest moral endeavor of man. The merits of his works had been *de congruo*.

A man may even earn more merits than are necessary for his salvation. This is the case if he is willing to follow, in addition to all the commandments of the Gospel, also the *evangelical counsels*. The supererogatory works of Christ and the saints have created a treasury of superabundant merits, the *thesaurus supererogationis meritorum*. The treasury is at the disposal of the pope and administered by the priests for the benefit of the souls in purgatory.

This brief outline of the order of salvation clearly indicates that the religious life of Roman Catholicism does not center in faith but in love and good works. Consequently no actual certainty of salvation is attainable. The pious is always kept in suspense as to his final destiny. No wonder, therefore, that the grandest hymn of the Middle Ages is not a hymn in praise of victorious faith but an expression of fear and apprehension: *Dies irae, dies illa*.

2. All the lines of interest in medieval theology converge in the teaching concerning the Sacraments. This was conditioned by a twofold interest: the practical concern of the individual to have salvation presented to him in a tangible form, and the hierarchical tendencies of the age to tie inseparably the salvation of the individual to the Church. Thus the sacraments became at one and the same time a means of grace and a means to rule.

Since the term *sacramentum* had been used in the preceding centuries for any significant religious act, the exact number of the sacraments had remained undetermined. To baptism and the Eucharist Abelard added confession and extreme unction, and his pupils added matrimony. These five sacraments were also recognized by Hugo, while Robert Pullus (d. 1150) attained the same number by omitting extreme unction and matrimony, and including penance and ordination. Through a combination of these finally the number seven was reached. Since Peter Lombard this is the established number which received official sanction at the council of Florence in 1439.

The Franciscans upheld Augustine's definition of a sacrament as a visible sign of an invisible grace. Thomas, however, made the sacramental matter the vehicle of grace except in case of ordination. In this sacrament, according to him, the power spiritual proceeds from the officiating bishop.

In each sacrament the matter, the visible element, is distinguished from the form, the words used in the rite. (The two terms have retained a connotation from Platonian philosophy: *materia* signifies the unformed substance of a thing, *forma* its shaping energy. Wood, e.g., first exists as an unshaped matter, and then formed into a table, a chair, etc. by the *forma* (idea) of the respective object. Thus in the Eucharist, bread and wine are the unformed matter till the words of the institution do change them into the sacramental body and blood of Christ.)

The primary effect of the sacrament is to restore to man his original righteousness through impartation of the redemptive merits of the Saviour. To this is added in the case of the three sacraments which cannot be repeated, baptism, confirmation and ordination, the communication of a character *spiritualis,* i.e., an indelible, indestructive mark imprinted for all time on the human soul. This strange conception has served as a convenient means to uphold the belief in the unity and sanctity of the Church in spite of prevailing dissensions and unbelief among the baptized and the undeniable unworthiness of many priests.

The validity of the sacraments depends exclusively on a virtue inherent in themselves, i.e., they are effective *ex opere operato.* The only requirement is that the officiating priest has the intention to do what the Church does, and that likewise the recipient, in order to participate in the blessing of the sacrament, must have the disposition of faith and not be in the state of mortal sin.

The individual definitions of each sacrament, as contained in the papal bull *Exultate Deo* of 1439, are chiefly based on Thomas Aquinas and are on the whole still authoritative in the church of Rome.

The matter of baptism is a triple immersion in or aspersion by water; its form is the words: "I baptize thee in the name of the Father, and of the Son, and of the Holy Ghost." Inasmuch as it confers upon the recipient the justifying grace, his sins, original as well as actual, are forgiven, their guilt and punishment are removed. The baptized is made a saint in the kingdom of God in spite of the fact that a tinder, *fomes peccati* remains, which might at any moment be kindled into a flame.

Confirmation is the anointing of the baptized with consecrated chrism, signifying the communication of the Holy Ghost to make him a strong and perfect Christian. In the ancient Church, as to the present time in the East, it was connected with the rite of baptism and administered by the priest, while in the church of Rome the ordinary minister now is the bishop. The matter of this sacrament is holy chrism, its form: "I sign thee with the sign of the cross, and confirm thee with the chrism of salvation, in the name of the Father, and of the Son, and of the Holy Ghost."

Theological speculation as well as practical piety culminates in the doctrine of the Eucharist, which is both a sacrament and a sacrifice. In the mass Christ descends from heaven into the elements of bread and wine, and at the same time, the priest offers Christ up to God. The mass, therefore, is a continual daily repetition of the sacrifice of Christ on Calvary. Its matter is bread and wine, its form the words of the institution.

According to Thomas the substance of the elements is changed to be the same as that of the celestial body of Christ. The accidental properties, however, remain unchanged. Thus the elements become essentially the body of Christ, though not with respect to the dimensions of His body and blood. This change is effected by virtue of the sacramental words when they are properly recited by a consecrated priest.

Since the whole Christ was held to be present in each of the elements the ever growing tendency to withhold the cup from the laity became gradually, though slowly the established custom of the Church.

The fact that the sacramental conception of the Eucharist became in thought and practice secondary to its being thought of as a daily sacrifice, not instituted for eating and drinking, but for adoration and worship, greatly contributed to an ever increasing aggrandizement of the sacerdotal hierarchy. The exhibition of the sacramental Christ is

e mass and in eucharistic processions (*Corpus Christi* festivals since 1264) turned out
be the greatest display of sacerdotal power.

The effect of the sacrament consists in the strengthening of sanctifying grace and
e remission of venial sins. As a sacrifice the Eucharist is a propitiatory, effectual
lation for the various benefits of those present or absent, living or dead.

With respect to penance the scholastics distinguished the sacrament of penance from
e Christian virtue of repentance. Whereas this virtue is a permanent requirement, the
ecessity of the sacrament is limited to certain periods only, i.e., to remove mortal sin
d to assure the communicant of the absence of such before holy communion.

The history of penance is long and intricate.[1] The severe discipline of the ancient
hurch had gradually been mitigated. Public penance proved distasteful to the northern
eople. It, therefore, was gradually supplanted by personal confession in private to the
riest. The earliest trace of this is found in monasteries of Cassianus (fifth century) in
outhern Gaul. From the monastic discipline the practice was transferred to the secular
ergy, and then to the laity. It was welcomed by the laity to quiet the fear of punish-
ent, purgatory and hell. On the one hand, it deepened the consciousness of sin, but it
so weakened the morality, since confession became habitual, and since the conception
ecame universal that through intercessions and satisfactions punishment for sin could
e absolved. The old order of contrition, confession, satisfaction and absolution was
anged to let absolution precede satisfaction. The confession itself was looked upon
forgiving the sins, the satisfaction as the means of escaping temporal punishments for
ns and acquiring merits. Whoever neglects penitential works must suffer in purga-
ry but whoever neglects repentance and confession is irrevocably lost. The attach-
ent of a positive value to satisfactions for removing punishment for sin naturally led
their classification as good works, procuring merit where there was no sin which
equired no compensation.

As soon as a real value became attached to satisfactions, exchanges, transfers, reduc-
ons, substitutions, attenuations, redemptions or commutations, a traffic in spiritual
dulgences by the Church became a logical development. Money payments were accepted
r the performance of penances, and the hiring of others to do works of penance for a
nner was permitted. The first indulgences appeared in Southern France in the eleventh
entury;[2] the first plenary indulgence was granted in 1040, by Benedict IX. Indulgences,
cording to the official interpretation, only remit the canonical punishments connected
ith sin; but the erroneous conception that they forgive sin proved only too popular
d worked disastrously in the continuation of the practice.

The acts of the penitent are the matter of this sacrament: the contrition or the
ttrition (Thomas) of the heart, the confession before the priest, and the satisfaction
rough penitential works. The words of the priest: "I absolve thee," constitute its form.
he forgiveness of sin is not obtained through the contrite disposition of the sinner, but
dependent on the keys of the Church. To confess at least once a year at Easter was
ade obligatory by Innocent III in 1215.

About 888, the Church of the West began to emphasize the ancient custom of
nointing the sick. Soon this practice received a sacramental character inasmuch as it
as connected with the remission of sins and was considered a substitute for penance.

---

[1] O. D. Watkins, *A History of Penance*, 1920.
[2] A. M. Lepicier, *Indulgences, Their Origin, Nature and Development*, 1895.

The matter of extreme unction is consecrated olive oil with which the priest who admin isters it anoints the eyes, ears, nostrils, lips, hands, feet and loins of the sick in immedia danger of death. Its form is the accompanying prayer: "Through this holy unction an His most precious mercy may the Lord forgive thee all thy sins of sight, etc." The effe of extreme unction is the healing of the soul by the remission of venial sin and cleansin from the remains of sin, and if God sees fit also the restoration of health to the body.

The last two sacraments exclude each other: the recipient of ordination is prohibite to marry and vice versa. Ordination is instituted to rule the Church, matrimony t multiply its membership.

Through seven successive acts of blessing the power and grace to rule and to pe form the sacred duties of the Church are bestowed upon the recipient of ordinatio This sacrament is administered by the bishop, and it imparts an indelible character. Th matter is found in the rites of the laying on of the hands and the anointing, and th handing over of the paten and chalice. The words of the consecrating bishop constitut the form: "Receive authority to offer sacrifice in the Church for the living and th dead, etc. Receive the Holy Ghost; whosoever sins you remit, they are remitted unt them, etc."

No teaching is as inconsistent and vacillating as the statements concerning matr mony. Contrary to all the other sacraments, in the case of the sacrament of matrimon the recipients are its agents; for matrimony itself, not the benediction of the pries constitutes the sacrament. Consequently the form is found in the mutual consent of th contracting parties. Its matter is left undefined. Its effect is the impartation of sanct fying mutual love which enables husband and wife to bear with each other's weakne and to procreate and educate their children in fear and love of God. As a sacramen matrimony is indissoluble. It may, however, be repeated in case of the death of on of the contractors. In spite of the contradictory teachings regarding matrimony, it sacramental conception has helped to preserve for it a holy place in the world of asceti and monastic ideals, and the requirement of a voluntary, mutual consent and the restric tion placed upon family intermarriage have proved to be of greatest importance i the civilization of the West.

Chapter Nine

CHURCH AND STATE IN THE FOURTEENTH AND FIFTEENTH CENTURIES

1. Thomas had, for the first time, assigned the pope a place in dogmatics in which he set forth the infallibility and unrestricted sovereignty of the pope over Church and state.[1] At the second council at Lyons in 1274 official sanction was given to this doctrine. In the notorious papal bull of 1302, *Unam sanctam,* Boniface VIII only formulated what had been taught and approved, but in a way that proved offensive to his time: the pope possesses both swords, the spiritual and the secular, and the unconditioned submission to the pope is necessary for eternal salvation. His boisterous claims, however, were supported by two jurists, the Italian monk Augustines Triumphus,[2] and the Spaniard Alvarus Pelagius.[3]

But Western Europe was by no means ready to surrender. Boniface met with the most disgraceful disaster. He was taken prisoner by the French king, and this incident ushered in one of the most ignominious periods in the history of the papacy (the Babylonian captivity of the Church, 1305-1377; the great schism, 1378-1415).

2. During the later Middle Ages Europe was in the transition from barter economy to money and credit economy, and the Holy See became the foremost international money institute. The exploitation of individuals and peoples through the taxing system of the Church and through the trade with indulgences and the like, proved destructive to the morals of the Church and the national wealth of the European peoples. The opposition, therefore, became a national affair in Western Europe, which experienced at this time a rising tide of national consciousness. The awakening nationalism at the same time fostered a revival of the Carolingian idea of a national church. At first this movement became noticeable in England, which had never been under the charm and pressure of the romantic idea of the empire.

Occam was the first who contended against the claims of the papacy in the name of reason and the Scriptures.[4] Its very idea is against both reason and the Bible, which are fully harmonious. This criticism of the hierarchial system is something new and paved the way for the triumph of Calvinism in English history.

By far more radical than Occam was Wyclif (d. 1384).[5] According to him, the power which the pope claims for himself does properly belong to the poor and pious who are united in a national church. This is to be ruled by the law of Christ which is contained in the infallible Bible.

On the continent these revolutionary ideas were proclaimed by John Huss, who

---

[1] *Summa,* II, II, 9. 1, a, 10 (22, p. 10).

[2] *Summa de Potestate Ecclesiae,* first edition, 1474.

[3] *De Planctu Ecclesiae,* first edition, 1474.

[4] *Dialogus inter Magistrum et Discipulum de Imperatorum et Pontificum Potestate* and other political writings are edited by Goldast, *Monarchia* II, Frankfort, 1614, and R. Scholz, 1914.

[5] His works have been edited by the Wyclif Society, vols. 1-19, 1884-1922.

died for them in 1415. [6] After his death, his followers tried to enforce them with the sword and the torch.

The same tendencies toward a national church were felt in Spain and notably in France (the Pragmatic Sanction of Bourges, 1438). Through the French influence the national conception of the Church prevailed at the three great councils of reform.

The collapse of the imperial power (the interregnum, 1254-1273) greatly strengthened the self-consciousness of the federated princes and cities in Germany and Italy. After its restoration it was the Emperor Ludwig of Bavaria (1314-1347), who was engaged in a life-long ardent struggle against the unbridled claims of the Church. His allies in this conflict were the German cities, the Italian Ghibelins (Dante), a minority party of the Franciscans which was at odds with the hierarchy over the mendicant principle of their order, and the famous writer Marsilius of Padua, professor at Paris. In his diatribe *Defensor Pacis* (first edition, Basel, 1522) Marsilius clearly set forth the principle of popular sovereignty in both Church and state. The pope is only the first and supreme officer of the Church, but as a fallible human being responsible to the whole Church, which consists of the clerics and the laity, men and women, to be judged according to the only infallible authority, the Bible, by a general council to which the Church has delegated her power.

These conciliar ideas over against the curial conception of the Church were most persistently defended, as stated above, by French scholars of the Sorbonne, such as Conrad von Gelnhausen, Henry von Langenstein, Peter D'Ailli and John Gerson. Their efforts resulted in three great attempts at practical reform: the councils at Pisa, in 1409, at Constance, in 1414-1418, and at Basel, 1431-1449. At the fifth session of the council at Constance the conciliar conception of the Church was solemnly approved. Nevertheless the revived papacy soon defied the conciliarists openly and boldly.

3. The social standard of the lower classes deteriorated, especially as the result of the spread of money as a means of exchange and the intrusion of the ego-centered Roman law. Pessimism prevailed and kindled revolutionary communistic ideas as well as ardent apocalyptic expectations.

The influence which the Church had lost over the state she tried to regain over the people. New churches were built; the number of the clerics and monks increased enormously; the traffic in relics flourished; the importance of the sermon received new emphasis; [7] the Bible was translated and printed in the popular idiom. [8]

A sad counterpart of this is the spread of superstition. Through Thomas Aquinas the belief in witches found its way into Christian dogmatics, and Pope Gregory IX put the Dominicans in charge of the cruel judicial process of the inquisition.

4. As to the upper classes, the Renaissance in Italy constitutes the most conspicuous movement. It was initiated by the poets Petrarca (d. 1374) and Boccaccio (d. 1375). As its name indicates it was a rebirth, i.e., of the philosophical and cultural ideas of the Graeco-Roman civilization. The thriving force of the movement is found in the desire to proclaim and to enjoy the innate rights and values of human nature. Thus the Renaissance produced the greatest artists like Michelangelo, and the most notorious criminals such as Rodrigo, the later Pope Alexander VI, and his son Cesare Borgia. The

[6] His works are edited by W. Flajshans, 1903 ff. Cf. M. Spinka, *Huss and the Czech Reform*, 1940.
[7] G. R. Owst, *Preaching in Medieval England*, 1350-1450, 1926.
[8] For a fuller discussion on this important material compare M. Reu, *Luther's German Bible*, 1934.

anti-Christian tendencies of the movement were repressed for a time by the reawakening of an intense interest in religion through the Reformation; but as an undercurrent they came again to the surface towards the end of the seventeenth century in Western Europe. As a cultural and aesthetic movement, it celebrated its greatest achievements in the field of literature and art. It invaded the very ranks of the upper hierarchy, even the Vatican. The popes of the fifteenth century were in thought and deed Greek despots. They were not disciples of the lowly Man of Nazareth, much less His vicars. The noblest of the Renaissance men is Michelangelo in whose poetry a truly evangelical ring is manifest.

Less radical than the Renaissance in Italy was the Humanistic movement as represented at Paris, Oxford, and the German universities. Its interest greatly helped to discredit the subtle method of scholasticism and to arouse a new interest in the ancient languages. Reuchlin, the greatest scholar of Hebrew, published his first Hebrew grammar in 1506, and in 1516 Erasmus' first edition of the Greek New Testament came off the press. Men of a similar disposition were Laurentius Valla, who criticized the so-called *Constantinian Donation,* Marsilio Ficino, and Giovanni Pici della Mirandola in Italy, the Cardinal Ximenes in Spain, John Colet and Thomas Morus in England, Ulric von Hutten in Germany. But either their insight into the corruption of the Church or their interest in a thorough reform was too superficial. And in the end, the common tenets of Greek philosophy bound them all to the church of Thomas Aquinas. The Church, therefore, could bear them all, the Borgias as well as Erasmus, but not Martin Luther. The Church excommunicated him, while murderers and adulterers, sceptics and scoffers in clerical robes could remain in her fold.

Chapter Ten

THEOLOGY AND PIETY IN THE LATER MIDDLE AGES

Literature: Sources: DUNS SCOTUS, edited by WADDING, 13 vols., 1639; re-edited by VIVES, 26 vols., 1891 ff.; BRADWARDINE'S works in *Anglia Sacra*, vol. i, 1691; BIEL, edited by STEINBACH. 1488 ff.; ECKHART, edited in part by FRANZ PFEIFFER in *Deutsche Mystiker des 14. und 15. Jahrhunderts.*, vol. 2, 1857; also in *Die Klassiker der Religion*, vols. 14-15, 1919; a new complete edition is under way, published by the Kohlhammer Verlag, Stuttgart, Germany. TAULER, in *Deutsche Texte des Mittelalters*, vol. 11, 1910; SEUSE, edited by KARL BIHLMEYER, 1907; by W. LEHMANN, 2 vols., 1911; RUYSBROECK, edited by J. B. DAVID, 6 vols., 1858-69; GOCH, in *Bibliotheca Reformatoria Nederlandia*, vol 6, 1909; WESEL, in *Monumenta Medii Aevi*, vol. I, 1757; WESSEL, published at Groningen, 1614; GREGOR OF RIMINI, *Lectura in I et II Librum Sententiarum*, 1482; C. HORSTMAN, *Works of Richard Rolle and His Followers*, 1895. ERASMUS, edited by BEATUS RHENANUS, 3 vols., 1540 and by JOHN CLERICUS, 10 vols., 1703-06; for the works of Occam, Wyclif and Huss see the previous chapter, footnotes 4-6, also T. BRUCE BIRCH, *The De Sacramento Altaris of William of Occam*, 1930 (Latin Text and English Translation). Studies: W. F. HOOK, *Lives of the Archbishops of Canterbury*, vol. 4, 1865 (on Bradwardine); KARL ULLMANN, *Reformatoren vor der Reformation*, 1841 f., 2nd edition, 1866; P. S. ALDER, *The Age of Erasmus*, 1914; P. SMITH, *The Age of Erasmus*, 1920.

1. The Englishman JOHN DUNS SCOTUS (d. 1308) marks the turning point in medieval scholasticism.[1] Over against the Aristotelian tenets in the system of Thomas, Duns Scotus stands out as the representative of the older Platonian-Augustinian school of thought. Concerning the problem of the *universals* he teaches that the genus is inherent in the individuals (*universalia in re*). But his realism is modified by his emphasis on the individuality of a thing, and by the stress which he laid on experience as a source of human knowledge. Endowed with a remarkable keenness of mind (*doctor subtilis*), Duns Scotus discovered and laid bare the weakness and defects in the theology of Thomas. Thus the peaceful alliance of theology with philosophy which Thomas had achieved in his *Summa*, was allotted but a brief duration of life. Duns Scotus distinguishes, at least in principle, between philosophical knowledge and the religious approach to an assurance of metaphysical entities. He, therefore, rejects the intellectual, speculative method of his Dominican rival. With him theology is a practical science. He concedes very little to logical demonstration. The fruition of the Godhead is effected not through the intellect but through the will. Thus he discredited a very forceful tenet of the scholastic age, and reintroduced a principle which proved very effective in shaping the theology which was to come. But in spite of this genuine Augustinian trend of thought, Duns Scotus remained within the approved limits of the traditional Semi-Pelagian interpretation of the great African theologian.

For the loss of the emphasis on the speculative foundations of theology, the student of Duns Scotus is compensated by his stress on the authority of Scriptures and the Church as dependable warranters of religious truth. Since it is, however, the Church which has approved and authorized the exact extent and content of the Scriptures, her authority remains with him of foremost importance.

The interpreter of Duns is handicapped by the subtlety of his terminology, and the

---

[1] C. R. S. Harris, *Duns Scotus*, 2 vols., 1927.

apparent endeavor of his heterodox teachings behind the shield of orthodoxy. For good reasons Duns Scotus could be called an *Abelard redivivus*. But he was by far too shrewd to commit himself openly as did that great savant of the twelfth century. [2]

Although Duns Scotus may occasionally define God, like Thomas, as the *infinite being*, it is the voluntaristic conception of Augustine which prevails in his theology. His conception of God bears all the characteristics of what we now call the *otherness* of God. In this respect Duns Scotus marks a milestone toward the rediscovery of the personal God of the Bible. God is pure will dominating the world. While Thomas said that *God wills the good,* Duns Scotus contended that *Whatever God wills, is good.* This absolute will of God is limited only by His own goodness or by the nature of a thing. God may save, if He wills, the condemned Judas; but He cannot save a stone. A certain element of arbitrariness is thus imparted to the nature of God which prepared the way for the subtle and futile discussions of later theologians on the possibilities and probabilities in the plans of God. On the other hand, by this stress on the will of God, Duns Scotus disentangled the conception of God from the many logical necessities under which, for instance, Anselm had put the dealings of God with the world.

In accordance with this viewpoint Duns Scotus denies that Christ has rendered a *superabundant satisfaction* to God. The cause and reason for His merits are only the *divine acceptance,* the divine will to affix any estimate to whatever is done or suffered.

Duns Scotus, very unlike St. Augustine, applied the same voluntaristic principle to his teaching on anthropology. Original sin is defined as the loss of original righteousness. The natural powers of men are unimpaired. He can produce within himself the *attrition,* by which he will receive and merit, by a merit of congruity, the justifying grace. In this respect Duns Scotus is a true exponent of the Semi-Pelagian tradition in the Franciscan order.

The same holds true as regards his views on the sacraments. The Augustinian tradition of his order is well maintained by him in spite of his orthodox terminology. In the doctrine of the Eucharist, his real sympathies are with the theory of consubstantiation. However, in order to avoid a seeming heterodoxy, Duns Scotus introduced into the discussion the theory of the *transsubstantiatio adductiva,* i.e., the earthly elements are not changed into the body and blood of Christ; rather some particles of them are annihilated by the sacramental union so that the sacramental Christ is coexistent with the bread and wine in the Eucharist.

2. The respective followers of Thomas and Duns Scotus now form two opposite schools of thought: The Thomists and the Scotists. Both schools produced men of great scholarship. The dominating figure of the fourteenth century is WILLIAM OCCAM (d. 1349 at Munich), who was, like Duns Scotus, an Englishman and member of the Franciscan order. In his theological development he started with the Scotist theology of his order. But his theology developed into a system of its own. This is marked by a survival of Nominalism, and Occam was considered the modernist of his day.

The revival of Nominalism had started with the Thomist Durandus de Porciano and the Scotist Peter Aureoli. But it was Occam who secured for it its dominating influence at the Sorbonne and at most of the universities in Germany. According to Occam, all knowledge is derived from intuitive observation of the individual thing.

[2] Cf. the divergent opinion of modern scholars on his teaching concerning the universals. While some have called him a Nominalist, others have defined his position as excessive realism. Seeberg, *DG, III⁴,* 569 f.

It is only by way of logical abstraction that the intellect creates a generic conception (*conceptualism*), a common name, to designate it. This conception may be called a *universal,* but it has no reality outside the concrete thing. The human intellect, however, substitutes a name (*terminus*) for this conception (*terminism*).

Occam combined in his nature, even more so than his countryman Duns Scotus, that which is typical of the Anglo-Saxon race, a critical radicalism and a practical conservatism. He shared with his time the disposition of the sceptics as regards the demonstrability of the Church's doctrines. He did not shrink from openly attacking the hierarchy (cf. the previous chapter). Nevertheless, he wanted to remain a loyal son of Rome. Since, however, the papacy was not sacrosanct to him, the authority of the Bible was a far more practical matter to him than to Duns Scotus. Mainly through Occam the Bible became, at least in theory, the doctrinal authority of the fourteenth century. Whatever is not contained in the Scriptures, the Christian is not bound to believe. The Scriptures are truth, because they are inspired. Inspiration is conceived of as a dictation by the Holy Spirit. In practice, his Biblicism remained ineffective, since he, too, continued to work under the illusion of the age that the doctrines of the Church are identical with the teachings of the Bible.

In the doctrine of the Eucharist, Occam tried hard to overcome the idea of a quantitative relationship between the body of Christ and the earthly elements. In his treatise *De Sacramento Altaris,* he devotes much time and effort to prove that a thing may lose its attribute of quantity without losing its essential identity. As the rational soul is locally inseparable from man, but as a whole present in the whole of man as well as in every part of him, so "the entire body of Christ is really contained under the whole host and under each part of the host." [3] As to the Biblical basis to the theory of transubstantiation Occam expresses openly his honest doubts. Nevertheless, he defends it, simply in obedience to the Church. "Although it is expressly set forth in the canonical Scriptures that the body of Christ is to be offered to the faithful under the species of bread, yet that the substance of the bread is really converted or transubstantiated into the body of Christ is not found expressed in the canon of the Bible; but this doctrine is believed to have been divinely revealed to the Holy Fathers, or to have been proved from passages of the Bible by a diligent and skillful examination." [4]

Occamistic Modernism held the field in theology, almost unrivaled, for nearly a hundred years. Its stronghold on the continent was the Sorbonne at Paris. Peter d'Ailli and Gerson, the most prominent and influential leaders of the great movement at reform of the Church *in her head and members,* were its professed followers. In Germany it was Gabriel Biel (d. 1495), professor at Tuebingen, who made Occamism live longer there than in any other country of Western Europe. Biel's pupil, John Nathin, in turn taught Martin Luther the Occamistic theology of his master at the University of Erfurt.

According to Biel faith is an "act of the intellect proceeding under the command of the assenting will." But he denies man the absolute assurance of his being in the state of grace. Rather, as man always striving struggles on, he may hope that God will grant him what he believes.

3. As time advanced the hair-splitting subtleties of Nominalism, its empty negative

---

[3] Occam-Birch. *De Sacramento Altaris,* p. 189.
[4] *Ibid.,* p. 173.

criticism, and its futile attempt at reform could no longer command the interest of the younger generation. After 1450 a return to the teachings of the *Ancients* (Thomas and Duns Scotus) became apparent. More and more Thomas especially was looked upon as the normative exponent of Catholic doctrine. The theologian of this group who is best known among Protestants is the Thomist friar Thomas Vio (Cajetanus), the papal envoy to confer with Luther at Augsburg in 1518. Spanish theologians of the next century put the finishing touch to the work of these Ancients from whom the hierarchy recruited its brain trust during the threatening crisis of the sixteenth century.

However, neither the rationalization of the Church's doctrine in the system of Thomas, nor the unintelligible positivism as advocated by Duns Scotus and the Nominalists could satisfy the genuinely religious need of the times. Thus again there was breaking forth a stream of outspoken religious subjectivism as in the eleventh and twelfth centuries. Historically *the rise of the new mysticism* is to be traced back to the female monasteries which had been placed under the spiritual supervision of the Dominican order. The new mysticism, therefore, is Thomistic in principle, although the Aristotelian outlook was broadened by Platonic and Neo-Platonic principles which reached the West through the writings of the Areopagite and John Scotus Erigena. For this reason the Dominican mysticism in Germany and the Netherlands was to some extent more philosophical (in danger of pantheism) and less Biblical than the Bernardian type of mysticism. It showed little interest in the historical foundations of Christianity. Its interest was centered in the emancipation of the soul, its illumination and blissful communion with God. But the German mystics were genuine occidentals with a deep appreciation of an active life of duty, some of them ranking foremost in the history of Christian preaching. As a church movement the mystics did not depart in any marked degree from the teaching and practice of the Church. In stressing the religious experience of the individual, the movement stands out as a forceful champion of the empirical tendencies of the age.

In the fifteenth century the movement became general. It now made its influence felt on the lay piety. Although the hierarchy had succeeded in wiping out mystic-sectarian lay organizations like the Catharists, Albigenses and the Sect of the Free Spirit, it could not kill the spirit of these movements. Even the Waldensians survived the inquisition and papal excommunication. In the century preceding the Reformation such lay organizations as *The Brothers of the Common Life* became the foster soil for mystic speculation and practical piety.

4. Among the most eminent of the Dominican mystics are: (a) Meister Eckhart (d. 1327) (B. F. MULLER-THYM, *The Establishment of the University of Being in the Doctrine of Meister Eckhart,* 1939). The inquisition brought charges of pantheism against him, and the bull of the pope issued two years after his death declared "twenty-eight of his propositions to be pantheistic in nature, seventeen heretical, and eleven dangerous." (b) Henry Seuse (Suso), the poet among the mystics. (c) John Tauler. His mysticism is more truly evangelical and Jesus-centered. (d) John Ruysbroeck (V. SCULLY, *A Medieval Mystic: John Ruysbroeck,* 1910; E. UNDERHILL, *Ruysbroeck,* 1915). (e) Thomas à Kempis (d. 1471), the alleged author of *The Imitation of Christ,* which has had the most marvelous circulation of all devotional literature. And finally (f) the anonymous author of *German Theology,* which was edited by Luther in 1516, and re-edited in 1518. Luther's praise of the book will hardly stand the test of

facts. He seems to have been misled by its serious devotional fervor. As regards its contents, the book is thoroughgoing Neo-Platonism.

Mystic piety also experienced a revival in England and other European countries. In England this type of piety was greatly fostered by such saints as Richard Rolle (d. 1349), Walter Hilton (d. 1396), who wrote *The Scale of Perfection* and Juliana of Norwich (d. about 1414), author of *Revelations of Divine Love*. Through the anonymous book, *The Cloud of Unknowing,* English mysticism became thoroughly tinged with the sentiment of Neo-Platonism. (E. UNDERHILL, *Mysticism*, 1905, pp. 285 ff.; W. RALPH INGE, *Studies of English Mystics*, 1910; *The Cloud Unknowing* was edited by Underhill in 1912; *Revelations of Divine Love* by G. WARRACK in 1901 and by G. TYRELL in 1902; *The Scale of Perfection* by FATHER DALGAIRNS in 1908.)

5. The emphasis on the will of God in Nominalistic theology, as well as the serious searching after personal religious experience, also fostered a revival of genuine Augustinian thought. The Pelagian tenets in contemporary theology are defied; the absolute necessity of divine grace is again set forth. Consequently, the doctrine of predestination receives a new emphasis, and Augustine's definition of the Church as the *congregatio praedestinatorum* is renewed.

Most eminent among this group are the distinguished English scholar Thomas Bradwardine (d. 1349), and the Augustinian friar Gregory of Rimini (d. 1358) (Cf. C. STANGE on the high estimate of Gregory by Martin Luther—*Studien zur Theologie Luthers,* I, 13 ff., 1928).

To this school of thought also belong the so-called *forerunners of the Reformation:* Wyclif, Huss, Goch, Wesel and Wessel. But the name is hardly justifiable. True enough, all of them felt disturbed over the corruption of the Church; they all hailed bitter charges of resentment against the numerous abuses of the Church, or openly attacked some of its doctrines: (Wyclif denounced transubstantiation as something worse than paganism; the words of institution are to be taken tropically or figuratively. He denied the necessity of the sacrament of penance, and he assailed the sale of indulgences as blasphemy. Cf. H. B. WORKMAN, *John Wickliffe,* 2 vols., 1926). However none of them was able to strike with the axe at the root of the evil; for every one, without exception, remained under the influence of the scholastic definition of grace as *gratia infusa,* and under the legalistic conception of the Gospel as a new law.

6. Since the general tendencies and importance of the Renaissance have been discussed in the previous chapter, a few remarks on the theology of ERASMUS may suffice in concluding the discussion on the Middle Ages. [5]

In regard to the problem of the freedom of the human will, Erasmus is an outright Pelagian. In his teaching on grace, he accepts formally the scholastic terminology; objectively, however, there is apparent a wide gap between him and the scholastics. The infusion of grace through the sacraments has no place in his system. The conception of grace is reduced to a divine ethical stimulus derived from the example of Jesus. As for the rest, there are a number of very interesting points in his world of thought. He took a critical position toward the *homoousios* of the ancient Church, and toward the sacrament of penance. On the Lord's Supper he favored the symbolical interpreta-

---

[5] J. A. Faulkner, *Erasmus,* 1908. P. Smith, *Erasmus, A Study of His Life, Ideals and Place in History* 1923; J. Huizinga, *Erasmus,* 1924. E. Emerton, *Desiderius Erasmus of Rotterdam,* 1899; J. J. Mangan, *Life, Character and Influence of Desiderius Erasmus of Rotterdam,* 2 vols., 1927; A. Hyma, *Erasmus and the Humanists* 1930.

on. He accepted the inspiration of the Scriptures as it had been set forth by the later scholastics; but he attributed only a diversified authority to the books of the New Testament. He also taught that the Church is under divine obligation to keep the Sabbath. Staying in the old church, Erasmus may be looked upon as a forerunner of the Catholic Modernists. Luther's evangelical position was thoroughly unsympathetic to him.

We have come to a close of our brief discussion of medieval theology. In summarizing its tendencies we may say with A. Nygrén that medieval theology lived on the Augustinian Caritas-synthesis." [6] Medieval theology, as we have shown, is a theology of merit, speculation, and mysticism. There are to the pious of that age the three "heavenly ladders" to make possible the soul's ascent to God. When we say that medieval theology is a theology of merit we ought, of course, not to omit to say that it is also a theology of grace. But as Nygrén remarks, "it is characteristic of it that it regards as one these two things which, in the Evangelical view, are simply exclusive of each other" (p. 403). This shows to us the lasting impression which Augustine has made upon the whole Middle Ages. The Catholic doctors are neither Pelagians promulgating an outright Eros-type of religion, nor are they followers of the New Testament with its emphasis on God's Agape. They are rather disciples of Augustine in whose thought Eros and Agape are merged into the synthesis of *Caritas*. [7] At the close of the Middle Ages this synthetic character of Christianity was seriously challenged, first by the revival of Classical learning in which the Eros-type gained new momentum, and secondly, in the Reformation with its stress on *Agape*. God is to Luther *Agape* who in Christ Jesus establishes fellowship with man on our own level. This revolutionary change in Christian thought is to be discussed in the following Book.

[6] *Agape and Eros*, Part II, Vol. II, 391 ff.
[7] Cf. our Chapter XI.

BOOK THREE

The Reformation

Chapter One

LUTHER AS REFORMER

Literature: Luther's theology, in the individual streams which have contributed to
orm the structure of what we understand by doctrinal Protestantism in the form of
Lutheranism, is so comprehensive and so rich that it is impossible here to give a propor-
onate view of the titles which ought to be mentioned if the directory were to be
omplete.

For this present purpose we shall content ourselves with giving the following information on important literature concerning Luther and his world of thought.

1. *The Works of Luther in Comprehensive Collections.* There are seven collections. Omitting
the earlier Works not in use any longer, we mention three which serve the Church of today: (1)
The *Walch edition* of 24 quarto-volumes (1740-53), prepared by J. G. WALCH of Jena. This
ork was republished in America by the Concordia Publishing House, St Louis (1880-1910).
Here Luther's Latin writings are translated into German. (2) The *Erlangen Edition* (1826-1857),
with 67 octavo-volumes, gives first Luther's German writings; then follow his Latin writings of
8 volumes. The 14 volumes translated into English by J. N. LENKER (1903 ff.) follow this
Erlangen edition. These are a selection of writings with the view of serving especially the exegete,
the preacher and the catechist. (Lenker died 1929.) (3) The *Weimar Edition*, begun 1883 ff.
nd considered the "pinnacle of achievement" in the publication of Luther's writings, is nearing
its completion. It follows the chronological order. To these must be added the editions of *Luther's
Letters,* viz. DE WETTE, ENDERS (now in the Weimar Edition).
2. Among the *Collections of the selective type* we mention the *Braunschweig-Berlin edition* of
volumes (1905) by BUCHWALD, KAWERAU, KOESTLIN and others, supplemented by 2 closing
volumes. On this background we have the *Works of Martin Luther,* an English edition in six
volumes, pub. A. J. Holman Company and the United Lutheran Board of Publication. It represents
an improvement over the German edition naturally, because more volumes of the Weimar Edition
were available for use. We mention also *Luther's Correspondence* (a selection), edited and trans-
ated by PRESERVED SMITH and C. M. JACOBS, 1913 and 1918 (United Lutheran Publication
House, Philadelphia, Pa.).
3. Among the *Biographies of Luther* we mention first the two volume work by J. KOESTLIN,
Martin Luther, sein Leben und seine Schriften, 1875; the 5th edition was revised by G. KAWERAU,
902. Another work of outstanding value is that by H. BOEHMER, *Luther im Licht der neueren
Forschung,* 1st ed. 1904; 5th ed. 1918. It was translated into English from an earlier edition by
HUTH, 1916. E. S. G. POTTER gave us a new translation from the 5th much revised and enlarged
dition. Dial Press, New York. We mention also A. C. MCGIFFERT, *Martin Luther, the Man
and His Work,* 1911. W. KOEHLER, *Luther und die deutsche Reformation,* 1916. O. SCHEEL,
Martin Luther, Vom Katholizismus zur Reformation, 2 vols., 1917-1921. Scheel stimulated the
investigations on *Luther in the years of his development.* (See below, I, 10). P. KALKHOFF,
Luther und die Entscheidungsjahre der Reformation, 1917. G. RITTER, *Luther,* 1925. J. MAC-
KINNON, *Luther and the Reformation,* 4 vols., 1925 ff. E. BONAIUTI, *Lutero e la reforma in
Germania,* 1926. There are also many popular writings on the life and work of Luther. For a
view of these see a special section in the work of M. REU, *Thirty-five Years of Luther Research,*
1917, with additions in his *Kirchliche Zeitschrift,* 1933, No. 9 ff. On Luther's conflict with
Zwingli see the literature to our chapters 2 and 3.

4. In the following our interest must be chiefly in matters pertaining to the History of Do
trine. Our special reference must be to the outstanding works on this subject by A. HARNACI
F. LOOFS[4], R. SEEBERG[3], and F. WIEGAND. For conservative theology the work by THEODOSIL
HARNACK in *Luther's Theologie,* 2 vols., 1862, 1886; rev. 1927, is of value. And added to thes
works must be the following two, which are to be mentioned in our discussion: W. WALTHER, *D*
Erbe der Reformation im Kampf der Gegenwart, 3 parts, 1903-09, and also K. HOLL on *Luthe*
1923 and 1927 in *Gesammelte Aufsaetze zur Kirchengeschichte.* We shall make special use c
Luther's Lectures on Romans, 1515 and 1516, as published by J. FICKER. Below, sub II, there wi
also be reference to P. DREWS, *Disputations of Luther between 1535 and 1545.* Luther's writin*
will be quoted after the Erlangen (E) and the Weimar (W) editions.

Note: DR. WILHELM PAUCK of the Chicago Seminary read a very valuable paper befor
a session of the American Society of Church History in New York (Dec. 1940) on *The Histor*
ography of the German Reformation During the Past Twenty Years, which was published in *Churc*
History of that date by the American Society of Church History.

I. GENERAL OBSERVATIONS

In this chapter the author of this volume does not claim to be more than an edite
of thoughts from great Luther scholars.

1. The First Steps along Doctrinal Lines. Excepting some lonely voices of th
spiritualistic type and the messages of Wyclif and Huss as precursors of the Reforma
tion there had been no concerted criticism of the doctrine of the Church. The reform
atory movements in the outgoing Middle Ages were directed against evils and abuse
pertaining to pretensions and morals of the clergy and to church government. Th
cry of the language of the Reforming Councils of the fifteenth century was for a *reforma*
tion in head and members. But with Luther and Zwingli the criticism turned decisivel
to the doctrinal foundations. And this appeared with such a religious and theologica
depth and with such an energetic offer of a remedy in the form of an evangelical systen
of theology that the movement of a reformation of the Church, first of all in doctrine
could no longer be resisted. But even when Luther arose and became the reformer i
was without any intention on his part; an occasion offered itself when his conscienc
urged him to protest against an abuse of the indulgences. Providentially this protest i*
the form of ninety-five theses nailed on the door of a church in Wittenberg, started the
movement on its way. Looking back upon his life, Luther himself declared: "God led
me on like a horse whose eyes have been blindfolded that he may not see those whe
are rushing toward him." He added: "A good work is seldom undertaken or accom
plished through wisdom or foresight—everything must be accomplished in the midst o
error or ignorance." [1]

As to the fact of Luther's gradual development as a reformer, see below, No. 11.

2. The Middle Ages were marked by a constant *confusion of the spiritual interest*
with those of a secular nature.

Neither the state nor the Church was free to act upon the foundations peculiar te
and characteristic of itself. Each had to consider the interests and the demands of the
other. It was difficult for the Reformation entirely to extricate itself from this situation
Luther, although very insistent upon the separation of Church and state, found it neces
sary to put the government of the young Church into the hands of the princes whe
then functioned through *consistories.* He looked upon them as chief members of the
Church (*praecipua membra ecclesiae*). He meant this to be a temporary conditio
only and to cease when the members of the Church would be sufficiently matured te

---

[1] *E, 57, 31 f.*

ake over the government themselves. Articles XVI and XXVIII of the *Augsburg Confession* later expressed the principle of separation of Church and state.

3. Neither Renaissance nor Humanism nor Spiritualism had the inner strength necessary to evercome the old and to usher in the new age. Either their will and thought were not serious and deep enough to shatter the Catholic system of the Middle Ages, or else they denied in an unhistorical manner every connection with the past. Thus the new development depended upon the Reformation initiated by Luther—that broad movement which in its first prophetic stage worked itself out with an unprecedented force. The Lutheran Reformation brushed aside *Humanism,* the child of the Renaissance, which through an aesthetic rationalism wanted to overcome the ills of the age by a regeneration of the world through the spirit of classicism and by blending religion with paganism, seeking a reform of Christianity by removing its dogmas or stripping them of their supernatural features and reducing religion to moralism.[2] The Lutheran Reformation, likewise, discredited *Socinianism* which was an endeavor to use the Bible in constructing a rationalistic body of doctrines, unitarian in nature. It renounced the Socinian teaching of God which rejected Christ's divinity, declining an objective conception of the atonement and making justification a moral process. *Spiritualism* in the form of Anabaptism also was brushed aside by the powerful development of that conservative Reformation.[3]

4. *The Reformation was in keeping with the deeply religious interest that inspired the Middle Ages.* As was stated that interest now became doctrinal. And soteriological orientation was the dominating note. What attracts our attention especially is the intensity of religious thought in that age. For a comparison we refer to the ecclesiastical legislation on repentance in the Middle Ages and to the various forms of repentance, which are observed in the monastic period of Luther's life. Luther turned against the traditional view of repentance as connected with the institution of indulgences.[4] He assailed the pardoning power of the pope, the validity of indulgences for the dead, the Roman theory of abundant merits from Mary and the Saints supplementing the merit of Christ, availiable for money, as the basis for the forgivenes of sins. The believers, so Luther said in one of his ninety-five theses, must learn that their whole life must be a repentance. In the place of repentance as a sacrament with meritorious works he substituted his new conception of faith and justification. Good works in the form of a "new obedience" will follow faith as the confidence (*fiducia*) in forgiveness through Christ; but these works must never have the significance of *satisfaction*. Repentance as mere *attrition* has no value; evangelical *contrition* will be coupled with faith. The full oral confession must not be forced by laws, because, "who can understand his errors?" (Psalm 19: 12). Luther, at an early period, recognized the impossibility of confessing all mortal sins (*W*. I, 322; 2, 60; 6, 162, 545). The thought then soon occurred to him, that we are really under obligation to confess our sins only to God (*W*, 6, 158 f.), and that the confession required by the Church is but a human ordinance (8, 152 f.). Hence we can confess to whomsoever we will; we are free to omit confession to man altogether, if we but confess to God (8, 161, 182, 175, 181, Erl. Ed. 28, 248, 302; 29,

---

[2] Read R. Seeberg's description in *DG,* IV³, pp. 35 f.
[3] For a brief description of this movement see our *Story and Significance of the Augsburg Confession,* pp. 14 ff. Cf. in Vol. II of our work Chapt. IV "The Theology of the Inner Light."
[4] For the sources in Luther's writings, see the enumeration of *loci* in R. Seeberg, *History of Doctrine,* II, 235-242.

353; 10, 401; 23, 86 f.). From this position Luther never wavered, although he alway
warmly commended voluntary private confession (W, 8, 168, 173, 176, 178; 6, 54
E, 23, 26 f.; 28, 249, 250, 308) (Cf. Seeberg as frequent guide to us in references t
Luther's works).

5. Lutheran writers have characterized the Lutheran Reformation as simply a *return
ing to apostolic conditions.* It is true that Luther, like the other reformers, aimed a
a return to Scriptural principles. But it is a mistake to think that the Lutheran Reforma
tion had simply an aim of re-establishing former conditions; it was rather a furthe
development of Christian doctrines. It received much of its content from men an
from conditions which had their existence long after the apostolic times. In the ancien
Church we think of the influence of Irenaeus, Origen, Athanasius, the Cappadocian
Tertullian and Augustine; and in the Middle Ages of the influence of men like Anselm
St. Bernard and some of the scholastics. The heritage from the religious experienc
of the Church was also important. Much of the best in the Reformation must be trace
to what was received through the aim of supplying the religious needs of the soul.

There was something in the Lutheran Reformation which makes the Church tha
has resulted from this movement very universal and ecumenical in character. "In tha
deep religious experience through which Luther gave birth to the material principl
of the Reformation it was not the German but rather the human in him that cam
to an expression. In his devout struggle after a sense of peace with God he had gon
down to those profound depths where incidentals and particulars are forgotten an
where one is on a level with the very elements of human nature. His prophetic geniu
touched the very heart-strings of human interests and human passions and struck
theme of universal appeal. In his search after a merciful God and the assurance o
forgiven sin he rose far above all circumstances of time and place. That is why hi
experience can be universally valid wherever human consciences can be awakened t
a sense of sin." Lutheranism is deeply human: "It has the most complete regard fo
personality, the most thorough appreciation of man as man." "It was no accident tha
the epoch-making book on *Christian Liberty,* that splendid paean of personality whic
restored man to his God-given dignity, came from the pen of the founder o
Lutheranism." [5]

6. *Luther was much attracted by the writings of the Mystics* whose thoughts h
had followed from the age of Augustine through Saint Bernard down to the school
men. He liked the practical emphasis of the German Mystics on the way to God, thei
translation of the ideas of the dogmaticians into practical religious truths expressed i
the mother tongue; also the religious and evangelical depth which was found in writing
such as *The Imitation of Christ* by Thomas à Kempis, the sermons of John Tauler an
in the *Theologia Germanica* which Luther published in 1516. But his aversion t
quietism, his vivid sense of personality in God and man and his strong ethical interes
kept him from embracing mysticism in its peculiar character. [6]

7. *The Augustinian and Pauline character of the Lutheran Reformation is con
spicuous.* Luther withdrew from Thomas Aquinus and Duns Scotus, and expressed hi
agreement with Augustine's monergism of grace by stress upon the inability of man t
bring about the new spiritual life in his own natural powers. It even led him into

[5] This quotation is from Dr. A. R. Wentz in V. Ferm's book, *What Is Lutheranism?* See pp. 72 ff.
[6] For a very scientific discussion on this subject see Loofs, *Leitfaden zur DG,* pp. 636, 691, 693.

eterminism such as he asserted in his *De Servo Arbitrio* against Erasmus (1524). The agreement with Augustine, then, led him further back to a study of St. Paul. Thus e came to write his lectures on Romans (1515-16) and in 1521 Melanchthon ollowed with the publication of his *Loci* which was essentially a treatment of Paul to the Romans. This gave to the Lutheran Reformation that decidedly Pauline and augustinian character in opposition to Pelagianism and to Semi-Pelagianism in all its orms.

8. *Luther witnessed the Bankruptcy of Scholasticism.* He found himself unable o keep company with the humanists, but he delighted in their attacks upon scholasticism, although differing from them in the type of their polemics. While he himself occasionally moved in scholastic forms of thought, as for instance in an Occamistic explanation of the ubiquity, he turned decidedly against what the scholastics taught on freedom of the will, grace, faith, righteousness, works, merits. He accused Thomas Aquinas of being responsible for the *dominance of Aristotle,* and with this in mind he called him *the devastator of the pious doctrine* (*W,* 8, 127). He used to say that nobody will become a theologian except he undertakes it without Aristotle. The scholastics were o him unsafe leaders in matters of the Gospel and the essentials of salvation. We eturn once more to the specifically religious character of the Lutheran Reformation cf. *sub.* 4).

The historians are attracted to Luther himself as reformer. His reformation grew ut of experiences in his own soul. We need only to think of how much he wrote on epentance and assurance of salvation. Soteriology was the central interest in his reformation. His leading question was: How shall I find a gracious God? We see this interest in his sermons, catechisms, yea, in all his writings. The purely speculative features of theology had no interest for him. He dealt with fundamentals: God's holiness, His love, man's sinfulness, law and gospel, Christ, faith, justification. To this he was led by his own experience and by his conception of repentance.

In Luther's system we observe the purity of the religion of redemption to which we referred as one of the leading interests in the construction of the History of Doctrine.[7]

Luther was a prophet, a real religious genius, "with a wonderful faculty of realizing in the clear depth of his own experience all the emotions and needs of his age" (Seeberg). His message was a response to questions which the people asked in their own hearts.

9. It is interesting to trace *the development of Luther as a reformer.* The times were ripe for the birth of the principles of the reformation, but they had to be experienced in the soul of some forceful personality before they could become dynamic for subsequent ages. The chosen instrument was Martin Luther. His development was gradual. This is overlooked by many who speak and think of Luther. The reformation must be studied as an experience of the Church in the leading factors of that great movement. In recent years Luther research has turned with much energy to the study of the young Luther.[8]

---

[7] See our own introduction, beginning in Chapter One, Book One.

[8] As to literature, cf. H. v. Schubert, *Luther's Fruehentwicklung,* 1916; see also K. Holl, *Luther,*[2] 1923, pp. 11 f.; Seeberg, *DG* IV[3], 80 ff.; J. Ficker, *Luther's Vorlesungen ueber den Roemerbrief* in 1515-16, 1908; 5. Oergel, *Vom jungen Luther,* 1889; W. Koehler, *Luther's Werden in Prot. Monatshefte,* 1907; O. Scheel, *Dokumente zu Luthers Entwicklung,* 1911 and 1912; the same, *Die Entwicklung Luthers bis zum Abschluss der Vorlesungen ueber den Roemerbrief. Hefte des Vereins fuer Reformationsgeschichte.* No. 100, 1910. O. Ritschl, *Luthers Entwicklung bis 1519* in *Int. Wochenschriften* No. 33, 1910. H. Boehmer, *Der junge Luther,* 1925. R. H. Fife, *The Young Luther,* 1928.

Doctrinally, the earlier Luther may be seen in the time between 1513-1517. He
we have his transition from the Middle Ages. R. Seeberg in his *DG,* Vol. IV, 2nd ar
3rd eds., devotes pp. 80-125 to the study of Luther's teaching in its original form
Luther has arrived at new thoughts on sin, law, the gospel, Christ, faith, justification, t
sacrifice in the mass, the seven sacraments, the authority of the Church; but on oth
things he was still Roman Catholic. Then, in a following chapter he shows to whic
further positions in the interpretation of the Gospel Luther arrived after the nailir
of the 95 theses, in consequence of his public conflict with the official Church over t
matter of repentance. These additional new thoughts pertained particularly to fait
works, law and gospel, sin and grace, justification, atonement. But even from 1517 o
the development of Luther continued in many ways: up to 1520 he still invokes
Peter. Up to about 1528, he prayed to St. Ann and to Mary. On the Lord's Suppe
in 1519, and later, his opposition to Rome moved him to expressions in which
avoided the clear testimony to the Real Presence. The opposition to the "Enthusiast
then led him to the necessity of taking a stand for the realistic features in the doctrir
of the Eucharist. So we see that Luther, under the influence of historical motives, foun
himself in a continuous state of doctrinal development; that is, errors to the right an
to the left taught him the truth of Scripture.

   10. The Lutheran Reformation was conservative: History of Doctrine and partic
larly Symbolics has always taken note of Luther's conservatism with regard to t
Church's tradition in matters of practice, in liturgy and like matters.

   "The net gains of ancient times are not ignored. The Reformation was not an effort
establish a new interpretation of Christianity or to fashion a new type of Christian thought, b
simply to move forward upon the best results of previous history, to rise above the potency
Roman forms and the intellectual charm of Greek speculations and gather the original essence
Christianity about a new center, namely, the gracious will of God as revealed in Christ. Wit
unswerving consistency Luther hammered into pieces the Roman conception of merit and wit
inexorable logic pointed out that all human righteousness is incomplete and that even the divir
renewing of man is incomplete in this life. The hope of salvation can never rest on anything th
man is or may become. Man needs God, and the way of salvation begins above. And so Luthe
built up his entire system about the gracious will of God, who is greater than our heart in th
he forgives us our sins through the merits of Christ. Our entire being, present and future, res
solely on the merciful will of God." [9]

   To return to the occasion for this quotation we recall Luther's position: Preserv
what is good, because in all matters of church practice nothing that is good can b
against Scripture. Luther always refused to lose *the net gains of ancient times.* Th
position has brought to the Lutheran Church the oft repeated charge of *half-way refo
mation.* Against this criticism note the care that has always been taken, even in matte
of practice, to profess the Gospel and to eliminate all work-righteousness and all humar
istic negation of grace. The Reformed Churches have been inclined to an opposit
principle which reads: Keep only what is expressly commanded in Scripture (Puritar
ism). Here the fear prevails that the human elements, the created things, in thei
service of symbolizing or communicating the divine and the spiritual, may take th
place of what is to be taught or to be communicated and that it may develop into a
idolatry, or into a magical mediation of the spiritual. [10]

   In doctrinal respects also we observe the conservatism of Luther. He accepted th

---

[9] A. R. Wentz, in V. Ferm's book, *What Is Lutheranism?* 1930, pp. 84 f.
[10] Cf. our *Story and Significance of the Augsburg Confession,* p. 141.

umenical creeds of Christendom. The *AC* refers to the Nicene and the Apostolic
reeds as documents of authority (cf. Arts. I and III). Luther regarded even the Atha-
sian Creed with its Chalcedonian Christology concerning the two natures of Christ and
e relation of them to each other so highly that he wrote: "It has been composed in such
way that I do not know whether anything more important and glorious has been
ritten since the time of the Apostles" (*E*, 23, 251 ff.). From his standpoint of a
ersonal union of the two natures he further developed their relation to each other. [11]
ikewise he accepted from Augustine the doctrine of man's natural depravity and the
sult from this condition with regard to the will. [12] His soteriology starts with the
ugustinian heritage, but steering clear of Augustine's confusion of justification and
nctification he re-interpreted Paul and established a relation between these two topics
soteriological interest. This secured for the troubled sinner the Gospel of certainty of
s salvation, which lies in his teaching of a forgiveness through justification by faith.
t the same time it safeguarded the holiness of life as fruit from the root.

11. Luther's theology was established upon the principle of an *Organic Union
etween the Divine and the Human:* God is present for our salvation in and through
hrist.

Luther saw this organic union between God and Christ in the *incarnation of the
ogos* as expressed by the trinitarian relation. [13]

He saw it also in the *personal union of the two natures* of Christ: His humanity
articipating in the attributes of His divinity (*genus majestaticum*). Zwingli warned
im of docetism. [14] Melanchthon, later, spoke of Brenz's *De Duabus Naturis* as "Heching
atin" (referring to the peculiar dialect of a little town). But Luther was established
his conviction on the organic relation between the divine and the human. On this
atter he felt himself in harmony with the Christology of Cyril of Alexandria, and not
ith that of Theodore of Mopsuestia and Nestorius. Art. VIII of the *Formula of Concord*,
speaking for Luther, carefully points out the Scylla and Charybdis to both sides.

a. Luther maintains a similar organic union, as that existing between the divine
nd human, in connection with the *means of grace.* In this sense the Bible *is* to him the
Word of God and does not just contain the Word. We notice the same idea in his
onception of the sacrament.

b. He sees this organic relation of the divine and the human also in the relation
etween the *invisible and visible* Church. To him there are not two churches, one
nvisible and one visible. Both are together in an organic relation; not like to circles
ide by side, but one circle is within the other.

Failing to see in Luther this emphasis on the organic union in all these respects,
e would miss the proper estimate of his theology. Here was the ultimate source of
is difference from the Zwinglian Reformation.

12. The Relation between Church and State. On this subject we shall have occasion
o refer to the position of Luther when we come to discuss the *Theology of Zwingli* (in
hapter II of Zwingli and in Chapter VI of Calvin). For a temporary review of the prac-

---

[11] See the *AC*, Art. III and the *FC*, Art. VIII.

[12] *AC*, Arts. II and XVIII; *FC*, Art. II.

[13] Compare in this work, on the ancient Church our chapter on the Trinity (IX); also in our *Introduction
the Symbolical Books of the Lutheran Church*, pp. 115-121; and in our *Churches and Sects of Christendom*,
age 187 f.

[14] Cf. our *Introduction²*, etc., p. 139, on Art. III of the *AC*.

tical interest involved, see our discussion of "The Kingdom" in our *Story and Significan* *of the Augsburg Confession*, 1930, pp. 137 ff. For an extensive discussion of Luthe principles on Church and state we must refer to our *Churches and Sects of Christendo* pp. 215-222.

13. *The Significance in Luther's New Discovery in the "Sola Fide."* In the followi two sections we shall epitomize a few paragraphs from a German Luther scholar, Walt Dress.

First: *Luther's Fundamental Point.* Peace for the troubled heart by reliance up the grace of God in Christ, *through faith alone*, as Paul teaches— this is the fundamen interest in Luther's emphasis. Here Luther is guided by a twofold observation:

a. Every special striving of a man to do something for his salvation, in which the had been so much in the life of Luther, comes to nothing. It proceeds from himself a ends in himself. It is a desire for his own perfection, and thus, he concludes, man mak an idol of himself. But God finds a way to man by offering him His grace freely. He man can do nothing but simply accept this grace in faith.

b. This grace as a free gift offers to the seeking sinner a certainty of his salvatio because he needs not ask: To what degree of perfection have I attained? The way faith is a sure way. Luther puts it into the words: "Thou hast as much as thou belie est." [14a] It also includes the reality in the facts of revelation: Only so far as we a required of God, do we know anything of Him.

Thus the *first* use of the *sola fide* serves to do away with all striving after merito ousness and with all sacramental magical dispensation of salvation: and the *second* u puts to naught all dependence on the rational proofs of philosophy and all inclinatio to metaphysics and speculation. Religion and theology are placed each on its own fee The foolishness of the Gospel becomes the wisdom of God unto salvation. [15]

Second: *The Natural Results from Luther's Principle for Civilization.* There w an anticipation of modern problems:

a. These religious perceptions just mentioned were of the utmost significance f the entire civilization. The limitation of the Church to its peculiar task of preachir the Gospel emancipated science, literature, state and law from the legalistic tutelage the hierarchy; it endowed them with the consciousness of their autonomous destiny, ar created therewith the foundation for the development and variety of modern culture.

b. Furthermore, the principle of the freedom of conscience, which was systematica advanced by the Reformation, and the doctrine of man's earthly vocation (*Beruf*), whic was first developed by Luther in its breadth and depth—these were the two gre channels in which the new culture was enabled to unfold itself with that freedom whic was needed for its development. [16]

c. The Influence of Luther upon Literature and Philosophy is also observable: German literature he gave not only its common language, but also an inexhaustib richness of graphic pictures and idiomatic expressions. And profound, too, was th influence of Luther's thought upon philosophy in its rational as well as in its speculati tendencies. German Idealism, to which both of those elements contribute, cannot thought of apart from the Lutheran Reformation. For it was the Reformation whic

---

[14a] *Tandum habes quantum credis.* W, 595, 5; 40, 1; 40, 444, 1 f.

[15] See our discussion of Professors Karl Holl and W. Walther on the meaning of Justification by Faith, belo sub II, 5. Cf. our *Churches and Sects of Christendom*, p. 198.

[16] See more of this below, II, 6, on the "Evangelical Ideal of the Christian Life."

drew its significance of the *personal life* from the religious life and established the unique value of personality far more forcibly than the Renaissance had done. It was the Reformation which called for a joyous and affirming, not a calm and stoical, relation to the destiny which God gives; and it was the Reformation which pointed emphatically to the pre-eminence of the will in human action (Drews). Thus even Schopenhauer adhered firmly to a thought of Luther and made it the basis of his system, when he discovered the nature of man in his unconscious will and when he interpreted it as evil. And other instances could be pointed out which show the influence of Luther upon literature and philosophy (Dress).

14. *Nygrén on Luther* (*Agape and Eros*, Part II, Vol. II, 463 ff.). Luther, according to Nygrén, accomplished a "Copernican revolution" in the history of Christian thought in this, that he insists "in opposition to all egocentric forms of religion, upon a purely theocentric relation to God" (p. 463). "Against the egocentric attitude which had come to mark the Catholic conception of love, Luther sets a thoroughly theocentric idea of love" (p. 465). Love in Luther's thought is concerned not with man's love for God, but strictly with the love with which God loved us, that means that Luther rediscovered the great paradox of the New Testament according to which God is willing to establish fellowship with men on our own level, on the level of sin, not of self-made holiness. "Our fellowship with God, then, rests for us on the basis not of holiness but of sin; and for God, upon His entirely unmotivated, groundless love, which justifies not the man who is already righteous and holy, but precisely the sinner (Enders I, 1884, 29; *W*, I, 370, 9). There is no other justification than the justification of the sinner, no other fellowship with God, than that on the basis of one's own sin and the groundless Divine love. In this sense, the justified Christian man is *simul justus er peccator* (*W*, 40, 1, 368)—in himself a sinner, but justified and taken into fellowship with God by the Divine love—that is, he is treated as only a man who is in himself righteous ought, in human judgment, to be treated. With this Luther renews the primitive Christian Agape tradition, which at an earlier stage was interrupted in the Church, and restores Jesus' message of fellowship with God—'I have not come to call the righteous, but sinners' (Mark 2: 17)—and Paul's gospel of the justification of the sinner" (p. 469).

II. HIGH POINTS IN LUTHER'S WORLD OF THOUGHT

Note: This section is to a considerable extent a contribution from Prof. W. Dress (formerly assistant to the late Dr. Reinhold Seeberg in the Berlin University). The translation is by my former literary assistant, the Rev. Paul M. Brosy, S.T.M. There are also incorporated in this section quite a number of gems out of the constantly changing famous *Luther Lectures* by PROFESSOR PAUL ALTHAUS of Erlangen who generously placed a typewritten copy of his lectures at my disposal. As much as possible we shall mark these extracts from Dr. Althaus with the letter "A" in parentheses; most thoughts from Dr. Dress are marked by the letter "D" in parentheses.

1. Luther's Conception of God.

a. His opposition to Scholasticism. If we desire to understand entirely that which was new in Luther's world of thought, we must start with the point which the medieval scholasticism set forth as the center of every theology—the conception of God. All theological structures must find a criterion in this conception.

b. In two *different directions* scholasticism had come to a conclusion with regard to the concept of God. (1) It sought to prove by means of speculative philosophy the absoluteness of God; it portrayed God as blissfully resting in Himself and enjoying

Himself. And (2) the idea of God was moulded into a system of legalistic moralism: God and man were placed on the same level as two contracting parties in an agreement. The requiting God could be decisively influenced in His action by the deeds of men.

For Luther it was impossible to bring these two modes of thought into a lasting wedlock. Either God is almighty and all-effective, or He is not God. The Almighty God, however, stands as the Lord of the world and of history, challenging the will of every man who He claims entirely for Himself. The Roman Catholic differentiation between the "commands" which unconditionally obligate every man and the "evangelical counsels" which need to be followed only by those who wish to attain to a special perfection—such a differentiation collapses. The holy God wishes the entire heart of man, and as He is perfect He also wants to lead man to perfection. Thus the unqualified command simply to love God and our neighbor (Matthew 22: 37 ff.) is once more set forth in its original rigor.

Thereby is rejected a doctrine of God thought of in metaphysical conceptions. At the same time, a purely religious thought of God is established. The greatness of God is known in His moral superiority which desires moral perfection in man also. Thus it is that every moral defect—no matter how insignificant—and every negligence in love —no matter how petty—must provoke the wrath of the Holy God and separate us from Him. But Luther digs still deeper. It is not to be thought that man prepares his approach to God through manifold laborious and pious deeds, and that hence morality forms the presupposition of religious relationships. The opposite is true. We are invited to listen to the foolish preaching of the Gospel, so obnoxious to the feeling of man: The holy God anticipates sinful man, God's goodness overcomes all human sin, God in His heart of hearts is defined as "pure love" (E, 14, 49), "merciful will" (e.g. E, 7, 68), "pure beneficence" (E, 7, 159). And His grace is free, not conditioned upon merits. (W, 43, 607, 37). All work-righteousness is thereby excluded. The fact is that God saves no one but the sinner, instructs none but the simple and ignorant, enriches none but the poor vitalizes none but the dead. (D)

Luther, therefore, made a sharp-cut distinction between the philosophical approach to a knowledge of God and the religious-theological way to assurance. Philosophy, in being occupied with a rational investigation of God's essence and nature, fails to attain its objective, for human reason after the fall is unable to understand God, nor does such a speculation afford any comfort to man. If God, according to the human intellect, is being considered the sole cause of the universe, the idea of God and the devil is blended into one conception of a horrifying, monstrous being.[17] Luther never loses sight of the fact that it is the sinful man who is searching for God. Theology, therefore, is a practical science in the eyes of the Reformer, to help man in his distress of sin and guilt. God who is hidden from the eyes of the sinner (Deus absconditus) revealed Himself to man in Christ Jesus who is the Deus incarnatus (W, 18. 644 f., 689). In Christ crucified there is a true knowledge of God; in Him we behold what God is: a furnace of love (W, 36. 424 f.).

To designate the two ways Luther used the term theologia gloriae and theologia crucis.[18] The theologians of glory are vain sophists. Having set their mind on high things such as God's infinite power, wisdom, justice, etc., they despise God in His

17 W 37. 455, 458; 461; 40. 1, 77, 99, 174, 607 f.; 43. 179, 459; E 16. 200 ff.
18 Heidelberg Disputation, E 1, 383 ff.; cf. W. von Loewenich, Luther's theologia crucis,² 1933.

ffering, weakness and foolishness. But "professing to be wise, they become fools" (Rom.
: 22). For the cross is the power of God unto salvation. [19] Faith is the only correlation
 God's revelation in Christ, the humble and suffering servant of God. Thus, Luther
d away with any kind of a human merit. In the state of faith, man is merely receptive,
ffering God to work. The door is closed to intellectualism and moralism as well as to
ysticism in their respective attempts to know and to find God. (A)

c. *God's Wrath and Love in Co-operation.* The doctrine of God's wrath receives a
onderful spiritual depth in Luther's theology. For Luther learned, according to Isaiah
8: 21 (Vulgate), to understand God's wrath as God's *strange work* (*Fremdes Werk,*
pus alienum, W, 3, 246, 19; 42, 356, 23)), with the help of which God pursues His
roper work (*eigentliches Werk, opus proprium*) of love. Thus the question of the
ntithesis between God's righteousness which punishes and His righteousness which
estows grace, or, to put it differently, the question as to how the free mercy of God
n be united with His stern righteousness, was comprehended to its depths and answered.
uther did not consider God's wrath as only a reflection in man's consciousness, as was
nce thought. [20] It is really there in all its fearfulness, shattering the sinner, for His
rath is the necessary affirmation of His righteousness over against the awfulness of
uman sin. God's wrath, therefore, is an eminently ethical reaction. [21] Aside from
Christ the divine wrath is a severe reality for the world, but in Christ God's wrath is
onquered (cf. the grand Lutheran hymn: "O Lamb of God, most holy, on Calvary slain
nd suspended . . . all sin hast Thou borne for us, else would despair reign o'er us. Have
nercy on us, O Jesus!").

In like manner Luther's conception of hell is to be explained. Under the influence
f the divine law man experiences the wrath of God in his conscience. The pangs of a
ad conscience are the very nature of hell. If the devil would have no guilty conscience,
ven he would be in heaven (*E, Op. Lat.,* 10, 375). But this purely inwardness of hell
s merely pre-eschatological. After the final manifestation of God's glory on the day of
udgment godless man as a whole, in his soul and body, must bear the eternal wrath
f God (*E,* 41. 319). (A)

d. *God All-operative?* Thus God is experienced as the One who is steadfastly
ctive, as the one who alone is operative in the whole creation. If man has recognized
Him in His works of grace, then he recognizes Him also in the world. And it is just
n this uninterrupted activity of grace that Luther sees the action that is worthy of God
n the proper sense. "Almighty is He, so that nothing but His might alone operates in
ll things and through all things and over all things. . . . The little word 'mighty' must
ot mean here a quietly resting Might, such as we mean when we say that a temporal
ing is mighty, although he sits still and does nothing; but it is an operative might and
onstant activity which moves and works without pause. For God rests not, He works
vithout cessation" (*W,* 7, 574). "All creatures are God's masks and He disguises
vhom He desires to let co-operate with Him and help Him do all kinds of things which
He can do and even does without their assistance" (*E,* 11, 115). "He is everywhere
resent, in death, in hell, among the fiends, yet, even in their hearts. For He has made
verything and He rules everything, so that it must do what He wills" (*W,* 19, 219,

---

[19] *Ergo in Christo crucifixo est vera theologia et cognitio Dei,* Thesis XX.

[20] Seeberg, *DG,* IV², 176.

[21] Different from Rudolph Otto's conception of the *mysterium tremendum* as something impersonal in his well
nown book, *The Holy.*

31). Thus the divine miracle is not primarily an unexpected supernatural intervention in the customary drift of things. The daily course of the world itself with its abundance of living movements and operative powers is the greatest miracle of all. (D)

This, however, does not mean that, in the eyes of Luther, man's activity is eliminated. Although God could create fruit out of the ground without plowing and sowing, and perpetuate the human race without the sexual life of man, it is His will and design to perpetuate His works through the toil and labor of human beings. But the relationship between God's operative power and our work is not a matter of necessity. God is at freedom to work whenever He wants. Yet we are bound to comply with His plan in order to obtain the necessaries of life. As the little children will not receive any gift from St. Nicolaus, unless they pray and hang up their stockings at night, so likewise we shall not be provided with these necessaries unless we work. But our work, like the suspended stockings of the children, is not the means of bringing forth food out of the earth, it only is the *conditio sine qua non*.[22]   (A)

2. *The Meaning of Christ for Luther.*

a. As to the *Person of Christ*, Luther wholeheartedly embraced the Christological dogma of the ancient Church. This is not to be looked upon as a deplorable survival of scholastic tenets in his thinking, as Ritschl and his followers once thought. Rather Luther's conception of Christ is the necessary correlation to his idea of justification. In the interest of redemption Luther's Christ "is separate from sinners and higher than the heavens." The genuine redemptive theology of Athanasius is revived in Luther's teaching of Christ. We may be assured under the weight of sin and guilt that we have "a brother in heaven Who is at the same time the Son of God" (*E*, 1. 193; *W*, 49, 282). "The man Jesus is the *Deus incarnatus*, the Eternal Word, the unique revelation and manifestation of the Father." "God desires to be known only through Christ; He is the mirror, the means, and the way by which we recognize God" (*W*, 40. 1, 602, 5). "Whoever does not find or receive God in Christ, shall at no time and in no place have or find God outside of Christ" (*W*, 50. 267, 6). To be more exact: through the medium of Christ's humanity God will show Himself to us (*E*, 7. 68; 10. 181; *W*, 40. 1, 77, 1). Hence we may appreciate Luther's strong interest in the unity of both natures, which followed necessarily from his fundamental view and as a consequence of the eucharistic conflict. True God and true man are together one person of which union the teaching of the *communicatio idiomatum* will follow.[23] It was not metaphysical speculation that prompted him to uphold the decision of the Fourth Ecumenical Council, it was simply his genuinely religious desire to read the heart of God out of the earthly life of Jesus. Cf. his hymn: *"All praise to Thee, Eternal Lord"* (*Gelobet seist du, Jesus Christ*). (Cf. below I, 2). (A)

b. The work of Christ. The Man Jesus reveals to us two different things: (1) He shows us the spiritual sense of the Law and makes the magnitude of God's demands entirely clear. (Drews, *Disput.*) (2) He shows us in His human deeds and sufferings the loving-will of God in a visible manner. And this is his *proper office*, to declare grace and the forgiveness of sins. (Drews, 300.) But Christ's significance is not exhausted in mere announcement of grace and forgiveness. He brings us peace, not by preaching as did the Apostles, but by *granting* it. He gives us grace and forgiveness of sins, He makes us living and righteous. He frees us from death and from sins. But those are

---

[22] *W*. 12. 442, 1 ff.; 17, 2, 192; 20. 272, 24; 31.1, 435.
[23] W. Dress referring to P. Drews, *Luther's Disputations*, p. 586.

vine works which the creature cannot do; even the angels are unable to perform them. These works belong to the highest creative majesty and permit us to experience that Christ is true God (*W*, 40, 1; 81, 2 ff.). (D)

Luther's teaching of the suffering of Christ is nothing but a grand prelude on the love of God (Althaus). First, Christ suffers His death vicariously as a punishment for man's sin. On the cross He realizes Himself the wrath of God. "For God cannot be well-disposed nor gracious to sin, nor can He take away His wrath and punishment until payment and satisfaction have been made for it" (*E*, 11, 290). If this work of reconciliation makes it possible for God to forgive, then the divine activity of Christ becomes revealed positively to us in redemption and regeneration. For the death of Christ is followed immediately by the resurrection. Good Friday and Easter are closely united in Luther's thinking. The *Christus miserabilis* of Anselm is blended into one picture with the *Christus gloriosus* of Byzantine theology. Luther has not written a single passion hymn; but his Easter hymns are a meditation on both the suffering and the exalted Lord.[24] Christ's resurrection announces not only that guilt and punishment have been removed but also that *the night of sin is ended (Ibidem)*. It is here that Christ displays His creative power in the real sense, by giving us *also the Holy Spirit that we may imitate Him and begin to stifle and to slay sin* (*E*, 14, 161 f.), Christ Himself operates in us as the exalted Lord and fights in us against sin (*W*, 1, 364, 23 f.; 3, 433, 3). We are attracted by these words from a hymn by Luther, which in prose may be expressed as follows: "Lean on me and thou shalt succeed. I give myself for thee and will fight thy struggle. For I am thine and thou art mine. And where I remain, there thou shalt be. No enemy shall separate us!" [25] This is a most beautiful expression of Luther's conception of Christ's redemptive work. (A)

3. Law and Gospel

a. Luther was very outspoken on the *distinction between Law and Gospel*. The Law commands, the Gospel gives. This means that we have Law and Gospel in the New Testament as well as in the Old Testament. In the words of Christ and Paul there is much Law (cf. the Sermon on the Mount and the Epistles) and in the Old Testament there is much Gospel (the many promises of grace).

b. Significance of the Law. It reveals our sinfulness, frightens, distresses us and thus prepares us for the gospel of grace. From this standpoint Luther eliminates from the *Law proper* the Jewish *law code* or the Mosaic Law in its national features and the ceremonial elements. But even the moral law as a demand when it first comes to man never brings to him a free and joyous doing of the good. Man feels rebellion, resistance. It only discloses his depraved condition. But for this very reason we need the Law. Luther turned energetically against the Antinomians (Agricola 1527, 1537). Even after the new life has taken a beginning we need the Law (1) to show us the will of God and (2) to deepen our repentance.

c. Significance of the Gospel. The Gospel as free gift must go together with the Law as demand and as guide. It is the remedy of the sickness (*E*, 14, 14). It gives man the spirit to keep God's commands from the impulses of the heart. It begets in him an infinitely rich love so that he cannot do otherwise than live and act according to God's

---

24 "Christ Jesus lay in death's strong bands." Cf. the Lutheran *Common Service Book*, No. 110.

25 "*Er sprach zu mir, Halt dich an mich, es soll dir jetzt gelingen; ich geb' mich selber ganz fur dich, da will ich fuer dich ringen. Denn ich bin dein und du bist mein, und wo ich bleib, da sollst du sein; uns soll der Feind nicht scheiden.*"

will. And this is an experience that goes through the whole life of the Christian. Ther
is judgment, the inward struggle, the comfort of the Gospel and joyous yielding. I
reminds us of what we saw above (B, 1) namely, that in God wrath and love combine

4. *Man as Being in Need of Law and Gospel.* On this point Luther has a ver
important message.

a. Man's Personal Sin. With gifted sight Luther saw the nature and the drivin,
strength of human personality and drew far-reaching psychological perceptions therefron
for a teaching on sin. As to the question of the origin of sin, Luther's teaching remain
strictly *infralapsarian.* Through the fall of Adam sin entered into the world, and i
him all have sinned. For the paternal sperm conveys the corruption from generation t
generation (*E,* 10, 304; 11, 246; 19, 15).

Over against the psychological understanding of "flesh" in the Middle Ages, Luthe
turned back to the language of St. Paul: *flesh* expresses a religious judgment over th
whole of man (of his body, soul and spirit) (*W,* 40, 2, 83; 84; 111 f.). He recognize
that in the soul there is not a quiet capacity for the good or for the bad—a tinde
(*Zunder* or *fomes*) as the scholastics had taught; but that the soul, always loving o
hating, is in movement, behind which there is a restless craving, a sinning will whicl
always and in all things desires itself. "Man can do nothing but seek only his ow.
and love himself above all things; that is the greatest of all things. Thus in what i
good and virtuous, man seeks himself, that is, that he may please himself." [26] "For self
will is the deepest and greatest evil in us and nothing is dearer to us than our own will
(*W,* 2, 105, 9; 4, 384, 15 ff.). Now, this self-will (*voluntas propria*) or concupiscenc
is the original sin (Ficker, *W,* 11, 189, 23) which penetrates our entire spiritual life
We all know that it is simply unconquerable (*W,* 1, 35, 36). For the self-seeking wil
often without our being conscious of it, lays hold of our best resolutions, especially o
those in the religious sphere. When we love God for the sake of His gifts or our ow.
profits, or because of our salvation and eternal blessedness, or from the fear of hell, ther
we love Him, not for His sake, but for our own sake with the impure love of con
cupiscence; that is to say, original sin knows how to insinuate itself as secret self-lov
into our very noblest thoughts (Ficker, II, 139, 20). It has already been said that Luthe
throughout does not fail to recognize that man carries within himself the consciousnes
of a higher destiny. But it is impossible to separate the better and the lower part i
man; both penetrate each other mutually, for the human soul is a living unity. An
the ever present unconscious will which stands behind every human action is th
self-will; so we must speak of a real depravity of nature (*corruptio naturae*).

b. The Question of Responsibility. Can this hereditary sin be charged to the indi
idual as a personal guilt, if it is given to him with his personal existence? The persona
existence is not a something which can be called to account; but the soul, which form
self anew with every decision of the will in its fundamental impulses, is responsible
for the direction which it gives to the will. It is certainly true that we are not compelle
to sin, that we do not sin against our own will, but our will is always at hand to assis
when we do something evil, even when we feel that we should and could have acte
differently (Cf. Drews, p. 279, 123, 126). For this reason Luther uses the significan
name of *personal* sin for original sin (Cf. *W,* 10, 1, 508, 20).

c. A Double Result. From this it follows, (1) that every differentiation betweer

---

[26] J. Ficker, *Roemerbrief,* II, 75, 8 ff.

enial and mortal sins collapses. Every sin separates us from God and places the sinner under the wrath and judgment of God. (2) It follows that sin can be characterized as unbelief, since only faith gives man a correct attitude toward God. (Cf. *W*, 3, 582, 7. icker II, 64, 23 ff. *E*, 12, 110, 111.)

5. *Luther's Doctrine of Justification.* (A review by the author. And cf. his *hurches and Sects of Christendom*, p. 198 f.)

On this subject there has been a deep-seated conflict between the Luther scholars f recent decades. The position is taken by R. Seeberg, K. Holl and others, that Luther's octrine of justification was different from what it has been represented to be by the onfessions under the influence of Melanchthon (*Augsburg Confession* and *Apology*). *ther Lutheran scholars, especially W. Walther and L. Ihmels, have denied this with uch energy.

What is the difference in brief? Walther's position is the one to which we have een accustomed in the traditional Lutheran Symbolics and Dogmatics where we learned at Luther had taught: Justification is a juridical act of God in which the believing nner, on account of Christ's merit is declared righteous through the forgiveness of sins nd by the imputation of Christ's righteousness.[27] But according to Holl (Seeberg t al.), Luther taught the justification of sinful man only in view of the fact that the elieving sinner will become righteous in the fellowship with God.

What is the religious interest in each case? (1) Walther's "synthetical" conception taking justification (*propter Christum, per fidem*) as an absolute and an uncon- itioned forensic act, offers a stronger basis to the really repenting and troubled sinner or the assurance of forgiveness and salvation. (2) Holl's *analytical* conception claims he advantage of being more consistent with God's holiness, the position being taken hat God cannot declare one who is not yet righteous to be actually just. And Holl has he interest of showing that Luther taught a justification which, while a declaration, is fter all to become real only in the religious experience of a developing righteousness.

In further discussing this problem let us say: We are not here dealing with the uestion of what the Scriptures say, nor with what the Symbolical Books teach, nor what utheran dogmatics has been teaching, but exclusively with the question: What were he thoughts of Luther? We must therefore follow these Luther scholars in their quota- ion of his writings and try to arrive at a conclusion as to who has interpreted him orrectly. Such an investigation, of course, cannot be completed from today to tomorrow, ut it is something in which Lutheran scholarship has to grow. Here we shall not aim o do much more than trace the argumentation on the two sides.[28]

It will be well to remember that the investigation of Holl in his essays on *Luther* as reference to Luther's lecture on the Letter to the Romans, 1515 (cf. Holl, p. 111). Quoting a sentence from article XX of the *Augsburg Confession,* he criticizes Melanchthon or having considered the doctrine of justification too much from the viewpoint of the omfort and confidence which man needs and experiences. He insists that the matter hould be considered first of all from the standpoint of the moral perfection of God. Here is the foundation of the difference between Walther and Holl (p. 114).

To Holl, justification in the conception of Luther is an act of grace, but at the same

---

[27] See our *Introduction to the Symb. Books of the Lutheran Church* on art. 4 of *AC*.

[28] For further reading on this subject see in our *Churches and Sects of Christendom* on *Justification*, chapters on Rome and 4 on the Lutheran Church. For a thorough discussion of the subject see W. Walther, *Symbolik*, p. 366 ff. Cf. A. Koeberle, *Quest for Holiness*, pp. 245 ff.

time an *estimate* (p. 117). He aims to harmonize two seemingly conflicting statement in that lecture of Luther on Romans in 1515, namely, the statement: "God regard the sinner as just, not because he is just, but he is just because he is so regarded by God (*Non enim quia justus est, ideo reputatur a deo, sed quia reputatur a deo, ideo justus es* (*W*, 1, 20, 16)", and the other statement: "Nobody is regarded just who does not fulfil the law through the work, but (*W*, 1, 20, 18) no one fulfills except he believes is Christ." Holl says that in the harmonizing of the seemingly conflicting statements of this kind lies the real problem of Luther's doctrine of justification.

Holl is opposed to Melanchthon's understanding of the sinner's apprehension of the righteousness of Christ by faith (*fide apprehendere Christum*, cf. A.C. Art. IV).

Melanchthon based the sinner's justification on Luther's teaching that Christ had satisfied the Law and that the believer now apprehends the merit of Christ by faith which God imputes for righteousness in his sight (*Augsburg Confession*, Art. IV). To this teaching of Art. IV, Holl opposes the second statement of Luther and insists that the righteousness which God recognizes must after all be man's own righteousness which God sees developing and which God wants to work out in the life of the justified. With this in mind Holl points to another expression of Luther, namely that the doers of the Law will be justified. [29]

What is it now that Walther is opposing in the interpretations of Holl?

Our reference is to an article in *Neue Kirchliche Zeitschrift*, 1923, No. 11. Walther begins his argumentation by pointing out that the aim of Holl is to defend Luther agains the old objection of the Romanists that he stood for an unethical conception of God namely in the teaching that God, in an act of forensic justification, declares a man to be righteous who is not actually righteous.

Walther objects that on the contrary Luther would have violated a real religious interest if he had taught that God justifies man because He sees what He can make of him, for we are justified because of Christ (*propter Christum*). And then Walther con tinues that even if in those quotations given above, at an earlier time, Luther should have meant to suggest Holl's conception (which *W* refuses to accept), we fail to find any thing confirmatory of such position in his later writings. True, the justified must have within him the desire to fulfill the law and the will to strive to do so, but justification is valid and complete simply because of Christ's passive and active obedience. [30]

Holl insists that there is a difference between Melanchthon in Art. IV of the *Augsburg Confession* on the one side, and Luther on the other. But Walther (p. 674) points to the fact that on the doctrine of justification the history of the Reformation knows of no conflict between Luther and Melanchthon. Luther especially would no have remained silent, if Melanchthon would have perverted this central doctrine of which he said in the Smalcald Articles: "Of this article nothing can be yielded or surrendered even though heaven and earth and all things should sink to ruin." (D)

More recently Karl Barth and his school have strongly opposed Holl's interpretation of Luther. For them the question is a side issue of their intense aversion to the ethicizing tenets in the theology of Ritschl. Also Althaus has expressed his disapproval of Holl and of his disciple E. Hirsch. [31] Although Althaus grants Holl that the term

---

[29] *W* 1, 20, 2 f.; cf. 40, 1; 397, 7. References by Holl.
[30] Cf. Walther, p. 671, with reference to *W* 40, 1, 402, 8.
[31] *Zeitschrift fuer Systematische Theologie*, 1923, pp. 107 ff. Cf. M. Reu, *Kirchliche Zeitschrift*, 1924 pp. 395 ff.

stificare may have in Luther's writings the double meaning of declaring just and of making just (in this respect there is no difference between Luther and Melanchthon till 1532), justification *propter Christum* always means the sinner's justification solely by virtue of Christ's perfect obedience to God. The attempt to make this *scandalon* acceptable to the modern mind, was, on the part of Holl, a deplorable lack of insight into the true nature of the sinfulness of mankind. On the other hand, we should, according to Althaus, by no means belittle Karl Holl's effort at emphasizing Luther's fervent desire for true holiness. [32]

In the act of justification the believer experiences the grace of divine predestination. As the sinner is justified by faith, so by faith he is assured of the eternal decree of God as a decree unto salvation. The *Deus absconditus* is no other God save the *Deus revelatus*. Since the divine revelation, however, can be apprehended by faith only, there always will remain some mysteries in God which are unfathomable for man. [33] (A)

6. *The Evangelical Ideal of the Christian Life.* Luther turned against the Aristotelian and scholastic ethics: It is not true that a good man is the result of so many single good deeds; but a really good man does good deeds with an inner necessity. [34] All depends on the entire attitude, on the whole direction of the will.

According to Luther true morality has two different marks. (1) It finds its norm in the unconditional divine Law of God, as it is impressed in the Scriptures, especially in the Decalogue and in the command to love God and one's neighbor, as also in the conscience: I am indebted to God for everything that I have. Thus ethical action is freed from all eudemonism and selfishness in the striving for advantages and even for virtues. Our duties are comprehended in the one duty, to honor and love God. Therefrom follows the (2) mark: No action, by compulsion, can please the unconditional demand of the divine Law. The right love must gush from the heart free and joyously, as a happy matter-of-course. What one should do (*das Gesollte*) must at the same time in all freedom be what one desires to do (*das Gewollte*).

The ethical strength of man breaks to pieces at this two-fold requirement. Man cannot attain to this perfect morality by his own efforts, because he is loaded with original sin. Justification which only contradicts openly all personal worthiness produces that genuine morality; in other words, only an ethic growing out of real religion can come up to the highest requirements, because it alone can realize the unconditional *Shall* as the joyful *Will*.

Out of the feeling of thankfulness there arises in man the desire to do God's will. It is indeed God Himself Who has begun in man His work of saving and Who puts the new pure will into the heart of the sinner. Christ Himself arises in the believer and operates in him through the Holy Spirit. [35] Therewith follows the inner certainty of action which understands the spiritual sense of the law and rejoices in it (Drews, p. 292), yea, which bears the law in itself and does what God wishes with Christian instinct, and indeed it does this every moment and without long choosing (*W*, 17, 1; 231, 5).

---

[32] Cf. Luther's *Sermon on Baptism* of 1519, and for a modern treatment of the subject Koeberle, *Quest for Holiness*, which has already been mentioned.

[33] Cf. Luther's writing of 1525 *De servo arbitrio;* also Loewenich, pp. 21 ff.

[34] *W*, 2, 492, 21: *Non iusta faciendo iustus fit, sed factus iustus facit iusta.*

[35] Cf. Drews. *Disput.*, p. 424. 268.

Good works follow from necessity from the union with God, just as a good tre must bear good fruits.

Therewith collapses all seeking after especially qualified works. Therewith is give also the love for our neighbor. For I can only show God my love by doing deeds o love to my neighbor. Not monastic works nor the spiritual works which the Churc urges upon a class is meant here; but the simple unadorned labor in the world is tha which God wishes.

Therefrom follows also a new idea of valuation of labor and vocation of whic we learned, p. 224 of our discussions. Labor is not a necessary evil to the Christia but a means which is given to man whereby he may operate in this world accordin to his aptitude. God Himself has comprehended daily labor in His Word and comman even the most insignificant and despised. "Ought not a heart to spring and run, whe it goes to work and does what is commanded of it?" (*W,* 30, I, 149, 17 ff.). (D

Marriage also receives an entirely new evaluation by Luther. His idea of marriag is removed equally both from monastic asceticism and sentimental romanticism. T beget and to bear children is truly a divine office (*W,* 42, 125). Sexual desire is nc evil in itself; but since the fall of Adam it is contaminated with sin. In this respec there is no difference between married and unmarried people (*W,* 40, 2, 38). Husban and wife, therefore, are constantly in need of God's forgiveness. And God will graciousl forgive, for He wants His creation to be preserved. Father and mother in taking upoi themselves all the toil and care of their children are rendering God a better service tha the monk or nun in the pious self-imagination of their profession (*E,* 2, 13; 5, 84 ff 100 f.). (A)

7. *The State is different* from the inner love-fellowship of the kingdom of Go where the principle of voluntariness obtains; in the state there is harsh compulsion. I consequence of this the office of the state is only a secular office, for one may not forc conscience and one may not let anyone else force conscience. Still there may be exhibite a positive relation between state and Church or the kingdom of God. The state produce the external righteousness and provides by means of might and law that men in thei corporate civil life are afforded the condition for developing a culture. Now since th Christians are ever in the minority, the state serves external righteousness which enforce itself with civil power, so that the wicked are kept from destroying the Christians an the Gospel with them. Thus viewed, the state performs a service for the Church t which the Church responds by placing at the state's disposal good citizens who do no think of their own weal but of that of the whole corporate body. But further: Sinc the state really does a work of love when it takes charge of the defenseless, it can b characterized as the *left hand of God's Kingdom* (*W,* 50, 2, 26, 21 ff.).

8. *Luther's Conception of the Church.*

Luther's conception of the Church is a true reflection of his teaching on justification As justification is proclaimed by a word and accepted by faith, thus the Church, accordin to Luther, is constituted by the Word and realized in the communion of the believers The Gospel—the Word of God—is the Church's life and substance (*W,* 7, 721, 9). A believers we need fraternal fellowship, in which each bears the other's burden, and eacl receives from the other. "For spiritual goods are, according to their nature, fellowship goods" (Holl, p. 96). God wishes to meet, not only me, but all men. And while H obligates individuals, He creates His kingdom out of the individuals who are under th ominion of His Spirit. This kingdom, as a spiritual factor, is invisible (Cf. *W*, 4, 81, 2). It reveals itself only to faith. But it nevertheless is just as truly there, as is God Who operates in our hearts. The Church is holy, because the Spirit holds sway in it and Christ rules in it (*W*, 40, 1; 69). It is still to be realized more and more, insofar as God lets His kingdom build itself in and through sinful men. Membership in the invisible Church can be given only through faith, through personal relation to Christ as the Head of the Church (Cf. *W*, 6, 295 ff.).

As now the kingdom of God arises where the Word of God becomes operative in men, so the declaration of grace must be made in a manner which is palpable to man. That is to say, the *invisible* Church demands a *visible* Church which dispenses the Word and Sacraments and thereby creates the members for the invisible Church. The office of this visible Church is therefore only the preaching of the Gospel and the administration of the Sacraments. The student of Luther, however, should be cautious with respect to the terms *visible* and *invisible* Church. They do not designate two different churches; they only express two different attributes of one and the same Church.

This mark of the visible Church supplied Luther with the critique of the Catholic ecclesiastical system. A sacramental-magical dispensation of salvation is not the task of the Church. There is no divine ecclesiastical law; just as little is there a justification for a hierarchically graduated *order* of ecclesiastical offices on the basis of special ordinations. For all men are equal before God and receive the same entire and undivided divine grace. Therefore every man is a priest before God (Cf. *W*, 8, 247 f.). Luther's interest was centered in the succession of believers (*successio fidelium*).

But, with the conception of the general priesthood of believers, there must be established emphatically the necessity of the ecclesiastical office. For although each has within himself the right to preach, still the public proclamation must be transferred to a special one to preach to the congregation; and this for the sake of order. Only the right to preach publicly differentiates the preacher from the rest of the parishioners. But if a congregation can call a pastor, it can also depose him, if he teaches falsely or is not equal to the tasks of his office.

The jurisdictions of state and Church are sharply distinguished from each other. The secular authority, if it be Christian, has its power direct from God, it is even in possession of the general priesthood. The Church does not have to prescribe to the government what it has to do. On the other hand, the secular authority may not meddle in the affairs of the Church. One can compel nobody to believe; therefore the Church must be founded entirely on the voluntary principle. The interference of the electoral government in the church-visitation of 1528 was only an expedient which was founded, not upon any right, but only upon the Christian duty of the sovereign. (D)

9. Word and Sacraments. The members of the *invisible* Church are gathered through the preaching of the *visible* Church. For "the Word of God cannot be without God's people. Again, God's people cannot be without the Word of God" (*E*, 25, 360). But the visible Church preaches the Word of forgiveness and administers the Sacraments. Thereby, in contrast to the Catholic Church which wants to infuse grace in a physical manner, the chief emphasis falls upon the Word. The Spirit operates, and this is energetically emphasized against the spiritualistic tendencies, only through the Word and in the Word, as this Word awakens faith and at the same time becomes the bearer of the entire revelation for the awakened faith (Cf. *W*, 18, 136, 9 ff.; 139, 18 ff.).

The Word also makes the Sacrament. For neither the water in Baptism nor the bread and wine in the Eucharist mean anything, unless the Word of God gives them significance (*W*, 47, 33, 20 ff.). Thus the Sacraments address themselves to faith which trusts in the promises given in the words of institution. The Sacraments are nothing else "than signs which serve and stimulate faith. . . without which faith they are of no profit" (*W*, 2, 686, 1 f.). They take effect, not by being done (i.e., *ex opere operato* as the Catholic view has it), but by being believed (*W*, 6, 533, 12). Accordingly only those Sacraments can be regarded as genuine which are founded in the Scripture on the Word of the forgiveness of sins. The Scripture, however, knows only of Baptism and the Eucharist. At first repentance was also named as a Sacrament, but soon Luther spoke of it as being simply the return to baptism (*regressus ad baptismam*).

The meaning of Baptism in Luther's mind may be developed under two concepts (1) It is a sign of the bond between God and man. Thus, by being accomplished once and for all, it assures man of God's unchangeable and gracious disposition which forgives and will continue to forgive sins and grants in the new birth His Spirit for the purpose of regeneration and sanctification. It "begins from that very hour to make man new pours God's grace and the Holy Spirit into him, and begins to slay nature and sin" (*W*, 2, 730, 26). But (2) Baptism also obligates man to mortify the old Adam daily "so that a Christian life is nothing else than a daily baptism" (*W*, 30, 1; 220, 22) From this view there follows, against false work-righteousness, the rite of infant baptism as an evidence of the gracious will of God.

The Eucharist is the Sacrament of fellowship. While it unites the faithful with Christ Who has won forgiveness and salvation for them, it also unites the faithful so that they love one another and bear one another's burdens. To Luther this meant not only that the effects of Christ are present, but also that He Himself is present in a personal fellowship with His own. So Luther espoused the doctrine of the Real Presence which teaches that under the bread and wine the body and blood of Christ are really present (Cf. *W*, 8, 440, 35 ff.). Thus it is possible for us to comprehend Luther's conflict with Zwingli, who held to the symbolical conception and with the interpretation of the Supper as a memorial feast. In the Supper, men do not act, but God acts. Just as Luther found the divine activity of Christ in His human deeds, so the *communicatio idiomatum* leads to the doctrine of the Real Presence. For inversely, the divine attributes are transferred to the man Jesus, and as a result the actual presence of the glorified body is maintained. But there is a modification. "He is everywhere, but He does not desire that you should seek Him everywhere; but where the Word is, there seek for Him, and you will rightly find Him" (*W*, 19, 492, 22).

10. The Word and the Scriptures.

Jesus Christ as the Word of God revealed God to men. In the history of the man Jesus, God became manifest to us. We know of the earthly life of Jesus only through the Scriptures. The content of the Bible is Christ. He is the organizing principle of Scripture.

To this outward Word God adds the inner Word, for the historical Jesus is active and ever present as the exalted Lord through the Spirit.

By the term *Word of God* Luther has reference primarily to the living Word a preached in the Church (*E, Op. Lat.*, 19, 243). But the truth of this Word is conditioned by its dependency upon the written word. Compare his energetic struggle against the *nthusiasts* who stood for a *theology of the inner light* (*E*, 49, 87; 45, 350) and against Zwingli whose symbolical interpretation of the words of the institution was, in the eyes of Luther, an impious attempt at mastering the Bible in the name of reason.

The Bible is for Luther the only authority. To say that the Church takes precedence over the Bible, because she existed before the canon of the Scriptures was complete, is as foolish as if you would hold John the Baptist in greater honor than Christ because of John's temporal precedence over Christ (*E, Op. Lat.*, 1, 90 ff.).

Formally Luther followed the terminology of the later Middle Ages (*via moderna*) in speaking of the Holy Spirit as the author and writer of the Bible (*W*, 7, 638; 8, 584; 4, 532 and many other passages). But side by side with these statements there are other passages showing a somewhat liberal attitude when it came to discussing the Biblical canon. For instance, Luther rejected the belief in the Solomonian authorship of Ecclesiastes (*E*, 62, 128); the book of Esther he rather wished to see eliminated from the Old Testament on account of its hyper-nationalistic Jewish sentiment (*E*, 62, 131). In the New Testament Luther revived the ancient differentiation between the *Homoogoumena* and the *Antilegomena* (*E*, 63, 154). In the various prefaces to the books of the New Testament (edition of 1522) Luther rejected the twice repeated denial of repentance of those fallen after baptism in Hebrews 6: 4-6 and 10: 24-31, and that Esau "found no place for repentance, though he sought it carefully with tears" (12: 17) is incompatible with the Gospel and St. Paul (*E*, 63, 155). The statement in James that Abraham was justified by works (2: 21 ff.) he considered a straight contradiction to St. Paul and all the other Scriptures (*E*, 63, 156 ff.). With respect to Revelation he offers the criticism that its obscure language is out of harmony with the lucid speech of Peter, Paul and Christ Himself (*E*, 63, 169 f.). In the later edition of 1545, however, Luther reveals a more friendly attitude to Revelation presenting an interpretation in the way of the continuous-historical method (*E*, 63, 158 ff.). These few statements may suffice to show that Luther was not altogether opposed to the modern method of lower and higher criticism. It was natural for Luther as reformer to re-examine the extent of the Canon and even to feel a responsibility in this direction. The quoted statements were not serious deliverances, but simply questions, one may say a groping for light regarding questions which seriously troubled his mind. His uncertainty as to the real solution of the extent of the Canon did not affect his certainty of Scripture inspiration. Different from Calvin who left to his followers a profession on the composition of the Canon neither Luther nor the Confessions of his Church have left to Lutheranism any such statement. How is this to be explained? (1) It was not a troubling question. (2) A declaration to make the deliverances of those two councils in the *fourth* century (Carthage and Laodicea) final for all times would have been equal to making church councils seats of absolute authority for the future. Luther believed in Scripture authority for the establishment of Confessions of Faith and for the preaching of the Gospel. For this there are very many clear testimonies in his writings. The question of the extent of the Canon, however, must not be confused with the question as to the relation of the divine and the human in the inspired Scriptures (*theopneustos*) of the Old and New Testament. This relation of the divine and the human element in Sacred Scripture, comparable to the relation of the Divine and Human in the person of Christ, was to Luther and should be to the Church, a mystery, a matter of Faith. [36] It was to him a matter of

[36] Cf. our *Churches and Sects of Christendom*, 1940, pp. 199 f.

faith. In his admission of the human element in Scripture he could go very far. So fc
instance when he could say with regard to the allegoric interpretation of the name Haga
(Gal. 4: 25) that the proof is too weak ("zum Stich su schwach"); and of I Peter 3: 1
that at this place Peter has gone "below the apostolic spirit." [Quoted by Kahnis (Do₁
matik, I, 272 ff.) and referred to by W. Rohnert, Dogmatik, p. 87.] For critical exam
ination on the part of those inclining to go too far in claiming that Luther was
champion of liberal views in his attitude to Scripture it may be profitable to read th
little monograph by W. ROHNERT, Was lehrt Luther von der Insipration der Heilige
Schrift? 1890.

Chapter Two

ZWINGLI AND HIS THEOLOGY

Sources: Zwingli's Works, edited by SCHULER and SCHULTHESS, 8 vols., Zurich 1828 ff. The ew critical edition of Zwingli's works within the *Corpus Reformatorum* (CR), begun 1905, was dited by EGLI, FINSLER, W. KOEHLER, FARNER, BLANKE and V. MURALT. Vols. 88 ff. Berlin 1905 ff. n the Sch. and Sch. Ed. the Latin writings are separated from the German at the close; in the *New Critical Edition* all is arranged chronologically. The very laborious work, in this chapter nd the next, of locating the quotations from Schuler and Schulthess (Zw. Works) in the new dition of the CR constitutes a credit that must be given to Mr. A. G. Van Dyke, at this time a udent in Princeton Theological Seminary. Our reference to Zwingli's "Works" always means the ld edition by Schuler and Schulthess.

The *literature* here enumerated has been gathered not with regard to what has been presented n the body of the succeeding discussion but with regard to what students may want to include n extensive reading on Zwingli as the pioneer of the Swiss Reformation in its pre-Calvinistic :age. Even in the Reformed Churches, Zwingli is much less known and studied than Calvin. wingli's Reformation was national; Calvin's was international and universal. This accounts for ae many titles in German on Zwingli's side.

Before beginning with an enumeration of that larger literature we may help the student by ointing him to some reading of easier orientation. In this class belong the Encyclopedias, all f them; all the *Histories of Doctrine:* A. HARNACK and F. LOOFS (with only a few pages), . WIEGAND and G. P. FISHER. KARL MUELLER, Reformed professor at Erlangen, is of importance ecause of his very searching book on *Symbolik,* 1896 (pp. 376-408; 433-444). Attention may lso be called to the writings on the Swiss Reformation by J. I. GOOD, *The History of the Swiss 'eformed Church Since the Reformation,* 1917. R. SEEBERG, *English* ed., but especially his latest erman editions of 1917 and 1920 (with some 30 pages) are of much value. The summarizing eferences to Zwingli in my *Churches and Sects of Christendom,* 1940, (pp. 264-279, cf. p. 32), ill be helpful for orientation.

Life and Doctrines of Zwingli: E. ZELLER, *Das theologische System Zwinglis,* 1853. K. B. IUNDESHAGEN, *Beitraege zur Kirchenverfassungsgeschichte,* 1864, I, 136 ff. MOERIKOFER, *luldreich Zwingli nach den urkundlichen Quellen,* 1867-69, 2 vols. G. FINSLER, *Ulrich Zwingli,* 873. J. H. KURTZ, *Church History,* II, 1394, par. 130-132. R. STAEHELIN, *Huldreich Zwingli: ein Leben und Wirken,* 1895 and 1897, 2 vols. G. FINSLER, *Zwingli Bibliographie,* 1897. IOELLER-KAWERAU, *Kirchengeschichte,* III³, 44 ff., 1907. Articles on Zwingli in *PRE,* XXII, 81 f; XXI, 774 ff., 1908. PAUL TSCHACKERT, *Entstehung der lutherischen und der reformierten .irchenlehre,* 1910, pp. 228-257. P BURCKHARDT, *Huldreich Zwingli: eine Darstellung seiner 'ersoenlichkeit und seines Lebenswerkes,* 1918. W. WALKER, *Church History,* 1918, pp. 359-366. V. KOEHLER, *Ulrich Zwingli und die Reformation in der Schweiz,* 1919. G. P. FISHER, *History f Christian Doctrine,* 1919, pp. 285-290. W. KOEHLER, *Ulrich Zwingli,* 1920. The same V. KOEHLER, *Zwingli und Luther, ihr Streit um das Abendmahl,* 1924, (of special importance, f. Chapter III). Art. by W. KOEHLER on *Zwingli* in *RGG,* V. 2151 ff., 1931. L. P. QUALBEN, l *History of the Christian Church,* 1933.

Special Discussions (valuable monographs): A. W. DIECKHOFF, *Die evangelische Abends- ahlslehre im Reformationszeitalter,* I, 1854. W. CUNNINGHAM, *The Reformers and the Theology f the Reformation,* Edinburgh, 1886. B. USTERI, *Darstellung der Tauflehre Zwinglis,* 1882, pp. 05-284. A. SCHWEIZER, *Zwinglis Bedeutung neben Luther,* 1884. B. USTERI, *Zwingli und rasmus,* 1885. R. SEEBERG, *Begriff der Kirche,* I, 78 ff., 1885; cf. English edition II, 315 ff.; also)G, IV, 369 f., 373 ff. A. RITSCHL, *Die christliche Lehre von der Rechtfertigung und Versoehnung,* 889, I, 165 ff. M. STAUB, *Das Verhaeltnis der menschlichen Freiheit zur Gotteslehre bei M. uther und H. Zwingli,* 1894. NAGEL, *Zwinglis Stellung zur Schrift,* 1896. C. VON KUEGELGEN,)ie Ethik Zwinglis, 1902. W. HASTIE, *The Theology of the Reformed Church in Its Fundamental 'rinciples,* Edinburgh, 1904. J. KREUTZER, *Zwinglis Lehre von der Obrigkeit,* 1909. C. PORTER- IELD KRAUTH, *The Conservative Reformation,* Philadelphia, 1872. P. WERNLE, *Das Verhaeltnis er schweizerischen zur deutschen Reformation,* 1918. The same author, *Der evangelische Glaube ach den Hauptschriften der Reformatoren,* II, 1919.

In English there are two works of high grade: (1) SAMUEL MACAULEY JACKSON with the tle *Huldreich Zwingli, the Reformer of German Switzerland,* New York, 190%. (2) SAMUEL

239

SIMPSON, *Life of Ulrich Zwingli, the Swiss Patriot and Reformer*, New York, 1902 (more popula than Jackson's book but scholarly and independent). The New Schaff-Herzog Encyclopedia say "The only thorough study of Zwingli's theology is by AUGUST BAUR, *Zwingli's Theologie. Ih* Werden und ihr System," 2 vols., Halle, 1885-89.

The following evaluation of Zwingli is largely a contribution from my literar assistant through a number of years, the Reverend Paul M. Brosy of Goshen, Indiana, a that time postgraduate student in Hamma Divinity School for his Master of Sacre Theology. J. L. N.

I. ZWINGLI AND LUTHER CONTRASTED

Calvin wrote in 1540 to Farel the following significant words concerning Zwingl and Luther: "If they are compared with each other, you yourself know how greatl Luther excels." [1] He was correct in noting the pre-eminence of Luther. But the tw men ought not to be compared. They may be contrasted, for they are antipodal me "quite unlike in temperament, cast of mind, and culture." Individualities are incom mensurable; especially is this the case with personalities of far reaching influence. Wer comparisons in order, we should feel constrained to say that in his religio-political activ ities Zwingli was far closer to Savonarola, while in some fundamental philosophico theological principles he was near to Calvin.

1. Zwingli had the *humanistic approach.* It was a time when the atmosphere wa heavy with humanism. [2] Just as humanism had turned for help to the treasures o antiquity—its ideals, philosophy, art, literature, original texts, so Zwingli was led t revert to the Bible and the early patristic writers. To him the Bible became a divin law by which the conduct of the individual, the ethics of the state, and the practice o the Church were to be regulated. He did not become a Reformer as the result of havin passed through soul-renewing experiences proceeding from a consciousness of sin, repen ance, and grace, as was the case with Luther. It was his *classical and Biblical studie* which made him what he was. And Zwingli ever remained the moderate Biblica humanist. Loofs remarks that "the humanistic-philosophical basis of his conception o Christianity continually cropped out more and more in his systematic writings." [3] Thi is correct. [4] Zwingli's "humanistic-philosophical" cast of mind stands out clearly al through his doctrinal system. We see it in his use of the Bible, in his wold-view, in hi desire for the strict independence of the spiritual and earthly spheres, in his doctrine o sin, in his Christology, in his attitude towards the sacraments, and in his view of Churcl and state. And so "the root of all these differences between Zwingli and Luther is t be found in the fact that Luther's understanding of the Holy Scripture was conditione chiefly by his religious experience, while that of Zwingli was conditioned in grea measure by his humanistic training" (*Loofs*, p. 799). This explains the intellectual moralistic tone in Zwingli's conception of Christianity.

2. Zwingli's *scope of reformatory activity* was from the first much larger than tha of Luther. Zwingli had learned to know men and life before he became a student o

---

[1] *Si inter se comparantur, scis ipse quanto intervallo Lutherus excellat.* See Herminjard, *Correspondence de Reformateurs francais*, vol. vi, 191. Cf. also A. Lang, *Johannes Calvin* (1909), p. 64 (No. 99 of *Schriften de Vereins fuer Reformationsgeschichte*). See also Gieseler, *Church History*, III, 2 p. 171, note 44.

[2] Erasmus was the exponent of the humanistic tendencies of the age. For a brief characterization of humanism see our *Story and Significance of the Augsburg Confession.* Luth. Literary Board, 1930, pp. 13 f.

[3] *DG⁴, Leitfaden zum Studium der Dogmengeschichte*, p. 796.

[4] See also W. Koehler in *RGG²*, V. 2156.

e Scriptures. Thus it was natural for him to include commonwealth and government
his reformatory endeavors. He followed *theocratic ideals*. In this he was akin to
ews later developed by Calvin. Luther suggested that state and Church might be
rought together in a case of necessity, but Zwingli believed that they belonged together
naturally as body and soul in man. In other words, Zwingli advocated a union of
hurch and state. According to him the secular power should supervise the discipline
the Church; at the same time the Bible of the Church was to be the law-code of the
overnment. The validity of the civil law depends upon its conformity to the Scrip-
res. Should the government fall short of being a Christian government, revolution
ould then be the program of the day. [5]

Zwingli's political activity was not limited to the direction of his native city, nor
the affairs of Switzerland, but in correspondence with Landgrave Philip of Hesse he
as engaged in political schemes of the widest and most daring character. Charles V
as to be dethroned, Philip of Hesse to be made emperor of Germany, the Roman
atholic king of France was to be used as an ally, and the fleet of Venice was to be
cluded in the combination. [6] If Luther had known of these plans he would never
ave met Zwingli in the Colloquy of Marburg (1529). It was difficult even for the
lector of Saxony to convince Luther that it was the duty of the Protestant princes to
eet Emperor Charles V with armed resistance were he to move against the Smalcald
ederation to crush the power of Protestantism. Luther stood upon the position that the
ospel needs no carnal weapons. Zwingli fell in the battle of Kappel (1531), clothed
the armor of a soldier. In the monument at Worms he is shown standing with the
ible in one hand and the sword in the other. This illustrates strikingly the contrast
etween Zwingli and Luther.

3. There has been a great deal of argument as to *whether Zwingli was dependent
pon Luther or not.* [7] Zwingli himself refused to be called a pupil of Luther, insisting
nat he had begun to preach the Gospel in 1516. [8] But Zwingli was acquainted with all
ne writings of Luther after 1518. [9] He had especially followed with interest the works
f Luther subsequent to the Leipzig Disputation of 1519. [10] It was from this time on
nat the humanist Zwingli became more consciously a reformer and that he was reli-
iously deepened (Wiegand). Many of his expressions on sin, repentance and recourse
the grace of God in Christ sound to the reader like thoughts of Luther. [11] In his
67 Schlussreden" (Articles of Belief) there are many echoes of Lutheran ideas. For
nstance: the independence of the Gospel from the official Church (Art. 1);[12] Christ
s the only way of salvation (Arts. 2-5); [13] the insufficiency of our own works; only
nsofar as they are the works of Christ are they good works (Arts. 7, 8, 14). [14]

---

[5] *Schlussreden*, Theses 34-43.

[6] Lenz, *Zwingli und Landgraf Philip*, in *Zeitschrift fuer Kirchengeschichte*, III, 28 ff., 220, 429 ff. Seeberg,
ng. ed., II, 318. Paul Tschackert, *Entstehung*, 254.

[7] See Loofs, 794-796. Seeberg, Eng. ed., II, 308; German ed., IV³, 356. Compare especially the references
f these two writers to Usteri and Staehelin. Cf. Kawerau in Moeller's *Church History*, Vol. III.

[8] *Uslegung, 18, Works*, I, 253 ff.; III, 489, 543. *CR*, LXXXIX (Zw., II), 144; *CR*, XCII (Zw., V),
2-14; *CR*, XCII (Zw., V), 712-18.

[9] Cf. Staehelin, *Works Suppl.* p. 15, *CR*, XCIV (Zw.,VII, 138 f).

[10] *Works*, VII, 83; *CR*, XCIV (Zw., VII), 195; cf. Staehelin, I, 166 ff.

[11] Cf. *Works*, I, 11; *CR*, LXXXVIII (Zw., VIII), 103 f.

[12] *Works*, I, 153, 176; *CR*, LXXXIX (Zw., II), 21-27; *CR*, XCIV (Zw., VII), 365 ff.; *CR*, XCIV (Zw.,
II), 460 ff.

[13] *CR*, LXXXIX (Zw., II), 27-51.

[14] *CR*, LXXXIX (Zw., II), 53-64, 73 f.

Zwingli likes to emphasize his independence of Luther: "I am not ready to be the name of Luther, for I have received little from him. What I have read of his writin is generally founded in God's Word." [15] But Zwingli could not avoid being influenc by such a writing as Luther's Commentary on Galatians. R. Seeberg remarks: "Zwing started with the Erasmian ideas of reformation. This led him to the Scriptures. B it was Luther's range of ideas that continually guided him in his interpretation. At th central point of his apprehension of religious truth, Zwingli is dependent upon Luther."

At the same time it is true that Zwingli, in his independency of thought, did n take over all the fundamental thoughts of Luther. For this he was too critical. T humanistic-philosophical basis of his whole conception of Christianity asserted itse more and more, especially also in his systematic writing.

4. The question has been raised as to the *religious orientation of Zwingli*. It h been criticized that Zwingli's reformation was lacking in the truly religious motiv which meant so much in the work of Luther. There are grains of truth in this statemen We have referred to his humanistic tendencies. The difference between the two me along this line is seen in points such as the following: (a) Luther would not part wit infant baptism, because baptism is the only means of bringing children to their Lor and Saviour; Zwingli stressed the reason that it was a means of supplying members fc his *people's church*.[17] (b) Luther emphasized the doctrine of justification by fait because it brought peace to his soul; Zwingli stressed it because it was a weapon fc destroying the Romish works of merit. (c) Luther made much of the Sacrament because they were to him veritable channels of grace; Zwingli retained them as outwar marks of the Christian because Christ had instituted and commanded them. And y while all this and more must be admitted it should not be overlooked, that in the la analysis it was Zwingli's religious thoughts, as expressed in his conception of God, c predestination, of the Church and on the conditions of salvation that provided the drivin power of his reformatory work. He was different from Luther in the building of h theological system.

5. *What then was Zwingli's significance for the cause of the Reformation?*

a. It must be admitted that he never had the commanding position occupied b Luther. To the day of his death Luther remained the decisive authority for those wh were associated with him Even the hand of death did not chill his marvelous potenc His theological and religious influence was rather augmented with the passage of th years. With Zwingli it was different. He had indeed many sympathizers, men lik Oecolampadius, Leo Jud, Haller, Bullinger, and others; but they never considered him a their leader. In his presence they felt themselves to be independent theologians an thinkers.

b. Neither can the literary production of Zwingli be compared with the funda mental significance of the writings of both Luther and Calvin. True, Zwingli wrot much, and he wrote beautifully and well. "In Zwingli's writings there runs a mus whose loins are girt-up. Learned ballast is lacking. An unrestrained rhetorical dictio holds the reader to the subject in a living manner from beginning to end. Rooted firml in the present, the practical man wrote not for libraries but for living men whom h

[15] *Works* I, 254; CR LXXXIX (Zw. II), 145-46.
[16] Eng. ed., II, 308. W. Koehler, special Zwingli scholar, does not think of denying Zwingli's dependenc on Luther (cf. *RGG*, V).
[17] Zwingli was the pioneer in what the churchmen of Europe today understand by *Volkskirche*.

ished to influence." [18] But, says the same writer, "his writings procured for him no
al spiritual leadership. They are all hastily manufactured products of the moment.
ne may marvel at the literary fruitfulness of Zwingli in the years from 1522 to 1531;
it not one of his writings possesses monumental features" (*Ibid.* 229).

c. In more recent times, historians of the liberalistic trends have praised Zwingli
being the pioneer of modernistic ideas among the Reformers. It was done already
y Richard Rothe (d. 1867) with his interest in a *Kulturprotestantismus.* W. Dilthy
d. 1912), and E. Troeltsch (d. 1923), professors of philosophy at the Berlin university,
ere outspoken in this observation. But here we want to call special attention to the
ritings, quoted in our literature on *Huldreich Zwingli* by Professor W. Koehler
1923), now in Heidelberg University, himself Reformed and a great admirer of Zwingli.
leasured by present-day tenets of Modernism we know, of course, that Zwingli believed
1 the fundamentals of conservative Protestantism, including the divinity of Christ and
lis atonement as a vicarious sacrifice. But the traits in his system that were different
rom the positions of Luther, Melanchthon, Calvin, Bullinger, Bucer *et al.*, were bound
) attract attention of a later Protestantism of the more liberal tendencies. There is his
:ress upon reasonableness as a criterion of truth and his special interest in the things
ertaining to this side of eternity, which was a symptom of his Humanism. Luther's
nterest in Humanism was limited to the formal matters in which this movement was
t to aid the Gospel (such as the languages); Zwingli kept a continued interest in
Iumanism as such. At a time when the other Reformers looked upon the Scriptures
s the only source of truth, Zwingli co-ordinated with the Bible at many occasions the
leas of classical antiquity, insisting that Christianity has no exclusive claim upon what
s true and good. Christianity was to him the most perfect religion; still he insisted
hat the pagans had real religion and the opportunity to make themselves pleasing to
50d. To Luther there was a fundamental dividing line between Christianity and pagan-
sm, a chasm that cannot be bridged; Zwingli bridged it with a wider conception of
eligion, which he put as a *tertium quid* and as solution of a problem above Christianity
nd paganism. To Zwingli it was not the sinfulness and guilt of man's natural condition
hat invited divine grace, but rather the fact that he was the crown of creation and
ccupied an important place in God's Cosmos (Koehler). And so many historians go
ll along the line of Zwingli's teachings in order to point him out as the herald of the
nodern tendencies. Below (II, 3), we shall have occasion to touch upon another of
hese peculiar tenets in Zwinglianism.

II. ZWINGLI'S THEOLOGY ON SOME CHARACTERISTIC POINTS

1. *The Holy Scriptures.* We have referred to Zwingli's humanistic estimate of the
criptures (sub 3) and have noted the legalistic use made of the Bible as a law of life.
We must add the following: Zwingli saw *no contrast between the Law and the Gospel,*
nd hence failed to differentiate properly between them. To him, the Law, like the
50spel, is a revelation of God's gracious will. Considered in itself, the Law does not
)ossess any condemnatory character. How different this from Luther's conception.
Together with Melanchthon and other colaborers, Luther laid bare the great contrast
)etween the Law and the Gospel by showing that the Law kills, while the Gospel makes

---

[18] Tschackert, *Entstehung,* 257.

alive; that the Law condemns while the Gospel saves; that it is the office of the Law to convince us of our sin, while in the Gospel we have the source of cleansing.

2. *The Doctrine of God.* It is here that we touch upon the great centrality in Zwingli's system. The point of orientation—the point of departure—for Zwingli's entire structure of thought is this very doctrine. If we should seek for a word by which to characterize his system succinctly, we should instantly hit upon the word "theological." Zwingli's system is theocentric; it is certainly not Christocentric, anthropological, nor soteriological. Zwingli would brook no meddling with the absolute sovereignty of God. Here then we have a monotheism very strict and unbending. Zwingli had been driven to this position by his disgust at the pagan worship of the relics and images at the shrine of Einsiedeln. His diametrical reaction to this was to make the doctrine of God the center and core of all his thinking.

What then is God? He is the *first moving Cause, the Absolute Causality* which occasions and cares for all things by His providence. Nothing ever happens by accident or by free will. At first the Lutheran reformers used much the same language. As a consequence of this determinism Zwingli declared that all evil, as well as all good, is due to the causality of God. This includes the fall of Adam into sin. But God cannot be accused of sin, since he does not stand under the Law. Thus, "If in man there is absolutely no free counsel, then we are compelled to confess that thefts, murders, and all sorts of crimes are done by divine providence. For thus, I say, we acknowledge providence as caring for and accomplishing all things" (*Works,* IV, 113). Nevertheless "one and the same deed, say adultery or murder, is no crime, insofar as it is the work of God its author, mover, and instigator; but insofar as it is the work of man, it is a crime and sin. For the former is not bound by the law, but the latter is indeed condemned by the law. For what God does, He does without hindrance; the other does it by an entirely evil inclination" (*Works,* IV, 112). "Hence it is that, although God in the beginning knowingly and providently formed man who was to fall, nevertheless at the same time He decided to reveal His Son in human nature that He might repair the fall" (*Works,* IV, 5).

3. *Zwingli's View of Sin* was largely colored by his humanism. "Original sin," he said, "is nothing but the defects of Adam." "It is the infirmity and defect of shattered nature"—"a defect which one derives from birth without his own fault." [19] This inherited sin is a "sickness" (*morbus est et conditio*), but not a guilt. It is not injurious for the children of Christian parents, not even for pagans, if they belong to the elect. He admits that it is the root of all individual sins and that it makes self-redemption impossible.[20]

4. *Election.* Since God is the Absolute Causality who occasions all things, He is therefore the cause of an *objective election* which is *unconditional, unchangeable and eternal.* "It is election which saves" (*Works,* IV, 122, 123), even though the elect person dies before faith has been granted to him. Hence it was easy for Zwingli to conclude that God's election is not confined to the limits of Christendom; it extends to and includes not only the Old Testament saints, but even such classified heroes and worthies as Hercules, Theseus, Socrates, Aristides, Antigonus, Numa, Camillus, Cato, the Scipios, etc. (*Works,* IV, 55). "In short, from the very beginning of the world up to its consummation there is not a faithful soul, whom you will not see there with God" (*Works,* IV,

---

[19] II, 287; *CR* XCI, (Zw. IV), 307.

[20] On Zwingli's estimate of original sin in further detail, see *Works* III, 231; *CR* XC (Zw. III), 761-62. And compare the above mentioned writing of W. Koehler.

55). Luther while believing in God's justice and love and in ways past human understanding, could see no such positive teaching in Scripture.

The difference between Luther and Zwingli on the subject of election should be carefully noted. Luther espoused a *subjective* election which was intimately and inseparably connected with faith and justification: "Hear the Incarnate Son, and predestination will offer itself spontaneously." Zwingli on the other hand advocated an *objective* election resting solely upon an arbitrary divine decree. The value of the doctrine of election for Zwingli was that by it "are abolished both free-will and merit." Thus he felt that by one stroke he had cut off the head of the "Roman dragon of meritorious works." But it landed him on the position of a relentless determination: The believer recognizes that his works are really God's works and that he "is only an instrument and tool by which God works." [21] For a detailed description of Zwingli's views of providence, election and predestination, by pointing to the sources, see Seeberg's description in his Eng. ed., II, 313, as cited.

5. *Faith*. Taking his works as a whole, faith with Zwingli had only a peripheral significance. He connected it with election as a confirmatory sign for the elect, while Luther yoked it with repentance and justification. For Zwingli election does not depend upon the presence of the faith; but faith follows election and betokens the same to the elect. "The free election of God does not follow faith, but faith follows election. For those, who have been elected from eternity, have certainly been elected before faith" (*Works*, IV, 7) Thus the elect are informed of their election by means of God-instilled faith, and are thereby assured of their salvation. Luther thought of faith as a means to salvation: "By faith are ye saved"; Zwingli looked upon faith as a sign of election and an assurance of salvation. It is true that Zwingli emphasized also the doctrine of justification; but he never had Luther's deep religious interest in that doctrine. Zwingli saw in it a good prophylactic against Romish works of merit.

6. *Christology*. In treating of the Person of Christ Zwingli adhered strictly to his world-view which distinguished rigidly between the divine and the human. Tschackert says: "The Chalcedonian Christology with its sharp separation of the divine and human natures in the God-Man suited Zwingli, and, what is more, suited him especially well" (*Entstehung*, p. 246). It is true that while separating the two natures he maintained the unity of the Person of Christ. He argued that the distinct properties and works of the two natures do not disrupt the unity of the Person any more than body and soul constitute two persons in man (*Works*, IV, 3). Nevertheless he distinguished so strictly between the two natures that in the mind of the Lutherans he laid himself open to the charge of Nestorianism. Christ, after his ascent, is omnipresent only according to His divinity, but according to His humanity He is now limited to a definite locality in heaven. In this language we miss the appreciation of the organic relation of the two natures in the living historic person of Christ. This divisive Christology[22] was to appear with great force in the disruptive conflict over the Eucharist.

In order to explain why it is that the Scripture often speaks of one nature of Christ in terms of the other nature or ascribes the properties of one nature to the entire Person, Zwingli in his conflict with Luther introduced his theory of the *Interchange* or *Alloeosis* —a figure of speech (*phrasis loquendi*) by which the Scriptures say one thing, but mean

---

[21] I, 276; CR LXXXIX (Zw. II), 180-1.
[22] *Works* II. 2. 67, 71; CR XCII (Zw. V), 922 ff.

another. Against this method of interpretation Luther turned with sharp criticism (see him quoted in the *FC,* art. 7, 39 and 40).[23]

7. *The Church.* The true Church, the body of Christ and communion of believers is composed of the "elect who have been predestinated to eternal life by the will of God" (*electi qui dei voluntate distinati sunt ad vitam aeternam*). This Church of the elect is known to God alone. Faith enables the elect person to perceive his own membership in this Church, but he remains ignorant of who the other members may be (*Works,* VI, 8). There are then in reality *two Churches:* the *visible* Church which is composed of all who name Christ and profess Him by using the Sacraments of the Church, and the *invisible* Church which comprehends only the elect. Luther, too, believed in a visible and an invisible aspect of the Church; but he considered the *visible* Church to be that preparatory institution in which, by means of Word and Sacrament, members are created for the *invisible* Church. Zwingli failed to establish any intimate connection between the two Churches. This was due to his doctrine of election and also to his philosophical world-view.

8. *The Sacraments.* Christ the Head of the Church has instituted certain *rites* which are to be performed by His Church—Baptism and the Eucharist. But the question is whether they are really means of grace. According to Zwingli the Sacraments can communicate nothing to the elect, for these are already assured of their election and salvation by their faith, and this certainty is strengthened for them by Christ the *infallible pledge.* But for what, then, were the Sacraments instituted? "The sacraments are given," said Zwingli, "as a public witness to that grace which each one possesses already in private, *Sacramenta dari in testimonium publicum ejus gratiae quae quique privato prius adest*" (*Works,* IV, 10). By partaking of the Sacraments the individual church member thereby professes his membership. The Sacraments thus are signs of union and allegiance by public profession. They are *Eidespflichte.* Hence they are sacrificial and not sacramental in significance. The sacrament has no supernatural content: it is rather an external symbol of something which has already been accomplished inwardly.

Baptism, in particular, is the rite in which "the body is washed with the purest element; but by this it is signified that we have been gathered by the grace of divine goodness into the assembly of the Church and of the people of God, in which we must live uprightly and purely" (*Works,* IV, 11). Baptism is thus only a sign and symbol of an inner regeneration.

The *Eucharist* also is a sign and symbol. At first Zwingli stood under the influence of Erasmus, the aristocratic humanist who was very anxious at all times to maintain at least a semblance of identity with the approved doctrine of the Church. Both held to a certain "real presence" of the Body of Christ. But at the same time the position was taken that the common people only, the "simple minded," had need of the sacrament. W. Koehler, in his book of 850 pages on *Zwingli and Luther* (*Their Conflict on the Eucharist*) 1924, has given us a very exhaustive discussion of Zwingli's development as to his view on the Supper. A change is not noticeable in his correspondence and in thesis eighteen of his *Schlussreden,* 1523.[24] Koehler speaks of four factors which have contributed to bring about a change in the view of Zwingli: (1) the famous letter of

[23] Cf. Seeberg, II, 321; *CR* XCII (Zw. V), 925; also Tschackert, *Entstehung,* p. 247.
[24] Cf. Koehler, pp. 16-61.

he Dutch humanist Honius laid before Luther, suggesting that the words "this is my body" be taken in the meaning of "this signifies;" (2) the teaching of Karlstadt, and as a result of it (3) Luther's increasing emphasis on the Real Presence, and (4) Zwingli's break with Erasmus, which removed him more decisively from the views of Romanism. It was especially the letter from Honius that made a deep impression on Zwingli. He felt it as "flesh of his own flesh." Under the impact of this letter and the other factors referred to Zwingli began to develop what is known as the symbolical interpretation of the Supper. On the previous stage of development he had already begun to look upon the Eucharist as a *Gemeinschaftsmahl* with Christ and fellow believers. More and more he stressed faith as the special constituent factor of the Supper. Christ in His humanity is present "not in essence and reality," but only "by the contemplation of faith." That is to say: Christ is present only by means of the imaginative or pictorial power of faith. The external eating and drinking are only appendages of the inward eating and drinking. The outward transaction is a pictorial representation of the inward reality. The Eucharist is an act of profession and allegiance whereby we confess that we are adherents of Christ and members of His Body. Then it is chiefly a memorial which we celebrate in remembrance of Christ's death and by which we show forth His death. And finally it is a thanksgiving (*Eucharistia*) to God for the gift of His Son and His redeeming work.

Zwingli, being guided by several considerations, kept away from any doctrine of a "real presence": (1) Scripture declares that "the flesh profiteth nothing" (John 6:63 f.). As a matter of fact, his whole argument revolves about this particular passage of the New Testament. (2) His world-view would not permit any such close conjunction of the heavenly and the earthly. (3) His Christology maintained that the humanity of Christ was limited to a definite place in heaven. In His divinity, of course, Christ is omnipresent in heaven and upon earth; but in His humanity He is limited to the conditions of creature. He cannot be present in the Supper according to His human nature because in this He is tied to "the right hand of God" in heaven. Here Calvin, later, found himself in agreement with Zwingli. The cases in Scripture where the divine attributes such as omnipresence, omnipotence, and omniscience are predicated of Christ's humanity must be interpreted by the *alloeosis*. (See above, paragraph 6 and compare in our *Introduction to Symbolical Books*,[2] 1926, p. 139.) Zwingli's caricatures of those who believed in the real presence are very coarse. He called such people "flesh-eaters" and "blood-drinkers," and he referred to the Lutherans in words which compared them to the Israelites who longed after the fleshpots of Egypt.[25]

9. *At the Marburg Colloquy* (1529) there were differences between Luther and Zwingli outside of the one on the Lord's Supper. But Zwingli, at that time, accommodated himself to the well known positions of Luther to such an extent that he subscribed to the Marburg Articles in which there was a codification of so many points of agreement. Further, history showed that in this they had been too optimistic. Luther was not able to accept Zwingli's hand of fellowship because under the circumstances this would have been a declaration on his part that he looked upon the disagreement concerning the Lord's Supper as a matter of indifference—a *syncretismon,* as called by Zwingli with the advice to ignore it. But it is a mistake to believe that Luther's attitude expressed an unfriendly feeling toward the Zwinglians. In a thorough investigation

---

[25] See Chapter III on the *First Conflicts over the Lord's Supper*, paragraphs 10 and 11.

Hans von Schubert, predecessor of Professor W. Koehler in the Heidelberg University
has pointed out the peaceful, cordial and hopeful mood in which Luther found himself
at the close of this colloquy. The much quoted remark, "Ye have another spirit than
we," was a purely objective statement and not spoken in the spirit of an invective. In
letters written at that time, for instance to his wife, Luther expressed hope for a growing
union to extend also to the difference on the Lord's Supper.[26]

In another place we have tried to summarize briefly the difference between Zwingli
and Luther, and we shall quote it at this place as a close to our discussion of this chapter
on Zwingli and his Theology: "There was (1) the relation of the two natures in the
person of Christ. Here Zwingli inclined to the Nestorianizing, side-by-side relation
between the divine and the human in the historic Christ, after the fashion of the old
Antiochian School (Theodore of Mopsuestia). Luther, on the other hand, stood for the
organic, personal union, following the Alexandrian School (Cyril). There was (2) the
difference on the Word. Zwingli emphasized the 'inner' Word with a concession to
tenets of the Anabaptists, which made Luther stress the written and spoken Word. There
was (3) an actual difference on man's natural depravity. Zwingli would admit only a
weakness in man which does not become real sin until it results in sinful acts. Luther
insisted that this natural, sinful condition is the real, special sin of mankind. This difference affected (4) the conception of infant baptism. To Zwingli baptism was a badge
of recognition as a Christian, a kind of initiation into the Church. To Luther it was a
sacrament of regeneration, of forgiveness of sin and of an imputation of Christ's righteousness. With large agreement (5) on justification by faith and good works there was on
the part of Zwingli a humanistic approach to the inner problems of religion which made
for fundamental differences from Luther's doctrine of sin and grace." (Neve, *Story and
Significance of the Augsburg Confession*, p. 46.) In addition there was then that "unconscious difference," as quoted from W. Koehler.

---

[26] Schubert, *Bekenntnisbildung und Religionspolitik*, 1529-1530. Cf. W. Gussmann's article *Luther in Marburg*, in "Allg. Ev. Luth Kirchenzeitung." (Leipzig 1929) No. 33 and 34.

Chapter Three

THE FIRST CONFLICT OVER THE LORD'S SUPPER

Literature: The references concerning Zwingli have always been to SCHULER and SCHULTHES, 8 vols., 1828 ff., but we must keep in mind that on Zwingli the New Critical Work of 10 vols., s part of the *Corpus Reformatorum* (CR), is near its completion. The student will take note of he service by A. G. VAN DYKE, to which we referred under "Literature" to Chap. II, of connecting he old quotation with those in the new edition of Zwingli in the CR. As to Luther's part in this onflict we quote from the *Weimar* (W) or from the *Erlangen* (E) edition. Both sides in this onflict, naturally, have had their advocates. On the Lutheran side, special attention is called to A. W. DIECKHOFF, *Die evangelische Abendmahlslehre in Reformationszeitalter,* I (1854); also to W. WALTHER *in Neue Kirchl. Zeitschrift,* 1896, pp. 794-819, 917-936. Cf. R. SEEBERG, *Hist. of Doctrine,* IV³, p. 318 f. On the Reformed side we have, besides able writers in the Zwingli biogra-hies, the Heidelberg Professor W. KOEHLER, *Zwingli und Luther, ihr Streit um das Abendmahl,* I (1924), an important work because of its critical examination of all previous investigations in this ield. He added a critical review of the Marburg Colloquy (1928). Cf. generally the Histories f Doctrine, especially HAGENBACH, LOOFS, R. SEEBERG, WIEGAND. The student will pardon the uthor for taking the liberty to refer also to his own book, *The Lutherans in the Movements for Church Union,* 1921. Additional literature in the footnotes.

1. The sharp controversy on the Lord's Supper between Luther and Zwingli (1524 :o 1528) was to some extent *a revival of the difference* between the realistic and the spiritualistic conception at various times in the history of the Church. In the ancient Church we have the realistic conception of Irenaeus (and his predecessors); then later :hat of Cyril of Jerusalem, of Cyril of Alexandria and of the conservatives of their age. On the other hand we have the symbolical view in the spiritualizing position of Origen and the rationalizing Antiochians. It may seem strange that we find Augustine on the symbolical side. However, to arrive at right conclusions regarding Augustine compare our Bk. I, Chapter XII, sec. 2 on the *Sacraments in the Ancient Church.* But the develop-ment was toward realism and even to transubstantiation. So it was in the East (John of Damascus) and also in the West (Gregory the Great). Then in the ninth century Radbertus re-emphasized transubstantiation by maintaining a "real presence" of the Body of Christ in the Supper, while Ratramnus had taken the position that under the veil of the bread the spiritual Body of Christ existed. Two centuries later Berengar risked to teach that bread and wine merely signify the Body and Blood of Christ. But the official Church forced him to say that under the act of consecration bread and wine change into the Body and Blood of Christ.

2. Luther had been a believer in the realistic conception of the Eucharist from the beginning, although he admits that there was a time in his development when he, in his antipathy to the pope, might have been open to some kind of symbolical interpretation. [1] But he had regard for the theory of William Occam, which he

---

[1] Luther's Works E, 53, 274. See his letter to the Strassburgers, 1524.

249

soon began to teach, arriving at an interpretation of his own, namely that in the eating of the bread the Body of Christ is at the same time truly received.

3. *Luther as interpreted by his followers.* He had no intention to teach a gross carnal eating of the Body of Christ in the Eucharist. This is seen from his agreement with Bucer's statement at the adoption of the Wittenberg Concord (1536), which included a rejection of the "impanation." [2] The *Formula of Concord,* later with an appeal to Luther, also rejected "the Capernaitic thoughts of the gross and carnal presence and insisted upon "the spiritual, supernatural, heavenly mode, according to which Christ is present in the Holy Supper." [3] It speaks of an "oral eating and not in a gross, carnal Capernaitic, yet in a supernatural, incomprehensible way" (7, 64). This teaching of the *Formula of Concord* was in actual agreement with Luther's own words (1538) "As nobody sees, touches, eats or chews the Body of Christ in a way as we see and chew visibly other flesh; for what we do to the bread is attributed to the Body of Christ because of the sacramental union between bread and body." (*W,* 26, 442 ff.) There is a real manducation of the bread, but with the bread the communicant receives the Body of Christ. It was the persistent symbolical interpretations of Luther's opponents on this point that forced him to occasional unacceptable expressions of an oral receiving of the Body in terms of a "manducation," as, for instance, in the instruction which he gave Melanchthon when he was to meet Bucer in Cassel (1534), preparatory to the drafting of the Wittenberg Concord (*E,* 2, 822). The receiving of the Body, in sacramental union with the bread, *cum ore,* became to Luther and the Lutherans in this conflict, the test of an honest acceptance of the "real presence," which then, later, was expressed in the *Formula of Concord.*

4. Together with this teaching we must hold before us the fact that to Luther the *purpose of the sacrament, its spiritual gift,* was the strengthening of the faith, the assurance of the forgiveness of sins and a help needed in the struggle with sin.[4] It is not just a theory for doctrinal consistency. Cf. the fitting remark of A. Nygrén: "Luther's view has often been construed as an attempt to steer a middle course between these two extremes, the magical and spiritualistic; against the former he denies any miraculous transformation, while he still insists, against the latter, upon the real presence of Christ in the Lord's Supper. Such an interpretation, however, in no way touches Luther's real meaning. He did not regard his view of the Lord's Supper as a *via media,* nor the two ways which he attacked as two opposite extremes. Rather than opposites, they are simply different expressions of one and the same thing. Both are examples of the same false way of salvation; in both cases the Lord's Supper, which is Christ's condescension to us, is transformed into an attempt on our part to mount up to God."[5]

5. *The Christological Basis for the Real Presence of Christ's Body.* As Zwingli based his rejection of the real presence upon his Christology, according to which Christ in His humanity cannot be omnipresent upon earth, so Luther undertook to base his teaching upon his own Christology. He stressed the personal union of the two natures in Christ and taught in the so-called *genus majesticum* of the *communicatio idiomatum,* that the human nature of Christ participates in the attributes of the divine nature and can, therefore, be present in the Supper. (*W,* 23, 141; 26, 324, 332, 340 f.)

---

[2] See Seeberg, Eng. ed., II, 75; cf. the reference to the statement in the *Formula of Concord,* see our Chapter VIII, 14.
[3] See the "Solid Declaration" of the *FC,* art. 7, 105.
[4] *W.* 23, 259; 26, 478 f.
[5] *Op. cit.,* Part Two, Vol. II, 478.

Luther had arrived at the need of teaching a *personal union of the two natures of Christ,* in such a manner that the *genus majestaticum* be admitted, that is the participation of Christ's human nature in the attributes of the divine nature. His leading consideration was that otherwise we would not have an atonement wrought by Christ as God-man. Read his words (quoted also in our above mentioned *Introd.,* p. 139): "If the devil should persuade me that in Christ a mere man was sacrificed and died for me, then I would be lost; but if I can attach to it the importance that Christ died for me as real God and man then such doctrine will outweigh and destroy sin, death and hell and all misery." When Zwingli met him with his theory of the *alloeosis*[6] then Luther warned: "Beware, beware, I tell you of the *alloeosis;* it is a mask of the devil! For in the end it constructs a Christ, after which I would not like to be a Christian; a Christ whose sufferings and life do not mean more than that of an ordinary saint." (*W,* 26, 321, 323, 342.)

It is not correct when Philip Schaff and others have said that Luther's Christology was developed for the need of a support for the doctrine of the "real presence." Luther's conception rested upon the broader consideration, the validity of Christ's redemption. But he saw in it at the same time a basis for the real presence in the Supper. His interest was in the presence of the God-man. He wanted the Church to be able to maintain the historic Christ, the whole Christ in both of His natures; He Who on the cross worked for us grace and forgiveness of sins, is present in the Eucharist and His Body is received as a pledge and a seal for the forgiveness of sins.

The writings of Luther are full of expressions on the personal union of the two natures and the emphasis upon the religious interest attached to it.[7]

6. The *"Right Hand of God."* Zwingli taught that after Christ's ascension His human nature does not participate in the attributes of the divine nature and is therefore confined to the "Right Hand of God in heaven." Luther replied that this cannot be a local place in heaven, a "golden chair" at the Father's right side, but it must be generally the realm of His omnipotent power. (*W,* 23, 131 ff.)

7. *On Christ's actual presence, His special presence and the Real Presence* Luther had thoughts such as the following: If God is present "everywhere in all things" (*W,* 23, 133, 143) then the same must be said of the Christ whose divinity is in a personal union with His humanity. (*W,* 23, 145.) But we are justified in speaking of a "special presence" of the ascended Christ for us *where His word tells us that He is* (*W,* 19, 492). In the same way we speak of a "Real Presence" in the sacrament of the Lord's Supper where He has promised to be present in the bread (*W,* 30, 1, 223 f., 225).

8. *Luther on the Real Presence in the Language of the Scholastics:* In order to lead away from a grossly material manner of Christ's presence in the Supper to a more Biblical conception, Luther made use of scholastic distinctions which he had learned in the school of Wm. Occam and G. Biel. He referred (1) to the local or "circumscriptive" presence which has reference to special relations. In this way Christ walked upon the earth. But this is not the way of His presence in the Supper. Then there is (2) a "definitive" form of presence by which was meant an incomprehensible presence, reminding of the way in which Christ came forth from the grave and entered a room through closed doors. And finally (3) there is the "repletive" way of a presence,

---

[6] *Works,* II, 68, CR XCII (Zw. V), 925.
[7] *W* 23, 141; 26, 324, 332, 340; 23, 139 f., 147 f.; 33, 153 f.; 26, 321; 33, 154 f.; 47, 199; 50, 589.

described simply as an omnipresence which is supernatural. In one of these last two modes it is that we must think of the presence of Christ in the supper. Luther did not succeed in making the mystery clear for the comprehension of reason. Nor did he really aim at that. What he wrote was written in defense against Zwingli's accusation of the absurdity of a Real Presence.[8] To Luther the "sacramental union," which was no consubstantiation, was a mystery, a matter of faith. He wrote (1527) "How it can be possible that he is present in the bread we do not know, must not know. We must believe God's Word and not dictate to Him manner and measure. With our eyes we see the bread, but with our ears we hear that there is the Body" (*W*, 23, 87). Zwingli wrote in defense of his position to F. Lambert and to the people of Strassburg, 1524,[9] including a letter to Alber in Reutlingen. Luther also wrote to the Christians at Strassburg, 1524.[10] Both sides were anxious to win the South Germans to their side. This explains the divided and mediating type of M. Bucer and his associates under the *Tetrapolitana* and the attitude of Calvin, in friendship with Melanchthon.

9. *Similarity and Difference between the Views of Occam and Luther:* Occam, as a Nominalist, in his *De Sacramento Altaris*, was not interested in the presence of Christ's Body as a quantity. The body might be reduced to a mathematical point and still be the Body of Christ, really present as the soul is everywhere present in the body.[11] So Luther suggested the thought that the presence of the Body of Christ in the Supper should not be thought of in the sense in which "straw is in a stack and bread in a basket." (*W*, 19, 341.) But Luther was different from Occam and Biel in this that he was not interested in the "speculative inference postulating a certain Something that may figure as the Body of Christ in the Lord's Supper"; his was the religious interest that the same historical Christ as God-man who wrought our redemption is present, and (against Zwingli) is present not just by imagination or spiritually, but in reality.

10. *The Conflict between Luther and his Opponents:* We referred in the preceding chapter (sub 8) to the suggestion of Honius to Luther that Christ's words "this is my body" should be interpreted by "it signifies." Of this Zwingli had learned in 1524, and the position of Honius appealed to him. Then followed (1524) Karlstadt's well known artificial interpretation: Christ had pointed to his own body to be given into death (not to the bread) when He said in the words of institution: "This is my Body." The preachers of Strassburg addressed letters of inquiry on this matter to both Luther and Zwingli. Luther, in a letter of 1524, warned them against Karlstadt and his associates (*E*, 53, 274; *W*, 15, 394), and then (1525) wrote his *Wider die himmlischen Propheten*. Zwingli published a large correspondence on this subject.[12] Then followed Bugenhagen (1525) with an attack upon Zwingli.[13] Zwingli replied.[14] Next followed Oecolampadius with a large book on the genuine words of the Lord: *This is my Body* (1525), dedicating it to the South German (Suabian) preachers. (*W*, 19, 447 f.) Soon Brenz, on Luther's side, published fourteen letters of those Suabian preachers in his *Syngramma Suevicum* (1526).[15]

---

[8] Cf. *W*, 26, 327, 329 f., 336 f. 26, 33.
[9] *Works*, III, 615-626. *CR*, XCV (*Zw.*, VIII), 261-278, III, 591-603. *CR*, XC (*Zw.*, III), 335-354.
[10] *W*, 15, 394.
[11] Cf. p. 212.
[12] See *Zw. Works*, III, 615-626; 591-603; 327-356.
[13] *Contra Novum Errorem*, *W*, 19, 447.
[14] *Works*, III, 604-614. *CR*, XCI (*Zw.*, IV), 558-576.
[15] German in the Walch's ed. of Luther's Works.

So far this agitation had not been directly a conflict between Luther and Zwingli although each referred to the other in occasional remarks. But the excitement in southern Germany was on the increase. In April, 1527, Zwingli sent to Luther a personal letter accompanied by an *Expositio Eucharistiae* and two other articles on the subject.[16] But Luther had already proceeded to direct public attack on Zwingli and published his sharp writing against the "enthusiasts" under the title: *Dass diese Wort Christi 'Das t mein Leib' etc., noch fest stehem.*[17] This drew the reply from Zwingli of June, 527.[18] Then in March, 1528, Luther published his famous *Grosses Bekenntnis vom Abendmahl Christi.*[19] Zwingli and Oecolampadius closed the controversy with a common reply.[20] This is a succinct account of that historical conflict.

11. At Marburg where Landgrave Philip of Hesse had invited both sides to discuss he differences (1529, Oct. 2),[21] Zwingli made as large concessions as possible to the Lutherans. Before parting he signed articles that were drafted by Luther on the leading doctrines (Trinity, Christ, original sin, faith justification, word, baptism, Eucharist, civil government).[22] On the Lord's Supper there was agreement in the demand of both kinds, in the rejection of the mass, in the assertion that the spiritual partaking of Christ's Body and Blood is "especially necessary for every Christian." In Art. 15, however, profession was made that they had not at this time agreed whether the true Body and Blood of Christ are bodily in the bread and wine. But, as we have shown[23] there was outside of the Lord's Supper, between Luther and Zwingli, a considerable sphere of disagreement. See pp. 266 ff. of the latter work. This was a fact that was more felt than really seen. And Luther was right when he said to Zwingli that there was a difference of spirit" that stood between them; Luther's hopefulness for a future union s reflected in his correspondence. He wrote home to his wife a beautiful letter full of optimism that at Marburg they had experienced large agreement and that there was ground for the hope of a developing harmony.[24] Zwingli wrote at the same time his impression of his opponent: "Luther, impudent and contumacious was vanquished . . . although that in the meanwhile he declared that he was unconquered."[25] It was soon known that the Marburg Colloquy had brought no union. But further endeavors were to be made.

12. The so-called "Schwabach Articles," in their confessional significance, will be described in the next section (Chap. IV). At this place, therefore, we need just a brief reference to these articles in so far as they have to do with the controversy on the Lord's Supper. They were prepared in June, before the Marburg Articles, and were to serve as a basis for the union to be effected between the South German or "Upper German"

---

[16] Zw. *Works*, VIII, 39-41; III, 459-562. *CR*, XCVI (Zw., IX), 78-81. *CR*, XCII, (Zw., V), 562-758.

[17] *W*, 23, 38-380; *E*, 30, 19-150.

[18] *Works*, II, 16-93. *CR*, XCII (Zw., V), 805-977.

[19] *E*, 30, 151-373; *W*, 26, 261-509.

[20] *Works*. II, 94-223.

[21] Cf. W. Koehler's reconstruction *Das Marburger Religionsgespraech*, published in *Schriften des Vereins fuer Reformationsgeschichte*, 1929.

[22] "The Marburg Articles" are given in German by Kolde, *Die Augsburgische Konfession mit Beilagen* (1896); in English translation by H. E. Jacobs, *Introduction to the Symbolical Books of the Lutheran Church*, Vol. II.

[23] In our *Story and Significance of the AC*, 1930, (pp. 43 f.) and also in our larger work, *Churches and Sects of Christendom*, (1940), 266 f.

[24] See *W*, 28, 669; also von Schubert, in *Zeitschrift fuer Kirchengeschichte*, 1908, p. 354, cf. his book. *Bekenntnisbildung und Religionspolitik*, 1910.

[25] Translated from Zwingli's *Works*, VIII, 370; *CR*, XCVII (Zw., X) 318; and quoted by R. Seeberg. See the Eng. ed. of his *History of Doctrine*, II, 330.

cities and the Lutherans in the North (Saxons and Brandenburgians). But when th
meeting was held (after the Marburg Colloquy) it was found that the two parties coul
not agree on the Lord's Supper. The South was under the influence of Zwingli and Buce

13. The *Augsburg Confession,* likewise to be discussed in Chapter IV, deals i
Art. X with the Lord's Supper. We must here take note of the controversy touchin
the formulation of this article. Melanchthon was in harmony with Luther in stressin
the real presence. The text of the brief articles to be read before Emperor Charles `
was as follows: *"Of the Supper of the Lord, they teach, that the Body and Blood of Chris*
are truly present, and are distributed to those who eat in the Supper of the Lord; an
they disapprove of those that teach otherwise." Landgrave Philip of Hesse wanted
change in this article so that the Zwinglians also could subscribe. [26] But the Lutheran
and with them even Melanchthon could not be moved. [27] One reason for him lay i
the general revolutionary character of the Zwinglian movement. So the language c
the article was left in its original formulation. But it seems that the rejectory phras
had been purposely put into the mildest form (*improbant* instead of the customar
damnant). Later, after the death of Zwingli (1531), particularly under the influenc
of Bucer (since 1535) and that of Calvin, Melanchthon, changed his policy and bega
more and more to feel himself out of harmony with Luther on this subject. In th
editions of the *AC* of 1540 and following years (*Variata*) he did remove the tw
phrases: "truly present" and "disapprove of those who teach otherwise," and made Ar
X to read as follows: "On the Lord's Supper they teach that with the bread and win
the Body and Blood of Christ are presented (*exhibiantur*) to those that eat (*vescentibus`*
in the Lord's Supper." But the *Variata* came into discredit, and the Lutherans returne
to the *Editio Princeps* of 1531. [28]

14. The *Wittenberg Concord* of 1536 represents an attempt at a union betwee
the two sides. Zwingli had died (1531). The Swiss had lost their leader. Marti
Bucer, the great compromise theologian at Strassburg, labored incessantly to bring abou
a union with Wittenberg, which was also to include the followers of Zwingli. Melanch
thon supported him. Bucer spoke of a "sacramental presence" of Christ's Body an
Blood in the Supper. While Luther was suspicious of a spiritualistic interpretation o
this phrase he yielded upon the basis of the following formula offered by Bucer: *"Tha*
the true Body and the true Blood of Jesus Christ are truly present and are offered." A
the final meeting in Wittenberg, after a conversation on the differences and the union
Melanchthon drew up articles of agreement. Against the pleading of Bucer that th
people of Strassburg felt deeply against a teaching according to which the Body of Chris
is received also by unbelievers Luther remained unyielding in insisting that the spiritua
gift was independent of the faith or unbelief of the recipient, still he permitted the othe
side to make the artificial and unmaintainable distinction between *unbelievers* and
unworthy. [29] The text of the Wittenberg Concord is contained in the *CR,* 3, 375 ff. It i
translated into English in Jacobs' *Book of Concord,* Vol. II, 253. We miss it in Schaff'
Creeds of Christendom. The first articles deal with the Lord's Supper. The first article say

---

[26] See T. Kolde, *Aelteste Redaktion der Augsburger Konfession,* pp. 40 ff.

[27] Cf. *CR,* II, 83, 103. *Dogmata habent intolerabilia.*

[28] On all this see Neve, *Introduction to the Symbolical Books of the Lutheran Church,*² 95, 221; cf. O. Zoeckler
Die Augsburgische Konfession (1870), also M. Reu, *The Augsburg Confession* (1930).

[29] Cf. Gruenberg in *PRE,* III, 609, line 50. Cf. Kolde in the *PRE,* XXI, 394, line 38. Koestlin-Kawerau
*Martin Luther,*⁵ II, 340.

that with (*cum*) bread and wine Christ's Body and Blood are truly and essentially present, offered and received. The second article rejects impanation and the existence of the body outside of the action in the sacrament. The third teaches the real presence independent of the worthiness of the servant of the Church and of the recipient, as long as the administration takes place according to the institution of Christ. The "unworthy receive the sacrament to their judgment."

But the Wittenberg Concord failed in effecting a permanent union. In February, 1536, about three months before the Wittenberg Concord was signed, the first Helvetic Confession was composed. [30] Bucer himself had a part in the construction of it. There was no admission of the real presence although there was a noticeable approach to Bucer's Confession, the *Tetrapolitana*. The point of interest is: What did Bucer mean when three months later he agreed to the terms of the Wittenberg Concord? [31]

Luther did his utmost in his personal attitude to win the Swiss to the Wittenberg Concord. Up to two years before his death he abstained from all controversy against the Zwinglians in the hope that a union on the basis of the real presence might develop.[32] But he found that his silence was more and more interpreted as an abandonment of his former position. Even Schwenkfeldt prided himself with being upon common ground with him.[33] In addition to this he saw his own colaborer Melanchthon, becoming interested in the compromise endeavors of Bucer. Our reference is to articles drawn up by these two men for introducing the Reformation in the city of Cologne (1544).[34] In 1543 Luther had already announced: "After so many Confessions which I have published I must send out one more; I shall do it soon and it will be my last." [35] The document appeared in September, 1544, under the title, *Kurtz Bekenntniss D. Martin Luthers vom Heiligen Sakrament*. [36] In very sharp language he rejects the teaching of Karlstadt, Zwingli, Oecolampadius and Schwenkfeldt and points his finger at "their disciples in Zuerich and wheresoever they are." This publication meant the entire failing of the Wittenberg Concord. [37]

---

[30] Schaff, *Creeds*, I, 388 f.; *PRE*, XXI, 392, 45.

[31] See the text of the First *Helv. Conf.* in Schaff's *Creeds*, III, 211 ff. Cf. Seeberg, II, Eng. ed., 390; Koestlin-Kawerau, II, 354.

[32] See in Neve, *Lutherans in the Movement for Church Union*, the footnote 30 on page 12.

[33] *CR*, III, 983 ff.; IV, 797.

[34] Koestlin-Kawerau, II[5], 581. *CR*, V, 313 f., 293, 304.

[35] Enders, Luther's *Briefwechsel* (1915), Vol. XVI, 5 ff.

[36] See this "Brief Confession of the Lord's Supper" in *E*, 32, 396 ff.; in *W*, 54.

[37] On the whole history of the Wittenberg Concord, see Neve, *The Union Movements*, chapter one, which was a paper read before the American Society of Church History in New York.

Chapter Four

MELANCHTHON THE COLABORER OF LUTHER

Literature: The Works of Melanchthon by BRETSCHNEIDER AND BINDSEIL in the *Corpus Reformatorum* (CR), vols. 1-28, 1834 ff. Since 1910 a *Supplement on Melanchthon* to vol. 1 by O. CLEMEN has been added, 1926. As to further literature we add MELANCHTHON'S *Loci Communes* in their original form by PLITT-KOLDE, since 1864, four editions up to 1924. J. A. F. KNAAKE, *Melanchthons Einleitung in die Lehre des Paulus*, 1904. F. GALLE, *Versuch einer Characteristic Melanchthons als Theologen*, 1840. HERRLINGER, *Die Theologie Melanchthons*, 1879. K. HARTFELDER, *Melanchthon als Praeceptor Germaniae* 1889. R. SEEBERG, *Die Stellung Melanchthons in der Geschichte der Kirche und Wissenschaft*, 1897 (*Aus. Rel. und Gesch.* 1, 277 ff.). O. KIRN, article in PRE, XII, 513 ff. G ELLINGER, in *RGG* III, 2082. O. RITSCHL, in *Dogmengeschichte des Protestantismus*, 1908, vols. 1 and 2. J. W. RICHARD, *Confessional History of the Lutheran Church*, 1909. THEO. SCHMAUK, *The Confessional Principle*, 1911. Cf. our *Introduction to the Symbolical Books of the Lutheran Church*,[2] 1926, pp. 84 ff.; *Story and Significance of the Augsburg Confession*, 1930, pp. 31 ff.; *Lutherans in the Movements for Church Union*, 1921, pp. 5 ff., 40 ff.

1. *Melanchthon's Natural Relation to Luther*. The Church Historian Gieseler called Melanchthon the *female principle of the Reformation*. The following rhyme has found circulation regarding the natural relation of Luther and Melanchthon: "*Was der Martin kuehn begonnen, hat der Philip fein gesponnen und in rechten Schick gebracht*." (What Martin boldly began, this Philip finely spun and gave it the proper form.)

Luther with all the depth of his religious genius was not at his best when it came to guarded theological definition. This we see in the *Smalcald Articles*. Such language surely was not fitting at the Augsburg Diet. Luther himself said of his coworker: "I was born for warring with factious spirits (*Rotten*) and devils. For this reason my books are stormy and warlike. To me it has fallen to uproot trees, to clear away thorn and brush, and to fill up mudholes. I am a rough pioneer who has to blaze the trail and even up the path. But Magister Philip proceeds quietly and with a clean hand: building, planting, sowing and watering with pleasure according to the rich gifts with which God has endowed him." [1] He had the didactical gift for method, form and system. Up to the end of his life Melanchthon was asked to formulate the results of the many conferences and colloquies into tangible and maintainable statements.

2. On the other hand he was a man of *irenic disposition*, he was easily ready for concessions to serve the cause of union and tranquility. This was a trait which often worried not only Luther but also many of his colaborers, and occasionally hindered the right development of things. Reaction against this conciliatory trait in Melanchthon started the development of anti-Melanchthonian factions which later were consolidated with strong leadership in most difficult and trying situations. This was observable especially in the controversies after Luther's death. The report of these belongs in our Chapter VII on the *Formula of Concord* where we must treat of these matters in detail. The changes of the *Augsburg Confession* in the Variata editions, 1540 ff., were outstanding instances of later disturbances through Melanchthon's concessions. But long before this final conflict, we can trace the effects of this irenic trait of Melanchthon even previous

---

[1] Cf. *PRE*, Vol. XII, 528.

and during the Augsburg Diet and continuing into the days of the Smalcald con-
ention (1537).

Such misapplied irenics brought new troubles instead of peace. The career of
Melanchthon toward the end of his life, especially after Luther's death, was filled with
ndless conflicts. After Calvin's mediating conception of the Lord's Supper had been
dopted by the followers of Zwingli, Melanchthon changed his attitude in the con-
overy on this matter, and his pupils, the *Philippists,* did not co-operate with the
utherans in that conflict in which German Lutheranism had to struggle for its very life.
here was much politics in these movements with frequent absence of the Christian
pirit on both sides. The further doctrinal details of this situation must be studied in
ur Chapter VII on the *Formula of Concord* (see *Crypto-Calvinistic Controversies*).

In addition there were related controversies on *Justification* (Osiander) and espe-
ally the one on the *Necessity of Good Works for Salvation* (Amsdorf against George
Major) in which Melanchthon was appealed to. (See in Chapter VII on the *FC.*)

3. *Melanchthon's Loci. Loci* meant to Melanchthon *Leading Conceptions,* in German *Leitbegriffe* (Kirn). This little book, first published in 1521, was written in Latin
nder the title *Loci Communes Rerum Theologicarum.*[2] It was the first dogmatics of
e young Protestant Church. It is said that during the lifetime of its author it had
one through 80 editions. This book exercised a great influence by establishing truly
vangelical conceptions among the clergy. Luther praised it as being "immortal." A
ading Roman theologian, J. Cochlaeus, said that because of the superior beauty of
Melanchthon's style and his skill in the quotations of Scripture this book was "more
ernicious than even Luther's writing on the *Babylonian Captivity.*"[3]

Later followed two entirely new prints, one in 1525, and another in 1543, which
xpressed certain changes especially pertaining to the doctrine of the will in the process
f conversion. In 1517, Melanchthon had come from Tuebingen to Wittenberg with
n aversion to scholasticism, because it was based on Aristotle. This aversion accounts
or the absence in the first edition of the *Loci* of Humanism with its philosophical ap-
roaches to the study of religion. Later, beginning already with 1523, about the time
f Luther's conflict with Erasmus, there is noticeable in Melanchthon a growing inclina-
on to return to certain ideals of Humanism. He began to question the correctness of
uther's conception of man's will, feeling that something really good should be admitted
n the natural man, a natural high endowment, although this be hindered by an inherited
weakness which must be overcome by the aid of the Holy Spirit. His observations during
e visitation of the churches between 1523 and 1529, taught him the need of preaching
e Law, not only for terrifying the sinner into the seeking of grace which he continued
o teach in Luther's manner after Paul to the Galations, but by insisting on the use of
he Law as a *guide* through the Christian life, as it was taught in article VI of the
Augsburg Confession. But his careful stress upon the continued need of the Law brought
gainst him the attacks from the Antinomians (Agricola, Cordatus). But on this matter
n itself, there was no disagreement between Melanchthon and Luther, as we shall see in
Chapter VII of this section.

The *Loci* of Melanchthon had much to do with preparing him for the later task
f writing the *Augsburg Confession.* Here he showed his remarkable gift for formu-

---

[2] The print in use for the first edition of the *Loci* is the one by Plitt-Kolde; see our literature.
[3] *Confutatio adv. Did. Faventium,* 1534, last page.

lating and stating in clear language the teachings of the Reformation. The book ha
grown out of the author's interpretation of Paul's *Letter to the Romans*.[4] In the *Intro
duction* he insisted that the Scripture alone, unmixed with philosophy, establishes article
of faith. With Luther he ignores the metaphysical teachings of the Trinity: "For
condemn metaphysical theories because I think that it is a great peril to subject celestia
mysteries to the methods of our reason."[5] In Luther's own way he dwelt on the com
bination of ideas involved in justification and the new repentance such as law and gospe
sin and grace. Faith he considered to be trust (*fiducia*), not mere assent to somethin
known; its correlate is justification. There is no room for merit. The Christian is fre
from the driving and from the accusation of the law. Melanchthon at that time ha
still Luther's determination in pointing to the necessity with which everything in th
life of man must occur according to the original plans of the omnipotent God. But i
this he later found a bearing in which he was guarded against making God the cause c
sin and at the same time could profess with Luther that man cannot, without the Hol
Ghost, effect his own regeneration. In articles XVIII and XIX of the *Augsburg Con
fession* he had purposely avoided a discussion of predestination.[6]

We heard of Melanchthon's gradually developing disagreement with Luther on man'
will in the process of conversion, which he expressed first in his 1535 edition of th
Loci, and we took note of how this change, beginning with 1523, had gradually devel
oped.[7] The student will ask why it is that this change is not especially noticeable i
the *Augsburg Confession* at the time of its delivery in 1530-31. The answer must b
that Melanchthon's later synergistic view had not yet crystallized itself into a dogma
At Augsburg Melanchthon knew also that on this point, where the teaching of Luthe
had been so decisive and on which he had so many adherents, he would not be justifie
in incorporating his own personal views into so important a document. But in 1535
in his *Loci,* he recognized three causes of conversion: The Word, the Holy Spirit, an
the human will. He speaks of a freedom of the will that man had retained by whicl
he has the power of applying himself to grace (*facultas se applicandi ad gratiam*).[8] Int
this category of changes with a doctrinal significance belong also certain expressions an
passages in articles XVIII, IV, V, and XX in the *Variata* edition of the *Augsburg Con
fession* of 1540 with its emphasis upon repentance and good works in a manner charac
teristic of synergism and corresponding with the new edition of Melanchthon's *Loci* o
1535.[9] From 1535 on Melanchthon labored for a certain co-operation of the human an
the divine factor in conversion. Prof. P. Tschackert points out some striking deviations o
the *Variata* from the *Invariata*. In article V of the Confession, where the *Invariata* reads
"through Word and Sacrament . . . the Holy Spirit is given," there the *Variata* says
'When we comfort ourselves (*erigimus nos*) through faith, then simultaneously (*simul*)
the Holy Spirit is given us." Again in article V the *Variata* has this sentence, "Whe
we hear or consider the Gospel, or use the Sacraments and comfort ourselves (*no.
consolamur*) through faith, then simultaneously (*simul*) the Holy Spirit is working."
Note the repeated use of the word *simul*. In article XVIII of Free Will, the *Invariata* says

---

[4] Note in our literature the publication by Knaake on this subject.
[5] Plitt, *Augustana*, p. 64. *CR* 1, 305.
[6] Cf. our *Introd. to the Symb. Bks.*[2], pp. 277 ff. For a convenient study we refer to R. Seeberg, *DG*, IV[3], 442 n.
[7] *CR* I, 688.
[8] *Loci* 1535, 1543; *CR* 21, 659 ff.
[9] O. Zoeckler, *Die Augsb. Konfession*, p. 37.

spiritual righteousness is worked by the Holy Ghost who is received in the heart through
the Word of God." Here the *Variata* says: "But spiritual righteousness is effected in us
when we are assisted (*adjuvamur*) by the Holy Spirit." The same word *adjuvati* is also
put into article XX. So Melanchthon, after changing his conviction concerning Free
Will, "put his own private theology into the *Variata.*"[10]

4. *Melanchthon's Earliest Contribution to Religious Education* should not be passed
by. It belongs to the engagements which have prepared him for authorship of the
Augsburg Confession.[11] It was in the years between 1525 and 1529 that official visitations of the churches were ordered to investigate the religious condition of the congregations in Saxony by the elector who functioned with authority of a bishop in need.
Melanchthon was among the men commissioned to conduct this investigation. An
alarming state of affairs was discovered. The religious ignorance and moral condition
not only of the common people but also of many of the clergymen was appalling. In
order to meet the situation in an orderly way and to make these visitations as fruitful as
possible, Melanchthon was instructed by the elector to draw up articles to guide the
church officers and ministers and their superintendents in the needed reform. This
document was published in 1528.[12] It was the first official form for teaching the fundamentals of the Christian religion. As such it was a pioneer to Luther's Catechism and
to the Augsburg Confession. But as a church order (*Kirchenordnung*) it dealt also
with principles of church discipline and public education. The creation of this document belonged to the permanently functioning elements in the evolution of the
Reformation.

5. *Melanchthon and the Augsburg Confession.* By the time of the drafting of this
great document (1530) Melanchthon was eminently prepared for his task. He had
been present at the Leipzig disputation of Luther with Eck (1519) and had clarified
his mind on Scripture as the authority of religion, a principle which he expressed even
before Luther declared it.[13] During thirteen years of struggle for the fundamentals of
the Reformation (the time which Schaff calls the *prophetic period*) he had enjoyed the
daily fellowship of Luther and together with him had witnessed the growth of Wittenberg into an international university. In order to hear Luther and Melanchthon and to
learn the Gospel, students of that day were flocking to Wittenberg from all countries.
Coming from Sweden, Norway, Denmark, from the Baltic provinces, from Poland,
Hungary, from France and England, we find all these coming teachers and preachers of
their respective countries at the feet of Luther and Melanchthon, the *praeceptor Ger-
maniae.* (Note in our literature K. Hartfelder's book.) The writing of the *Loci* and of
the *Articles for Visitation* and the preparation, jointly with Luther, of the so-called
Schwabach Articles (see our Chapter V), the observation of Luther's separation from
Humanism and from the Pelagianism of his day (*Campanus*), and the elimination of
Spiritualism with its theology of the *Inner Light,* also the problems included in the
Zwinglian movement—all this had been a great school for fitting and enabling Melanch-
thon for writing the *Augsburg Confession,* this *Magna Charta* of Protestantism in gen-
eral and of Lutheranism in particular.[13a]

---

[10] P. Tschackert, *Enstehung,* p. 291.
[11] H. Lietzmann edited his *Unterricht der Visitatoren.*
[12] The title was *Unterricht der Visitatoren als die Pfarrherren im Kurfuerstentum zu Sachsen.* See its text in
the CR, vol. 26, 41 ff.; cf. Richter, *Kirchenordnungen,* 1, 82 ff.
[13] *RGG*[2], III, 2075.
[13a] Cf. our *Story and Significance of the Augsburg Confession,* chapters 2 and 3.

In the next Chapter, presenting a brief view of the earliest of the Lutheran Confessions, we shall also give a condensed view of the theology of the *Augsburg Confession*. Outstanding among the doctrinal interests of Melanchthon in connection with the *Augsburg Confession,* were the distinctions from Zwingli and the Anabaptists concerning the Eucharist. His consideration finally led him into the publication of the *Variata* edition of 1540 ff., where he removed from article X on the Lord's Supper the two phrases *truly present* and *we disapprove of those who teach otherwise* (cf. Chapt. V), substituting the sentence of the *Variata: De coena Domini docent quod cum pane et vino exhibeantur corpus et sanguis Christi vescentibus in coena Domini.* This alteration did not appear in the German text of the Confession. In English it would read: "Concerning the Supper of the Lord they (the churches of the Reformation) teach that with the bread and wine there are presented (*exhibeantur*) to those that eat, the body and blood of Christ in the Supper of the Lord." [14]

6. *"Melanchthonianism."* It will be of interest in this connection to reprint from our *Lutherans in the Movement for Church Union,* pp. 40-43 the following: "By Melanchthonianism we understand the doctrinal elements in the teachings of Melanchthon on which he departed from the teachings of Luther." At present the historian characterize as *Melanchthonianism* also the growing inclination of Melanchthon to write theology after the methods of scholasticism.

But in this discussion we must confine ourselves to matters in which Melanchthon approached Bucer and Calvin, the Lord's Supper and the person of Christ. We have to keep in mind that Melanchthon had no doctrine of the Eucharist of his own. It was in his nature to evade the controversy rather than to solve the problem. He preferred to leave conflicting principles untouched. There is something eclectic about him.[15] It cannot be said that he ever adopted Calvin's doctrine of the Lord's Supper, especially not its characteristic formulas of the exaltation of the believing soul into heaven and of the communication of Christ's humanity to the believer through the Spirit.[16] Neither did he reject it. But his approach to Calvin is in the conception of a personal presence of Christ in the Supper. This he had adopted from Bucer. He liked this conception because he thought that he could use it as a formula for union. We must agree when Stahl says: "Melanchthon's conception of a general presence of Christ in the Supper is after all Calvin's doctrine not openly expressed. There is no middle doctrine between Luther and Calvin. As soon as the Lutheran view is abandoned the Calvinistic view of a personal presence seems the only one that is left. Calvin, Bucer, Melanchthon mark only different theological types of Calvin's doctrine." A characteristic of the Bucero-Melanchthonian expressions is their elasticity. As to the real doctrine which Melanchthon held for himself historians are not agreed. Kirn[17] calls attention to the fact that the pupils of Melanchthon have interpreted their teacher differently on this subject (Peucer different from Hemmig and Major). But the fact that Melanchthon supported Hardenberg in Bremen[18] and that through his written estimate (*Gutachten*) he was instru-

---

[14] For a critique see our *Introduction to the Symb. Bks. of the Luth. Church,* pp. 101-111, and pp. 219-223 also our monograph *Are We Justified in Distinguishing between an Altered and an Unaltered Augsburg Confession* Luth. Lit. Bd., Burlington, Iowa.

[15] Stahl, *Die Luth. Kirche und die Union,* p. 108 f.

[16] *Institutiones* IV, 17, 9, 10, 18.

[17] *PRE* XII 526, 20.

[18] *PRE* vol. 7, 412, *CR* 9, ff.

ental in confirming Elector Frederick III in views[19] that took the Palatinate over to Calvinism shows that between the doctrines of Luther and Calvin he favored Calvinism. He himself did not make the choice, because he saw the salvation of German Protestantism in a tenacious adherence to his unionistic formulas. He refused to go beyond the expression of Paul, I Cor. 10:16, that the bread is "the communion of the Body of Christ." In article X of the *Augsburg Confession,* in the *Variata,* he uses the preposition *um.* This can have the signification "by means of"; when so interpreted it is Lutheran. But it may also mean "simultaneously" or "in connection with"; when so understood it is Calvinistic. The oral reception of the Body of Christ and its reception also by the unworthy offer the test as to which significance is accepted. Melanchthon rejected the oral receiving of Christ's Body.[20]

It will be of interest to add a few lines on Melanchthon's followers as a party. Melanchthonianism as an organized party[21] suffered severe defeat in the drama that took place in Saxony.[22] This defeat at that time was not merely the result of the severe polemics of the stricter Lutherans, but it had its source in the lack of character and positiveness of the Melanchthonian position. Kawerau remarks that Philippism remained *etwas Halbes.* Melanchthon's doctrine of the Lord's Supper lacked in biblical foundation and dogmatic completeness. It could appeal to those only with an indifferent attitude of mind. And the Christology of the Melanchthonians falls short in that it refuses to draw logical consequences from admitted premises. Melanchthonianism in the point under consideration was too neutral. Kawerau calls attention to the fact that after the introduction of the *Formula of Concord* wherever Melanchthonianism still persisted there came forth no scholarship that could be compared with the literary productions of Concordia Lutheranism.[23]

For the time being Melanchthonianism was defeated through the very general adoption of the *Formula of Concord* and the publication of the *Book of Concord,* yet it was by no means dead. Germany, consisting of many different independent dominions and principalities, secured to Melanchthonianism safe places of refuge. As characteristic of that age we read that Dr. Polykarp Leyser at a disputation in Wittenberg tore the picture of Melanchthon from the wall and threw it to the ground. Where subscription to the *Formula of Concord* was refused, Melanchthonianism as a rule found a field for its influence.

An important instrument through which Melanchthonianism kept exercising an influence with practical results was the *Augsburg Confession* in the *Variata* edition. It served as an instrument for the introduction of a milder Lutheranism or even a complete Calvinism in many territories.

7. *Melanchthon on Sources and Norms of Truth.* Theology, distinct from other sciences, has its object and its authority in the revelation of Scripture. Melanchthon did not use Scripture for building a speculative system (like Origen, the Scholastics, later Schleiermacher, Biedermann, Dorner, and many of the conservatives of the 19th century) but his was the dogmatics of the *Loci:* the teachings of Scripture simply co-ordinated

---

[19] *Ibid.* 9, 960 ff.
[20] *Ibid.* 9, 1046.
[21] Cf. *PRE,* 15, 323.
[22] See in our Chapter VII the Crypto-Calvinistic Controversy. Cf. our *Union Movements,* p. 84.
[23] *PRE* 15, 329, 55. For a fitting and very practical description of Melanchthonianism, by the late Dr. E. J Wolf (Gettysburg), see our *Churches and Sects of Christendom,* p. 598.

under topics which indicated the fundamentals of religion. He does not have a defined doctrine of inspiration, because he believed in that as a self-evident fact.[24] He accepted as standards of truth the symbols of the ancient Church and had much faith in the resolutions of the Ecumenical Councils. To these authorities he added the teaching of Luther, which he saw expressed in the Lutheran Confessions. He believed that the teaching of the Wittenberg School was a true expression of the faith of the believers in all ages.[25] We cannot here follow his endeavors to relate the teachings of these sources and authorities of truth.[26]

8. *On Melanchthon's Conception of Justification* (with special regard to the historical controversy between the late Professors Walther and Holl), see our chapter on the Roman Catholic Church in our *Churches and Sects of Christendom* and also in Chapter I on Luther in this Book III.

9. *Conclusion:* In the form of the following *post scriptum* notes we shall now add a closing estimate of Melanchthon even though this cannot strictly claim to be History of Doctrine.

After Luther's conflict with Erasmus (1525), Melanchthon felt that he wanted to withdraw from lecturing on theology. He was really a philologian who had been pressed into the teaching of theology by Luther. He had never been ordained, nor was he a doctor of theology. But his elector appointed him to a special theological professorship thus retaining this talented man for the university at Wittenberg.

Melanchthon became famous as a professor and was styled the *Praeceptor Germaniae*. As was already stated, Melanchthon together with Luther attracted students from many countries so that Wittenberg was looked upon as an international university of Protestantism. The publication of J. Hausleiter, *Aus der Schule Melanchthons,* in which he describes the theological disputations and achievements during the years 1546 and 1560, gives us an impression of the academic activity of Melanchthon. He also organized many other universities for work in all branches of science. One may say that in many directions he controlled the university studies.

He must also be credited with having led German Humanism into the channels of Protestantism. He did this by bringing science and faith into the closest unity. Thus the history of German Humanism came to be distinct from that of Italy where Humanism was lost in skepticism and atheism.

In the history of the Reformation Melanchthon will ever be chiefly remembered as the colaborer of Luther, especially at the time when confessional statements were to be drafted. Of the hard judgments against him in the later years of his life when he yielded at moments when a firm and positive attitude was the need of the hour we shall read in Chapter VII in the discussion of the Formula of Concord. But the conciliatory and mediating trait in Melanchthon, as a sympton of his peculiar type of humanism, was bound to reassert itself later in the age of syncretism and in the ages of union endeavors in Germany, England and America. This is a matter which we have analyzed with regard to many relations and situations in our *Lutherans in the Movements for Church Union,* and again in our *Churches and Sects of Christendom.*[27]

---

[24] *CR,* 15, 175; 21, 632.
[25] *CR,* XI, 728; 3, 291; 6, 57, 72, 73, 92; 7, 398; 11, 272, 326; 8, 49; 28, 369. References by R. Seeberg, *DG,* IV³.
[26] Consult R. Seeberg as referred to.
[27] See the Tables of Contents and the Topical Indices.

As bearing upon the general result of these movements, we quote a judgment given
y the late Prof. Kahnis of Leipzig: "Philippism lacked in positiveness of character and
as therefore unable to speak the last word when the Formula of Concord was under
onsideration. Lutheranism alone had the theological force, the definiteness of doctrine,
he outspoken individuality, the consciousness of its right to exist, the courage of con-
iction, and the territorial solidity, that were necessary for this task." [28] Neither should
he following judgment by the same Lutheran scholar be overlooked in this connection:
It will always be the theological ideal of German Protestantism to combine with the
rm ground of Luther the scientifically progressive search for truth that characterized
Melanchthon."

---

[28] *Der innere Gang des deutschen Protestantismus* I. 55.

Chapter Five

THE EARLIEST CONFESSIONAL WRITINGS
OF LUTHERANISM

In order to do justice to the historical situation touching the particular symbols of Lutheranism as documents, a distinction must be made between two periods. The earlier of its Confessions (the *Catechism*, the *Schwabach Articles*, the *Augsburg Confession*, Melanchthon's *Apology* and the *Smalcald Articles*), are confessional expressions of the *prophetical* period of the Reformation. The *Formula of Concord* represents the doctrinal results of a long period of theological controversy within the Lutheran Church itself; it may be called the *didactical* period of the Reformation.

1. *THE SCHWABACH ARTICLES* are a document of closest relation to the *Augsburg Confession*. They were drafted in June, 1529, on instruction of the Elector of Saxony by the Wittenberg theologians, most probably by Melanchthon, with the assistance of Luther. [1] These articles were written before the *Marburg Articles* had been composed by Luther, as has been shown by H. von Schubert. [2] The intention was to use them as a basis for negotiations with the Upper German Cities, which were under the influence of Martin Bucer at Strassburg. Bucer, then, was mediating on the Lord's Supper between Luther and Zwingli. The articles did not accomplish the doctrinal union at the meeting in Schwabach, on October 16. Philip of Hesse was urging a political union of German Protestantism. Luther was opposed to such a union, because he saw in it an act of disloyalty to the rightful government, and the Elector of Saxony inclined more and more to a policy of non-activity toward the emperor. Nevertheless the Protestants of Northern Germany wanted to let their friends who leaned toward Bucer know what was their position confessionally, particularly on the Lord's Supper. An agreement was not reached. Still these *Schwabach Articles* had their value. At the Augsburg Diet (1530), they served Melanchthon as an important aid in the construction of the doctrinal elements of the *Augsburg Confession*. By these *Schwabach Articles* especially Melanchthon, at Augsburg, would always know on what points the Lutheran party at Augsburg was in agreement with Luther. Because of their political character this document had been kept secret until Luther published it while the Augsburg Diet was in session. The *Augsburg Confession* then obviously made these *Schwabach Articles* superfluous. But they were of far greater importance than were the *Marburg Articles*. That is why we mention them here. The *Schwabach Articles* are the first relatively complete confessional document of Lutheranism.

In these articles we have an actual contribution of Luther's thought material to the *Augsburg Confession*. The tone is decidedly polemical against Rome, as for instance in Article XV, where the prohibition of marriage and ordinary food and drink to priests, together with the urging of the monastic life and vows of every kind, are declared to be

---

[1] Luther, E, 24, 322 ff.

[2] *Zeitschrift fuer Kirchengeschichte*, 1908. Cf. the writer's *Introduction to the Symbolical Books*, 1926, pp. 88 f., and in *Story and Significance of the Augsburg Confession*, 1930, pp. 41 f.

othing but damnable doctrines of the devil. The mass is spoken of as the greatest of
ll abominations. In Article X there is strong emphasis upon the real presence of Christ's
3ody and Blood in the Eucharist, in opposition to "the other side."

The contents of the *Schwabach Articles* can be indicated here only by the topics
nder discussion, which are as follows: 1. The Trinity; 2. The Incarnation of the Son
f God; 3. The Work of Christ; 4. Original Sin; 5. Justification by Faith; 6. Faith, the
3ift of God; 7. The Preached Word; 8. The Two Sacraments; 9. Baptism; 10. The
Eucharist; 11. Private Confessions; 12. The Christian Church; 13. Christ's Return to
udgment; 14. The Government; 15. Monastic Vows and Other Prohibitions; 16. The
Mass; 17. Ceremonies of the Church. Space will not be taken here to point out the
natters in which the *Augsburg Confession* shows the influence of the *Schwabach Articles*.
Calinich and Knaake have gone into details on this subject. J. W. Richard in his
Confessional History has given a valuable summary particularly of the investigations by
Dr. Calinich.

Literature: The text of the *Schwabach Articles,* in German can be found at the follow-
ng places: E, 24, 322 ff., W, CR, 26, 139 ff. Conveniently accessible in TH. KOLDE, *Die
Augsburgische Konfession mit Beilagen,* 1896, p. 123 ff. Translated into English by H. E. JACOBS,
Symbolical Books of the Lutheran Church, Vol. II; also in the *Triglotta* of the Missouri Synod.
For *reviews of the situation* see J. KOESTLIN, *Martin Luther⁵* by G. KAWERAU, I, 199 f.;
SCHMAUK-BENZE, *The Confessional Principle,* 1911, (see index). J. L. NEVE, *Story and Sig-
nificance of the Augsburg Confession,* 1930, as referred to. The best review, based upon the
investigations by H. VON SCHUBERT and W. GUSSMANN and others, is given by M. REU in his
Augsburg Confession, 1930, pp. 9-37.

2. THE AUGSBURG CONFESSION of 1530 and 1531 was destined to become the
official confession of the Lutheran Church. There had been no plan, however, to estab-
ish a new dogma. In an epilogue to Part I (Article XXI) Melanchthon insisted there
had been no departing from the teachings of the "Catholic" Church as represented by the
Fathers, that is from Athanasius to about Leo the Great and perhaps to Gregory the
Great. The confessors wanted to take the position that errors in doctrine which had
crept in later and which never had been codified in a real creed, should not claim to be
Christian Catholic doctrine. As an example we may mention the Semi-Pelagianism of
he Middle Ages, which was sanctioned first by the condemnation of Gottschalk (853)
and later by the teaching of men like Thomas Aquinas and Duns Scotus. The decrees
of the Fourth Lateran Council (1215), also may furnish a list of teachings that were
Roman Catholic, but could not claim to be *Christian* Catholic in character. Of course,
here was much self-deception in the presumption that the early Church was in entire
harmony with the doctrinal positions of our Reformers. This must not surprise us when
we remember that church history at that time was yet in its swaddling clothes.[3] But the
plan of the Lutherans in giving account of themselves at Augsburg was to proceed on
he ground that they were in entire harmony with the teachings of the early Catholic
Church, and that their *apology,* as they first called their document, needed to refer only
o some abuses which they had removed. In other words, it was the plan to present to
he emperor only what the Confession deals with in its second part (Articles XXII to
XXVIII). So it came about that Melanchthon at first had his mind only on these
articles *on abuses.*

---

[3] On the changing views of Melanchthon in this respect see R. Seeberg, *History of Doctrine²,* Eng. ed., II,
50; cf. *CR,* 2, 217.

But the publication of Dr. Eck addressed to the emperor, charging the Lutheran
with the teachings of Zwingli, Karlstadt and the Anabaptists, convinced Melanchthon
and his assistants that the chief part of the Confession to be presented to the emperor
was to deal also with the *doctrine* of his group. So it came about that Articles I-XXI
which now constitute the chief part of the *AC*, were written.

Literature: The various editions of the *Augsburg Confession,* and their preparatory drafts were
published in the CR, 26, 97-776. As further literature we mention PLITT, *Einleitung in die
Augustana,* 2 vols. 1867-68. ZOECKLER, *Die Augsburg Konfession,* 1870, P. SCHAFF, *Creeds of
Christendom.* TSCHACKERT, *Die unveraenderte Augsburgische Konfession,* critical ed., Latin and
German, comparing the various editions, 1901. KOLDE, in J. T. MUELLER'S *Symbolische Buecher*
beginning with the 10th edition. For Germany, MUELLER'S *Symb. Buecher* has been replaced
(since 1930) by a work edited by the Evangelische Kirchenausschuss. T. KOLDE, *Die aeltest*
Redaktion der Augsburgischen Konfession, with Melanchthon's original introduction. NEVE, *The*
Augsburg Confession, popular and featuring events of Church History; also *A Guide to the Augs*
burg Confession, for students of theology and confined to problems of Symbolics, 1927. The latter
is a revised and augmented form of pp. 83-307 of the same author's *Introduction to the Symbolical*
Books of the Lutheran Church,[2] 1926 (widely used as guide in theological seminaries). Con
tributions by Geo. J. Fritschel. This book covers the interpretation of all confessional writings in
the Lutheran Church. Future editions will embrace the results of recent studies. Its outstanding
part (pp. 115-307) constitutes an interpretation of the articles of the *Augsburg Confession.* Cf
also the author's *Story and Significance of the Augsburg Confession.* Excepting the last mentioned
book, all three editions offer interpretations of the text. W. VOLLRATH, *Das Augsburger Bekenntnis*
1930 (discussion of contents on the basis of its history). M. REU, *The Augsburg Confession,* 1930.

In the 21 doctrinal articles of the Confession a certain systematic arrangement is
observable. Article I begins with God and Article XVII closes the body of doctrines with
Christ's Return for Judgment; Articles XVIII, XIX and XX were added to supplement
certain groups of previously discussed articles which the following topical organization
will show:

FIRST

Article I on the trinitarian relation in the *Godhead,* and III on the *Son of God* with par
ticular regard to the incarnation and Christ's states of humiliation and exaltation, with the saving
object of His work of reconciliation, may be subsumed under Luther's phrase in the *Smalcald*
Articles when he speaks of *the article of the divine majesty,* on which at that time there was no
conflict. [5]

SECOND

The *anthropological, including the hamartological interest* of the Confession is dealt with in
Article II on man's natural depravity, defined as a condition in which man is born "without fear of
God and without trust in God and with concupiscence," and is characterized as "truly sin" (*vere*
sit peccatum), and bringing "eternal death," if there is not a regeneration "through baptism and
the Holy Ghost." This "organic basis" for Lutheran theology (Zoeckler) is asserted against the
Pelagians and Roman Catholic Semi-Pelagians who deny that original sin is truly sin "and who to
obscure the glory of Christ's merit and benefits argue that man can be justified before God by his
own strength and reason."

Next, in Article XVIII, the question is discussed, what influence has this natural depravity had
on man's will? While retaining a certain outward freedom even in moral things, in matters of civil
righteousness (*in rebus civilibus*), he lost through the fall the "power without the Holy Ghost, to
work the righteousness of God, that is spiritual righteousness" (*justitia spiritualis*). "This righteous
ness, if experienced by the regenerated, is wrought in the heart (*haec fit in cordibus*) when the
Holy Ghost is received through the Word." Article II of the *Formula of Concord, On Free Will*
offers an elaboration on this subject.

Article XIX on the Cause of Sin, finally, affords a postscript to the Confession before its
delivery[6] and supplements Article II by insisting that while God created and preserves man the cause
of sin must not be sought in God, but *"in the devil and ungodly men."*

---

[4] Complete on all introductory matters.
[5] As to detailed interpretation of these two articles see our *Introduction to the Symbolical Books.*[2]
[6] See our *Introd.*[2], p. 93, on basis of Kolde, *Aelteste Redaktion,* p. 61.

THIRD

Articles IV, VI and XX offer the *Central Doctrine of Man's Salvation*. Article IV of *Justification*, which can be traced through the whole Confession as the fundamental interest, teaches against Pelagianism and Semi-Pelagianism (1) "that men cannot be justified before God by their own strength, merits or works," but (2) *are* freely justified for Christ's sake through faith (*propter Christum, per fidem*) when they believe that they are received into favor and that their sins are forgiven for Christ's sake, who, by His death, hath made satisfaction for our sins." And as a postscript, just before delivery, the statement was added: This faith God imputes for righteousness in His sight. Romans 3 and 4." [7]

Closely associated with the article on justification is Article VI *Of the New Obedience:* "This faith" (*fides illa*), spoken of in Article IV, is bound (*debeat*) "to bring forth good fruits." "It is necessary (*oporteat*) to do good works." They are not optional. Remember, however, they must be of the sort which are "commanded by God" (*mandata a Deo*); not the works of a self-chosen sanctity (*consilia evangelica*). The warning is attached: "But not that we should rely on those works to merit justification before God, for remission of sins and justification are apprehended by faith." "We are freely receiving remission of sins, without works, by faith alone."

Article XX on *Faith and Good Works*, a lengthy article constituting one-third of all the doctrinal articles (again a postscript to the first draft), confirms eloquently this fundamental doctrine of the Reformation. (In this connection read also in the *Formula of Concord* Articles III *Of the Righteousness of Faith*, IV *Of Good Works*, V *Of Law and Gospel*, and VI *Of the Third Use of the Law*.)

FOURTH

Articles V on *How Faith to Receive Justification Is Obtained*, IX *On Baptism*, X on *the Lord's Supper* (cf. Article XXIV *On the Mass* in Part II), and XIII *On the Use of the Sacraments*, point to Word and Sacraments as means of grace. In Article V they are called "instruments" for the Holy Ghost working "faith where and when it pleaseth God" (*ubi et quando visum est Deo*). This Augustinian phrase disappeared in Melanchthon's later Variata editions, indicating his development in the direction of synergism. [8] This article was directed against "the Anabaptists and others who think that the Holy Ghost cometh to men without the external Word, through their own preparation and works." [9]

Article IX did not aim at a complete doctrine of *Baptism*. Here the common ground with Rome was large. This statement was directed against the Anabaptists. They were also fundamentally out of harmony with the views of Zwingli. The Sacrament is spoken of as "necessary for salvation" (as to divine appointment). "Children are to be baptized." This and not more was said in the original draft which Luther saw (May 11th). But before delivery two statements of a general doctrine on Baptism were added (1) The principal thing is that "through baptism" the children or adults "are received into His grace." This is the objective significance: Not we offer to God (Melanchthon), but Baptism is "God's work" (Luther). At the same time (2) Baptism is not an *opus operatum*, therefore "through Baptism is offered the grace of God" (for receiving or rejecting). This is the subjective significance. [10]

Article X *On the Lord's Supper* (cf. in Part II, Article XXII *Of both Kinds*) is very brief. It reads "The Body and Blood of Christ are truly present and are distributed to those who eat the supper of our Lord; and they disapprove of those that teach otherwise." In his Variata of 1540 ff., Melanchthon omitted the two phrases "truly present" (*vere adsint*) and "they disapprove of those that teach otherwise" (*improbant secus docentes*). The omission of these two significant phrases was to serve as an invitation to the Protestants in the South now under Zwinglian influence and now under the influence of Bucer to join the Lutheran side. But gradually, with the ascendancy of Calvinism in conflict with Lutheranism, the Variata came into discredit, and the leaders of Lutheranism insisted upon subscription to the original form. [11]

Article XIII *On the Use of the Sacraments* serves a supplementary purpose. The element of truth in Zwinglianism is recognized: The sacraments being "marks of profession among men." But the statement is qualified: "Not only, but rather to be signs and testimonies of the will of God toward us to awaken and confirm faith in those who use them." The clarified view of the Lutheran

---

[7] Neve, p. 94. Kolde, as cited.

[8] See our *Introduction*, p. 170 f.

[9] For reading, see our *Introduction*, p. 172; also *Story and Significance*, pp. 14 ff.

[10] See our *Introduction*, pp. 201 ff.

[11] Here is not the place for telling this story. We refer to our detailed discussion in the following places: our Book III, Chapter III. Our *Introduction to the Symbolical Books*[2], pp. 101-11; 219-223. Our *Altered or Unaltered Augsburg Confession?* 1911 (a pamphlet of 43 pages), also our *Story and Significance*, pp. 87-96.

Church concerning the conception and use of the Lord's Supper is to be found in the *Formula* ‹
Concord, Article VII.

FIFTH

Between Articles X *On the Eucharist* and XIII *On the Use of the Sacraments* we have in X
On Confession and XII *On Repentance,* two articles of preparatory significance for the sacrament
In the Variata, Melanchthon changed the order and wrote in XI *On Repentance* and in XII *O*
Confession. This being good logic, we may here follow that order:

Repentance: (1) Against the *Anabaptists* of that time the position is taken that grace can b
lost. (2) Against the *Perfectionists* it is taught that sinlessness cannot be attained on this side c
eternity. (3) The position of the old *Novatians* (including the Montanists) is rejected, wh
"would not absolve such as had fallen after baptism though they returned to repentance." (4) C
special importance is the *definition of repentance* in opposition to that of *Rome* (contrition c
heart, oral confession, satisfaction through good works). The Lutheran definition reads: "No
repentance consists properly of these two parts: One is contrition, that is, terrors smiting the cor
science through the knowledge of sin; the other is faith, which, born of the gospel, or of absolutior
believes that for Christ's sake sins are forgiven, comforts the conscience and delivers it from terror
Then good works are bound to follow, which are the fruits of repentance (cf. Article VI). [12]

Confession to God will follow true repentance. But the burden of this article is on *privat*
confession as opposed to Rome's *auricular* confession with that enumeration of sins, which is nc
commanded because it is impossible really to distinguish between *mortal* and *venial* sins. Priva
confession also "Must not be forced" (*Schwabach* and *Marburg Articles*). It may be made to
friend, and it should be retained because of the spiritual help derived from it. [13]

SIXTH

The Church (Article VII and the introduction to Article VIII), the Ministry (V, VIII, XIV, c
in Part II, Article XXVIII, *Of Ecclesiastical Power*), and the Attitude to Traditional Usages in th
Church (Article XV; cf. in Article XXVIII: *The Power of the Keys and the Jurisdiction of Bishops*
1. *The Church.* The brief Article VII is fundamental. (1) The Definition reads: "Th
Church is the congregation of saints" (*congregatio sanctorum*). This means, as is said in Article VII
that the Church is *properly* (*proprie stricte dictu*) the congregation of saints and true believers.
In a wider sense (*large dictu*), the Church, as an outward organization, is associated with man
who are not saints. But against Rome with its conception of the Church as being fundamentall
and essentially an organization of good and bad, a *corpus mixtum,* the *AC* defines the Church as
membership of *saints.* And against the spiritualistic individualism of the Anabaptists it stressed th
Church as a *congregation.* It should also be noted here that in distinction from the conception c
the Reformed-Presbyterian Churches the Lutherans do not have church government as a third mar
of the Church. They do not believe that the Scriptures intended to communicate a form (for churc
government. (2) The Marks of the Church are seen in the *Gospel* being *rightly taught* an
the Sacraments *rightly administered.* This twice repeated *rightly,* a postscript before delivery of th
Augsburg Confession (cf. our *Introduction,* pp. 182-191; *Story and Signif.,* pp. 144-148), indicate
the ideal in the doctrinal presentation of the saving gospel. (3) Perpetuity is stressed: "Th
One Holy Church is to continue forever." Kingdoms may go out of existence, but against th
Church the gates of hell shall not prevail. (4) As to the Unity of the Church "it is enoug
to agree concerning the doctrine of the Gospel and the administration of the sacraments." It is nc
"necessary that human traditions, rites and ceremonies, instituted by men, should be everywhe
alike." This last statement finds application to the contents of Articles XV and XXVIII (see below)
Note: All this and the following discussion presupposes an actual existence of the Churc
strictly speaking (*proprie*). The One Holy Church, as is declared in the *Apology* (*Book a*
Concord, p. 165, 20), is not a Platonic state, not an "imaginary Church which is to be foun
nowhere," not an abstract conception, but saints "in all the world, in various kingdoms, island
lands and cities, from the rising of the sun to its setting, who have truly learned to know Chris
and His Gospel." [14]
2. *The Ministry:*
A. Its Activity, Article VIII: Since there may be *many hypocrites and evil persons* in th
Church externally considered (*late dictu*) there may also be some in the ministry. In such case
the administration of the sacraments does not lose its validity, as was taught by the Donatists. Fc

[12] On these four points see our *Introduction,* pp. 232-240.
[13] On Confession, as preparation for the Eucharist, see also Article XXV of Part II.
[14] See our *Introduction,* p. 196-198.

both the Sacrament and the Word are effectual by reason of the institution and commandment of Christ."

B. For the sake of good order and because in an officially recognized ministry there will be the guarantee not only for the ethical quality but also for a needed training. Article XIV teaches that "no one should publicly teach in the Church or administer the Sacraments unless he be *regularly called*" (*nisi rite vocatus*). [15]

3. Article XV, supplemented by sections in Article XXVIII, offers guiding thoughts concerning Rites and Usages not commanded by Scripture but which have grown out of the history of the Church. The approach to these discussions may be seen in the closing statement of Article VII: Nor is it necessary that human traditions, rites or ceremonies, instituted by men, should be everywhere alike." The problem of the *adiaphoron* is involved. Articles XV and XXVIII give an evangelical treatment of Sunday observance (carefully to be compared with Luther's discussion in his *Large Catechism*). The principles that should guide us in the observance or rejection of rites and usages in the Church are the following: (1) Ceremonies, divinely commanded, such as the sacraments, must be maintained. (2) With respect to ceremonies, not divinely commanded, there must be liberty. (See Article XXVII *On Monastic Vows*.) (3) Ceremonies, however, should not be multiplied (Article XXIII), because (a) they tend to obscure the doctrine of grace, (b) they may lead men to think lightly of the real commandments, (c) they may burden men's consciences. (4) Yet there are rites and usages which *ought to be observed*, namely, (a) such as are profitable for good order and helpful: as for instance, the observance of the Lord's Day on Sunday instead of Saturday, after the former practice has become the usage (Article XXVIII); (b) where it is dictated by charity, i.e., not to give offense; and (c) as added by the *Formula of Concord* (Chap. X) where it is our duty to profess the truth. [16]

SEVENTH

The *Augsburg Confession* has one article on Civil Affairs. It is Article XVI. Three points are here stressed: (1) Civil government is a divine institution. (2) It is right to hold property. (3) Marriage is pleasing to God. Most of the statements in this article are in explication of point 1 on government. In opposition to the Anabaptists of that day the Lutherans looked upon the government as the natural order. (*Apology*, Chap. VIII, Article XVI.) From this followed a fourfold attitude: (1) *obedience* to the government. This the Lutherans, different from the Reformed people, stressed to the exclusion of revolution. (2) Legitimacy of the different forms of *public redress;* wars, military service, capital punishment, oath "when required by the magistrates." (3) The right of Christians to bear *civil office* (different from the Presbyterian Covenanters). (4) Their right to "sit as judges, to determine matters *by the imperial and other existing laws* even if these should not be in harmony with Scripture. The underlying idea here is recognition of state and Church as separate spheres. Calvin, with Zwingli, said: "God's Word is the law of the nation. The state must execute the laws of the Church. In countries under Calvin's influence the position is taken: "Politics is applied Christianity." [17]

EIGHTH

Some of the Last Things (*Augsburg Confession*, Article XVII. Cf. *Apology*, in *Book of Concord*, pp. 299 ff.; *Large Catechism*, pp. 446 ff.).

1. The *conciliatory tendency* of the Lutherans at Augsburg to Rome must have led them to pass by the Roman teaching of purgatory which with the designation of the pope as antichrist was missed by Luther. [18]

Note: Luther wrote in the *Smalcald Articles* of the pope as "the very antichrist" (p. 320, 10). And again he said (p. 320, 39) that in 2 Thess. 2: 2 "The marks of the antichrist plainly agree with the kingdoms of the pope and his adherents." Did Luther really mean to make this conviction a dogma? On another occasion he wrote as follows: "To me there is no doubt any more that the pope with the Turk is the antichrist; believe what you will." [19]

2. The fundamental statement here is that "Christ shall appear for judgment and raise up all

---

[15] On questions herewith connected, see our *Introduction*, pp. 246-255. Note here the references to Article XXVIII of the *Augsburg Confession* and to Melanchthon's Appendix to the *Smalcald Articles* concerning the relation of pastors to bishops and the relation of the local congregation to synodical organizations.

[16] For a more complete discussion, see our *Introduction*[2], pp. 255-264.

[17] For reading see our *Introd.*, p. 264-270. In *Story and Signif.*, pp. 137-139 (on the "Kingdom").

[18] See his letter to Jonas in: Enders, *Luthers Briefwechsel*, VII, 133.

[19] E, 7, 184.

the dead; He shall give to the godly and elect eternal life and everlasting joys, but ungodly me and the devils he shall condemn to be tormented without end."

Note: It is interesting to observe that in a former draft of our Confession Melanchthon h written "that all deceased men shall be raised up with the same body in which they died." Th he changed to the present reading before the delivery of the documents.[20]

3. Origen's *Apokatastasis,* adopted by the Anabaptists and held by some Universalists, namel that "there will be an end to the punishments of the condemned," is here rejected.

4. The rejection of Chiliasm is put into the following words: "They condemn also others wl are now spreading certain Jewish opinions that before the resurrection of the dead the godly sha take possession of the kingdom of the world, the ungodly being everywhere suppressed."

5. In practical application Lutheranism rejects the following three positions: (1) that Chri will come for a reign of a thousand years before the revelation of antichrist and judgment da (against Heb. 9: 28; Matt. 25: 31); (2) that there will be, on this side of eternity, an ou wardly victorious kingdom of Christ upon earth (against John 18: 36); that we shall expect, o this side of eternity, a time when there shall be no struggle with the enemies of Christ and wi sin and when there shall be no cross to bear (against Acts 14:21, Matt. 16:24, Luke 18:8; 17:26

These are the topics of the *Augsburg Confession* from Article I *On God* to Article XVII *O Eschatology,* with supplementary articles from XVIII to XXI, also in Part II of Confession and i the same certain articles in the *Book of Concord.* Article XXI with an addition on the "Worship Saints" may be grouped with Article XVII because of the epilogue attached to it with its retre spective view over the whole of Part I of the Confession. It begins "This is about the 'sum our Doctrine,'" etc. (Cf. *Book of Concord,* p. 46.)

3. THE APOLOGY OF THE AUGSBURG CONFESSION, published by Mr LANCHTHON immediately after his return from the diet, became necessary because of th official reply to the Confession by the Roman theologians in their so-called *Confutatio* The detailed history belongs to Symbolics. (See a brief, yet comprehensive, review i our *Introduction to the Symb. Books,*[2] pp. 308-314.) The following few statemen may characterize the *Apology* historically: Its chief and permanent value consists in it being the oldest and most authentic interpretation of the *Augsburg Confession* by th author himself. The aim of the *Apology* was (1) to reject the claim of the Romanis that through the *Confutation* the *Confession* had been refuted; (2) to characterize th fundamental differences by tracing them back to the distinction on such terms as la and grace, sin and justification. The doctrine of justification by grace through faith i the pivot of Melanchthon's discussions. (3) Neither does he overlook some other point that needed further elucidation—the doctrine of the Church, the number of sacrament the mass, the invocation of saints, celibacy, etc. As to a summarizing view over th contents see Geo. J. Fritschel in our *Introduction,*[2] pp. 315-354.

Further Literature: The *Confutation* and MELANCHTHON'S *Apology,* in their original edition were published in the *Corp. Ref.,* Vols. 27 and 28, 1-326. PLITT, *Die Apologie der Augustan* 1873. J. FICKER, *Die Konfutation des Augsburgischen Bekenntnisses, ihre erste Gestalt und ihr Geschichte,* 1891. KOLDE, in J. T. MUELLER, *Symbolische Buecher,* beginning with 10th ec (1907). SCHAFF, *Creeds of Christendom,* Vol. I.

4. THE SMALCALD ARTICLES were occasioned by the need of the Lutherans t be prepared in case they should decide to attend the general Council, which the pop had promised to convene. They met at Smalcald, 1537. This time, Luther had preparec the articles. On the Lord's Supper he employed strongly realistic terms. It must b remembered that this was one year after the drafting of the Wittenberg Concord o 1536. Melanchthon in connection with Bucer was interested in toning down the realisti expressions on this subject hoping that a union, not only with the South Germans, bu

---

[20] Kolde. *Aelteste Redaktion.*

also with the Swiss might gradually be effected. Luther also wanted that union, but above all he was determined to safeguard the doctrine of the Real Presence. At first he had written "that under bread and wine there be the true body and blood of Christ in the Supper." But, as we know from comparison of his autograph text with the received text, he crossed that out and wrote: "We hold that bread and wine in the Supper are the true body and blood of Christ, and are given and received not only by the godly, but also by wicked Christians."

Literature: See the connected history on all of this in KOLDE'S contribution to J. T. MUELLER'S *Symbolische Buecher:* also NEVE, *Introduction to the Symb. Bks.,* where we have tried to present the essentials of this rather complicated history in ten brief paragraphs, p. 354 ff. *Luther's autograph text,* in the library of the Heidelberg University, was published by K. Zangemeister. SCHAFF, *Creeds,* vol. I.

5. This section on the *earlier Confessions* must not be closed without calling special attention to the *TRACTATUS OF MELANCHTHON,* appended to the *Smalcald Articles.* In the *First Part,* Melanchthon rejects the *divine right* of the superiority of the pope over all the bishops and pastors; also the pope's so-called "divine right" of the two swords, i.e. his unconditioned power in spiritual and worldly things. The *Second Part,* on the power and jurisdiction of bishops was especially practical because the question of the Lutherans everywhere was: What is our relation to the bishops who claim jurisdiction over us? Melanchthon does not reject an episcopacy as long as it does not claim to be of divine right; from this standpoint there is no difference between bishops and pastors; an ordination by the pastor in his Church is just as valid as that by a bishop. When, therefore, the regular bishops prosecute the Gospel and refuse to ordain proper ministers, then any church has the right to ordain its own ministers. For wherever there is the Church there is also right and duty to preach the Gospel. Yet ordination is no sacrament, but a solemn public confirmation of the one who has been called to preach the Gospel. Schaff calls this *Tractatus* of Melanchthon, adopted at Smalcald, *a theological masterpiece for that age.* (*Creeds,* Vol. I) Here we have "for the first time a doctrine of the papacy and of the authority in the Church, that is founded upon Scripture and history" (Tschackert).

Note: The catechisms of Luther can be omitted from this review because as manuals for catechetical instruction they are not *Confessions* in quite the same sense as are those that have been discussed.

APPENDIX

The Reformed Confessions under the Influence of Zwingli. In this present chapter the chief discussion had to be on the *Earlier Confessions of Lutheranism.* On the *Formula of Concord* there will be a special chapter, after we have received a view of Calvin and his work.

At this place we shall list *the oldest Confessions* which grew out of the Swiss Reformation. They do not have the importance for the Reformed Church as has the *Augsburg Confession* for the Lutheran Church. The interest of the Reformed Churches is in their later Confessions which stood under the influence of Calvin's movement. Four Confessions of the Swiss Reformation under Zwingli have to be mentioned:

(1) *The 67 Articles or Conclusions,* 1523; (2) *The Ten Theses of Berne,* 1528; (3) *The Confessions of Faith to Emperor Charles V,* 1530; (4) *The Exposition of the*

Christian to King Francis I, 1536, edited by Bullinger.   For a lucid discussion of their doctrinal contents we refer to PHILIP SCHAFF, *Creeds*, 1, 369-384.   Cf. our description of Zwingli's Theology in our Bk. III, Chap. II and our literature there given.

Then there are a few Confessions which aimed at a mediation between the followers of Luther and those of Zwingli, chiefly under the influence of M. Bucer: (1) *The First Confession of Basle*, 1534; (2) *The First Helvetic Confession*, 1536; (3) *The Second Helvetic Confession*, 1566.   Schaff calls this last mentioned Confession "the last and best of the Zwinglian family."   He describes its contents in *Creeds*, Vol. I, 390-420.

Chapter Six

BUCER, CALVIN AND THE CONFESSIONAL STANDARDS OF CALVINISM

I. MARTIN BUCER

Literature: PRE, III, 603 ff. Cf. XXIII, 291 f. *The New Schaff-Herzog Encyclopedia. RGG,* , 1294 ff. Cf. *The Dictionary of Biographies.* A. Lang, *Der Evangelienkommentar M. Bucers und die Grundzuege seiner Theologie,* 1900. G. KLINGENBERG, *Das Verhaeltnis Calvins zu Bucer,* 1912. G. ANRICH, *Reformation of Martin Bucer,* 1914. J. L. NEVE, *the Lutherans in the Movements for Church Union,* 1921 (pp. 7-17). W. KOEHLER, *Zwingli und Luther,* I, (Conflict on the Eucharist) 1924. H. EELLS, *Martin Bucer and the Conversion of John Calvin,* 1924; also *The Genesis of Martin Bucer's Doctrine of the Lord's Supper,* 1926. W. PAUCK, with view on *De Regno Christi,* wrote on MARTIN BUCER'S *Conception of the State* (*Princeton Theological Review,* January, 1928), which was enlarged into a book of 208 pages under the title: *Das Reich Gottes auf Erden, Eine Untersuchung zur englischen Staatskirche des 16. Jahrhunderts,* 1930. The Histories of Doctrine, especially: R. SEEBERG, *DG,* IV², 551-556; English ed. II, 390-394.

Martin Bucer (1491-1551) was an Augustinian monk as Luther had been. Since 1518 he was a follower of the Reformation. Later he became the Reformer of Strassburg. His residence in Upper Germany on the Rhine, so near Switzerland, brought him into contact first with theological influences from Zwingli and his group and later with Calvin. It made him the type of mediating theologian for which he is known in history. In 1549, on account of the Counter-Reformation, he was forced to leave Strassburg and accept the invitation of Cranmer to come to England as professor at Cambridge where he soon became an influential factor in the Protestant circles of that country.

Several things attracted the English reformers to Bucer: (1) His mediating position on the Lord's Supper was bound to appeal to them. In this matter he had enjoyed the confidence of Philip of Hesse, and had been untiringly active in efforts of mediating between the Cities of the South and the Lutherans of Northern Germany. While the Augsburg diet was in session he was the leading theologian to formulate the *Tetrapolitana* with its mediatory position regarding the Eucharist. (2) He was endowed with a fine gift to regulate the practical things of the Church, like Bugenhagen in the North, and he organized the Protestant Churches in numerous cities in Upper Germany. (3) In connection with this practical inclination he approached to a considerable extent the peculiar ideals of Christian life, which came to be characteristic of Calvin's reformation. Especially in his book *De Regno Christi,* dedicated to King Edward of England, he developed a conception of the relation between Church and state which is strongly suggestive of the ideas of Calvin (cf. W. Pauck).

Note: Space permits of but very brief reference to the part which Bucer played in the endeavor to bring about a union between Luther and the orphaned Zwinglians and his own followers in the South. The movement resulted in the Wittenberg Concord of 1536, which was drafted by Melanchthon and signed by Luther, Melanchthon, Bugenhagen, Myconius and others on behalf of the Lutherans and by Bucer, Capito, Aulbert on the other side. The text (Latin) will be found in the *Corpus Reformatorum,* III, 375 ff.; English in H. E. JACOBS' *Book of Concord,* II, 253 ff. For a full description of the whole historical situation see NEVE, *Union Movements* (reprint from the *Lutheran Quarterly,* Jan. 1918 to July 1921, cf. Chapter One, which is prefaced by a complete literature).

Bucerism, however, like Zwinglianism, lost its identity as an independent movement; it became a stepping stone to Calvinism. As a theologian Bucer was fundamentally influenced by Luther and, while mediating on the Supper, and differing from Luther on Church and state, as also in his teaching of a double predestination, his soteriological conceptions (sin, grace, justification and sanctification) are formed in agreement with Luther or Melanchthon. In summary it should be noted (1) that it was largely Bucer, in connection with Melanchthon, who transmitted Luther's conception of Christianity to Calvin; and (2) that it was Bucerism, with Melanchthonism, that prepared the way for the German Reformed Church as its exists today (especially along the Rhine) and which put upon these churches the peculiar stamp of a mild Calvinism in the Eucharist, evading, however, the double predestination in Calvin's form of emphasis. It must be admitted, however, that Bucer, influenced by Calvin, had taught the double predestination. [1]

II. JOHN CALVIN. A SURVEY OF HIS THEOLOGY WITH SPECIAL REGARD TO HIS DIFFERENCES FROM LUTHER

Literature: CALVIN'S *Works* are gathered in the *Corpus Reformatorium* (CR) *beginning with* Volume XXIX and filling 59 volumes. Our reference will be chiefly to Volumes XXIX and XXX which contain his *Institutes* (*Institutiones Religionis Christianae*). Volume XXXVI of the *Corpus Reformatorum* contains special theological discussions and Volume XXXIII his catechism. In our quotations and references we follow the 6th edition of ALLEN'S abbreviated English translation from CALVIN'S last (1558) edition of the *Institutes*. There is also an English edition of Calvin's works in 51 volumes, 1843-1855, by the CALVIN TRANSLATION SOCIETY.

Biographies and Estimates: H. HENRY, *John Calvin,* 3 vols., 1835 ff. E. STAEHELIN, 2 vols., 1863. E. DOMERGUE, *Jean Calvin,* 7 vols. (in French); 1899-1927. W. WALKER, *John Calvin,* 1906. H. VON SCHUBERT, *Calvin,* 1909. K. HOLL, *J. Calvin,* 1909. A. LANG, *Johannes Calvin,* 1909, which is No. 99 in the *Schriften des Vereins fuer Reformationsgeschichte.* R. C. HUNT, *Calvin,* 1933. Among the Histories of Doctrine see especially F. LOOFS, FISHER, SHELDON, THOMASIUS-SEEBERG, R. SEEBERG, *DG,* IV³, 551-644 (including the English translation of the older edition). Also P. TSCHACKERT, *Die Enstehung der lutherischen und der reformierten Kirchenlehre,* pages 381-446.

On some special features in the significance of Calvin's teaching see DOMERGUE in an appendix to the above mentioned work where he gives a view of the extensive literature on Calvin which appeared about 1909. Regarding his conception of the relation between Church and state, on which the interest has been intense, the following publications may be mentioned: F. W. KAMPSCHULTE, *J. Calvin, seine Kirche und sein Staat in Genf,* 1869 and 1899. G. BEYERHAUS, *Studien zur Staatsanschauung Calvins,* 1910. H. HUSHERR, *Der Staat in Calvins Gedankenwelt,* 1923. On other matters of special interest see the footnotes.

1. The extent of Calvin's Influence in the Protestant World justified a review of Calvin as a theologian. The Protestants in France and Holland became followers of Calvin. After the reception of Bucer in England and with so many of the English and Scotch Protestants at the time of Queen Mary as refugees in Geneva, it was only natural that Protestantism as developing in Great Britain should side with the theology of Calvin. Our chief interest here is in Puritanism and the Westminster and Scotch Confessions. As to the much debated question concerning the *real presence* in the Lord's Supper, the Thirty-nine Articles of the confession of the Anglicans also stand noticeably on Calvin's side of the dividing line between Lutheranism and Calvinism. Even in Germany, the land of the Lutheran Reformation, large contingents came under the influence of Calvin. The Palatinate adopted the Heidelberg Catechism (1581). Anhalt, Hesse, Lippe, Bremen and even the Hohenzollern with their constantly growing political influ-

---

[1] Seeberg, *DG,* IV², 444.

ence fell in line. Calvin had a following also in the East around Koenigsberg.[2] There were Reformed in the Rhineland, added to Prussia in 1814. In the neighboring countries also were adherents to Calvin's type of Protestantism (Czecho-Slovakia, Hungary). This brief review gives us an impression of Calvin's sphere of influence. Surely in a History of Christian Doctrine Calvin must be studied in connection with his characteristics as a Reformer, the topics of his theology and the historical evolution of his type.

2. *Calvin's Significance.* Calvin as churchman and theologian absorbed the oldest heritage of the Reformed Church from her original reformer, Zwingli, by effecting a doctrinal agreement with his followers, now under the leadership of Bullinger. This was done in the *Zurich Consensus (Tigurinus)* of 1549.[3] The biographer of Calvin, E. Staehelin, pronounces this confessional document "the solemn act by which the Zwinglian and Calvinistic reformations were joined in everlasting wedlock as the one great Reformed Church." (2, 121.) Still, Calvin was not a follower of Zwingli. He called his original purely symbolical conception of the sacraments, particularly on the Lord's Supper, "profane,"[4] and he labored to deepen it. While there is a noticeable approach to Zwingli in the *Consensus,* yet in substance we have here the teaching of Calvin after the manner of Bucer's mediation. The position upon which Calvin settled was that peculiar mediating type of theology of which Bucer had been the chief representative.[5] This, then, is Calvin's historical significance: He succeeded in putting the stamp of his theology on all the various Protestant teachings in Western Europe which had hesitated to include among their tenets Luther's realism, his distinction between Law and Gospel and his conception of a separation of Church and state. By so doing he gradually united all the diverging tendencies within the Reformed Churches, and by further development of these tendencies he made them into a new type of Protestant Christianity.

3. *His Particular Endowment.* Calvin was the greatest among the theologians of the Reformed group. He was not such a prophet as was Luther, who left to the Church much uncoined gold, so that generation after generation continues to study his writings, seemingly without exhausting them. Calvin, like Melanchthon, succeeded in actually coining his own theological thought. Calvin can be studied, exhausted and mastered. He was not creative in the sense that he produced a new world of religious thought. In the main he worked with the ideas of Luther, Augustine and others. But, as Seeberg remarks: "He possessed the wonderful talent of comprehending any given body of religious ideas in its most delicate refinements and giving appropriate expression to the results of his investigations."[6] He was the greatest exegete of the Reformation period, excelling Luther in keen logical thought. He surpassed him and also Melanchthon in the gift of systematizing the new conception of Christianity, which had been brought to light through the Reformation. As a man of the second generation of Reformers he had a distinct advantage over Luther, Zwingli and Melanchthon—the advantage of perspective. But with him that large view over the whole situation was a native gift. In addition to this, he had a remarkable ability for organization and with it, the Frenchman's gift for ruling.

---

[2] For a brief review of all these developments see the writer's book on *The Union Movements,* pp. 19 ff.; 110 ff.

[3] Schaff, *Creeds,* 1, 472.

[4] *CR, XXXIX,* 438.

[5] Cf. A. Lang on *Bucer,* pp. 5 ff., 371 ff.; the same on *Calvin,* p. 47.

[6] *Hist'y of Doctr.,* Eng. II, 394.

Calvin was a Christian statesman. As such he modified and applied in his own way the principles of Protestant religion to the needs of locality and time. Since he lived and labored in a republic, he became the type of an aristocratic republican. This made him the ideal of the Anglo-Saxon in Great Britain. As to America, however, the consistent development into democracy caused this part of Calvin's endowment to be felt as something foreign. Luther turned early from the study of jurisprudence to that of theology. But Calvin was a perfectly trained lawyer. This may account to some extent for his legalistic conception of Christianity to which we must refer. In this respect he reminds us of Tertullian, the father of Roman Catholicism.

4. Relation to the German Reformers. Calvin never met Luther, but he was thoroughly familiar with his writings, and he accepted his teachings in most of the so-called fundamentals. His estimate of him was high. In a letter addressed to Farel, 1551, he said: "If they (Luther and Zwingli) are compared, you yourself know how far Luther excels." [7] Shortly before Luther's death he addressed him as *his most honored father.*[8] Luther, in 1539, wished Calvin well and sent him greetings through Bucer. Especially during the years of his banishment from Geneva and his stay at Strassburg (1538-1541), Calvin inclined strongly to Lutheranism. This attitude was cultivated to a considerable degree by his personal acquaintance and friendship with Melanchthon whom he met at the colloquies at Worms and Regensburg, 1540 and 1541. Calvin was spoken of as an "Upper-German Lutheran."[9]

Later this cordial relationship between Calvin and Lutheranism broke up in consequence of a new conflict over the Lord's Supper. It came about in this way: Following the agreement in the Wittenberg Concord of 1536 between the Lutherans of Northern Germany and Bucer who thought that he could win the Upper German Cities and the orphaned Zwinglians at Zuerich, Luther had desisted from all further controversy on the Eucharist, hoping that a union on this much controverted subject would develop. But Bucer found that he had been too optimistic; he was unable to move the Upper German Cities, not to speak of the Zuerich theologians, into an unreserved recognition of the Wittenberg Concord. Instead of this, Calvin, 1549, succeeded in effecting that union with the former followers of Zwingli reported above and to which Bucer himself and the Cities in the South agreed. Reports were circulated that Luther, because of his silence, had yielded his doctrine of a *real presence.* In addition to all this Luther's own Melanchthon had begun to show the effects from the fellowship and correspondence with Calvin, and from his late co-operation with Bucer. The mediating doctrinal basis for the introduction of the Reformation in Cologne, prepared by Melanchthon with Bucer, revealed the situation.[10] This was the moment when Luther—two years before his death—decided to publish as a final testimony for the *real presence* of Christ's body in the Eucharist his *Brief Confession of the Supper.*[11] With very bitter words against Karlstadt, Schwenkfeld, the Swiss Reformation and its followers *wherever these may be,* Luther confirmed his old teaching as he had given it in his writings against Zwingli in that *Grosses Bekenntniss vom Abendmahl,* in 1528.

---

[7] *CR,* XXXIX, 24.

[8] See A. Lang, *Johann Calvin,* 1909, p. 67.

[9] See E. Troeltsch, *The Social Teachings of the Christian Churches,* English translation 1931, II, 579.

[10] See Koestlin-Kawerau, *Martin Luther* II, 582 ff.

[11] *Kurz Bekenntniss vom Abendmahl,* 1544.

Note: Luther was convinced that his conception of the Supper was the teaching of Scripture, that it was in harmony with the Church's doctrine of a personal union of the two natures of the God-man. In it all Luther acted in harmony with his principle of realism, which permeates his whole system. We see it in his conception of the Word as a means of grace just as much as in his teaching of the sacrament. It is observed especially in the Lutheran teaching on Baptism.[12] Lutheranism in the constituent features of its doctrinal and practical life is an organism. The difference on the Supper is just one symptom of a general difference.

Luther's final Confesson of 1544 was very embarrassing to Calvin who on the basis of the Bucerian formulas had developed a doctrine of the Supper, which, while deeper than that of Zwingli, stood opposed to the Lutheran conception. See Calvin's letter:[13] "I have said that I would regard him (Luther) as a servant of Christ even if he should scold me as a devil." And after Luther's death (Nov. 28, 1552) he wrote to Melanchthon whose friendship he did not want to lose: "You can imagine how painful it would be for me to find myself estranged from the man (Luther) whom I love and honor more than any other and whom God not only adorned with incomparable gifts but whom He, as His most prominent servant, entrusted the administration of the highest things." [14] But with all these pleasant words, Calvin was very determined in the rejection of Luther's teaching on this point.

In 1552, with a publication by J. Westphal, the Lutherans began their polemical activity against Calvin.[15] Calvin at first ignored this and other attacks, but finally he replied in two successive writings.[16] A heated controversy was in progress with many theologians of both sides participating. Calvin replied in a third and last writing.[17] This whole controversy brought further embarrassment to Melanchthon. In his *Ultima Admonitio* Calvin made the statement that he had received the *Augsburg Confession* in the sense in which it had been interpreted by its own author (Melanchthon), meaning by that the altered edition of 1540 ff., which he, with others, had subscribed to at the colloquy in Worms, 1540.[18]

5. We saw that Calvin rejected the Zwinglian view of the Eucharist as "profane." [19] On the other hand, he indulged in the most bitter denunciation when he came to discuss the Lutheran teaching of the real presence. This doctrine was to him a papistic invention, frivolous, and utterly absurd, and the mind of the Lutherans seemed to him "awfully infatuated with the delusions of Satan" (Inst. IV, 17. 18 f., 24 f.). What then was Calvin's own teaching? Vaguely speaking Calvin seems to be pending somewhere between Luther and Zwingli. But toward which of these two positions is he leaning?

In the recent controversy on the Lord's Supper in German theology, Reformed theologians have charged their Lutheran opponents that they do not fairly deal with Calvin inasmuch as they do not make enough of the real distinction between Calvin and Zwingli. We shall let the Reformed theologian Niesel[20] present in brief outline Calvin's teaching on the Lord's Supper:

---

[12] Cf. the writer's *Story and Significance of the Augsburg Confession*, p. 136; and his book on the *Union Movements*, pp. 169-173.

[13] *CR*, XXXIX, 774.

[14] *CR*, XLII, 416.

[15] The title was *Farrago Confuseanarum*, etc., 5 vols. For a characterization of the work, see Kawerau in PRE, XXI, 186.

[16] *Defensio*, etc., and *Secunda Defensio*, etc. See *CR*, XXXVII, I ff. Cf. *PRE*, XXI, 187.

[17] *Ultima Admonitio*, etc. See *CR*, XXXVII, 137 ff.; cf. *PRE*, XXI, 188.

[18] *PRE*, XXI, 187 ff.

[19] *CR*, XXXIX, 438.

[20] *Kalvins Lehre vom Abendmahl*[2] 1935, p. 16.

In his controversy with Westphal, Calvin has finally come to his own concerning
the Eucharist. He laid down the result of this conflict in his edition of the *Institutes*
of 1559, Book Four, chapter seventeen, paragraphs twenty to thirty-four. To this chapter
most of our quotations bear reference.

Niesel agrees that Zwingli's conception did not satisfy Calvin (pp. 33 ff.). In the
view of Calvin, this writer says, "the sacred mystery of the Supper consists of two parts:
the corporeal signs . . . and the spiritual truth, which is at the same time typified and
exhibited by these symbols." This truth, he goes on to say, includes three particulars:
"the signification, the matter of substance, which depends upon the signification, and the
virtue or effect which follows from both" (11). "The signification consists in the promises," i.e. the words of the institution, "Given for you and shed for you, for the forgiveness of sins." These promises of Christ are interwoven with the sign (*ibid*). When
we hear those promises, "we may certainly conclude that the virtue of that life-giving
death will be efficacious with us" (1). The matter or substance of the Supper is "Christ,
with His death and resurrection" (11). The effect consists of "redemption, righteousness, sanctification, eternal life, and all the other benefits which Christ confers upon us"
(*ibid*).

It is evident that these statements have a close resemblance to Luther's views of
the Supper. In clear words Calvin brings out his spiritual-physical conception of the
sacrament: "If, by the breaking of the bread, the Lord truly represents the participation
of His Body, it ought not to be doubted that He truly presents and communicates it"
(10). In all these expresssions Calvin is in close harmony with Luther. The difference
between the two Reformers becomes apparent as soon as we inquire concerning the
modus praesentis (Niesel, pp. 54 ff.). For at the same time, Calvin lays emphasis on
the fact that the earthly elements are merely figures and symbols, that "Christ is not
attached to the element of bread" (12). Bread and wine are token and pledges (1) to
seal and confirm His promises that His flesh is meat indeed, and His blood drink indeed
(4). The *hoc est* in the words of the institution merely have a metonymic meaning.
"As bread nourishes, sustains, and preserves life of the body, so the body of Christ is
the only food to animate and support the life of the soul" (3).

Calvin, no less than Luther, bases his view ultimately on a metaphysical argument.
In the interest of the true humanity of the risen Lord, Calvin feels compelled to reject
Luther's teaching of a local relation of the body of Christ to the bread. The Lord on
the day of His ascension was actually removed from one place to another (27). Calvin
has "not the least doubt that Christ's body is finite, according to the invariable condition
of a human body, and is contained in heaven" (12). Therefore it would be "derogatory
to Christ's celestial glory" to represent Him "as brought under the corruptible elements
of this world" (18). The ubiquity of Christ's body is decidedly denied. Calvin has no
place in his Christology for a participation of Christ's human nature in the attributes of
His divinity, for the *genus majestaticum* (Niesel, p. 84 f.). How then does Calvin
bridge the distance between heaven and earth, Christ and the Church? This he has
effected by the third person of the Holy Trinity, the Holy Spirit. "The Spirit unites
things which are separated by local distance" (10). He is the "channel by which all
that Christ Himself is and has is conveyed to us" (12). And since the Spirit has His
work naturally only in the believing, Calvin is further led to deny the Lutheran teaching
of the receiving of Christ's body also by unworthy communicants (*manducatio indig-*

orum). "I deny," he says, "that it (the Body of Christ) can ever be eaten without the taste of faith" (33). "It is certainly offering an insult, and doing violence to Christ, to attribute to Him a body ... distributed to unbelievers" (*ibid.*). With equal determination Calvin contends that believers receive elsewhere by faith all they receive at the Lord's table (IV, 14. 17), and that we Christians receive nothing beyond that which was received by the saints under the Old Testament (IV, 14. 23).

Calvin is indeed pending somewhere between Luther and Zwingli. To be more exact, he has his place somewhere in the company of Augustine, to whom there are ample references in his discussion on the Eucharist (cf. Niesel, p. 2 f.). Calvin's teaching is neither purely symbolical (Zwingli), nor realistic (Luther), but essentially spiritual. Cf. our *Churches and Sects of Christendom*, pp. 322-327.)

6. In his teaching on *Baptism* Calvin again deepened the very superficial conception of Zwingli. He overcame it through his thoroughly Augustinian and Lutheran conception of man's natural and inherited depravity (see below, 7, a). He writes in his *Institutes:* "Those who have imagined that Baptism is nothing more than a mark or sign by which we profess our religion before men, as soldiers wear their insignia of their sovereign as a mark of their profession, have not considered that which was the principal thing in Baptism." [21] Calvin then speaks of the positive gifts of this sacrament. These he then sums up in "the promise of remission of sins, mortification of the flesh, spiritual vivification and participation of Christ." [22]

It will be necessary both to contrast and to compare Calvin with Luther. To avoid a misunderstanding on the part of many, we first make the following statement: Calvin as well as Luther, while believing in infant baptism, had no thought of limiting the spiritual effect to the moment of baptismal administration; this effect was to both of them for life and through life, as long as the soul feels the need of grace. We have seen articles by Lutheran pastors addressing to their readers the searching question: Are you using your baptism as a means of grace? Calvin speaks of the promise in baptism, he also says that in his own life, although he had been "blind and unbelieving for a long time," this promise "always remained steady, firm and true." [23]

Still, there is on the subject of baptism a marked difference between Calvin and Luther. This appears when the question is asked how these benefits from baptism are communicated and received? Is it by the Holy Spirit *through the sacrament of baptism itself as a means of grace,* or is it through the Holy Spirit *by or rather in connection with baptism as an illustration and a pledge?* Luther had written in his Small Catechism in answer to the question "What benefits does baptism confer?" "It worketh forgiveness of sins, delivers from death and the devil, and gives everlasting salvation to all who believe, as the words and promises of God declare." Speaking on what was to him the heart of baptism he says: "It is not the water, indeed, that produces these effects, but the Word of God which accompanies and is connected with the water, and our faith which relies on the Word of God connected with the water. For the water, without the Word of God is simply water and no baptism. But when connected with the Word of God, it is a baptism; that is, a gracious water of life and a 'washing of regeneration' in the Holy Ghost as St. Paul says to Titus in the third chapter, verses 5-8," etc.

[21] *Inst.* IV. 15. 1. IV. 15. 1-6.
[22] IV. 15. 16.
[23] IV. 15. 17.

Over against this definition of Luther we shall now give the following compre hensive definition by Calvin in his *Institutes:* "He as truly and certainly performs thes things (the benefits) internally on our souls as we see that our bodies are externall washed, immersed and enclosed in water. For this analogy or similitude is a most certai rule of sacraments; that in corporeal things we contemplate spiritual things, just as i they were placed before our eyes, as it has pleased God to represent them to us by sucl figures: not that such blessings are bound or enclosed in the sacrament, or that it ha the power to impart them to us; but only because it is a sign by which the Lord testifie His will, that He is determined to give to us all these things: nor does it merely fee our eyes with a bare prospect of the symbols, but conducts us at the same time to th thing signified, and efficaciously accomplishes that which it represents." [24]

The chief interest of Calvin, pertaining to Baptism as to the Supper, is in th pedagogy of the rite, in the promise of grace, and in the assurance that God will do wha by symbols and analogies He promises to the elect. The benefits are not communicatec through the work of the Word as being in any *necessary connection* with baptism.[2] "Baptism, in the Calvinistic sense, has clearly only representational, symbolical, and con firmatory significance." [26] To Calvin, baptism is a means of grace in the pedagogica sense. This can be seen in the many analogies which he employs in chapter 14 (or the sacraments in general) and 15 (on baptism in particular) of his *Institutes.* It i seen not only in the above quoted definition, but in many other places: "It *resembles* legal instrument—properly attested—by which God assures us (the elect) that all our sin are cancelled, effaced and obliterated so that they will never appear in His sight, not come into His remembrance, nor be imputed to us." [27] "It *shows* us our mortification in Christ and our new life in Him" (*Ib.* 4). "It affords us a *certain testimony* that we are not only engrafted in Christ's life and death, but are so united with Him as tc be partakers of all His benefits" (*Ib.* 5). "Of this regeneration we have *an earnest* in baptism" (IV, 15, 12). One marvels at the wealth of religious thought and the orien tation in Scripture that comes to expression here as everywhere in Calvin's *Institutes* But with all the religious depth of his symbolism and his stress on the work of the Word, in connection with the "representational, symbolical and confirmatory" significance of the baptismal act, he could not bring himself to agree with Luther that the "baptismal act" is the communicating means of grace used by the Holy Spirit in the case of this fundamental sacrament in the Christian's life. This stress upon the pedagogical feature which Luther had also which is Scriptural in a number of respects, should not exclude the realistic meaning of baptism, which was at home in the Church from the beginning

Calvin's definition of a sacrament in general to which he devoted a preparatory chapter (14) is wider than that of Luther. He identified without qualification the circumcision of the Old Testament and John's baptism with Christian baptism.[28] He defined baptism as a "testimony of the grace of God toward us, confirmed by an outward sign, with a reciprocal attestation of our piety towards Him." [29] Baptism was to Calvin,

---

[24] *Inst.,* IV, 15, 14.
[25] *CR,* XXXVII, 118 f.
[26] Geo. W. Richards, *The Heidelberg Catechism,* 1913, p. 89.
[27] *Inst.,* IV, 15, 1.
[28] *Inst.,* IV, 14, 23; IV, 15, 7, 8.
[29] IV. 14. 1.

ne might say, a sermon of God's grace in the form of a promise which is confirmed by water as a sign or a seal.

Calvin, while a strict supernaturalist, was fundamentally averse to the mystery which n Lutheranism appeared in the doctrine of the personal union between the divine and he human natures of Christ, in the union between the spiritual and the corporeal elements of the means of grace and, connected herewith, in the inner identity of the o-called *invisible* and *visible* Church. Calvin, in agreement with Zwingli and following he old Antiochean line of Christological thought (Theodore of Mopsuestia), in contrast o Luther who had his orientation in the Alexandrian Christology (Cyril), sought to olve the mystery by a certain rationalizing process of analyzing, which left the visible nd the invisible to be thought by itself, which dissolves the mystery.

7. *Predestination.* Calvin taught the double predestination (*gemina praedestinatio*): o salvation and to damnation. His own definition of this *decretum horribile*[30] as he imself called it, (III, 21, 5) reads as follows: "Predestination we call the eternal decree of God, by which he has determined in Himself what He would have to become of every ndividual mankind. For they are not all created with a similar destiny; but eternal life s foreordained for some and eternal damnation for others. Every man, therefore, being created for one or the other of these ends, we say, he is predestinated either to life or o death." To Calvin, more outspokenly than by Augustine, the double predestination o reprobation as well as to life is clearly taught in Scripture. In his *Institutes* he devotes a special chapter to this proof (III, 22).

Calvin's double predestination was closely connected with his conception of God's *general providence*. The fact is that the former is nothing but the application of the latter. The eternal predestination of all either to life or death is the working out of God's general providence. This providence has as *its aim* the glory of God and at the same time the salvation of the elect. But this same providence carries with itself the damnation of the non-elect.[31]

To this teaching of Calvin must be added the fact that he thought of God as having planned before creation. He not merely foresaw the fall of the first man and the ruin of posterity in him, but He arranged it all by the determination of His own will. "This (the condemnation of all men), not being attributable to nature, it is evident, must have proceeded from the wonderful counsel of God." "I inquire again, how it came to pass that the fall of Adam, independent of any remedy, should involve so many nations with their infant children in eternal death, but because such was the will of God. . . . It is an awful decree, I confess. But no one can deny that God foreknew the future final fate of man before He created him and that He did foreknow it because it was appointed by His own decree. . . . God not only foresaw the fall of the first man, and the ruin of posterity in him, *but also arranged all by the determination of His own will.* . . . It belongs to His power to rule and govern all things by His hand." [32] C. Hodge puts the following construction upon this *"infralapsarian"* view of Calvin: "God, with the design to reveal His own glory, that is the perfections of His own nature, determined first to create the world; secondly, to permit the fall of man; thirdly, to elect from the mass of fallen men a multitude, whom no man can number, as vessels of mercy," etc.[33]

---

[30] *Inst.*, III, 23, 7.
[31] *Inst.*, III, 24, 1-14.
[32] III, 23, 7.
[33] *Systematic Theology* II, 316. Calvin rejects the idea of a mere "permission," III, 23, 8.

This is the so-called infralapsarian type in the teaching of Calvin himself as compare
with the "supralapsarian" form in the *Second Helvetic Confession,* in the *Decrees o*
Dort, in the *Westminster* and *Scotch Confessions.*

We should also call attention to Calvin's insistence that as to the means of grac
for man's illumination, regeneration and justification only the elect receive the call effe
tively (*specialis vocatio*) while the non-elect either do not hear the Word, or if they d
hear it, remain indifferent and blind: "The supreme Lord, therefore, by depriving o
the communication of His light, and leaving in darkness those whom He has reprobate
makes way for the accomplishment of His predestination." And in the following sectio
we read: "Nor can it be disputed that such to whom God determines not to enlighte
He delivers His doctrine involved in enigmatical obscurity that its only effect may be t
increase their stupidity." [34]

Still, man himself is responsible: "Their perdition depends on the divine predestina
tion in such a manner that the cause and matter are found in themselves." [35] Calvi
was settled upon the position that God Himself is inwardly working in the acts of ev
men as well as in those of the good. Still while He uses the evil for His purposes, H
never commands it.[36] Man himself has the responsibility: "Man falls . . . according t
the appointment of divine providence, but he falls by his own fault." [37] The Christia
believer must resist all temptation of wanting to solve the mystery involved in this doubl
and seemingly contradictory statement: "To be ignorant of things which is neither pos
sible nor lawful to know is to be learned; an eagerness to know them is a species o
madness." [38] At the same time Calvin wanted the doctrine of the double predestinatio
to be preached because to him it is taught in Scriptures as was mentioned above.

Note: Calvin's doctrine of predestination, however, in the supralapsarian form, was accepte
only in Geneva. There it became incorporated in the *Geneva Consensus* of 1552. But large par
of the Reformed churches continue to hold to it in the form which it received in the *Canons o*
Dort and the *Westminster Confession.* It has kept alive the teaching of grace and a fear of Go
which struggles for an attitude of trust in God's providence. Arminianism as a rationalizing facto
tends to a latitudinarianism with dangers as described in Book IV, Chapter II.

8. *Other Tenets of Interest in the Teaching of Calvin.* His conception of Go
received attention in our review of his doctrine of predestination. However, there are a
few topics on which a brief report must be added:

a. On *original sin* Calvin voiced altogether the convictions of Luther and Melanch
thon: He spoke of "an hereditary depravity and corruption of our nature . . . producing
in us those works which Scripture calls works of the flesh." With Paul he calls it "sin"
and its outcroppings are called "fruits of sin." "It is not to be understood as if we
though innocent, were undeservedly loaded with the guilt of his (Adam's) sin; but we
are all subject to a curse in consequence of his transgression. . ." "And therefore infant.
themselves . . . though they have not yet produced the fruits of their iniquity, yet they
have their seed within them . . . and therefore cannot but be odious and abominable to
God" "This depravity never ceases in us, but is perpetually producing new fruits. . ."
"Our nature is not only destitute of all good, but is so fertile in all evils that it canno

---

[34] *Inst.,* III, 24, 12, 13.
[35] III, 23, 8.
[36] Seeberg, *DG,* IV³, 577, referring to *Inst.* I, 18, 4; II, 4, 2.
[37] *Inst.,* III, 23, 8.
[38] III, 23, 10.

:main inactive." He agrees to the term "concupiscence" which means that "everything
a man, the understanding and will, the soul and body, is polluted." [39]   This is Lutheran
nd anti-Zwinglian.

b. Regarding *Christ and His Work:* Calvin has the Chalcedonian conception of the
wo natures in Christ.   But with Zwingli he refused Luther's development of that doc-
ine in the *communicatio idiomatum,* particularly the participation of Christ's humanity
a the omnipresence of his divinity (*genus majestaticum*).   Calvin believed firmly in
ne principle: *Finitum non est capax infiniti.*

In order to be our Saviour Christ needed to be God-man. He had to suffer as man
f we are to participate in the fruit of His suffering. But He had to be God in order
> overcome death.   Calvin presented the work of Christ in the scheme of the threefold
ffice: prophet, high priest and king, as this had first been done by Eusebius of Caesarea.
Ie did not see the efficacy of Christ's redemptive work in an inner law, but he based it
pon God's free will that it should be so. [40]

c. Justification and Sanctification. Calvin took justification in the forensic meaning:
God declares the sinner just for Christ's sake. [41] He based the justification of the sinner
xclusively upon the historic redemption of Christ, not upon the moral renovation
ffected through the Spirit of Christ.   But he taught that in reality the work of sanctifi-
ation connects itself immediately with justification: "Christ, therefore, justifies no one
vhom He does not also sanctify." [42]   Calvin is very careful in balancing the religious
nd the moral interests.   Man's new religious attitude to God rests alone upon His justi-
ication, but what he wants to teach is that no one experiences this justification without
imultaneously receiving the spirit of Sanctification.   Calvin has fine gems of thought
a his argumentation on this subject.   As a reformer of the second generation he could
ake advantage of the discussions and controversies provoked by the earlier statements
>f Luther and Melanchthon on all the pertinent matters.   The matured thoughts of
Lutheranism on these things must be sought in the *Formula of Concord.* [43]

d. The Preaching of the Word as a Means of Grace. The position is taken in agree-
nent with Zwingli that God can also without previous preaching influence the soul
hrough His Spirit. Luther had been so very outspoken in his protest against Zwingli
ind the Anabaptists on this matter.   The words of Calvin, addressed indirectly to the
Lutherans, read as follows: "But they do not consider that when the apostle makes hear-
ng the source of faith, he only describes the ordinary economy and dispensation of the
Lord, which He generally observes in the calling of the people; but he does not prescribe
a perpetual rule, precluding His employment of any other method; which He has cer-
ainly employed in the calling of many to whom He has given the true knowledge of
Himself in an internal manner, by the illumination of His Spirit, without the intervention of any preaching." [44]   The question is whether that which seems to be an immediate revelation has not after all in some way been mediated through the revelation from
the Word.

---

[39] *Inst.,* II, 1, 8.
[40] III, 11, 12.
[41] III, 11, 23.
[42] III, 16, 1.   Compare our discussion of Luther upon this subject, Book III, Chap. I.
[43] For a very helpful guide through the ideas of Calvin on the various topics here referred to see Seeberg,
DG, IV², 584-602.   Cf. the *Eng. Ed.,* II, 401-405. See also Troeltsch, *op. cit.,* II, 580.
[44] *Inst.,* IV, 16, 19.

The real character of Calvin's teaching on the means of grace, particularly of th
Word, appears in the distinction he makes between (1) the external (universal) Wor
which goes to all but touches the non-elect without the inner persistent influence o
the Spirit and (2) the inner effective Word that converts, sanctifies and saves the elect.[45]
This distinction expresses Biblical truth when connected with the teaching of the un
versality of grace, but it is likely to fall outside of evangelical thought when used as a
explanation of the double predestination. Calvin, even more than Luther, stressed th
sacraments as being essentially the Word.

e. The *Church* was to Calvin first of all the number of the elect in all ages.[46] Bu
since predestination, as a rule, will work itself out in connection with the work of th
Word, therefore the Church became to Calvin also the congregation of believers tha
gather around Word and Sacrament. Thus he would speak with Zwingli of an "invisible
Church which is holy, and of a "visible" Church with many hypocrites.[47] It should als
be noted that Calvin was in full agreement with Luther on the objectivity of the Churcl
He said: "I know very well, thank God, that the true efficacy of the sacrament does nc
depend upon the worthiness of him who dispenses it.[48]

Certain differences from Luther appear when we study Calvin's views on the "Churc'
which is visible to man."[49] The Lutherans, who followed Luther in his peculiar way o
combating the spiritualism of the Anabaptists with their radical objection to the though
of a visible Church, were slow in following the Reformed theologians in using the term
"visible" and "invisible." As with regard to the person of Christ, the means of grace
the call, predestination, they held to a conception of an organic union of the spiritua
and the corporeal which has not been favored by Reformed theology, so they did als
with regard to the Church: they wanted to safeguard the conception in which the "in
visible" and the "visible" Church are essentially One Church with a difference only in
two aspects. The *Augsburg Confession* in articles VII and VIII avoids these two terms. I
later exchange of thought with the Reformed theologians the Lutherans also would us
them; but care was taken to speak with proper qualification; the Church "properl
speaking;" or the Church in the "narrower" and "wider" sense.[50] Calvin also calls it th
"universal" Church.[51] In reading the *Institutes* on this subject[52] one marvels at th
comprehensiveness of Calvin's view over all the essentials of the Church which he pic
tures in the language of Scripture and of an experience in which he draws largely fron
Luther and Melanchthon.

f. *Church Organization.* In the matter here indicated Calvin developed a funda
mental difference from Luther. Not only the work of the pastors as ministers of th
Gospel, but a certain organization for the administration of doctrine, cultus and disciplin
in the Church was made a matter of divine right and was regarded as a command o
Scripture. The examples of a church government in the Scriptures, which to Luthe
merely indicated that the gifts of the Spirit in the congregation of believers must worl

---

[45] III, 24, 8; 21, 7.
[46] IV, 1, 7, 8.
[47] *CR*, XXIX, 542. *Inst.*, IV, 1, 7.
[48] See *Briefe*, I, 6, 57, 76, 271.
[49] *Inst.*, IV, 1, 7, 8.
[50] Cf. Neve, *Intr. to Symb. Books*[2], pp. 195-198.
[51] *Inst.*, IV, 9.
[52] IV, 1, 9 ff.

emselves out in a Christian order for the edification of souls, were to Calvin so many
aragraphs of a divine command.[53]

Note: It has been a matter of debate whether the episcopal, or the presbyterian or the con-
regational form of church government was clearly typified by example of Scripture. No wonder
erefore that in denominational history all three of these forms have made their appeal. To Luther
d Melanchthon the question of church government was an adiaphoron. Within the Lutheran
hurch of today, owing to history and conditions, the one or the other of these forms either rules
tirely or prevails in the main. The fact that all the historical churches in their organization
ve taken precaution to counteract the disadvantages of their adopted form of government shows
at here is a field in which there must be freedom. From this standpoint the presbyterian form
hich Calvin introduced also can claim its right.

In the last edition of his *Institutes,* in his *De ecclesia potestate* (Book IV), Calvin
xpressed himself on the powers of the Church in his theory of church government.
n Geneva it was composed of laymen in co-operation with the pastors, perpetuating
self by co-optation; and it was to deal with matters of doctrine, cultus, and discipline.
t had no right to make new dogmas,[54] but it was charged with watching over the funda-
entals[55] and over "a truly evangelical service." [56]

g. Church Discipline. It was a further duty of Calvin's presbytery in Geneva to
dminister discipline after Matthew 18: 15-17.[57] From history we know how this rule
unctioned. A leading principle was the honor and glory of God. "Above all, the
onor of God is maintained in punishing crimes." [58] Within five years, under the the-
cracy situation in Geneva, from 1542-1546, seventy-eight persons were exiled, and
fty-eight were condemned to death. This was at a time when that city had about 20,000
nhabitants.[59] Calvin admonished not to treat the guilty with undue severity.[60] For
xample, he would have had Servetus executed by the sword rather than by the more
orturous fire.

Calvin's mistake was his refusal to recognize the freedom of conscience. In his
ealing with teachers of false doctrine within the Church, Christ speaks of excommuni-
ation after previous brotherly admonition; but neither He nor the apostles have com-
anded that they are to be put to death. Calvin's practice was a return to medieval
ethods which Luther had characterized ironically with the remark: "With a death
entence they solve all argumentation" (*Mit dem Tode loesen sie alle Argumente*).
uther admitted that there might be cases where in the interest of tranquility troublesome
ersons may be banished from the country. But he was opposed to bodily punishment
or heresy.[61] These were his words: "Heresy can never be restrained with force. It must
e grasped in another way. This is not the sort of battle that can be settled with the
word. The weapon here to be used is God's Word. If that does not decide, the decision
ill not be effected by worldly force, though it should drench the whole world with
lood. Heresy is a thing of the soul; no steel can cut it out, no waters can drown it.

[53] IV, the whole of chapter 3
[54] IV, 8, 10.
[55] *CR,* LXXVII, 307.
[56] *Inst.,* IV, 10, 1. 5. 8. 27 ff
[57] IV, 11, 1.
[58] *CR,* XLI, 76.
[59] Tschackert, p. 386. R. Staehelin in *PRE,* III, 668.
[60] *Inst.,* IV, 12, 8; II, 2.
[61] Luther wrote to Brenz, 1529: *Man soll keine falschen Lehrer toeten; es ist genug, dass man sie verweise.*
e must not kill false teachers; it is enough to send them out of the country. Enders, *Luther's Correspondence,*
211.

God's Word alone can destroy it." [62] It should here be remarked that regarding t execution of Servetus, Melanchthon was in agreement with Calvin.[63] In the history Lutheranism we have the execution of N. Krell.[64] Here however political conditio contributed to the tragedy. As to the death of Servetus it must be kept in mind that was the outcome of a theocratic situation. The government acted in agreement wi Calvin.[65]

h. Relation between Church and State. To Calvin, the Church is an institution divine right (*de jure divino*) and as such serves for the salvation of souls. To Luth the Church is essentially the congregation of saints gathering around the means of grac and as such becomes an institution only *de jure humano.* Calvin stresses the independen of the Church from the state.[66] It was on Calvinistic territory in England and Ameri where this idea of Calvin was first developed and realized. But Calvin taught that t state, in addition to its duty of safeguarding peace and order, must see to it that t right kind of doctrine and worship be maintained, and also that the sins against the fir table of the commandments be punished. He demanded that the state conform its law to the divine law.[67] The ministers of the Church are chiefly the ones to say what is t right religion. Calvin naturally could not allow the state to settle Church matters upc the basis of its principles.[68] The officers of the Church were thus to be the judges state affairs involving religion and morals. This then was the situation: in spite of t admission that the state is sovereign and must be obeyed as long as this can be do without sin,[69] yet the Church dictated to the state in matters of religion and morals an demanded that the state help Christianize the world and permeate the social order an the whole civilization with the ethical principles of Christianity—with force where th becomes necessary. Zwingli had stressed the same principle. Thus the overthrow Roman Catholic practice of using the state for realizing the ideals of the Church aga came into Protestantism by the back door.

i. Calvin sought a field for the activity of his followers also in the sphere of *soci economy.* Trade and industry were to be used for God's glory. Here Calvin and h followers can claim successes which Lutheranism never had. A large part, however, the explanation of the interest and successes of the peoples under the influence of Calvi ism must be sought in the fact that the West of Europe along the Atlantic (Hollan France, and England as seafaring countries) was commercially far more developed tha was Germany and the central states of Europe. Wealth is easily followed by a highe articulation of the cultural interests. Seeberg calls attention to the fact that under centr European conditions, as in Poland, Hungary and Germany, Calvinism did not have th same success. Outstanding Luther scholars, such as H. Boehmer and R. Seeberg empha ically protest against the picture of Luther's ethics which Troeltsch has drawn as the basi

---

[62] *Luther's Works, W* 11, p. 268. See also Luther's *Address to the German Nobility,* translated by Wace an Bucheim, p. 75.

[63] *CR,* VIII, 326; 9, 763.

[64] See our *Union Movements,* p. 28 ff. Cf. *PRE,* XXI, 85 ff. Kurtz, Eng. Ed., par. 141, 13.

[65] Calvin's demand for the punishment of heretics was reflected in the *Second Helvetic Confession,* 30; also the *Gallic Confession* 30; also in the *Hungarian Confession* 5, 32.

[66] *Inst.,* IV, 11, 5.

[67] IV, 20, 2. 20. *CR,* XXXIII, 354. This was adopted in the strictly *Calvinistic Belgic Conf.* 36, and t *Hungarian Conf.* 5, 32.

[68] *Inst.* IV, 20, 3. *CR,* XLI, 76.

[69] *Inst.* IV, 20, 22 ff.

f Luther's social ideas. Seeberg calls this picture *ganz verzeichnet*, i.e. badly mis-rawn.[70]

j. From Calvin's view of the relation between Church and state we may separate *Calvin's philosophy of the state and particularly his views of the relation of the citizens › the sovereign.* To the individual citizen Calvin preached loyalty even in cases where ›vereigns are tyrants and neglect their duty. His reason is that "they have their govern-ment only from Him" (God),[71] and that it is the "Most High" who "removeth Kings nd setteth up Kings and giveth (the kingdom) to whomsoever He will." (*Ibid.* 26.) Ie says "We shall not hesitate to regard the most iniquitous tyrant with the honor due › the station in which the Lord has deigned to place him." (*Ibid.*) Calvin cited Scrip-ıre to be observed so that "seditious thoughts may never enter our minds" (27). With egard to the government of cruel tyrants he says: "Nothing remains for us than to serve nd to live" (28). Again: "For us it is to obey and suffer" (31). It is in this paragraph ׳here Calvin says: "This observation I always apply to private persons." One exception nly he will admit and even stress: "If they command anything against Him it ought ₁ot to have the least attention; nor, in this case, ought we to pay any regard to all that .ignity attached to magistrates" (32). But after these instructions for private persons .ave been given he now added the following very significant paragraph which in certain ituations, especially in countries of Calvinistic influence, has determined political history. ›alvin writes (*Ibid.* 31): "If there be, in the present day, any magistrates appointed for he protection of the people and the moderation of the power of kings such as were, in ncient times, the Ephori, who were a check upon the kings among the Lacedaemonians, ›r the popular Tribunes upon the Consuls among the Romans, or the Demarchi upon the ‹enate among the Athenians; or with power such as perhaps is now possessed by the Three Estates in every kingdom when they are assembled; I am so far from prohibiting ׳em, in the discharge of their duty, to oppose the violence and cruelty of kings, that I ffirm that, if they connive at kings in their oppression of the people, such forbearance ׳volves the most nefarious perfidity, because they fraudulently betray the liberty of their ›eople, of which they know that they have been appointed protectors by the ordination ›f God."

In the Netherlands, in Scotland, in England, and in America, then, appeared the ituations in which that citizenship of a "lower government" functioned in judgment of ׳e higher government. Zwingli, who had also preached obedience to the government,[72] ￼ade provisions for revolutions in case of unfaithfulness to the "rule of Christ." He ꭉcognized authority in the sovereignty of the people. The majority has the right to ￼ethrone godless kings.[73]

9. Calvin's Authorities for Christian Doctrine.

a. The Nature of Calvin's Biblicism. Having completed our review of Calvin's ￼eology with special regard to his difference from Luther, we shall now close with a ￼rief review of the authorities from which he drew or by which he was guided in the rection of his system.

<hr>
[70] See Troeltsch, as referred to, pp. 554 ff. Seeberg *DG*, IV³, 276 ff. H. Boehmer, *Luther*, English trans-ation. Of special interest for Lutheran thought and work on this subject is volume 2 of W. Elert's *Morphologie es Luthertums*, 1932 (first volume 1931 on matters of faith). Here the author discusses the nationalities of ￼utherans, their family life, their conception of the state, their attitude to politics, war, to the classes of society, ￷ the economic problems in all directions. This volume must be read together with the one by Troeltsch.
[71] *Inst.* IV, 20. 25.
[72] *Works,* ed. Schuler and Schulthess, I, 156. 449.
[73] I, 370; cf. IV, 42, 59.

As with Luther, the Scriptures were to Calvin the only source and norm of Christian truth. [74] They are divinely inspired. By inspiration Calvin means essentially a dictate of the whole content of the Bible. [75] To this teaching of a verbal inspiration of the book as such he added as a support his doctrine of a "testimony of the Holy Spirit" (*testimonium Spiritus sancti*).[76] Against the Roman Catholic view that the Bible had received its authority through the Church Calvin taught a "directly communicated inner testimony which gives us a certainty of the Scriptures' authority that stands above all human logic" (Tschackert). [77] Calvin, like Luther, was an opponent of the Anabaptists with their theology of the "inner light." Against them Calvin now had to show the difference between the testimony of the truly divine Holy Spirit and the easily misleading human spirit. This he did by continuing to establish himself on the verbal inspiration of the Scriptures. [78] In general it must be said that Calvin stresses Scripture as a book of laws from heaven that is to be obeyed to the letter. He went beyond Luther by offering a doctrine of the canon, carefully describing its composition. [79] Several of the Reformed Confessions have followed him by giving a list of the Biblical books. [80]

It was this way of viewing the Bible as a divine code of laws in the form of a definite collection that has become embarrassing also for the perfectly reverent and legitimate historical investigation of the sacred writings in the field of Biblical introduction and criticism. [81]

b. Calvin agreed with the Lutherans in the adoption of the ecumenical creeds, "for they contain nothing but the pure and natural interpretation of the Scriptures." [82] The Scriptures themselves, of course, must remain the real norm by which all later doctrines are to be judged, but these old creeds, Calvin says, will stand the test.[83]

10. Calvin's Humanism.

There must be a few remarks on a certain humanism which colored the theology of Calvin.[84] His commentary to Seneca's *De clementia* indicates his interest and inclination. The form of his writings shows the balance and moderation of the humanists. He also betrays influences from the "biblicistic" features of the humanism of Erasmus and from other sources. He combined scholarship with religion, culture with morality. This, in a way, had been Melanchthon's aim although he had been making practical use of it only in his organization of the university studies. Zwingli was a decided follower of humanism. But Calvin's strong inclination to Luther and Melanchthon kept him from sacrificing any of the evangelical essentials. Humanism, however, was to him not just a means of interpreting the Bible as with Luther, but a new world of moral culture, to which he felt himself attracted. His Lutheran opponents in the succeeding centuries of

---

[74] *Inst.*, III, 21, 3.

[75] IV, 8, 6, 9.

[76] See 2nd ed. of the *Institutes* in CR, XXIX, 299; XXX, 56 ff. Cf. 3rd ed., I, 3, 7; 9, 3.

[77] Historically considered, this teaching represents a combination of views in the later Middle Ages with thoughts of Luther.

[78] Seeberg, *ibidem*.

[79] IV, 8, 6.

[80] *Gallic Conf.*, 3. Belgic, 4. Anglican, 5. *Westminster*, I, 1 f.

[81] Cf. P. Tschackert, pp. 394 ff. Cf. our *Union Movements*, p. 171 ff.

[82] *Inst.*, IV, 9, 8.

[83] I, 8, 3; II, 16, 18. Occasional remarks of a critical nature, which he has uttered, must not be taken to detract from his fundamental agreement with the teaching of these symbols. Cf. Tschackert, p. 395 ff.

[84] See *Union Movements*, pp. 83 ff., 102 ff. Here the special reference is to Seeberg, DG, IV², 558 ff.; cf. 629 f.

onflict have always dwelt upon this trait in Calvin and Calvinism. [85]   In studying the iffering traits in Luther and Calvin, attention has been called to the fact that Luther was a friend of German mysticism; Calvin spoke in decidedly disapproving terms of the Deutsche Theologie" which was a leading representation of German Mysticism. [86]   But his has been observed, that in the aim of making the deeply mystical thoughts of Luther more tangible, Calvin, like Melanchthon, has rationalized or, let us say in the case of Calvin, spiritualized the more deeply religious tenets of Luther.

III. Brief Review of the Confessional Standards of the Reformed Churches

Literature: PHILIP SCHAFF, *Creeds,* I, Ch. 7; III, Part 2.   R. SEEBERG, *DG,* IV³, 644 ff. and 48 ff.   On Calvin's *Institutes* see E. KLOTSCHE, *Christian Symbolics,* 1929, 194 ff.

1. CALVIN'S *Institutes (Institutiones religionis christianae)* in the matured form of its third edition of 1559 may be called in general the real bond of union between the followers of Calvin.   This does not include the supralapsarian forms of his double predestination.   The first edition of 1536 followed Luther's catechism; the second edition of 1539, written in Strassburg and trebled in size, was intended as a handbook for students.   In this edition he began with the inspiration of Scripture to which he added the inner testimony of the Holy Spirit.   He also introduced the completed double predestination (in opposition to Melanchthon who evaded predestination).   The third edition presented the systematically rounded form of this great work.[87]

2. The First Reformed Writings (under influences from Bucer and Zwingli).

In the years after the delivery of the *Augsburg Confession* (1530), especially after the death of Zwingli (1531), a number of Confessions came into existence, which generally expressed the Zwinglian type of teaching, and yet aimed at not losing too much touch with Lutheranism.

a. In this class of documents belongs the *Tetrapolitana,* the Confession of the four cities of Strassburg, Constance, Memmingen and Lindau.   This Confession (23 articles) was delivered to Charles V at the Augsburg Diet, July 9, 1530.   The authorship belongs to the Strassburg theologians Bucer and Capito.   These men had been under the influence of both Luther and Zwingli, but wanted their Confession to be "neither Lutheran nor Zwinglian."   The phraseology in the article on the Lord's Supper sounds Lutheran: "The true Body and the true Blood is truly received as food for the soul."   But this meant, according to the *Strassburg Apology,* that "Christ is truly present and received in the Supper." [88]

b. The agreements arrived at by the synod held at Bern (1532), which was directed by Capito, also show the union tendency in the language on the Lord's Supper.   Zwingli's doctrine is deepened and supplemented.   The sacraments are not just signs, but they are at the same time a secret power.   The believer receives Christ's Body and Blood by

[85] Cf. Loescher, *Historia Motuum* II, 187 ff.   See H. Schmidt, *Geschichte der synkretistischen Streitigkeiten,* 1846, pp. 14 to 16.
[86] *CR,* XLV, 441 ff.
[87] All editions are found in the *Corp. Ref.* For a full description of the contents see Tschackert, pp. 394. Cf. Koestlin, in *Theologische Studien und Kritiken,* 1868, 417 ff.
[88] Cf. *PRE,* XIX, 561, line 47 ff.   See the text in *Bekenntnisschriften der reformierten Kirche,* edited by Mueller (1903), pp. 55-78.   Cf. A. Paetzold, *Die Konfutation des Vierstaedterbekenntnisses* (1900).

which he is fed spiritually just as the mortal body is fed by bread and wine (Chapter XX, cf. XXII). Here we notice clearly the transition to Calvin's theory. [89]

c. The *Confession of Basle,* prepared by Oswald Myconius, 1534, which is an expansion of a deliverance by Oecolampadius, [90] also belongs to this class. The Strassburgers were not quite satisfied with the section on the Lord's Supper, charging that it would be a communion without Christ.

d. The First Helvetic Confession of 1536, composed by Bullinger, Myconius and others, has its significance in that it is, as Schaff remarks, "the first Confession which represented the faith of all the Reformed cantons of Switzerland." [91]

3. Next follow the Confessions under influence of Calvin's theology. The details of their history and significance belong to Symbolics. Here we must not do more than enumerate.

a. First to be mentioned is the *Zurich Consensus* of 1549 (Tigurinus), in which Calvin took over the Zwinglian Reformation. (We repeat Staehelin's remark: "The solemn act by which the Zwinglian and Calvinistic Reformation joined in everlasting wedlock.")

b. Among the many others there are: (1) *The Second Helvetic Confession* of 1566, which rejected the "hypothetical universalism" of Amyraldus and reaffirmed the double predestination; (2) *The Heidelberg Catechism* in Germany, 1563; (3) *The Westminster Confession* in Great Britain, 1647. These have been or will be spoken of in other connections.

c. Special mention must be made of the *Canons of the Synod at Dort* (1618-19), and its counterpart, the *Confession by Episcopius* (1620), which reaffirmed the 5 articles of remonstration by the Arminians. The special interest in this case was in the bitter conflict in Holland over Calvin's double predestination. (See Book Four, in our Vol. II, Chapter II.)

Calvin was a Reformer of the second generation. So it came that he saw himself before the task not, first of all, to lay the doctrinal foundations which had been the chief work of his predecessors, but to organize and to establish, and to reach out into new territories. A large part of Calvin's interest was in law and order and discipline. But, didactically also, he succeeded in his *Institutes* in casting all the religiously practical principles of the Reformation independently into a theologically systematized form.

The author of this volume should not be expected to duplicate what he has discussed rather extensively regarding the "Reformed and Presbyterians" in his recently published book *Churches and Sects of Christendom,* 1940. Furthermore, in Volume Two of this present work the Chapters II and III on Arminianism in *Holland* and *England* will be supplementary to this present discussion on Calvinism.

---

[89] See in *PRE,* II, 621, line 34 ff.
[90] Cf. *PRE,* II, 426, 40.
[91] See the text in 27 articles, German and Latin, in Schaff. *Creeds,* III, 209-31.

Chapter Seven

CONTROVERSIES IN THE LUTHERAN CHURCH AND THEIR SETTLEMENT IN THE FORMULA OF CONCORD

1. For Orientation. It will be remembered that in the ancient Church the first simple Rules of Faith, as expressed in the so-called Apostles' Creed, were soon developed into the speculatively stated definitions of the *Symbolum Quicunque* (Athanasian Creed). In like manner "the great prophetic age of Protestantism was followed by a didactic age." [1] Controversies were bound to arise. They came in the form of deep-going conflicts which caused divisions among the Lutherans and made settlements necessary. Many of the controversies, which lasted for almost thirty years (1548 to 1577), were not edifying in character. But they were necessary for the final establishment of Lutheranism. "Pathological" reviews, such as are given by Jacob Planck in his *Entstehung des protestantischen Lehrbegriffs* (1781-1800), are out of place in our discussion. What we need to remember is that the Lutheran Church will always aim to find her bond of unity in the *pure doctrine* of the Word. The controversies, which we now purpose to review, represented the endeavor of the Lutheran Church to achieve this kind of unity.

For special reading the student is referred to the chapter by Geo. J. Fritschel in our *Introduction to the Symbolical Books of the Lutheran Church,*[2] pp. 401-444.

JACOB ANDREAE (pupil of Brenz and one of the special adherents of Luther) and MARTIN CHEMNITZ (pupil of Melanchthon) were the chief authors of the *Formula of Concord.* Their work was finished 1577. It was promulgated in the *Book of Concord,* on the 25th of June, 1580 (the day of the delivery of the *Augsburg Confession*).

As to standards for the doctrinal deliverances, the *Formula of Concord* recognized: (1) The Scriptures as the only source of Christian life and doctrine; (2) the Ecumenical Symbols as confessions of the ancient Church; (3) the *Augsburg Confession* "as symbol of our time"; interpreted by the *Apology* and the *Smalcald Articles,* with the *Catechisms of Luther* as *popular presentations of the same doctrine.*

The *Formula of Concord* presents itself in two parts: I, in the Epitome (*People's Ed. of the BC,* English, pp. 491-532); II, in a Comprehensive Summary (pp. 532-671). In consists of twelve articles, dealing exclusively with differences among the Lutherans in the post-Reformation age.

The Irenic Tendency is noticeable. Where errors were to be pointed out (in cases such as controversies with Flacius, Osiander, Agricola, Major, Amsdorf, Strigel, Melanchthon), the names of the teachers were not mentioned. It was to be a formula of *concord* on the basis of Luther's theology. Luther's name alone is mentioned. The chief aim was to bring about a union between the *Gnesio-Lutherans* (Flacius and others) and the Melanchthonians. After many years of vain efforts for union by the princes and theologians (between 1555 and 1570), Andreae together with Chemnitz succeeded in the task (between 1573 and 1577). See the narrative by Geo. J. Fritschel in our *Introduction,* mentioned above, pp. 410-418.

The result of the publication of the *Formula of Concord* was the prevailing of Luther's theology, chiefly with regard to the matters on which Zwingli and his followers, Bucer with his union endeavors, and Calvin, had expressed an opposite position; but also with regard to teachings in which Melanchthon or his followers (Philippists) had taken a different position from Luther. For a

---

[1] Seeberg, English ed., II. 363.

brief and convenient view over the whole range of these differences, which our Chapter is to discuss in details, the student will find in the brief review which Geo. J. Fritschel has presented in our *Introduction*.

The first reply by the Reformed to the *Formula of Concord* came from the *Newsted Admonition* (1581) (*Neostadiensium Admonitio*),[2] followed later (1607) by HOSPINIAN'S *Concordia Discors*, to which J. HUTTER replied in his *Concordia Concors* (1614).

2. Our Plan of Discussion. We can best find our way through the apparent chaos of controverted issues by organizing our material as Thomasius and Tschackert have done and by dealing (1) with the controversies affecting, in a special way, the heart of Lutheranism—namely, the Antinomian and the Osiandrian conflicts; (2) with the controversies bearing upon the conflict between Lutheranism and Melanchthonianism or Philippism—namely the Adiaphoristic, the Majoristic, and the Synergistic conflicts; (3) with the controversies which cleared up the relation between Lutheranism and Calvinism—namely, the Crypto-Calvinistic conflict over the Lord's Supper and the Person of Christ; to which we shall add the discussion of Predestination. The settlement of all these agitations was finally reached in the Formula of Concord.

Literature: We cite the following literature for further reading: R. SEEBERG, *History of Doctrine,* English ed., 1905, II, 363-390; German, IV,[3] 1920, 530 ff.   G. P. FISHER, *History of Christian Doctrine* (1906), pp. 291-297.   P. TSCHACKERT, *Entstehung der luth. und der ref. Kirchenlehre* (1910), pp. 477-564.   LOOFS, *Dogmengeschichte,*[4] pp 912-931.   F. H. R. FRANK, *Theologie der Konkordienformel* (4 volumes), 1858 ff.   G. THOMASIUS, *Das Bekenntnis der ev. luth. Kirche in der Konsequenz seines Prinzips* (1848).   O. RITSCHL, *Dogmengeschichte des Protestantismus,* 4 vols., 1908-1927.   GEO. J. FRITSCHEL, *The Formula of Concord* (1916). Article in the *PRE,* 732 ff., FRANK-SEEBERG. T. BENTE in the *Triglotta,* 1921.

I. CONTROVERSIES BEARING ON THE SPECIFICALLY LUTHERAN PRINCIPLE

A. THE ANTINOMIAN CONTROVERSIES

1. In order to understand *the first outbreak of this controversy* we must refer to what Luther had taught in his *Freedom of the Christian Man.* The believer is free from the Law as an outward authority; the Gospel furnishes the needful impulse for good works. In answer to the question as to how repentance is brought about, Luther's reference was to the Gospel—a teaching which was grossly misapplied by many in the Peasants' War of 1524. But along with this teaching on the freedom of the Christian man, Luther had preached (beginning with 1517, and not beginning after his experience with the peasants, cf. Tschackert, p. 479) the need of the Law as the chief instrument for working repentance. He had warned against an under-estimation of the Old Testament and had spoken of Moses as the *father of all prophets.*

2. John Agricola of Eisleben seized upon the one side of this teaching of the great Reformer and caused the first outbreak of the Antinomistic controversies.[3] In his *Instructions for the Visitation of the Saxon Churches* (1527), Melanchthon had written "that the ministers should also preach the Law in order to bring people to repentance." As a result, he was attacked by Agricola who contended that repentance is produced not by the Law, but by the Gospel. Luther sided with Melanchthon. Ten years later Agricola staged the real controversy by attacking Luther himself. He maintained that there is no

---

[2] See our *Introduction,* p. 186, and closing paragraph of this chapter.
[3] For a monograph on "Johann Agricola" see Kawerau, Berlin, 1881; also his article in *PRE,* I, 249 ff., cf. 585 ff.: see also Tschackert, 479 ff.; and Fritschel, 166f.

eed whatever for the preaching of the Law: "The Decalogue belongs to the hall of justice, not to the pulpit;" "Man is overpowered by the kindness of God, and thereupon renounces his former life and shrinks from incurring the displeasure of his heavenly Father."[4] Six public disputations were held by Luther. Although Agricola revoked, he never really gave up his views. He felt that he was called to establish, against Luther, the real doctrine of free grace.[5]

3. *A second Antinomistic controversy* arose through such men as A. Poach and A. Otto, of whom the latter stood on the side of Amsdorf. They gave utterance to statements like these: "The best art of the Christian is to know nothing of the Law;" "Evangelical preachers must preach the Gospel and not the Law;" "Law, good works, and new obedience do not belong to the kingdom of God, but to the world, to Moses and the dominion of the pope." This type of radicalism received its answer in the following historical statements which are reminiscent of Luther in his second disputation with Agricola: "The Law of God has a threefold duty—(1) to produce outward righteousness among the ungodly through threats and promises (*usus legis politicus*); (2) to produce contrition in the heart of the sinner so that in the terrors of conscience he will accept the grace of God offered to him in Christ (*usus legis paedagogicus*); (3) to serve the converted Christian as a guide and a canon in the doing of works 'commanded by God' (*mandata a Deo*, cf. *Augsburg Confession*, article VI) (*usus legis didacticus*)."[6]

4. In Article V the *Formula of Concord* undertook to solve the difficulty by defining the terms *repentance* and *Gospel*. The Law, in its strictest sense, is the divine revelation of God's will, His wrath, and His punishment of sin and unbelief (17-19). The Gospel, in its strictest sense, is the divine revelation of God's grace in atonement, forgiveness, and salvation (20). Everything that threatens and condemns is *Law;* and everything that comforts and offers grace is *Gospel*. These two were preached from the beginning and must be preached to the end (21-26).

Article VI of the *Formula* introduced a special discussion of the *Third Use of the Law*. It shows the need of the Law after conversion. We follow the summarizing statements of Fritschel: The Law is indispensable for holiness of life; if Chrisians were perfectly renewed, they would not need the Law; but since renewal has only begun and they still have the Old Adam, they need also the Law and its instructions, warnings and punishment (7-9).

A distinction is made between *the works of the Law and the fruits of the Spirit:* (1) The Law demands newness of life, but gives no power to produce it; the Gospel brings the Holy Spirit and renews men's hearts, instructs them through the Law, admonishes and, if they sin, punishes them (11-14); (2) The unregenerate can produce only the works of servants, while the regenerate, as children of grace, produce works as the fruits of the Spirit (15-17).

Why do believers still need the Law? Without it they would improvise works of their own. Furthermore, they need to be reminded of their imperfection (20-21).[7]

[4] Seeberg, English edition II, 251.
[5] See Kawerau and Seeberg, *ut supra;* Fritschel, 167; Tschackert, *Entstehung*, 480-483.
[6] Fritschel, 168; cf. Tschackert, 488; also our *Introd. to Symb. Bks.*, 412 f.
[7] Compare Seeberg II, 385 f. See also our *Introd. to the Symb. Bks.*, 395, 412-413.

B. THE OSIANDRIAN CONTROVERSY

Literature: On the history and literature regarding A. Osiander, first at Nuremberg and later at Koenigsberg, consult the various Church Histories and Encyclopedias. Osiander has found a special biographer in Prof. W. MOELLER (Elberfeld, 1870), whose article in *PRE* has been brought up to date by Tschackert. For a review of the whole literature see TSCHACKERT *Entstehung*, p. 489. On the conflict, consult SEEBERG, English ed., II, 369 (*DG*, IV³, p. 496 ff.) also FRITSCHEL, *Formula of Concord*, 154 ff.

1. Osiander confounded justification and sanctification. His special teaching on justification is part of a comprehensive system. (For a convenient review of this system we refer the student to Seeberg, English ed., II, 370 ff.). On the doctrine of justification he regarded himself as being, in the main, on the Lutheran side against Romanism. But he objected to a mere imputation of Christ's righteousness as the basis of the sinner's adoption. This does not mean that he did not have Luther's doctrine of atonement. In fact, he taught that Christ, by His innocent sufferings, had endured "the wrath of God and obtained for us the forgiveness of sins;" also that He had "fulfilled the Law purely and perfectly for us and for our benefit, in order that it might not be imputed to us, nor we be accursed because we do not in this life perfectly fulfill the Law." But, approaching the views of mysticism, he taught that justification through faith is a process of becoming righteous by the indwelling of the divine nature of Christ in the believer. Osiander emphasized the *Christ in us,* while Luther had established himself upon the *Christ for us* as the source of man's renewal.

F. Stancaro, an Italian, introduced the view that Christ is our righteousness according to His human nature only.

2. In Article III the *Formula of Concord* was obliged to make a pronouncement upon these matters because of the controversy which arose. Concerning Justification through Faith the *Apology* is quoted with its evaluation of this article as "the chief in the entire Christian doctrine without which no poor conscience has any firm consolation, or can know aright the riches of the grace of Christ" (6). Emphasis is placed on the following items: (1) "Our righteousness rests not upon one or the other nature of Christ, but upon His whole Person Who alone, as both God and Man, is in His entire and most perfect obedience our righteousness" (55); (2) The *most perfect obedience* of Christ, which was manifested *in doing and suffering* (14-15),[8] constitutes the merits of Christ which God imputes to us for righteousness (30); this is justification which is defined as meaning, *to absolve for the sake of Christ* (17). (3) But this justification is apprehended by faith, not because faith is the beginning of the new life, but because it is the receptive organ which appropriates the merit of Christ (13, 31). (4) But faith, which apprehends justification, cannot be without true contrition.[9] This explains the beginning of a life of sanctification (*inchoata renovatio*) which must and will of necessity now follow. This "incipient righteousness or renewal is," however, "incomplete and imperfect in this life because of the flesh" and, therefore, we cannot stand before God upon this ground; the only safe ground is "the righteousness of the obedience, suffering and death of Christ which is imputed to faith" (32).

---

[8] This was the beginning of the terms "active" and "passive" obedience in the teaching of the Church. Cf. footnote in Seeberg, English ed., II, 371.

[9] In the narrower sense, cf. our interpretation of Art. XII of the *Augs. Conf.* Cf. A. Koeberle, *Quest for Holiness*, pp. 92-94, *Excursus;* E. Hirsch, *Die Theologie des Andreas Osiander*, 1919; H. W. Heidland, *Die Anrechnung des Glaubens zur Gerechtigkeit*, 1936, pp. 134 ff.

II. The Conflicts of Lutheranism with Melanchthonianism

or

The Adiaphoristic, the Majoristic, and the Synergistic Controversies, and Their Settlement in the Formula of Concord

A. The Adiaphoristic or Intermistic Controversy [10]

1. After having defeated the Smalcald Federation of the Protestant princes (1547), Charles V was now ready to restore the unity of the Church. The *Augsburg Interim,* which had been drafted by a Roman theologian of the old school and finished by Bishop John Pflug in company with John Agricola (then court-preacher at Brandenburg, was published on May 15, 1548. It contained twenty-five articles which all the churches of Germany, Romanist as well as Protestant, were to accept as an interimistic measure until a General Council could be held to accomplish the final settlement. For Saxony the *Augsburg Interim* was worked over into the *Leipzig Interim.*

2. The character of this *Leipzig Interim* becomes apparent when we consider its contents.[11] The doctrine of *Justification* was impregnated with the teaching of an *infused righteousness. Faith* was removed from its central position in the order of salvation and counted among the virtues which merit reward. The teaching on the *power and authority of the Church* amounted to this, that the Lutheran pastors must place themselves under the sovereignty of the Roman bishops. In *matters of worship,* the Mass was restored with practically all the abandoned ceremonies (the Seven Sacraments, the worshiping of images, fasting, even the *Corpus Christi* procession). The Catholic Encyclopedia (VII, 77) characterizes the *Interim* in the following words: "The points of doctrine were all explained in the sense of the Catholic dogma, but couched in the mildest and vaguest terms; and wherever it was feasible, the form of the concept approached the Protestant view of those subjects. In matters of ecclesiastical discipline two important concessions were made to the Protestants, viz., the marriage of the clergy and the communion under both kinds."

A remark of Lindsay (*The Reformation in Germany,* p. 390) is interesting at this point: "Nothing that Charles ever undertook proved such a dismal failure as this patchwork creed made from the snippets from two Confessions. However lifeless creeds may become, they all—the real ones—have grown out of the living experience of their framers, and have contained the very life-blood of their hearts as well as their brains. It is a hopeless task to construct creeds as the tailor shapes and stitches coats."

3. Melanchthon, Bugenhagen and the rest of the Wittenberg theologians were now under the jurisdiction of Elector Maurice who had joined the Emperor and had contributed to the defeat of the Smalcald Federation. By permitting *the Interim to pass without protest* they became guilty of grave offence against the Church. It was a time when in other parts of Germany some four hundred clergymen were driven from their homes because of resistance, many of whom were also imprisoned. Melanchthon's inner attitude was expressed when he was first approached by Maurice. He wrote: "I will not

---

[10] O. Ritschl, *op. cit.,* II, 328 ff.

[11] The text is given by Bieck. *Das dreifache Interim,* Leipzig, 1721. Cf. the article *Adiaphora* in *PRE,* I, 172 ff.; the works on the *History of Dogma* by Seeberg, Loofs; also Tschackert, *Entstehung,* p. 505-514; Fritschel, *Formula of Concord,* pp. 25, 41, 215.

encumber my conscience with this book" (*CR*, VI, 839). But as soon as it became too dangerous to protest, his action conformed to the following principle: Do the best you can under these present circumstances and save as much as you can. The result of this attitude toward the *Interim* was that the Lutherans lost confidence in Melanchthon and became distrustful of his school, the *Philippists*.[12]

Note: Although it means trespassing upon the specific field of Church History, we cannot resist quoting here from a few letters which were addressed to the conscience of Melanchthon. Corvinus, who had been imprisoned for three years because of his writing against the *Interim*, pleaded with Melanchthon (in Latin): "Oh, my Philip, Oh, I say, our Philip, return through the immortal Christ to the former candor, to the former sincerity, to the former constancy! Do not make the minds of our people languish by your fright and half-heartedness! . . . You must not be the cause of such immense offenses within the Church! Do not permit your so excellent writings, words, acts, by which you have done so wonderfully much for the Church and schools, to be turned in such a way through that fault of disregard, innovation, moderation! Think of how much courage your plans give on the one hand to the opposition, and on the other hand how it robs our side! We pray that, mindful of your profession, you and your Wittenberg men would conduct yourselves as you did in the beginning of this matter, that is, that you would think, speak, write and do what becomes Philip, the Christian teacher, not the court-philosopher."

On July 22nd, Caspar Aquila had written to Melanchthon: "Thou holy man, reply and breath, defend the Word and Name of Christ and His glory, which is the highest possession on earth, from that virulent sycophant." (This concluding allusion was to Agricola who was the Protestant party in the framing of the *Interim*.)

Calvin also expressed his censure in a letter which lacerated Melanchthon's heart. He wrote: "Your condition is another one than that of many; for it is more disgraceful for the leaders or standardbearers to tremble than for the mass of soldiers to flee." [13]

4. *Matthias Flacius*, professor of Hebrew at Wittenberg and a former pupil of Melanchthon, was the chief leader of the opposition against the *Interim*.[14] Such men as Amsdorf, Wigand, Westphal and others were associated with him at Magdeburg, the city of refuge. The Lutheran congregations everywhere suffered especially from the introduction of the old Roman ceremonies to which they offered a passive resistance. The Interimists had made the declaration that such ceremonies are *adiaphora*, i.e., neither commanded nor prohibited, *Mitteldinge;* and therefore fall into the category of freedom as to practice in the Church. It was at this point that Flacius began his attack upon the Wittenbergers in his publication, *De veris et falsis Adiaphoris* (1549). He proceeded upon the self-same principles which Melanchthon had established in the *Augsburg Confession* (articles XV and XXVIII) and in the corresponding articles of the *Apology*. See the discussion in our *Introduction to the Symbolical Books of the Lutheran Church*,[2] pp. 255-264. But he emphasized the fact that circumstances may arise, under which *adiaphora* may cease to be such. The existing situation made Flacius see that the whole heritage from Luther was at stake together with the fundamental positions of the Reformation on justification, good works, repentance, the Church, and the ministry. In view of this danger Flacius sounded a warning against making any concessions whatever, even in the matter of ceremonies. He established himself squarely upon the principle, which Lutheranism has adopted, that in the case of conflict regarding the truth, and where offence might be given, nothing is an *adiaphoron* (*Nihil est adiaphoron in casu confessionis et scandali*).[15]

---

[12] See article by Kawerau in *PRE*, XV, 322-331.

[13] Quotations by Fritschel, *Formula of Concord*, pp. 46-49.

[14] See the description of his course in our *Introduction*, pp. 402 and 407. For fundamental literature on Flacius we refer the student to his biographer W. Preger, *Matthias Flacius Illyricus*, 2 volumes (1859, 1861); also the article in the *PRE*, VI, 82-92, by G. Kawerau.

[15] Cf. O. Ritschl, I, 356 ff.

5. It was this last-mentioned thought of Flacius upon which Article X of the *Formula of Concord* concentrated the Church's interest. The discussion is limited to *adiaphora* of a churchly nature (which was different from the discussion at the time of Pietism, when it was about matters of pleasure and recreation). In other words, it centered around the use or non-use of ceremonies in the Church. Such as are "contrary to God's Word, these are not to be regarded *adiaphora*" (5). "Likewise when there are useless, foolish spectacles that are profitable neither for good order, nor Christian discipline, nor evangelical propriety in the Church, these also are not genuine *adiaphora* or matters of indifference" (7). But there are *genuine adiaphora or matters of indifference* (2, 8). Is the Church, then, free to do as it pleases? Answer, "At a time of confession, at a time when the enemies of God's Word desire to suppress the pure doctrine of the holy Gospel, the entire Church, yea every Christian, but especially the ministers of the Word as the presidents of the congregations of God, are bound according to God's Word to confess the doctrine and what belongs to the whole of religion, freely and openly, not only in words, but also in works and with deeds; and that then, in this case, even in such *adiaphora*, they must not yield to the adversaries. . . ." (10).

3. THE MAJORISTIC CONTROVERSY

1. The *Leipzig Interim* had also omitted Luther's *sola fide,* had emphasized *the necessity of Christian virtues for salvation,* and had even stressed the reward merited by good works. In a controversy with Nikolaus von Amsdorf who was a strict follower of Luther, George Major, a pupil of Melanchthon, maintained that "good works are necessary to salvation, since no one is saved by wicked works and no one without good works." While such a statement grew out of a desire to defend the attitude of the Wittenberg theologians toward the *Interim,* it was also calculated to establish the profound connection between faith and the new life. Amsdorf declared that the statement could be defended only by a "Pelagian, a Mameluke, and a denier of Christ." Flacius also became a participant in the controversy, and made the assertion that the gift of the Holy Spirit is only "an appendage, consequence, and supplement of grace." Amsdorf even went so far as to say that "good works are injurious to salvation" and that "God does not care for works," meaning by this, of course, if there is any reliance on them for salvation. Even Luther had occasionally expressed himself in that way. Melanchthon simply emphasized the necessity of the *new obedience* as in Article VI of the *Augsburg Confession,* and advised that the qualifying term for salvation be used only in connection with faith. Amsdorf's party, which was strictly Lutheran, disowned his (Amsdorf's) statement and insisted that the new obedience must proceed from the inward impulses of the new heart.[16]

2. In Article IV *Of Good Works* the FC starts on the basis of Article VI of the *Augsburg Confession, Of the New Obedience,* and records the following points of agreement between the Lutheran theologians: (1) It is the will of God that believers shall walk in good works which, however, must not include the works of self-chosen sanctity, but only such as are *commanded by God;* (2) Works pleasing to God can be done only by persons who through faith are reconciled with God and renewed by the

---

[16] As to the fundamental literature in the writings of that time, see the quotations in Seeberg, II, 364 f.; Cf. Tschackert 514-518; Fritschel, 161 f.; Wiegand, 137; Loofs, 898. The student should observe the close relation of this conflict with the Antinomistic Controversies which we treated before.

Holy Ghost, or as Paul says (Eph. 2: 10), "Created anew in Christ Jesus to good works." The works of such persons are good notwithstanding the imperfections of the works. Although the works of *civil righteousness,* as done by the unconverted, are commendable before the world and are indeed required and rewarded by God in this world, nevertheless they are regarded by God as sinful and impure, i.e., stained with sin, because of the persons performing them. (Cf. *Augs. Conf.,* Article XVIII, with the *Formula of Concord,* Article IV.) (3) Faith, therefore must be the *mother and source* of truly good works. Note the quotation from Luther (4, 10-12).

The *Formula* then proceeds to the matters of controversy between the *Philippistic and the Lutheran parties.* It says first that, although emphasis is placed upon the necessity of doing good works, this must not be interpreted to mean that good works are to be done under compulsion and coercion instead of evangelical freedom. The emphasis upon the necessity of good works is simply to indicate "the arrangement made by God's immutable will to which we are debtors" (14, 16-20).

Next, the *Formula* takes up the *controversy between Major and Amsdorf.* (1) It says that it cannot be admitted "that to believers good works are needful for salvation, so that it is impossible without good works to be saved." Such a teaching would conflict with the exclusive particles *alone* and *only,* in the article on justification and salvation; for, in the language of Paul, these particles ascribe everything *alone* to the grace of God and the merit of Christ. A contrary teaching would rob tempted and troubled consciences of the comfort of the Gospel, etc. (22-29). (2) Then, after stating with strongest emphasis that it is false to teach that salvation cannot be lost by wilful sins (31-33), the *Formula* says that it must not even be taught that good works are necessary for the retention of righteousness and salvation, because Paul says (Romans 5: 2) that the *sola fides* has not only access to grace, but is itself the beginning, middle and end (34). (3) Finally, Amsdorf's proposition "that good works are injurious to salvation," is rejected, "because it is stated in so absolutely false and offensive a manner whereby discipline and decency are impaired. . . ." (39). This much, however, is admitted: "If anyone should wish to introduce good works into the article of justification, or rest his righteousness or trust for salvation thereon, in order to merit God's grace and thereby be saved, to this we say . . . that to such a man his works are not only useless and a hindrance, but also *injurious.* But the fault is not in the good works themselves, but in the false confidence placed upon the works" (37).

C. THE SYNERGISTIC CONTROVERSY

1. We know of Melanchthon's disagreement with the strict Lutherans in regard "to the condition of man's will in the experience of his conversion." In his *Loci* of 1535, he emphasized the point that original sin has not deprived man of the faculty to make right decisions when incited by the influences of grace. As to spiritual righteousness, there is no faculty in man's will capable of producing something new; but the will of man is able to assume an attitude and give assent, when this *new* makes its advance to him. Thus Melanchthon arrived at the constantly repeated formula of the three *concurring causes* in the process of conversion: the Word of God, the Holy Spirit, and man's will which is not entirely inactive, but which struggles against its own infirmity. [17]

---

[17] *CR* XXI. 276; cf XXI. 658.

schackert remarks correctly: "The ethical motive of Melanchthon is altogether respect-ble, but in the formulation of his thesis he was unfortunate. For the divine work and he human attitude must not be thought of in the form of an addition of co-ordinated actors" (*Entstehung,* p. 521). Lutheranism is very sensitive when it comes to its Augustinian monergism of grace in conversion.

2. *The Synergistic expressions* of the *Leipzig Interim* have presented a strong appeal o many theologians who cannot be charged with desiring to surrender anything of the *ola gratia,* as can be seen from the utterances of such men as J. Pfeffinger and Victor Strigel. The *Interim* said, "God does not deal with man as with a block, but He draws aim in such a way that his will also co-operates." [18] Pfeffinger adopted the phrase of the *three efficient causes,* and said of the third of these—namely, the will of man—that it does not resist, but adapts itself to the working of the Spirit. He said that there must be something within us which explains why some assent and others do not (In his *Proposiones de libero arbitrio,* 1555). In public disputation with Flacius (1560) Strigel said that sin has not been abolished and has not destroyed free will, but only depraved it; the will acts in its own way in conversion, with a peculiar *mode of action,* so that no inward transformation can be real except the will has also given its assent. To use the words of Seeberg (p. 368), Strigel "conceives of the natural man as only bound, wounded and hindered by sin. . . . Although it be but weakly, yet the will of man co-operates; its attitude toward grace is not simply passive, but only '*more passive than active.*'" [19]

3. After the conflict with Pfeffinger had been opened by publication from N. Amsdorf and J. Stolz (1558), it was Flacius who, in his disputation with Strigel, again became the champion of the strict Lutherans. He acknowledged a co-operation of the will which, however, did not begin until after the actual moment of conversion. *Conversion is wrought exclusively by the Holy Spirit* in such a way that man is entirely passive. Man is converted as an *objectum conversionis,* even when his will *raves and howls.* "God alone converts man—He does not exclude the will, but every efficacy or operation of it." [20]

4. It was natural that the discussion should run over into the doctrine of *original sin.* In that disputation Strigel had used the illustration of the magnet: "When the magnet is touched with the juice of garlic it loses its quality of attraction, and after it is touched again with the blood of an animal, the attraction is restored." "But all the time," says Strigel, "the magnet does not cease to be a magnet." Thus original sin is merely accidental to man and his will. At this point Flacius stepped forward with the assertion that original sin is not accidental, but is the essential substance of man. The essential nature of man has been itself transformed by sin. Here he used the most extreme expressions: "The image of God has been replaced by the true and living image of the devil (*ad imaginem Satanae transformatus*), the nature of man has been distorted into a diabolic nature, and every point of attachment to divine influences has been lost." [21] Fritschel says: "In order to do justice to Flacius, we must go back to his phraseology and grasp his real meaning. He distinguishes between two kinds of *substances:*

---

[18] Bieck, *Das dreifache Interim,* p. 326 f.
[19] *Disputatio inter Flacium et Strigelium,* p. 232.
[20] See the references in Seeberg, English ed., II, 368, to *Disputatio, etc.,* pp. 43, 71, 100, 118, 131, 178, 233. Seeberg remarks that Strigel approached the problem from the standpoint of the "formal freedom," while Flacius started with the "material" bondage of the will.
[21] See his *Clavis Scripturae,* II, p. 651 ff.

the *substantia materialis* and the *substantia formalis*." [22]   But almost all of Flacius
friends among the strict Lutherans turned against him because of that *Manichaea*
statement which he refused to retract.

5. *The Formula of Concord* devoted its first two articles to a rather thorough dis
cussion of these matters. We begin with a review of the contents of Article II. (1)
Original sin, which Luther called the *natural* or *personal* sin, is estimated as being a
corruption of nature which is the *root of all other sins,* "so that we are by nature children
of wrath, death and damnation, unless delivered therefrom by the merit of Christ."
"What this hereditary evil is, no reason knows and understands; but, as the Smalcald
Articles say, it must be learned and believed from the revelation contained in the Scrip
tures." This depravity extends especially to "the highest, principal powers of the soul
in understanding, heart and will." It shows itself in this "that now, since the fall, man
receives by inheritance an inborn wicked disposition, an inward impurity of heart, wicked
lusts and propensities" (1-12). (2) Next, all Pelagian and Pelagianizing errors are
rejected which teach: (a) that original sin is only a debt without corruption (Zwingli)
(b) that evil lusts are not sins, but natural conditions, and that original sin is not really
a condemning sin; also that nature is incorrupt and perfect (Pelagius and the Scholastics)
(c) that original sin is only a slight blemish, an external impediment, and that man
has not entirely lost all power in spiritual things (Synergists) (16-25). (3) Next, a
distinction is drawn between *nature* and *sin* (cf. Art. XIX of the *Augsburg Conf.*). A
proofs of this distinction, references are made (a) to the article of *creation*—God create
man, but not sin (34-42); (b) to the article of *redemption*—Christ assumed human
nature, but not original sin (43-44); (c) to the article of *sanctification*—God cleanse
us from sin, but we retain our nature (45); (d) to the article of *resurrection*—we shall
rise with our nature, but without sin (46-47). From all this we see that it is erroneous
to identify nature with sin (48-49).[22] (4) Finally, instruction is given as to the use of
terms: (a) The term *nature,* is ambiguous—it may mean the essence, body and soul of
man, but it has also been used to describe the vicious quality of his nature; (b) The
term *original sin* has also been used in different senses—as the *deep corruption of human
nature (Smalcald Articles)* and occasionally also as meaning *sinful from the beginning*
(Luther) (52-53); (c) Finally, as to the disputed terms *substance* and *accident,* it is
declared that between these "there is no mean, so that everything which is there must
be either *substance,* i.e., an independent essence, or *accident,* i.e., an incidental matter
which does not exist by itself essentially, but in another independent essence, and can
be distinguished therefrom" (54). The appeal is to Augustine who spoke as follows:
"Original sin is not the nature itself, but an incidental defect and damage in the nature"
(55). But this original sin, as an *accident,* is described as "an unspeakable evil and such
an entire corruption of human nature that in it and all its internal and external powers
nothing pure and good remains; but everything is entirely corrupt, so that on account
of original sin, man is in God's sight truly spiritually dead and, with all his powers, has
died to that which is good" (60). This strong language was used in order to ward off
Flacianism as well as Synergism. The special discussion of Synergism is taken up in the
following article.

Article II of the *Formula* naturally lays the chief emphasis on the settlement of the

---

[22] For further explanation along this line see Fritschel, *Book of Concord,* 134 f.; also our *Intr. to the Symb.
Bks.,* p. 220. Compare Seeberg, English ed., II, 369; also Preger II, 199 ff., 322 ff. Kawerau in *PRE* XIX, 99.

ynergistic conflict. The Formula limits itself to a discussion of the ability of the under-
tanding and will of the unregenerate man in his conversion and regeneration: that is,
whether, when the Word of God is preached and the grace of God is offered, he can,
rom his own powers surviving since the fall, prepare himself for grace, assent thereto,
nd accept the same (2).

On the basis of a large quotation from Scripture (8-16) the position is taken "that
n spiritual and divine things the intellect, heart and will of the unregenerate man cannot in any way, by their own natural powers, understand, believe, accept, think, will,
begin, effect, do, work, or concur in working anything; but they are entirely dead to good,
and corrupt; so that in man's nature, since the fall, there is before regeneration not the
east spark of spiritual power remaining by which of himself he can prepare himself for
God's grace, or accept the offered grace, or for and of himself be capable of it, or apply
or accommodate himself thereto, or by his own powers be able of himself, as of himself,
o aid, do, work, or concur in working anything for his conversion, either entirely, or
n half, or in even the least or most inconsiderable part; but he is the servant of sin
(John 8: 34; Eph. 2: 1; 2 Tim. 2: 26). Hence the natural free will, according to its
perverted disposition and nature, is strong and active only with respect to what is dis-
pleasing and contrary to God" (7, cf. Scripture references in 17).

The degree to which the natural man's will is in bondage in spiritual things is thus
described: "The Holy Scriptures compare the heart of the unregenerate man to a hard
stone which does not yield to the one touching it, but resists; and to a rough block, and
o a wild, unmanageable beast" (19). In a quotation from Luther we have once more
he words that "in spiritual and divine things, which pertain to the salvation of the soul,
man is like a pillar of salt, like Lot's wife, yea, like a log and a stone, like a lifeless statue.
. . For man neither sees nor perceives the fierce and terrible wrath of God on account
of sin and death, but he continues even knowingly and willingly in his security. . . .
yea, all teaching and preaching are lost upon him, until he is enlightened, converted, and
egenerated by the Holy Ghost" (20-21).

The monergism of divine grace is established by a large Scriptural quotation of a
very convincing nature (26) and by further quotation from the *Augsburg Confession,
Apology, Smalcald Articles,* and the *Catechisms* (30-41).

The instrument that is employed to effect man's conversion is the Word in the form
of Law and Gospel, which "breaks our hearts and draws man so that through the preaching of the Law he sees his sins and God's wrath, and experiences in his heart true terrors,
repentance, and contrition . . . and, through the preaching and consideration of the Holy
Gospel concerning the gracious forgiveness of sins in Christ, a spark of faith is kindled
in him, which accepts the forgiveness of sins . . ." (54). But the natural man has the
power to thwart the work of the Holy Ghost through the Word and render it devoid
of results. (57-58)

The power of man to resist takes us back to that description of the natural man as
a "stone or a block." His resistance shows that "a man before his conversion is still a
rational creature" (59), and God has a "way of working in a man, as a rational creature,
quite different from his way of working in another creature that is irrational, or in a
stone or block" (62). "The Lord draws the man whom He wishes to convert . . . in
such a way that his understanding, in place of being darkened, becomes enlightened,
and his will, in place of being perverse, becomes obedient" (64).

Then follows a description of the will of man after he has been converted, enlightened, and renewed. Now "it is certain that, through the power of the Holy Ghost, we can and should co-operate, although still in great weakness" (63-65). Man has now come into a condition in which he "wills what is good and 'delights in the Law of God after the inward man' (Romans 7:22), and henceforth does good to such an extent and as long as he is impelled by God's Spirit, as Paul says (Romans 8: 14), 'For as many as are led by the Spirit of God, they are the sons of God' ... The converted man does good spontaneously, as David says" (Psalm 110:4) (63, 64).

The new life remains beset with imperfections (64, 68). Paul's experience of "another law in my members warring against, etc." (Romans 7: 22 f.) is quoted (64) and, further, it is said: "For since we, in this life, receive only the first-fruits of the Spirit and the new birth is not complete but only begun in us, the combat and struggle of the flesh against the spirit remains even in the elect and truly regenerate man." "There is a great difference perceptible ... among Christians in that one is weak and another strong in the Spirit" (68).

With regard to backsliding we read: "When the baptized have acted against conscience, allowed sin to prevail in them, and thus have grieved and lost the Holy Ghost in them, they need not be rebaptized, but must again be converted" (69).

Among the *errors rejected* we call special attention to statements on Pelagianism (75), Semi-Pelagianism (76), Synergism (77-78), and a peculiar form of holiness (81).

III. CONTROVERSIES CLEARING UP THE RELATION BETWEEN CALVINISM AND LUTHERANISM

A. ON THE LORD'S SUPPER AND ON THE PERSON OF CHRIST

1. The Westphal Controversy.

The publication of the *Consensus Tigurinus* in 1549, served as "the solemn act by which the Zwinglian and Calvinistic reformations were joined in everlasting wedlock as the one great Reformed Church." [23] Previous to this the Lutherans were not generally aware of the fact that Calvin stood opposed to the Real Presence as it had been expressed in the Wittenberg Concord. In fact, he was regarded as an "Upper German Lutheran" (*ein oberdeutscher Lutheraner*).[24] But the spread of Calvinism to France, Holland and England, and the subtle suggestion of the Calvinistic conception of the Eucharist in Germany, particularly in the Palatinate and in Saxony, moved Joachim Westphal, a prominent minister in Hamburg, to sound an alarm. He issued a publication in which he revealed the existing difference between Calvin and Luther on the Eucharist; and warned the Lutheran Church of the undermining influences which were at work.[25] With the development of such circumstances Calvin replied three times.[26]

---

[23] Staehelin, *Johann Calvin*, II, 121.

[24] Cf. Loofs[4], 877, 879; also Thomasius-Seeberg, II, 547.

[25] The title was *Farrago Confuseanarum*, etc., 5 volumes. For a characterization of the work, to which others were added in quick succession, see Kawerau in *PRE*, XXI, 186, 36 ff.

[26] See his *Defensio*, etc., in *CR* of 1555, XXXII, 1 ff.; also his *Secunda Defensio* in XXXII, 41 ff.; and his *Ultima Admonitio* in XXXII, 137 ff. It was in this last publication that Calvin said he received the *Augsburg Confession* in the sense in which it had been interpreted by its own author. By this he meant the *Variata* edition to which he and others had subscribed at the Colloquy of Worms, 1540. See our *Union Movements*, p. 24; PRE, XXI, 187, line 59; Kawerau in Moeller's *Kirchengeschichte*, III, 141; Salig. *Augsb. Konf.*, I, 491; Staehelin, *Joh. Calvin*, I, 234; *CR*, IV, 33 ff., XLIII, 305. We can see how the Lutherans, in their struggle with Calvinism, were driven to demand the recognition of the Unaltered Edition of the *Augsburg Confession* of 1531. See our *Introduction²*, pp. 101 ff., 219 ff.

Westphal has been severely criticized by the union-theologians for his focusing of he Church's attention upon the fundamental difference between Calvin and Luther on he Eucharist.[27] But G. Kawerau, himself a mediating historian, says correctly: "If he had not done it, some one else would." [28] Certainly there was something vital that needed o be cleared up. It opened the eyes of Lutheran Germany to the silent propaganda which was being spread in behalf of Calvin's doctrine on the Eucharist. It further revealed he disappointing fact that Melanchthon and his followers were quite willing to exchange Luther's teaching for that of Calvin. The difference between the two conceptions was beclouded by the use of Bucero-Melanchthonian phraseology. All this was part and parcel of a plan to crowd Lutheranism out of Germany and to supplant it with another ype of Protestantism.

Note: The controversy, which was opened by Westphal, spelled the beginning of the end of Calvin's dominion over Germany; [29] or at least, it limited it to a narrower territory. [30] Calvin certainly deceived himself as to the vitality of the old Lutheran position, when he fancied Westphal's publications to be of no account and accordingly replied quite superciliously.

The case of Frederick III in the Palatinate reveals the situation. When the Lutheran estates at the Diet of Augsburg, in 1564, accused him of having broken the Augsburg Religious Peace Treaty of 1555 by introducing Calvinism, he replied that he had never read Calvin, that he did not know what Calvinism was, and that he still adhered to the *Augsburg Confession* (*Variata*). And yet, a year before, he had publicly introduced the *Heidelberg Catechism!* This showed that the Lutheran Church was in a struggle for its very existence. It also indicated the necessity of insisting upon subscription to the *Unaltered Augsburg Confession.* [31]

2. The report on the controversies in Bremen and in the Palatinate must be limited here to their doctrinal features.

a. Hardenberg of Bremen came from the humanistic circles and had been in association with some of Calvin's followers. His strictly Lutheran associate, Timan, took sides with Westphal. Hardenberg corresponded a great deal with Melanchthon, and when driven to a definite statement, he rejected Luther's doctrine of the Real Presence, refusing to accept by oath the Tenth Article of the *Augsburg Confession.* He declared that he could accept the Bible only. The *Augsburg Confession,* he maintained, was the product of the time which was composed to please the emperor and the pope. To his mind this was particularly true of Article X which impressed him as containing too much of the Roman doctrine of transubstantiation. He published the alleged assertion of Luther that he had done too much in the Eucharist controversy. So Bremen was lost to the Lutheran Church and was regularly represented at the Synod of Dort. [32]

b. The Palatinate was lost to Lutheranism through Elector Frederick III who took his country over to Calvinism (1561). This was an especially severe blow to the Lutheran Church. The elector had made a personal study of the different views of the Lord's Supper. When he asked Melanchthon for his opinion in the matter, Melanchthon

[27] See, for instance, H. Dalton, *Miscellanen,* 1905, p. 302 ff.
[28] *PRE,* XXI, 186, line 60.
[29] Kruske, *Joh. von Lasco und der Abendmahlsstreit,* 1901, p. 83.
[30] Kawerau in *PRE,* XXI, 186, line 57.
[31] See our *Union Movements,* p. 25, lines 29 f.
[32] On the whole history see Kurtz, *Church History,* English ed., par. 144, 2; German ed., 1906, par. 152, 2. Moeller-Kawerau, *Kirchengeschichte,* III, 1907, p. 306. Hering, *ut supra,* I, 204-212. Also the article on "Hardenberg" in *PRE,* VII, 408 ff.

replied: "It is not difficult, but dangerous, to answer." [33]   The elector decided in favor of the introduction of Calvinism. Z. Ursinus and C. Olevianus were instructed to write the *Heidelberg Catechism*. The church service was *reformed*. Altars, baptismal fonts and paintings were removed, and the organs were silenced. The opposing ministers were driven from the country, and Reformed ministers from other countries were called to take their places. [34]

3. *The Synod at Stuttgart* (1559), under the leadership of Brenz, had adopted the following confessional statement which may be looked upon as an expression of the faith that was generally held by the Church of Germany at that time on the Eucharist. (1) In the Supper there are distributed with the bread and wine, through the power of Christ's words of institution, the true Body and Blood of Christ, truly and essentially, to all who receive them by eating and drinking. (2) The substance of the bread and wine is not changed, neither are they symbols; but as they are present substantially, so also is the substance of the Body and Blood of Christ present, which is distributed and received with the bread and wine. (3) The Body and Blood are in no state of mixture with the earthly elements, neither are they locally included in them; but they are present, as described by the Word of Christ; wherefore there can be no Sacrament outside of its use (*extra usum non esse sacramentum*). (4) Christ is everywhere according to Ephesians 1: 21 ff., 4: 10; His Body is therefore not confined to one place, but in divine majesty is omnipresent in a supernatural, divine way; His presence in the Supper is therefore not made impossible by His Ascension and Session at the right hand of the Father, but rather confirmed thereby. (5) The godless and unbelievers also receive the Body and Blood of Christ; but they are judged, not vivified, by the Sacrament. [35]

4. *The Crisis in Saxony.* The Crypto-Calvinistic agitations were also extended to Electoral Saxony where Melanchthon and his school at Wittenberg had been working into the hands of Calvin with all kinds of machinations. [36] To be fair historically, it must be admitted that there was an element of self-defense on the part of the Philippists (Melanchthon having passed away in 1560).[37] The Flacianists were setting the stage for the destruction of the Philippists whose aim was, under the guise of general Bucero-Melanchthonian terms, to displace Luther's doctrine of the Real Presence and install Calvin's conception. [38] The anonymous publication of 1574, *Exegesis Perspicua,* finally brought the Philippistic plan into the open daylight. A great protest arose with the result that the Philippists were driven from Wittenberg and their leaders imprisoned. It was this bit of drama that kept Saxony in the rank and file of the Lutheran Churches. [39]

5. *The Exegesis Perspicua* gives us a glimpse into the theology and plans of the Melanchthonian party. We quote largely from Geo. J. Fritschel's *Formula of Concord,* 189-193.

Regarding the *Person of Christ* it is emphasized that the two natures "are unmixed also in the glorified Christ," that His Body up to the day of judgment remains a human

---

[33] *CR*, IX, 960.

[34] Kurtz, English ed., par. 144, 1; German ed., 1906, par. 152, 1. Moeller-Kawerau, III, 301 ff. As to the responsibility of fanatical Lutherans cf. article "Heshusius" in *PRE*, VIII, 8 ff.; also George J. Richards, *Heidelberg Catechism*, 1913, p. 39 ff.

[35] Seeberg, *DG*, IV², 509 f.

[36] Read Kurtz, English ed., par. 141, 1; German ed., 1906, par. 161, 4, 10, 13. Fritchel, *Formula of Concord*, pp. 52, 177, 181, 183 ff.

[37] See Kawerau in *PRE*, XV, 327, 44.

[38] *Ibid.*, XV, 328, 5.

[39] Fritschel, *Formula of Concord*, 181 ff. Moeller-Kawerau, III, 290 ff.

body—except that before His death it was a natural body, while now it is a spiritual body. Over against Luther's emphasis upon the personal union of the two natures of Christ it is urged that Christ suffered according to His human nature only, and is omnipresent according to His divine nature alone.

Upon this basis it is insisted that His presence in the Eucharist is only a presence of His divine nature, the human nature being in heaven and hence far removed from us. Still it may be said that a communication of Christ's Body takes place, but this means that Christ Himself is present for believers and is willing to make them His members. This presence might even be called a substantial presence, that is, Christ is present just as really as is the Holy Spirit in His work. "The communication in the Sacrament is a spiritual, and not a bodily one. This spiritual communication is the spiritual union of Christ's divinity with us, and not a communication of Christ's Body." On the words of institution this statement is made: "As Christ had spoken, before the institution of the Sacrament, of His efficiency within the disciples, they knew that this ceremony was to be a seal of this promise and not a real gift differing from the Gospel," etc. "Luther was drawn into the Eucharist controversy by those who considered the Sacrament merely visible signs and tokens of human profession (Zwingli). The other side (Reformed) saw the error of this leader. But the Lutheran side (in attacking the former and abandoned error) continued to fight against those that now teach better. It retained some ideas which arose from transubstantiation, and refused to abandon them. Luther had already fallen into this mistake, but more have those that came after him."

Practical suggestions are offered in the *Exegesis Perspicua Controversiae de Coena:* "We must not adhere too tenaciously to the founder of Protestantism (Luther), but must allow room for the better insight which came later (Melanchthon, Calvin)." Reference is made to the flourishing condition of the Church in Reformed countries. Schools and congregations prosper there, and there is a truly Christian life. Their doctrine agrees with that of the ancient Church. They have a great number of martyrs. . . . Until a synod has definitely decided the controverted points, the doctrine of ubiquity and of the eating of Christ's Body by the ungodly should be dropped, and a definite formula should be used: "The bread is the communion of the Body of Christ." In more detailed statements we should use the expressions and explanations of Melanchthon. These are better than the terms used in the *Augsburg Confession;* for when he wrote the *Augsburg Confession,* he did not see as clearly as he did later.

Such was the *Exegesis Perspicua.* Although is was published anonymously, its author was Joachim Curaeus of Glogau (ed., Scheffer, Marburg, 1853).

6. *Retrospective Review of Melanchthonianism.*

The silence of Melanchthon in the Westphal, Bremen and Palatinate controversies won for him and his followers the name of *Crypto-Calvinists.* Melanchthon was greatly embarrassed by the Westphal controversy which revealed how he had expressed himself when Luther was still alive and again later after he had entered into fellowship with Bucer and Calvin.[40]

We must ask the student to read again what we wrote on Melanchthon's attitude in the conflict on the Lord's Supper in this Book III, Chapter IV, section 6. The literature for considering this whole question is large. We should not overlook the thorough and impartial investigations of Otto Ritschl in his *Dogmengeschichte des Protestantismus,*

---

[40] *PRE,* XXI, 188.

Vol. IV: *Das orthodoxe Luthertum im Gegensatz zu der Reformierten Theologie,* pp. 14 ff.; cf. Vol. I, 279 ff.

Melanchthonianism as an organized party[41] suffered a severe defeat in the drama that took place in Saxony, as we have indicated above. This defeat was not merely the result of the fierce polemics of the strict Lutherans, but it had its source also in the lack of character and positiveness of the Melanchthonian position.[42] Melanchthon's expressions on the Eucharist were lacking both in Biblical foundation and in dogmatic completeness. They could appeal only to those with an indifferent attitude of mind. The Christology of the Melanchthonians falls short in that it refuses to draw logical conclusions from admitted premises. In the points under consideration Melanchthonianism was too neutral; it lacked in positiveness. Kawerau calls attention to the fact that after the introduction of the *Formula of Concord,* wherever Melanchthonianism still persisted, there came forth no scholarship that could be compared with the literary productions of *"Concordia Lutheranism."* [43]

7. The *Formula of Concord* deals with the questions under discussion in Articles VII (Eucharist) and VIII (Person of Christ) and from the viewpoint of the personal union of the two natures in Christ, also in Article IX (Descent to Hell).

a. In Article VII the *Formula* uses painstaking care to guard the interpretation of Article X of the *Augsburg Confession* on the *Lord's Supper* by describing the kind of "real presence" which Luther meant in his controversy with his opponents and in his agreement with the "Upper Germans" in the Wittenberg Concord (9-16). The *Catechism* and especially the *Smalcald Articles* are referred to (17-27). The Bodily Presence is taught on the basis of the words of institution (46-59). Thus it is taught that, on account of the sacramental union between the earthly elements and the heavenly gifts, Christ's Body and Blood are truly and essentially present and are received with the bread and wine. It is not, however, a "physical or earthly presence" (5, 6; cf. 17). From such a view of the Real Presence it follows that communicants receive the Body of Christ *with the mouth* (*ore*) *which however does not mean a Capernaitic eating* (*manducation*), for it takes place in a supernatural, incomprehensible, heavenly way. Along with this sacramental mode of receiving Christ's essential Body by worthy and unworthy communicants, there goes also a spiritual reception by faith alone, which can also take place outside of the use of the Sacrament (15, 16; 41, 42; 63-66). The pious, indeed, receive the Body and Blood of Christ as an infallible pledge and assurance that their sins are surely forgiven, and that Christ dwells in them and wishes to be efficacious in them (63, 44). The discussions in this article are so thorough and exhaustive that all loopholes for the vagueness of Melanchthon, the mediating suggestions of Bucer and the definitions of Calvin, are completely stopped. There can be no mistake, henceforth, as to the distinction between Lutheranism and Calvinism. To have made this clear in every respect is the significance of this article.

b. But the *Formula of Concord* carried its decisions back to the doctrine of the *Person of Christ,* where the cause of the difference had already appeared in the controversy between Luther and Zwingli. The latter had taken the position that, according to His Body, Christ can not be present in the Supper, because omnipresence belongs to

---

41 *PRE*, XV, 323, 15.
42 Kawerau remarks that Philippism remained *etwas Halbes. Ibid.,* 329, 51.
43 *Ibid.,* XV, 329, 55.

the divine nature only. Calvin agreed with Zwingli. Here the *Formula,* in its system of the *unio personalis* and the *communicatio idiomatum,* teaches also the *genus majes-taticum* according to which there are communicated to Christ's human nature certain attributes of the divine nature (omnipotence, omnipresence, omniscience); so that the whole Christ, in one undivided Person, can be and is present where in the Word He promises to be present (16, 17). This doctrine is proved by quotations from the Scriptures (54-59). As to the question whether such a communication is possible or not, the *Formula* answers characteristically: "No one can know better or more thoroughly than the Lord Christ Himself" (53).[44]

c. In the brief Article IX on the "Descent to Hell," we can see again the Lutheran emphasis upon the personal union of God and Man in Christ: "The entire person, God and Man, after the burial, descended into hell, conquered the devil, destroyed the power of hell, and took from the devil all his might."

B. ON PREDESTINATION

Literature: THOMASIUS, *Das Bekenntnis der ev. luth. Kirche in der Konsequenz seines Prinzips,* p. 216 ff. A. SCHWEIZER (Ref.) *Die protestantischen Zentraldogmen,* I, 418 ff. THOMASIUS-SEEBERG, *Dogmengeschichte,* II, 623 ff. F. FRANK, *Theologie der Koncordienformel,* IV, 121 ff. J. FICKER, article on *Zanchi, PRE,* XXI, 607 ff. P. GRUENBERG (Ref.), article on *Marbach, PRE,* XII, 245 ff. LOOFS, *DG,* 925. R. SEEBERG, *DG,* IV³, 527 ff., 546 ff. F. WIEGAND, II, 138, 143. FRITSCHEL, *Formula of Concord,* 217-225. P. TSCHACKERT, *Entstehung d. luth. u. ref. Kirchen-lehre,* 559-564.

1. The incorporation of this topic in the *Formula of Concord* can be traced to a number of reasons. (1) We refer to those earlier inner conflicts of Luther when, in the struggle for the assurance of salvation, he feared that he was not among the elect and that the gift of grace was not for him. At that time it was Father Staupitz who taught him to turn from his brooding over the *eternal decrees* to a consideration of the *wounds of Christ* in which God has revealed His heart to the sinner. (2) But Luther was deeply interested in Augustine; he became a champion of this church father's doctrine of predestination, when he was attacked by Erasmus on the matter of the *Free Will.* But the conflict soon subsided. Melanchthon changed noticeably, as can be seen in the stronger emphasis he placed upon a certain freedom of the will with regard to things spiritual. Luther never abandoned his emphasis on Augustine's monergism of divine grace in salvation, because of the comfort it offers the soul when in need of assurance. He did not, however, discuss the theory of it. During the lifetime of Luther and Melanchthon the Lutherans were never provoked to a controversy with the Calvinists over the teaching of a double predestination (also for reprobation) which was expressed in the *Institutes* of Calvin (Chap. VI). They evidently feared that the controversy might expand to such dimensions as to become uncontrollable. (3) The historical occasion for the incorporation of Article XI in the *Formula* must be seen: (a) in the way in which Flacius and a few of his followers had been emphasizing the *substantial* corruption of man and God's choice of a few from this *massa perditionis* for salvation; and

---

[44] Space does not permit us to present the Christology of Brenz and Chemnitz, which really should be studied in this connection. On Brenz see Seeberg. English ed., II, 374; his *DG,* IV³, 514-517. Tschackert, *Entstehung,* 540 ff. The title of the publication is *Bekenntnis und Bericht der Theologen in Wuerttemberg,* etc., published in Pfaff, *Acta et Scripta Eccles. Wirteb.,* Tueb. 1720, p. 276 ff. Melanchthon called it "Hechinger Latein." On the contribution of Chemnitz in his *De Duabus Naturis* (1571); see Seeberg, English ed., II, 575-577; *DG,* IV³, 522-526. Also Tschackert, 543 f.; and Wiegand, 139.

(b) in a special controversy on Predestination between the Lutheran Professor J. Marbach and the Reformed Professor X. Zanchi. Zanchi taught all the features of Calvin's predestination. Among them was this: "The elect receive the true faith only once, after which they cannot lose the Spirit and fall from Christ. With the unregenerated part of their being only can they sin—not with their whole soul and their whole will." [45] Marbach, however, insisted that, in dealing with predestination, we should not begin from above, that is, with the eternal decree (*a priori*), but from below, that is, with the effects of God's election (*a posteriori*), because in this way it would be easier for the Christian to use this doctrine for his spiritual comfort.

2. By means of a formula of union agreed upon at Strassburg in 1563, a temporary settlement was effected whereby recognition was given to a special predestination and to the universal significance of the work of Christ and the call. Theoretically, the contradiction between these two statements is not capable of solution; but practically it can be overcome if the individual Christian will cling to the gracious will of God in Christ and seek here the assurance of his election. Seeberg, whom we are following in these remarks, points out very correctly in his last edition (Vol. IV, 529) that a perfectly consistent execution of the doctrine of predestination always runs up against two things: (1) against the dangerous consequences that attend such a doctrine (moral laxness or despair); and (2) against certain Biblical expressions on the universality of God's grace for man's salvation. And Seeberg adds the following remark: "We can escape the above-mentioned contradiction only in two ways—either by rejecting special predestination which however would have to be at the danger of falling into Semi-Pelagianism, or simply by abandoning the universal significance of the work of Christ and of the call." Later Lutheranism did not find the courage to attempt either of these solutions.

3. As to the expression of the *Formula of Concord* in this matter, we can do no better service for the reader than to quote from Dr. Geo. J. Fritschel whose book, *The Formula of Concord* (pp. 219-225), we have mentioned quite frequently.[46]

I. INTRODUCTION

No *public* controversies have occurred concerning this article. (The Strassburg controversy was a local affair.) But there is a great diversity of expression in the discussion among Lutheran theologians. Hence this article has been inserted to preclude future strife. (1-2)

II. DEFINITIONS AND BRIEF SUMMARY

First: The Distinction between "Foreknowledge" and "Predestination." *Foreknowledge* extends to all creatures, both good and bad (3-4), and to all things. But it is not the source or cause of evil things; on the contrary, it sets a limit and measurement to evil, and regulates it for good (6). The source of all evil is the wicked wills of the devil and of man (7). *Predestination* extends only to the good, namely, the children of

---

[45] Loescher, *Historia Motuum,* III, 30.

[46] The Lutheran Church in America has passed through severe controversies on Predestination and Conversion which have lasted over a full generation, but which are now approaching a final settlement. (See Neve-Allbeck on the *History of the Lutheran Church in America*), 1934. In these controversies Dr. Fritschel has had a vital part, both at conferences and through a large literary activity. He has been a life-long student of article 11 of the *Formula of Concord.* His outline offers a very convenient guide. The numbers of the paragraphs are those of the text of the article.

God (5). And it is the source which procures, works, helps and promotes whatever belongs to salvation. It is the rock upon which our salvation is founded (8).

Second: How must Predestination be considered? (a) It must not be considered *a priori;* for then the idea might arise that God foresaw how many are to be saved or lost; or, God held a review and decreed that this one shall be saved, and that one shall be damned (9). From this mode of consideration arises either false security or else despondency (10-11). But all doctrines of God lead to the opposite results, viz., contrition, faith, good works (12). (b) It must be considered *a posteriori,* as comprehending the whole plan of God pertaining to our redemption (1-2), the call (3), righteousness (4), and salvation (5-8, 13-22). This must not be considered abstractly (in itself), but concretely (in its reference to the individual believer), how and in what manner God would execute His plan. And all this must be taken together as the simple and correct doctrine of predestination (24).

III. A More Detailed Statement

A. The Presentation of Chemnitz

First: For salutary use the explanation must also show how I can know who are the elect (25).

Second: The Details. (a) The source of what we know about predestination is not reason, is not the Law, is not evidence, but only revelation (26). (b) It has been revealed through the call (27). (c) Both the Law and the Gospel are universal (28). (d) God's call is earnest, and we should accept it (29). (e) Hence the elect are those described as sheep, hearers, believers, sanctified, those who hunger and thirst (30). (f) Their sonship or adoption is attested to them by the Holy Spirit (31). (g) Finally, God has promised in the future to finish the work begun (32).

Third: We should concern ourselves with this revealed will of God and strive to enter in at the narrow gate, and not trouble ourselves about the secrets of God's eternal will (33).

Fourth: The Doctrine of Reprobation. (a) It is not God's will that any should perish, as if God's will were contradictory (35-36). (b) God offers His grace universally (37). (c) God's grace is truly present and active in the Word; but it is not God's will that those should be elect who despise, reject, blaspheme and persecute His Word (39). (d) God has decreed to reject those who harden themselves, etc. And this is the reason why many are called and few are chosen (40) For few accept the Word, many reject it (41). Few of the latter retain it; many become backsliders (42). The reason for this is not God's predestination, but man's perverse will.

Fifth: The practical test of this doctrine by comparing it with other doctrines. (a) It affirms the doctrine of justification through faith alone (43). (b) It overthrows both the doctrine of Pelagianism and that of Synergism (44). (c) It shows the eternal interest of God in my personal salvation (45). (d) It shows that my salvation rests in the strong hand of God (46-47). (e) It shows, amid temptations and crosses, that God purposes to lead every Christian through the cross to the crown (48-49). (f) It shows that there will always be a Church (50). (g) It contains powerful admonitions and warnings (51a). In short, it stands the test outlined in 12 (cf. 51b).

Sixth: The Secrets of God's Wonderful Ways. Besides these revealed things, God has kept concealed much that must and will remain unknown to us, though the curiosity of man busies itself most about it (52-53)—1. The number of those who will enter heaven and hell; God knows it, but it is not revealed to us (54-55); 2. The time of each individual's conversion and return (56); 3. God's ways of mercy and punishment in the case of backsliders (57-62). In all things which go beyond these limits, we remain silent and do not challenge God's ways, but imitate Paul who excludes all vain questions by his doxology, "O the depths of the riches," etc. (63-64).

B. The Presentation of Andreae

First: The doctrine of Predestination must be considered in Christ. (1) For we have been predestined in Christ (Eph. 1: 4). (a) The Father directs us to Him; (b) The Son calls us to Himself; (c) The Spirit brings us no other message. Hence the Holy Trinity points to Christ as the Book of Life, in which we should look for our predestination (65-66). (2) Christ proclaims our eternal election in the words, "Repent ye and believe," "Everyone that seeth the Son and believeth," "God so loved the world," etc. (67). (3) This proclamation is to be preached universally (68). (4) The Holy Spirit works true faith in the hearers (69). (5) Whoever would be saved should hear Christ who invites all (70). (6) Hence we should repent and believe and entrust ourselves entirely to Him (71-72). (7) The Holy Spirit impels the elect (believers) to good works; we should not resist this impulse, but exercise all Christian virtues (73). (8) The Holy Spirit bears witness to them (74). (9) For the future God has promised His grace to His children, and will forgive their sins in daily repentance (75).

Second: It is true that no one can come to Christ except the Father draw him. (1) The Father does not draw directly, but through the Word and Sacraments. (2) God does not want man to wait for a direct drawing outside of the Means of Grace. (3) God uses the ordained means and thereby draws the sinner from the jaws of hell into His kingdom (76). (4) Hence every sinner should repair to the Means of Grace, assured that God draws through them (77).

Third: That only a few are saved is the fault of those who reject salvation. (1) They hear the Word and despise it (78). (2) The devil makes them vessels of dishonor; God finds them as such and makes them vessels of honor, if they repent and believe; but He punishes impenitent sinners (79-82). (3) God often punishes sin by hardening the hearts of the obdurately impenitent, as we see in the case of Pharaoh (83-86).

Fourth: The Test of this Doctrine. (1) It gives all glory to God and His eternal mercy(87-88). (2) It does not produce either despondency or frivolity (80-90). Any doctrine which produces these is false (91-92). (3) Hence we will retain this plain, correct and useful interpretation, and will shun all acute discussions, and reject all contrary doctrines (93).

Note: For the benefit of the students who would like to see *another organization for studying the contents of the Formula of Concord* we shall give here a brief extract from the organization followed by Geo. J. Fritschel in our *Introduction to the Symbolical Books of the Lutheran Church.*[2] The Roman numbers, in the following, refer to the articles of the *Formula of Concord* and the Arabic numbers to the pages in our *Introduction to the Symb. Books:*

1. *Adiaphoristic* (Art. X, 407, 438): Whether concerning Romanist rites and ceremonies, in face of threatening persecution, concessions should be made for the time being (Melanchthon opposed by Flacius).

2. *Osiandristic* (III, 408, 425): Whether in place of the juridic conception of justification, Osiander's teaching of Christ, the personified righteousness, overshadowing all unrighteousness and inspiring to good works should be accepted (Melanchthon and Flacius against Osiander).

3. *Majoristic-Amsdorfian* (IV, 408, 427): Whether good works are necessary for salvation. (Conflict between Lutherans and Philippists).

4-5. *Antinomian* (V and VI, 428, 429): Whether the law is necessary in the process of conversion. (The position of Agricola rejected by Luther).

6-7. *Synergistic* (II and XI, 292, note 1; 440 ff.): On free will and predestination. (Melanchthon and the Philippists opposed by Flacius).

8. *Flacian* (1, 409, 420): The overstatement by Flacius: Original sin substantial, instead of only accidental in the nature of man.

9-11. *Crypto-Calvinistic* (VII, 409, 430; VIII, 409, 436 ff.; IX, 409, 438 ff.). On the Lord's Supper and the Person of Christ

12. *Various Sects* (XII).

IV. CONCLUDING ESTIMATE OF THE FORMULA OF CONCORD

The significance of the Formula of Concord may be summed up in the following manner.

1. It represents the development of Lutheran doctrine as we find it in the latter part of the Reformation Age. Theological reflection on the fundamental principles of the Reformation had produced divisions, which may be taken as a revelation of the German mind in its never-ending search for truth with which there goes the inclination toward individualism and factionalism.[47]

2. As regards *Calvinism* the adoption of the *Formula of Concord* and the pretty general consolidation of German Lutheranism in the *Book of Concord,* for that day, put a stop to the further conquest of Lutheran territory by Calvinism which remained limited, in the main, to its original influence in the South and to the West along the Rhine. Through the *Augsburg Confession* as interpreted in controverted matters by Luther's *Concordia Theology,* on the one side, and by the *Heidelberg Catechism* with all the Reformed Confessions as its background, on the other side, the consciousness of Lutheranism and Calvinism as two distinct churches of Protestantism was decisively expressed. From now on—not earlier—we have the names *Lutheran and Reformed* as adopted by the churches themselves. The name *Lutheran* had been used by Rome since 1520, to designate that which adhered to the Reformation cause. With the introduction of Calvinism into the Palatinate the distinction is made between *Lutherans* and *Calvinists.* After 1585 the followers of Luther began to call themselves *Lutherans.* But the followers of Calvin refused to have the name *Calvinists* and used the title Reformed instead. The purpose for desiring this latter name was to indicate that they as a church were aiming to reform German Lutheranism from the Romish leaven within her.[48]

3. In our introductory notes of this chapter we spoke of the conciliatory and irenic character of the Formula of Concord in all the endeavors of bringing about harmony

---

[47] Cf. R. Seeberg, *DG,* IV³, 550.

[48] See on this subject H. Heppe, *Ursprung und Geschichte der Bezeichnung reformierte und lutherischer Konfession,* 1859. Moeller-Kawerau, *Lehrbuch der Kirchengeschichte,* III³ (1907), 300. G. W. Richards, *The Heidelberg Catechism* (1913), p. 44. Neve, *Union Movements* (1921), pp. 34-36. Cf. our *Churches and Sects of Christendom* (1940), The Name "Lutheran," pp. 175 ff.

within Lutheranism. It gave expression to a consensus already inaugurated. It accomplished the purpose which it had in view. This included the elimination of Calvinism. While this had become a necessity it must not be overlooked that in very many points of evangelical Christianity Calvin, with his great gifts of theological interpretation, was fundamentally a follower of Luther. In certain articles of difference the *Formula of Concord* took position against Melanchthon, but outside of this it was in perfect harmony with the leading thoughts of Melanchthon's theology, which permeated all Lutheran teaching (cf. the *Augsburg Confession* and its *Apology*). The difference between Calvin and Melanchthon was this: Melanchthonianism was merely an influence within Lutheranism while Calvinism was in process of becoming a new and independent church with the program of eliminating historic Lutheranism. While the *Formula* succeeded in its purpose it is at the same time to be admitted that it did not succeed, in every respect, in reducing the rich prophetic theology of Luther to formulated expression. R. Seeberg, somewhere, observes correctly that while Calvin had the good fortune to see the whole of his theology adopted by his followers, much of the gold which Luther left to the Church remained uncoined. It is a constant object for study up to this day.[49]

4. Among the replies to the *Formula of Concord* by the Reformed, the *Newsted Admonition* (*Neostadiensium Admonitio*) was especially significant, for two reasons: (1) This book, covering 455 quarto pages, was written with great thoroughness by Zach. Ursinus, one of the authors of the *Heidelberg Catechism*. (2) It was written at the instruction of Count Casimir, of Neustadt in the Palatinate, and published in the name of the Newsted theologians. These theologians at first labored for a Melanchthonian middle type of Protestantism, but in fact they found themselves entirely on the side of Calvin, agreeing with him even in the doctrine of Predestination although not pressing this point to the extent it was done in other countries.

An impression of the *Newsted Admonition* may be had by a mere quotation of the captions to the twelve chapters: (1) The person of Christ, a review of the true doctrine. (2) The Lord's Supper, a review of the true doctrine. (3) Refutation of the false accusation of our churches with regard to false dogmas. (4) The authority of the Augsburg Confession. (5) The true meaning of the Augsburg Confession. (6) Regarding the authority of Dr. Luther. (7) Concerning the unjust condemnation of our doctrine on the Book of Concord. (8) Proof of false assertions in the Book of Concord. (9) Proof of contradictions in the Book of Concord. (10) The procedure of the theologians in bringing about concord, and the part of a Christian magistrate in church controversies. (11) The inconvenience in the carrying out of this concord. (12) An epilogue on the true method for establishihg Christian concord in the churches. (See on these matters *Lutherans in the Movements for Church Union*, pages 34-36. Cf. Meusel, *Kirchlichen Handlexikon*, IV, 756).

---

[49] R. Seeberg, English ed., II, 389 f. German ed., Vol. IV³, 549 f. Tschackert, *Entstehung*, pp. 569-572.

Chapter Eight

THE AGE OF STRICT ORTHODOXY IN
THE LUTHERAN CHURCH

Literature: A. THOLUCK, *Der Geist der luth. Theologen Wittenbergs im Verlaufe des 17. Jahrh.,* 1852. The same: *Das akademische Leben des 17. Jahrh.,* 1853. The same: *Das Kirchliche Leben des 17. Jahrh.,* 1861. J. KUNZE in his article in the *PRE* (III, 653, line 24) remarks: "Tholuck's judgment betrays the narrow position of the pietistic-unionistic school." PHILIP SCHAFF, *Creeds* (I, 349 ff.), follows Tholuck too uncritically. The *PRE* of the 3rd ed. in many pertinent articles, supervised by ALBERT HAUCK, has aimed to do justice to this age. As further literature we mention: K. F. A. KAHNIS, *Der innere Gang des deutschen Protestantismus,* 2 vols., 3rd ed., 1874; Vol. I, 57-163, furnishes very interesting reading on this subject. O. RITSCHL, *Dogmengeschichte des Protestantismus,* 4 vols., 1908-1927, must have special mention. I acknowledge gratefully also an unpublished discussion for my personal use by Dr. OTTO RITSCHL himself, which I have here used in connection with other materials. Among the latter I refer to my book *The Lutherans in the Movements for Church Union,* especially to Chapter IV on *The Age of Syncretism,* 1921; *also to* W. ELERT, *Morphologie des Luthertums,* Vol. I, 1931; and to H. SASSE, *Here We Stand,* 1937.

Introductory Remarks. The *Corpora Doctrinae* in the Lutheran Church (1560-1580) represents the time when the various dominions of Germany tried independently to create and to safeguard a unity in matters of doctrine.[1] In the *Book of Concord* (1580), the Lutherans finally arrived at a common collection of symbolical writings, intended as an authority for all Lutheran territories. The age of intense interest in the achieved doctrinal unity of the Lutheran Church prevailed up to the pietistic movement which was the time when the new philosophy gradually ushered in the Rationalism of the eighteenth century. The Reformed Church had a similar age of orthodoxy, which began with the Synod of Dort (1619). It was counteracted by an early yielding to the irenical principles in the controversy pertaining to the distinction between Fundamentals and Non-fundamentals, especially however by the inroads of Arminian thought upon the Calvinistic system. The Lutheran age of orthodoxy was of considerably longer duration than that of the Reformed. It lasted about a century. In this Chapter we must aim to study the doctrinal characteristics of this age within the Lutheran Church; concerning developments in the Reformed camp we will have occasion to give information in our Volume Two, Book IV, Chapters II, on "Arminianism in Holland" and III, on "Arminianism in England."

1. The Lutherans of Anti-Melanchthonian Persuasion must here have brief mention, because after the death of Luther they were the men who, unconsciously, took first steps in creating a foundation for the age of a strict Lutheran orthodoxy. The most significant among their leaders were: Nikolaus von Amsdorf (1483-1565), Nikolaus Gallus (1516-1570), Johannes Wigand (1523-1587), Matthaeus Judex (1528-1564), Joachim Westphal (1510-1574) and, outstanding among them all, Matthias Flacius Illyricus (1520-1575). When Luther was still living we find Amsdorf and others of this group to be watching Melanchthon. Their charge against him was that he was mixing Luther's

---

[1] For a brief review, cf. our *Introduction to the Symbolical Books of the Luth. Ch.*, pp. 29 f.

doctrines with philosophical thought. Later, as we have seen in our preceding Chapter (VII), charges were especially made against his yielding attitude to the Leipzig *Interim* and to other positions or tendencies of Melanchthon or the *Philippists* (Synergism and Crypto-Calvinism). Otto Ritschl declares with much emphasis that it was the faithful protest of these Lutherans and especially of Flacius in those days of the *Interim* (1548-1552) which saved Protestantism.[2]

Flacius and many Lutheran theologians and pastors, as refugees with him, were besieged by Maurice of Saxony in the city of Magdeburg. Maurice, himself a Lutheran, had made common cause with Charles V in the Smalcald War (1548) in order to win for himself the electorate of Saxony. But Maurice, son-in-law of the imprisoned Philip of Hesse, having decided to espouse the cause of German nationalism which the emperor was aiming to weaken, marched suddenly against the unprepared emperor. This ended unexpectedly the career of Charles V. The Augsburg Religious Peace Treaty of 1555 followed; it secured for the adherents of the *Augsburg Confession* the right to exist. But it was the unarmed resistance of those besieged Lutherans and their literary polemics which convinced Maurice and those about him of a spirit in Lutheranism that could be overcome neither by diplomacy nor by force.

2. *As Special Founders* of the strict Lutheran orthodoxy of the Seventeenth Century which are here to be discussed, we must point to a succeeding group of leading theologians. The most prominent among these was Martin Chemnitz (1522-1580). Others were Tilemann Hesshusen (1527-1588), David Chytraeus (1530-1600), Nikolaus Selnecker (1530-1592) and Jakob Andreae (1528-1590). These men held to Luther's type of theology in the main; they were, however, not as outspoken against Melanchthon as were the followers of Flacius.[3] They felt that as theologians they were very much indebted to Melanchthon. Chemnitz erected his great work, the *Loci Theologici,* published 1591 after his death, upon Melanchthon's *Loci* which continued to be used in the schools until it was supplanted by Leonhard Hutter's *Compendium Locorum Theologicorum* (1610).

3. *The Union of Divided Lutheranism* became the great task of this last-mentioned group. The doctrine of the ubiquity of the human nature of Christ had been taught by Luther in his conflict with Zwingli on the *real presence* (1528). Johannes Brenz (1499-1570), the Reformer of Wuerttemberg and its influential leader for fifty years had revived speculatively this doctrine in his work on the personal union of the two natures in Christ (1561). In a controversy on this subject the followers of Melanchthon at the Wittenberg University declined the ubiquity while the Wuerttembergers now under the theological leadership of Andreae, insisted upon it. In a co-operation between Andreae and Chemnitz, as pupil of Melanchthon, and supported by Selnecker, Chytraeus, and some others, it came to the agreement expressed in article 8 of the *Formula of Concord* (1577), concerning the person of Christ, which constitutes a theological compromise between the ubiquity of Brenz and the *multivolipresence* of Chemnitz. The *Formula of Concord,* in the entirety of twelve articles covered all the controverted confessional prob-

---

[2] Cf. his vol. 2, 357 ff. We shall give the quotation from Ritschl at the close of our chapter. The reader will not overlook that this author of the four volumes on the *Dogmengeschichte des Protestantismus,* who was professor at the University of Bonn in the Rhinelands, the university which was established to be the oustanding school for the most consistent type of the Prussian Church Union (the so-called *Consensus Union,* cf. the Topical Index) was the son and biographer of the late Professor Albrecht Ritschl of Goettingen. Surely, he will not be taken as a Lutheran partisan when we quote him below on the seventeenth century Lutherans.

[3] Cf. Otto Ritschl, *op. cit.* II, 388 ff., 359 ff., 365 ff., 371 ff.

lems of that day. This has been described in our preceding Chapter (VII). And three years later, 1580, it was republished in a *Book of Concord* together with the three so-called *Ecumenical Symbols,* the *Augsburg Confession* of 1531 and its *Apology,* Luther's *Smalcald Articles* with its *Appendix* by Melanchthon and the *Smaller* and the *Larger Catechisms* of Luther. With this event the Lutheran Church received a doctrinal unity which constituted the basis for the gradual development of the large theological literature during the *age of orthodoxy.* It also gave to Lutheranism the confessional consciousness as a Church. This was an important event in Church history.

4. *Discussions following the Formula of Concord.*

a. The student must be asked to read about the reply of the *Reformed Theologians to the Formula of Concord in the "Newsted Admonition."* This historical situation has been described extensively in the writer's book on the *Union Movements,* pp. 34-36; also in his *Introduction,*[2] pp. 186 and 401 ff. The separation between the Lutherans and the Reformed as distinct Churches of Protestantism had become final. In chapters three and four of our book on the *Union Movements,* we have reviewed nine historical endeavors, covering a century and a half, to bring about a union between the Lutherans and Reformed. All failed. Later, 1817, the Prussian King Frederick William III, finally did promulgate the Union, but confessional reaction made it necessary to change the absorptive character of this union to a mere confederate union (1834). This is a story that must be studied in another connection.[4] Here our attention must not be diverted from the theological discussions during this age of strict orthodoxy.

b. Before beginning a review of the theological labors of the age here under observation, mention must be made of *two* great works of the previous period. The one was the *Magdeburg Centuries* (1559-1574) published in 13 volumes under the editorship of Flacius. It was "a history of the Church according to centuries." The first three volumes represent a work on *Biblical Dogmatics* by Wigand and Judex.[5] In itself it was intended as a counter-production to Melanchthon's *Loci.* The second of these great works, a real classic, was Chemnitz's *Examen Concilii Tridentini* (4 vols. 1565-1573). It was a most searching work concerning the errors of Romanism.[6]

c. Nine years after publication of the *Formula of Concord,* at and after the colloquy between the Lutherans and the Reformed in Montbeliard (1586), a comprehensive insight was received into the fundamental difference between them on the *doctrine of predestination.*[7] Calvin taught a double predestination: of some for eternal life and others for reprobation. At first there was considerable hesitation in the camp of the Reformed to accept this doctrine. It was bound to affect the seriousness of the general call. Art. XI of the *Formula,* while insisting that our actual salvation is the result of predestination, had refused to teach a predestination unto death. But due to the influence of Beza, the Calvinistic doctrine of a double predestination found favor and through the Canons of Dort (1618-1619) became recognized dogma.[8] This event revived the discussion also among the Lutherans. It was remembered that Luther in his conflict with Erasmus (1524) had taught a double predestination, although referring the thought of reprobation to the secretly working God into whose doings man must not pry. (The

---

[4] See our *Union Movements,* pp. 110 ff., also our *Churches and Sects of Christendom,* 1940, pp. 593 ff.
[5] *Syntagma,* etc., 1560-1563. Cf. O. Ritschl, I, 140 f.
[6] Later, 1634-1637, a like work of 4 vols., *Confessio Catholica,* came from the pen of J. Gerhard.
[7] O. Ritschl, IV, 129 ff.
[8] See in our Vol. II, Book IV, Chap. II, on *Arminianism in Holland.*

Deus absconditus.) Melanchthon, being led by the same motive, simply taught that he who has been justified should also believe in his predestination for eternal life. This teaching was received more and more by orthodox Lutheranism. The decisive word in this matter was spoken by a leading dogmatician of that day who had also written much along exegetical lines, Aegidius Hunnius (1550-1603). Against the particularism of the Reformed teaching of a double predestination, on the one hand, and against S. Huber's virtual elimination even of the idea of a real election, on the other hand,[9] Hunnius made God's eternal election dependent upon the divine foreknowledge of those who come to accept in true faith God's universal grace.[10] The settlement upon this position then led the Lutherans, especially after the decrees of the Synod at Dort, to severe attacks on the Calvinists (pp. 151 ff.). They pointed out the fundamental difference regarding the conception of God between the two Churches. To Calvin and his Reformed followers God was essentially and pre-eminently the jealous guardian of His own glory; as everything else in the world, so also the reprobation of some and the election of others is a means for God's glorification.[11] The Lutherans, on the other hand, in their fundamental position upon the universality of grace, held to the conviction which Luther had acquired in the hard struggle of his soul, namely that the analysis of God's essence consists in His unselfish goodness and love, in which He wants to give eternal salvation to all men if only they are willing to accept His grace. With their attacks from this standpoint, the Lutherans pointed to the Calvinistic particularism in the conception of the call and even insisted that it included the teaching that Christ had not died for all men, a charge which the Reformed always vigorously protested. This one controversy on predestination crowded into the background the interest in other topics of disagreement.

 d. Other topics of disagreement with the Reformed were: (1) the old difference between the realistic or the symbolical conception of the Lord's Supper. (2) Herewith connected was the relation of the divinity and the humanity in the person of Christ: the Lutherans taught that with the incarnation of the *Logos* the divinity had communicated its attributes to the human nature (*communicatio idiomatum realis*); the Reformed followed Zwingli in his statement that in Scripture the one God-man, in the possession of His two natures, is sometimes spoken of as God and sometimes as man. He is just *called* either the one or the other (*communicatio idiomatum verbalis*).[12] Calvin also had refused here to follow Luther.

 In addition to this warfare against the Reformed there was the continued conflict with Rome. Gerhard published his *Confessio Catholica* of four volumes (1634-1637), comparable to the above mentioned great work of Chemnitz. Anabaptism and like tendencies of the spiritualistic type, as also the Unitarianism in the form of the Socinianism of that age, were strongly combatted.

 The irritation of the Lutherans was chiefly toward the Reformed. What was the reason? The Lutherans felt that their own territory had been invaded. The Palatinate was lost to Calvinism. In 1563 we have the publication of the *Heidelberg Catechism.* In Saxony where the pupils of Melanchthon at the Wittenberg University stood opposed

---

[9] According to him, even the godless, who are ultimately lost, are included in God's decree of election.
[10] Cf. O. Ritschl, IV, 143 ff.
[11] Cf. in this volume our Chap. VI on Calvin with reference to his *Institutes.*
[12] See our *Introduction*², p. 139.

communicatio idiomatum and *ubiquity,* which in that day were the shibboleths of genuine Lutheranism, the publication of the *Exegesis Perspicua* (1574) revealed the fact that the mediating and noncommittal attitude of Melanchthonism might become a stepping-stone to Calvinism. A Crypto-Calvinistic propaganda was in progress at many places. Reaction against the separation of Lutheranism from Calvinism in the *Formula of Concord* (1577) was soon one of the moving factors in that widely spread propaganda.

Hesse (1581-1592) and Anhalt (1595-1647) also became centers for this agitation. The city of Bremen (1581-1595) and also Lippe (1602) were *converted* to Calvinism. Then, through influences from the Palatinate and from Hesse, Elector Sigismund of Brandenburg, the Hohenzoller, turned to the Reformed and soon began to work for the conversion of his people (1613). It was in the movements at Anhalt that the term *Reformed* as a name for the adherents of Calvin in Germany first came into use. All these conversions had for their declared object the *reformation* of Lutheranism from the remnants of Romanism. [13] Lutheranism with its realistic conceptions in the heritage from Luther was pictured as very coarse compared with the more polished views of Calvinism and the pliability and the humanism of the Melanchthonian school. It was favored at the courts and by the princes. These, as the rule, were forcing either a *reformation* or a union with Calvinism. Historical Lutheranism was to be crowded out of Germany. If the work was begun by conferences, then these were dominated by the princes in such a way that the Lutheran side had no chance. This was one reason why the seventeenth century Lutherans looked upon Calvinism of that time as their most dangerous opponent and even hesitated to join the conferences with the Reformed theologians. In addition to this political reason it must be kept in mind, of course, that to Luther and to the followers of his principles the differences between the Wittenberg and the Zurich-Geneva Reformations have never been matters of indifference. It should not be overlooked that to Calvin himself the differences between himself and Luther were of greatest importance, as must be judged from many statements in his *Institutes.*

5. *Further Controversies and Developments which have marked this Age of Orthodoxy* (Cf. H. Sasse, *Here We Stand,* 1937, Chap. III).

a. The Inspiration of Scripture as a teaching was at home among the fathers of the ancient Church. See Book I, Chap. VI. The writings of the Canon were used as source and as norm of truth. Augustine already had given expression to Luther's principle that Scripture interprets itself (*scriptura sui ipsius interpres*). All the Reformed theologians of the outgoing Middle Ages believed in the sole authority of Scripture. Its inspiration was generally accepted. The traditional teaching of the Church was held to be true because of its agreement with Scripture. Cf. the positions of Biel, D'Ailly and many others. Occam was courageous enough to turn the *quia* into a *quatenus,* namely, by insisting that only in so far as dogmas are supported by Scripture can they claim to be authoritative.[14] The revolutionary thought in the stand of Luther at the Leipzig Disputation was the assertion that the official Church was teaching things out of harmony with Scripture as the exclusive standard of truth.

As to the extent of the Canon, however, Luther personally found himself in a critical attitude to the *antilegomena* of the New Testament (Hebrews, James, Jude, Apocalypse),

---

[13] See our *Union Movements,* pp. 36-40.
[14] Cf. Seeberg, *DG,* III⁴, 722 ff.

taking offense especially at James 2: 24. This matter of the extent of the Biblical Cano
was to him an unsolved problem which engaged his thought into the last years of h
life.[15]   Once in Luther's writings, however (W, VI, 95), we find that he aime
to reconcile Paul and James, although the reference here was to James 2: 17 an
not also to 2: 24.[16] Melanchthon, following his own conservative trait in matters (
tradition, was averse to all critical expression regarding the Canon.[17] But among tl
representatives of Lutheran orthodoxy until down to Aegidius Hunnius and Matthi;
Hafenreffer the critical attitude of Luther to certain books of our present Canon ;
maintained in a varying degree.[18]   Still, Luther, with Melanchthon, Brenz and all th
leaders was painstaking in conforming all doctrine to the testimony of Scripture.
was largely because of Luther's strong emphasis upon the Word of God that the Churc
after him is even today spoken of as the *Church of the Word*.

This takes us to the manner of Scripture inspiration. On this question there wa
among the Reformers an absence of unity and clarity. Bullinger was the first Protestar
theologian to attempt in a monograph a connected and detailed doctrine of Bibl
inspiration (1538). Calvin, in the second edition of his *Institutes* (1543), settled th
extent of the Canon and taught verbal inspiration: "The sacred writers received thei
messages through a *dictate* of the *words* by the Holy Spirit."[19]

The high estimate that Luther and Melanchthon held of the Word as source an
standard for truth did not cause them also to offer a formal doctrine of inspiration. Thei
entire teaching presupposed their belief in the inspiration of Scripture. Calvin stresse
the Scriptures as a book of laws and rules for conduct and belief. The divine verba
inspiration as such occupies his interest as a safeguard for truth and life. M. Bucer i
his commentary to the Gospel (1536), and H. Bullinger in a monograph (1538), ha
preceded Calvin with deliverances of a like nature, although the *verbal* inspiration wa
not yet mentioned. The Lutheran group of Reformers, even where the significance o
certain verbal expressions is pressed, have a different way of writing on the subject.

Twelve years after the publication of Bullinger's monograph on the Scriptures[20]
Lutheran of the Melanchthonian school, George Major, also wrote a monograph. Not
the title which read *De origine et autoritate Verbi Dei*, Wittenberg, 1550, and compar
it with Bullinger's title. There is no intention here to discredit the title of Bullinger
many Lutherans have written legitimately under the same title—later when the questior
of the relation of God's Word to the Bible was in need of ventilation. But attentior
must be called to the inclination of the Reformed theologians (Bucer, Bullinger, Calvin
the Reformed Confessions) to write and to theorize on the Bible *as a book* and th
inclination of the Lutheran Reformers to center their interest first of all on the *Wora
of God*. Melanchthon, in his first edition of the *Loci*, during the years of special conflic
with Rome, was very outspoken in stressing with Luther the need to follow the Scriptures. He believed in their inspiration as we have seen above, although rarely referring
to it. In carefully worded definitions he wrote first of the Old Testament and then o

[15] O. Ritschl, I, 71 referring to P. Drews, *Disputations of Dr. Martin Luther*, 1895, p. 714 with reference
to a disputation in 1543.
[16] See O. Ritschl, as cited.
[17] Cf. *op. cit.*, I, 116 f. See the *Apology* in the *Book of Concord*, 124 ff. *CR*, XXV, 590 ff.; XXI, 842.
[18] F. Kropatscheck, *Das Schriftprinzip der luth. Kirche*, Vol. 1, 1904. J. Leitpoldt, *Die Kritik des Reforma-
tionszeitalters am neutestamentlichen Kanon* in *Deutsch-Evangelische Blaetter*, 1906, pp. 773-789.
[19] *CR*, XXIX, 631. XXX, 849. Cf. the *Institutes* of the last (3rd) ed., IV, 8, 6, 9.
[20] *De Scripturae Sanctae Autoritate, Certitudine, Firmitate et Absoluta Perfectione*, 1538.

he New in the 1543 edition of the *Loci*.[21] Melanchthon did not speak of inspiration, he simply said that God had willed that His revealed Word should be left to us in writing.[22] The interest of Melanchthon was in the revealed *Word* (*verbum, omne verbum, universum verbum Dei*, the *totam doctrinam a Deo nobis traditum*).[22a] In conformity with Luther he settles upon Law and Gospel as the special *Word* in the Word. Guided by this thought he even risks the distinction between the essential substance in Scripture dealing with that fundamental topic, and other (historical) materials which do not all have the same significance.[23] The Scriptures were to him the reliable record of divine revelation in which we must have confidence because the "prophets in the O. T. were teachers immediately called by God" (*doctores immediate vocati a Deo*) and because the "apostles in the New Testament were immediately called by Christ" (*doctores . . . immediate vocati a Christo*). The reliability of the Old Testament message was confirmed by the *testimony of miracles* as that of the New Testament *by the testimony of the Holy Spirit and by miracles.*

The position of J. Brenz, reformer of Wuerttemberg (d. 1570), was similar to that of Luther and Melanchthon. It is of interest to note that in a critical estimate of the Calvinistic *Confessio Gallicana* at the Poissy Conference (1561), he had himself commissioned to criticize that in Article III of this Confession the letters of James and Jude, as also the Book of Revelation are spoken of as belonging to the Canon.[24] J. Wigand and M. Judex, belonging to the *Gnesio-Lutherans*, both joint publishers of the *Syntagma* (1560), which was practically a part of the introduction to the *Magdeburg Centuries*, did not yet speak of a verbal inspiration of Scripture. But, following the Church father Eusebius, they looked upon the Acts of the Apostles, all Epistles of Paul and the two first Epistles of John and Peter, as trustworthy writings on the Holy Spirit's work through the apostles, without speaking of special inspiration. It was declared that these authentic writings, together with the specially inspired Gospels, are to be used for reliable articles of faith. As less certain they considered the *Antilegomena*. In their critique of the Epistle of *James* they follow Eusebius and join with Luther pointing especially to its departure from the analogy of apostolic teaching, criticizing particularly that while mentioning Christ it does not speak of his work and that the author calls himself a *servant* (*doulos*). Against Jude also is mentioned that "he does not call himself apostle but only servant; also that (cf. v. 14) he admits that he had lived after the time of the apostles." From tradition he quotes the story of the struggle of the archangel Michael with the devil for the body of Moses, and also speaks of the prophecy of Enoch, while all such things have no mention in the reliable books of the Old Testament. As to Hebrews, they observe the non-Pauline authorship, pointing to the fact that Heb. 2: 3 f. does not agree with Gal. 1: 12, and that the teaching in chapters 6: 1-6 and 10: 26 concerning those fallen from grace that they cannot return through repentance agrees neither with Paul nor the other apostles and is in conflict with Matthew 11: 28. Second Peter and the two brief letters by John are taken to be genuine. The Book of Revelation in the New Testament is not to be discredited, because it is not out of harmony with the

---

21 *CR*, XXI, 1099.
22 *CR*, XV, 531; XXVIII, 437.
22a *CR*, XV, 1312.
23 See his *Enaratio in Ecclesiasten* of 1550 in *CR*, XIV, 94.
24 In the following we quote by extracting from O. Ritschl's *Dogmengeschichte des Protestantismus*, I, 133 ff.

analogy of faith (cf. p. 137). The review here given by O. Ritschl is of interest because it shows how early Lutheranism groped and struggled for a concept of Scripture and the Canon.

Among the Lutheran theologians it was Flacius who first spoke of the verbal inspiration of Scripture, and following him it was Johann Gerhard who developed this into a Protestant dogma. Different from his co-laborers Wigand and Judex who had spoken only of the New Testament, Flacius stepped into a discussion of the inspiration of Scripture as a whole, including also the Old Testament. The writing in which this was done is his *Clavis Scripturae,* 1674.[25] To Flacius the Holy Spirit was the real author of Scripture. Still he spoke eloquently of Paul's art of oratory and of John's style but through their individuality it is the Holy Spirit that speaks. We are here continuing to review the situation after O. Ritschl, *Dogmengeschichte des Protestantismus,* I, 142 ff. He says that the thought of a mechanical process does not fit the situation. Rather is the whole consciousness of the sacred writer filled with an enthusiasm produced by the Spirit. The student will feel the need of following the references of our author to the special sentences in his quotations (p. 143 to 147). The matter of the Hebrew vowels, which Flacius did not mention, offered difficulties in the explanation of reality (see Ritschl, p. 148). To Flacius the relation of the divine and the human in the concept of inspiration was that of an organic union which has always been characteristic of Lutheranism. In the Neo-Lutheranism of today we meet the statement that the Scriptures are at the same time wholly human and wholly divine. It is a dynamic relation between the divine and the human, resulting in a mutual *perichoresis*—a thought concerning which Luther and his followers were in deep inner agreement with the New Alexandrian School in the ancient Church.

It must not be overlooked that Chemnitz and the contemporary theologians, although not speaking of *verbal* inspiration, taught very emphatically the inspiration of all the canonical books of both Testaments. But there had been no occasion for developing it into a standard teaching excepting in heated conflict with Rome, with Bellarmin especially. But J. Gerhard found the poise needed for treating the subject systematically. He did it in his *Locus de Scriptura,* 1610. Like Flacius he took his position on the declaration that in Scripture it is God, the Holy Spirit, who speaks, and that therefore Scripture is *theopneustos* (II Tim. 3: 16). The writers are *amanuenses* (See Gerhard's *Locus* as cited, at several places Cf. p. 55). Between Scripture and the Word of God there is declared to be no essential difference. He followed the Reformed theologian A. Polanus in extending the inspiration to the punctuations in the Hebrew vowels. Among the later dogmaticians of the seventeenth century it was especially J. A. Quenstedt (d. 1688), who completed the dogma on inspiration of Scripture in the Lutheran Church of that age. It was he who furnished the outline for discussion of the problem by the three propositions: (1) The holy writers received an outward and an inner impulse from the Holy Spirit for writing (*impulsus ad scribendum*). (2) The Holy Spirit also gave them the materials and the words (suggestio rerum et verborum). (3) He led them in such a way that they were guarded against error (*directio divina*). Much of what was said in connection with this discussion in that age was not maintainable. The "outward and inner impulse" was spoken of in such a way that there was little room for considering the historical occasions and motives that had brought into existence

---

25 Cf. his biographer J. W. Preger, *Matthias Flacius Illyricus, Clavis* etc., edited by J. Musaeus, 1659-61.

o many of the Biblical writings. There was an insistence on "verbal" inspiration and ɔn "inerrancy" (not to be ignored), but they went too far in establishing principles with egard to purely outward and non-religious matters. However, looking at the situation rom present-day conservative positions we may say that the above-mentioned three ɔoints in Quenstedt's propositions could become very acceptable to an evangelically conservative theology of today if the truth revealed in Holy Scripture is looked upon, ɪot as something that came to earth unmediated, as with a cloudburst, or by mechanical ɪnanipulation, but in a history of redemption in a variety of ways: under a wonderful *providentia specialissima*, with God's own hand electing, calling, moving and directing ɪn a peculiar development. This would bring the seventeenth century orthodoxy very ɪear to the Erlangen theology in the heritage of which, consciously or unconsciously, so ɪnany of the Lutherans of today stand.[26]

The late Marburg Professor A. F. C. Vilmar, in his lectures on Dogmatics (published 1874, recently re-edited), wrote interestingly on those three propositions of Quenstedt: "To these sentences," he says, "nothing needs to be opposed, provided we ːeep in mind that the Apostles, in their writing, stood under no *other*, especially under ɪo *higher* influence of the Holy Spirit than they had received for their ministry of ːeaching. There was no special influence for their writing that they did not have for ːheir teaching." (See page 98.) And it was "their Christian experience, exclusively, in connection with the Church, which gives to the Holy Scriptures that irresistible and constantly renewed confirmation (*Beglaubigung*, pp. 99 ff.)." These statements of Vilmar (d. 1868), a strong witness for an evangelical Lutheranism, were out of agreement with ːhe special builders of the dogma of Bible inspiration in the seventeenth century (Flacius, Gerhard, Hutter, Quenstedt, Calov, Hafenreffer, Huelsemann, Baier, Dannhauer, Koenig, Hollaz).

Neither would these men have been in agreement with that leader of nineteenth century Lutheranism in Leipzig, Professor C. E. Luthardt (d. 1902), when concerning the ɪnethod in Dogmatics he made the following statements: "We shall not put the doctrine ɔf Holy Scripture and its inspiration at the head of the system of doctrine (*Glaubens-'ehre*), as it has been the custom, but we shall make it an integral part of the whole system where it has its own logical place." "Our certainty begins with Christ Himself. While the certainty of Scripture inspiration is an essential part in the structure of doc-ːrine it is not itself the real foundation of the structure. For it is not because of Scripture ːhat we believe in Christ, but in connection with our faith in Christ we also believe in ːhe Scriptures; because it is He of whom Scripture testifies. Otherwise our faith in Christ would rest upon an intellectual procedure of proving truth, or upon a commandment of Scripture, while the real foundation of faith must be an inner conviction of the thing itself, a testimony of the conscience." [27] This is Erlangen theology. These statements ɔf both Vilmar and Luthardt are out of tune with the position of the seventeenth century ːheologians. As to the quotation from Luthardt the question will be asked by true believers in Christ and His salvation whether the Word of God, preached or written, does not have originally and fundamentally—different from all non-Biblical communica-ːion—an influence, an appeal, a converting and regenerating power. This is the teaching

---

[26] See our *Churches and Sects of Christendom*, p. 242. Note there especially our reference to J. C. K. Hofmann, *Weissagung und Erfuellung* (Prophecy and Fulfillment), 1841-1844, and his *Schriftbeweis* (Scripture Proof), 2 vols., 1852-1856.

[27] Luthardt, *Die Christliche Glaubenslehre*[2], 1906, 72.

of Scripture in many places, and it is in harmony with the Christian experience of the true believers all through the ages. It must not be overlooked, of course, that Luthardt, in the above quoted passages, speaks of the system in Dogmatics and not generally of the Holy Spirit's work in creating the Christian life.

FOR FURTHER ORIENTATION

Note: I trust my readers will bear with me in the evident inadequacy of method concerning the following *interpolated* section. For a work of this nature there are moments when a conspectus (*Zusammenschau*) of divers developments can claim a place—exceptionally.

We shall mention several works outside of the seventeenth century Lutheran Dogmaticians which have at the head of their systems the doctrine of Scripture Inspiration in an especially developed form; and then we shall also note the passing of Dogmatics into other types. There is a difference in method, but back of it there may be a difference also in the use made of Scripture in the building of the dogma.

H. Schmid, *Die Dogmatik der Evangelisch-Lutherischen Kirche*, 1843, is widely known. This book of one volume, in a very concentrated form, had seven German editions (up to 1893). It was translated into Swedish, and also into English with a third edition in 1899 (by C. A. Hay and H E. Jacobs and published by the Lutheran Publication Society in Philadephia). The sub-title in literal translation from the German reads: "Verified from the original sources." The reference is to the Lutheran Dogmaticians of the seventeenth century and their use of Scripture.

Outstanding in its influence as a work on Dogmatics in the second half of the nineteenth century was F. A. Philippi, *Kirchliche Glaubenslehre,* six small volumes, some of these with three editions (1854-1890). This work belongs to the Lutheranism before the Erlangen movement. It strongly opposed some of the specific principles of the latter. Volume I, from pp. 125 to 246, discussed the Scriptures as the source of Dogmatics, stressing their verbal inspiration. (Cf. O. W. Heick in our Volume Two.)

Also to be mentioned as belonging to this class is W. Rohnert, *Die Dogmatik der Evangelisch Lutherischen Kirche,* 1902. One volume, 640 pages, very lucidly written. Rohnert was author also of the two monographs: *Die Inspiration der Heiligen Schrift und ihre Bestreiter; Was lehrt Luther von der Inspiration der Heiligen Schrift?* In this Dogmatics the Inspiration of Scripture has its place at the head of the system and is discussed on pages 41-117.

Concordia Lutheranism in America has produced several works on Dogmatics. There is the purely Biblicistic *Outline of Doctrinal Theology* by A. L. Graebner, 1910, Concordia, St. Louis, Mo. Also the *Evangelisch Lutherische Dogmatik* by A. Hoenecke, at the seminary of the Wisconsin Synod, now Thiensville, four volumes, 1909. This work, complete and scholarly, is characterized by dignified objectivity. Especially outstanding is *Die Christliche Dogmatik,* by F. A. O. Pieper, (Dr. Walther's successor in Concordia, St. Louis), three large volumes, 1917. Both of these last named works present in their initial volume, as the special foundation of the system, a very extensive discussion of Scripture as the only source of Dogmatics. Pieper's discussion covers in Vol. I the pages 233 to 370. The Inspiration of Scripture alone fills pages 262 to 370. This Dogmatics has been called a revival (*Nachbluete*) of the old Lutheran dogmatics. But it is very much modernized in the form of its presentation. This can be observed especially in its remarkable *Lebendigkeit der Fragestellung* and with its keen polemics against all forms of theological liberalism. In connection with this three-volume work of Pieper, and based upon this work, in English, we mention the ably written *Christian Dogmatics* by Prof. J. T. Mueller, in St. Louis, a Handbook of Doctrinal Theology for Pastors, Teachers and Laymen, in one volume, 665 pages, 1934. The three-volume work of Pieper has now been published in an English translation by Prof. W. Albrecht, 1941. The print is in mimeotype only, produced by the Concordia Supply Company, Concordia Seminary, Springfield, Illinois, with an omission of many of the footnotes.

Note: It should here be added that in 1872 C. F. W. Walther republished C. Loeber's *Dogmatics* of 1711 (used for decades in the seminaries at Springfield, Ill. and Dubuque, Ia.); also that in 1844 the seminary in Neuendettelsau (Germany) republished for use in America the *Epitome Credendorum* of N. Hunnius, edited by Dean Brandt (3rd ed. by F. Bauer, 1870). W. Loehe, with his deep interest in the Lutheran Church in America, had this book translated into English (1847). It should also be added that Dr. Walther, about 1879, arranged for a large new edition of Baier's *Compendium Theologiae Positivae,* 1886, which was used in Concordia Seminary at St. Louis.   ,

In other Lutheran bodies of various synodical names in America we have a number of authors with works on Dogmatics. The first was S. Sprecher, at Springfield, Ohio, with his *Groundwork of a System of Evangelical Lutheran Theology,* 1879. He stressed, in the meaning of the older Pietism, the theology of experience versus the dogmatics of confessionalism. It was planned as a "groundwork" for succeeding volumes which have not appeared. Cf. the interesting review by C. G. Stork in the *Lutheran Quarterly,* Oct. 1879. As succeeding works we mention: M. Valentine, Gettysburg, *Christian Theology,* two vols., 1906; R. G. Weidner, *Monographs on Dogmatics,* Maywood Seminary, 1905-1915. H. E. Jacobs, Mount Airy (Philadelphia), *A Summary of the Christian Faith,* 1919; A. G. Voigt, Columbia, S. C., *Biblical Dogmatics,* 1917 f. (2nd ed. 1925 with title "Between God and Man"); C. E. Lindberg, Rock Island, Ill., *Christian Dogmatics, with Notes on the History of Doctrine,* 1922, the first publication had been in Swedish, 1898; J. A. Singmaster of Gettysburg, *A Handbook of Christian Theology,* 1927; E. Hove, Norwegian Lutheran Church, *Christian Doctrine,* 1931; J. Stump, Minneapolis, *The Christian Faith,* 1932.

Some of these writings bear upon themselves the marks of influences from certain leading conservative works which have appeared on the other side of the Atlantic, having had their orientation chiefly in some outstanding positions of the Erlangen School. After F. H. Frank's work on *Christian Certainty,* 1873, it was chiefly C. E. Luthardt's *Kompendium der Dogmatik,* in eleven editions (from 1865 to 1914) which was an outstanding guide. Recently this work has been revised for a new edition by Professor R. Jelke—Dr. M. Reu, among others, co-operating (in the 12th and in the 13th edition). We referred before to Luthardt's *Christliche Glaubenslehre gemeinverstaendlich dargestellt,* 1898 and 1906. Then there was the above mentioned *Dogmatik* by Vilmar, 1874, recently republished. For a full review, in brief mention, of all authors on Protestant Dogmatics, see Luthardt (Jelke), *Kompendium der Dogmatik,* pp. 46-48. It was a leading trait of the Erlangen School to speak of the Inspiration of Scripture as closely related to the Incarnation of Christ and his work of redemption. Cf. A. von Oettingen, *Lutherische Dogmatik,* 1897, 3 vols. Here Dogmatics appears as an exhibition of a developing organism of grace and truth (See Vol II, 334-372). It is in

harmony with this position that in America Dr. H. E. Jacobs, in his *Summary*, and
Dr. A. G. Voigt, in his *Biblical Dogmatics,* discussed the doctrine of Inspiration late
in the book in sections dealing with the work of the Holy Spirit. It may here be men
tioned that Professor M. Reu is about ready to publish his continually revised and
amplified monographs on dogmatical subjects in a work which is to have the title
"Christian Dogmatics." From the sections that have appeared so far, we know it will
be a Dogmatics fundamentally Biblicistic in character. For further discussion of the
theological situation along this line see Volume Two by Dr. O. W. Heick in his review
of *Continental Theology.*

b. The controversy concerning the *Distinction between Fundamentals and Non
Fundamentals* was another topic of discussion in this age. In Volume Two, Section
in our description of George Calixtus and the Syncretistic Controversies, we shall dea
with this old problem in post-Reformation theology. Here we shall offer only a few
historical sidelights for students who desire to choose this field for special study. I shall
be careful to point to the special places in the four volumes on the *Dogmengeschichte
des Protestantismus* by Otto Ritschl, where he has written on this subject. The litera
ture in his footnotes contains most valuable titles for such a study. The two men who
may be called the pioneers in the study of this subject were the Wittenberg theologian:
Aegidius Hunnius and Leonhard Hutter (1563-1616). After them the development
issued into the Syncretistic Controversies in connection with the names which are to be
mentioned below. The theological atmosphere for the special interest in this and related
subjects had been created by Flacius and later by John Gerhard in the Jena University
the author of the *Loci Theologici* in 9 volumes (1610-1622).[28] In the construction of
this great work there were observable the influences from Melanchthon. As to its con
tents the Dogmatics of the age was fundamentally Biblicistic, following the verbal inspira
tion of Scripture.[29] The leading interest, however was in the Scripture thoughts which
are related to the doctrine of justification.

This led the theologians to the inquiry concerning the Fundamentals and Non
Fundamentals of Scripture. In this question the Reformed of Holland and of England
were also intensely interested. This one interest became the topic of theological work
for centuries in all Protestant communities. The argumentation in Germany at that
time issued in a long conflict between the irenically inclined George Calixtus, professo
at the former Helmstedt University, and the strictly Lutheran theologians, chiefly at the
Wittenberg, Jena and Strassburg Universities. The outstanding leaders in these "Syn
cretistic Controversies," on the Lutheran side, were Abr. Calovius (1612-1686), J. Huelse
mann (1629-1661) and J. C. Dannhauer (d. 1666).[30]

c. *Other Doctrinal Interests. The Unio Mystica.* The aim of the strictest among
Lutherans in their striving for purity of doctrine was at an absolute unity of the Faith
Syncretism was generally rejected. But the failing of Calovius to see his *Consensu
Repetitus* of 1664 accepted (cf. our *Union Movements,* p. 106) made it clear that the
Lutheran Church of that time was not willing to add further Confessions to the *Book of*

[28] Cf. O. Ritschl, *DG,* pp. 142 ff.
[29] *Ibid.* I, 168 ff.; cf. IV, p. 300.
[30] For an historical estimate of Calixtus, see our book on the *Union Movements,* pp. 82 to 86. In O. Ritsch
see IV, pp. 365. In our *Union Movements* this controversy has been reviewed, pp. 86 to 109. An extende
extract is given in this work, Vol. Two, Chapter I; concerning England the review is continued in Chapter III. I
the work of O. Ritschl, as cited, compare I, p. 240, and in the same volume the whole of Chapter LXVII dea
with this subject.

Concord. The longer the lapse of time the more it was seen also that there were differences in the Lutheran Church between groups and theologians, which could not be regulated by discipline. We shall indicate a few of such cases and refer the reader to places where he can go for further information: (1) We refer to the *krypsis* theory of the Wuerttemberg theologians concerning the divine majesty of Christ during His earthly life against the *kenosis* position which, in varying expressions, has been maintained in Lutheranism (1624).[31] (2) There were protests also against J. Arndt (1555-1621) on account of the features of mysticism which he introduced into Lutheranism. It paved the way for the Pietistic movement and even contributed to a new locus in Dogmatics, the *unio mystica,* which under leadership of Huelsemann and Calovius went beyond what Luther and Melanchthon had taught of a sacramental union. These theologians taught a mysterious union taking place between the pious souls and divinity.[32] Ritschl, in his work, has most interesting observations along this line. He insists that Calovius, by incorporating into his system the exercise of faith as trust, which he takes as an effect of the mystical union, was obliged to cover the intellectualistic adulteration of the original Lutheran doctrine of justification.[33]

d. The Method of these Lutherans had become more and more that of the revived Aristotelian scholasticism of J. Zabarella of Padua in Italy (1532-1580). In this Melanchthon had already made the beginning by employing the syllogistic method of leading to conclusions. He was followed especially by J. Wigand and soon also by J. Gerhard, N. Hunnius (in his Latin work), Huelsemann, Calovius and Quenstedt. With this method went a thoroughness, exactness and a comprehensiveness concerning details, which kept the student from seeing the inner religious connections. It had been the unfailing gift of Luther never to lose from sight the leading essentials and their religious significance. It is this whole observation which has resulted in the judgment of present-day historians that Melanchthon, who has always received either praise or criticism for his irenic attitude in the divisive problems during the Reformation age, was at the same time responsible for the introduction of the scholastic method during the age of Lutheran orthodoxy.

e. But the Type of This Scholastic Theology Could Not Maintain Itself. After a reign of about a hundred years, at the end of the seventeenth century, it had spent its force as a method, even though the theological system in more reasonable form has continued for centuries to influence the practical teachings within Lutheranism. This can be observed in the best of its many catechisms, in many of its handbooks for Dogmatics and in very much of its devotional literature. In the new theology since Schleiermacher the seventeenth century theology of the *Loci* was abandoned.[34]

As to its scholastic method, then, and other features characteristic of that age, the seventeenth century theology ceased to function and had to leave the field to other theological tendencies. It was in itself a species of rationalism; not of the Socinian type, as was historic Rationalism, but in its method of argumentation with that constant appeal to reason. A contributory factor to the discrediting of the seventeenth century

---

[31] See the *Lutheran Cyclopedia,* pp. 260 f.; O. Ritschl, as cited, IV, pp. 188 ff.

[32] Cf. O. Ritschl, IV, 193 ff., 213 ff. Other Lutheran theologians fell in line and developed the *unio mystica* into a recognized topic in theology. J. A. Quenstedt (1617-1688) and D. Hollaz (1648-1713). Cf. *op. cit.,* IV, 223 ff.

[33] See his argumentation, IV, 218 f.

[34] See in our Book V, Chapter Two, our long discussion of Schleiermacher, and in our *Churches and Sects of Christendom,* pp. 226 ff.

Lutheranism later was its intolerance to all theological dissent. At the outbreak of the Thirty Years War, for instance, there could be military co-operation against Roman Catholicism for the defense of Protestantism only where a confessional union with the Reformed had been established! When the Thirty Years War drew to its close, in which Germany suffered miseries beyond description, many of the more intelligent citizens took deep offense at the unbearable exaggerations in the theological controversies between the Protestants. True, the inroads of Calvinism upon Lutheran Germany, aggravated by the many union movements which were forced by the princes, made the Lutherans confessionally nervous. They had to struggle for the life of their church. Now they should have adorned their good cause with Christian charity. The form of their polemics cannot be commended and would be impossible today. But there is truth in what P. Tschackert, an irenic historian of the last generation, said: "In the rough hull of their orthodoxy they preserved the religious contents of the Reformation and handed them to posterity." [35] But it should not be denied that the Lutheranism of that age was in need of correctives.

I shall close this chapter with the following from Otto Ritschl in the first of his four volumes on *Dogmengeschichte des Protestantismus* (pp. 11 ff.):

"Since about two centuries, but especially since the existence of the evangelical Union, no theological *Richtung* of the old Protestantism has been treated more unjustly than the truest and most genuine followers of Luther, the 'Gnesio-Lutherans' of the sixteenth and the 'orthodox' Lutherans of the seventeenth centuries. . . Without their energetic and forceful work the Protestantism of Germany would not have stood up against Rome's counter-reformation. . . . But what is the objection to these theologians of original Protestantism? The answer is that they conducted an inconsiderate polemics against all their opponents. . . But who ever has written against his opponents with more determination than Luther? Why, now, must the polemical character of the old Protestant orthodoxy serve as a reason against the religious value of this polemic and its recognized significance for the preservation of German Protestantism? . . In what an unbiased spirit have not historians like Loofs taken care of men like Nestorius and Pelagius. . . The gift of historical adaptation to sentiments of others should not be so sacrificed in Protestant History of Doctrine."

---

[35] *PRE³*, III, p. 643. For a completion of this description see our *Union Movements*, pp. 108 f., and read in Vol. II of this work (Chapter I) our treatment of "Calixtus and the Principles of Syncretism."

Chapter Nine

DOCTRINAL DEVELOPMENTS WITHIN
ROMAN CATHOLIC THEOLOGY

Literature: See the Histories of Doctrine by which we have been guided in this volume. See, further, K. WERNER, *Geschichte der Katholischen Theologie seit Trient bis zur Gegenwart*, 1889. A. EHRHARD, *Katholisches Christentum und Kirche Westeuropas*. (Cf. *Kultur der Gegenwart* I, IV, 1,² pp. 298 ff.) J. SCHEUBER, *Kirche und Reformation, Katholisches Leben im 16, und 17. Jahrhundert*,⁴ 1917. MARTIN CHEMNITZ, *Examen Concilii Tridentini*, 1565 f. R. MUMM, *Die Polemik des Martin Chemnitz gegen das Konzil von Trient*, 1905. P. TSCHACKERT'S article on *Council of Trent in PRE* (A. HAUCK'S *Realencyclopaedie*, etc.³), XX, 99 ff. and C. MIRBT'S article on the *Vatican Council* in the same work, XX, 445 ff. K. D. SCHMIDT, *Studien zur Geschichte des Konzils von Trient*, 1925. On both subjects cf. the *Catholic Encyclopedia*. *Canones et Decreta Concilii Trid.* edited by RICHTER and SCHULTE, 1853. *Concilium Tridentinum* in 12 volumes, published by the Goerresgesellschaft, 1901 ff. For a convenient Text of the Creeds and Decrees of Trent (Latin and English) see SCHAFF'S *Creeds: First*, the Historical Introduction, Vol. I, 83-191; *Second*, Texts of the Creeds and Decrees, Vol. II, 77-271. CARL MIRBT, *Quellen zur Geschichte des Papstums*,⁴ 1924. H. RUECKERT, *Die Rechtfertigungslehre auf dem tridentinischen Konzil*, 1925. KATH. WERKE: I. VON DOELLINGER, *Ungedruckte Berichte und Tagebuecher zur Geschichte des Konzils von Trient*, 1876. A. PRUMBS, *Die Stellung des Trienter Konzils zu der Frage nach dem Wesen der heiligmachenden Gnade*, 1909. A. MAICHLE, *Das Dekret de editione et usu sacrorum librorum*, 1914; same, *Der Kanon der biblischen Buecher und das Konzil von Trient*, 1929.

The following two treatises on the Councils of Trent and of the Vatican have been prepared by Dr. O. W. Heick, author of Book II on the Middle Ages.*

I. CATHOLIC THEOLOGY IN THE SIXTEENTH CENTURY.
THE COUNCIL OF TRENT—1545-1563

1. Strange as it seems, during the Middle Ages the Roman Church with few exceptions was without definite universally binding dogmas. In scholasticism we see represented only the private teachings of the theologians. Toward the end of the Middle Ages, the scholastics were split up in different schools with extremely divergent tendencies. At the eve of the Reformation it was the sentiment of the Curialistic party that the usages of the Roman Church are the expression of divine truth (Harnack). For that reason there was generally no inclination for a settled dogma. The *fides implicita*, the disposition readily to believe what the Church believes, was predominant and greatly favored by the highest authorities. Even the religiously awakened circles took little interest in theology and dogma. Their only aim was to bring about a personal revival of Christian faith and practical reform within the Church. Then came the Reformation. It created not only for its own religious life a dogmatic expression, it also compelled Roman Catholicism to turn toward dogmatic problems and to formulate its own doctrines against Protestantism.

2. A number of theologians, engaged in controversies with the Reformation, represented a "Reform Catholicism" which was ready to concede several points to Protestant-

---

* *Note*: The student will hold in mind that the essentials of Roman Catholic Theology in historical development, have been reviewed in Book Two on the Middle Ages, and that the following presentations, together with something additional in Volume Two, are of supplementary significance. Cf. also our *Churches and Sects of Christendom*, 1940 (Chapter Two).

ism. These theologians adhered strictly to the cardinal Roman Catholic viewpoints and rejected sharply the Protestant doctrines. They differed, however, from the older controversialists on account of the deep feeling for the problems stirred up by Luther and in their endeavor to do justice to them in positive statements.[1] We mention especially John Driedo (d. 1535), A. Pighius (d. 1542), John Gropper (d. 1559) and Contarini (d. 1542). These men discussed the authority of the Scriptures and the Church and their mutual relation. But they treated mainly of Freedom and Sin, Grace and Justification, and the Sacraments.

3. While the men just mentioned kept comparatively close to Augustinianism and Thomism, the more liberal school, which was connected with Semi-Pelagianism of the Franciscan theology, was greatly strengthened by the Jesuit Order then coming into prominence. An original theological significance cannot be attributed to Ignatius Loyola (d. 1556). Only certain formulas and methods of his *Spiritual Exercises* are new. Through them he strengthened the authority of the Church, especially the papacy. Owing to the fact that he endeavored to render man's relation to Christianity and the Church as convenient as possible, Ignatius was compelled to lower the moral standards. For this reason the Jesuit Order became the instigator of the Moralist controversies in the succeeding centuries.

4. After the Religious Treaty of Augsburg in 1555, the Roman Catholic Church realized the necessity to begin with the settlement of its dogma. This occurred at the Council of Trent. The historical significance of this Council is valued equally high both by Protestant and by Catholic theologians. Harnack's judgment is significant: "The Decrees of Trent are the shadows of the Reformation. That it was given to Catholicism to understand itself, to give expression to its distinctive character, and to rescue itself from the uncertainties of the Middle Ages, was a debt it owed to the Reformation" (Vol. VII, 3d ed., 36). Seeberg states: "The significance of the Decrees of Trent consists in elevating the medieval theology to a dogma. This Council has indeed quite extensively settled the doctrinal contrasts within the Church, and thereby formed a basis for the future development of Roman Catholicism. The *Tridentinum* put an end to all attempts at an understanding between the churches. Only from now on the breach became definite and irreparable."[2] The Roman Church historian F. X. Funck has this to say: "No less important was its dogmatic effect inasmuch as it settled the Roman Catholic doctrine with reference to those points that were endangered by the Reform movement, and as it put an end to eventual doubts. The Council assumes a highly important position; in a sense, it laid the foundation to modern Roman Catholicism."[3]

5. The Decrees of the Council are, for the greater part, the outcome of a lengthy controversy. Consequently, they are the result of compromises whereby the theology of the Thomists gained a slight superiority over its Nominalistic rival by virtue of the authority of Augustine. In questions where no agreement could be reached, it was thought expedient either to condemn the opponents by means of negative statements, or to observe complete silence. The History of Doctrine must mainly content itself with presenting the settled doctrinal Decrees. These are reprinted in the *Canones et Decreta Concilii Tridentini,* edited by Richter and Schulte *et al.* All of the more important

---

[1] Seeberg, IV[3], 734 ff.

[2] IV[3], 755 f.

[3] *"Katholisches Christentum und Kirche in der Neuzeit"* in *Kultur der Gegenwart,* I, 4, p. 224.

Decrees are also included by Mirbt, *Quellen zur Geschichte des Papstums*. The most important Decrees treat of the Scripture and Tradition, of Sin, Grace and Justification, and of the Sacraments.

6. During the Fourth Session the Decree on the *Canon of the Scriptures* was settled. Here the discussion centered chiefly around the question concerning the authoritative sources of the Christian truth. As such are mentioned the Scriptures and Tradition. Until then Roman Catholicism had not stated their mutual relation dogmatically. In spite of the actual superiority of Tradition, the first place had been assigned theoretically to the Scriptures. As a safeguard against Protestantism the Scriptures and Tradition are now completely co-ordinated. Both are inspired. The extent of the Canon is strictly determined by the enumeration of every single writing that belongs to it. The Apocrypha of the Old Testament are declared canonical. The Vulgate is decreed to be the authentic text. Also the interpretation of Scripture remains a prerogative of the Church. Only such sense of Scripture is to be acknowledged to which the *Holy Mother Church has adhered and still adheres.* The interpretation of Scripture is above all contained in the consensus of the Church Fathers. This interpretation relates to faith and morals only so that in purely grammatical and historical matters a certain freedom was not abolished by the *Tridentinum.*

The exact content and extent of Tradition was left undecided, preserving for the Church freedom of adding and removing according to the exigencies of circumstances. This device left the Church unhampered to reject in the future Protestant teachings even then when it is impossible to furnish arguments from the Scriptures or from the tradition of the past.

7. The Fifth Session settled the Decree on *Original Sin.* In view of contrasting opinions existing within Catholicism, a clear decision was not arrived at. It remained undecided whether man through the fall had lost his righteousness in which he was created or only the *donum superadditum.* Adam's sin extends to all men by propagation not merely by imitation. Through Baptism not only the guilt is remitted, but all wherein sin truly consists is wholly rooted up. The concupiscence remaining in the baptized cannot be called sin in the strictest sense of the term. Sin has only weakened but not extinguished man's free will. The controverted question between Franciscans and Dominicans regarding Mary's relation to original sin was not answered.

8. The long drawn out Sixth Session dealt rather searchingly on the main issue with Protestantism, the doctrine of Justification. (Cf. our more detailed discussions in *Churches and Sects of Christendom*, chap. 2 on Rome.) Justification is defined as the "translation from the standing in which man was born as a son of the First Adam into the standing of grace and adoption of the children of God." This translation runs through *several stages:*

(*a*) In the beginning the prevening grace is effective in man through the Word. He perceives the call of God as intended for him "to which he may assent and with which he may co-operate." This co-operation, however, it is claimed, is not to bear the character of a merit, so that there is no support of the Nominalist's theology of a real *meritum de congruo.* On the other hand, this also means that the *sola gratia* of the Reformation is likewise rejected.

(*b*) This first stage is followed by the second, namely *Justification* itself, the really justifying stage. Justification "is not merely the forgiveness of sins, but also sanctification and renewal of the inward man by a voluntary acceptance of grace and of gifts whereby the unrighteous is made righteous." The forensic conception of justification is condemned as a Protestant heresy. The actual moral change of man not only belongs to justification, it is its main element.

(c) Subjectively, therefore, "justification cannot be effected by faith alone, hope and love must accompany it. Faith is but the foundation and root of human salvation. For faith does not perfectly join us to Christ nor make us living members of His body, unless hope and love are added to it." This inward psychico-moral disposition is infused into men through the sacraments, particularly through Baptism. The Pauline *sine operibus* (Rom. 3: 28), which was at first taken into consideration, was passed over when the Decree was finally drawn up.

(d) The co-operation of man in his justification becomes evident through the statement that justification is capable of being increased by man's concurrent effort and good works. These human acts merit eternal life, but only because they are in themselves gifts of God.

(e) In basing justification upon faith and good works, absolute certainty of present and final pardon can never be attained. The Council evades a positive attitude to the assurance of salvation, but rejects the Protestant conception of assurance as vain and heretical. The real Catholic frame of mind is a disposition of the soul composed of fear and hope (Gregory I). Accordingly there is no assurance of election except through special revelation. Justification may be lost but can be regained through the Sacrament of Penance.

9. The settlement on the *Decree of the Sacraments* occurred during the Seventh Session. With regard to the doctrines of the sacraments sharp contrasts were just then in evidence among the theological schools in Roman Catholicism. According to the teachings of the Thomists, grace is embedded in the sacraments. Certain sacraments press upon man a spiritual and indelible character. According to the Scotists, an inward spiritual power runs parallel to the external act. In order to conceal this discord, the Council refused to make a positive statement concerning the doctrine of the sacraments but satisfied itself with anathematizing the doctrine of the opponents. The medieval decrees of the Council of Florence on the sacraments are followed as closely as possible. The *Seven Sacraments* are, in the words of the Council, instituted by Christ; they are necessary for salvation; they contain the grace which they confer upon the non-resisting, and they are effective *ex opere operato*. Three of them impress upon the soul a distinctive character (Baptism, Confirmation and Ordination).

(a) The Decrees on Baptism and Confirmation do not furnish anything of importance. In regard to the Eucharist the Council declared itself decidedly in favor of transubstantiation. "By the consecration of bread and wine a conversion takes place of the entire substance of the bread into the Body of Christ, and of the entire substance of the wine into the substance of His Blood." Consequently, the Body of Christ is present also *extra usum,* and the consecrated wafer is an object of veneration. The denial of the cup to the laity is justified by the theory that in every particle the whole Christ is present, and that therefore the eating of the bread alone communicates the full Supper.

(b) Closely related to the Lord's Supper is *the Mass,* which is of supreme importance to the Roman Catholic Church. The theory of the sacrifice of the Mass was dealt with not before the Twenty-second Session (September 17, 1562). The anathema is pronounced upon those who deny the Mass to be a true and proper sacrifice. There occurs, so it is claimed, an unbloody and representative repetition of the sacrifice once rendered upon the Cross. "The object of the sacrifice of the Mass then is the body of Christ offered on the Cross. Likewise is Christ the subject Who instituted the sacrifice because He wished to remain priest forever. On the other hand, the Church or the priest, is in some way also to be looked upon as one who offers the sacrifice. But the historic sacrifice of the Cross always remains the essential thing, the continued existence and power of which is to find expression in the sacrifice of the Mass." [4]

(c) The extraordinary importance given to *Penance* at the rise of the Reformation compelled the Council to deal with the Sacrament of Penance in an especially searching manner. It is decreed that penance is a sacrament instituted by Christ Himself (John 20: 22). All three traditional parts of the sacrament are declared to be necessary for obtaining salvation. The cardinal conviction of the Reformation is rejected: namely that it is sufficient to have "a terror-stricken conscience, and faith awakened by the gospel." Attrition is described as a preparation for grace to be received in the sacrament which changes attrition into contrition. The special auricular confession of all mortal sins is required. Absolution is a juridical act in which the priest in God's stead not only forgives sin, but also inflicts the satisfying penalties. The satisfaction which forms the third part of the Sacrament of Penance, though not intended to absolve from guilt, proposes to take upon itself the penalties inflicted by the priest in order that sin become ever more odious to man, and that man rid himself from his sinful habit.

(d) Closely related to these satisfying penalties are the *Indulgences*. They were dealt with shortly before the close of the Council during the Twenty-fifth Session. Indulgences are designated as a "usage which is beneficial to the Christian people." The existence of a number of abuses is admitted, especially the opinion as if absolution could be obtained for money without the sacrament. This last Session also recognized the effect of the Church upon *Purgatory* through intercessory prayers and the sacrifice of the Mass.

(e) In dealing with the Sacrament of *Extreme Unction* during the Twenty-fourth Session the Council canonized only the viewpoint so far upheld by the Church. During the same Session *Marriage* was declared a Sacrament, yet the greater merit of the virgin state is maintained.

(f) During the discussion of the Sacrament of *Ordination* in the Twenty-third Session, contrasting opinions were asserted much as held by the Conciliarists and Curalists of the fourteenth and fifteenth centuries. The peculiar standing of the priesthood, as effected by ordination, was maintained over against the Protestant conception of the common priesthood of all believers. A superiority is granted to the bishops, not on the basis of a different kind of ordination, rather in view of the fact that the bishops are the successors of the Apostles. The relation of the pope to the bishops was not definitely settled by the Council. The designation of the pope as *Vicar of Christ,* was omitted, although planned at first. Even in the introductory formula of the Decrees of the Council the authority of the Council and the papal authority as represented by the papal legates are co-ordinated without any clear distinction, "The most holy ecumenical and general Tridentine Synod rightly assembled in the Holy Spirit and presided over by the three legates of the Apostolic See, etc."

---

[4] Seeberg, IV³. 795.

The Council, however, assigned the publication of the Decrees and the execution of a number of Canons to the pope, thereby acknowledging his superiority over the Council. Still it took more than three centuries of a development, subject to many changes, before the papal dogma, which was left unsettled by the *Tridentinum,* was formulated by the *Vaticanum.*

II. The Dogmatic Development in the Roman Catholic Church from the Decrees of Trent to the Vatican Council (1563-1872)

1. In the centuries following the Council of Trent three great theological controversies stirred the Roman Catholic Church. There was, *first,* the controversy between Curialism and Conciliarism. This controversy involved two problems: (a) the question of the divine rights of the bishops as independent from the pope and the Councilar rights as superior to the pope; (b) the question of Catholic tradition, whether the extent and content of Tradition shall be determined by the principle of Vincentius of Lerins [5] or by papal decrees. *Second,* there was the controversy between Augustinianism and Jesuitic Pelagianism, and *third,* the controversy regarding Probabilism. These three controversies have a close bearing one upon the other. At bottom they formed a unity. On that account the Vatican Council decided all three with one stroke. The party distinguished by its Curialistic, Pelagian and Probabilistic tendencies proved the victor.

2. When Pius IV sanctioned the decrees of Trent in the bull *Benedictus Deus* of July 26, 1564, he showed clearly his authority as superior to the Council, for its decrees became valid only through the confirmation by the pope. This was pointed out still more definitely in the so-called *Professio Fidei Tridentini,* drawn up at Rome in the year 1564, which states the confessional oath of the Roman Catholic clergy in the following form: "I recognize the Catholic and Apostolic Church as the mother and teacher of all churches, and solemnly vow and swear faithful obedience to the pope at Rome, the successor of Peter, the blessed prince among the apostles, and the vicar of Jesus Christ" (Mirbt,[4] pp. 338-340). Still more clearly defended was this papal decision in the *Catechismus Romanus* of 1566. Though Christ is the invisible Lord of the Church, "yet the visible one is he who as his legitimate successor occupies the Roman See of Peter, the prince among the apostles." The authority of the pope is independent of the authority of the councils, "for authority is granted to the pope not by any synod or other human institution, but by divine right" (Cf. Mirbt,[4] p. 345).

3. At the beginning of the seventeenth century the Jesuit Cardinal Bellarmin became the defender of the Tridentine Council, especially over against the brilliant Protestant criticism of Martin Chemnitz. As a real champion of the papal claims he formulated them in almost the same terms in which the *Vaticanum* accepted them. In matters of faith and morals the pope can claim infallibility. Bellarmin decided also the second question concerning the relation of the pope to the bishops in the sense that the bishops have their authority not immediately from Christ, as the successors of the Apostles, but mediately through the pope. As to the secular claims of the Church, Bellarmin held to a mediating view. While he defended the right of the pope to depose governments which are contrary to the welfare of the Catholic Church, he asserted not a direct, but indirect power (*potestas indirecta*) in the papacy in temporal matters. This

[5] The criterion of Catholic and reliable tradition is that which was believed *everywhere, always and by all.*

view, though at first rejected at Rome, was generally accepted by the Curialistic party.

4. Not before the lapse of two full centuries, during which Conciliarism successfully repelled Curialism, could these opinions officially prevail as dogma. The criticism of the secular claims of the popes was especially outspoken in France, where royal power became the foremost opponent of papal authority, and engaged the services of the bishops. The *Declaratio Clerici Gallicani* of 1682, states this in the first article: "To the holy Peter and his successors, to the Vicar of Christ, and to the Church itself God has granted authority in spiritual things pertaining to eternal life, not in civil and temporal affairs. The kings and princes are, therefore, by divine right subject to no authority of the Church in secular affairs. They can neither mediately nor immediately be deposed by the power of the keys held by the Church." The fourth article states: "The pope has also the highest authority in matters of faith, and his decrees apply to all churches and every church in particular; still, his decision is not incapable of reform, unless the assent of the Church has been added." (Mirbt,[4] p. 390.)

These conceptions became more and more generally known during the eighteenth century. It was then that the papacy and its chief support, the Jesuits, saw their strongest decline. The main argument against infallibility and the universal episcopate of the pope was summarized by the suffragan Bishop Nicolas von Hontheim (d. 1790) in his book written under the assumed name Febronius, which bears the title *De Statu Ecclesiae e Legitima Potestate Romani Pontificis* (1763). On the basis of this book the four German archbishops declared at the Conference of Ems in the so-called *Ems Punctation* that the bishops in the past used their divinely ordained power, and that all infringements which the Roman Curia had usurped on the basis of the forged *Pseudo-Isidorian Decretals* should be rejected. This position was defended at the Synod of Pistoja (1786), but most emphatically rejected by the papacy. (Mirbt,[4] p. 414.)

5. In the nineteenth century the papacy saw for various reasons, mostly political, a decided rise and increase of its power. The general Romanticist viewpoint, with its recollection of the past, also aided the authority of the pope. It was defended particularly in France in the book of the Comte de Maistre, *On the Pope and Papacy*. Pius IX (1846-1878) thought the time had come for raising the papal claims to a church dogma. The way had already been prepared for them by promulgating the doctrine of the *Immaculata Conceptio Mariae* (1854), which the pope alone had raised to a dogma without the assent of a council. (Mirbt,[4] p. 446.)

6. The Vatican Council convened by Pope Pius IX in 1869, dealt foremost with the *fides catholica*. Natural revelation with its necessity for proving by rational means a number of Christian truths, like faith in God, is strongly emphasized; likewise its task to refute the modern materialistic and pantheistic errors which the pope had summarized before this together with many other errors, in the so-called *Syllabus* of 1864. (Mirbt, p. 450 ff.) The strong rational character of Catholicism is restored in the style of the old apologists and in the sense of the Thomist scholastics. There is a co-ordination of natural and supernatural revelation which is equally reposed in the Scriptures and Tradition. The Vulgate and the interpretation of the Scriptures by the Church in the sense of the *Tridentinum* is recognized. (Mirbt,[4] p. 456 ff.)

The real effectual work of the Vatican Council consists in the formulation of the *Constitutio de Ecclesia Christi* which contains the doctrines on the "establishment, perpetuity, and nature of the sacred apostolic primacy" (Mirbt,[4] p. 461 ff.) To the pope alone, as the successor of Peter and the vicar of Christ, belongs plenary power which is *immediate* and *truly episcopal*. All bishops receive their authority only through and from the pope. Consequently the pope is the real universal bishop in all dioceses. The bishops are only his representatives who are permitted to discharge the duties of their office in communion with him and depending on him. These settlements effected completely the absolute monarchial constitution of the Church. In the chapter *On the Infallible Jurisdiction of the Roman Pontiff* papal infallibility is defined as a divinely revealed dogma: "that the Roman pontiff when he speaks *ex cathedra*, i.e. when, in discharging his office as pastor and teacher of all Christians, he, by virtue of his supreme apostolic authority, defines, by the divine assistance promised to the blessed Peter, a doctrine pertaining to faith and morals which is to be held by the whole Church and he exercises that infallibility by which the divine Redeemer wished His Church to be instructed in defining a doctrine pertaining to faith or morals. Therefore such definitions of the Roman Pontiff are of themselves, not through the assent of the Church, immutable" (Mirbt,[4] p. 473).

7. In order neither to underestimate nor to overestimate the importance of this settlement the following must be considered. The point of importance lies in the definite victory of Curialism over Conciliarism. The pope makes dogmatic decisions *ex sese*, by virtue of his own power, not through the assent of the Church. The Council thus lost every dogmatical importance in the sense of the ancient, mediaeval, and even of the Tridentine Council. There is transferred to the pope an infallibility which however the Roman Church has always claimed. What really occurred within Catholicism was the shifting of the seat of infallibility from a group to an individual. The infallibility of the pope does not refer to him as a private person, to his personal thoughts and actions. It is rather limited by a number of stipulations: (1) The pope must function as the supreme teacher of all Christendom and make a decision valid for the entire Church, not only for a single diocese. (2) These decisions must relate to faith and morals, not to any practical questions of Church administration or purely secular problems. (3) The decision must bear the character *ex cathedra*. This limits the infallibility to such a decision which bears the marks given under No. 1 and No. 2. All these stipulations are so elastic that it is extremely difficult to determine when the pope exercises his power of infallibility. In the half century since the *Vaticanum* not a single decision has borne the character of infallibility, neither the demand of the so-called *Modernists Oath*, nor the drawing up of the new *Corpus Juris Canonici*. In practice, therefore, the infallibility of the pope is positively much less important than negatively, since it eliminated the council as a factor attributing to dogmatic development.

8. Before the doctrinal development of Catholicism was formally completed by the *Vaticanum*, several decisions were made concerning the questions that had been controversial for a long time.

(a) There was above all the doctrine of Grace and Election, or, in the historical sense, the problem to what extent the Roman Catholic Church after the Reformation could recognize Augustine. There arose during the centuries after the Reformation once more a strong Augustinianism which was, however, more and more decidedly condemned. Michael Bajus (1513-1589), professor at Louvain, defended a number of Augustinian theses, eg., that the neutral will is sinful without the help of God; that the concupiscence is sin in the strictest sense; that no human being is without sin, not even the Virgin

Mary. This position was condemned by Pope Pius V, in 1567. (Mirbt,[4] p. 347 f.) Much more important was the restoration of Augustinianism by the Bishop of Ypres, Cornelius Jansen (d. 1638). In his book *Augustinus,* published after his death, Jansen showed strong Biblical, anti-scholastic and anti-Jesuit tendencies and represented essentially the doctrine of Augustine. Pope Innocent X condemned in the year 1653 five theses of Jansen which had been contested by the Jansenists as belonging to him. (Mirbt,[4] p. 383.) The controversy was resumed and became stronger once more when Paschasius Quesnel (d. 1719) renewed the Jansen theses. Then Clement XI sharply condemned the Augustinian sentences in his bull of 1713 *Unigenitus* (Mirbt,[4] p. 395 ff.) The condemned sentences 1-43 deal with the utter depravity of the sinner who is free only to do evil beyond the irresistible grace; the sentences 44-71 move along the thought that love only corrects human will. Both groups of the condemned sentences contain the Augustinian-Jansenist conception of sin and grace. The bull *Unigenitus* means a landmark of supreme importance in the history of Catholicism, the renunciation of the most precious treasure of the Augustinian inheritance.[6]

(*b*) While the Church of Rome rejected genuine Augustinianism, she became progressively more lenient toward Pelagian tendencies. An outstanding leader in this Pelagianizing movement was the Jesuit scholar L. Molina (1536-1600). In his *Concordia* he made the attempt to offer a logical explanation of the problem of grace and free will, of foreknowledge, providence and predestination. Man is free, he maintained, in every state of life. In spite of original sin he possesses freedom "not only with reference to ethical good and evil in his natural actions, but also in his supernatural salutary works in which divine grace co-operates with his will." In opposition to Pelagius he taught that God is the First Cause of salvation with the free will of man as a *causa secunda.* To harmonize freedom of will with the eternal decrees, he based the latter on the foreknowledge of God. The decrees he maintained, presuppose a special knowledge (*scientia media*) in the light of which God infallibly foresees the attitude which man's will will assume, and guided by this foreknowledge God determines what kind of grace He shall give him.

Since the teaching of Molina was contrary to the celebrated authority of Thomas, controversy was bound to follow. The chief leader of the Thomistic opposition was Dominicus Bañez (1528-1604).[7]

Likewise, the lax medieval Franciscan ethics gained a new momentum in the teachings of the Jesuits. The papal decisions of 1665 and 1666 disapproved only the extreme consequences of the Jesuit morals. In the next century these were being restored to their full propensities through the work of Alphons Maria de Liguori (1696-1787) who was promoted a *Doctor Ecclesiae* by a decree of Pope Pius IX on May 23, 1872 (Mirbt, p. 468). Also the dogmatization of the "Immaculate Conception," December 8, 1854, meant a victory of the Franciscan-Jesuit theology over against the Augustinian-Thomistic school: "Mary is from the first moment of conception kept free from all guilt of original sin." It is thus evident that the development of Catholicism both as to its formal principle (authority of tradition and papal infallibility) as well as to its material principle (Pelagian conception of sin and grace) issued into a dogmatics and ethics which stand in a decided opposition to Augustinianism and Protestantism.

---

[6] Seeberg, IV[3], 866 f.

[7] Cf. G. Schneemann, *Die Entstehung und Entwickelung der thomastisch-molinistischen Kontroverse,* 1879; see also the *Catholic Encyclopedia* X 436 ff.

Sources and Works with Suggested Abbreviations

ANF   *Ante-Nicene Fathers,* ed. by A. Roberts and J. Donaldson, American reprint revised by A. C. Coxe, prefixed to the Schaff and the Schaff-Wace ed. of the Oxford ed., 1885 ff.

APNF   *Ante-Nicene, Nicene and Post-Nicene Fathers,* 1886-1890.

BC   *Book of Concord,* 1580. For convenient use, *H. E. Jacobs,* (Peoples Edition), Philadelphia, 1911. Compare *Concordia Triglotta* (Latin, German and English), St. Louis, 1921. Best and most up to date critical edition: *Die Bekenntnisschriften* d. ev. luth Kche., by Deutsche Evangelische Kirchenausschuss, 1930, Goettingen (Vandenhoek und Rupprecht).

BKV   *Bibliothek der Kirchenvaeter.* German translation. (Catholic.) Kempten. (BKV²) First Ed., 1869-1886.

Calvin   In *CR,* 29-86. His *Institutes,* 1558. His *Writings, English,* 1843-55. Cf. page 275.

CE   *Catholic Encyclopedia,* New York, 1913 ff.

C. Cath.   *Corpus Catholicorum,* 1903 ff. Paris, Louvain and Washington. 112 vols. up to 1940. Will be complete in about 5 times as many volumes.

CR   *Corpus Reformatorum.* Writings of Melanchthon (Vols. 1-28), Calvin (29-87) and Zwingli (88 ff.). Publication of CR, since 1834 ff.

CSEL   *Corpus Scriptorum Ecclesiasticorum Latinorum.* Vienna. Since 1866.

DG   *Dogmengeschichte.* (The Histories of Doctrine).

Gr. Chr. Schr.   *Die griechischen christl. Schriftsteller der ersten drei Jahrhunderte,* ed. by the Academy of the Berlin University. Since 1897.

HD   *History of Doctrine.*

HG   DG⁴, 1840 (Hagenbach, K. R.).

Harnack   A. von Harnack. *DG, German, 4th and 5th editions, 1927; HD, English from 3rd ed.; Grundriss, 6th ed., 1922.*

HE   Hastings, *Encyclopedia.* Since 1928.

Hefele²   K. J. von Hefele, *Conciliengeschichte,* 1855-1890 ff.

IE   *International Encyclopedia,* 1927.

JTS   *Journal of Theological Studies,* 1900.

Kl. T.   *Kleine Texte,* ed. by H. Leitzmann. Since 1902.

Klotsche   E. Klotsche, *HD.,* 1926.

Kurtz   *Church History* by J. H. Kurtz. German, 14th ed. by N. Bonwetsch and P. Tschackert, 1906; English ed., tr. by J. MacPherson, 1888 ff. With recent reprint.

Loofs   *Leitfaden zum Studium der DG⁴.* 1906.

Luther   Works: Erl. Ed. (E); Weim. Ed. (W). Cf. page 217.

Mansi   J. D. Mansi, *Sacrorum Conciliorum . . . Collectio.* Old print, 1798; new print, 1903.

MSG	J. P. Migne, *Patrologiae Cursus Completus. . . . Series Scriptoresque Ecclesiae Graecae,* 1857-1904.
MSL	Migne, *Series Latina,* 1844-1904.
Moeller, Ch. Hist.	W. Moeller, *Lehrbuch der Kirchengeschichte,* Vol. I, 1889; tr. into English; re-written by H. von Schubert (English), 1902.
Mueller, Ch. Hist.	K. Mueller, Kirchengeschichte (in its latest ed.).
Nygrén	Anders Nygrén, *Agape and Eros,* Eng. ed., 3 vols., 1938 ff.
NSH	*The New Schaff-Herzog Encyclopedia of Religious Knowledge,* 1908-1912. Following the PRE.
Oxford Ed.	*Oxford Library of Church Fathers,* publ. under direction of Pusey, Keble and Newman. In 48 vols. 1837-1845.
PNF	*Post-Nicene Fathers,* part of the APNF (see ante).
PRE	*Realencyklopaedie fuer Protestantische Theologie und Kirche,* 3rd. ed. by A. Hauck. 24 vols., 1896-1913.
Rinn	*Dogmengeschichtliches Lesebuch,* edited by H. Rinn, 1910.
RGG	*Die Religion in Geschichte und Gegenwart, 2nd edition,* 1932.
Seeberg	Reinhold Seeberg: *Handbuch der DG¹,* 1898; English translation from first German and part of second ed. by C. Hay. The third German ed., 1920-23 (DG³). (Of the double volume IV A and B the Section A, under influence of the Luther Renaissance, was published in a 4th edition by the author.) *Grundriss,* 5th ed., 1927.
SBA	*Sitzungsberichte der Akademie der Wissenschaften in Berlin.*
TU	*Texte und Untersuchungen zur Geschichte der altchristlichen Literatur,* ed. by O. von Gebhardt and A. von Harnack. Since 1882.
T & St.	*Texts and Studies. Contributions to Biblical and Patristic Literature,* ed. by J. A. Robinson. Since 1891.
Thomasius-Bonwetsch	*DG* by S. Thomasius, Vol. I, revised by N. Bonwetsch, 1886 ff. Vol. II, revised by R. Seeberg, 1889.
Wiegand	F. Wiegand, *DG* in two small vols., 1912-1919. Also a popularized ed. of three small vols., 1928-29.

INDEX